My
iPhone®
for Seniors
FIFTH EDITION

Brad Miser

My iPhone® for Seniors, Fifth Edition

Copyright © 2019 by Pearson Education, Inc.

ISBN-13: 978-0-7897-6030-2

ISBN-10: 0-7897-6030-4

Library of Congress Control Number: 2018961279

1   18

Trademarks

Warning and Disclaimer

Special Sales

Editor-in-Chief
Brett Bartow

Executive Editor
Laura Norman

Marketing
Stephane Nakib

Director, AARP Books
Jodi Lipson

Development Editor
Charlotte Kughen

Managing Editor
Sandra Schroeder

Project Editor
Mandie Frank

Copy Editor
Charlotte Kughen

Indexer
Ken Johnson

Proofreader
Debbie Williams

Editorial Assistant
Cindy Teeters

Designer
Chuti Prasertsith

Compositor
Tricia Bronkella

Contents at a Glance

To access the online chapters, go to informit.com/myiphoneseniors5e and click the Downloads tab below the book description. Click the link to download the chapter.

Table of Contents

To access the online chapters, go to informit.com/myiphoneseniors5e and click the Downloads tab below the book description. Click the link to download the chapter.

About the Author

Brad Miser has written extensively about technology, with his favorite topics being the amazing "i" devices, especially the iPhone, that make it possible to take our lives with us while we are on the move. In addition to *My iPhone for Seniors*, Fifth Edition, Brad has written many other books, including *My iPhone*, Twelfth Edition. He has been an author, development editor, or technical editor for more than 60 other titles.

Brad is or has been a sales support specialist, the director of product and customer services, and the manager of education and support services for several software development companies. Previously, he was the lead proposal specialist for an aircraft engine manufacturer, a development editor for a computer book publisher, and a civilian aviation test officer/engineer for the U.S. Army. Brad holds a bachelor of science degree in mechanical engineering from California Polytechnic State University at San Luis Obispo and has received advanced education in maintainability engineering, business, and other topics.

Brad would love to hear about your experiences with this book (the good, the bad, and the ugly). You can write to him at bradmiser@icloud.com.

Dedication

To those who have given the last full measure of devotion so that the rest of us can be free.

Acknowledgments

To the following people on the *My iPhone for Seniors* project team, my sincere appreciation for your hard work on this book:

Laura Norman, who is my current acquisitions editor and who was the development editor on many prior versions. We developed the original concept for *My iPhone* together (many years ago now!) and she works very difficult and long hours to ensure the success of each edition. Laura and I have worked on many books together, and I appreciate her professional and effective approach to these projects. Thanks for putting up with me yet one more time! Frankly, I have no idea how she does all the things she does and manages to be so great to work with given the incredible work and pressure books like this one involve!

Charlotte Kughen, my development and copy editor, who helped craft this book so that it provides useful information delivered in a comprehensible way. Charlotte is an extremely professional and skilled editor, and somehow manages to be very pleasant to work with at the same time. That is indeed a rare combination. Thanks for your work on this book!

Karen Weinstein, the technical editor, who caught a number of mistakes I made and who made useful suggestions along the way to improve this book's content.

Mandie Frank, my project editor, who skillfully managed the hundreds of files and production process that it took to make this book. Imagine keeping dozens of plates spinning on top of poles and you get a glimpse into Mandie's daily life! (And no plates have been broken in the production of this book!)

Chhavi Vig, my associate sponsoring editor, who coordinated the many files among the different people who worked on this book to make sure everyone had what they needed, when they needed it.

Chuti Prasertsith for the cover of the book.

Cindy Teeters, who handles the administrative tasks associated with my books. Cindy does her job extremely well and with a great attitude. Thank you!

Que's production and sales team for printing the book and getting it into your hands.

We Want to Hear from You!

As the reader of this book, *you* are our most important critic and commentator. We value your opinion and want to know what we're doing right, what we could do better, what areas you'd like to see us publish in, and any other words of wisdom you're willing to pass our way.

We welcome your comments. You can email or write to let us know what you did or didn't like about this book—as well as what we can do to make our books better.

Please note that we cannot help you with technical problems related to the topic of this book.

When you write, please be sure to include this book's title and author as well as your name and email address. We will carefully review your comments and share them with the author and editors who worked on the book.

Email: feedback@quepublishing.com

Reader Services

Register your copy of *My iPhone for Seniors* at informit.com/que for convenient access to downloads, updates, and corrections as they become available. To start the registration process, go to quepublishing.com/register and log in or create an account.* Enter the product ISBN, 9780789760302, and click Submit. Once the process is complete, you will find any available bonus content under Registered Products.

*Be sure to check the box that you would like to hear from us in order to receive exclusive discounts on future editions of this product.

Figure Credits

© thatsmymop/Shutterstock

© annika09/123rf.com

© Ermolaev Alexander/Shutterstock

© Georgios Kollidas/Shutterstock

© Kovalchuk Oleksandr/Shutterstock

Using This Book

This book has been designed to help you transform an iPhone into *your* iPhone by helping you learn to use it easily and quickly. As you can tell, the book relies heavily on pictures to show you how an iPhone works. It is also task-focused so that you can quickly learn the specific steps to follow to do lots of cool things with your iPhone.

Using an iPhone involves lots of touching its screen with your fingers. When you need to tap part of the screen, such as a button or keyboard, you see a callout with the step number pointing to where you need to tap. When you need to swipe your finger along the screen, such as to browse lists, you see the following icons:

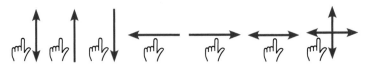

The directions in which you should slide your finger on the screen are indicated with arrows. When the arrow points both ways, you can move your finger in either direction. When the arrows point in all four directions, you can move your finger in any direction on the screen.

To zoom in or zoom out on screens, you unpinch or pinch, respectively, your fingers on the screen. These motions are indicated by the following icons:

When you need to tap twice, such as to zoom out or in, you see the following icon:

If you use an iPhone 6s/6s Plus or later model, you can use pressure on the screen to activate certain functions. The following icons indicate when you should apply some pressure (called a Peek) or slightly more pressure (called a Pop):

Sometimes, you should touch your finger to the screen and leave it there without applying pressure to the screen. The following icon indicates when you should do this:

When you should rotate your iPhone, you see this icon:

As you can see on its cover, this book provides information to help you use iPhone models that can run iOS 12. These models are 5s, SE, 6, 6 Plus, 6s, 6s Plus, 7, 7 Plus, 8, 8 Plus, X, Xs, Xs Max, and Xr. Each of these models has specific features and capabilities that vary slightly (and sometimes more than slightly!) from the others. Additionally, they have different screen sizes with the SE being the smallest and the Xs Max model being the largest.

Because of the variations between the models, the figures you see in this book might be slightly different than the screens you see on your iPhone. For example, the iPhone X has settings that aren't on the 5s or SE. In most cases, you can follow the steps as they are written with any of these models even if there are minor differences between the figures and the screens on your iPhone.

When the model you're using doesn't support a feature being described, such as the Display Zoom that is on the iPhone 6, 7, and 8 but not on earlier or later models (such as the X), you can skip that information.

The most "different" models of iPhone that run iOS 12 are what I refer to throughout the book as the "X models," which are the iPhone X, Xs, Xs Max, and

Xr. These models don't have the Touch ID/Home button that earlier models have. These also use Face ID instead of Touch ID when user authentication is required, such as when you unlock the phone. These are the models that are primarily used for the tasks throughout this book. Where there are variations on tasks with other models (such as using the Touch ID/Home button instead of Face ID), you see those differences noted in the text.

Models that have a Touch ID/Home button are referred to (cleverly I must say) as "non-X" models. While the X models are fairly similar, some of the non-X models have a bit more variation. For example, the iPhone 7 Plus and iPhone 8 Plus have dual cameras on the backside (which enable additional photographic capabilities, such as portrait mode), the other non-X models have only one camera on the backside.

Fortunately for this book's purposes, most of the tasks you need to do are the same or very similar among all the models. (When there is a difference, it is called out so you'll know.) So, no matter which iPhone model you use, this book helps you make the most of it.

If you review this book's Table of Contents, you see that some chapters are provided online. You can download these elements by performing the following steps:

1. Use a web browser to go to www.informit.com/myiphoneseniors5e.

2. Click the Downloads tab.

3. Click the content you want to download. The content opens in a web browser window.

4. Download the content to your iPhone, computer, or other device. You can then read that content using a PDF viewing application, such as iBooks or Acrobat Reader.

Getting Started

Learning to use new technology can be intimidating. Don't worry; with this book as your guide, you'll be working with your iPhone like you've been using it all your life in no time at all.

There are several ways you can purchase an iPhone, such as from an Apple Store, from a provider's store (such as AT&T or Verizon), or from a website. You may be upgrading from a previous iPhone or other type of cell phone, in which case you are using the same phone number, or you might be starting with a completely new phone and phone number. However you received your new phone, you need to turn it on, perform the basic setup (the iPhone leads you through this step-by-step), and activate the phone.

If you purchased your phone in a physical store, you probably received help with these tasks and you are ready to start learning how to use your iPhone. If you purchased your iPhone from an online store, it came with basic instructions that explain how you need to activate your phone; follow those instructions to get your iPhone ready for action.

For this book, I've assumed you have an iPhone in your hands, you have turned it on, followed the initial setup process it led you through, and activated it.

With your iPhone activated and initial setup complete, you are ready to learn how to use it. This book is designed for you to read and do at the same time. The tasks explained in this book contain step-by-step instructions that guide you; to get the most benefit from the information, perform the steps as you read them. This book helps you learn by doing!

As you can see, this book has quite a few chapters. However, there are only a few that you definitely should read as a group as you get started. You can read the rest of them as the topics are of interest to you. Most of the chapters are designed so that they can be read individually as you move into new areas of your iPhone.

After you've finished reading this front matter, I recommend you read and work through Chapter 1, "Getting Started with Your iPhone," Chapter 2, "Using Your iPhone's Core Features," and Chapter 3, "Setting Up and Using an Apple ID, iCloud, and Other Online Accounts" in their entirety. These chapters give you a good overview of your iPhone and help you set up the basics you use throughout the rest of the book.

From there, read the parts of Chapter 4, "Customizing How Your iPhone Works," and Chapter 5, "Customizing How Your iPhone Looks and Sounds," that are of interest to you (for example, in Chapter 5, you find out how to change the wallpaper image that you see in the background of the Home and Lock screens). Tasks covering how to protect your iPhone with a passcode and how to have your iPhone recognize your face (for Face ID) or fingerprints (for Touch ID) to unlock it and to make purchases from the iTunes Store (tasks that are covered in Chapter 4) should be high on your priority list. Chapters 4 and 5 are good references whenever you need to make changes to how your iPhone is configured.

After you've finished these core chapters, you're ready to explore the rest of the book in any order you'd like. For example, when you want to learn how to use your iPhone's camera and work with the photos you take, see Chapter 13, "Taking Photos and Video with Your iPhone," and Chapter 14, "Viewing and Editing Photos and Video with the Photos App."

You'll soon wonder how you ever got along without one!

1

Getting Started with Your iPhone

Your iPhone is one of the most amazing handheld devices ever because of how well it is designed. It has only a few external features you need to understand. For most of the things you do, you just use your fingers on your iPhone's screen (which just seems natural), and the iPhone's consistent interface enables you to accomplish most tasks with similar steps.

Getting to Know Your iPhone's External Features

Take a quick look at the iPhone's physical attributes. It doesn't have many physical buttons or controls because you mostly use your fingers on the screen to control it. X models have different external features than non-X models do, so refer to the figure and description that most closely match your iPhone.

X models look like this:

4:32

Camera

Dual cameras
(backside)

Mute switch

Side button

Volume
buttons

Speakers and microphone

Lightning port

- **Cameras**—X models (except the Xr) have multiple cameras. The one on the front at the top near the center of the phone is the TrueDepth camera that you use for Face ID, selfies, and Animojis (Animated Emojis). It has two cameras on the back near the top of the phone. These enable you to capture all sorts of photos and video, including types that models with one camera on the backside can't, such as telephoto zoom and portraits. When you take photos or video, you can choose the cameras on either side of the phone.

- **Side button**—Press this button once to lock the iPhone's screen and put it to sleep, and press it again to wake the iPhone from Sleep mode. When you hold it down for a couple of seconds, you activate Siri. When you press it twice, you can use Apple Pay, download apps from the App Store, and more. Quickly press this button and either Volume button quickly to take a screenshot. Press and hold this button and either Volume button to turn the phone off or make an emergency call.

- **Mute switch**—This switch determines whether the iPhone makes sounds, such as ringing when a call comes in or making the alert noise for notifications, such as for an event on a calendar. Slide it toward the front of the iPhone to hear sounds. Slide it toward the back of the iPhone to mute all sound. When muted, you see orange in the switch.

- **Volume buttons**—Press the upper button to increase volume; press the lower button to decrease volume. These buttons are contextual; for example, when you are listening to music, they control the music's volume, but when you aren't, they control the ringer volume. When you are using the Camera app, pressing either button takes a photo. You also use these in combination with the Side button to perform various actions (refer to the Side button description).

- **Lightning port**—Use this port, located on the bottom side of the iPhone, to plug in the EarPods or connect it to a computer or power adapter using the included USB cable. There are also accessories that connect to this port. The Lightning port accepts Lightning plugs that are flat, thin, rectangular plugs. It doesn't matter which side is up when you plug something into this port.

- **Speakers and microphone**—The iPhone's speakers and microphone are located on the bottom edge of the case. If you are having a hard time hearing (because of background noise for example), holding this edge to your ear can help.

Non-X models look like this:

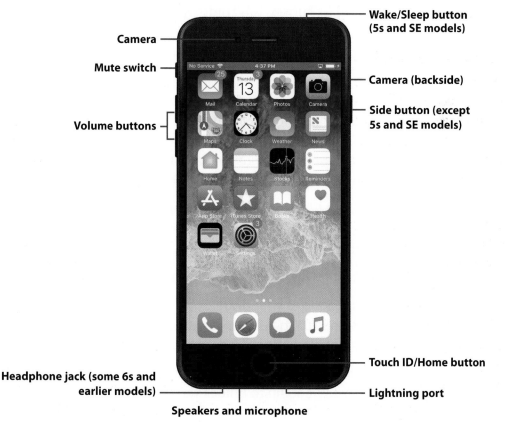

- **Cameras**—One of the iPhone's cameras is located on its backside near the top-left corner (the 7 Plus and 8 Plus have two cameras there and take photos similar to the X models); the other is on the front at the top near the center of the phone. When you take photos or video, you can choose the cameras on either side.

- **Side button**—Press this button (on the 5s and SE this is called the Sleep/Wake button and is located on the top of the phone instead of on the side) to lock the iPhone's screen and put it to sleep. Press it again to wake the iPhone from Sleep mode. You also use this button to shut down the iPhone and to power it up.

- **Mute switch**—This switch determines whether the iPhone makes sounds, such as ringing when a call comes in or making the alert noise for notifications, such as for an event on a calendar. Slide it toward the front of the iPhone to hear sounds. Slide it toward the back of the iPhone to mute all sound. When muted, you see orange in the switch.

- **Volume**—Press the upper button to increase volume; press the lower button to decrease volume. These buttons are contextual; for example, when you are listening to music, they control the music's volume, but when you aren't, they control the ringer volume. When you are using the Camera app, pressing either button takes a photo.

- **Lightning port**—Use this port, located on the bottom side of the iPhone, to plug in the EarPods or connect it to a computer or power adapter using the included USB cable. There are also accessories that connect to this port. The Lightning port accepts Lightning plugs that are flat, thin, rectangular plugs. It doesn't matter which side is up when you plug something into this port.

- **Headphone jack (5s, SE, 6/6 Plus, and 6s/6s Plus)**—Some earlier models have a standard 3.5 mm jack that can be used for headphones (such as the older EarPods) and powered speakers.

- **Touch ID/Home button**—This button provides multiple functions.

The Touch ID sensor recognizes your fingerprint, so you can simply touch it to unlock your iPhone, sign in to the iTunes Store, use Apple Pay, and enter your password in Touch ID-enabled apps.

It also serves as the Home button. When the iPhone is asleep, press it to wake up the iPhone; press it again to unlock the iPhone (if you have Touch ID enabled, this also enters your passcode; if not, you have to manually enter the passcode to unlock the phone). When the iPhone is awake and unlocked, press this button to move to the all-important Home screens; press it twice quickly to open the App Switcher. Press and hold the Home button to activate Siri to speak to your iPhone. When you quickly press it and the Side button, you take a screenshot. You can also configure it so you can use it to perform other actions, such as pressing it three times to open the Magnifier.

So Many iPhones, So Few Pages

The iPhone is now in its twelfth generation of software that runs on multiple generations of hardware. Each successive generation has added features and capabilities to the previous version. All iPhones run the iOS operating system. This book is based on the current version of this operating system, iOS 12. iOS 12 is compatible with the following models: 5s, SE, 6, 6 Plus, 6s, 6s Plus, 7, 7 Plus, 8, 8 Plus, X, Xs, Xs Max, and Xr. If you don't have one of these models, this book helps you see why it is time to upgrade, but most of the information contained herein won't apply to your iPhone until you do.

There are also differences even among the models of iPhones that can run iOS 12. For example, the iPhone 7 Plus, 8 Plus, and X models (except Xr) have dual cameras on the backside that provide additional photographic features, including telephoto and portrait photographs. Models with only one camera on the backside can't take these types of images.

This book is primarily based on the X models. If you don't use one of these models, there might be slight differences between what you see on your iPhone and the steps and figures in this book. These differences aren't significant and won't stop you from accomplishing the tasks as described in this book.

Important differences are noted in the text. For example, instead of unlocking X models by pressing the Side button and looking at the screen (with Face ID enabled), you unlock non-X models by pressing the Home button and using your finger to unlock it with Touch ID.

Are You X or Non-X?

Because there are so many models of iPhone that run iOS 12, I group them into two groups to make referring to them easier. I refer to the X, Xs, Xs Max, and Xr as the X models (clever of me I know). I refer to the 5s, SE, 6, 6 Plus, 6s, 6s Plus, 7, 7 Plus, 8, and 8 Plus as non-X models. It's easy to tell which group a phone belongs to because X models don't have a Touch ID/Home button while non-X models do. When there is a significant difference between these two groups, you see information for each in the text.

Getting to Know Your iPhone's Software

You might not suspect it based on the iPhone's simple and elegant exterior, but this powerhouse runs very sophisticated software that enables you to do all sorts of great things. The beauty of the iPhone's software is that it is both very powerful and also easy to use—once you get used to its user interface (UI for the more technical among you). The iPhone's UI is so well designed that after a few minutes, you might wish everything worked so well and was so easy to use.

Using Your Fingers to Control Your iPhone

Apple designed the iPhone to be touched. Most of the time, you control your iPhone by using your fingers on its screen to tap icons, select items, swipe on the screen, zoom, type text, and so on. If you want to get technical, this method of interacting with software is called the multi-touch interface.

Going Home

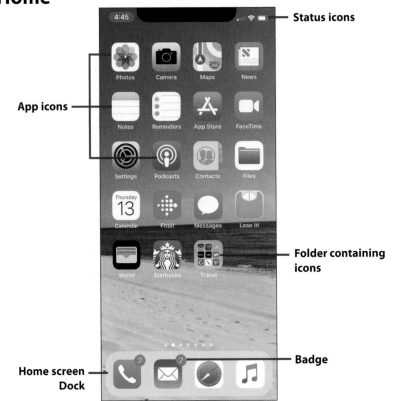

Status icons

App icons

Folder containing icons

Badge

Home screen Dock

Almost all iPhone activities start at the Home screen, or Home screens, to be more accurate, because the Home screen consists of multiple pages. When your iPhone is unlocked and you are using an app, you can move to a Home screen by swiping up from the bottom of the screen (X models) or pressing the Touch ID/Home button (non-X models). You move to the Home screen automatically any time you restart your iPhone and unlock it. Along the bottom of the Home screen (or along the side on an iPhone Plus model when held horizontally) is the Dock, which is always visible on the Home screens. This gives you easy access to the icons it contains; up to four icons can be placed on this Dock (these icons can be folders containing groups of icons). Above the Dock are apps that do all sorts of cool things. Your iPhone comes with a number of preinstalled apps and as you install your own apps, the number of icons on the Home screens increases. To manage these icons, you can organize the pages of the Home screens in any way you like, and you can place icons into folders to keep your Home screens tidy. At the top of the screen are status icons that provide you with important information, such as whether you are connected to a Wi-Fi network and the current charge of your iPhone's battery.

Touching the iPhone's Screen

Tap an app's icon to launch it

The following figures highlight the major ways you control an iPhone:

- **Tap**—Briefly touch a finger to the iPhone's screen and then lift your finger again. When you tap, you don't need to apply pressure to the screen, simply touch your finger to the screen and lift your finger off again immediately. For example, to open an app, you tap its icon.

- **Double-tap**—Tap twice. You double-tap to zoom in on something; for example, you can double-tap on a web page to view something at a larger size.

- **Swipe**—Touch the screen at any location and slide your finger on the screen (you don't need to apply pressure, just touching the screen is enough). You use the swipe motion in many places, such as to browse a list of options or to move among Home page screens. Whatever you are swiping on moves in the direction that you swipe.

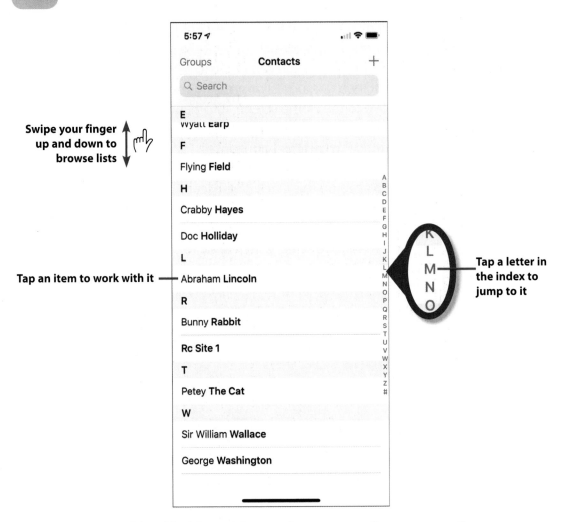

Swipe your finger up and down to browse lists

Tap an item to work with it

Tap a letter in the index to jump to it

- **Drag**—Touch and hold an object and move your finger across the screen without lifting it up; the faster you move your finger, the faster the resulting action happens. (Again, you don't need to apply pressure, just make contact.) For example, you can drag icons around the Home screens to rearrange them.

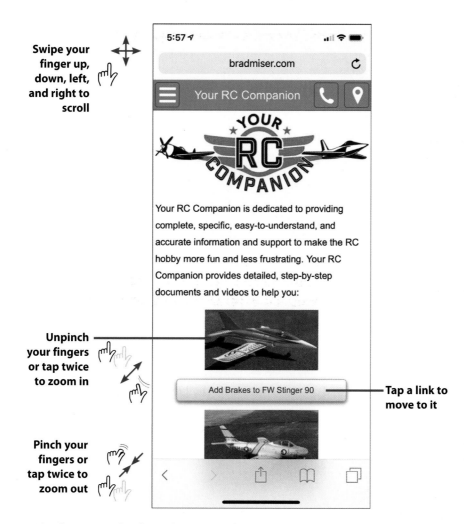

Swipe your finger up, down, left, and right to scroll

Unpinch your fingers or tap twice to zoom in

Tap a link to move to it

Pinch your fingers or tap twice to zoom out

- **Pinch or unpinch**—Place two fingers on the screen and drag them together (pinch) or move them apart (unpinch); the faster and more you pinch or unpinch, the "more" the action happens (such as a zoom in). When you are viewing photos, you can unpinch to zoom in on them or pinch to zoom out again.

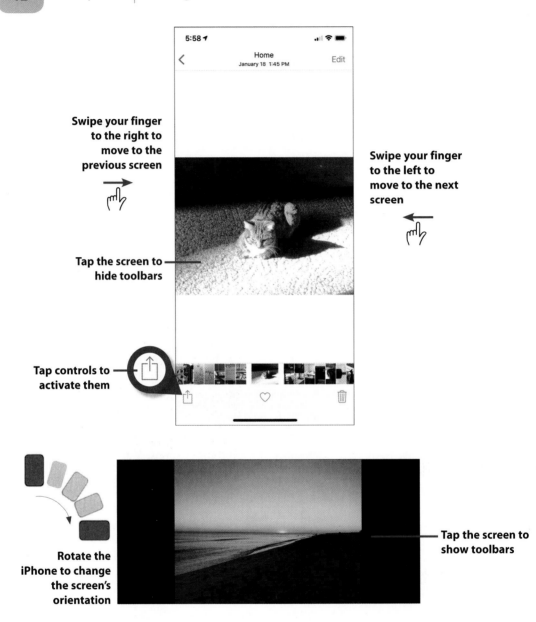

Swipe your finger to the right to move to the previous screen

Swipe your finger to the left to move to the next screen

Tap the screen to hide toolbars

Tap controls to activate them

Rotate the iPhone to change the screen's orientation

Tap the screen to show toolbars

- **Rotate**—Rotate the iPhone to change the screen's orientation.

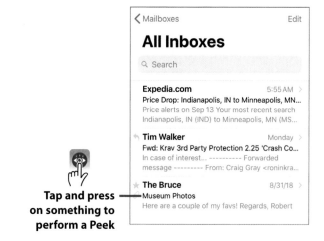

Tap and press on something to perform a Peek

Swipe up on a Peek to reveal menus with actions you can select to perform them

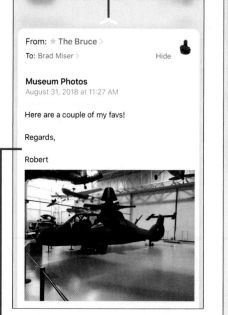

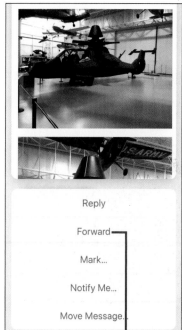

A Peek is a quick way to look at something without actually opening it

When you swipe up on a Peek, you get a menu; tap an action to perform it

- **Peek**—On an iPhone that supports 3D Touch (iPhone 6s and later models), you can take action on something by applying pressure to the screen when you touch it. When you are looking at a preview of something, such as an email, touch and put a small amount of pressure on the screen to perform a

Peek. A Peek causes a window to open that shows a preview of the object. You can preview the object in the Peek window; if you swipe up on a Peek, you get a menu of commands related to the object. For example, when you perform a Peek on an email and then swipe up on the Peek, you can tap Reply to reply to the email.

Tap and press on something to perform a Peek

Press slightly harder on a Peek to perform a Pop

When you perform a Pop, the object opens in the associated app

- **Pop**—When you are looking at a Peek, apply slightly more pressure on the screen to perform a Pop, which opens the object in its app. For example, you can perform a Peek on a photo's thumbnail to preview it. Apply a bit more pressure (a Pop) on the preview to "pop" it open in the Photos app (for example, if you want to edit by cropping your finger out of the photo).

Working with iPhone Apps

When you tap an app's icon, it opens and fills the iPhone's screen

The reason an iPhone is so useful is because it can run all sorts of applications, or in iPhone lingo, *apps*. iPhones come with a number of preinstalled apps, such as Phone, Mail, Safari, and so on, but you can download and use thousands of other apps, many of which are free, through the App Store. You learn about many of the iPhone's preinstalled apps as you read through this book. And as you learned earlier, to launch an app, you simply tap its icon. The app opens and fills the iPhone's screen. You can then use the app to do whatever it does.

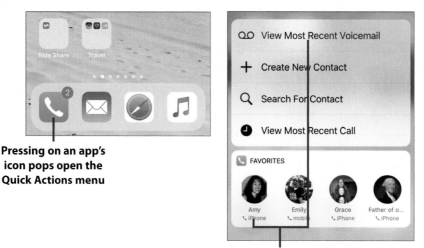

Pressing on an app's icon pops open the Quick Actions menu

Tap a Quick Action to perform it

On an iPhone that supports 3D Touch (iPhone 6s and later models), you can press on an app's icon to open its Quick Actions menu; tap an action to take it. For example, when you open the Quick Actions menu for the Phone app, you can quickly place calls to people you have designated as favorites.

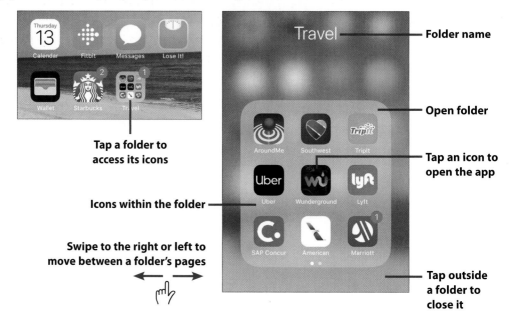

Tap a folder to access its icons

Icons within the folder

Swipe to the right or left to move between a folder's pages

Folder name

Open folder

Tap an icon to open the app

Tap outside a folder to close it

In Chapter 5, "Customizing How Your iPhone Looks and Sounds," you learn how you can organize icons in folders to keep your Home screens tidy and make getting to icons faster and easier. To access an icon that is in a folder, tap the folder. It opens and takes over the screen. Under its name is a box showing the apps it contains. Like the Home screens, folders can have multiple pages. To move between a folder's pages, swipe to the left to move to the next screen or to the right to move to the previous one. Each time you "flip" a page, you see another set of icons. You can close a folder without opening an app by tapping outside its box.

To open an app within a folder, tap its icon.

When you are done using an app, swipe up from the bottom of the screen (X models) or press the Touch ID/Home button (non-X models). You return to the Home screen you were most recently using.

When you move back to a Home screen, the app moves into the background but doesn't stop running (you can control whether or not apps are allowed to work in the background using the Settings app, which you use throughout this book). So, if the app has a task to complete, such as uploading photos or playing audio, it continues to work behind the scenes. In some cases, most notably games, the app becomes suspended at the point you move it into the background by switching to a different app or moving to a Home screen. In addition to the benefit of completing tasks when you move into another app, the iPhone's capability to multitask means that you can run multiple apps at the same time. For example, you can run an Internet radio app to listen to music while you switch over to the Mail app to work on your email.

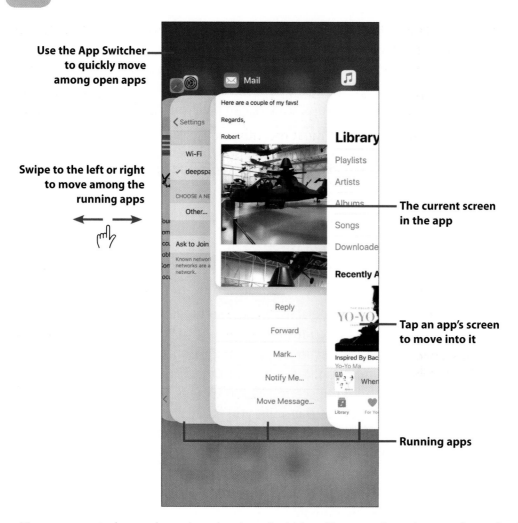

Use the App Switcher to quickly move among open apps

Swipe to the left or right to move among the running apps

The current screen in the app

Tap an app's screen to move into it

Running apps

You can control apps by using the App Switcher. To open it, swipe up from the bottom of the screen and pause toward the middle of the screen (X models) or press the Touch ID/Home button twice (non-X models). The App Switcher appears.

At the top of the App Switcher, you see icons for apps you are currently using or have used recently. Under each app's icon, you see a thumbnail of that app's current screen. You can swipe to the left or right to move among the apps you see. You can tap an app's screen to move into it. That app takes over the screen, and you can work with it, picking up right where you left off the last time you used it.

When you open the App Switcher, the app you were using most recently comes to the center to make it easy to return to. This enables you to toggle between two apps easily. For example, suppose you need to enter a confirmation number from one app into another app. Open the app into which you want to enter the number. Then open the app containing the number you need to enter. Open the App Switcher and tap the previous app to return to it quickly so that you can enter the number.

To close the App Switcher without moving into a different app, tap on the top or bottom of the screen outside any app's window or icon. You move back into the app or Home screen you were most recently using.

Swipe up on an app's screen to force it to close

In some cases, you might want to force an app to quit, such as when it's using up your battery too quickly or it has stopped responding to you. To do this, open the App Switcher. Swipe up on the app you want to stop. The app is forced to quit, its icon and screen disappear, and you remain in the App Switcher. You should be careful about this, though, because if the app has unsaved data, that data is lost when you force the app to quit. The app is not deleted from the iPhone—it is just shut down until you open it again (which you can do by returning to the Home screen and tapping the app's icon).

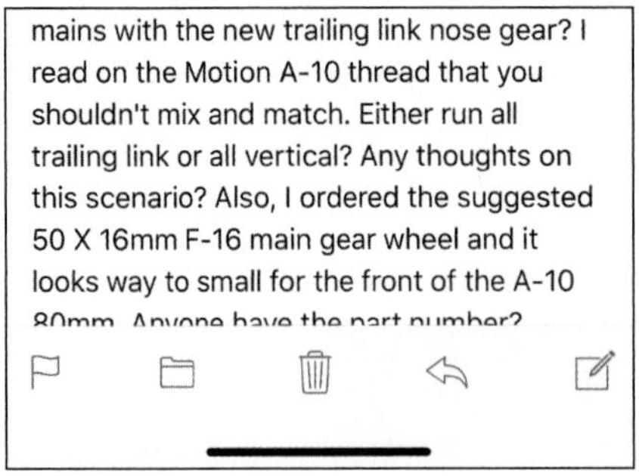

mains with the new trailing link nose gear? I read on the Motion A-10 thread that you shouldn't mix and match. Either run all trailing link or all vertical? Any thoughts on this scenario? Also, I ordered the suggested 50 X 16mm F-16 main gear wheel and it looks way to small for the front of the A-10 80mm. Anyone have the part number?

Swipe along the bottom of the screen to the left or right to change apps

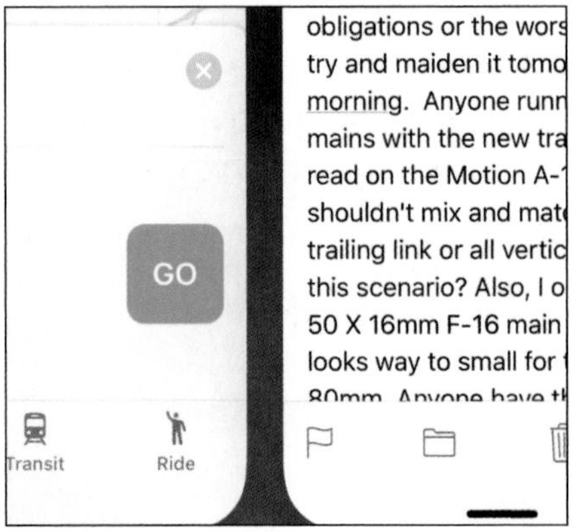

obligations or the wors try and maiden it tomo morning. Anyone runn mains with the new tra read on the Motion A-1 shouldn't mix and mat trailing link or all vertic this scenario? Also, I o 50 X 16mm F-16 main looks way to small for 80mm. Anyone have th

GO

Transit   Ride

Keep swiping until the app you want to use fills the screen

6:56

Indianapolis, Brownsburg...
May 19–29, 2017

Work with the app you switched to

Photos   For You   Albums   Search

On X models, you can quickly switch apps by swiping to the left or right along the bottom of the screen when you are working with an app (not while you are on a Home screen). You can swipe to the right to move into apps you were using earlier or to the left to move to apps you were using more recently. (If you are on a Home screen, swiping to the left or right moves among pages of the Home screen until you get all the way to the right in which case the Widget Center opens.)

Tap to return to the app you were previously using

Sometimes, a link in one app takes you into a different app. When this happens, you see a left-facing arrow with the name of the app you were using in the upper-left corner of the screen. You can tap this to return to the app you came from. For example, you can tap a link to a web page in a Mail email message to open the associated web page in Safari. To return to the email you were reading in the Mail app, tap the Mail icon in the upper-left corner of the screen.

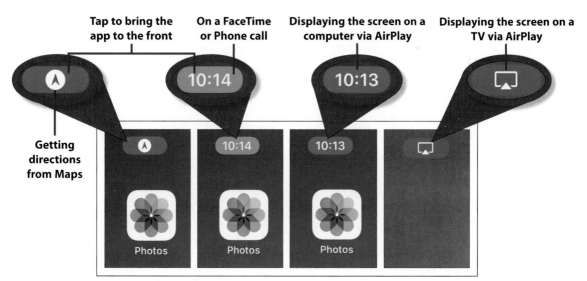

Getting directions from Maps

Tap to bring the app to the front

On a FaceTime or Phone call

Displaying the screen on a computer via AirPlay

Displaying the screen on a TV via AirPlay

As you read, an app can continue to work in the background. For example, if you are using Maps for turn-by-turn directions, you might switch to the Music app to choose different music. Even though you don't see Maps (because it has moved into the background), it continues to provide directions to you through both audible and visual means. In many cases, you can tell if an app is actively working in the background by the presence of the active app indicator in the upper-left corner of the screen (X models) or in a bar across the top of the screen (non-X models). This appears in different colors and provides various information depending on the app it is representing. For example, if you are on a FaceTime call and move FaceTime into the background, this indicator is green. You also see the current time.

In addition to providing you with information about the background activity, you can use this indicator to bring the background activity to the front. For example, if you are on a phone call using the Phone app and have switched to a different app, you can tap this indicator to return to the Phone screen.

Swipe all the way to the right to access widgets

Apps can provide widgets, which make it easy to work with those apps from the Widget Center. To access these widgets, swipe all the way to the right from a Home screen or from the Lock screen (more on this later). You see widgets for various apps. Swipe up or down the screen to browse all the widgets available to you. Tap Show Less to collapse a widget or tap Show More to expand it. Tap something inside a widget to use that app. For example, tapping a favorite in the Phone widget places a call to that person. You learn more about how to use widgets in Chapter 2, "Using Your iPhone's Core Features" and how to configure the Widget Center in Chapter 4, "Customizing How Your iPhone Works."

When you tap something on the Widget Center, you move into the associated app to complete the task. To close the Widget Center without moving into an app, swipe to the left to return to the first page of the Home screen.

Using the Home Screens

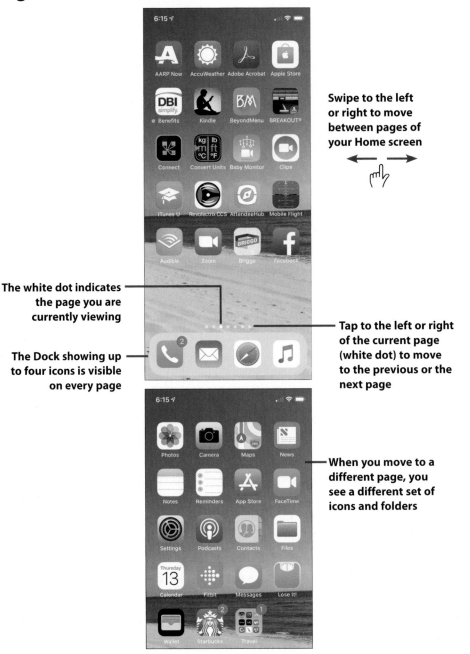

Swipe to the left or right to move between pages of your Home screen

The white dot indicates the page you are currently viewing

Tap to the left or right of the current page (white dot) to move to the previous or the next page

The Dock showing up to four icons is visible on every page

When you move to a different page, you see a different set of icons and folders

Previously in this chapter, you read that the Home screen is the jumping-off point for many of the things you do with your iPhone because that is where you access the icons you tap to launch things such as apps you've saved there.

The Home screen has multiple pages. To change the page you are viewing, swipe to the left to move to later pages or to the right to move to earlier pages. The dots above the Dock represent the pages of the Home screen; the white dot represents the page being displayed. You can also change the page by tapping to the left of the white dot to move to the previous page or to the right of it to move to the next page. (As described earlier, when you swipe all the way to the right or tap the first white dot, you open the Widget Center.)

Using the iPhone Plus's Split-Screen

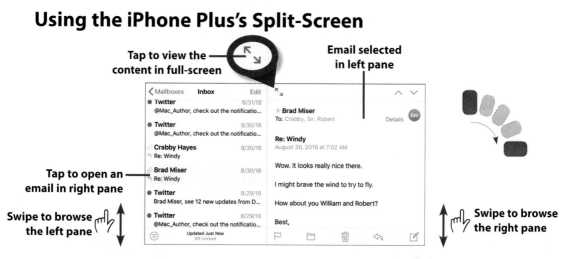

Tap to view the content in full-screen

Email selected in left pane

Tap to open an email in right pane

Swipe to browse the left pane

Swipe to browse the right pane

When you hold an iPhone Plus in the horizontal orientation, you can take advantage of the Split-screen feature in many apps (not all apps support this). In Split-screen mode, the screen has two panes. The left pane is for navigation, whereas the right pane shows the content selected in the left pane. The two panes are independent, so you can swipe up and down on one side without affecting the other. In most apps that support this functionality, there is an icon you can use to open or close the split screen. This icon changes depending on the app you are using. For example, when you are using Safari to browse the Web, tap the Bookmark icon to open the left pane and tap it again to close the left pane (while the left pane is open, you can select bookmarks and see the associated web pages in the right pane). As another example, in the Mail app, you tap the Full Screen icon (two arrows pointing diagonally away from each other) to open or close the left pane.

Preinstalled apps that support this functionality include Settings, Mail, Safari, and Messages; you see examples showing how Split-screen works in those apps later in this book. You should hold your iPhone Plus horizontally when using your favorite apps to see if they support this feature.

Dock

Home screen pages

When you hold an iPhone Plus horizontally and move to the Home screen, the Dock moves to the right side of the screen and you see the Home screen's pages in the left part of the window. Though this looks a bit different, it works the same as when you hold an iPhone vertically.

Working with the Control Center

The Control Center provides quick access to a number of very useful controls.

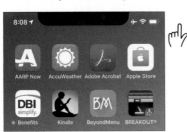 

Swipe down from the upper-right corner of the screen to open the Control Center (X models)

Swipe up from the bottom of the screen to open the Control Center (non-X models)

Open the Control Center by swiping down from the upper-right corner of the screen (X models) or swiping up from the bottom of the screen (non-X models). You can open the Control Center while you are on any Home screen, on an app screen, or on the Lock screen (if your iPhone is asleep, you need to wake it).

Control Center Tip

Some apps have their own Dock at the bottom of the screen. When you are using such an app on a non-X model, make sure you don't touch an icon on the Dock when you are trying to open the Control Center because you'll do whatever the icon is for instead. Just swipe up on an empty area of the app's Dock and the Control Center opens. On the iPhone X, this isn't an issue because you swipe down from the upper-right corner of the screen instead.

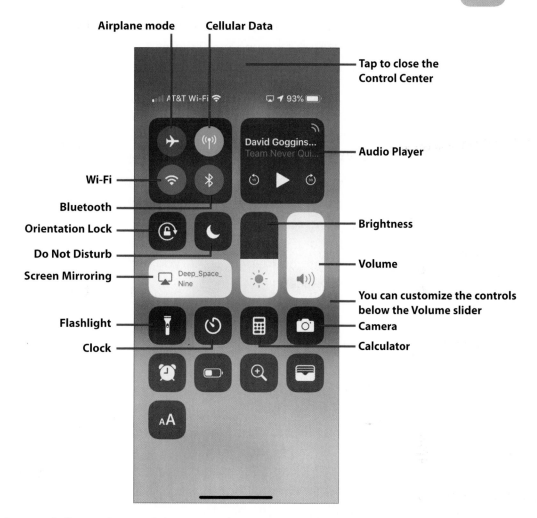

Airplane mode   Cellular Data

Tap to close the
Control Center

AT&T Wi-Fi   93%

David Goggins...
Team Never Qui...   Audio Player

Wi-Fi

Bluetooth

Orientation Lock   Brightness

Do Not Disturb

Screen Mirroring   Deep_Space_
Nine   Volume

You can customize the controls
below the Volume slider

Flashlight   Camera

Clock   Calculator

In the top-left quadrant of the Control Center are icons you can use to turn on or turn off important functions, which are Airplane mode, Cellular Data, Wi-Fi, Bluetooth, Orientation Lock, and Do Not Disturb mode. To enable or disable one of these functions, tap its icon, which changes color to show its status. When the function is enabled, the buttons have color, such as blue, orange, or green. To disable a function, tap the icon so that it becomes gray to show you it is inactive. For example, to lock the orientation of the iPhone's screen in its current position, tap the Orientation Lock icon so it becomes white with a red icon. Your iPhone screen's orientation no longer changes when you rotate the phone. To make the orientation change when you rotate the phone again, tap the Orientation Lock icon to turn it off again.

You learn about the Airplane and Do Not Disturb modes later in this chapter. Wi-Fi and Cellular Data are explained in Chapter 2. You learn about using Bluetooth in the Chapter 15, "Working with Other Useful iPhone Apps and Features."

In the upper-right quadrant, you see the Audio Player. You can use this to control music, podcasts, and other types of audio that are playing in their respective apps (you learn about the Music app in the Chapter 15).

Just below the Audio Player are the Brightness and Volume sliders. You swipe up or down on these to increase or decrease the screen's brightness and the volume of whatever you are hearing on your phone. It is handy to be able to get to either of these controls quickly. For example, when someone is scanning your phone's screen, such as when you are boarding a plane, you might be asked to make the screen brighter so it can be scanned more easily. Just open the Control Center and swipe up on the Brightness slider and then tap outside the Control Center to close it. (Remember to lower the brightness again because having the screen very bright increases the rate at which battery power is used.)

The controls above the first row of four icons are always on the Control Center; you can't change them in any way. However, below those is a section of controls you can change. By default, you see the Flashlight, Clock, Calculator, Camera, and others in this area. Like the icons toward the top of the screen, tap these icons to perform the associated action, such as using the iPhone's flash as a flashlight, or opening an app—the Clock app, for example. You can configure the controls that are in this area by adding, removing, and organizing them; you learn how to configure your Control Center in Chapter 4.

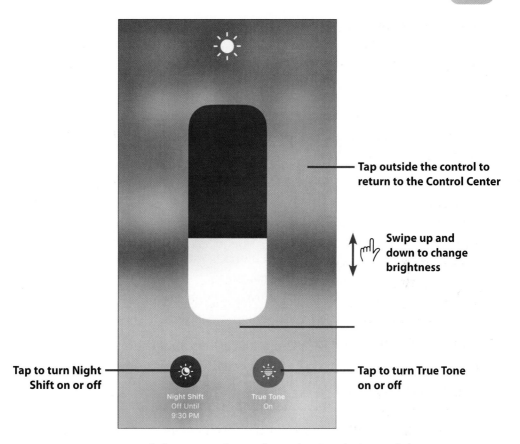

Tap outside the control to return to the Control Center

Swipe up and down to change brightness

Tap to turn Night Shift on or off

Tap to turn True Tone on or off

Night Shift
Off Until
9:30 PM

True Tone
On

When you press on some of the controls, such as the Brightness slider, you see additional options. You should press the controls you use to see what options are available. For example, when you press the Brightness slider, you see a larger slider and have access to the Night Shift and True Tone icons (you learn about Night Shift in Chapter 5).

When you're done using the Control Center, tap anywhere on the screen except on one of its icons to close it.

Examples of using the controls on the Control Center are provided in several places throughout the rest of this book.

Working with the Notification Center

Your iPhone has a lot of activity going on, from new emails to reminders to calendar events. The iOS notification system keeps you informed of these happenings through a number of means. Visual notifications include banners and badges. Alert sounds can also let you know something has happened, and vibrations make you feel the new activity.

Visual notifications let you know when something of interest has happened, such as an event on your calendar

Individual notifications (onscreen alerts, sounds, or vibrations) arrive with the activity with which they are associated such as new emails, messages, and updated information from apps. For example, you can have banner notifications and a sound when you receive new text messages.

You learn how to work with the notifications your iPhone uses in Chapter 2. Because there is likely to be a lot of activity on your iPhone, you want to customize the notifications you receive so you are aware of important information but not distracted or annoyed by less important activity; configuring notifications is explained in Chapter 4.

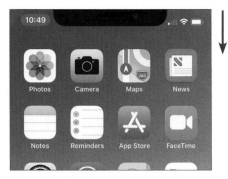

Swipe down from the top center of the screen to open the Notification Center when your iPhone is unlocked

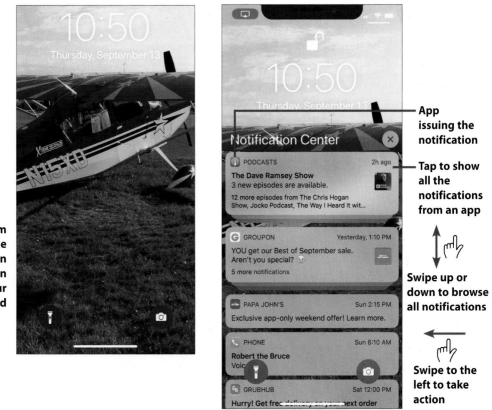

Swipe up from the middle of the screen to open the Notification Center when your iPhone is locked

App issuing the notification

Tap to show all the notifications from an app

Swipe up or down to browse all notifications

Swipe to the left to take action

You can also access groups of notifications on the Notification Center, which you open by swiping down from the top center of the screen when your iPhone is unlocked or swiping up from the middle of the screen when it is locked. The Notification Center opens and displays notifications grouped by day and the app from which they come. Notifications from the same app are "stacked" on top of each other so you can see more notifications on the screen.

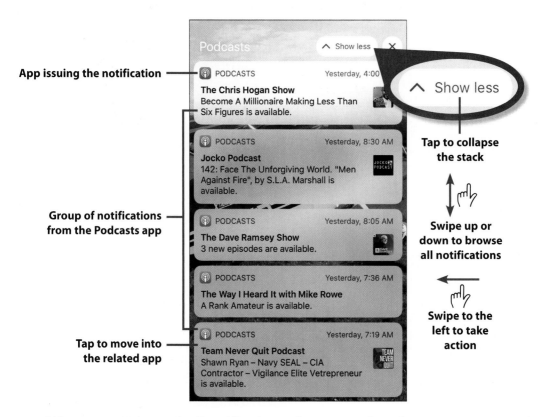

When you tap a stack of notifications, they expand so that you can see each notification in the stack. You can work with the individual notifications in the stack or you can collapse the stack again by tapping Show less.

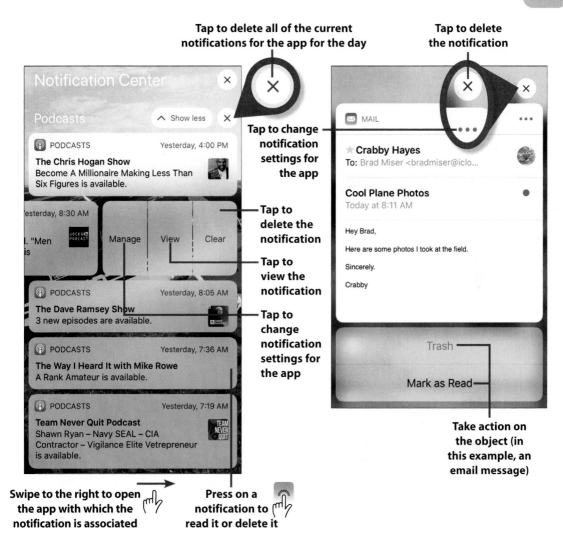

Tap to delete all of the current notifications for the app for the day

Tap to delete the notification

Tap to change notification settings for the app

Tap to delete the notification

Tap to view the notification

Tap to change notification settings for the app

Take action on the object (in this example, an email message)

Swipe to the right to open the app with which the notification is associated

Press on a notification to read it or delete it

You can read the notifications by swiping up and down the screen. You can work with the notifications on the Notification Center just as you work with individual notifications (see Chapter 2). For example, on an iPhone with 3D Touch, press on a notification to pop it open to read more of it or to take action on it; press a little harder to open the associated app. On iPhones without 3D Touch, tap a notification to move into the associated app.

When you swipe to the left on a notification, you can tap Clear to delete the notification or View to open it. If you swipe to the right on a notification, you open the app that generated it (if your iPhone is locked, you need to unlock it to move into the app). If you press on a notification, it opens in a window that enables you to read the notification, such as an email, and take action on it.

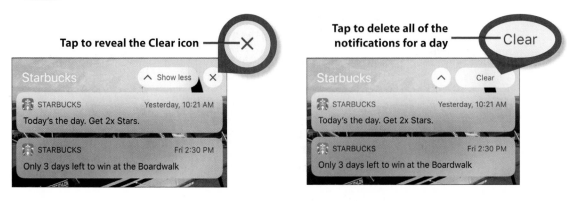

Tap to reveal the Clear icon

Tap to delete all of the
notifications for a day

You can remove all the current notifications from an app by tapping Delete (x) on its group of notifications and then tapping Clear.

To close the Notification Center when your iPhone is unlocked, move back to the Home screen by swiping up from the bottom of the screen (X models) or pressing the Touch ID/Home button (non-X models). When the iPhone is locked, just press the Side button to put the phone to sleep to hide the Notification Center.

Using Siri Suggestions

Earlier, you learned how to access apps from the Home page and App Switcher. Your iPhone can make recommendations about apps that you might want to use based on those you have most recently used, your current activity, and even your location. Sources of information, such as websites, contacts, and other information on your iPhone can also be suggested. This is done through SIRI SUGGESTIONS.

To use SIRI SUGGESTIONS, swipe down from about three-quarters up the screen

You can see these suggestions by swiping down from about three-quarters up the screen (if you swipe down from the top, you open the Notification Center instead). In the APPLICATIONS section, you see the apps being suggested. Tap an app to open it. You can show more apps by tapping Show More, or if the panel is already expanded, tap Show Less to show fewer apps.

At the top of the screen is the Search bar, which you can use to search your phone (this is covered in Chapter 2).

In the suggested search section, you can tap a suggested search to run it (this is also covered in Chapter 2).

If you don't want to use any of the apps shown or perform a search, tap Cancel to return to the previous screen.

Using the Do Not Disturb Mode

All the notifications your iPhone uses to communicate with you are useful, but at times, they can be annoying or distracting. When you put your iPhone in Do Not Disturb mode, its visual, audible, and vibration notifications are disabled so that they won't bother you. For example, the phone won't ring if someone calls you unless you specify certain contacts whose calls you do want to receive while your phone is in this mode.

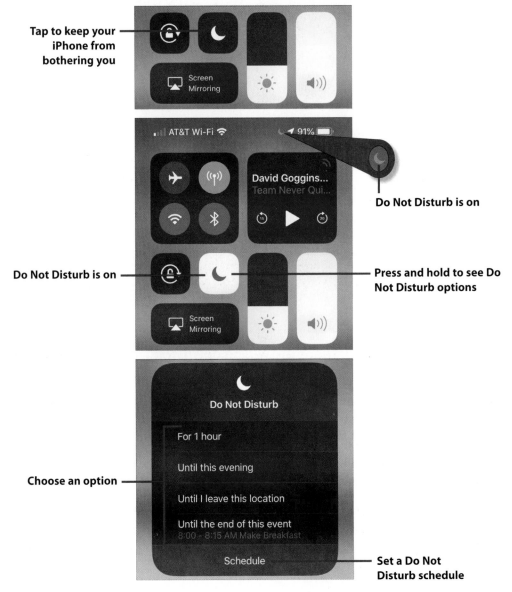

Tap to keep your iPhone from bothering you

Do Not Disturb is on

Do Not Disturb is on

Press and hold to see Do Not Disturb options

Choose an option

Set a Do Not Disturb schedule

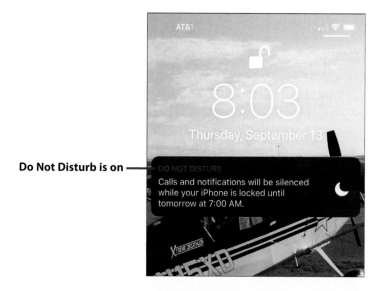

Do Not Disturb is on

To put your iPhone in Do Not Disturb mode, open the Control Center and tap the Do Not Disturb icon. It becomes purple and the Do Not Disturb: On status appears at the top of the Control Center. Your iPhone stops notifications. The Do Not Disturb status icon appears at the top of the screen so you know your iPhone is silent.

If you press on the Do Not Disturb icon, you see options, such as For 1 hour, Until this evening, Until I leave this location, Until the end of the current event, and so on. Tap an option to activate it You can tap Schedule to set a Do Not Disturb schedule.

When Do Not Disturb is active, you see its current status on the Lock screen. On non-X models, you also see the Do Not Disturb icon on the status bar at the top of the screen (see "Understanding iPhone Status Icons" later in this chapter).

To make your notifications active again, tap the Do Not Disturb icon so it is gray; your iPhone resumes trying to get your attention when it is needed, and the Do Not Disturb status message disappears from the Lock screen. Of course, Do Not Disturb turns off automatically if it is set to do so, such as at a specific time or when an event ends.

In Chapter 4, you learn how to set a schedule for Do Not Disturb so that your iPhone goes into this mode automatically at certain times, such as from 10 p.m. to 6 a.m. You can also configure certain exceptions, including whose calls come in even when your iPhone is in Do Not Disturb mode.

Using Airplane Mode

Although there's some debate about whether cellular devices such as iPhones pose any real danger to the operation of aircraft, there's no reason to run any risk by using your iPhone's cellular functions while you are on an airplane. (Besides, not following crew instructions on airplanes can lead you to less-than-desirable interactions with the flight crew.) When you place your iPhone in Airplane mode, its cellular transmitting and receiving functions are disabled, so it poses no threat to the operation of the aircraft. While it is in Airplane mode, you can't use the phone, the Web, Siri, or any other functions that require cellular communication between your iPhone and other devices or networks. You can continue to use Wi-Fi networks to access the Internet and Bluetooth to communicate with Bluetooth devices.

Tap to put your iPhone in Airplane mode

To put your iPhone in Airplane mode, open the Control Center and tap the Airplane mode icon. All connections to the cellular network stop, and your iPhone doesn't broadcast or receive any cellular signals. The Airplane mode icon becomes orange, and you see the Airplane mode status icon at the top of the screen.

This iPhone is in Airplane mode

Tap to turn Airplane mode off

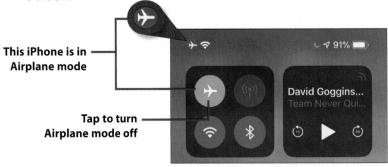

In Airplane mode, you can use apps that don't require a cellular connection; for example, you can connect to a Wi-Fi network to work with email or browse the Web.

To turn off Airplane mode, open the Control Center and tap the Airplane mode icon; it becomes gray again and the Airplane mode status icon disappears. The iPhone resumes transmitting and receiving cellular signals, and all the functions that require a cellular connection start working again.

Meeting Siri

Siri is the iPhone's voice-recognition and control software. This feature enables you to accomplish many tasks by speaking. For example, you can create and send text messages, reply to emails, make phone calls, get directions, and much more. (Using Siri is explained in detail in Chapter 11, "Working with Siri.")

When you perform actions, Siri uses the related apps to accomplish what you've asked it to do. For example, when you create a meeting, Siri uses the Calendar app.

Siri is a great way to control your iPhone, especially when you are working in handsfree mode.

Your iPhone has to be connected to the Internet for Siri to work. That's because the words you speak are sent over the Internet, transcribed into text, and then sent back to your iPhone. If your iPhone isn't connected to the Internet, this can't happen and Siri reports that it can't connect to the network or simply that it can't do what you ask right now.

Using Siri is pretty simple because it follows a consistent pattern and prompts you for input and direction.

Siri is ready to do your bidding

What can I help you with?

Activate Siri by pressing and holding the Side button (X models) or pressing and holding the Touch ID/Home button non-X models) until you hear the Siri chime. If so configured (see Chapter 11), you can say "Hey Siri" to activate it, too. And, if those ways aren't enough, you can press and hold down the center part of the buttons on the right EarPod wire.

All of these actions put Siri in "listening" mode, and the "What can I help you with?" text appears on the screen. This indicates Siri is ready for your command. (Although when you use "Hey Siri" to activate it, the onscreen text is skipped and Siri gets right to work.)

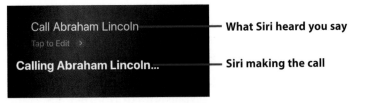

Call Abraham Lincoln ———————— **What Siri heard you say**
Tap to Edit >

Calling Abraham Lincoln... ———— **Siri making the call**

Speak your command or ask a question. When you stop speaking, Siri goes into processing mode. After Siri interprets what you've said, it provides two kinds of feedback to confirm what it heard: It displays what it heard on the screen and provides audible feedback to you. Siri then tries to do what it thinks you've asked and shows you what it is doing. If it needs more input from you, you're prompted to provide it and Siri moves into "listening" mode automatically.

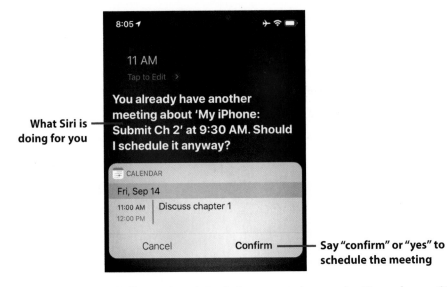

What Siri is doing for you —

8:05
11 AM
Tap to Edit >

You already have another meeting about 'My iPhone: Submit Ch 2' at 9:30 AM. Should I schedule it anyway?

CALENDAR
Fri, Sep 14
11:00 AM | Discuss chapter 1
12:00 PM

Cancel   Confirm ———— **Say "confirm" or "yes" to schedule the meeting**

If Siri requests that you confirm what it is doing or make a selection, do so. Siri completes the action and displays what it has done; it also audibly confirms the result.

Siri isn't quite like using the computer on the Starship Enterprise on *Star Trek*, but it's pretty darn close. Mostly, you can just speak to Siri as you would talk to someone else, and it is able to do what you want or asks you the information it needs to do what you want.

Using Shortcuts

Like Siri, shortcuts are a way to get things done quickly and easily. There are two basic kinds of shortcuts: shortcuts Siri creates for you automatically and shortcuts you create using the Shortcuts app.

Shortcuts are nice for those tasks that you frequently do. For example, suppose you regularly call William Wallace on his iPhone. If he has multiple phone numbers, you could use Siri to call him by saying, "Call William Wallace iPhone," to call him on his iPhone. With shortcuts, you don't even need to work that hard. You could create the phrase "Will" and when Siri hears you say it, the call is placed.

You can perform a shortcut by speaking its phrase

As you perform tasks, Siri automatically creates shortcuts for you. To be able to use Siri shortcuts, you need to activate them by establishing phrases that trigger them; this is covered in detail in Chapter 11.

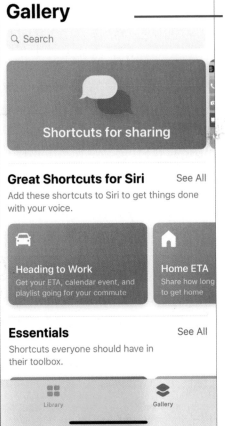

Use the Shortcuts app to combine multiple tasks that you can accomplish by speaking one phrase

To be even more efficient, you can combine multiple tasks under one shortcut. For example, you might want to get directions to your office (to account for traffic conditions), send a text letting co-workers know you are on the way, and start a podcast to listen to. You could accomplish all these jobs by speaking one phrase. To build this type of shortcut, you use the Shortcuts app, which is explained in Chapter 4.

Understanding iPhone Status Icons

At the top of the screen, you see icons that provide you with information, such as if you are in Airplane mode, whether you are connected to a Wi-Fi or cellular data network, the time, whether the iPhone's orientation is locked, the state of the iPhone's battery, and so on. On X models, you see these icons on each side of the "notch" in the center of the screen, on the Control Center, and on the Lock screen. On non-X models, you see these icons across the top of the screen, on the Control Center, and on the Lock screen. The following table provides a guide to the most common of these icons. You won't see all of these icons on all models. For example, you don't see the battery percentage status icon on X models; you have to use the Widget or Battery screen in the Settings app to see this information.

Icon	Description	Where to Learn More
.ıll	Signal strength—Indicates how strong the cellular signal is.	Chapter 2
AT&T	Provider name—The provider of the current cellular network.	Chapter 2
LTE	Cellular data network—Indicates which cellular network your iPhone is using to connect to the Internet.	Chapter 2
📶	Wi-Fi—Indicates your phone is connected to a Wi-Fi network.	Chapter 2
Wi-Fi	Wi-Fi calling—Indicates your phone can make voice calls over a Wi-Fi network.	Chapter 2
🌙	Do Not Disturb—Your iPhone's notifications and ringer are silenced.	Chapters 1, 4
*	Bluetooth—Indicates if Bluetooth is turned on or off and if your phone is connected to a device.	Chapter 15
79%	Battery percentage—Percentage of charge remaining in the battery.	Chapter 16
▭	Battery status—Relative level of charge of the battery.	Chapter 16
▭	Low Battery status—The battery has less than 20% power remaining.	Chapter 16
▭	Low Power mode—The iPhone is operating in Low Power mode.	Chapter 16
🔒	Orientation Lock—Your iPhone's screen won't change when you rotate your iPhone.	Chapter 1

Icon	Description	Where to Learn More
	Charging—The battery in the iPhone is being charged.	Chapter 16
	Location Services—An app is using the Location Services feature to track your iPhone's location.	Chapter 4
	Airplane mode—The cellular transmitting and receiving functions are disabled.	Chapter 1

Turning Your iPhone Off or On

You seldom need to turn your iPhone off, but you might want to shut if off if you aren't going to be using it for a while or for troubleshooting purposes. How you turn it off depends on the type of phone you have.

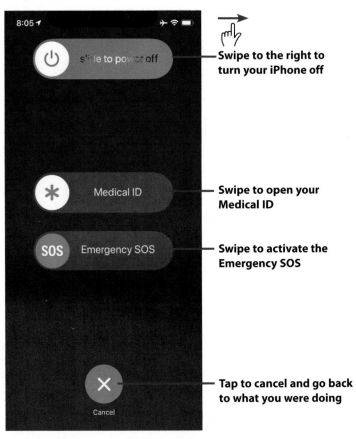

Swipe to the right to turn your iPhone off

Swipe to open your Medical ID

Swipe to activate the Emergency SOS

Tap to cancel and go back to what you were doing

On X models, press and hold the Side button and either Volume button. Several sliders appear on the screen; swipe the top slider to the right.

On non-X models with a Side button, press and hold the Side button down until the power off slider appears. Swipe to the right on that slider to shut the phone down.

On non-X models with a Sleep/Wake button, press and hold that button down until the power off slider appears. Swipe to the right on that slider to shut the phone down.

To restart your iPhone, press and hold the Side button (or Sleep/Wake button) until the Apple logo appears on the screen, and then let go of the button.

After it starts up, assuming you have a passcode, you see the Enter Passcode screen. Enter your passcode to start using your phone; once your passcode is entered correctly, you move to the Home screen. (Even if you have Face ID or Touch ID enabled to unlock your phone, you must enter your passcode the first time you unlock it after a restart.)

If you don't have a passcode configured (you should have a passcode configured to protect your information), you move directly to the Home screen when the phone starts and it's ready for you to use. Keep in mind, if you do not have a passcode configured, your phone is vulnerable to anyone who gets hold of it.

See Chapter 4 for information about configuring a passcode, Face ID, and Touch ID.

Sleeping/Locking and Waking/Unlocking Your iPhone

When your iPhone sleeps, it goes into a Low Power mode to extend battery life. Some processes keep working, such as playing music, whereas others stop until your iPhone wakes up. Almost all of the time, you'll put your iPhone to sleep rather than turning it off because it's much faster to wake up than to turn on. Because it uses so little power when it's asleep, there's not much reason to shut it down.

Also, when you put your iPhone to sleep, much of its functionality can't be used until it is unlocked; you can do a number of tasks, such as using widgets and viewing notifications, while the iPhone is awake, but locked. If you configure your iPhone to require a passcode to unlock, this also protects your information. Even when the iPhone is locked, you can receive and work with notifications, such as when you receive emails or text messages. (See Chapter 4 to configure which notifications you see on the Lock screen; see Chapter 2 for the details of and how you can interact with them.)

To put your iPhone to sleep and lock it, press the Side button (on an iPhone 5s or SE, use the Sleep/Wake button). The screen goes dark.

When an iPhone is asleep/locked, you need to wake it up to use it. You can do this in several ways: touch the screen (X models), press the Side button (or Sleep/Wake button), touch or press the Touch ID/Home button (non-X models), or simply raise the iPhone (on models that support the Raise to Wake feature). The Lock screen appears.

This iPhone is awake and unlocked

Swipe down from the top-right corner of the screen to open the Control Center (X models)

Control audio that is playing

Swipe to the right to access widgets

Swipe to the left to take photos or video

Swipe up from the middle of the screen to open the Notification Center

Swipe up from the bottom of the screen to unlock the phone (X models)

Press to use the flashlight app (X models)

Press to take photos or video (X models)

You can do quite a lot of things directly on the Lock screen:

- If you want to use app widgets, swipe to the right to open the Widget Center.

- To access the Notification Center, swipe up from the middle of the screen.

- Open the Control Center by swiping down from the upper-right corner of the screen (X models) or swiping up from the bottom of the screen (non-X models).

- Take photos or video (press the Camera icon on X models or swipe to the left on all models).

- Control audio playback (when audio is playing the controls appear on the Lock screen).

- Activate the flashlight (X models).

When you are ready to use apps or access your Home screens, you need to unlock your iPhone. How you unlock your iPhone depends on its state and the model you are using.

To unlock an X model, swipe up from the bottom of the screen. If the phone is just asleep (not locked), you move directly to the last screen you were using. If the phone is locked, what you do next depends on whether you have Face ID enabled.

If you have Face ID enabled and are looking at the screen, the phone unlocks as soon as you swipe up. If you aren't looking at the screen when you swipe up, you see the Face ID prompt on the screen; when you look at the screen, and your face is recognized, the phone is unlocked.

Enter your passcode to start using your iPhone

If you don't have Face ID enabled, if you aren't looking at the screen (or aren't being recognized for some reason), or you have just restarted the phone, enter your passcode at the prompt to unlock your iPhone.

If you have a non-X model with Touch ID configured to unlock it (see Chapter 4), wake the phone and then press the Touch ID/Home button with a finger whose fingerprint has been stored for use. When your fingerprint is recognized, your iPhone unlocks and you can start using it.

If your non-X Model iPhone doesn't have Touch ID configured or doesn't support Touch ID, to unlock it, press the Touch ID/Home button and enter your passcode to unlock your phone.

Be Recognized

To use Face ID or Touch ID, you need to train your iPhone to recognize your face or the fingerprints you want to use. You were prompted to configure Face ID or Touch ID when you started your iPhone for the first time. You can change or add Face ID or Touch ID at any time; see Chapter 4 for the details.

However you unlock the phone, when it unlocks, you move to the last screen you were using before it was locked.

If you don't use your iPhone for a while, it automatically goes to sleep and locks according to the preference you have set for it (this is covered in Chapter 5).

The Time Is Always Handy

If you use your iPhone as a watch the way I do, just wake it up. The current time and date appear; if you don't unlock it, the iPhone goes back to sleep after a few seconds.

Working with Face ID or Touch ID

You can use Face ID or Touch ID to quickly, easily, and securely provide a password or passcode in many different situations, such as unlocking your iPhone, downloading apps from the App Store, signing into an account in a banking or other app, and so on.

The First Time

The first time you do something after Face ID or Touch ID is enabled, such as downloading an app, you might still be prompted to enter your Apple ID or other password. The next time you perform that action, you can use Face ID or Touch ID to complete it.

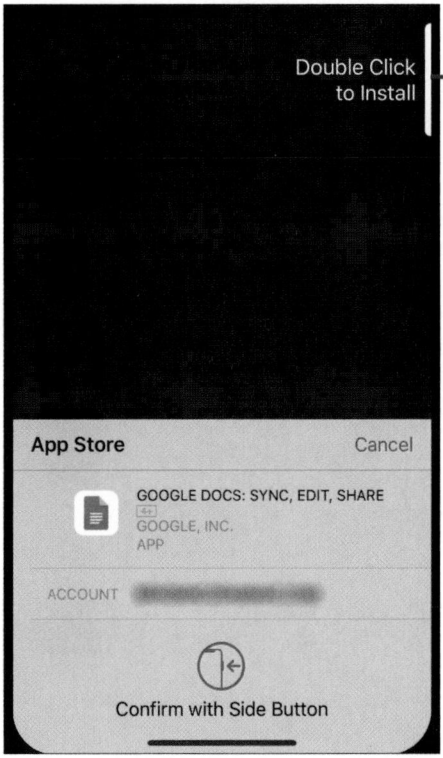

Double Click to Install — **Press the Side button twice to start the download**

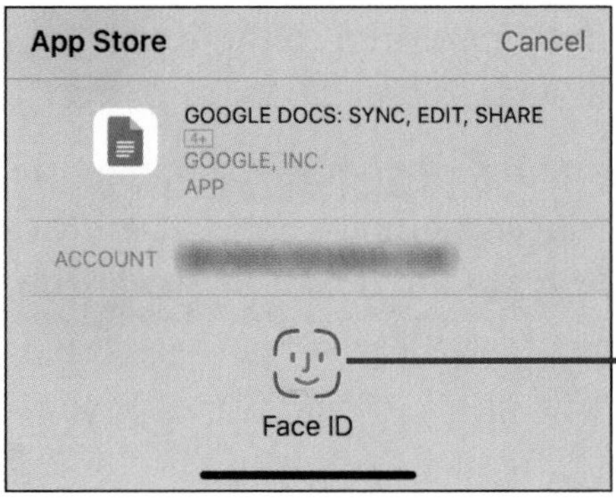

App Store   Cancel

GOOGLE DOCS: SYNC, EDIT, SHARE
4+
GOOGLE, INC.
APP

ACCOUNT

Confirm with Side Button

App Store   Cancel

GOOGLE DOCS: SYNC, EDIT, SHARE
4+
GOOGLE, INC.
APP

ACCOUNT

Face ID — **When your face is recognized, the app is downloaded and installed on your iPhone**

For example, to download an app using Face ID, move to the app's screen in the App Store app and tap Get (or the price if there is a license fee). At the prompt, press the Side button twice and look at the phone. When your face is recognized, the app is downloaded and installed.

Using Face ID in other situations is similar. If you see the Face ID prompt, look at the phone. In other cases, you won't see the prompt and the action you are performing is completed as soon as your face is recognized.

The First Time, Part 2

The first time you sign into an app, such as a banking app, that supports Face ID or Touch ID, you're prompted to allow that app to use Face ID or Touch ID to enter your password. If you allow it, you can sign into the app by just looking at the phone on the log-in screen or by pressing the Touch ID/Home button. If you don't allow it, you need to manually enter the password to be able to access your account.

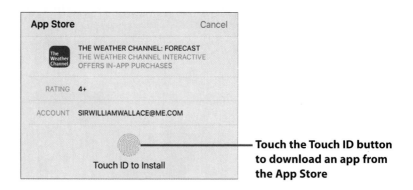

Touch the Touch ID button to download an app from the App Store

Using Touch ID is only slightly more difficult than using Face ID. When prompted to do so, touch a recorded fingerprint to the Touch ID/Home button. The resulting action is completed, such as downloading an app from the App Store.

If you don't have the settings configured to enable you to use Face ID or Touch ID or you use an app that doesn't support Touch ID or Face ID, you need to provide your password when prompted to do so. Whatever action you were performing is completed.

Setting Volume

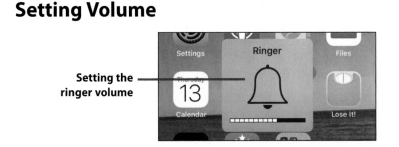

Setting the ringer volume

To change the iPhone's volume, press the up or down Volume button on the side of the iPhone. When you change the volume, your change affects the current activity. For example, if you are on a phone call, the call volume changes, or if you are listening to music, the music's volume changes. If you aren't on a screen that shows a Volume slider, an icon pops up to show you the relative volume you are setting and the type, such as setting the ringer's volume. When the volume is right, release the Volume button.

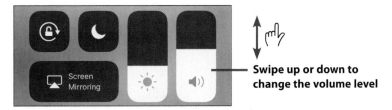

Swipe up or down to change the volume level

You can also use the Volume slider on the Control Center to change the volume level.

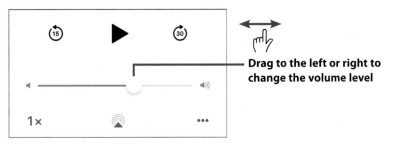

Drag to the left or right to change the volume level

When you are using an audio app, such as the Podcasts app, you can also drag the volume slider in that app to increase or decrease the volume. Drag the slider to the left to lower volume or to the right to increase it.

When you use the iPhone's EarPods, you can change the volume by pressing the upper part of the switch on the right EarPod's wire to increase volume or the lower part to decrease it.

To mute your phone's sounds, slide the Mute switch, located on the left side of the phone, toward the back of the phone. You see an on-screen indicator that the phone is muted and you see orange within the Mute switch on the side of the iPhone; notification and other sounds won't play. To restore normal sound, slide the switch toward the front of the phone.

Unintentional Muting

If your phone suddenly stops ringing when calls come in or doesn't play notification sounds that you think it should, always check the Mute switch to ensure it hasn't been activated accidentally or that you forgot that you had muted your iPhone. (There's no indication on the screen that the iPhone is currently muted, so you have to look at the switch to tell.)

Connect to the Internet via Wi-Fi or a cellular network

Use the Settings app to configure your iPhone

Notifications, such as badges, keep you informed

Use the iPhone's great text tools in many apps

Take advantage of an Internet connection in many different apps

Print email and other documents from your phone

In this chapter, you learn to use some of your iPhone's core features. Topics include the following:

→ Getting started
→ Working with the Settings app
→ Connecting to the Internet using Wi-Fi networks
→ Connecting to the Internet using cellular data networks
→ Securing your iPhone
→ Working with text
→ Using widgets
→ Searching on your iPhone
→ Working with Siri Suggestions
→ Working with notifications
→ Printing from your iPhone

Using Your iPhone's Core Features

In Chapter 1, "Getting Started with Your iPhone," you learned how to interact with your iPhone, including navigating Home screens, using apps, locking and unlocking the phone, swiping to open and close things, and zooming in or out. In this chapter, you learn to use some of the iPhone's "core" features, meaning those that apply across multiple apps and functions of your phone.

Getting Started

Here are the core features and concepts you learn about in this chapter:

- **Settings app**—The iPhone's Settings app is where you do almost all of your phone's configuration, and you use it frequently throughout this book.

- **The Internet**—Your iPhone has many functions that rely on an Internet connection; most of the apps you use either require or can use a connection to the Internet to do what they do for you. For example, to send and receive email, your iPhone has to be connected to the Internet.

- **Wi-Fi**—Wi-Fi stands for Wireless Fidelity and encompasses a whole slew of technical specifications around connecting devices together without using cables or wires. Wi-Fi networks have a relatively short range and are used to create a Local Area Network (LAN). The most important thing to know is that you can use Wi-Fi networks to connect your iPhone to the Internet. This is great because Wi-Fi networks are available in many places you go. You probably have a Wi-Fi network available in your home to which you can connect your iPhone, too. (If you connect your computers to the Internet without a cable from your computer to a modem or network hub, you are using a Wi-Fi network.)

- **Cellular data networks**—In addition to your voice, your iPhone can transmit and receive data over the cellular network to which it is connected. This enables you to connect your iPhone to the Internet just about anywhere you are. You use the cellular network provided by your cell phone company. There are many different cell phone providers that support iPhones. In the United States, these include AT&T, Sprint, T-Mobile, and Verizon. You don't need to configure your iPhone to use the cellular data network, as it is set up from the start to do so.

- **Security**—Connecting your iPhone to the Internet enables you to do lots of useful, and sometimes amazing, things with it. But that connection does come with some risk because of the sensitive information you store on your iPhone and the tasks you perform with it. The good news is that you can protect your information with a few relatively simple precautions.

- **Text**—You enter text on your iPhone for many different purposes, including sending messages and emails and writing notes. You can type text using the iPhone's amazing onscreen keyboards. You can also dictate text wherever you might need to create it. The iPhone has many features to help you make the text you enter "just right." For example, text is automatically checked for correct spelling and the Predictive Text feature suggests text you might want to enter with just a tap.

- **Widgets**—Widgets are "mini" versions of apps installed on your iPhone that you can access easily and quickly from the Widget Center (you saw an introduction to this in Chapter 1).

- **Search**—Your iPhone has a lot of information on it. This includes apps, emails, music, and much more. The iPhone's Search tool enables you to find what you want to work with quickly and easily.

- **Siri Suggestions**—You frequently want to "go back" to something you were using recently, such as an app or a search. The Siri Suggestions tool presents these recent items to you so that you can return to them with a single tap. Siri can also learn from what you do and make suggestions about what you might find useful; for example, when you correct a text message that you've dictated, Siri can make suggestions about what you might have intended to say.

- **Notifications**—The iPhone's notification system keeps you informed about activity in which you may be interested, such as new emails, events, app updates, and so on. There are a number of types of these notifications that you experience. Visual notifications include alerts and badges. Alert sounds can also let you know something has happened, and vibrations make you feel the new activity.

- **Print**—The paperless world has never become a reality—and probably never will. Fortunately, you can print emails, documents, and other content directly from your iPhone.

Working with the Settings App

Aptly named, the Settings app is where you configure the many settings that change how your iPhone looks, sounds, and works. In fact, virtually everything you do on your iPhone is affected by settings in this app. As you use and make an iPhone into *your* iPhone, you frequently visit the Settings app.

Using the Settings App on Any iPhone

You can work with the Settings app on any iPhone as follows:

1. On the Home screen, tap Settings. The Settings app opens. The app is organized in sections starting at the top with your Apple ID information followed by Airplane Mode, Wi-Fi, Bluetooth, and Cellular.

2. Swipe up or down the screen to get to the settings area you want to use.

3. Tap the area you want to configure, such as Sounds & Haptics (iPhone 7 or later) or Sounds (earlier models).

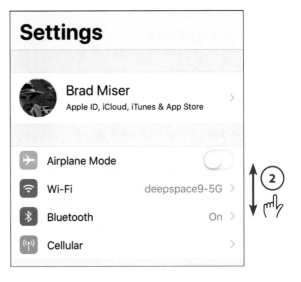

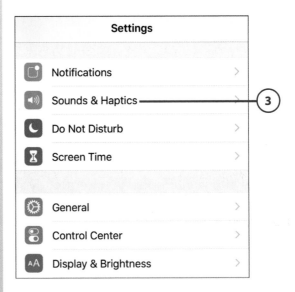

(4) Use the resulting controls to configure that area. The changes you make take effect immediately.

(5) When you're done, you can leave the Settings app where it is (it remains there when you come back to it) or tap the Back icon (<), which is always located in the upper-left corner of the screen (its name changes based on where you are in the app), until you get back to the main Settings screen to go into other Settings areas.

Searching for Settings

You can quickly find settings you need by searching for them:

(1) Move into the Settings app. (If you aren't on the main Settings screen, tap the Back icon (<) until you get there.)

(2) Tap in the Search bar; if you don't see the Search bar, swipe down from the top of the Settings screen until it appears.

(3) Type the setting for which you want to search. As you type, potential matches are shown on the list of results. Matches can include a settings area, such as Sounds & Haptics, or specific settings, such as the ringtone and vibrations used when you receive a call.

(4) Tap the setting you want to use.

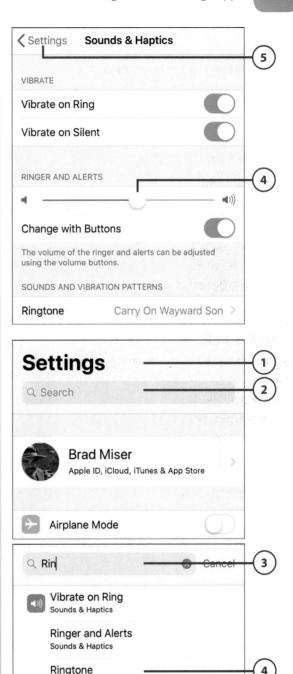

(5) Configure the setting you selected in the previous step.

⟨ Back   **Ringtone** ──────── (5)

Vibration   Alert ›

STORE

Tone Store

Download All Purchased Tones

This will download all ringtones and alerts purchased using the "bradmacosx@mac.com" account.

RINGTONES

✓   Carry On Wayward Son

Using the Settings App on an iPhone Plus

When you hold an iPhone Plus in the horizontal orientation and use the Settings app, you can take advantage of the Split-screen feature as follows:

(1) Hold the iPhone Plus so it is horizontal.

(2) Tap the Settings app to open it. In the left pane, you see the areas of the Settings app that you can configure. In the right pane, you see tools you can use to configure the selected setting. The two panes are independent, making navigation easier than with other iPhones.

(3) Swipe up or down on the left pane until you see the function, feature, or app you want to configure.

Settings pane   Selected setting   Tools to configure the selected setting

4 Tap the function, feature, or app you want to configure, such as Sounds. Its controls appear in the right pane.

5 Swipe up or down on the right pane until you see the specific setting you want to change.

6 Tap the setting you want to configure, such as Ringtone. Its controls appear in the right pane.

7 Use the tools in the right pane to configure the setting you selected in step 6. These work just as described in the previous task and throughout this chapter except that you move within the right pane instead of changing the entire screen.

8 To move back through the screens in the right pane, use the Back icon (<), which is labeled with the name of the screen you came from.

9 Tap another area in the left pane to configure it. As you can see, the split screen makes it very easy to quickly switch between areas in the Settings app.

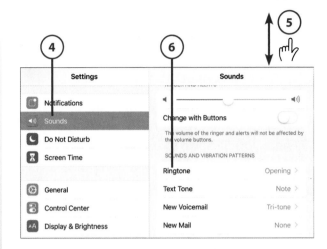

Connecting to the Internet Using Wi-Fi Networks

Your iPhone is designed to seamlessly connect to the Internet so apps that use the Internet to work, such as Safari to browse the Web, are always ready when you need them. Wi-Fi networks provide fast Internet connections and you usually have an unlimited amount of data to work with, so you don't have to worry about paying more based on how you are using your iPhone. Because of their speed and unlimited data (usually), Wi-Fi networks are the best way for your iPhone to connect to the Internet.

Wi-Fi networks are available just about everywhere you go, including homes, offices, hotels, restaurants, and other locations. Fortunately, it's very easy to connect your iPhone to the Wi-Fi networks you encounter. (And, if there isn't a Wi-Fi network available, your iPhone uses its cellular data network to connect to the Internet, which is covered later in this chapter.)

Almost all Wi-Fi networks broadcast their information so that you can easily see them with your iPhone; these are called *open networks* because anyone who is in range can attempt to join one because they appear on Wi-Fi devices automatically. The Wi-Fi networks you can see on your iPhone in public places (such as airports and hotels) are all open. Likewise, any Wi-Fi networks in your home or office are very likely to be open as well. To connect your iPhone to an open network, you tap its name and then enter its password (if required).

Your iPhone remembers Wi-Fi networks you've connected to previously and joins one of them automatically when available; these are called *known networks*. For example, if you have a Wi-Fi network at home and another in your office, when you change locations, your iPhone automatically changes Wi-Fi networks.

If your iPhone can't connect to a known network, it automatically searches for other Wi-Fi networks to join. If one or more are available, a prompt appears showing the networks available to your iPhone. You can select and join one of these networks by tapping its name on the list of networks and entering its password (if one is required, you need to obtain it from the source of the network, such as a hotel or restaurant).

If no Wi-Fi networks are available or you choose not to connect to one, your iPhone automatically switches to its cellular data connection (covered in "Connecting to the Internet Using Cellular Data Networks" later in this chapter).

Connecting to Open Wi-Fi Networks

To connect your iPhone to a Wi-Fi network, perform the following steps:

1. On the Home screen, tap Settings. Next to Wi-Fi, you see the status of your Wi-Fi connection. It is Off if Wi-Fi is turned off, Not Connected if Wi-Fi is turned on and your phone isn't currently connected to Wi-Fi, or the name of the Wi-Fi network to which your iPhone is connected.

2. Tap Wi-Fi.

3. If Wi-Fi isn't enabled already, slide the Wi-Fi switch to on (green) and your iPhone searches for available networks. A list of available networks is displayed in the CHOOSE A NETWORK section (it can take a moment for all the networks available in the area to be shown). Along with each network's name, icons indicating whether it requires a password (the padlock icon) to join and the current signal strength (the radio waves icon) are displayed.

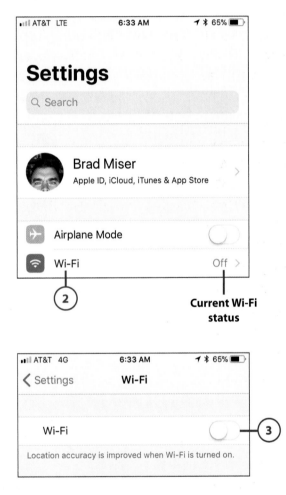

Current Wi-Fi status

Quick Access to the Wi-Fi Switch

You can quickly turn Wi-Fi on or off using the Control Center, which you can open by swiping down from the upper-right corner of the screen (X models) or swiping up from the bottom of the screen (non-X models). If the Wi-Fi icon (it looks like the signal strength indicator on the Wi-Fi Setting screen) is blue, Wi-Fi is on. Tap that icon to turn Wi-Fi off (the icon becomes gray). Tap it again to turn Wi-Fi on and reconnect to a known network. See Chapter 1 for more information about working with the Control Center.

4 Tap the network you want to join. Of course, when a network requires a password, you must know that password to be able to join it. Another consideration should be signal strength; the more waves in the network's signal strength icon, the stronger the connection.

5 At the prompt, enter the password for the network you selected. If you aren't prompted for a password, skip to step 7. (You're likely to find networks that don't require a password in public places; see the next section for information on these types of networks.)

6 Tap Join. If you provided the correct password, your iPhone connects to the network and gets the information it needs to connect to the Internet. If not, you're prompted to enter the password again. After you successfully connect to the network, you return to the Wi-Fi screen.

7 Review the network information. The network to which you are connected appears just below the Wi-Fi switch and is marked with a check mark. You also see the signal strength for that network.

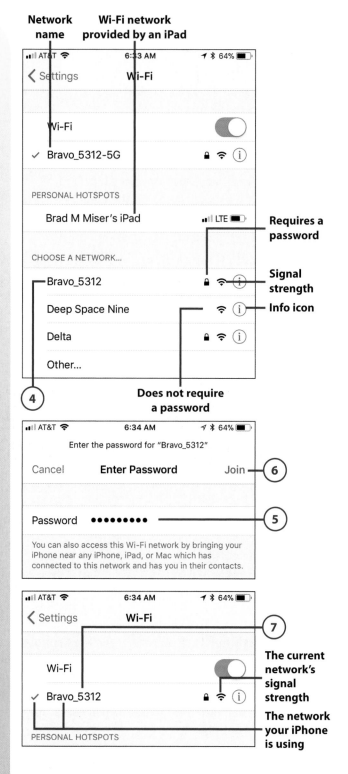

Network name

Wi-Fi network provided by an iPad

Requires a password

Signal strength

Info icon

Does not require a password

The current network's signal strength

The network your iPhone is using

8) Try to move to a web page, such as www.bradmiser.com, to test your Wi-Fi connection. (See Chapter 12, "Surfing the Web," for details.) If the web page opens, you are ready to use the Internet on your phone. If you are taken to a login web page for a Wi-Fi provider rather than the page you were trying to access, see the next task. If you see a message saying the Internet is not available, there is a problem with the network you joined. Go back to step 4 to select a different network.

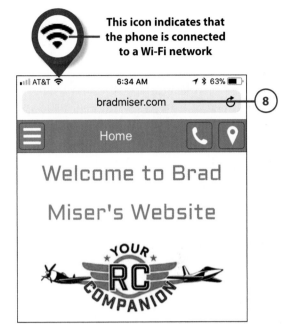

This icon indicates that the phone is connected to a Wi-Fi network

>>>Go Further
CONNECTING TO WI-FI NETWORKS

As you connect to Wi-Fi networks, consider the following:

- **Typing passwords**—As you type a password, each character is hidden by a dot in the Password field except for the last character you entered, which is displayed on the screen for a moment. Keep an eye on characters as you enter them because you can fix a mistake as soon as you make it rather than finding out after you've entered the entire password and having to start over.

- **Changing networks**—You can use these same steps to change the Wi-Fi network you are using at any time. For example, if you have to pay to use one network while a different one is free, simply choose the free network in step 4.

- **Be known**—After your iPhone connects to a Wi-Fi network successfully, it becomes a known network. This means that your iPhone remembers its information so you don't have to enter it again. Your iPhone automatically connects to known networks when it needs to access the Internet. So unless you tell your iPhone to forget a network (explained later in this chapter), you need to enter its password only the first time you connect to it.

- **Security recommendation**—If you are connected to a network that doesn't use what Apple considers sufficient security, you see the words "Security Recommendation" under the network's name. If you tap Info (i) for that network, you see its Info screen. At the top of that screen, you see the type of security the network is using and a recommendation about the type of security it should use. If the Wi-Fi network comes from a router or modem you own or rent, contact your Internet service provider, such as a cable company, to learn how the security provided by that router or modem can be reconfigured to be more secure. If the network is in a public place or business, you just have to use it as is (unless you can contact the administrator of that network to see if better security is available).

- **Have a network, but no Internet**—If you successfully connect to a network, but there is an exclamation point on top of the signal strength icon, the network you are connected to might not have a current Internet connection. Sometimes, that's because you need to provide some additional information to reach the Internet (as described in the next section). At other times, it's because the network has lost its connection to the Internet. You'll need to get that connection restored (such as by contacting your provider) before you can use that network to connect to the Internet. (If you are working with a network inside your home or business that you control, try resetting the modem, which usually involves unplugging the modem, waiting for about 30 seconds, and plugging it in again. This often solves the issue and should be the first thing you try, even before contacting your provider.)

- **Personal hotspots**— iPhones and iPads can share their cellular Internet connection (how to do this is covered in a later Go Further sidebar) with other devices by providing a Wi-Fi network to which you can connect your iPhone. The icons for these networks are a bit different, being two connected loops that indicate the network is from a hotspot. You can select and use these networks just like the other types of networks being described in this chapter. The speed of your access is determined mostly by the speed of the device's cellular data connection. Also, the data you use while connected to the hotspot's network counts against the data plan for the device to which you are connected.

Connecting to Public Wi-Fi Networks

Many Wi-Fi networks in public places, such as hotels or airports, require that you pay a fee or provide other information to access the Internet through that network; even if access is free, you usually have to accept terms and conditions for the network to be able to use it.

When you connect to one of these public networks, you're prompted to provide whatever information is required. This can involve different details for different networks, but the general steps are the same. Follow the instructions that appear.

Better Safe Than Sorry

Many public Wi-Fi networks have very limited or no security. This means the information being transmitted from your iPhone to the Internet (and vice versa) is susceptible to being intercepted by hackers and others who are looking for personal information. It's best practice not to use these networks for sensitive information, such as to access your bank account or other areas where you don't want to run any risk of your information being compromised. They are perfectly fine for browsing the Web, email, and other such activities.

Following are the general steps to connect to many types of public Wi-Fi networks:

1. Move to the Settings screen.

2. Tap Wi-Fi.

3. Tap the network you want to join. You move to that network's Log In screen. Follow the onscreen prompts to complete the process. This often involves selecting a connection option and providing payment or identification information, as this example of connecting to a hotel's Wi-Fi network shows.

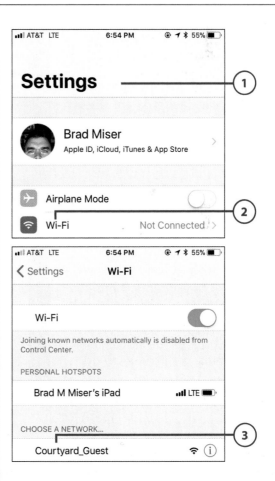

(**4**) Choose the connection option you want to use.

(**5**) Provide the information required to join the network, such as a last name and room number. If a fee is required, you have to provide payment information (if you are in a hotel, the fee is added to your room charges). In many cases, you at least have to indicate that you accept the terms and conditions for using the network, which you typically do by checking a check box.

(**6**) Tap the icon to join the network. This icon can have different labels depending on the type of access, such as Connect, Authenticate, Done, Free Access, Login, and so on.

(**7**) Tap Done (if required).

(**8**) Try to move to a web page, such as www.wikipedia.org, to test your Wi-Fi connection (not shown in a figure). (See Chapter 12 for details.) If the web page opens, you are ready to use the Internet on your phone. If you are taken to a login web page for the Wi-Fi network's provider, you need to provide the required information to be able to use the Internet. For example, when access is free, as it is at most airports, you usually just have to indicate you accept the terms of use for that network.

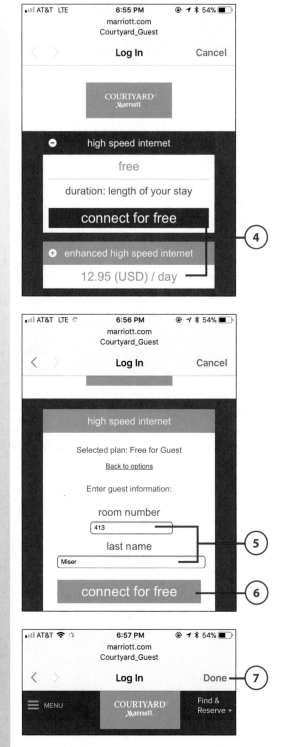

No Prompt?

Not all public networks prompt you to log in as these steps explain. Sometimes, you use the network's website to log in instead. After you join the network (step 3), your iPhone is connected to the network without any prompts. When you try to move to a web page as explained in step 8, you're prompted to log in to or create an account with the network's provider on the web page that appears.

A Closed Network

Some Wi-Fi networks are *closed*, which means they don't broadcast their names. Closed networks aren't listed in the CHOOSE A NETWORK section on the Wi-Fi screen. To be able to access a closed network, you need to know its name, its password, and the type of security it uses. With this information in hand, tap Other in the CHOOSE A NETWORK section. Then type the network's name. Tap Security, choose the appropriate type, and tap Other Network. Enter the network's password and tap Join. After you join them once, closed networks become known so you have to enter all of this information only the first time you use that network.

Disabling Automatic Prompting

When your iPhone can't find a known network—meaning one that you've used before—it presents a prompt showing you the currently available networks. You can use this prompt to select and join one of these networks. This can be useful because you don't have to use the Settings app to find a network to which you are going to connect; instead, you can just tap a network at the prompt to join it.

However, this automatic prompting for networks can be as annoying as it is helpful. It is helpful in that your iPhone prompts you when it comes into range of a network it doesn't know, which can make it easier to know when a network is available to you. It can be annoying when you are moving around a lot because what you are doing can be frequently interrupted by the prompt, even if you don't want to connect to one of the available networks. For example, when you walk through an airport, the prompt can appear multiple times as you move between networks.

To disable automatic network prompting, perform the following steps:

1. Open the Settings app and move to the Wi-Fi screen.

2. Set the Ask to Join Networks switch to off (white). To connect to unknown networks, you need to use the Settings app as described in the previous tasks because your iPhone no longer automatically prompts you to join unknown networks. (Remember that it still joins known networks, meaning those you have used before, automatically.)

Forgetting Wi-Fi Networks

As you learned earlier, your iPhone remembers networks you have joined and connects to them automatically as needed; these are known networks. Although this is mostly a good thing, there are times when you no longer want to use a particular network any more. For example, when in an airport, you might decide to connect to a network for which you have to pay for faster Internet access, or you might prefer to access the Internet using cellular service. Each time you move through that airport, your iPhone connects to that network again automatically, which might not be what you want it to do.

To have your iPhone forget a network so it doesn't automatically connect to it in the future, do the following:

1. Move to the Wi-Fi screen in the Settings app.

(**2**) Tap Info (i) for the network that you want your iPhone to forget. (You can forget a network only if you are or have previously been connected to it.)

(**3**) Tap Forget This Network.

(**4**) Tap Forget in the resulting prompt. Your iPhone stops using and forgets the network. You return to the Wi-Fi screen. If another known network is available, your iPhone connects to it automatically. If a network you've forgotten is still in range of your iPhone, it continues to appear in the CHOOSE A NETWORK section, but your iPhone no longer automatically connects to it. You can re-join a forgotten network at any time, just as you did the first time you connected to it.

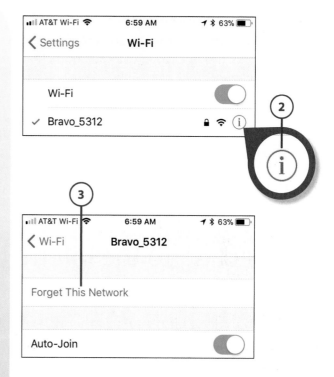

Forget Versus Auto-Join

When you forget a network, your iPhone stops connecting to it automatically and erases the network's password so you have to enter it again if you want to re-join that network. If you just want to stop automatically joining the network but keep its password on your iPhone, set the Auto-Join switch to off (white) instead of performing step 3. Your iPhone stops automatically connecting to that network, but you can re-join it at any time by tapping it on the CHOOSE A NETWORK list (you don't have to re-enter the password as you do if you forget a network).

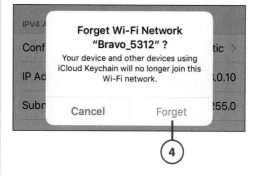

Cell Phone Provider Wi-Fi Networks

Many cell phone providers also provide other services, particularly public Wi-Fi networks. In some cases, you can access that provider's Internet service through a Wi-Fi network that it provides; often, you can do this at no additional charge. So, you can take advantage of the speed a Wi-Fi connection provides without paying more for it. You connect to these networks just like any other by selecting them on the network list. What happens next depends on the specific network. In some cases, you need to enter your mobile phone number and then respond to a text message to that phone number. Check your provider's website to find out whether it offers this service and where and how you can access it.

Connecting to the Internet Using Cellular Data Networks

When you don't have a Wi-Fi network available or you don't want to use one that is available (such as if it has a fee or is slow), your iPhone can connect to the Internet through a cellular data network.

The provider for your iPhone also provides a cellular data connection your iPhone uses to connect to the Internet automatically when you aren't using a Wi-Fi network (such as when you are in a location that doesn't have one). (Your iPhone tries to connect to an available Wi-Fi network before connecting to a cellular data connection, because Wi-Fi is typically less expensive and faster to use.) These cellular networks cover large geographic areas and the connection to them is automatic; your iPhone chooses and connects to the best cellular network currently available. Access to these networks is part of your monthly account fee; you choose from among various amounts of data (ideally, you can choose an account with unlimited data) per month for different monthly fees.

Most providers have multiple cellular data networks, such as a low-speed network that is available widely and one or more higher-speed networks that have a more limited coverage area.

The cellular data networks you can use are determined based on your provider, your data plan, the model of iPhone you are using, and your location within your provider's networks or the roaming networks available, when you are outside of your provider's coverage area. The iPhone automatically uses the fastest connection available to it at any given time (assuming you haven't disabled that option, as explained later).

In the United States, the major iPhone providers are AT&T, Sprint, T-Mobile, and Verizon. There are also other smaller providers, such as Virgin Mobile. All these companies offer high-speed Long Term Evolution (LTE) cellular networks (these are also referred to as true 4G networks) along with the slower 4G and 3G networks. In other locations, the names and speeds of the networks available might be different.

The following information is focused on LTE networks because I happen to live in the United States and use AT&T as my cell phone provider. If you use another provider, you are able to access your provider's networks similarly, though your details might be different. For example, the icon on the Home screen reflects the name of your provider's network, which might or might not be LTE.

This iPhone is connected to a high-speed LTE cellular network

LTE high-speed wireless networks provide very fast Internet access from many locations. (Note: LTE networks might not be available everywhere, but you can usually access them near populated areas.) To connect to the LTE network, you don't need to do anything. If you aren't connected to a Wi-Fi network, you haven't turned off LTE, and your iPhone isn't in Airplane mode, the iPhone automatically connects to an LTE network when available. When you are connected to the LTE network, you see the LTE indicator at the top of the iPhone's screen. If you can't access the LTE network, such as when you aren't in its coverage area, the iPhone automatically connects to the next fastest network available, such as 4G. If that isn't available, it connects to the next fastest and so on until it finds a network to which it can connect if there is one available. If it can't connect to any network, you see No Service instead of a network's name; this indicates that you currently can't connect to any network, and so you aren't able to access the Internet.

One thing you do need to keep in mind when using a cellular network is that your account might include a limited amount of data per month. When your data use exceeds this limit, you might be charged overage fees, which can be very expensive. Most providers send you warning texts or emails as your data use approaches your plan's limit, at which point you need to be careful about what you do while using the cellular data network to avoid an overage fee. Some tasks, such as watching YouTube videos or downloading large movie files, can chew up a lot of data very quickly and should be saved for when you are on a Wi-Fi network to avoid exceeding your plan's monthly data allowance. Other tasks, such as using email, typically don't use very much data.

Unlimited Data

Fortunately, most of the major providers now offer unlimited data plans for a reasonable fee. If you don't already have an account with unlimited data, check with your provider periodically to see if an unlimited data plan is available. As competition has increased among cell providers, unlimited data plans have become more common and less expensive in many areas. If other cell providers are available to you, check to see if they offer unlimited data plans; if so, you can consider changing providers or using a competitor's plan to lower the cost of your plan. Having an unlimited data plan is good because you don't need to worry about overage charges from using more data than your plan allows.

An App for That

Various apps are available in the App Store that you can install on your iPhone that monitor how much data you are using. These apps are a good way to know where your data use is relative to your plan's monthly allowance so that you can avoid an overage situation (of course, if you have an unlimited plan, you don't need to worry about it). To get information on finding, downloading, and installing apps, see the section "Using the App Store App to Find and Install iPhone Apps" in Chapter 4, "Customizing How Your iPhone Works." (To find an app for this purpose, search for "data monitoring app.")

When you move outside your primary network's geographic coverage area, you are in roaming territory, which means a different provider might provide cellular phone or data access, or both. The iPhone automatically selects a roaming provider, if there is only one available, or allows you to choose one, if there is more than one available.

When you are outside of your primary provider's coverage area, roaming charges can be associated with calls or data use. These charges are often very expensive. The roaming charges associated with phone calls are easier to manage, because it's more obvious when you make or receive a phone call in a roaming area. However, data roaming charges are much more insidious, especially if Push functionality (where emails and other updates are pushed to your iPhone from the server automatically) is active. And when you use some applications, such as Maps to navigate, you don't really know how much data is involved. Because data roaming charges are harder to notice, the iPhone is configured by default to prevent data roaming. When data roaming is disabled, the iPhone is unable to access the Internet when you are outside of your cellular network, unless you connect to a Wi-Fi network. (You can still use the cellular roaming network for telephone calls.)

You can configure some aspects of how your cellular network is used, as the following task demonstrates. You can also allow individual apps to use, or prevent them from using, your cellular data network. This is especially important when your data plan has a monthly limit (if you have an unlimited plan, you don't need to bother).

In most cases, the first time you launch an app, you're prompted to allow or prevent it from using cellular data. At any time, you can use the Cellular Data options in the Settings app to enable or disable an app's access to your cellular data network.

The options you have for configuring how your iPhone uses its cellular data connection depend on the provider your iPhone is connected to and the model of iPhone you use. For example, if you live in the United States and use Sprint as your cellular provider, the Cellular screens in the Settings app look a bit different than the figures in this section (which are based on AT&T's service). Regardless of the specific options you see on your phone, the basic purpose is the same, which is to configure how your iPhone uses its high-speed network and to enable and disable roaming.

Configuring Cellular Data Use

The following steps show configuring cellular data use on an iPhone using AT&T in the United States; you can use similar steps to configure these options on an iPhone from a different provider:

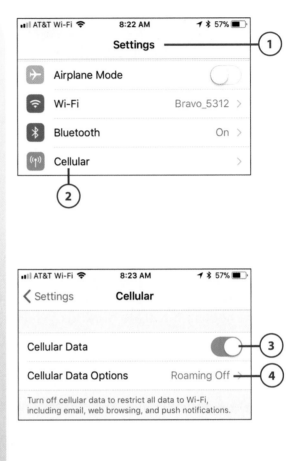

(1) Open the Settings app.

(2) Tap Cellular.

(3) To use a cellular Internet connection, set the Cellular Data switch to on (green) and move to step 4; if you don't want to use a cellular Internet connection, set this switch to off (white) and skip the rest of these steps. To use the Internet when the Cellular Data switch is off, you have to connect to a Wi-Fi network that provides Internet access.

(4) Tap Cellular Data Options.

(5) To configure the high-speed network, tap Enable *high-speed network*, where *high-speed network* is the name of the high-speed network your provider has. With some providers, this is a switch that enables or disables the high-speed network; set the switch to be on or off and skip to step 8 (if you set the switch to off, the iPhone can't use the higher-speed network, but can use slower networks).

More Cellular Data Control

You can quickly turn cellular data on or off from the Control Center. For example, if you want to stop using cellular data (perhaps you are reaching the cap of your cellular data plan), you can open the Control Center and tap the Cellular Data icon to disable cellular data use. Tap the icon again to enable it. (When the icon is green, cellular data is enabled.)

(6) To disable the high-speed network, tap Off; to use it for both voice and data, tap Voice & Data; or to use it only for data, tap Data Only. (When you enable the high-speed network for voice, the quality of the sound of your calls might be better.)

(7) Tap the Back icon (<).

(8) If you want to allow data roaming, slide the Data Roaming switch to the on (green) position. With some providers, Roaming is an option instead of a switch; tap Roaming and use the resulting switches to enable or disable roaming for voice or data and then tap the Back icon (<). You should usually leave Data Roaming off so that you don't unknowingly start using roaming (which can lead to high fees) should you be moving around a lot. You can then enable it as needed so you know exactly when roaming is on.

(9) Tap the Back icon (<).

(10) Use the controls in the *PROVIDER* section, where *PROVIDER* is the name of your provider, to configure how the cellular service interacts with other services, such as to enable Wi-Fi calling, calls on other devices, and so on. These settings are explained in Chapter 7, "Communicating with the Phone and FaceTime Apps."

(7)

AT&T Wi-Fi 🛜	8:23 AM ✈ ✶ 56% 🔋
<	**Enable LTE**

Off

Voice & Data **(6)**

Data Only

Using LTE can load data faster and improve voice quality.

(9)

AT&T Wi-Fi 🛜	8:23 AM ✈ ✶ 56% 🔋
< Cellular	

Enable LTE   Voice & Data >

Data Roaming   ⚪ **(8)**

(10)

AT&T Wi-Fi 🛜	8:23 AM ✈ ✶ 56% 🔋
< Settings	**Cellular**

AT&T

Wi-Fi Calling   On >

Calls on Other Devices   On >

Carrier Services   >

Set Up Personal Hotspot

Share your iPhone internet connection with your computer and iOS devices via Wi-Fi, Bluetooth, or USB.

11 Swipe up the screen until you see the CELLULAR DATA section. This section enables you to allow or prevent individual apps from accessing a cellular data network. To limit the amount of data you use, it's a good idea to review this list and allow only those apps that you rely on to use the cellular data network. (Of course, if you are fortunate enough to have an unlimited cellular data plan, you can leave cellular data for all the apps enabled.) This list can be quite long if you have a lot of apps stored on your iPhone.

12 Set an app's switch to on (green) if you want it to be able to use a cellular data network to access the Internet.

13 Set an app's switch to off (white) if you want it to be able to access the Internet only when you are connected to a Wi-Fi network.

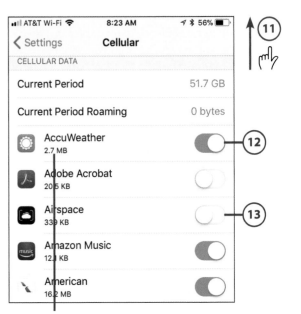

Amount of data the app has used since last reset

14 Set the Wi-Fi Assist switch to on (green) if you want your iPhone to automatically switch to its cellular connection when the Wi-Fi connection is weak. If you have a limited cellular data plan, you might want to set this switch to off (white) to minimize cellular data use. If you have an unlimited plan, you should leave this on.

15 If you want to access files on your iCloud drive when you aren't using a Wi-Fi network, set the iCloud Drive switch to on (green). If you set this switch to off, files are synced the next time you connect to a Wi-Fi network. Like the other areas, if you have an unlimited data plan, you can leave this enabled, but if you do have a limit, you might want to disable it.

•ıll AT&T Wi-Fi 🛜	8:24 AM	➹ ✳ 56% ▬

‹ Settings　　　**Cellular**

806 MB

System Services　　　　　　23.7 GB >

Uninstalled Apps　　　　　　139 KB

Wi-Fi Assist　　　　　　　　　⬤━━ **14**
81.7 MB

Automatically use cellular data when Wi-Fi connectivity is poor.

iCloud Drive　　　　　　　　　⬤━━ **15**

When not connected to Wi-Fi, use cellular network to transfer documents and data.

CALL TIME

Current Period　　　　　2 Days, 22 Hours

Lifetime　　　　　　　　2 Days, 23 Hours

Reset Statistics

Last Reset: Sep 25, 2016 at 4:58 AM

>>>Go Further
MORE ON CELLULAR DATA

Using a cellular network to connect to the Internet means you seldom have to be without a connection unless you choose to be. Here are some things to keep in mind as you keep connected:

- **Unlimited data but limited speed**—Under an unlimited data plan, some providers limit the speed at which your cellular data service operates if you pass a threshold amount of data used that month. You can continue to use all the data you want, but the performance of the connection might be slower. Check your plan's details to see what the threshold is and what speed reduction is applied. You probably won't hit that threshold unless you watch a lot of video on your phone, but it's good to be aware of such limitations on your account.

- **GSM versus CDMA**—There are two fundamental types of cellular networks, which are GSM (Global System for Mobile Communications) or CDMA (Code-Division Multiple Access). The cellular provider you use determines which type of network your iPhone uses; the two types are not compatible. GSM is used by most of the world whereas some very large carriers in the United States (such as Verizon and Sprint) use CDMA. There are differences between the two, which is why you might see different cellular options than shown in the figures here (which show the options for AT&T, which uses GSM). If your iPhone uses CDMA, you see the International CDMA switch on the Roaming screen. If your phone has poor performance when you are roaming in different countries, set this switch to off (white).

- **Cellular data usage**—In the Cellular Data section, you see how much data you've used for the current period and how much you've used while roaming. This can help you see where your use is compared to your monthly plan allowance (if you have a monthly plan allowance of course) so you know whether you are getting close to exceeding that allowance (thus incurring overage charges). This isn't proactive at all, as you have to remember to check the information. If you are concerned about data use, you're better off getting an app with more active monitoring, as discussed earlier in this chapter in the "An App for That" note.

  If you tap System Services, you see the data usage for core system functions, such as Time & Location, Messaging Services, and Siri. This can be useful information to see how much data these services use, especially when you are in a roaming situation. You can limit the data use by some of these services by not accessing the related function; for example, you can turn off Siri to prevent it from using cellular data.

- **Higher-speed networks use more power**—Using a higher-speed network, such as an LTE network, also uses somewhat more battery power than using a slower network. If getting the absolute maximum time on a charge is important, you might want to disable the high-speed network.

- **Apps' cellular data use**—Just under each app's name in the CELLULAR DATA section, you see how much data the app has used since the counter was reset. This number can help you determine how much data a particular app uses. For example, if an app's use is shown in megabytes (MB), it's used a lot more data than an app whose use is shown in kilobytes (KB).

- **Cellular data use reset**—You can reset all of the statistics on the Cellular screen by swiping up until you reach the bottom of the screen and tapping Reset Statistics. Tap Reset Statistics again.

- **Personal hotspot**—The iPhone can be a personal hotspot, which is when it provides an Internet connection to computers or other devices through its cellular data connection. This is useful when you are in a location where you can't connect a computer or other device to a Wi-Fi or cellular network with Internet access (or don't want to spend the money to do so) but can access the Internet with the iPhone's cellular data connection.

  There are a lot of caveats to this service, including whether your provider offers it, additional costs, and so on. Check with your provider to see if the personal hotspot feature is supported and if there are additional fees to use it. If it is provided and the fees are acceptable, this is a good way to provide Internet access to other devices when a Wi-Fi or cellular connection either isn't available or is too expensive.

  First, add the personal hotspot service to your cellular account. Second, move to the Cellular screen in the Settings app, and then tap Set Up Personal Hotspot or Personal Hotspot (if you don't see either option, your provider doesn't offer personal hotspot service). Follow the onscreen prompts to complete the configuration of the personal hotspot; the details depend on the specific provider you are using. After your iPhone is configured as a hotspot, it can share its Internet connection with other devices. To allow access to the Internet through your phone's hotspot, provide the name of its network and password (which are both automatically generated when you enable the hotspot) to the people you want to allow to use your hotspot.

Securing Your iPhone

Even though you won't often be connecting a cable to it, an iPhone is a connected device, meaning that it sends information to and receives information from other devices, either directly or via the Internet, during many different activities. Some are obvious, such as sending text messages or browsing the Web, whereas others might not be so easy to spot, such as when an app is determining your iPhone's location. Whenever data is exchanged between your iPhone and other devices, there is always a chance your information will get intercepted by someone you didn't intend or that someone will access your iPhone without you knowing about it.

The good news is that with some simple precautions, the chances of someone obtaining your information or infiltrating your iPhone are quite small (much less than the chance of someone obtaining your credit card number when you use it in public places, for example). Following are some good ways to protect the information you are using on your iPhone:

- Always have a passcode on your iPhone so it can't be unlocked without entering the passcode. Configuring a passcode is explained in Chapter 4.

- Use Face ID (X models) or Touch ID (non-X models) to make entering your passcode and passwords much easier and more secure. Configuring Face ID and Touch ID are also explained in Chapter 4.

- Never let someone you don't know or trust use your iPhone, even if he needs it "just for a second to look something up." If you get a request like that, look up the information for the person and show him rather than letting him touch your iPhone.

- Learn how to use the Find My iPhone feature in case you lose or someone steals your iPhone. This is explained in the Chapter 16, "Maintaining and Protecting Your iPhone and Solving Problems," on this book's website (see the back cover for the information you need to access it).

- Never respond to an email that you aren't expecting that directs you to click a link to verify your account. If you haven't requested some kind of change, such as signing up for a new service, virtually all such requests are scams, seeking to get your account information, such as username and password, or your identification, such as full name and Social Security number. And many of these scam attempts look like email from actual organizations. For example, I receive many of these emails that claim, and sometimes even look like, they are from Apple. However, Apple doesn't request updates to account information using a link in an email unless you have made some kind of change, such as registering a new email address for iMessages. Legitimate organizations never include links in an email to update account information when you haven't requested or made any changes.

  To reinforce this concept, there are two types of requests for verification you might receive via email. The legitimate type is sent to you after you sign up for a new service, such as creating a new account on a website, to confirm that the email address you provided is correct and that you are really you. If you make changes to an existing account, you might also receive confirmation request emails. You should respond to these requests to finish the configuration of your account.

If you receive a request for account verification, but you haven't done anything with the organization from which you received the request, don't respond to it. For example, if you receive a request that appears to be from Apple, PayPal, or other organizations, but you haven't made any changes to your account, the email request is bogus and is an attempt to scam you. Likewise, if you have never done anything with the organization apparently sending the email, it is also definitely an attempt to scam you.

If you have any doubt, contact the organization sending the request before responding to the email.

- If you need to change or update account information, you can go directly to the related website using an address that you type in or have saved as a bookmark using the Safari app. This protects you because it ensures you can move directly to the legitimate website rather than clicking a link that might take you to a fraudulent website.

- Be aware that when you use a Wi-Fi network in a public place, such as a coffee shop, hotel, or airport, there is a chance that the information you send over that network might be intercepted by others. The risk of this is usually quite small, but you need to be aware that there is always some level of risk. To have the lowest risk, don't use apps that involve sensitive information, such as an online banking app, when you are using a Wi-Fi network in a public place.

- If you don't know how to do it, have someone who really knows what they are doing set up a wireless network in your home. Wireless networks need to be configured properly, so they are secure. Your home's Wi-Fi network should require a password to join.

- For the least risk, only use your home's Wi-Fi network (that has been configured properly) or your cellular data connection (you can turn Wi-Fi off when you aren't home) for sensitive transactions, such as accessing bank accounts or other financial information.

- Never accept a request to share information from someone you don't know. In the Chapter 15, "Working with Other Useful iPhone Apps and Features," you learn about AirDrop, which enables you to easily share photos and lots of other things with other people using iOS devices. If you receive an AirDrop request from someone you don't recognize, always decline it. In fact, if you have any doubt, decline such requests. It's much easier for someone legitimate to confirm with you and resend a request than it is for you to recover from damage that can be done if you inadvertently accept a request from someone you don't know.

- Only download apps through Apple's App Store through the App Store app on your iPhone. Fortunately, the way the iPhone is set up, you have to do something very unusual to install apps outside of the App Store. As long as you download apps only as described in this book, you are free of apps that can harm your information because Apple has strict controls over the apps that make it into the App Store. (Downloading apps is explained in Chapter 4.

Reality Check

Internet security is a complex topic, and it can be troublesome to think about. It's best to keep in mind the relative level of risk when you use your iPhone compared to other risks in the physical world that most of us don't think twice about. For example, every time you hand your credit card to someone, there is a chance that that person will record the number and use it without your knowledge or permission. Even when you swipe a credit card in a reader, such as at a gas station, that information is communicated across multiple networks and can be intercepted. (For example, there have been numerous compromises of credit card information at a number of well-known retailers.) If you take basic precautions like those described here, the risks to you when you are using your iPhone are similar to or less than the other risks we all face in everyday life.

My recommendation is to take the basic precautions, and then don't worry about it overly much. It is a good idea to have identity theft insurance in case your information is compromised, which can happen whether you use an iPhone or don't use one. Try to find an insurance company that assigns someone to do the work of recovering for you should your identity be stolen because that can be very time-consuming and difficult.

Working with Text

You can do lots of things with an iPhone that require you to provide text input, such as writing emails, sending text messages, and so on. There are a couple of ways you can enter text, the most obvious of which is by typing. The iPhone's keyboard is quite amazing. Whenever you need it, whether it's for emailing, messaging, entering a website URL, performing a search, or any other typing function, it pops up automatically.

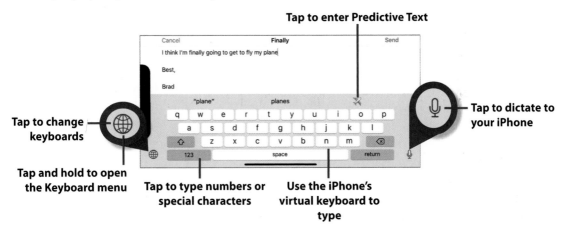

Tap to enter Predictive Text

Tap to change keyboards

Tap to dictate to your iPhone

Tap and hold to open the Keyboard menu

Tap to type numbers or special characters

Use the iPhone's virtual keyboard to type

To type, just tap the keys. As you tap each key, you hear audio feedback (you can disable this sound if you want to) and the key you tapped pops up in a magnified view on the screen. The keyboard includes all the standard keys, plus a few for special uses. To change from letters to numbers and special characters, just tap the 123 key. Tap the #+= key to see more special characters. Tap the 123 key to move back to the numbers and special characters or the ABC key to return to letters. The keyboard also has contextual keys that appear when you need them. For example, when you enter a website address, the .com key appears so you can enter these four characters with a single tap.

Working with Predictive Text

You can also use Predictive Text, which is the feature that tries to predict text you want to enter based on the context of what you are currently typing and what you have typed before. Predictive Text appears in the bar between the text and the keyboard and presents you with three options. If one of those is what you want to enter, tap it and it is added to the text at the current location of the cursor. If you want to enter the middle option, tap the Space key; that word is entered followed by a space so you can keep typing. If you don't see an option you want to enter, keep typing and the options change as the text changes. You can tap an option at any time to enter it. The nice thing about Predictive Text is that it gets better at predicting your text needs over time. In other words, the more you use it, the better it gets at predicting what you want to type. And, it can even suggest phrases based on what you are typing; tap the phrase to enter it. You can enable or disable Predictive Text, as you see shortly.

Predictive Text Need Not Apply

When you are entering text where Predictive Text doesn't apply, such as when you are typing email addresses, the Predictive Text bar is hidden and can't be enabled. This makes sense because there's no way text in things such as email address-es can be predicted. When you move back into an area where it does apply, Predictive Text becomes active again.

Working with Keyboards

The great thing about a virtual keyboard like the iPhone has is that it can change to reflect the language or symbols you want to type. As you learn in Chapter 4, you can install multiple keyboards, such as one for your primary language and more for your secondary languages. You can also install third-party keyboards to take advantage of their features (this is also covered in Chapter 4).

By default, two keyboards are available for you to use. One is for the primary lan-guage configured for your iPhone (for example, mine is U.S. English). The other is the Emoji keyboard (more on this shortly). How you change the keyboard you are using depends on whether you have installed additional keyboards and the orientation of the iPhone.

If you haven't installed additional keyboards, you can change keyboards by tap-ping the Emoji key, which has a smiley face on it.

If you have installed other keyboards, you change keyboards by tapping the Globe key.

Each time you tap this key (Globe if available, Emoji if there isn't a Globe), the keyboard changes to be the next keyboard installed; along with the available keys changing, you briefly see the name of the current keyboard in the Space bar. When you have cycled through all the keyboards, you return to the one where you started. If you have only two keyboards installed, such as one for your main language and the Emoji keyboard, tap the Emoji icon (the smiley face) to use emojis or the ABC key to enter letters and numbers.

The Keys, They Are A-Changin'

The keys on the keyboard can change depending on the orientation of the iPhone. For example, when you have more than one keyboard installed and hold the iPhone vertically, the Emoji key disappears and you see only the Globe key. Not to worry though, you can still get to the Emoji keyboard by tapping the Globe key until the Emoji keyboard appears, or by opening the Keyboard menu and tapping Emoji. When you have installed additional keyboards and hold an iPhone Plus horizontally, you see both the Globe and Emoji keys. Tap the Emoji key to switch to that keyboard or the Globe key to cycle through all the keyboards.

Tap to configure keyboards and text options

Tap a keyboard to use it

You can also select the specific keyboard you want to use and access keyboard and text options by touching and holding on the Globe key (or the Emoji key, if you don't see the Globe key). The Keyboard menu appears. Tap a keyboard to switch to it. Tap Keyboard Settings to jump to the Keyboards screen in the Settings app where you can configure keyboards and enable or disable text options (these settings are covered in Chapter 4).

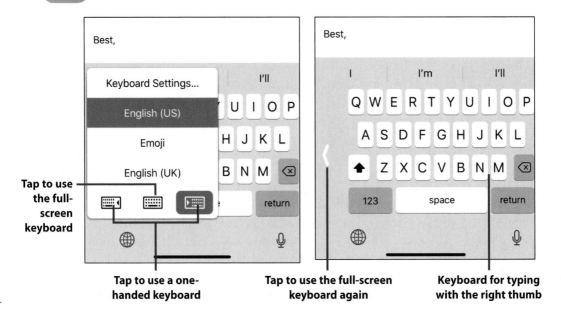

Tap to use the full-screen keyboard

Tap to use a one-handed keyboard

Tap to use the full-screen keyboard again

Keyboard for typing with the right thumb

Because you often type on your iPhone while you are moving around, it has a one-handed keyboard (this needs to be enabled via the Keyboard settings covered in Chapter 4). This keyboard "squishes" all the keys to the left or right side of the screen to suit typing with a thumb. To use a one-handed keyboard, touch and hold the Globe or Emoji key to open the keyboard menu (this only works when the iPhone is held vertically). Tap the left or right keyboard; the keyboard compresses toward the side you selected and you can more easily tap its keys with one thumb. To return to the full-screen keyboard, tap the right- or left-facing arrow that appears in the "empty" space on the side of the screen not being used for the keyboard or open the Keyboard menu and tap the full-screen keyboard.

Using Emojis

Tap an emoji to enter it ──

Swipe to browse emojis

Tap to return to the previous keyboard

Tap to see emojis you've used frequently

Tap to see groups of emojis

Emojis are icons you insert into your text to liven things up, communicate your feelings, or just to have some fun (if you don't have this keyboard installed, see Chapter 4). You can open the Emoji keyboard by tapping its key (the smiley face), by tapping the Globe until it appears, or by selecting it on the Keyboard menu. You see a palette containing many emojis, organized into groups. You can change the groups of emojis you are browsing by tapping the icons at the bottom of the screen. Swipe to the left or right on the emojis to browse the emojis in the current group. Tap an emoji to enter it at the cursor's location in your message, email, or other type of document. To use an emoji you've used often, tap the Clock icon to see emojis you've used frequently; you'll probably find that you use this set of emojis regularly so this can save a lot of time. To return to the mundane world of letters and symbols, tap the ABC key.

Predictive Text suggests emojis too

The Predictive Text feature also suggests emojis when you type certain words; just tap the emoji to replace the word with it.

Emoji Options

If you tap and hold on some emojis, you see options. For example, if you tap and hold on the thumbs-up emoji, you see a menu with the emoji in different flesh tones. Slide your finger over the menu and tap the version you want to use. The version you select becomes the new default for that emoji. You can go back to a previous version by opening the menu and selecting it.

Emojis Galore

Emojis are very widely used in text messages because you can communicate a lot with a single icon. The Messages app enables you to access many kinds of emojis through the apps you can install within the Messages app itself; these are often called stickers, but they work the same way as emojis. See Chapter 9, "Sending, Receiving, and Managing Texts and iMessages," to learn how to add and use sticker apps within the Messages app.

What's Your Typing Orientation?

Like many other tasks, you can rotate the iPhone to change the screen's orientation while you type. When the iPhone is in the horizontal orientation, the keyboard is wider, making it easier to tap individual keys, and you have access to more keys. However, you see fewer lines of text. When the iPhone is in vertical orientation, the keyboard is narrower, but you can see more of the typing area. So, try both to see which mode is most effective for you.

Correcting Spelling as You Type

If you type a word that the iPhone doesn't recognize, that word is flagged as a possible mistake and suggestions are made to help you correct it. How this happens depends on whether or not Predictive Text is enabled.

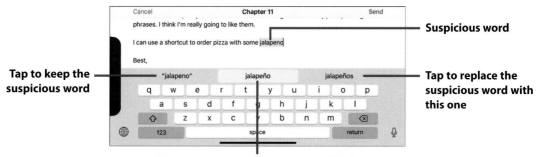

Suspicious word

Tap to keep the suspicious word

Tap to replace the suspicious word with this one

If you tap the space key, the suspicious word is replaced with this one

If Predictive Text is enabled, potential replacements for suspicious words appear in the Predictive Text bar. When you tap the space key, the suspicious word is replaced with the word in the center of the Predictive Text bar. Tap the word on the far left to keep what you've typed (because it isn't a mistake) or tap the word on the right end of the bar to enter it instead of what you've typed.

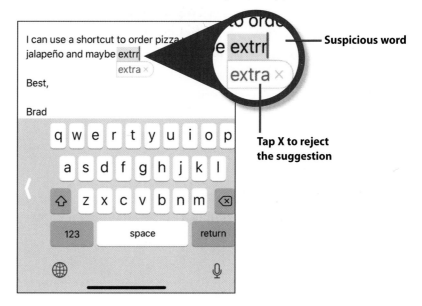

Suspicious word

Tap X to reject the suggestion

If Predictive Text isn't enabled, a suspicious word is highlighted and a suggestion about what it thinks is the correct word appears in a pop-up box. To accept the suggestion, tap the space key. To reject the suggestion, tap the x in the pop-up box to close it and keep what you typed. You can also use this feature for short-hand typing. For example, to type "I've" you can simply type "Ive" and iPhone suggests "I've," which you can accept by tapping the space key.

Typing Tricks

Many keys, especially symbols and punctuation, have additional characters. To see a character's options, tap it and hold down. If it has options, a menu pops up after a second or so. To enter one of the optional characters, drag over the menu until the one you want to enter is highlighted, and then lift your finger off the screen. The optional character you selected is entered. For example, if you tap and hold on the period when you are writing text, you can select an ellipsis (…). If you tap and hold on the period when you are typing a web or email address, you can select .com, .edu, so on.

Your Own Text Replacements

You can create your own text shortcuts so you can type something like "eadd" and it is automatically replaced with your email address. See Chapter 4 for the details.

By default, the iPhone attempts to correct the capitalization of what you type. It also automatically selects the Shift key when you start a new sentence, start a new paragraph, or in other places where its best guess is that you need a capital letter. If you don't want to enter a capital character, simply tap the Shift key before you type. You can enable the Caps Lock key by tapping the Shift key twice. When the Caps Lock key is highlighted (the upward-facing arrow is black), everything you type is in uppercase letters.

Options, Options

Using the Keyboards screen in the Settings app, you can enable or disable text-related functions, such as Auto-Capitalization. See Chapter 4 for details.

Editing Text

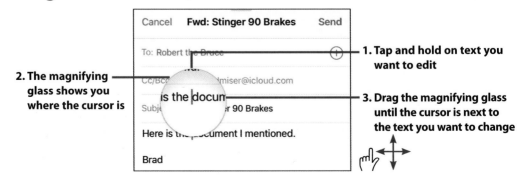

1. Tap and hold on text you want to edit

2. The magnifying glass shows you where the cursor is

3. Drag the magnifying glass until the cursor is next to the text you want to change

To edit text you've typed, touch and hold on the area containing the text you want to edit. A magnifying glass icon appears on the screen, and within it you see a magnified view of the location of the cursor. Drag the magnifying glass to position the cursor where you want to start making changes, and then lift your finger from the screen. The cursor remains in that location, and you can use the keyboard to make changes to the text or to add text at that location, or you can make a selection on the menu that appears.

Using 3D Touch with Text

When you are using an iPhone that supports 3D Touch (6s and later models), you can apply slight pressure when you touch the screen to have the closest word selected automatically; it is highlighted in blue to show you that it is selected. To place the cursor without selecting words that are near your finger, just touch the screen without applying any pressure.

Selecting, Copying, Cutting, or Pasting Text

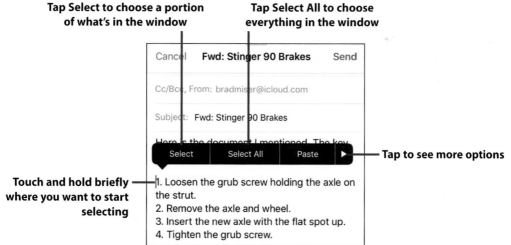

You can also select text or images to copy and paste the selected content into a new location or to replace that content. Touch and hold down briefly where you want to start the selection until the magnifying glass icon appears; then lift your finger off the screen. The Select menu appears. Tap Select to select part of the content on the screen, or tap Select All to select everything in the current window.

More Commands

Some menus that appear when you are making selections and performing actions have a right-facing arrow at the right end. Tap this to see a new menu that contains additional commands. These commands are contextual, meaning that you see different commands depending on what you are doing at that specific time. You can tap the left-facing arrow to move back to a previous menu.

Cancel   **Fwd: Stinger 90 Brakes**   Send

Cc/Bcc, From: bradmiser@icloud.com

Subject: Fwd: Stinger 90 Brakes

Here is the document I mentioned. The key

| Cut | Copy | Paste | Replace... | ▶ |

The blue markers indicate where the selection starts and stops

1. Loosen the grub screw holding the axle on the strut.
2. Remove the axle and wheel.
3. Insert the new axle with the flat spot up.
4. Tighten the grub screw.

Selected text

You see markers indicating where the selection starts and stops. (The iPhone attempts to select something logical, such as the word or sentence.) New commands appear on the menu; these provide actions for the text currently selected.

Cancel   **Fwd: Stinger 90 Brakes**   Send

Cc/Bcc, From: bradmiser@icloud.com

Subject: Fwd: Stinger 90 Brakes

Here is the document I mentioned. The key
steps are:

Magnified view of what you are selecting

1. Loosen the grub screw holding the axle on the strut.
2. Remove the axl **screw.**
3. Insert the new axle with the flat spot up.
4. Tighten the grub screw.

Drag the markers so that they enclose what you want to select

Selected text (in blue)

Drag the two markers so that the content you want to select is between them; the selected portion is highlighted in blue. As you drag, you see a magnified view of where the selection marker is, which helps you place it more accurately. When the selection markers are located correctly, lift your finger from the screen. (If you tapped the Select All command, you don't need to do this because the content you want is already selected.)

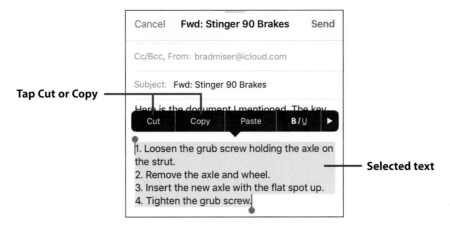

Tap Cut or Copy

Selected text

Tap Cut to remove the content from the current window, or tap Copy to just copy it.

Have I Got a Suggestion for You!

As you select different items, explore the menu to see commands that might be useful to you. These commands are contextual so they change based on what you have selected. For example, when you have a word or phrase selected, one of the suggestions might be Look Up, which opens Siri Suggestions for the word or phrase you selected. The results can include dictionary or Wikipedia entries, suggested apps, and so on. Tap Done to return to the text with which you were working. As you use your iPhone, check out the options on this menu because you'll find some very useful tricks tucked away there.

Format It!

If you tap **B**/U on the menu, you can tap Bold, Italics, or Underline to apply those formatting options to the selected text. You also can tap multiple format options to apply them at the same time. You might need to tap the right-facing arrow at the end of the menu to see this command, depending on how many commands are on the menu.

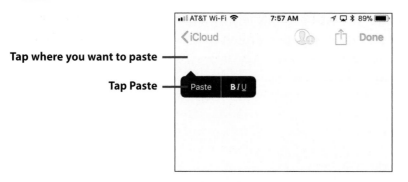

Tap where you want to paste ——

Tap Paste ——

Move to where you want to paste the content you selected; for example, use the App Switcher to change to a different app. Tap where you want the content to be pasted. For a more precise location, tap and hold and then use the magnifying glass icon to move to a specific location. Lift your finger off the screen and the menu appears. Then tap Paste.

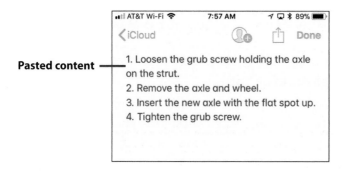

Pasted content ——

The content you copied or cut appears where you placed the cursor.

Correcting Spelling After You've Typed

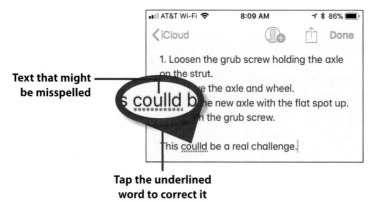

Text that might be misspelled ——

Tap the underlined word to correct it

The iPhone also has a spell-checking feature that comes into play after you have entered text (as opposed to the Predictive Text and autocorrect/suggests features that change text as you type it). When you've entered text the iPhone doesn't recognize, it is underlined in red.

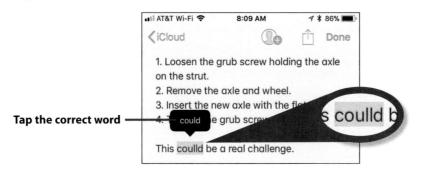

Tap the correct word

Tap the underlined word. It is shaded in red to show you what is being checked, and a menu appears with one or more replacements that might be the correct spelling. If one of the options is the one you want, tap it. The incorrect word is replaced with the one you tapped.

Contextual Menus and You

In some apps, tapping a word causes a menu with other kinds of actions to appear; you can tap an action to make it happen. For example, in the iBooks app, when you tap a word, the resulting menu enables you to look up the word in a dictionary. Other apps support different kinds of actions, so it's a good idea to try tapping words in apps that involve text to see which commands are available.

Undo

The iPhone has a somewhat hidden undo command. To undo what you've just done, such as typing text, gently shake your phone back and forth a couple of times. An Undo Typing prompt appears on the screen. Tap Undo to undo the last thing you did or tap Cancel if you activated the undo command accidentally.

Dictating Text

You can also enter text by dictating it. This is a fast and easy way to type, and you'll be amazed at how accurate the iPhone is at translating your speech into typed words. Dictation is available almost anywhere you need to enter text. (Exceptions are passcodes and passwords, such as for your Apple ID.)

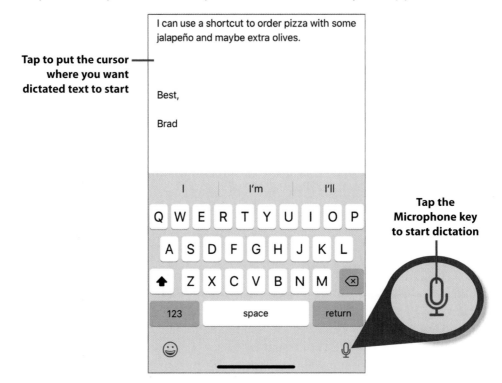

Tap to put the cursor where you want dictated text to start

Tap the Microphone key to start dictation

To start dictating, tap the Microphone key. The iPhone goes into Dictation mode. A gray bar appears at the bottom of the window. As the iPhone "hears" you, the line oscillates.

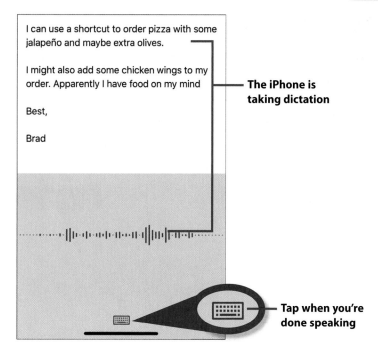

I can use a shortcut to order pizza with some jalapeño and maybe extra olives.

I might also add some chicken wings to my order. Apparently I have food on my mind

Best,

Brad

The iPhone is taking dictation

Tap when you're done speaking

Start speaking the text you want the iPhone to type. As you speak, the text is entered starting from the location of the cursor. Speak punctuation when you want to enter it. For example, when you reach the end of a sentence, say "period," or to enter a colon say "colon." To start a new paragraph, say "new paragraph."

jalapeño and maybe extra olives.

I might also add some chicken wings to my order. Apparently I have food on my mind!

Best,

Brad

The text you spoke

When you've finished dictating, tap the keyboard icon. The keyboard reappears and you see the text you spoke. This feature is amazingly accurate and can be a much faster and more convenient way to enter text than typing it.

You can edit the text you dictated just like text you typed using the keyboard.

Drawing in Text

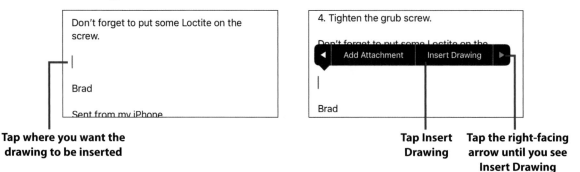

Tap where you want the drawing to be inserted

Tap Insert Drawing

Tap the right-facing arrow until you see Insert Drawing

You can use the iOS drawing tool to create and insert drawings that include shapes, text, colors, and other elements into places where you create text, such as emails. Tap in the window where you want the drawing to be. On the menu, tap the right-facing arrow until you see Insert Drawing and then tap that command.

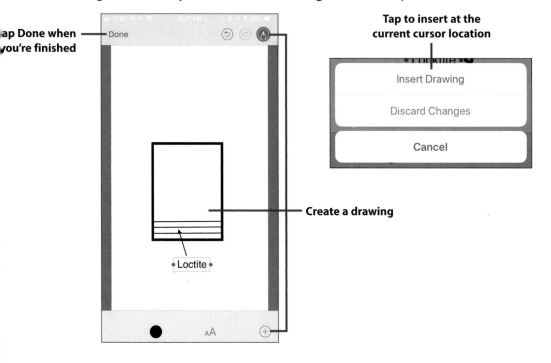

Tap Done when you're finished

Tap to insert at the current cursor location

Create a drawing

Use the drawing tool to create the drawing. Tap Add (+) to add shapes, lines, or text. Tap text to edit it. Tap Signature to sign your name. You can tap objects to select them to move or change them. You can use the format tools (color and font) to format objects. When you're done, tap Done. Then tap Insert Drawing to place the drawing where the cursor was located.

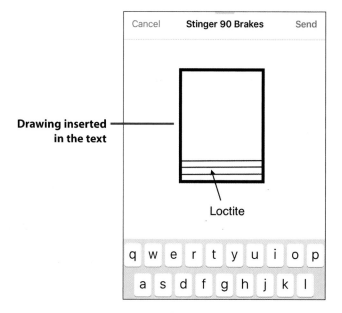

Drawing inserted in the text

When you move back to the text, you see the drawing you created. You can then complete what you were doing, such as finishing and sending an email message.

Using Widgets

Widgets are "mini" versions of apps installed on your iPhone that you can access easily and quickly from the Widget Center.

Swipe all the way to the right to open the Widget Center

You can open the Widget Center in a number of ways:

- Wake your iPhone and swipe to the right on the Lock screen.

- Move to a Home page and swipe all the way to the right.

- Swipe down the screen to open the Notification Center and then swipe to the right.

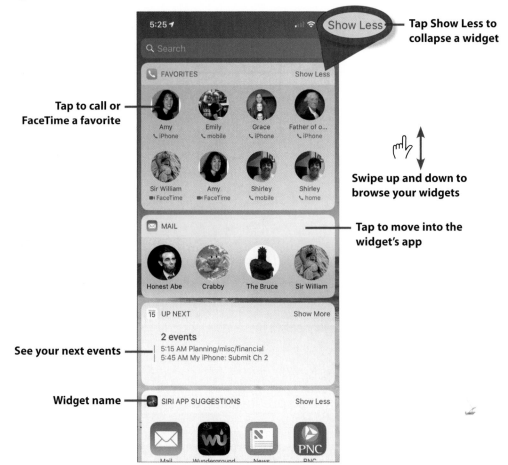

At the top of the Widget Center, you see the Search tool (more on this later). If you open the Widget Center from the Lock screen, you see the current time and date under the Search tool; if you open it from a Home screen, you don't see the date or time. Beneath that, you see widgets for apps installed on your iPhone. Swipe up and down the screen to browse your widgets.

Configuring the Widget Center

You can choose the widgets that appear in the Widget Center and the order in which those widgets are shown on the screen. See "Configuring the Widget Center" in Chapter 4 for the step-by-step instructions to configure your Widget Center.

Each widget provides information or functions based on its app. For example, you can use the FAVORITES widget to place phone calls using the Phone app or to make FaceTime calls to your contacts you've designated as Favorites (you learn how to do this in Chapter 7). You can see your daily calendar in the CALENDAR widget, get news in the NEWS widget, or listen to music in the MUSIC widget.

You can expand a widget to show all of its information or tools by tapping the Show More command or collapse it to a more minimal state by tapping the Show Less command.

You can interact with widgets in several ways. Some widgets provide information that you can view within the widget, such as CALENDAR, STOCKS, or UP NEXT. Some apps provide options you can tap to perform specific actions; these include FAVORITES and MUSIC. When you tap something within a widget, the associated app opens and either performs the task you indicated or shows more information about what you selected.

Some apps even have multiple widgets. For example, the Calendar app has the UP NEXT widget that shows you the next events on your calendar and the CALENDAR widget that shows the events on the current date.

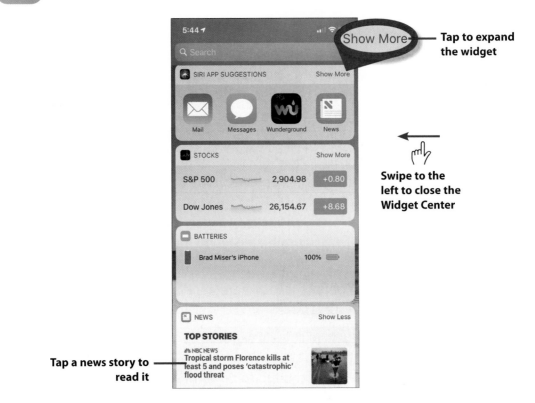

Tap to expand the widget

Swipe to the left to close the Widget Center

Tap a news story to read it

If you don't move into an app from a widget, you can close the Widget Center by swiping to the left. You move back to the screen you came from, such as a Home screen. If you do move into an app from a widget, you work with that app just as if you moved into it from a Home screen.

Searching on Your iPhone

You can use the Search tool to search your iPhone to find many different types of information, including locations, emails, messages, apps, and so on.

Swipe down from the center part of the screen to search your iPhone

There are a couple of ways you can start a search:

- Swipe to the right to open the Widget Center. The Search bar is at the top of the screen.

- On a Home screen, swipe down from the center of the screen. The Search bar appears at the top of the screen.

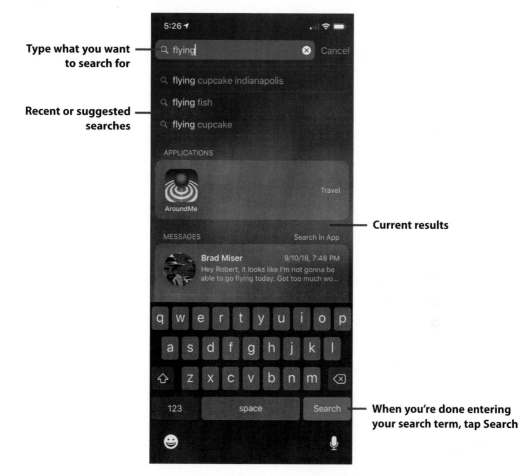

Type what you want to search for

Recent or suggested searches

Current results

When you're done entering your search term, tap Search

To perform a search, tap in the Search bar and type the search term using the onscreen keyboard. As you type, recent or suggested searches appear just below the Search bar; tap a search to perform it. Under the search list, you see the current items that match your search. If you don't tap one of the recent or suggested searches, when you finish typing the search term, tap Search to see the full list of results.

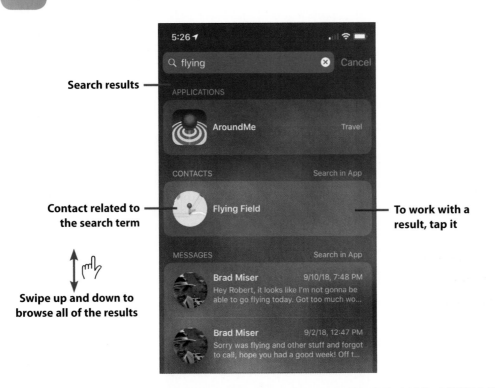

Search results

Contact related to the search term

To work with a result, tap it

Swipe up and down to browse all of the results

The results are organized into sections, such as CONTACTS, MAIL, MESSAGES, APPLICATIONS, MAPS, MUSIC, and so on. Swipe up and down the screen to browse all of the results. To work with an item you find, such as to view a location you found, tap it; you move to a screen showing more information or into the associated app and see the search result that you tapped.

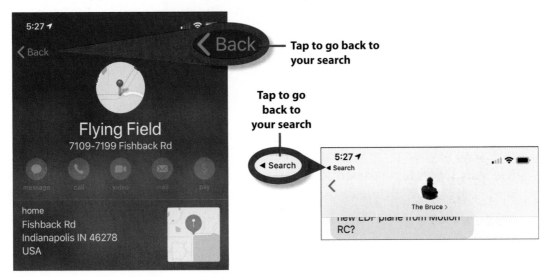

Tap to go back to your search

Tap to go back to your search

The results remain in the Search tool as you work with them. To move back to the search results, tap the Back icon (<) in the upper-left corner of the screen or tap Search (which you see depends on the result you tapped on).

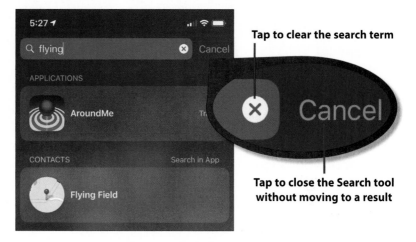

Tap to clear the search term

Tap to close the Search tool without moving to a result

The results of the most recent search are still listed. To clear the search term, tap Clear (x). To close the Spotlight tool without going to one of the results, tap Cancel.

Tell Me More

If one of the categories you find in a search has a lot of entries, you see the Show More command. Tap this to show more of the results for that category. Tap Show Less to collapse the category again. When you can search within an app, you see the Search in App text on the right side of the screen aligned with the results section; tap this to open the app and perform the search within that app.

Working with Siri Suggestions

Siri Suggestions can make it easy to get back to apps, searches, or other items you've used recently. Using Siri Suggestions can also lead you to useful things you weren't necessarily looking for. These suggestions show up in many different areas on your iPhone and you can access them directly at any time.

Swipe down from the center part of the screen to see Siri Suggestions

Tap to open an app

To access Siri Suggestions, swipe down from the center of a Home screen. Just under the Search bar, you see the SIRI SUGGESTIONS panel. This panel shows you apps you've used recently or apps that might be useful to you based on your location. For example, the Starbucks app may be suggested when you are near a Starbucks location. Tap an app to open it.

There's a Widget for That

You can also use the SIRI APP SUGGESTIONS widget in the Widget Center to quickly access recently used or suggested apps.

Siri Suggestions can also appear in other apps. Siri monitors your activity and "learns" from what you do in order to improve the suggestions it makes. These suggestions can appear in many different places, such as when you are entering email addresses in a new email, dealing with new contact information, performing searches, editing a text message, and so on. When you see a list of Siri Suggestions, you can tap the suggestion you want to use. For example, if it is an email address, that address is entered for you. If it is a search, the search is performed.

You can enable or disable the apps and services that Siri can access to make these suggestions; the information to do this is provided in Chapter 11, "Working with Siri." For example, if you don't want Siri to be able to make suggestions based on a specific app, you can disable the Search & Siri Suggestions setting for that app.

Working with Notifications

As you learned in Chapter 1, the iPhone's notification system keeps you informed of activity in which you may be interested, such as new emails, events, app updates, and so on. There are a number of types of these notifications that you will experience. Visual notifications include banners and badges. Alert sounds can also let you know something has happened, and vibrations make you feel the new activity.

You can determine which types of notifications are used for specific activity on your iPhone. This might be one of the most important areas to configure because you want to make sure you are aware of activity that is important to you, but too many notifications can be disruptive and annoying. So, you want to strike a good balance between being aware and being annoyed.

Notification Center

In Chapter 1, you learned how to use the Notification Center to work with groups of notifications. This can be a more efficient way to deal with notifications since you can access "batches" of them instead of dealing with each one individually. You might want to configure individual notifications for the activity that is most important to you and access the rest via the Notification Center.

Working with Visual Notifications

 — **Badge showing one new email**

Badges appear on an app's or a folder's icon to let you know something has changed, such as new email, messages, or invitations.

Badges are purely informational, meaning you can't take any action on them. They inform you about events so that you can take action on them, such as to download and install an update to your iPhone's iOS software or read new text messages.

Badges on Folders

In Chapter 5, "Customizing How Your iPhone Looks and Sounds," you learn how to organize apps in folders. When apps in folders have badges enabled, the badge you see on a folder is a total count of the badges on the apps within that folder. The only way to know which apps that are in the folders have badges is to open the folder so you can see the individual app icons and badges.

Alerts appear when activity happens that you might want to know about, such as receiving email or a calendar invitation. There are three types of alerts; each type is based on the location where the notification appears. Lock Screen notifications appear on the Lock screen. Notification Center notifications appear only in the Notification Center, and Banners appear on any screen when your iPhone is unlocked. As you learn in Chapter 4, you can select the types of notifications used by each app.

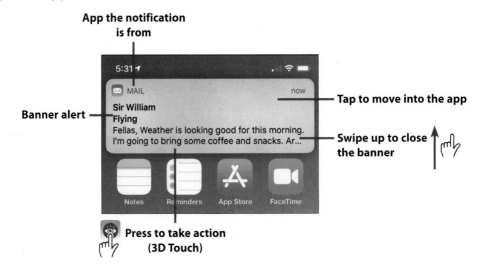

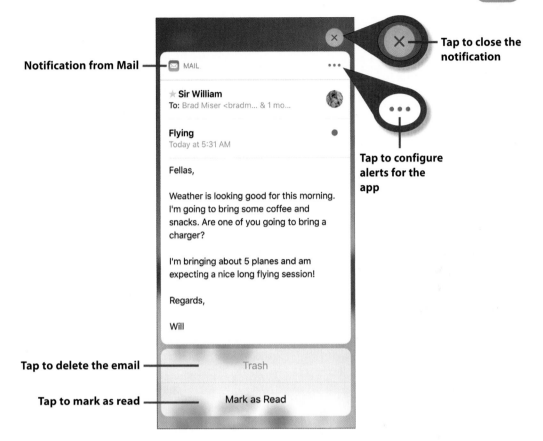

Notification from Mail

Tap to close the notification

Tap to configure alerts for the app

Tap to delete the email

Tap to mark as read

In addition to providing information for you, alerts enable you to take action related to the activity that generated the notification. For example, you can respond to a text message directly from its alert.

There are two types of banner alerts. Persistent banner alerts remain on the screen until you take action on them, which can be closing them, responding to them, and so on. Temporary banner alerts appear on the screen for a few seconds and if you don't take action on them, they rotate off the screen to get out of your way.

When your iPhone is unlocked, banner alerts appear at the top of the screen. They provide a summary of the app and the activity that has taken place, such as a new email or text message. When a banner appears, you can view its information; if it is a temporary banner, it rotates off the screen after displaying for a few seconds; if it is a persistent banner, you need to do something to cause it to disappear. You can tap it to move into the app to take some action, such as to read an email. You can swipe up from the bottom of the banner to close it. For some apps, such as Mail, you can press on the notification to open a menu of commands.

No 3D Touch?

If your iPhone doesn't support 3D Touch (it's not an iPhone 6s or later model), you can swipe down on a notification to take action on it, such as to reply to a text message.

Alert on the Lock screen

Press to take action (3D Touch)

Tap to close the alert

Tap to configure alerts for the app

New message

Reply to the message

Alerts can also appear on the Lock screen, which is really convenient because you can read and take action on them directly from that screen. If your phone is asleep, the alerts appear briefly on the screen and then it goes dark again (unless the phone is in Do Not Disturb mode in which case this doesn't happen); you can press the Side button or the Touch/ID Home button or raise your phone to see your alerts without unlocking the iPhone. You can swipe up or down the screen to browse the alerts.

To respond to an alert or take other action on it, press it to open it (3D Touch iPhones) or swipe to the right on it (non-3D Touch iPhones) and then take action, such as replying to a message. In some cases, you might need to unlock your phone to complete an action associated with an alert. In those cases, you're prompted to use Touch ID, Face ID, or your passcode to proceed.

Alerts and other notifications appear in the Notification Center, which you can open by swiping up on the Lock screen or swiping down from the top of the screen when your phone is unlocked. See Chapter 1 for the details about using the Notification Center.

Alert on the Notification Center

Group of notifications from the Podcasts app

Working with Other Types of Notifications

Sounds are audible indicators that something has happened. For example, you can be alerted to a new email message by a specific sound. You can choose global sound notifications, such as a general ringtone, and specific ones, such as a special ringtone when someone in your contacts calls you.

Vibrations are a physical indicator that something has happened. Like sounds, you can configure general vibrations, and you can also configure an app's vibration pattern for its notifications.

Notifications Can Be Annoying

A lot of apps are configured to get your attention by default so that you might be inundated with alerts or sounds. You can configure how and when you receive notifications, hear sounds, or feel vibrations so you are notified only to the extent you want to be. You can configure notifications globally using the Settings app. You can also configure notifications for a specific app by tapping the Options icon (…) that appears when you open an alert. This is a convenient way to configure alerts because you can do so as the alerts occur. Chapter 4 has all the details.

Printing from Your iPhone

You can print directly from your iPhone to AirPrint-compatible printers.

First, set up and configure your AirPrint printer (see the instructions that came with the printer you use).

It Depends

When you tap the Share icon, you might see a menu containing commands instead of the grid of icons shown in the figure. The way it appears is dependent upon the app you are using. If you see a menu, tap Print to move to the Printer Options screen.

AirPrint?

AirPrint is an Apple technology that enables an iOS device to wirelessly print to an AirPrint-compatible printer without installing any printer drivers on the iOS device. To be able to print directly to a printer via Wi-Fi, the printer must support AirPrint (a large number of them do). When an iOS device, such as your iPhone, is on the same Wi-Fi network as an AirPrint printer, it automatically detects that printer and is able to print to it immediately.

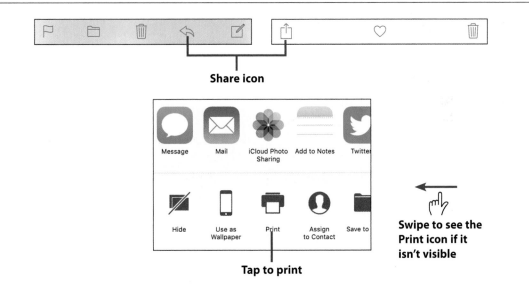

When you are in the app from which you want to print, tap the Share icon. Tap Print on the resulting menu. You might need to swipe to the left to expose the Print command. (If you don't see the Share icon or the Print command, the app you are using doesn't support printing.)

The first time you print, you need to select the printer you want to use. On the Printer Options screen, tap Select Printer. Then tap the printer you want to use. You move back to the Printer Options screen and see the printer you selected.

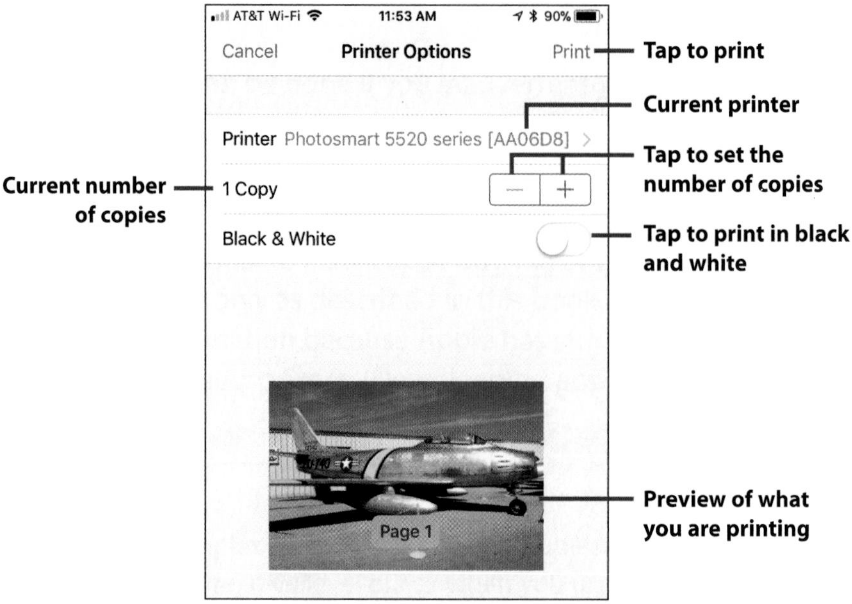

Tap − or + to set the number of copies; the current number of copies is shown to the left of the controls. You can use other controls that appear to configure the print job, such as the Black & White switch to print in black and white on a color printer; the controls you see depend on the capabilities of the printer you selected. Tap Print to print the document.

The next time you print, if you want to use the same printer, you can skip the printer selection process because the iPhone remembers the last printer you used. To change the printer, tap Printer and tap the printer you want to use.

Go here to configure and manage your Apple ID, iCloud, and other online accounts

Store app data (such as contacts) on the cloud using iCloud and other online services

Store files on the cloud

In this chapter, you learn how to configure an Apple ID on your iPhone and to set up various types of accounts, such as iCloud and Google, so that apps on your iPhone can access data stored on the Internet cloud. Topics include the following:

3

→ Getting started
→ Configuring an Apple ID
→ Configuring and using iCloud
→ Setting up other types of online accounts on your iPhone
→ Setting how and when your accounts are updated

Setting Up and Using an Apple ID, iCloud, and Other Online Accounts

Connecting your iPhone to the Internet enables you to share and sync a wide variety of content using popular online accounts such as iCloud and Google. Using iCloud, you can put your email, contacts, calendars, photos, and more on the Internet so that multiple devices—most importantly your iPhone—can connect to and use that information. (There's a lot more you can do with iCloud, too, as you learn throughout this book.) There are other online accounts you might also want to use, such as Google for email, calendars, and contacts as well as email accounts provided by your Internet Service Provider, such as a cable company.

To use iCloud and access other services provided by Apple, such as the App Store, iTunes Store, and iMessage, you need to have an Apple ID configured on your iPhone. The Apple ID connects the services Apple provides to you on all of your devices.

You need to configure these accounts on your iPhone to be able to use them; this chapter includes sections for several different online accounts you might want to use. Of course, you need to refer only to the sections related to the accounts you actually use.

This chapter also explains how to configure how and when your information is updated and demonstrates tasks you might find valuable as you manage the various accounts on your iPhone.

Getting Started

You can configure your iPhone to use various types of online accounts that offer different types of services and information. Here are some of the key terms for this chapter:

- **Apple ID**—An Apple ID enables you to access many Apple services, especially iCloud, and make purchases from the App Store, iTunes Store, and Apple's online store. An Apple ID also enables you to use iMessage to send and receive messages via the Messages app. An Apple ID is the "connector" between all your devices; it enables you to start tasks on one device, such as writing an email on your iPhone, and finish them on another, such as an iPad. Similarly, if you subscribe to Apple's Music Library, your Apple ID provides access to that music on each of your devices (iPhones, iPads, or computers).

- **iCloud**—This is Apple's online service that offers lots of great features that you can use for free; if you store a lot of information online, you might need to add storage to your account for an additional fee. It includes email, online photo storage and sharing, backup, calendars, Find My iPhone, and much more. This chapter explains how to set up iCloud on your iPhone; you find examples of how to use iCloud services in this chapter and throughout the rest of this book.

- **Family Sharing**—This Apple service allows you to share content with a group of people. (They don't actually have to be related to you.) For example, you can share music you download from the iTunes Store—when you set people up in your "family" group. This service is free.

- **Google account**—A Google account is similar to an iCloud account except it is provided by Google instead of Apple. It also offers lots of features, such as email, calendars, and contacts. You can use iCloud and a Google account on your iPhone at the same time.

- **Push, Fetch, or Manual**—Information has to get from your online account onto your iPhone. For example, when someone sends an email to you, it actually goes to an email server, which then sends the message to devices that are configured with your email account. You can choose how and when new data is provided to your phone. The three ways data gets moved onto your iPhone (Push, Fetch, Manual) are explained in "Setting How and When Your Accounts Are Updated" later in this chapter.

Configuring an Apple ID

An Apple ID is required to access Apple's online services, including iCloud, the App Store, iTunes, and the online store. You can access all of these services with one Apple ID.

An Apple ID has two elements. One is the email address associated with your account; this can be one provided by Apple or you can choose to use an address from a different service (such as Google Gmail). The other element is a password.

In addition to your email address and password, your contact information (such as physical address and phone number) and payment information (if you make purchases through your account, such as apps or storage upgrades) is also part of your Apple ID.

If you have used Apple technology or services before, you probably already have an Apple ID. If you don't already have one, obtaining an Apple ID is simple and free.

If you have any of the following accounts, you already have an Apple ID:

- **iTunes Store**—If you've ever shopped at the iTunes Store, you created an Apple ID.

- **Apple Online Store**—As with the iTunes Store, if you made purchases from Apple's online store, you created an account with an Apple ID.

- **Find My iPhone**—If you obtained a free Find My iPhone account, you also created an Apple ID.

Another way you might have already obtained an Apple ID is during the initial iPhone startup process when you were prompted to sign in to or create an Apple ID.

If you don't have an Apple ID, read the next section to obtain one. If you already have an Apple ID, move to "Signing into Your Apple ID" to learn how to sign into it on your iPhone. If you both have an Apple ID and have already signed into it on your iPhone, skip to the section "Changing the Personal Information Associated with Your Apple ID" to learn how to configure it.

Obtaining an Apple ID

If you don't have an Apple ID, you can use your iPhone to create one by performing the following steps:

1. On the Home screen, tap Settings.

2. Tap Sign in to your iPhone.

3. Tap Don't have an Apple ID or forgot it?.

4. Tap Create Apple ID.

5. Provide the information required on the following screens; tap Next to move to the next screen after you've entered the required information. You start by entering your birthday, providing your name, and so on. You are guided through each step in the process.

During the process, you're prompted to use an existing email address or to create a free iCloud email account. You can choose either option. The email address you use becomes your Apple ID that you use to sign in to iCloud. If you create a new iCloud email account, you can use that account from any email app on any device, just like other email accounts you have.

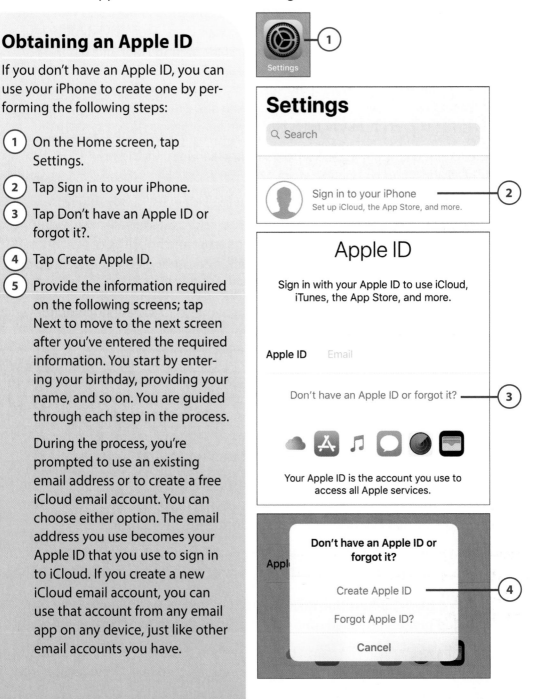

You also create a password, enter a phone number and verification method, verify the phone number you entered, and agree to license terms. When your account has been created, you sign into iCloud, which you do by entering your iPhone's passcode.

You might then be prompted to merge information already stored on your iPhone, such as Safari bookmarks, onto iCloud. Tap Merge to copy the information that currently is stored on your iPhone to the cloud or Don't Merge to keep it out of the cloud.

When you've worked through merging your information, you're prompted to sign in to the iTunes and App Stores to make sure your new account can work with those services, too. You can choose to review your account information now or skip it and configure it at another time.

When the process is complete, you're signed into your new Apple ID; skip ahead to "Changing the Personal Information Associated with Your Apple ID" to learn how to change its settings.

8:32

Cancel   Next

Birthday

Your birthday is used to determine which services to set up on this iPhone.

| Birthday | 7/22/64 |

⑤

April   19   1961
May   20   1962
June   21   1963
July   22   1964
August   23   1965
September   24   1966
October   25   1967

Signing In to Your Apple ID

You can sign in to an existing Apple ID on your iPhone by doing the following:

1. On the Home screen, tap Settings.

2. Tap Sign in to your iPhone.

3. Enter your Apple ID (email address).

4. Tap Next.

Settings

Q Search

Sign in to your iPhone ——— 2
Set up iCloud, the App Store, and more.

Cancel   Next —— 4

Apple ID

Sign in with your Apple ID to use iCloud, iTunes, the App Store, and more.

Apple ID   ▓▓▓▓▓▓▓▓▓▓ ——— 3

Don't have an Apple ID or forgot it?

5. Enter your password.

6. Tap Next. If you are using the same Apple ID on another device, you're prompted to enter the verification code sent to those devices. See the sidebar "Two-Factor Authentication" for more information.

7. Enter your verification code; if you weren't prompted to enter a code, skip this step.

8. Enter your iPhone's passcode. You might be prompted to merge existing information on the iPhone onto your iCloud storage.

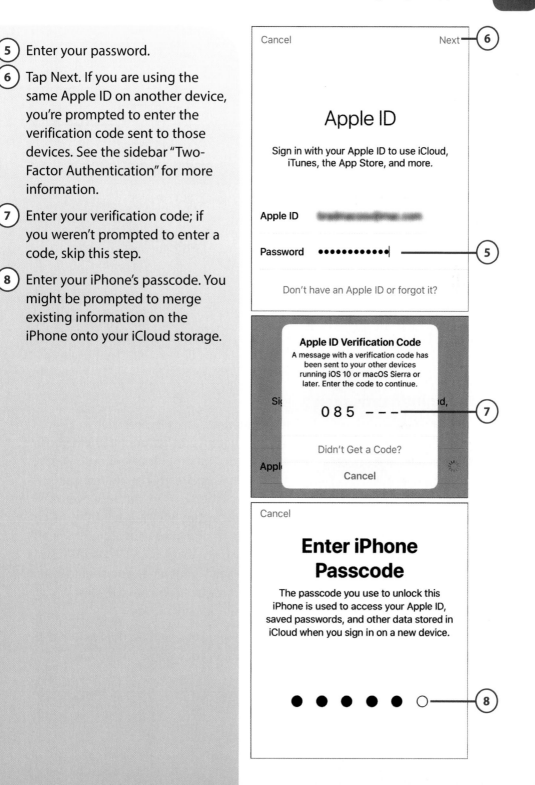

⑨ Tap Merge to copy information from your iPhone onto the cloud or Don't Merge if you don't want that information copied to the cloud. You might be prompted to perform this merge step more than once depending on the kind of information already stored on your iPhone. If you don't have any information that can be merged, you skip this step entirely.

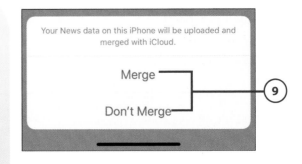

When you've finished these steps, you are signed in to your Apple ID and can configure it further using the information in the next section.

Two-Factor Authentication

Apple uses two-factor authentication for its services. This requires that you have two pieces of information to be able to access your Apple accounts. One is your Apple ID login information (email and password). The other is a verification code that is sent to other devices on which the Apple ID is already configured (called trusted devices). This makes using Apple services more secure because even if someone was able to get your Apple ID and password (which is unlikely), he would still need the verification code to be able to sign in to your account (meaning he would also have to be able to access another device on which your Apple ID is already configured, which is very, very unlikely). In general, you should use two-factor authentication when it is available (it requires you have at least two devices that can use your Apple ID, such as an iPhone and a Mac).

You can configure two-factor authentication for your Apple ID in the Password & Security settings, which are described in "Changing Your Apple ID's Password and Security Settings."

Changing the Personal Information Associated with Your Apple ID

When you create or sign in to your Apple ID, the personal information associated with your account is used on your iPhone. You can change this information on your phone, for example, if you want to change your contact information or how you pay for purchases from Apple. Following are the steps you can use to change the personal information associated with your Apple ID:

1. On the Home screen, tap Settings.

2. Tap your Apple ID, which appears immediately under the Search bar at the top of the Settings screen. The Apple ID screen has four sections. The top section shows your Apple ID and photo (if you have one) and provides access to your account's primary settings, which are contact information, payment and security, and payment and shipping information.

3. To set or change the photo associated with your Apple ID, tap the image shown just above your name.

4. Tap Take Photo to take a new photo for your Apple ID or Choose Photo to use an existing photo.

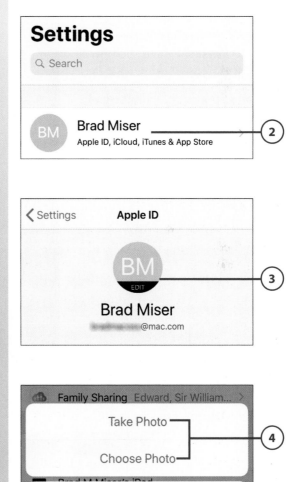

5 Use the resulting tools to configure the photo for your Apple ID (detailed information about working with the iPhone's photo tools is provided in Chapter 13, "Taking Photos and Video with Your iPhone," and Chapter 14, "Viewing and Editing Photos and Video with the Photos App"). When you're done configuring the photo, you return to the Apple ID screen and see the new photo at the top of the screen.

6 To change your contact information, tap Name, Phone Numbers, Email.

7 To change the name associated with your account, tap the name shown and edit it on the resulting screen; when you're done, tap Back to move to the previous screen (this step is not shown in the figures).

8 To change the email addresses with which you can be contacted in various apps, such as FaceTime, tap Edit.

Address Info

If an email address has the Info icon (i) next to it, you can tap that icon to verify the address so you can use it with your iCloud account.

9 To remove an address, tap its Unlock icon (-).

10 Tap Delete. That address is removed from the list and can't be used for associated apps.

11 To add more email addresses or phone numbers, tap Add Email or Phone Number.

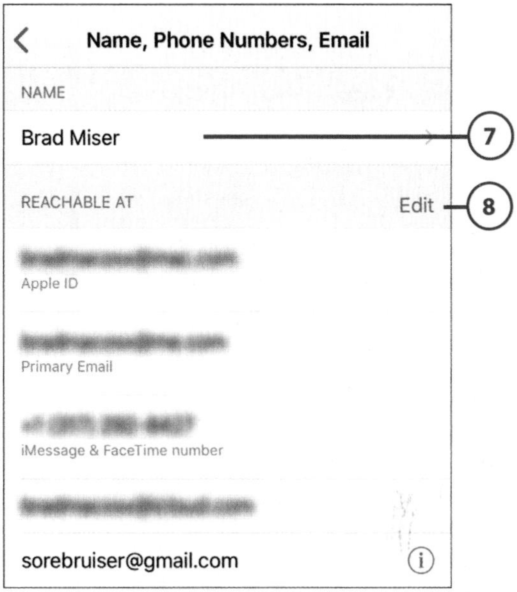

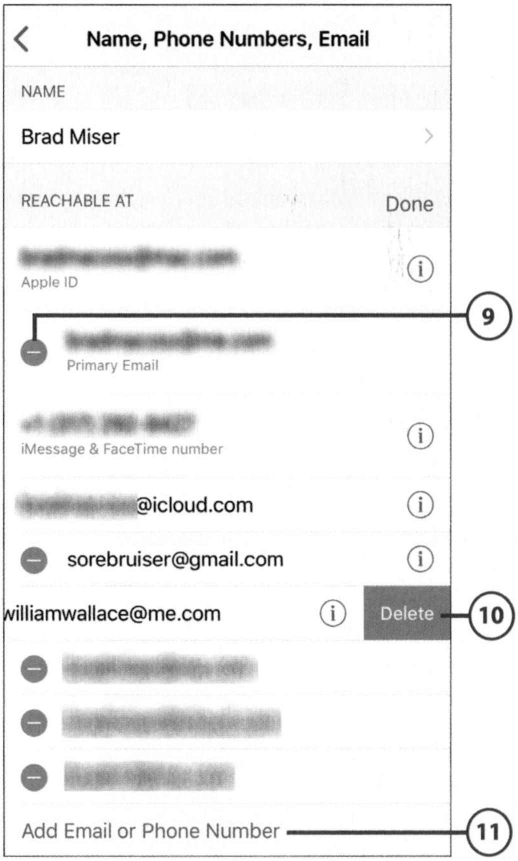

(12) Tap Add an Email Address to associate a new email address or tap Add a Phone Number to add a phone number. Follow the resulting steps to complete the process (not shown in the figures). For example, enter the new email and then respond to the verification email sent to the address.

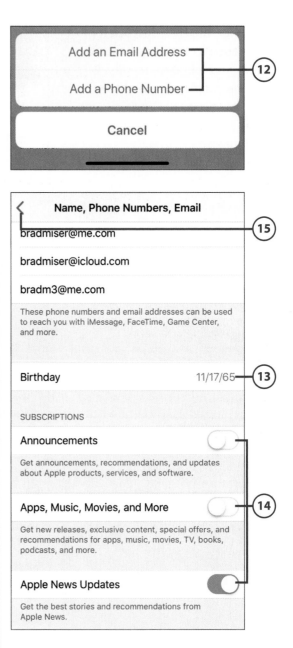

Done Is Done

When you make some changes, such as adding a new email address, you exit Edit mode automatically. You have to tap Edit again to make more changes. If a change you make doesn't automatically move you out of Edit mode, tap Done when you are finished making changes.

(13) If you need to change the birthday for your account, tap it and make the change on the resulting screen.

(14) To receive emails from Apple for various types of information, set the associated switch to on (green) or to prevent such messages from being sent, set the switch to off (white).

(15) When you're done making changes to your personal information, tap the Back icon (<).

Confirmations Galore

Many changes you make to your Apple ID, such as adding a new email address or changing security settings, result in you receiving confirmation emails and notifications from Apple on all of the devices tied to your account. These are helpful because they confirm the actions you are taking. If you ever receive such a notification but you haven't changed your account, carefully review it. In many cases, especially email notifications, these unexpected notifications are attempts to get your information for nefarious purposes. Don't respond to emails you don't expect even if they appear to be from Apple (if you make a change and then receive an email, that is expected). Instead, log in directly to your account on your iPhone or other device (such as a computer to log into the iCloud website) to make sure it hasn't been changed by someone else.

Changing Your Apple ID's Password and Security Settings

To access the security settings for your Apple ID, perform the following steps:

(1) Move to the Apple ID screen.

(2) Tap Password & Security.

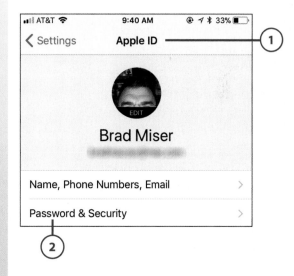

(3) To change your password, tap Change Password and follow the onscreen instructions to make the change. You need to enter your iPhone's passcode and then you'll be able to change the password.

(4) If two-factor authentication isn't currently enabled, tap Turn on Two-Factor Authentication and then tap Continue and follow the prompts to complete the process (not shown in the figures); if it is already enabled, you see the On status (as shown in the figure).

(5) To change the phone number used for account verification, tap Edit and use the resulting tools to delete or change existing numbers or add new ones.

(6) If you need a verification code for another device with which you are trying to access your Apple ID information, tap Get Verification Code. The code appears on the screen and you can enter that code on the other device to verify it; tap OK to close the code dialog.

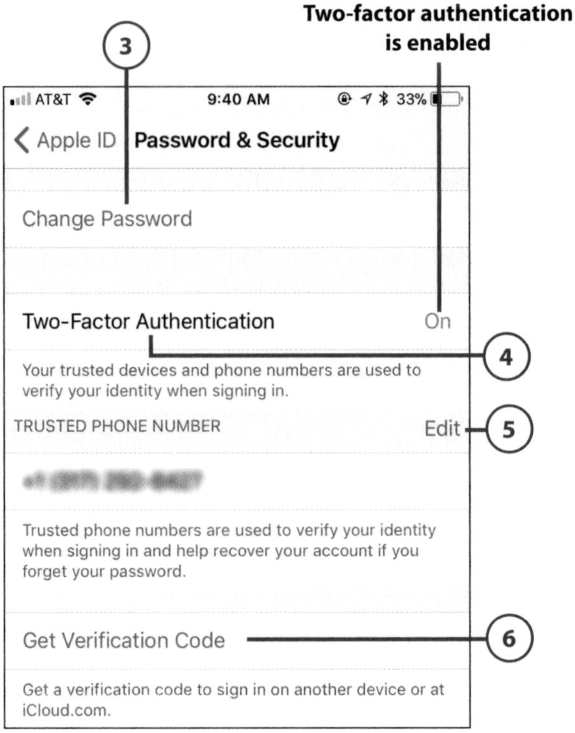

Two-factor authentication is enabled

(3)

.ıll AT&T 📶   9:40 AM   @ ✈ ⚹ 33% 🔋

‹ Apple ID | **Password & Security**

Change Password

Two-Factor Authentication   On

(4)

Your trusted devices and phone numbers are used to verify your identity when signing in.

TRUSTED PHONE NUMBER   Edit **(5)**

Trusted phone numbers are used to verify your identity when signing in and help recover your account if you forget your password.

Get Verification Code **(6)**

Get a verification code to sign in on another device or at iCloud.com.

Changing Your Apple ID's Payment and Shipping Information

To change the payment and shipping information for your Apple ID, perform the following steps:

(1) Move to the Apple ID screen.

(2) Tap Payment & Shipping.

(3) To change your payment information, tap the current payment method (which is what will be used for all purchases made under your account, such as from the App Store).

(4) Enter your passcode.

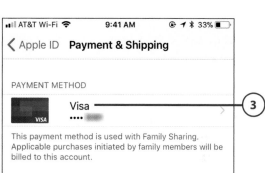

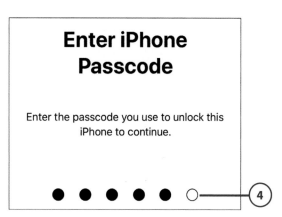

5 Use the fields on the resulting screen to provide or change your name, credit, or debit card information, and the billing address associated with the payment method.

6 Tap Save when you have updated the information.

Apple Pay Cash

In the middle of the screen, you see the balance in your Apple Pay Cash account. You can add money to this account so that you can send it to other people using the Pay Cash card in the Wallet app. Learn about this in "Working with the Wallet App," in Chapter 15, "Working with Other Useful iPhone Apps and Features."

7 If you haven't put in an address yet, tap Add a Shipping Address and enter the address, or if you've already entered one and want to change it, tap the current address.

8 Use the fields on the resulting screen to provide or change the address to which items you purchase from Apple should be delivered.

9 Tap Done when you have updated the information.

ıll AT&T Wi-Fi ⓦ   12:11 PM   @ ✦ ✱ 57% 🔋

Cancel   **Payment Details**   Save —— **6**

CARDHOLDER

First Name   Brad

Last Name   Miser

—— **5**

BILLING INFO

Number   2356 5236 9635 2356

Expires   08/2018

CVV   253

Phone   (555) 555-5555

APPLE PAY CASH

Apple Pay Cash
Balance $0.00

Your Apple Pay Cash balance can be used on any Apple Pay capable iPhone, iPad or Apple Watch signed in with your Apple ID.

SHIPPING ADDRESS

—— **7**

This shipping address will be used when you make Apple Store purchases.

ıll AT&T Wi-Fi ⓦ   12:11 PM   @ ✦ ✱ 56% 🔋

‹ Back   **Shipping Address**   Done —— **9**

First Name   Brad

Last Name   Miser

Company

Address   56790 Space Drive

Address   line 2

—— **8**

Configuring Services that Use Your Apple ID

In the center part of the Apple ID screen, you see tools you can use to configure iCloud (covered in "Configuring and Using iCloud" later in this chapter) and the iTunes and App Stores (covered in "Customizing How Your iPhone Works with Apps" in Chapter 4, "Customizing How Your iPhone Works"). The Share My Location feature enables your location to be shared with family and friends in various apps (such as Messages); on the Share My Location screen, you can enable or disable Location Sharing and see the people with whom your address is currently being shared. Family Sharing enables you to configure a group of people with whom you share content related to your Apple ID (such as music you purchase from the iTunes Store and apps you download from the App Store). You can use the Family Sharing option to configure your Family Sharing group and determine the access this group has to various elements associated with your account or phone (Purchase Sharing [apps], Apple Music, iCloud Storage, Location Sharing, and Screen Time).

Changing the Devices Using Your Apple ID

You will likely have more than one device that uses your Apple ID. For example, you might have an iPad on which you want to be able to access the same information as you can on your iPhone. You can get information about the devices currently using your Apple ID like so:

(1) Move to the Apple ID screen.

(2) Tap the device about which you want to get information.

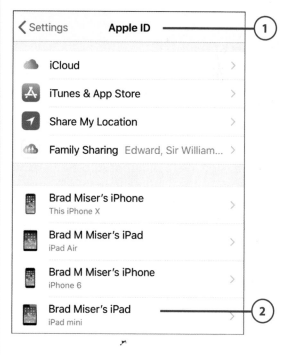

(3) Review the information about the device. For example, you can see if the device is being tracked by Find My iPhone/iPad and if it is being backed up to your iCloud account. (If the device is also an iPhone, you can enable or disable some iCloud functions from this screen.)

(4) If you don't recognize the device, tap Remove from Account and follow the onscreen prompts to disconnect the device from your Apple ID. You should also imme-diately change your Apple ID password.

```
< Apple ID        Device Info


                  Brad Miser's iPad
                Show in Find My iPhone


  ●  Find My iPad                    On

  🔄  iCloud Backup              Unknown     ── 3
  Last iCloud backup: 8/22/18 at 3:39 PM

  DEVICE INFO

  Model                          iPad mini

  Version                        iOS 9.3.5

  Serial Number                  ███████████

  This device is trusted and can receive Apple ID
  verification codes.


  Remove from Account  ────────────  4

  If you don't recognize this device, remove it and change
  your password.
```

Signing Off

If you don't want to continue accessing your Apple ID on your iPhone or you want to sign into a different Apple ID, tap Sign Out at the bottom of the Apple ID screen. If Find My iPhone is enabled, you need to enter your password and tap Turn Off to continue the process. You might be prompted to keep some informa-tion on your iPhone; if you choose to keep that information, it remains on your iPhone but is no longer synchronized to the information stored on the cloud. After you have completed the process, you can sign in to the same or a different Apple ID using the information in "Signing In to Your Apple ID" earlier in this chapter.

Configuring and Using iCloud

iCloud is a service provided by Apple that provides you with your own storage space on the Internet. You can store content from your iPhone, computer, or other devices in your storage space on the cloud, and because it is on the Internet, all your devices are able to access that information at the same time. This means you can easily share your information on your iPhone, a computer, and iPad, so that the same information and content is available to you no matter which device you are using at any one time.

Although your iPhone can work with many types of online/Internet accounts, iCloud is integrated into the iPhone like no other (not surprising because the iPhone and iCloud are both Apple technology). An iCloud account is part of an Apple ID; if you have an Apple ID, you also have an iCloud account.

An iCloud account is useful in a number of ways, including the following:

- **Photos**—You can store your photos in iCloud to back them up and to make them easy to share.

- **Email**—An iCloud account includes an @icloud.com email address (unless you choose to use an existing account instead). You can configure any device to use your iCloud email account, including an iPhone, an iPad, an iPod, or a computer.

- **Contacts**—You can store your contact information in iCloud.

- **Calendars**—Putting your calendars in iCloud makes it much easier to manage your time.

- **Reminders**—Through iCloud, you can be reminded of things you need to do or anything else you want to make sure you don't forget.

- **Notes**—With the Notes app, you can create text notes, draw sketches, and capture photos for many purposes; iCloud enables you to use these notes on any iCloud-enabled device.

- **Messages**—This puts all of your messages in the Messages app on the cloud so you can access them from all your devices.

- **Safari**—iCloud can store your bookmarks, letting you easily access the same websites from all your devices. And you can easily access websites currently open on other devices, such as a Mac, on your iPhone.

- **News**—iCloud can store information from the News app online, making reading news on multiple devices easier.

- **Stocks**—If you use the Stocks app to track investments, iCloud ensures you have the same investments in the Stocks app on all your devices.

- **Health**—This causes the information stored using the Health app to be available to multiple devices. For example, you might track information on your Apple Watch and want to be able to analyze it on your iPhone.

- **Wallet**—The Wallet app stores coupons, tickets, boarding passes, and other documents so you can access them quickly and easily. With iCloud, you can ensure that these items are available on any iCloud-enabled device.

- **Game Center**—This capability stores information from the Game Center app on the cloud.

- **Siri**—It can be helpful to manage Siri information on multiple devices; this setting puts that information on the cloud.

- **Keychain**—The Keychain securely stores sensitive data, such as passwords, so that you can easily use that data without having to remember it.

- **Find My iPhone**—This service enables you to locate and secure your iPhone and other devices.

- **iCloud Backup**—You can (and should) back up your iPhone to the cloud so that you can recover your data and your phone's configuration should something ever happen to the iPhone itself (such as losing it).

- **iCloud Drive**—iCloud enables you to store your documents and other files on the cloud so that you can seamlessly work with them using different devices.

- **App Data**—When iCloud Drive is enabled, you can allow or prevent individual apps from storing data there. For example, if use the iBooks app on an iPhone and an iPad, you can store its information on the cloud so that you always pick up reading where you left off when you change devices.

You can also manage your iCloud storage space, share your location, and configure some aspects of iCloud mail.

You learn about iCloud's many useful features throughout this book (such as using iCloud with your photos, which is covered in Chapter 14). The tasks in this chapter show you how to set up and configure other iCloud features you might want to use.

Multiple iCloud Accounts

You can have more than one iCloud account. However, you can be signed in to only one iCloud account on your iPhone at a time.

I'm In

To access your iCloud account, sign in to your Apple ID as described in "Signing In to Your Apple ID" earlier in this chapter.

Configuring iCloud to Store Photos

Storing your photos on the cloud provides many benefits, not the least of which is that the photos you take with your iPhone are automatically saved on the cloud so that you can access them from computers and other iOS devices (such as iPads), and your photos remain available even if something happens to your iPhone, such as if you drop it in water and it stops working. Using iCloud also makes it easy for you to share your photos with others. To configure your photos to be stored in iCloud, do the following:

1. Open the Apple ID screen.
2. Tap iCloud.
3. On the iCloud screen, tap Photos.

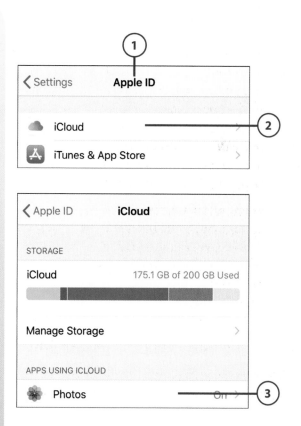

(**4**) To store your entire photo library on the cloud, set the iCloud Photos switch to on (green). This stores all of your photos and video in iCloud, which both protects them by backing them up and makes them accessible on other iOS devices (iPads, iPod touches, iPhones) and computers, (including Macs, Windows PCs, and via the Web).

(**5**) If you enable the iCloud Photos feature, tap Optimize iPhone Storage to keep lower-resolution versions of photos and videos on your iPhone (this means the file sizes are smaller so that you can store more of them on your phone), or tap Download and Keep Originals if you want to keep the full-resolution photos on your iPhone. In most cases, you should choose the Optimize option so that you don't use as much of your iPhone's storage space for photos. (You can still access the full-resolution versions on the cloud, such as to download them to a computer.)

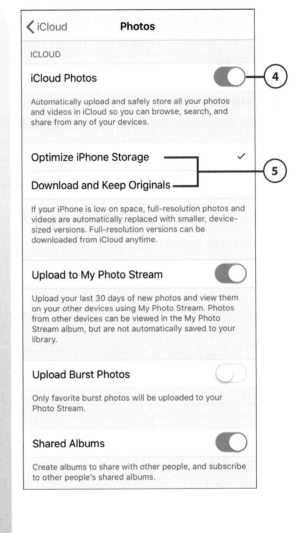

6. Ensure the Upload to My Photo Stream switch is on (green) (if you aren't using iCloud Photos, this switch is called My Photo Stream); if you disabled this, skip to step 8. Any photos you take with the iPhone's camera are copied onto iCloud, and from there they're copied to your other devices on which the Photo Stream is enabled. Note that Photo Stream affects only photos that you take with the iPhone from the time you enable it, whereas the iCloud Photos feature uploads all of your photos—those you took in the past and will take in the future.

7. If you want all of your burst photos (photos taken in sequence, such as for action shots) to be uploaded to iCloud, set the Upload Burst Photos switch to on (green). In most cases, you should leave this off (white) because you typically don't want to keep all the photos in a burst. When you review and select photos to keep, the ones you keep are uploaded automatically. (You learn more about burst photos in Chapter 14.)

8. To be able to share your photos and to access photos other people share with you, set the Shared Albums switch to on (green).

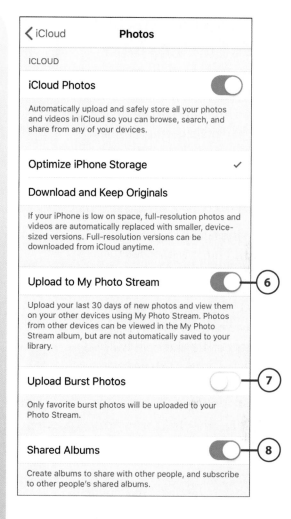

iCloud   **Photos**

ICLOUD

iCloud Photos

Automatically upload and safely store all your photos and videos in iCloud so you can browse, search, and share from any of your devices.

Optimize iPhone Storage   ✓

Download and Keep Originals

If your iPhone is low on space, full-resolution photos and videos are automatically replaced with smaller, device-sized versions. Full-resolution versions can be downloaded from iCloud anytime.

Upload to My Photo Stream   — 6

Upload your last 30 days of new photos and view them on your other devices using My Photo Stream. Photos from other devices can be viewed in the My Photo Stream album, but are not automatically saved to your library.

Upload Burst Photos   — 7

Only favorite burst photos will be uploaded to your Photo Stream.

Shared Albums   — 8

Create albums to share with other people, and subscribe to other people's shared albums.

Enabling iCloud to Store Information on the Cloud

As you learned earlier, one of the best things about iCloud is that it stores email, contacts, calendars, reminders, bookmarks, notes, and other data on the cloud so that all your iCloud-enabled devices can access the same information. You can choose the types of data stored on the cloud by performing the following steps:

(1) Move to the iCloud screen. Just below the Photos section are the iCloud data options. Some of these have a right-facing arrow that you tap to configure options, whereas others have a two-position switch. The types of data that have switches are Mail, Contacts, Calendars, Reminders, Notes, Messages, Safari, News, Stocks, Health, Wallet, Game Center, and Siri. When a switch is green, it means that switch is turned on and the related data is stored to your iCloud account and kept in sync with the information on the iPhone.

(2) To store data on the cloud, set an app's switch to on (green). You might be prompted to merge that information with that already stored on the cloud. For example, if you have contacts information on your iPhone already and want to merge that with the contacts already on the cloud, tap Merge. If you don't want the contacts currently stored on your iPhone copied to the cloud, tap Don't Merge instead.

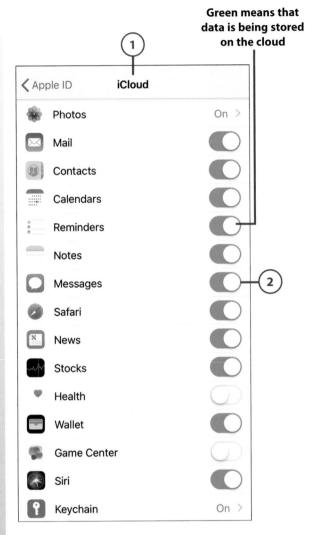

Green means that data is being stored on the cloud

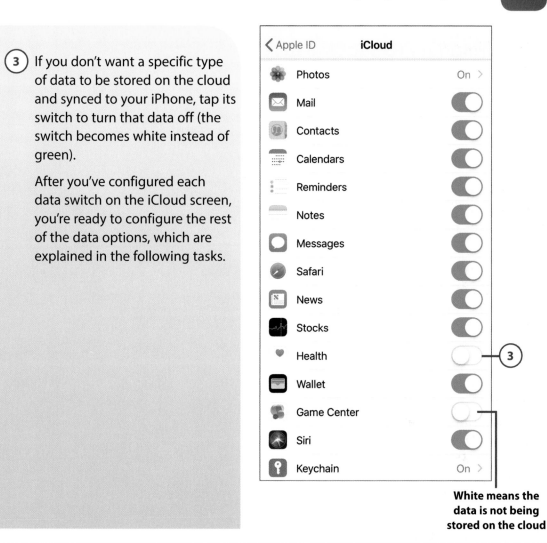

③ If you don't want a specific type of data to be stored on the cloud and synced to your iPhone, tap its switch to turn that data off (the switch becomes white instead of green).

After you've configured each data switch on the iCloud screen, you're ready to configure the rest of the data options, which are explained in the following tasks.

White means the data is not being stored on the cloud

To Keep or Not to Keep?

When you turn off a switch because you don't want that information stored on the cloud any more, you might be prompted to keep the associated information on your iPhone or delete it.

If you choose Keep on My iPhone, the information remains on your iPhone but is no longer connected to the cloud; this means any changes you make exist only on the iPhone. If you choose Delete from My iPhone, the information is erased from your iPhone. Whether you choose to keep or delete the information, any information of that type that was previously stored on the cloud remains available there; the delete action affects only the information stored on the iPhone.

Configuring Your iCloud Keychain

A keychain can be used to store user-names, passwords, and credit cards so you can access this information with-out retyping it every time you need it. Enabling keychain syncing through iCloud makes this information avail-able on multiple devices. For example, if you've configured a website's password on your keychain on a Mac, that pass-word is available in the Safari app if the keychain is synced via iCloud. Follow these steps to enable keychain syncing through iCloud:

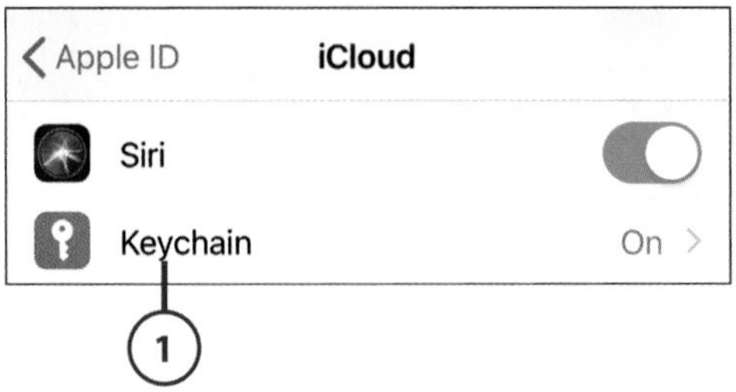

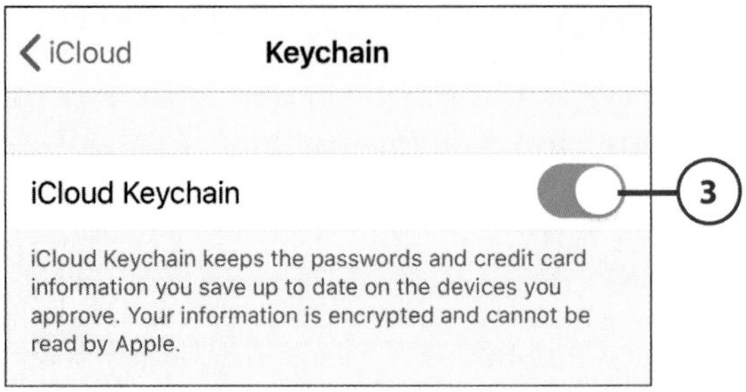

1. On the iCloud screen, tap Keychain.

2. If prompted to do so, enter your Apple ID password and tap OK (not shown in the figures).

3. Set the iCloud Keychain switch to on (green).

> ⟨ Apple ID   iCloud
>
> 🌟 Siri   ⬤⚪
>
> 🔑 Keychain   On ⟩
>
> ①

> ⟨ iCloud   **Keychain**
>
> iCloud Keychain   ⬤⚪ —③
>
> iCloud Keychain keeps the passwords and credit card information you save up to date on the devices you approve. Your information is encrypted and cannot be read by Apple.

Your Experience May Vary

How iCloud Keychain syncing is configured can vary based on the current status of your keychain. These steps assume your keychain is already configured on another device, such as a Mac, and your iPhone is connecting to that keychain. If you don't have any keychain syncing configured, you might see additional steps when you perform step 3. In that case, just follow the onscreen prompts to com-plete the process.

It's Not All Good

Proceed with Caution

If you store a lot of sensitive information in your keychain on a Mac, such as usernames and passwords to websites, credit cards, and such, be careful about enabling keychain syncing. When you enable this iCloud feature, all this data becomes available on your iPhone and can be used by anyone who can use your phone. Assuming you have a passcode to the phone, you are protected from someone using your phone without you knowing it, but if you let someone use your phone, they can also use your sensitive information. You might choose to leave keychain syncing off and just keep a minimum amount of sensitive information on your phone.

>>>Go Further

CONFIGURING FIND MY iPHONE

Find My iPhone enables you to locate and secure your iPhone if you lose it. This feature is enabled by default when you sign in to your iCloud account. You should usually leave it enabled so that you have a better chance of locating your iPhone should you lose it—or in case you need to delete its data in the event that you won't be getting the iPhone back. There are a couple of configuration tasks you can do for Find My iPhone:

- To disable Find My iPhone, open the iCloud settings screen and tap Find My iPhone. Set the Find My iPhone switch to off (white) and enter your Apple ID password at the prompt. You can no longer access your iPhone via the Find My iPhone feature.

- To send the last known location of the iPhone to Apple when power is critically low, open the Find My iPhone settings screen and set the Send Last Location switch to on (green). When your iPhone is nearly out of power, its location is sent to Apple. You can contact Apple to try to determine where your iPhone was when the battery was almost out of power.

Configuring Your iCloud Backup

Like other digital devices, it is important to back up your iPhone's data so that you can recover should something bad happen to your iPhone. You can back up your iPhone's data and settings to iCloud, which is really useful because that means you can recover the backed-up data using a different device, such as a replacement iPhone. Configure your iCloud backup with the following steps:

1 On the iCloud settings screen, tap iCloud Backup.

2 Set the iCloud Backup switch to on (green). Your iPhone's data and settings are backed up to the cloud automatically.

‹ Apple ID | iCloud

Siri

Keychain | On ›

Find My iPhone | On ›

iCloud Backup | On ›

1

‹ iCloud | Backup

BACKUP

iCloud Backup | **2**

Automatically back up data such as your accounts, documents, Home configuration, and settings when this iPhone is connected to power, locked, and on Wi-Fi. Learn more...

Back Up Now

Last successful backup: Yesterday at 2:27 PM

Back Me Up on This

You can manually back up your iPhone's data and settings at any time by tapping Back Up Now on the Backup screen. This can be useful to ensure recent data or settings changes are captured in your backup. For example, if you know you are going to be without a Wi-Fi connection to the Internet for a while, back up your phone to ensure that your current data is saved in the backup.

Configuring iCloud Drive

iCloud Drive, which is enabled by default, stores files (such as Keynote presentations) on the cloud so that you can work with those documents on any device. For example, you can create a Keynote presentation on a Mac and then access it on your iPhone to present it. To configure your iCloud Drive, perform the following steps:

1. On the iCloud settings screen, set the iCloud Drive switch to on (green).

2. Set the switch to on (green) for those apps that you do want to use the iCloud Drive to store data.

3. Set the switch to off (white) for any apps that you don't want to use your iCloud Drive.

‹ Apple ID	iCloud	
🔄 iCloud Backup	On ›	
☁ iCloud Drive	⬤	①
📖 Books	⬤	
📝 Pages	⬤	
📊 Numbers	⬤	②
📺 Keynote	⬤	
🎸 GarageBand	○	
⭐ iMovie	⬤	③
🎥 Clips	○	

Managing Your iCloud Storage

Your iCloud account includes storage space that you can use for your data including photos, documents, and so on. By default, your account includes 5 GB of free storage space. For many people, that is enough, but if you take a lot of photos and video and use iCloud Photos, you might find that you need more space. It is easy (and relatively inexpensive) to upgrade the amount of room you have on your iCloud Drive. You can use the STORAGE section on the iCloud settings screen to manage your storage space as follows:

(1) Move to the STORAGE section located at the top of the iCloud settings screen. Here you see a gauge that displays the amount of space you have and how that space is currently being used. The gray portion of the bar indicates how much free space you have; if this portion of the bar is very small, you might want to consider upgrading your storage space. The colored bars show the data being used by various types of data or apps, such as Photos.

(2) Tap Manage Storage. At the top of the resulting iCloud Storage screen, you see the same storage information as on the prior screen. Under that, you see the tools you can use to manage your storage.

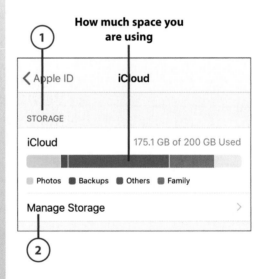

How much space you are using

STORAGE

iCloud   175.1 GB of 200 GB Used

Photos ● Backups ● Others ● Family

Manage Storage

(3) If you use the Family Sharing feature, tap Family Usage and use the resulting settings to enable the people in your sharing group to store content on your iCloud Drive.

(4) To change the amount of storage space available to you, tap Change Storage Plan and follow the onscreen prompts to upgrade (or downgrade) your storage.

(5) Swipe up the screen to review all of the apps that are currently using iCloud storage space.

(6) Tap an app to get details about how it is using iCloud space.

< iCloud   **iCloud Storage**

iCloud   175.1 GB of 200 GB Used

⬜ Photos ⬛ Backups ⬛ Others ⬛ Family

Family Usage   42 GB **(3)**

Change Storage Plan   200 GB **(4)**

☁ iCloud Drive   87.2 GB >

✳ Photos   31.6 GB >

🔄 Backups   7.5 GB >   **(5)**

💬 Messages   2.8 GB >

✉ Mail   2.6 GB

📊 Keynote   1.1 GB >

📄 Pages   115.7 MB > **(6)**

📖 iBooks   66.5 MB >

(**7**) If the app works with documents, you see the list of documents and how much space each is using (if it doesn't use documents, you only see a total).

Delete or Disable?

When you delete documents or data from your iCloud storage, it is removed from the cloud. This also means it is removed from every device using that data on the cloud. If you want the app to stop storing data on the cloud, but keep the data on the devices currently using it, prevent it from using iCloud storage as described in "Configuring iCloud Drive" instead.

(**8**) To remove documents and data from iCloud, tap Delete Documents & Data, Disable & Delete, or Delete Data. After you confirm the deletion, the app's data is deleted from your iCloud storage. (Of course, make sure you have this information stored in another location if you are going to need it again.)

‹ iCloud Storage **Pages**	
Pages Apple Inc.	
Documents & Data	115.7 MB
Delete Documents & Data	(**8**)

This will delete all app data from iCloud and all connected devices. This action can't be undone.

DOCUMENTS & DATA

Newbie Freewing F-15 Build Log_wo...	22 MB
plane_storage.pages	14.4 MB
Plane Test Stand.pages-tef	5 MB
bike_flyer.pages	4.7 MB
Sodexo-Tulsa School Dist- VFA Pro...	3.8 MB
Oshkosh 2013.pages	3.3 MB
FMS P-47 1700mm Review_v2.pages	3.3 MB
FMS P-47 1700mm Review.pages	3.3 MB

(**7**)

>>>Go Further

YET EVEN MORE iCLOUD CONFIGURATION OPTIONS

Most of the time, you can use your iCloud account just fine if you only configure it as described in the previous tasks. However, there are some other configuration options located at the bottom of the iCloud settings screen that you might want to use at some point:

- **Look Me Up**. Some iCloud-aware apps can look you up via your Apple ID; people who do this see your first and last names. You can tap Look Me Up to see which apps and people have accessed this information.

- **Mail**. Use this option to configure certain aspects of your iCloud email. These options are explained in Chapter 8, "Sending, Receiving, and Managing Email."

>>>Go Further

EMAIL ALIASES

One of the great features of iCloud is using email aliases. You can create alias addresses for specific purposes, such as avoiding spam or just to use an email address you prefer. Email sent to one of your aliases comes into your normal inbox. When you send email from an alias, it appears to be from the alias address, even though any aliases are still related to the same email account. You can create email aliases for your iCloud account using your iCloud website, available at www.icloud.com. Log in to your iCloud account, and then open the Mail app. Open the Mail Preferences dialog by clicking the gear icon and choosing Preferences. Then, click the Accounts tab, where you can create and manage up to three aliases.

Setting Up Other Types of Online Accounts on Your iPhone

Many types of online accounts provide different services, including email, calendars, contacts, social networking, and so on. To use these accounts, you need to configure them on your iPhone. The process you use for most types of accounts is similar to the steps you used to set up your iCloud account. In this section, you learn how to configure a Google account and an account that you might have through your Internet provider, such as a cable company.

Configuring a Google Account

A Google account provides email, contacts, calendar, and note syncing that are similar to iCloud and Exchange. To set up a Google account on your iPhone, do the following:

(1) On the Home screen, tap Settings.

(2) Tap Passwords & Accounts.

(3) Tap Add Account.

Settings

🅰	iTunes & App Store	>
▤	Wallet & Apple Pay	>
🔑	Passwords & Accounts	> ──(2)

< Settings **Passwords & Accounts**

🔑	Website & App Passwords	354 >
⌨	AutoFill Passwords	⬤

ACCOUNTS

iCloud
iCloud Drive, Mail, Contacts, Calendars and 9 more... >

Accruent
Mail, Calendars >

Gmail
Mail, Contacts, Calendars >

Your RC Companion
Mail >

indy.rr.com
Mail >

Add Account >

(3)

4. Tap Google.

5. Enter your Google email address.

6. Tap Next.

7. Enter your Google account password.

8. Tap Next.

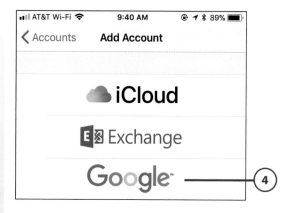

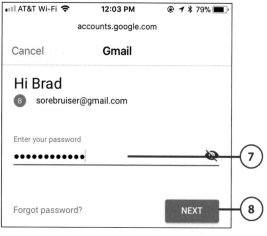

⑨ Enable the features of the account you want to access on the iPhone—which are Mail, Contacts, Calendars, and Notes—by setting the switch to on (green) for the types of data you do want to use or to off (white) for the types of data you don't want to use.

⑩ Tap Save. The account is saved, and the data you enabled becomes available on your iPhone.

●Ill AT&T Wi-Fi 📶	12:05 PM	⊕ ✈ ✱ 79% ▮▶
Cancel	**Gmail**	Save
✉ Mail		⬤
👥 Contacts		⬤
📅 Calendars		⬤
▭ Notes		◯

Advanced Google

Similar to iCloud and Exchange, a Google account has some settings you aren't likely to use, but it's good to know how to get to them in case you do. To access these settings, move to the Passwords & Accounts screen and tap your Google account. On the Gmail account's screen, you can change the types of data you are syncing by setting the switches to on or off. Tap Account, and then tap Advanced to see additional settings. Working with these is similar to working with iCloud. For example, you can determine where draft email messages are stored, such as on the Gmail server or on your iPhone.

You can't change the password for a Google account in the Settings app on your iPhone. You have to change the password elsewhere, such as by accessing your Google account via the Google website. After your Google password has been changed, you're prompted to enter the new password the first time your iPhone attempts to access your account.

Setting Up an Online Account that Isn't Built In

You can access many types of online accounts on your iPhone. These include accounts that are "built in," which include AOL, Exchange, Google, iCloud, Outlook.com, and Yahoo! Setting up an AOL, Exchange, Outlook.com, or Yahoo! account is similar to configuring a Google or iCloud account on your iPhone. Just select the account type you want to use and provide the information for which you are prompted.

There are other types of accounts you might want to use that aren't "built in." An email account included with an Internet access account, such as one from a cable Internet provider, is one example. Support for these accounts isn't built in to the iOS; however, you can usually set up such accounts on your iPhone fairly easily.

When you obtain an account, such as email accounts that are part of your Internet service, you should receive all the information you need to configure those accounts on your iPhone. If you don't have this information, visit the provider's website and look for information on configuring the account in an email application. You need to have this information to configure the account on the iPhone.

With the configuration information for the account you want to use on your iPhone in hand, you're ready to set it up:

(**1**) On the Home screen, tap Settings.

(**2**) Tap Passwords & Accounts.

Settings		
iTunes & App Store		>
Wallet & Apple Pay		>
Passwords & Accounts		>

(3) Tap Add Account.

(4) Tap Other.

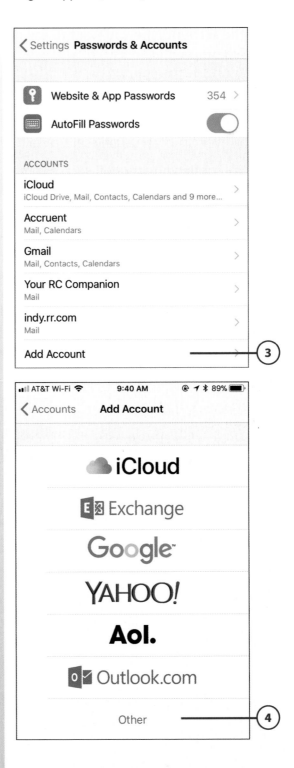

5 Tap the type of account you want to add. For example, to set up an email account, tap Add Mail Account.

6 Enter the information by filling in the fields you see; various types of information are required for different kinds of accounts. You just need to enter the information you received from the account's provider.

7 Tap Next. If the iPhone can set up the account automatically, its information is verified and it's ready for you to use (if the account supports multiple types of information, you can enable or disable the types with which you want to work on your iPhone). If the iPhone can't set up the account automatically, you're prompted to enter additional information to complete the account configuration. When you're done, the account appears on the list of accounts and is ready for you to use.

8 Configure the switches for the data sync options you see. For example, to use the account for email, set the Mail switch to on (green).

9 Tap Save. The account you configured is available in the related app, such as Mail if you set up an email account.

ᴧ AT&T Wi-Fi 🛜	12:11 PM	℗ ✓ ✳ 78% 🔋
‹ Add Account	**Other**	

MAIL

Add Mail Account ──────────── › ⑤

CONTACTS

Add LDAP Account   ›

Add CardDAV Account   ›

ᴧ AT&T Wi-Fi 🛜	12:12 PM	℗ ✓ ✳ 78% 🔋
Cancel	**New Account**	Next ── ⑦

Name   Brad Miser

Email   [redacted] ── ⑥

Password   ••••••••

Description   indy.rr.com

ᴧ AT&T Wi-Fi 🛜	12:14 PM	℗ ✓ ✳ 77% 🔋
Cancel	**IMAP**	Save ── ⑨

✉ Mail   🟢 ──┐
                      ⑧
▭ Notes   ◯ ──┘

Multiple Accounts

There is no limit (that I have found so far) on the number of online accounts (even of the same type, such as Gmail) that you can access on your iPhone. (You can only have one iCloud account configured on your iPhone at the same time.)

Configuring Social Media Accounts on Your iPhone

Social media apps are useful for doing things such as keeping in touch with others, sharing your opinions and reading the opinions of others, and exchanging photos. Examples of these types of social media include Facebook, Instagram, and Twitter. Your iPhone is ideally suited to these because you can easily download and configure these apps to work on your phone.

Unlike Google, iCloud, and other accounts that are configured through the Settings app, you configure your social media accounts directly in their apps.

To use a social media app, you perform the following three steps:

1. Download and install the app you want to use.

2. Configure the app to access your social media account.

3. Configure other settings for the social media app.

The steps to find and download apps are provided in Chapter 4. Examples of the second and third steps follow.

Facebook is one of the most popular social media channels you can use to keep informed about other people and inform them about you. Use these steps to download and configure Facebook on your iPhone:

1. Use the App Store app to download and install the Facebook app on your iPhone (see Chapter 4 for the details of working with the App Store app).

2. Tap the Facebook icon on a Home screen to open the app.

Already Signed In?

If you have previously signed into Facebook on the phone, you see that account on the opening screen. Tap the account shown. You're prompted to enter your password; when you do, you sign in and can jump to step 10.

Don't Have a Facebook Account?

If you don't already have a Facebook account, you can create one by tapping Sign Up for Facebook on the opening screen in the app or on the Log In screen. Follow the onscreen instructions to create a new Facebook account and log into it.

3. Tap in the Email or phone number field.

4. Enter the email address, phone number, or Facebook account name associated with your account.

5. Enter your password. (If you don't know your password, tap Forgot Password? and follow the onscreen instructions to reset it.)

6. Tap Log In.

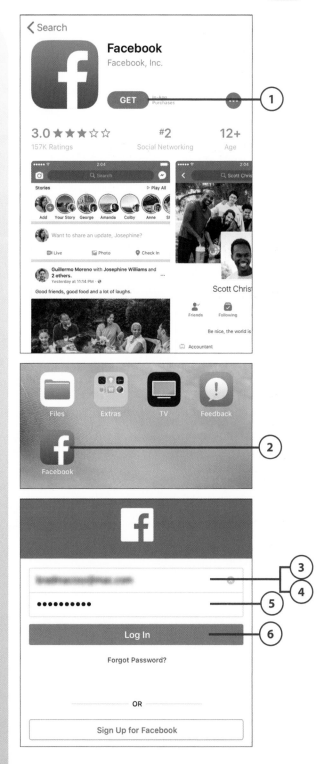

(7) If you want to receive notifications from Facebook, such as when someone posts on your Timeline, tap Allow; if you don't want these notifications, tap Don't Allow. (You can always change these notification settings as described in Chapter 4.)

(8) Use the Facebook app to post comments, add photos, and so on. You can use the app with its default settings. Perform steps 11 and 12 when you want to make changes to how the app works.

(9) Further configure the app by tapping Facebook on the Settings screen.

(10) Use the app's settings to configure how it works for you. For example, you can configure notifications, determine if it uses cellular data, and so on.

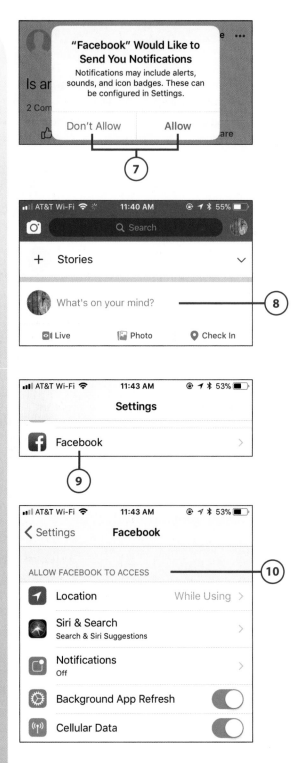

Setting How and When Your Accounts Are Updated

The great thing about online accounts is that their information can be updated any time your iPhone can connect to the Internet. This means you have access to the latest information, such as new emails, changes to your calendars, and so on. There are three basic ways information gets updated:

- **Push**—When information is updated via Push, the server pushes (thus the name) updated information onto your iPhone whenever that information changes. For example, when you receive a new email, that email is immediately sent (or pushed) to your iPhone. Push provides you with the most current information all the time but uses a lot more battery than the other options.

- **Fetch**—When information is updated via Fetch, your iPhone connects to the account and retrieves the updated information according to a schedule, such as every 15 minutes. Fetch doesn't keep your information quite as current as Push does, but it uses much less battery than Push does.

- **Manual**—You can cause an app's information to be updated manually. This happens whenever you open or move into an app or by a manual refresh. For example, you can get new email by moving onto the Inboxes screen in the Mail app and swiping down from the top of the screen.

You can configure the update method that is used globally, and you can set the method for specific accounts. Some account types, such as iCloud, support all three options whereas others might support only Fetch and Manual. The global option for updating is used unless you override it for individual accounts. For example, you might want your work account to be updated via Push so your information there is always current, whereas configuring Fetch on a personal account might be frequent enough.

Configuring How New Data Is Retrieved for Your Accounts

To configure how your information is updated, perform the following steps:

1. Move to the Passwords & Accounts screen of the Settings app.

2. Tap Fetch New Data.

3. To enable data to be pushed to your iPhone, slide the Push switch to on (green). To disable push to extend battery life, set it to off (white). This setting is global, meaning that if you disable Push here, it is disabled for all accounts even though you can still configure Push to be used for individual accounts. For example, if your iCloud account is set to use Push but Push is globally disabled, the iCloud account's setting is ignored and data is fetched instead.

4. To change how an account's information is updated, tap it. The account's screen displays. The options on this screen depend on the kind of account it is. You always have Fetch and Manual; Push is displayed only for accounts that support it.

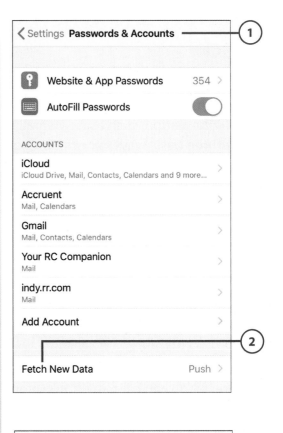

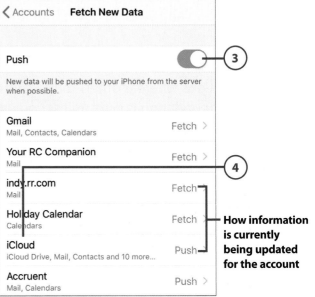

How information is currently being updated for the account

5 Tap the option you want to use for the account: Push, Fetch, or Manual.

If you choose Manual, information is retrieved only when you manually start the process by opening the related app (such as Mail to get your email) or by using the refresh gesture, regardless of the global setting.

If you choose Fetch, information is updated according to the schedule you set in step 9.

6 If you choose the Push option in step 5 and are working with an email account, choose the mailboxes whose information you want to be pushed by tapping them so they have a check mark; to prevent a mailbox's information from being pushed, tap it so that it doesn't have a check mark. (The Inbox is selected by default and can't be unselected.)

7 Tap Fetch New Data.

8 Repeat steps 5 through 7 until you have set the update option for each account. (The current option is shown to the right of the account's name.)

9 Tap the amount of time when you want the iPhone to fetch data when Push is turned off globally or for those accounts for which you have selected Fetch or that don't support Push; tap Manually if you want to manually check for information for Fetch accounts or when Push is off. Information for your accounts is updated according to your settings.

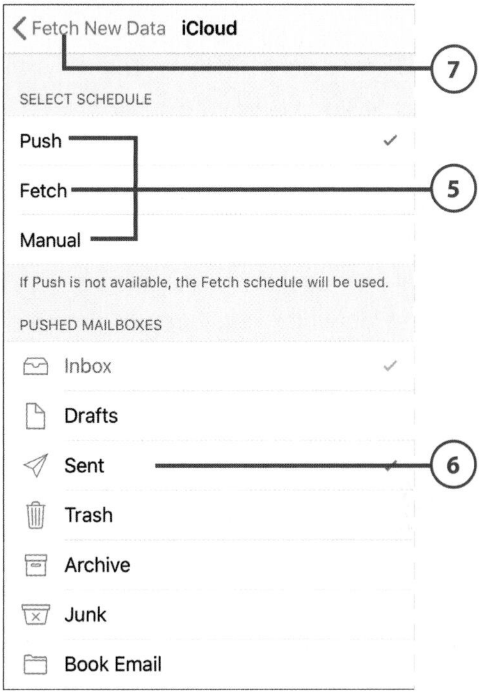

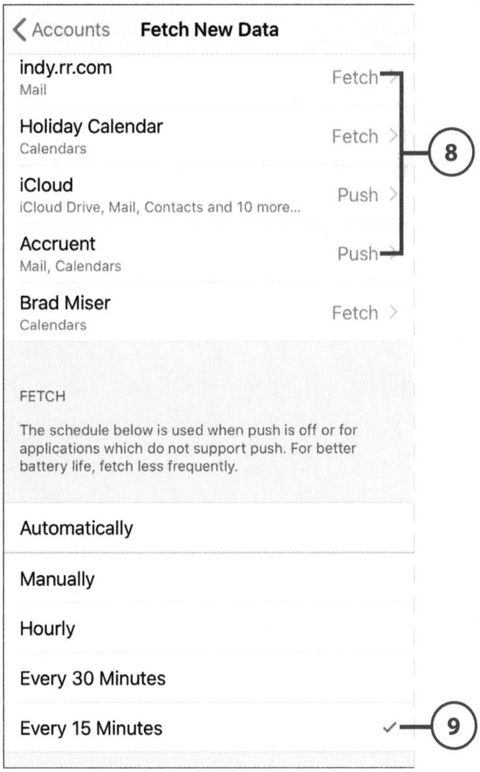

>>>*Go Further*

TIPS FOR MANAGING YOUR ACCOUNTS

As you add and use accounts on your iPhone, keep the following points in mind:

- You can temporarily disable any data for any account by moving to the Passwords & Accounts screen and tapping that account. Set the switches for the data you don't want to use to off (white). You might be prompted to keep or delete that information; if you choose to keep it, the data remains on your iPhone but is disconnected from the account and is no longer updated. If you delete it, you can always recover it again by simply turning that data back on. For example, suppose you are going on vacation and don't want to deal with work email, meeting notifications, and so on. Move to your work account and disable all its data. That data disappears from the related apps; for example, the account's mailboxes no longer appear in the Mail app. When you want to start using the account again, simply re-enable its data.

- If you want to completely remove an account from your iPhone, move to its configuration screen, swipe up the screen, and tap Delete Account. Tap Delete in the confirmation dialog box and the account is removed from your iPhone. (You can always sign in to the account to start using it again.)

- You can have different notifications for certain aspects of an account, such as email. See Chapter 2, "Using Your iPhone's Core Features," for the details about using notifications, and Chapter 4 for the steps to configure the notifications your online accounts use. For example, you might want to hear a different sound when you receive work emails versus those sent to your personal account.

- Although using Push is great because you always have the most current information on your iPhone, it has one certain and one potential drawback. The certain drawback is that it causes your iPhone to use more power, and so your iPhone runs out of power faster than it does if you set this to Fetch or Manually. The potential drawback is if you have a plan that has a limited amount of data each month; using Push consumes a lot more data than Fetch or Manually do and so can use more of your data allowance than you might want. As long as you keep an eye on your battery's status, using more power probably won't be a big deal. If you have an unlimited data plan, the extra data Push uses doesn't matter at all;

if you do have a limited plan, you need to consider whether using Push is worth the additional data it consumes.

- You can change how information is updated at any time, too. If your iPhone is running low on battery, disable Push and set Fetch to Manually so you can control when the updates happen. When your battery is charged again, you can re-enable Push or set a Fetch schedule.

Tap to personalize an iPhone to make it your own

Use shortcuts to perform a series of tasks by speaking a phrase

Install apps so you can do all kinds of useful and fun things with your iPhone

Configure notifications from apps so they provide the right amount of information at the right times

In this chapter, you learn how to make an iPhone into *your* iPhone by making it work the way you want it to. Topics include the following:

→ Getting started
→ Configuring notifications
→ Configuring Do Not Disturb
→ Configuring Screen Time
→ Configuring the Control Center
→ Configuring the Widget Center
→ Setting keyboard, language, and format options
→ Setting a Passcode and Face ID or Touch ID
→ Setting accessibility options
→ Customizing how your iPhone works with apps
→ Customizing how your iPhone works with shortcuts

Customizing How Your iPhone Works

You can configure the iPhone to make it work how you want it to. Taking the time to tailor your iPhone to your personal preferences and how you want to use it makes the iPhone easier and more fun to use.

Getting Started

As you've seen in previous chapters, the Settings app enables you to configure various aspects of your iPhone, such as connecting your iPhone to a Wi-Fi network and configuring iCloud and other online accounts. The Settings app provides many other configuration tools that you can use to tailor how your iPhone works to suit your preferences.

Perhaps the most important settings are related to the security of your iPhone, which you can configure by setting a passcode with facial recognition with Face ID or with fingerprint recognition using Touch ID; in addition to securing your iPhone, Face ID or Touch ID make your phone much more convenient to use. Also very important is configuring the notifications your iPhone uses so you get the information you need without being constantly bombarded; setting a Do Not Disturb schedule helps prevent your iPhone from bothering you when you don't want it to. You can use the Screen Time settings to put limits on how long and in what ways your iPhone can be used; this can be very useful if you share your phone with young people, and you want to make sure they don't spend too much time on the phone or that they don't do things you don't want them to.

You can also configure the Control Center, Widget Center, keyboards, privacy and location services options, and how content on your phone can be accessed.

Although the Settings app enables you to customize how your iPhone works in many ways, installing apps on your iPhone enables it to do so much more than it can "out of the box." You'll want to explore and download apps to completely customize how you use your iPhone; the possibilities of what your phone can do with apps are limitless!

And, new to iOS 12, is the ability to create shortcuts, which enable you to perform multiple tasks by speaking one phrase. Siri automatically creates shortcuts for you. And, you can use the Shortcuts app to create and manage your own shortcuts so that your iPhone does more while you have to do less.

Configuring Notifications

In Chapter 2, "Using Your iPhone's Core Features," you learned how to work with the various types of notifications your iPhone presents to keep you informed of important (and at times, not-so-important) information. Notifications can become distracting or overwhelming because the apps on your phone can provide notifications about all manner of things—incoming mail, messages, news updates, and so on. If an app manages a lot of activity, it can generate multiple notifications over a short period of time.

Using the Settings App to Configure Notifications

You can configure how apps can provide notifications and, if you allow notifications, which type. You can also configure other aspects of notifications, such as whether an app's notifications appear in the Notification Center or if they appear on the Lock screen. Apps can support different notification options; some apps, such as Mail, support notification configuration by account (for example, you can set a different alert sound for new mail in each account). You can follow the same general steps to configure notifications for each app; you should explore the options for the apps you use most often to ensure they work the best for you.

When you configure notifications for apps that support multiple accounts (such as Mail), you can configure notifications for each account separately. For example, you might want a different sound for new email sent to your iCloud account than the sound you hear for new email sent to your Google Gmail account.

When you configure notifications for an app that doesn't support different accounts, you configure all notifications for the app at the same time.

The steps in the following task show you how to configure Mail's notifications, which is a good example because it can include notifications for multiple accounts and supports a lot of notification features; the notification settings for other apps might have fewer features or might be organized slightly differently. When you configure notifications for an app that doesn't support accounts, you set all the options from one screen as opposed to using a different screen for each account used by that app. But configuring the notifications for any app follows a similar pattern as exemplified by the steps for Mail's notification settings.

To configure notifications from the Mail app, perform the following steps:

1. Tap Settings on the Home screen.
2. Tap Notifications.

(3) Tap Show Previews. As you may recall from Chapter 2, alerts from an app can contain a preview of the information related to the alert, such as part of an email message.

(4) To have alerts always show the preview, tap Always; tap When Unlocked to show previews only when your iPhone is unlocked; or tap Never to hide previews.

(5) Tap the Back icon (<).

(6) Tap Siri Suggestions. Siri can suggest shortcuts for apps so you can speak a phrase to do something in that app. On the Siri Suggestions screen, you see the apps installed on your iPhone. The switch next to each app determines if these sugges-tions can be made on the Lock screen. (You'll learn more about shortcuts in "Customizing How Your Phone Works with Shortcuts" later in this chapter and "Using Siri with Shortcuts" in Chapter 11, "Working with Siri.")

< Settings   **Notifications**

Show Previews   Always >   (3)

Notification previews will be shown whether iPhone is locked or unlocked.

< Back   **Show Previews**   (5)

Always   ✓

When Unlocked   (4)

Never

< Settings   **Notifications**

Show Previews   Always >

Notification previews will be shown whether iPhone is locked or unlocked.

Siri Suggestions   (6)

Choose which apps can suggest Shortcuts on the lock screen.

7 Set the switch to off (white) if you don't want Siri to suggest shortcuts for an app on the Lock screen; set it to on (green) if you do want to see these suggestions on the Lock screen. If you set an app's switch to off, Siri still creates shortcut suggestions for the app, you just won't see them on the Lock screen. (You can control whether Siri can make suggestions for the app using the Siri & Search settings as described in Chapter 11.)

8 Set the switches to off for other apps for which you don't want to see shortcut suggestions on the Lock screen.

9 Tap the Back icon (<). In the Notification Style section, you see all the apps installed on your phone. Along with the app name and icon, you see the current status of its notifications.

10 Swipe up or down the screen to locate the app whose notifications you want to configure. (The apps are listed in alphabetical order.)

11 Tap the app whose notifications you want to configure.

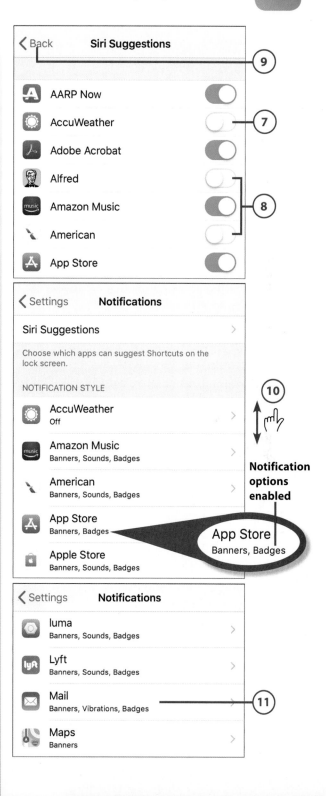

(12) If you want the app to provide notifications, set the Allow Notifications switch to on (green) and move to step 13. If you don't want notifications from the app, set the Allow Notifications switch to off (white) and skip to step 35.

(13) Tap the account for which you want to configure notifications; if the app doesn't support accounts, skip to step 15.

(14) If you don't want any notifications for the account, set the Allow Notifications switch to off (white) and skip to step 30. If you do want notifications for the account, set the switch to on (green) and continue to step 15.

(15) Tap the Lock Screen icon so it has a check mark if you want notifications to be visible on the Lock screen; if you don't want to receive notifications on the Lock screen, tap the Lock Screen icon so it doesn't have a check mark.

(16) Tap the Notification Center icon so it has a check mark if you want notifications to appear in the Notification Center.

(17) Tap the Banners icon so it has a check mark if you want to see banner notifications (which appear at the top of the screen).

(18) If you enabled Banners, tap Banner Style; if not, skip to step 22.

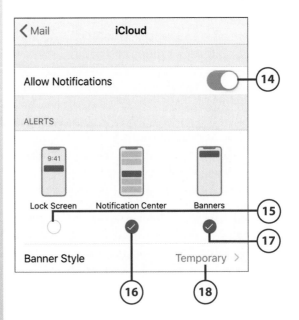

19 Tap Temporary if you want the alert banners to appear on the screen, remain there for a few seconds, and then disappear. Temporary banners keep you informed, but don't interrupt what you are doing.

20 Tap Persistent if you want the alert banners to remain on screen until you take action on them. For example, if the alert is for a calendar event, you might want it to be persistent so that it really gets your attention.

21 Tap the Back icon (<).

22 Tap Sounds.

23 Use the resulting Sounds screen to choose the alert sound and vibration for new email messages to the account (see "Choosing the Sounds and Vibratory Feedback Your iPhone Uses" in Chapter 5, "Customizing How Your iPhone Looks and Sounds," for the details about configuring sounds and vibrations).

24 Tap the Back icon (<).

21

‹ iCloud	**Banner Style**	
Temporary		✓
Persistent		

19
20

Banner Style	Temporary ›
Sounds	Bamboo ›

22

‹ iCloud	**Sounds**	
Vibration		Default ›

24

STORE

Tone Store

Download All Purchased Tones

This will download all ringtones and alerts purchased using the "bradmacost@mac.com" account.

23

ALERT TONES

None (Default)

Aurora

✓ Bamboo

Chord

Circles

Complete

Hello

(25) To display the app's badge (which shows the number of new items in that app or account), set the Badges switch to on (green). (If you set this to off [white] for an account, new items sent to that account won't be included in the count of new items shown on the app's badge.)

(26) Tap Show Previews.

(27) Tap Always (Default) if you always want previews to appear in notifications; When Unlocked if you want them to appear only when your iPhone is unlocked; or Never if you don't want previews to be displayed at any time.

(28) Tap the Back icon (<).

(29) Tap the Back icon (<).

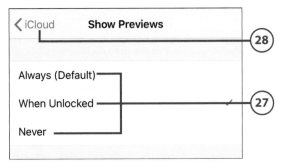

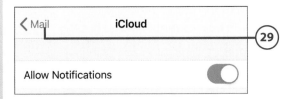

30 Configure notifications for the other accounts used in the app.

31 Configure notifications for VIP email and threads.

32 Tap Notification Grouping.

33 Tap Automatic if you want notifications grouped in the notification center automatically; tap By App if you want them to be grouped by the app they come from, or Off if you don't want them grouped at all (they appear individually in the Notification Center, assuming you've enabled them to appear there in step 16).

34 Tap the Back icon (<).

35 Tap the Back icon (<).

⟨ Notifications **Mail**

Allow Notifications

Your RC Companion
Badges

Gmail
Banners, Badges

indy.rr.com
Badges   **30**

iCloud
Banners, Sounds, Badges

iCloud
Banners, Sounds, Badges

Accruent
Badges

Notification options enabled

VIP
Banners, Vibrations, Badges

Thread Notifications
Banners, Vibrations, Badges   **31**

You can receive VIP and Thread Notifications even if other Mail notifications are turned off.

OPTIONS

Notification Grouping   Automatic >

34   **32**

⟨ Mail   **Notification Grouping**

Automatic   ✓

By App   **33**

Off

⟨ Notifications **Mail**

35

Allow Notifications

(36) Repeat steps 11 through 35 for each app shown on the Notifications screen. Certain apps might not have all the options shown in these steps while others might have more options, but the process to configure their notifications is similar.

(37) Swipe up until you reach the bottom of the screen.

(38) Configure any special notifications you see. What you see here depends on the country or region your phone is associated with. For example, where I live in the United States, the GOVERNMENT ALERTS section includes two notifications. AMBER Alerts are issued when a child is missing and presumed abducted, whereas Emergency Alerts are issued for things such as national crises, local weather, and so on. You can use the switches to enable (green) or prevent (white) these types of alerts, but you can't configure them.

More Options

Some apps provide notifications for the types of activity they manage. For example, the Calendar app enables you to configure notifications for upcoming events, invitations, and so on. Open the Notification Settings screen for the apps you use frequently to explore the notification options they offer.

>>>Go Further
NOTIFY THIS

Here are some other hopefully useful notification tidbits for your consideration:

- **VIPs**—Mail supports VIPs, which are people from whom email messages are treated specially, such as having a dedicated mailbox in the Mail app. You can apply specific notification settings to VIP messages using the VIP notification option. These override the notification settings for the email account to which messages from VIPs are sent.

- **Threads**—Mail can keep related messages together as threads. Like VIP messages, you can override Mail's notifications for messages that are part of threads using the Thread Notifications option.

- **Special sounds and vibrations for contacts**—You can override some app's sounds and vibration notification settings for individuals in your Contacts app. For example, you can configure a specific ringtone, new text tone, and vibrations for calls or texts from a contact. You do this using the contact information screen as explained in Chapter 6, "Managing Contacts."

- **Installed app not shown**—You must have opened an app at least once for it to appear on the Notifications screen.

- **Initial notification prompt**—The first time you open many apps, you are prompted to allow that app to send you notifications. If you allow this, the app is able to send notifications about its activity. If you deny this, the app isn't able to send notifications. You can always configure the app's notifications using the steps in this task regardless of your initial decision.

- **Lots of apps**—If you have a lot of apps or activity on your iPhone, notifications can become disruptive. It can take a little time to set each app's notifications, but making sure you receive only the notifications that are important to you prevents your iPhone from bothering you unnecessarily. For less important apps, have their notifications appear grouped only in the Notification Center so you can review them at your leisure. For more important apps, use banner alerts to make sure you are aware of the activity for that app.

Configuring Notifications from Notifications

As you receive notifications, you can configure the notifications from the app directly from a notification. This is convenient because you can configure notifications for apps as they happen, which sometimes makes it easier to decide which options you want to set.

How you do this depends on the type of notification you are working with. The steps to configure notifications from notifications follow:

(1) If you are starting from a notification on the Notification Center, move to step 2; if you are starting from a banner alert, skip to step 4.

(2) Swipe to the left on a notification or a group of notifications.

(3) Tap Manage and skip to step 6.

(4) If you have a phone that supports 3D Touch, press and hold on the notification; if you are using an older model, swipe to the left on the notification.

(5) Tap the Options icon (…).

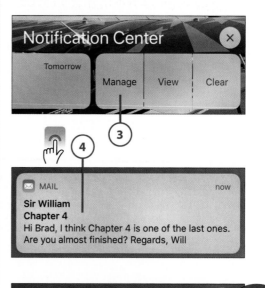

6 If you want the only notifications you receive to be on the Notification Center (no banners, sounds, or badge), tap Deliver Quietly. The notifications for the app and all its accounts are set to Deliver Quietly. Skip the rest of these steps.

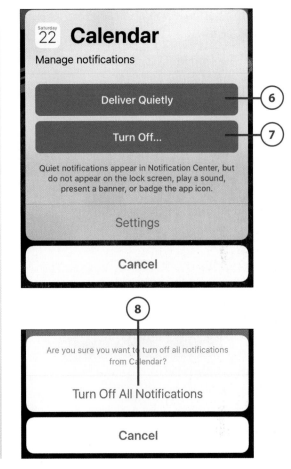

More on Managing Notifications from Notifications

If you set the notifications for an app to Deliver Quietly, you can restore them to their prior settings by opening the Manage notifications dialog and tapping Deliver Prominently. If you want to use the Settings app to configure the notification settings, tap Settings.

7 To turn off all notifications for the app, tap Turn Off.

8 Tap Turn Off All Notifications.

Configuring Do Not Disturb

As you learned in Chapter 1 "Getting Started with Your iPhone," the Do Not Disturb feature enables you to temporarily silence notifications; you can also configure quiet times during which notifications are automatically silenced by performing the following steps:

1. Open the Settings app and tap Do Not Disturb.

2. To activate Do Not Disturb manually, set the Manual switch to on (green). (This does the same thing as activating it from the Control Center as explained in Chapter 1.)

3. To configure Do Not Disturb to activate automatically on a schedule, set the Scheduled switch to on (green).

4. Tap the From and To box.

5. Tap From.

6. Swipe on the time selection wheels to select the hour and minute (AM or PM) when you want the Do Not Disturb period to start.

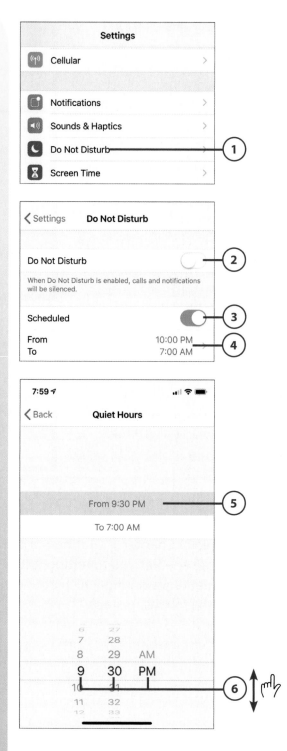

⑦ Tap To.

⑧ Swipe on the time selection wheels to set the hour and minute (AM or PM) when you want the Do Not Disturb period to end.

⑨ Tap the Back icon (<).

⑩ If the Do Not Disturb period is at night or at another time during which you really don't want to be disturbed, set the Bedtime switch to on (green). In addition to calls and notifications being silenced, the Lock screen is also dimmed.

⑪ If you want notifications to be silenced during the Do Not Disturb period only when your phone is locked, tap While iPhone is locked. Tap Always if you want notifications to be silenced regardless of the Lock status. This setting presumes that if your iPhone is unlocked, you won't mind taking calls or having notifications even if it is within the Do Not Disturb period because you are probably using the phone.

⑫ Tap Allow Calls From.

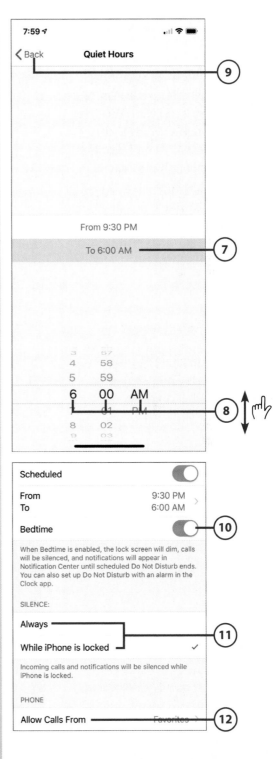

(13) Tap the option for the group of
people whose calls should be
allowed during the Do Not Disturb
period. The options are Everyone,
which allows all calls to come in; No
One, which sends all calls directly to
voicemail; Favorites, which allows
calls from people on your Favorites
lists to come through but calls from
all others go to voicemail; or one of
your contact groups, which allows
calls from anyone in the selected
group to come through while all
others go to voicemail.

(14) Tap the Back icon (<).

(15) Set the Repeated Calls switch to on
(green) if you want a second call
from the same person within three
minutes to be allowed through. This
feature is based on the assumption
that if a call is really important, the
person calling you will try again
immediately.

(16) Tap Activate in the DO NOT
DISTURB WHILE DRIVING section.

(17) To have Do Not Disturb activate
automatically when you are driving,
tap Automatically to have this based
on your iPhone's motion (once the
iPhone's accelerometer detects that
the phone has reached a particular
speed) or When Connected to Car
Bluetooth to have Do Not Disturb
active whenever your iPhone is
connected to your car's Bluetooth
system; to prevent this type of automatic activation, tap Manually.

(18) Tap the Back icon (<).

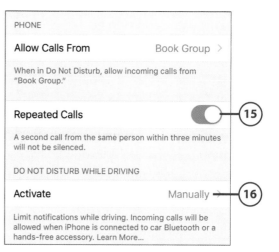

(19) Tap Auto-Reply To.

(20) Configure to whom you want automatic replies to be sent when Do Not Disturb is on (regardless of how it was activated) by tapping No One to prevent automatic replies; Recents to send replies to people on your recent lists (such as calls you have recently received); Favorites to send replies to your favorites; or All Contacts to automatically reply to anyone on your Contacts lists.

(21) Tap the Back icon (<).

(22) Tap Auto-Reply.

(23) Type the message you want to be automatically sent.

(24) Tap the Back icon (<). During the Do Not Disturb period or based on the DO NOT DISTURB WHILE DRIVING setting, your iPhone is silent, except for any exceptions you configured. Automatic replies are sent according to your configuration. When the scheduled Do Not Disturb period ends, your iPhone resumes its normal notification activity.

DO NOT DISTURB WHILE DRIVING

Activate   Manually >

Limit notifications while driving. Incoming calls will be allowed when iPhone is connected to car Bluetooth or a hands-free accessory. Learn More...

Auto-Reply To   Favorites > **(19)**

< Back   **Auto-Reply To**   **(21)**

No One
                                                         (20)
Recents

Favorites   ✓

All Contacts

Auto-Reply To   Favorites >

Auto-Reply   I'm not available. >

Your Favorites will receive this message when they text you, and may break through Do Not Disturb by sending "urgent" as an additional message.

(24)   **(22)**

< Back   **Auto-Reply**

I'm not available now but will be in touch shortly.   **(23)**

Configuring Screen Time

Screen Time enables you to both monitor and limit the time you or someone with whom you share your iPhone are using your iPhone in various ways. When Screen Time is active, it tracks how long you are using your phone and the tasks you are performing with it. You can also limit the use of the phone by configuring the following:

- **Downtime**. You can set a downtime during which only specific apps and phone calls will work. The idea is to help you limit the time you are on your phone.

- **App Limits**. Use this to place limits on the amount of time per day that certain types of apps will work, such as Social Networking. This can be helpful if you feel you are spending too much time with specific kinds of apps. Once the time limit is reached, the apps in the group that have limits are not available to use again until the next day.

- **Always Allowed**. You can select specific apps that are always available regardless of the other restrictions (such as App Limits).

- **Content & Privacy Restrictions**. These settings enable you to restrict the access to specific content and apps on your phone. Suppose you let other people borrow your iPhone but don't want them to use certain apps or to see data you'd rather keep to yourself. You can enable restrictions to prevent someone from accessing these areas. You can also restrict the use of apps, movies, music, and other content based on the age rating that the app or other content has.

You can enable or disable Screen Time and you can set a Screen Time Passcode that someone needs to be able to change the Screen Time settings; if you are configuring Screen Time for someone else, you should set a passcode to prevent him from accessing the Screen Time settings. You can also share your Screen Time information on all your devices that are configured with your iCloud account so you can see the total time you are spending on all your devices.

Configuring Downtime, App Limits, a Screen Time Passcode, and Screen Time Sharing

To configure Screen Time, perform the following steps:

(1) Open the Settings app and tap Screen Time.

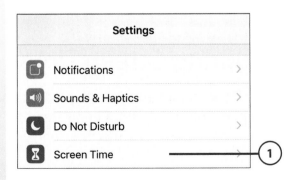

(2) Tap Turn On Screen Time.

(3) Tap Continue. (You have to do this step only when you perform step 2. When you are making changes to Screen Time when it is already active, you move directly from step 1 to step 5.)

(4) Tap This is My iPhone if you are configuring your own phone or This is My Child's iPhone if you want to have a "quick start" and configure all the details later. These steps show the This is My iPhone option because it shows you how to configure each element.

A Shortcut by Any Other Name

There are many options under the Screen Time settings, and it can take a while to work through all of them. The good news is that you don't have to tackle them all at once. If you want to take a shortcut, in step 4, tap This is My Child's iPhone instead of This is My iPhone. You are guided through steps to configure the most important Screen Time elements, which are Downtime, App Limits, and a passcode. After you've completed the This is My Child's iPhone option, you can use these steps to configure other elements, such as Content & Privacy Restrictions, as you want to increase the amount of limitations Screen Time places on your iPhone.

(5) If you want to schedule time that you won't use your iPhone, tap Downtime; if you don't want to use this, skip to step 10.

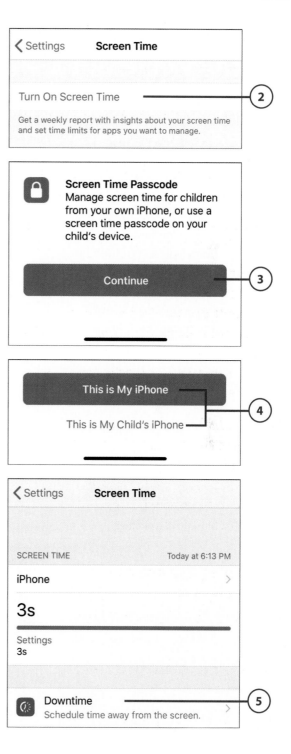

6 Set the Downtime switch to on (green).

7 Tap Start and use the resulting wheels to select the downtime's start time.

8 Tap End and use the resulting wheels to select the downtime's end time.

9 Tap the Back icon (<).

10 Tap App Limits. The first time you set App Limits, you jump directly to step 11. If you've configured App Limits before, tap Add Limit and then move to step 11 (not shown in the figures).

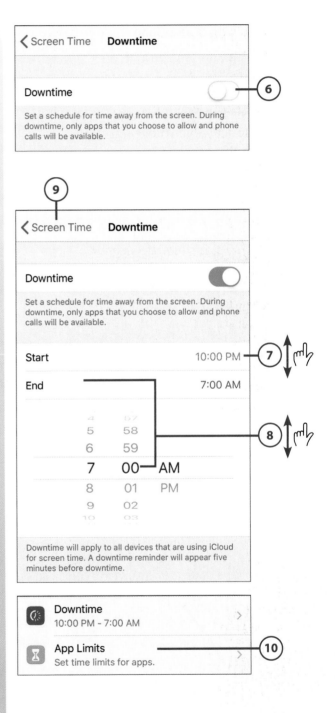

‹ Screen Time   **Downtime**

Downtime

Set a schedule for time away from the screen. During downtime, only apps that you choose to allow and phone calls will be available.

‹ Screen Time   **Downtime**

Downtime

Set a schedule for time away from the screen. During downtime, only apps that you choose to allow and phone calls will be available.

Start   10:00 PM

End   7:00 AM

4   57
5   58
6   59
7   00   AM
8   01   PM
9   02
10   03

Downtime will apply to all devices that are using iCloud for screen time. A downtime reminder will appear five minutes before downtime.

Downtime
10:00 PM - 7:00 AM

App Limits
Set time limits for apps.

11 Tap the groups of apps for which you want to set a time limit.

12 Tap Add.

13 Use the Time wheel to set the time limit.

14 If you want the limit to apply only to certain days, tap Customize Days and select the days on which you want the limit to be active (not shown on the figures).

15 To change the apps for which the limit applies, tap Edit Apps; on the resulting screen, tap apps whose circle is selected to remove them from the limit or tap apps whose circle isn't selected to add them to the limit. Then tap Add to return to the previous screen (these steps are not shown on the figures).

16 Tap the Back icon (<).

Cancel	**Choose Apps**	Add

CATEGORIES

All Apps & Categories

Social Networking
Messenger, Facebook, and 4 more

Games
BREAKOUT®, CSR Racing 2, and 1 m...

Entertainment
TV, Podcasts, and 13 more

< App Limits **Social Networking**

Time   1 hr

57
58
0   59
1 hour   0 min
2   1
3   2

Customize Days

App limits apply to all devices that are using iCloud for screen time. A notification will appear five minutes before the limit expires.

APPS & CATEGORIES

Social Networking
Messenger, Facebook, and 4 more

Edit Apps

Delete Limit

(17) To set more limits, tap Add Limit and repeat steps 11 through 16.

Change Your Mind

To remove a limit, move the App Limits screen and tap the limit you want to remove. Tap Delete Limit and then tap Delete Limit again. The limit is removed.

(18) Tap the Back icon (<).

(19) Tap Always Allowed.

(20) To enable an app to work during downtime or if it is included in an app limit, tap Add (+). The app moves to the ALLOWED APPS section and will open even if it is during downtime or if the app is under a limit.

(21) To put an app under downtime, tap Remove (–); then tap Remove at the prompt (not shown in the figure). The app moves to the CHOOSE APPS section and is controlled by downtime and a limit.

(22) Tap the Back icon (<).

Content & Privacy Restrictions

The Content & Privacy Restrictions section enables you to control access to types of content and other functions on your iPhone. See the next section for the details of configuring these options.

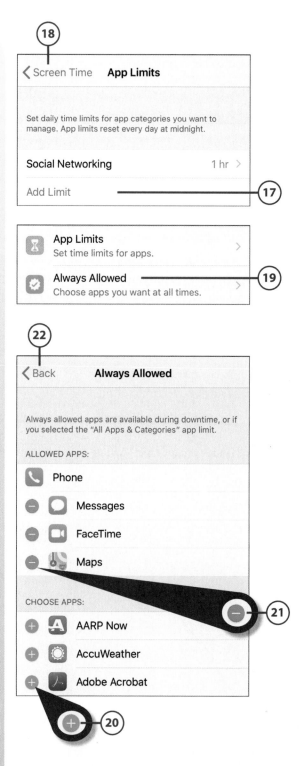

23 To configure a passcode to prevent changes to Screen Time settings, tap Use Screen Time Passcode; if you don't want to set this passcode, skip to step 26.

24 Enter the passcode you want to use.

25 Re-enter the passcode you want to use (not shown on figures).

26 If you want to include the time you are using all of the devices signed into your iCloud account, set the Share Across Devices switch to on (green). If you leave this switch off, Screen Time only tracks time on the iPhone.

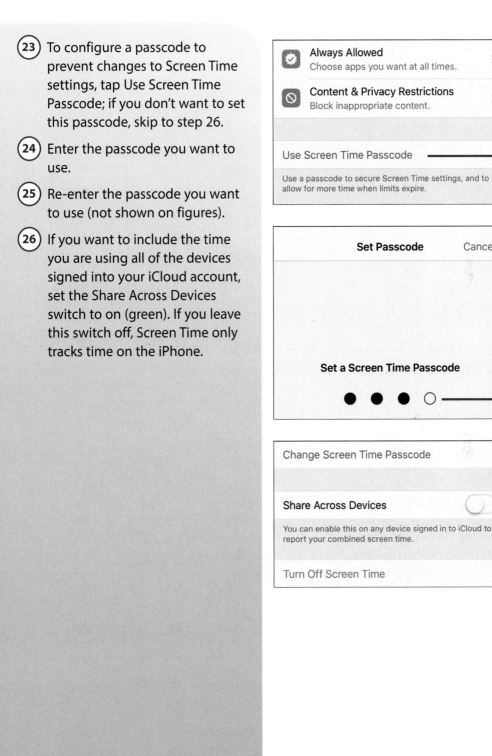

Always Allowed
Choose apps you want at all times.   >

Content & Privacy Restrictions
Block inappropriate content.   >

Use Screen Time Passcode ———————— **23**

Use a passcode to secure Screen Time settings, and to allow for more time when limits expire.

Set Passcode   Cancel

Set a Screen Time Passcode

● ● ● ○ ———————— **24**

Change Screen Time Passcode

Share Across Devices   ⬜ ——— **26**

You can enable this on any device signed in to iCloud to report your combined screen time.

Turn Off Screen Time

>>>Go Further
MORE SCREEN TIME

As you've seen, Screen Time helps you put various kinds of limitations on how your iPhone works. Following are a few more Screen Time pointers:

- If you set a Screen Time passcode, you need to provide it in order to make changes to settings, such as to change the Downtime period or to turn Screen Time off.

- If you use an iPhone that has a four-digit passcode (not recommended if your iPhone supports a six-digit passcode), don't set the Screen Time passcode to be the same as your iPhone's passcode. This is especially important if you give the iPhone passcode to someone who uses your iPhone or if you are setting Screen Time up on someone else's iPhone.

- If you want to stop using Screen Time, move to the Screen Time screen and tap Turn Off Screen Time. (You have to provide your Screen Time passcode to do this.) Tap Turn Off Screen Time at the prompt. You can re-enable it again by repeating these steps.

- If you want to change the configuration option for Screen Time, such as using the This is My Child's iPhone option instead of This is My iPhone, turn Screen Time off and start over.

Setting Content & Privacy Restrictions

To restrict access to content or apps, perform the following steps:

1. Use the steps in the previous task to move to the Screen Time Settings screen.

2. Tap Content & Privacy Restrictions.

3. Set the Content & Privacy Restrictions switch to on (green).

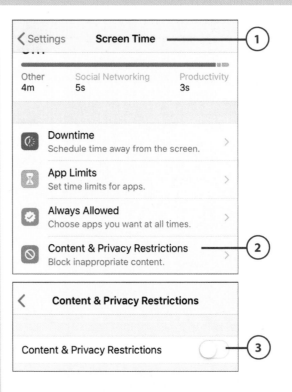

4 Tap iTunes & App Store Purchases.

5 Tap Installing Apps.

6 Tap Allow to allow someone using the phone to install apps or Don't Allow if you want to prevent apps from being downloaded.

7 Tap the Back icon (<).

8 If you want to prevent apps from being deleted, tap Deleting Apps, tap Don't Allow, and tap Back (<).

9 Set Allow to permit In-app Purchases or Don't Allow to prevent them. Some apps, especially games, allow you to make purchases while you are using the app. For example, you can buy additional levels for a game. To prevent in-app purchases, set In-app Purchases to Don't Allow. This is especially important if you let your phone be used by children or others who might inadvertently make purchases you don't want made.

10 If you want a password to be required for every purchase from the iTunes, App, or Book Store, tap Always Require. If you set Don't Require instead, the password is needed for only the first purchase; additional purchases within a relatively short time can be made without entering the password again. After that time passes, the password is required again.

11 Tap the Back icon (<).

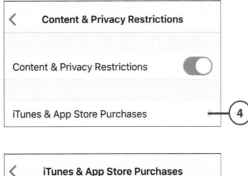

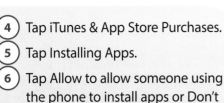

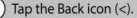

Screen Time Passcode Required

If you want to prevent certain tasks from being done, such as not allowing apps to be downloaded to the phone, make sure you have set a Screen Time passcode. If you don't have a Screen Time passcode, someone can move to the Screen Time Settings screen and re-enable a task you want to prevent. When a Screen Time passcode is set, you need to enter it to be able to make changes, which prevents others from changing these settings (unless you give them the passcode of course).

(12) Tap Allowed Apps. On this screen, you can allow or prevent Apple apps from being used. (You can't control the use of third-party apps that have been downloaded from the App Store.)

(13) Set an app's switch to off (white) to prevent it from being used (its icon doesn't appear on any Home screen).

(14) Tap the Back icon (<).

(15) Tap Content Restrictions if you want to prevent certain types of content from being accessed on the iPhone.

Content & Privacy Restrictions	⬤
iTunes & App Store Purchases	>
Allowed Apps	—(12)

< Back   **Allowed Apps**   (14)

✉	Mail	⬤
🧭	Safari	⬤
📷	FaceTime	○
📷	Camera	⬤
✴	Siri & Dictation	⬤	(13)
▭	Wallet	⬤
((·))	AirDrop	⬤
▶	CarPlay	○

★	iTunes Store	⬤
📖	Books	⬤
🎙	Podcasts	⬤
N	News	⬤

| Allowed Apps | > |
| Content Restrictions | —(15) |

(16) Tap Ratings For.

(17) Tap the country whose rating system you want to use for content on your iPhone.

(18) Tap the Back icon (<).

(19) If you want to prevent explicit content from being available in the Music, Podcasts, or News apps, tap Music, Podcasts & News and then tap Clean. Tap Back (<) to return to the Content Restrictions screen.

(20) To prevent music profiles and posts from being available in the Music app, tap Music Profiles & Posts and then tap Off. Tap Back (<) to return to the Content Restrictions screen.

(21) Tap Movies.

(22) Tap the highest rating of movies that you want to be playable (for example, tap PG-13 to prevent R and NC-17 movies from playing); tap Allow All Movies to allow any movie to be played; or tap Don't Allow Movies to prevent any movie content from playing. Prevented movie ratings are highlighted in red.

(23) To prevent movies from being streamed to the iPhone, set the Show Movies in the Cloud switch to off (white).

(24) Tap Back (<).

< Back   **Content Restrictions**

ALLOWED STORE CONTENT

Ratings For   United States →   **(16)**

< Back   **Ratings For**   **(18)**

Trinidad & Tobago

Tunisia

Turkey

Turkmenistan

Uganda

Ukraine

United Arab Emirates

United Kingdom

United States   ✓   **(17)**

ALLOWED STORE CONTENT

Ratings For   United States >

Music, Podcasts & News   Explicit →   **(19)**

Music Profiles & Posts   On →   **(20)**

Movies   Allow All Movies →   **(21)**

< Back   **Movies**   **(24)**

Don't Allow Movies

G

PG

PG-13

R   ✓   **(22)**

NC-17

Allow All Movies

Show Movies in the Cloud   ⬤   **(23)**

Whose Ratings?

The country you select in step 17 determines the options you see in the related steps because the restrictions available depend on the location you select. These steps show the United States rating systems; if you select a different country, you see rating options for that country instead.

(25) Tap TV Shows and use the resulting screen to set the highest rating of TV shows that you want to be playable. Tap Back (<) to return to the Content Restrictions screen.

(26) Use the Books option to enable or disable access to explicit books.

(27) Tap Apps and set the highest rating of app that you want to be available (for example, tap 12+ to prevent 17+ applications from working); tap Allow All Apps to allow any application to be used; or tap Don't Allow Apps to prevent all applications. Tap Back (<) to return to the Content Restrictions screen.

(28) Tap Web Content. You can use the Web Content screen to control the websites that can be accessed.

(29) Tap Limit Adult Websites to attempt to block pornographic and other such sites. This blocks many of such sites but might not block all of them. If you choose this option, tap Back (<) to return to the Content Restrictions screen and skip to step 34.

(30) Tap Allowed Websites Only to limit access to only the websites listed in the ONLY ALLOW THESE WEBSITES section. You see the default sites that are allowed.

Movies	R >
TV Shows	Allow All TV Shows (25)
Books	Explicit (26)
Apps	Allow All Apps (27)
WEB CONTENT	
Web Content	Unrestricted Access (28)

Web Content

WEB CONTENT
- Unrestricted Access (33)
- Limit Adult Websites (29)
- Allowed Websites Only (30)

Allow access only to the websites below.

ONLY ALLOW THESE WEBSITES:

(31) To remove a website from the list so it can no longer be visited, swipe to the left on it and tap Delete.

(32) To allow more websites to be visited, tap Add Website. On the Add Website screen, enter the title of the site and its URL (you can copy and paste it into the URL field). Tap Back (<) to move to the Web Content screen. You see the website you added and it can be visited using Safari.

(33) Tap Back (<).

(34) Use the Web Search Content and Explicit Language options to allow or prevent Siri from being used for web searches or for explicit language to be used.

(35) Use the controls in the GAME CENTER section to allow or prevent multiplayer games, friends to be added, or the screen to be recorded while using the Game Center.

(36) Tap Back (<).

Allow access only to the websites below.

ONLY ALLOW THESE WEBSITES:

Apple — Start

es (by BBC)   Delete — (31)

Discovery Kids

Disney

HowStuffWorks

National Geographic - Kids

PBS Kids

Scholastic.com

Smithsonian Institution

Time for Kids

Add Website — (32)

< Back   **Content Restrictions**

Music Profiles & Posts   On > — (36)

Movies   R >

TV Shows   Allow All TV Shows >

Books   Explicit >

Apps   Allow All Apps >

WEB CONTENT

Web Content   Allowed Websites Only >

SIRI

Web Search Content   Allow >
                                              — (34)
Explicit Language   Allow >

GAME CENTER

Multiplayer Games   Allow >

Adding Friends   Allow > — (35)

Screen Recording   Allow >

(37) Tap Location Services.

(38) To lock the Location Services in their current configuration, tap Don't Allow Changes and skip to step 45.

(39) To allow changes to be made on the Location Services screen, tap Allow Changes.

(40) To disable Location Services for all apps, set the Location Services switch to off (white) and tap Turn Off at the prompt. Apps that require Location Services to work won't work properly with this disabled. Skip to step 52.

(41) Tap Share My Location. You can share your location with others in several areas, such as the Messages app.

(42) To prevent your location from being shared, set the Share My Location switch to off (white) and skip to step 45. If you leave this switch on (green), move to the next step.

(43) Tap From and use the resulting Share Location From screen to select the device to be used to identify your location. You can choose any device signed into your iCloud account that has Share Location enabled. Tap Back (<) to move back to the Share My Location screen.

(44) If you use the Family Sharing feature, tap a person listed and tap Stop Sharing My Location to stop sharing your location with that person or tap Share My Location to share your location with that person.

(45) Tap Back (<).

Location Services

Using its GPS or network connection, your iPhone's Location Services feature can determine where the phone is. This is useful in many situations, such as in the Maps app when you want to generate directions. Lots of other apps use this capability, too, such as apps that provide you location-specific information (the Uber app uses it to determine your location when you request a ride, for example). However, you might not want some apps to be able to access this information.

(46) Swipe up and down the list of apps on the Location Services screen. These are all the apps that have requested access to your iPhone's location. Along the right side of the screen, you see the current status of Location Sharing for the app. Always means that the app can always access your location. While Using means the app can access your location information only while you are using it. Never means that using location information for the app has been disabled (some apps don't work properly when set to this status). Apps marked with a purple arrow have recently accessed your location; those that have done so within the past 24 hours are marked with a gray arrow. An outline purple arrow indicates that the app is using a geofence, which is a perimeter around a location that defines an area that is used to trigger some event, such as a reminder.

(47) Tap an app to configure its access to Location Services.

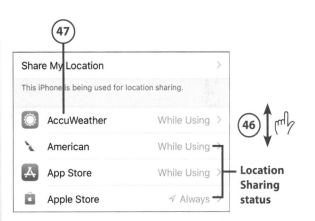

(48) Tap the status in which you want to place the app's access to your location. Some apps only have the Always or Never options, whereas others also have the While Using the App option.

(49) Tap Back (<).

(50) Repeat steps 46–49 for each app whose access to your location you want to configure.

System Services

At the bottom of the Location Services screen, you see the System Services option. Tap this to enable or disable Location Services for core iPhone function, such as Emergency Calling, Setting Time Zone, and so on. You probably won't want to disable Location Services for these features, but it's good to know where to do that just in case you decide to disable that feature.

(51) Tap Back (<).

(52) Use the settings below Location Services to determine whether apps can access information stored in each area and whether they should be locked in their current states. For example, you can prevent apps from accessing your calendars or photos. For each option you can choose Allow Changes to allow apps to access the information (such as in the Contacts app) or choose Don't Allow Changes to prevent apps from accessing the information or changes to be made.

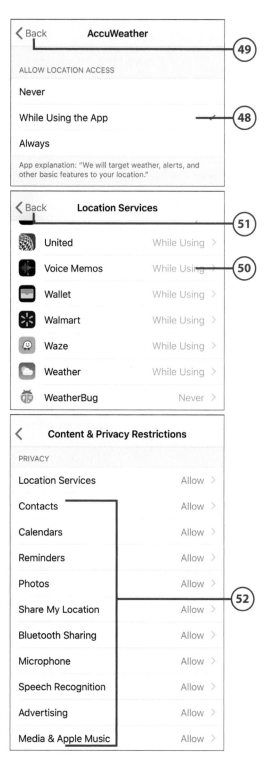

(53) Use the controls in the ALLOW CHANGES section to allow or prevent the actions you see. For example, if you set Account Changes to Don't Allow, the accounts currently configured on the Passwords & Accounts screen are locked in their current state and can't be changed. Or, if you set Cellular Data Changes to Don't Allow, the current configuration of cellular data use is locked as it is.

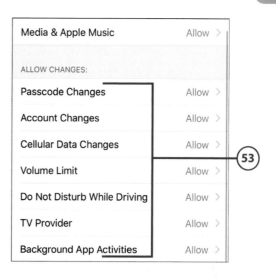

Media & Apple Music	Allow >
ALLOW CHANGES:	
Passcode Changes	Allow >
Account Changes	Allow >
Cellular Data Changes	Allow >
Volume Limit	Allow >
Do Not Disturb While Driving	Allow >
TV Provider	Allow >
Background App Activities	Allow >

(53)

>>>Go Further
PRIVACY, PRIVACY

You can configure privacy settings using the Privacy settings option on the Settings screen. You can configure the same set of Location Services options as you can on the Screen Time screen. You can also see the apps that are accessing features of your iPhone. For example, tap Speech Recognition to see which apps are using your iPhone's Speech Recognition capabilities.

Using Screen Time

Most of the options under Screen Time work automatically, such as the Downtime or App Limits. For example, when an app limit is reached, you won't be able to use the apps in that group until the following day.

You can use Screen Time to monitor your iPhone use as follows:

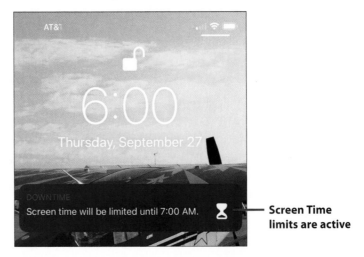

Screen Time limits are active

- When it is active, you see a notification on the Lock screen.

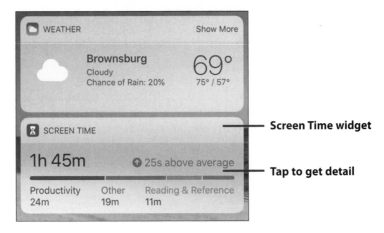

Screen Time widget

Tap to get detail

- You can use the Screen Time widget to get a quick view of your use. Tap the widget to get the full story in the Settings app.

- To get detailed information about your screen use, open the Screen Time screen in the Settings app or tap the Screen Time widget. At the top of the screen, you see usage information that includes total time and a breakout of how the time has been used (such as Social Networking).

- When you tap to get more detail, you can choose to view information for the current day or for the past week. The graph shows your use by the hour. Below that, you see individual activities; tap an activity to see its detail. If you swipe up the screen, you see additional information, such as the notifications you have received.

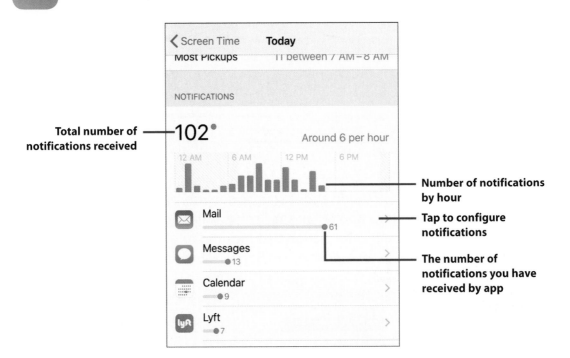

Total number of notifications received

Number of notifications by hour

Tap to configure notifications

The number of notifications you have received by app

- At the bottom of the screen, you see information about the notifications you receive; since there is the potential to receive so many notifications, this can be very useful information. You can see total notifications, notifications by day, and notifications by app. You can tap an app to configure its notifications.

Configuring the Control Center

As you learned in Chapters 1 and 2, the Control Center provides quick access to a number of your iPhone's features and tools. The top part of the Control Center screen always contains the same controls, but you can configure the controls toward the bottom of the Control Center by performing the following steps:

① Open the Settings app and tap Control Center.

2 To be able to access the Control Center while you are using apps, set the Access Within Apps switch to on (green). If you set this to off, you need to move back to the Home or Lock screen to use the Control Center.

3 Tap Customize Controls. The Customize screen has two sections: INCLUDE shows the controls installed in your Control Center, whereas MORE CONTROLS shows controls that are available for you to add to the Control Center.

4 To remove a control from the Control Center, tap its Unlock (–) icon.

5 Tap Remove. The control is moved from the INCLUDE list to the MORE CONTROLS list. It no longer appears on the Control Center.

‹ Settings   **Control Center**

Swipe down from the top-right edge to open Control Center.

Access Within Apps

Allow access to Control Center within apps. When disabled, you can still access Control Center from the Home Screen.

Customize Controls

‹ Back   **Customize**

Add and organize additional controls to appear in Control Center.

INCLUDE

- Flashlight
- Timer
- Calculator
- Camera
- Alarm
- Low Power Mode
- Magnifier
- Wallet
- Text Size

MORE CONTROLS

- Alarm
- Low Power Mode   Remove
- Magnifier

6 To add a control to the Control Center, tap its Add (+) icon. The control moves to the bottom of the INCLUDE list and is added to the Control Center.

7 Move a control higher on the Control Center by dragging its Order icon (three lines) up the INCLUDE list or move it lower by dragging its Order icon down the list. The top four controls on the list appear first in the customizable part of the Control Center; the next four are below those, and so on.

8 Repeat steps 4 through 7 until you have all the controls you want on the Control Center in the order you want them. The next time you open the Control Center, it reflects the changes you made.

Your Control Center Options Are Limited

There are more controls on the Control Center than you see on the Customize screen. You can't change some of the Control Center's options. For example, you always see the Airplane Mode, Cellular Data, Wi-Fi, and Bluetooth icons on the Control Center. The area you can customize is below the Screen Mirroring, Brightness, and Volume controls.

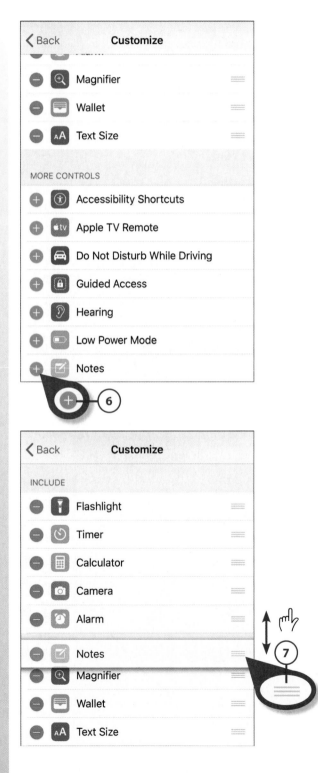

Configuring the Widget Center

As described in Chapters 1 and 2, the Widget Center provides quick access to widgets that enable you to take action or to view information. You can determine which widgets are shown in the Widget Center and the order in which those widgets appear on the screen; for example, you might want your most frequently used widgets to be at the top of the screen.

To configure the Widget Center, perform the following steps:

1. Open the Widget Center by moving to the Home screen and swiping all the way to the right.

2. Swipe all the way up the screen.

3. Tap Edit. You see the Add Widgets screen. This screen has two sections. At the top are the currently installed widgets; installed widgets have the Unlock (–) icon next to their icons. Toward the bottom of the screen, you see the MORE WIDGETS section that shows you available widgets that aren't currently in your Widget Center.

4 To remove a widget, tap its Unlock (–) icon.

5 Tap Remove. The widget is removed from your Widget Center and moved onto the MORE WIDGETS list.

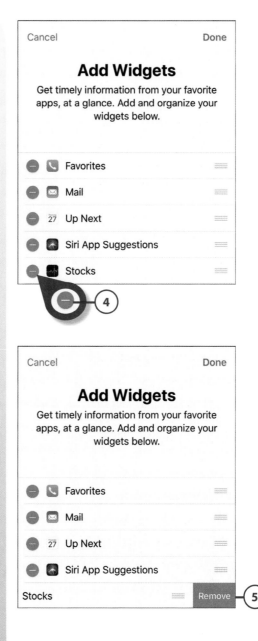

6 Swipe up the screen until you see the MORE WIDGETS section. Widgets that are new since the last time you viewed this list are marked with a blue circle.

7 To add a widget to the Widget Center, tap its Add (+) icon. The widget jumps up the screen to become the last widget on the list of widgets in the Widget Center. It appears at the bottom of the Widget Center.

8 To change where a widget appears in the Widget Center, drag its Order icon (three lines) up or down the screen. When it is in the position you want, take your finger off the screen and the widget is placed there.

9 Repeat steps 4 through 8 until the Widget Center contains the widgets you want to access, in the order in which you want them to be shown.

10 When you're done making changes to the Widget Center, tap Done. You return to the Widget Center and see the results of the changes you've made.

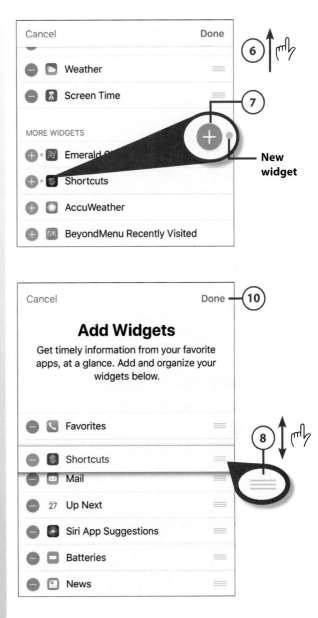

New widget

New Widgets

When new widgets become available, you see a message under Edit on the Widget Center screen. Tap this to move into Edit mode, so you can see the new widgets and add them to the Widget Center if you want to use them.

Setting Keyboard, Language, and Format Options

You'll be working with text in many apps on your iPhone. You can customize a number of keyboard- and format-related options so text appears and behaves the way you want it to.

Setting Keyboard Preferences

You use the iPhone's keyboard to input text in many apps, including Mail, Messages, and so on. A number of settings determine how the keyboard works.

1. On the Settings screen, tap General.

2. Swipe up the screen.

3. Tap Keyboard.

4. Tap Keyboards. This enables you to activate more keyboards so that you can choose a specific language's keyboard when you are entering text. At the top of the screen, you see the keyboards that are available to you.

5. Tap Add New Keyboard.

Fun in Text

The Emoji keyboard allows you to include a huge variety of smiley faces, symbols, and other icons whenever you type. The Emoji keyboard is active by default; however, if you don't see it on the list of active keyboards, you can use these steps to activate it.

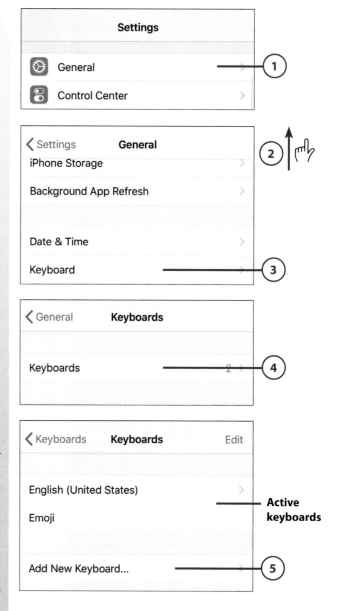

6. Swipe up and down the screen to browse the available keyboards.

7. Tap the keyboard you want to add.

8. Tap the keyboard you added in step 7.

9. Tap the keyboard layout you want to use. (Not all keyboards support options; if the one you are configuring doesn't, skip this step.)

10. Tap the Back icon (<).

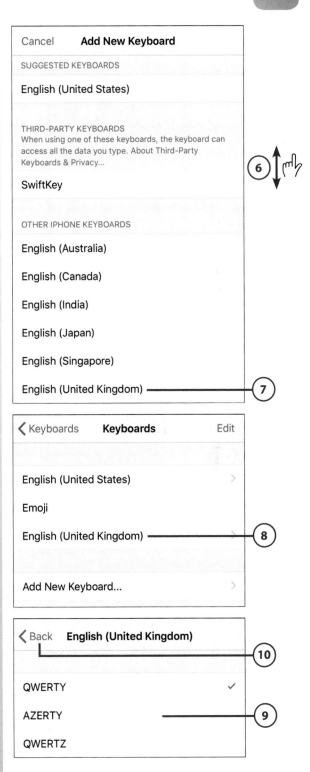

(11) Repeat steps 5–10 to add and configure additional keyboards.

(12) Tap the Back icon (<).

(12)

‹ Keyboards	**Keyboards**	Edit
English (United States)		›
Emoji		
English (United Kingdom)		›
Add New Keyboard...		›

(11)

>>>Go Further

THIRD-PARTY KEYBOARDS

You can install and use keyboards from third parties (meaning not Apple) on your iPhone. To do this, open the App Store app and search for "keyboards for iPhone" or you can search for a specific keyboard by name if you know of one you want to try. (See "Using the App Store App to Find and Install iPhone Apps," later in this chapter for help using the App Store app.) After you have downloaded the keyboard you want to use, use steps 1–5 to move back to the Keyboards Settings screen. When you open the Add New Keyboard screen, you see a section called THIRD-PARTY KEYBOARDS in which you see the additional keyboards you have installed. Tap a keyboard in this section to activate it as you do with the default keyboards. When you move back to the Keyboards screen, you see the keyboard you just activated. Tap it to configure its additional options. Then you can use the new keyboard just like the others you have activated. Make sure you check out the documentation for any keyboards you download so you take advantage of all of their features.

(13) Tap One Handed Keyboard.

(14) To be able to use the one-handed keyboard (which squishes all the keys toward one side of the screen), tap Left to place it on the left side or Right to put it on the right side of the screen; tap Off if you don't want to use the one-handed keyboard.

(15) Tap Back (<).

(16) To prevent your iPhone from automatically capitalizing as you type, set Auto-Capitalization to off (white).

(17) To disable the automatic spell checking/correction, set Auto-Correction to off (white).

(18) To disable the iPhone's Spell Checker, set the Check Spelling switch to off (white).

(19) To disable the Caps Lock function, set the Enable Caps Lock to off (white).

(20) To disable the iPhone's Predictive Text feature (see Chapter 2), set the Predictive switch to off (white).

(21) To prevent the iPhone from automatically trying to correct your punctuation, set the Smart Punctuation switch to off (white).

(22) To prevent the character you type from being shown in a magnified pop-up as you type it, set the Character Preview switch to off (white).

< General   **Keyboards**

Keyboards   2 >

Text Replacement   >

One Handed Keyboard   Off > —(13)

< Back   **One Handed Keyboard**   —(15)

Off
Left ———————————————————(14)
Right   ✓

If you have multiple keyboards enabled, you can quickly access one-handed keyboard options at the bottom of the input switcher menu by pressing and holding on the globe key.

One Handed Keyboard   Right >

Auto-Capitalization   ◯—(16)
Auto-Correction   ◯—(17)
Check Spelling   ◯—(18)
Enable Caps Lock   ◯—(19)
Predictive   ◯—(20)
Smart Punctuation   ◯—(21)
Character Preview   ◯—(22)
"." Shortcut   ◯

Double tapping the space bar will insert a period followed by a space.

Enable Dictation   ◯

About Dictation and Privacy...

(23) To disable the shortcut that types a period followed by a space when you tap the space bar twice, set the "." Shortcut switch to off (white). You must tap a period and the spacebar to type these characters when you end a sentence.

(24) To disable the iPhone's dictation feature, set the Enable Dictation switch to off (white). The microphone key won't appear on the keyboard and you won't be able to dictate text.

One Handed Keyboard	Right >
Auto-Capitalization	
Auto-Correction	
Check Spelling	
Enable Caps Lock	
Predictive	
Smart Punctuation	
Character Preview	
"." Shortcut	(23)

Double tapping the space bar will insert a period followed by a space.

Enable Dictation	(24)

About Dictation and Privacy...

Language Options

The keyboard options you see depend on the language being used. For example, if settings apply only to a specific language, you see them in that language's section.

Changing Keyboards

To delete a keyboard, move to the Keyboards Settings screen and swipe to the left on the keyboard you want to remove. Tap Delete. The keyboard is removed from the list of activated keyboards and is no longer available to you when you type. (You can always activate it again later.) To change the order in which keyboards appear, move to the Keyboards screen, tap Edit, and drag the keyboards up and down the screen. When you've finished, tap Done. (An explanation of how to switch between keyboards when you type is provided in Chapter 2.)

Creating and Working with Text Replacements

Text replacements are useful because you can use just a few letters to type a series of words. You type the replacement, and it is replaced by the phrase with which it is associated. To configure your text replacements, do the following:

(**1**) Move to the Keyboards screen as described in steps 1–3 in the previous task.

(**2**) Tap Text Replacement.

(**3**) Review the current replacements.

(**4**) To add a replacement, tap Add (+).

(**5**) Type the phrase for which you want to create a replacement.

(**6**) Type the shortcut you want to be replaced by the phrase you created in step 5.

(**7**) Tap Save. If the replacement doesn't contain any disallowed characters, it is created and you move back to the Text Replacement screen where you see your new text replacement. If there is an error, you see an explanation of the error; you must correct it before you can create the replacement.

(**8**) Repeat steps 4–7 to create other text replacements.

(**9**) When you've created all the replacements you want, tap Keyboards.

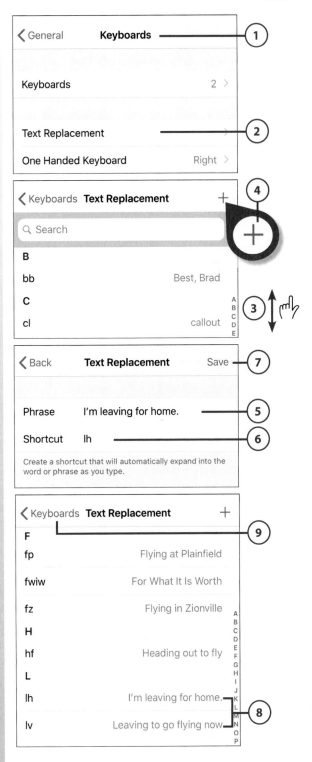

Shortcuts to Replacements

To change a replacement, tap it. Use the resulting screen to change the phrase or shortcut, and tap Save to update the replacement. To remove a replacement, swipe to the left on it and tap Delete. To search for a replacement, tap in the Search bar at the top of the screen and type the replacements you want to see; you can also use the index along the right side of the screen to find replacements. You can also tap Edit on the Shortcuts screen to change your replacements. And, yes, you can create a phrase without a replacement, but I don't really see much use for that!

Setting Language and Region Preferences

There are a number of formatting preferences you can set that determine how information is formatted in various apps. For example, you can choose how addresses are formatted by default by choosing the region whose format you want to follow.

(1) On the Settings screen, tap General.

(2) Swipe up the screen.

(3) Tap Language & Region.

(4) Tap iPhone Language.

(5) Swipe up and down the screen to view the languages with which your iPhone can work or tap in the Search bar and type a language you want to use to find it. The current language is marked with a check mark.

(6) Tap the language you want to use.

(7) Tap Done.

Settings
⚙ General ———————— (1)
▣ Control Center >

< Settings **General**
iPhone Storage > (2)
Background App Refresh >
Date & Time >
Keyboard >
Language & Region ———— > (3)

< General **Language & Region** Edit
iPhone Language English → (4)

Cancel **iPhone Language** Done — (7)
🔍 Search
English (US) ——————— (6) English (US)
Español (EE. UU.) Spanish (US) (5)
English (Australia) English (Australia)

8 Tap to confirm the change in language you indicated. Your iPhone screen goes dark while the iPhone switches to the new language. When it comes back, you return to the Language & Region screen, and the language you selected starts being used.

9 Tap Add Language.

10 Using steps 5–7, find and tap another language. This language is used when your primary and other languages can't be, such as on websites that don't support your primary language.

11 Tap Done.

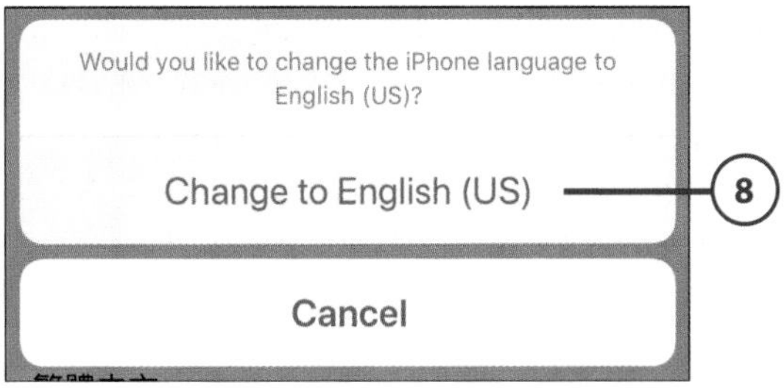

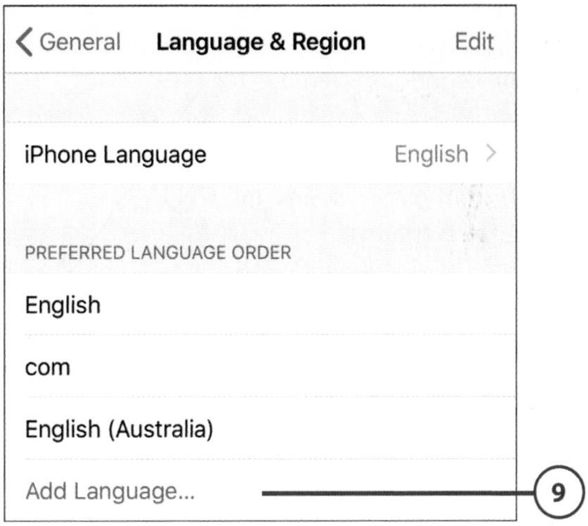

Would you like to change the iPhone language to English (US)?

Change to English (US) ————— **8**

Cancel

‹ General   **Language & Region**   Edit

iPhone Language   English **›**

PREFERRED LANGUAGE ORDER

English

com

English (Australia)

Add Language... ————— **9**

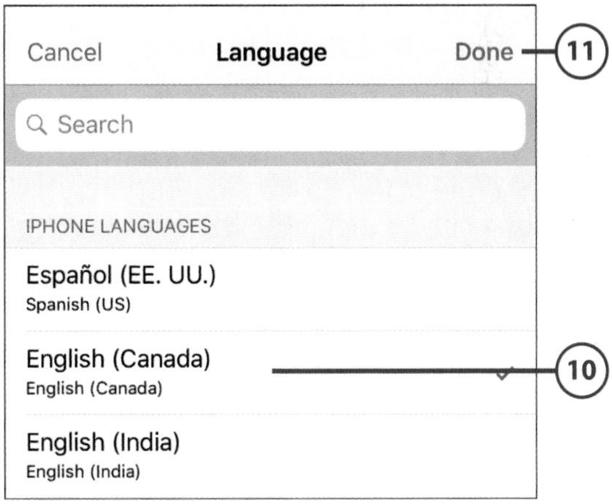

Cancel   **Language**   Done — **11**

Q Search

IPHONE LANGUAGES

Español (EE. UU.)
Spanish (US)

English (Canada) ————— **10**
English (Canada)

English (India)
English (India)

12 Tap the language you want to be primary to confirm it. The language you selected is configured and you move back to the Language & Region screen. The new language is shown on the list in the center of the screen.

Would you like to change the iPhone language to English (Canada)?

Change to English (Canada)

Keep English ——————— **12**

Cancel

Order, Order!
To change the order of preference for the languages you have configured, tap Edit, drag the languages up or down the screen to set their order, and tap Done to save your changes.

English (Canada)

Add Language... —————— **13**

Apps and websites will use the first language in this list that they support.

Region   United States >

14

13 To add more languages, tap Add Language and follow steps 10–12 to add more languages.

14 Tap Region.

15 Swipe up and down the regions available to you. The current region is marked with a check mark.

16 Tap the region whose formatting you want to use; if there are options within a region, you move to an additional screen and can tap the specific option you want to use.

17 Tap Done.

Cancel   **Region**   Done —— **17**

Q Search

Ukraine

United Arab Emirates

United Kingdom ——————— **16**

United States   A
                                      B
                                      C
Uruguay   D   **15**
                                      E
                                      F
Uzbekistan   G
                                      H
                                      I
V   J
                                      K
                                      L
Vanuatu   M
                                      N

(18) If you've changed the region, tap the language you want to use as the primary iPhone language. Your iPhone starts using the formatting associated with the region you selected.

(19) Tap Calendar.

(20) Tap the calendar you want your iPhone to use.

(21) Tap Back (<).

(22) Tap Temperature Unit.

(23) Tap the unit in which you want temperatures to be displayed.

(24) Tap Back (<).

(25) Swipe up until you see the bottom of the screen where there are examples of the format options you have selected, such as the time and date format.

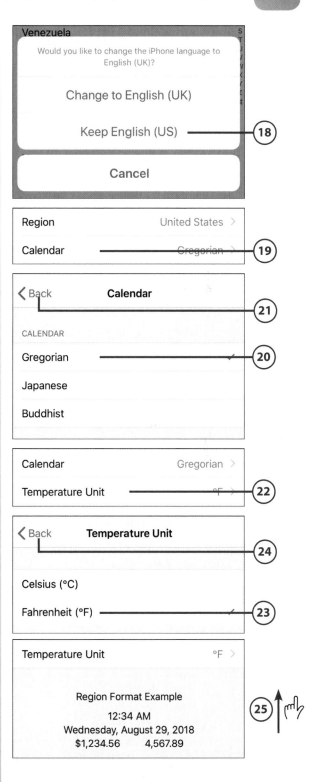

Setting a Passcode and Face ID or Touch ID

Your iPhone contains data you probably don't want others to access. You can (and should) require a passcode so your iPhone can't be unlocked without the proper passcode being entered. This gives you a measure of protection should you lose control of your phone.

X models of the iPhone support Face ID. This enables you to enter your iPhone's passcode and app passwords by simply looking at the screen. Non-X models support Touch ID, which performs the same functions, but instead of looking at your phone, you touch a finger to the Touch ID/Home button.

You need to configure these options on your iPhone to use them. If you have an X model, see "Configuring a Passcode and Face ID (X Models)." If you have a non-X model, see "Configuring a Passcode and Touch ID (non-X Models)."

Configuring a Passcode and Face ID (X Models)

You should configure a passcode to protect your iPhone and set up Face ID to make the passcode easier to use. Once you have enabled Face ID, you can use it for other types of ID validations, such as logging into your bank account.

To configure a passcode and Face ID, perform the following steps:

1. On the Settings screen, tap Face ID & Passcode.
2. Swipe up the screen until you see Turn Passcode On.
3. Tap Turn Passcode On.

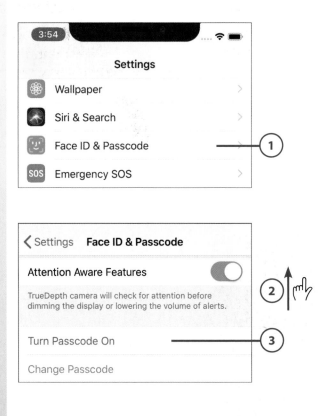

4. Enter a six-digit passcode.

5. Re-enter the passcode. If the two passcodes match, the passcode is set.

6. If you are prompted to enter your Apple ID password, do so and tap Continue. (Not shown in the figure.)

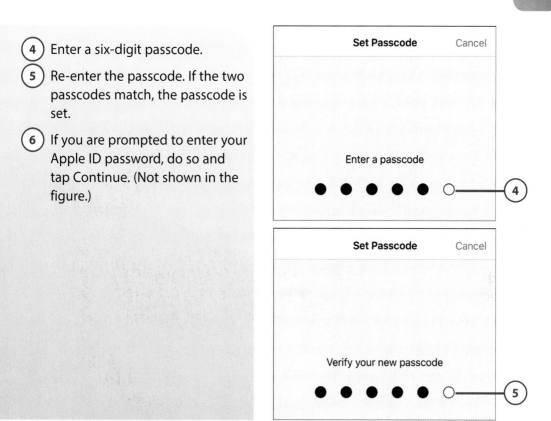

Already Have a Passcode?

When you first turned on your iPhone, you were prompted to create a passcode and to record your face for Face ID. If your iPhone already has a passcode set, when you perform step 1, you're prompted to enter your current passcode. When you enter it correctly, you move to the Face ID & Passcode screen, and you can make changes to the current passcode, replace the current face used for Face ID, and so on. In this case, you can skip directly to step 8. If you want to change your current passcode, tap Change Passcode and follow steps 4 and 5 to change it. Then, continue with step 6.

Are You Complex?

By default, your passcode is a simple six-digit number. If you want to have a more complex (and more secure) passcode, on the Create or Change Passcode screen, tap Passcode Options. You are prompted to create a new, complex passcode. You can choose Custom Alphanumeric Code, Custom Numeric Code, or 4-Digit Numeric Code (the latter is a less secure option, and I don't recommend it). Choose the option you want, and then follow the onscreen prompts to create it. The Alphanumeric Code option is the most secure, especially when you use a code that is eight characters or longer that includes both letters and numbers. The steps to set a complex passcode are similar to the six-digit passcode; the difference is that you use the keyboard and numeric keypad to configure the passcode instead of just the numeric keypad.

(7) Tap Set Up Face ID.

(8) Tap Get Started.

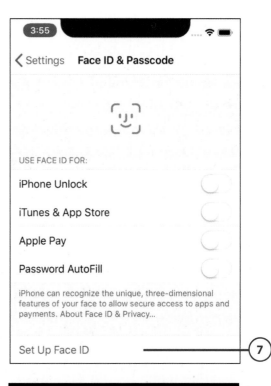

⑨ Look at the iPhone and position your face within the frame. When the iPhone recognizes a face being in the frame, it starts recording your face.

⑩ Move your head around in a circle. As you do, the green lines around the circle on the screen fill in, which indicates the part of the image that has been successfully recorded.

⑪ Continue moving your head in a circle until all of the green lines are filled in. When the process is complete, you see First Face ID scan complete appear on the screen.

⑫ Tap Continue. Record your face a second time.

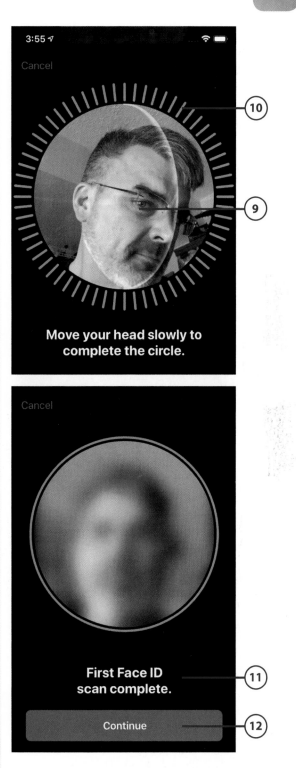

13 Rotate your head until the circle is enclosed by green lines. When the second image has been recorded, Face ID is now set up appears on the screen.

14 Tap Done. You return to the Face ID & Passcode screen.

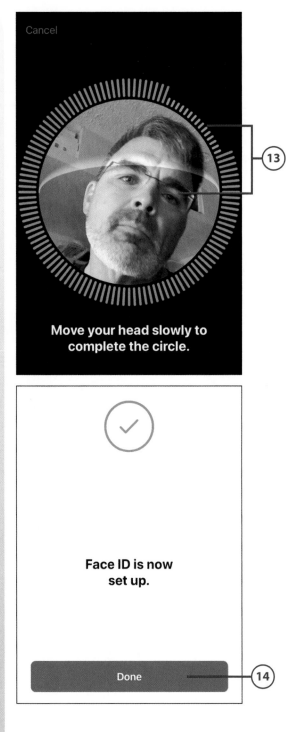

(15) If you don't want to use Face ID for one of the options shown in the USE FACE ID FOR section, set its switch to off (white). You'll need to enter the related passcode or password to complete an action if you disable Face ID for that action. For example, if you don't want to be able to use Face ID when you download apps, set the iTunes & App Store switch to off (white); you'll need to enter your Apple ID password when you download apps, instead of using Face ID.

(16) Tap Other Apps (you see this only after other apps have requested and been granted permission to use Face ID).

(17) To prevent one of the apps listed from using Face ID, set its switch to off (white).

(18) Tap the Back icon (<).

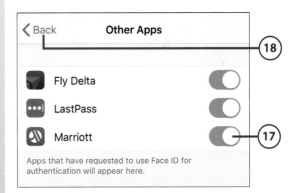

19 If you want to enable someone else to use Face ID with your iPhone, tap Set Up an Alternate Appearance and follow steps 8 through 14 to record the other person's face. You could also use this to capture an alternate appearance for yourself in the event your appearance changes so dramatically that it isn't recognized by Face ID; this would be unusual, however, since Face ID can handle changes in appearance due to haircuts, different cosmetic applications, and so on.

20 To replace the current Face ID, tap Reset Face ID and follow steps 8 through 14.

21 If you don't want the additional security offered by the Face ID system by verifying you are looking at the iPhone, set the Require Attention for Face ID switch to off (white). You should usually leave this set to on (green). However, if you wear sunglasses or Face ID isn't working for some other reason, try setting this switch to off to see if Face ID works better.

22 If you don't want the TrueDepth camera to check for your attention before the display is dimmed or the alert volume is lowered, set the Attention Aware Features switch to off (white). When this is on (green), if you are looking at the iPhone, the display won't be dimmed nor will the alert volume be lowered. This is useful because the iPhone can "tell" when you are looking at it so that it won't dim the screen or lower the volume automatically.

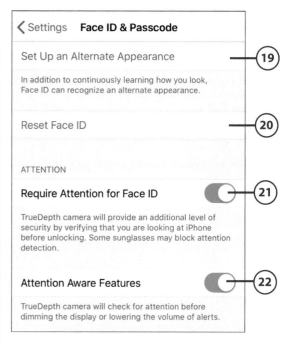

23 Swipe up the screen until you see the Voice Dial switch.

24 To prevent Voice Dial from working, set the Voice Dial switch to off (white). (Voice Dial enables you to make calls by speaking even if you don't use Siri.)

25 Use the switches in the ALLOW ACCESS WHEN LOCKED section to enable or disable the related functions used when your iPhone is locked. The options include Today View (the Today section of the Notification Center), Notification Center, Control Center, Siri, Reply with Message, Home Control, Return Missed Calls, and USB Accessories. If you set a switch to off (white), you won't be able to access the corresponding function when your iPhone is locked.

26 If you want the iPhone to automatically erase all your data after an incorrect passcode has been entered 10 times, set the Erase Data switch to on (green) and tap Enable at the prompt (not shown on the figure).

3:56

‹ Settings   **Face ID & Passcode**

Voice Dial

Music Voice Control is always enabled.

ALLOW ACCESS WHEN LOCKED:

Today View

Notification Center

Control Center

Siri

Reply with Message

Home Control

Return Missed Calls

USB Accessories

Unlock iPhone to allow USB accessories to connect when it has been more than an hour since your iPhone was locked.

Erase Data

Erase all data on this iPhone after 10 failed passcode attempts.

Data protection is enabled.

>>>*Go Further*

BE SECURE WITH FACE ID

Here are some additional tidbits to help you with your iPhone's security:

- **Face ID and Apps**—The first time you launch an app that supports Face ID, you're prompted to enable Face ID in that app. If you allow this, you can log into the associated account by looking at the screen at the prompt, just like unlocking your phone or using Apple Pay. You can change this setting by moving back to the Other Apps screen and change the app's switch to on (green) to enable Face ID or off (white) to disable Face ID for that app.

- **Automatic Erase**—When you have enabled the Erase Data function and you (or someone else) enter an incorrect passcode when unlocking your iPhone, you see a counter showing the number of unsuccessful attempts. When this reaches 10, all the data on your iPhone is erased on the next unsuccessful attempt.

- **Making Changes**—Any time you want to make changes to your passcode or Face ID settings, move back to the Passcode & Face ID screen by tapping Face ID & Passcode and entering your passcode. To disable the passcode (not recommended), tap Turn Passcode Off, tap Turn Off, and enter the passcode. To change your passcode, tap Change Passcode. Enter your current passcode and enter your new passcode twice. Your iPhone returns to the Passcode and Face ID screen, and the new passcode takes effect. You can change the other settings similar to how you set them initially, as described in the steps earlier in this section.

- **Require Passcode**—This setting applies only if you don't use Face ID and rely on just the passcode instead. You can use it to determine how much time passes when the phone goes to sleep and when it locks automatically. For example, if you set this to After 1 minute, if you start to use the iPhone within 1 minute of the time it went to sleep, you won't need to unlock it. If more than one minute has passed, you need to enter the passcode to unlock the phone.

- **Automatic Locking**—For security purposes, you should configure your iPhone so that it locks automatically after a specific amount of idle time passes. To do this, you use the Auto-Lock setting on the Display & Brightness settings screen as explained in Chapter 5.

Configuring a Passcode and Touch ID (non-X Models)

To configure the passcode you have to enter to unlock your iPhone and set up Touch ID, perform the following steps:

(1) On the Settings screen, tap Touch ID & Passcode.

(2) Tap Turn Passcode On.

(3) Enter a six-digit passcode.

Settings
Siri & Search   >
Touch ID & Passcode   >   —(1)
SOS Emergency SOS   >

Add a Fingerprint...
Turn Passcode On   —(2)

Set Passcode	Cancel

Enter a passcode

● ● ● ● ● ○ —(3)

Already Have a Passcode?

When you first turned your iPhone on, you were prompted to create a passcode and to record a fingerprint for Touch ID. If your iPhone already has a passcode set, when you perform step 1, you're prompted to enter your current passcode. When you enter it correctly, you move to the Touch ID & Passcode screen, and you can make changes to the current passcode, add new fingerprints, and so on. In that case, you can skip directly to step 5. If you want to change your current passcode, tap Change Passcode and follow steps 3 and 4 to change it. Then continue with step 5.

Are You Complex?

By default, your passcode is a simple six-digit number. If you want to have a more complex (and more secure) passcode, on the Create or Change Passcode screen, tap Passcode Options. You are prompted to create a new, complex passcode. You can choose Custom Alphanumeric Code, Custom Numeric Code, or 4-Digit Numeric Code (this is a less secure option, and I don't recommend it). Choose the option you want and then follow the onscreen prompts to create it. The Alphanumeric Code option is the most secure, especially if you use a code that is eight characters or longer that includes both letters and numbers. The steps to set a complex passcode are similar; the difference is that you use the keyboard and numeric keypad to configure the passcode instead of just the numeric keypad.

4 Re-enter the passcode. If the two passcodes match, the passcode is set.

5 If you have an Apple ID configured and are prompted to confirm it, enter your Apple ID password; if you don't have an Apple ID configured or aren't prompted to confirm it, skip to step 7.

6 Tap Continue.

7 Tap Require Passcode; when you use Touch ID to unlock your iPhone, you don't have an option for when the passcode is required, so if you are going to or already use Touch ID, skip to step 10.

8 Tap the amount of time the iPhone is locked before the passcode takes effect. The shorter this time is, the more secure your iPhone is, but also the more frequently you'll have to enter the passcode if your iPhone locks frequently.

9 Tap the Back icon (<).

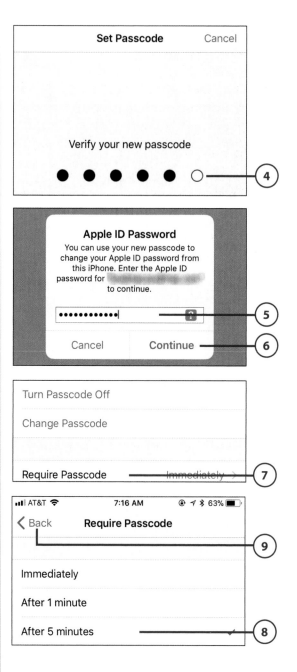

(10) If you have an iPhone 5s or later, tap Add a Fingerprint and continue to step 11; if you have a model that doesn't support Touch ID, skip to step 25.

(11) Touch the finger you want to record to the Touch ID/Home button, but don't press it. An image of a fingerprint appears.

(12) Leave your finger on the Touch ID/Home button until you feel the phone vibrate, which indicates part of your fingerprint has been recorded and you see some segments turn red. The parts of your fingerprint that are recorded are indicated by the red segments; gray segments are not recorded yet. This step captures the center part of your finger.

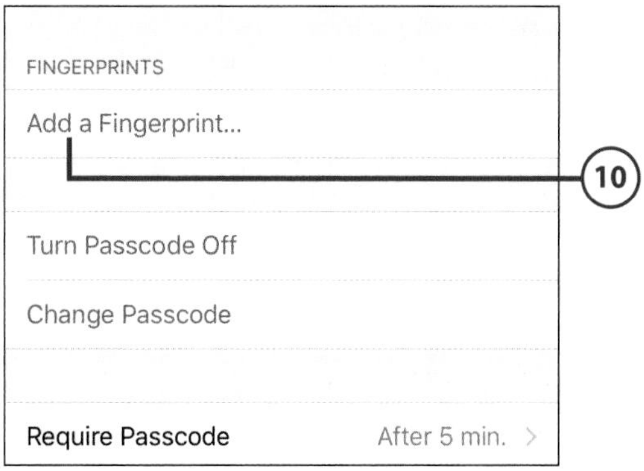

FINGERPRINTS

Add a Fingerprint...

(10)

Turn Passcode Off

Change Passcode

Require Passcode   After 5 min. >

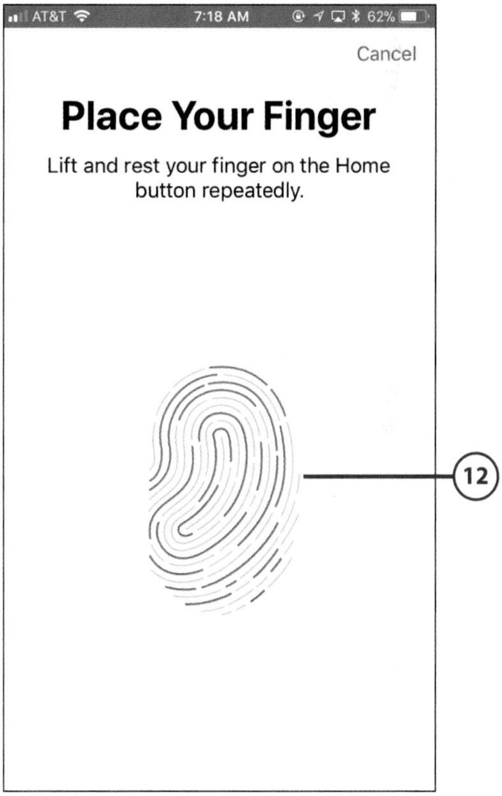

AT&T 🤖   7:18 AM   @ ✈ 🖵 ✳ 62% ▭

Cancel

Place Your Finger

Lift and rest your finger on the Home button repeatedly.

(12)

(13) Lift your finger off the Touch ID/
Home button and touch the button again, adjusting your finger
on the button to record other
parts that currently show gray
lines instead of red ones. Other
segments of your fingerprint are
recorded.

(14) Repeat step 13 until all the segments are red. You are prompted
to change your grip so you can
record more of your fingerprint.

(15) Tap Continue.

(16) Repeat step 13, again placing other areas of your finger to fill in more gray lines with red. This step captures the fingerprints more toward the edges of your fingers. When the entire fingerprint is covered in red lines, you see the Complete screen.

(17) Tap Continue. The fingerprint is recorded and you move back to the Touch ID & Passcode screen. You see the fingerprint that has been recorded.

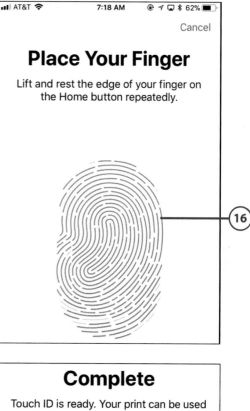

18 Tap the fingerprint you recorded.

19 Give the fingerprint a name.

20 Tap Back (<).

21 Repeat steps 10–20 to record up to five fingerprints. These can be yours or someone else's if you want to allow another person to access your iPhone.

FINGERPRINTS

Finger 1 ——————————— **18**

Add a Fingerprint…

22 To be able to use Touch ID to unlock your iPhone, ensure the iPhone Unlock switch is set to on (green).

23 If it isn't enabled already and you want to also be able to enter your Apple ID password by touch-ing your finger to the Touch ID/ Home button, set the iTunes & App Store switch to on (green). You need to enter your Apple ID password and tap Continue to complete this configuration.

AT&T   7:19 AM   62%

< Passcode Lock ——————————— **20**

Right Thumb ——————————— **19**

Delete Fingerprint

24 To use your fingerprint to make Apple Pay payments, set the Apple Pay switch to on (green). (Refer to Chapter 15, "Working with Other Useful iPhone Apps and Features," for more informa-tion about Apple Pay.)

25 To enable your passwords for various accounts to be entered with Touch ID, set the Password Autofill switch to on (green).

< Settings   **Touch ID & Passcode**

USE TOUCH ID FOR:

iPhone Unlock ——— **22**

iTunes & App Store ——— **23**

Apple Pay ——— **24**

Password AutoFill ——— **25**

FINGERPRINTS

Right Thumb

Add a Fingerprint… ——— **21**

26 Swipe up the screen until you see the Voice Dial switch.

27 To prevent Voice Dial from working, set the Voice Dial switch to off (white). (Voice Dial enables you to make calls by speaking even if you don't use Siri.)

28 Use the switches in the ALLOW ACCESS WHEN LOCKED section to enable or disable the related functions when your iPhone is locked. The options include Today View (the Today section of the Notification Center), Notification Center, Control Center, Reply with Message, Home Control, Wallet, Return Missed Calls, and USB Accessories. If you set a switch to off (white), you won't be able to access the corresponding function when your iPhone is locked.

29 If you want the iPhone to automatically erase all your data after an incorrect passcode has been entered 10 times, set the Erase Data switch to on (green).

30 Tap Enable.

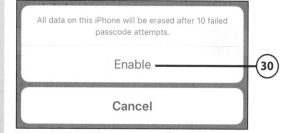

⟨ Settings   **Touch ID & Passcode**

Voice Dial   ⬤ —**27**

Music Voice Control is always enabled.

ALLOW ACCESS WHEN LOCKED: **26** ↑ 🖑

Today View   ⬤

Notification Center   ⬤

Control Center   ⬤

Reply with Message   ⬤

Home Control   ⬤

Wallet   ⬤

Return Missed Calls   ⬤

USB Accessories   ◯ —**28**

Unlock iPhone to allow USB accessories to connect when it has been more than an hour since your iPhone was locked.

Erase Data   ◯ —**29**

All data on this iPhone will be erased after 10 failed passcode attempts.

Enable ———**30**

Cancel

>>>Go Further

BE SECURE WITH TOUCH ID

Here are some additional tidbits to help you with your iPhone's security:

- **Touch ID and Apps**—The first time you launch an app that supports Touch ID, you're prompted to enable Touch ID in that app. If you allow this, you can log into the associated account by touching the Touch ID button, just like unlocking your phone or using Apple Pay. After you've enabled apps to use Touch ID, you can return to the Touch ID & Passcode screen to enable or disable Touch ID for specific apps.

- **Automatic Erase**—When you have enabled the Erase Data function and you (or someone else) enter an incorrect passcode when unlocking your iPhone, you see a counter showing the number of unsuccessful attempts. When this reaches 10, all the data on your iPhone is erased on the next unsuccessful attempt.

- **Making Changes**—Any time you want to make changes to your passcode and fingerprint settings, move back to the Touch ID & Passcode screen by tapping Touch ID & Passcode and entering your passcode. To disable the passcode (not recommended), tap Turn Passcode Off, tap Turn Off, and enter the passcode. To change your passcode, tap Change Passcode. You then enter your current passcode and enter your new passcode twice. You return to the Touch ID & Passcode screen, and the new passcode takes effect. You can change the other settings similar to how you set them initially as described in these steps. For example, you can add new fingerprints. To remove a fingerprint, move to the Fingerprints screen, swipe to the left on the fingerprint you want to remove, and tap Delete.

- **Require Passcode**—This setting applies only if you don't use Touch ID and rely on just the passcode. You can use it to determine how much time passes when the phone goes to sleep and when it locks automatically. For example, if you set this to 1 minute, and you start to use the iPhone within 1 minute of the time it went to sleep, you won't need to unlock it. If more than one minute has passed, you need to enter the passcode to unlock the phone.

- **Automatic Locking**—For security purposes, you should configure your iPhone so that it locks automatically after a specific amount of idle time passes. To do this, you use the Auto-Lock setting on the Display & Brightness settings screen as explained in Chapter 5.

Setting Accessibility Options

The iPhone has many features designed to help people who have hearing impairments, visual impairments, or other physical challenges to be able to use it effectively.

You can enable and configure the Accessibility features on the Accessibility Settings screen.

(1) On the Settings screen, tap General.

(2) Swipe up the screen until you see Accessibility.

(3) Tap Accessibility. The Accessibility screen is organized into different sections for different kinds of limitations. The first section is VISION, which includes options to assist people who are visually impaired.

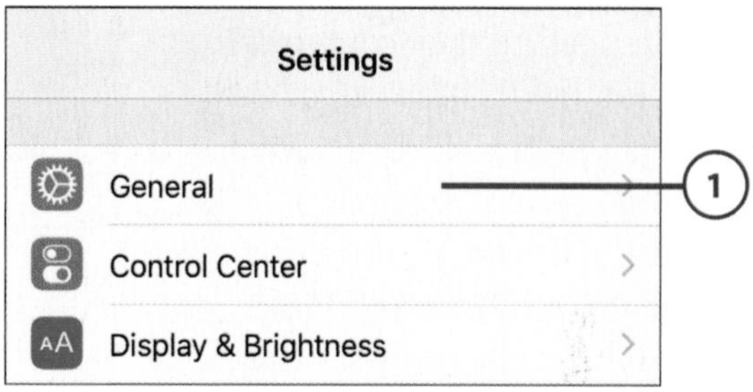

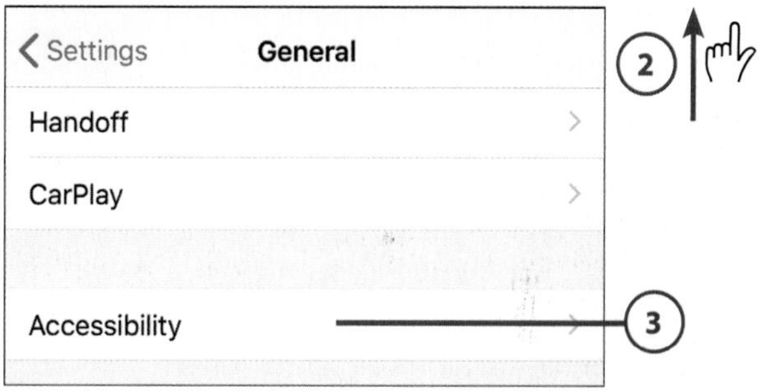

Settings

General ————————————→ **(1)**

Control Center >

AA Display & Brightness >

‹ Settings   **General**   **(2)**

Handoff >

CarPlay >

Accessibility ————————→ **(3)**

(4) Use the controls in the VISION section to change how the iPhone's screens appear. Some of the options include the following:

- **VoiceOver**—The iPhone guides you through screens by speaking their contents. To configure this, tap VoiceOver and set the VoiceOver switch to on (green) to turn it on. The rest of the settings configure how VoiceOver works. For example, you can set the rate at which the voice speaks, what kind of feedback you get, and many more options.

- **Zoom**—This magnifies the entire screen. Tap Zoom and then turn Zoom on. Use the other settings to change how the zoom works, such as whether it follows where you are focused on the screen or remains fixed.

- **Magnifier**—This feature enables you to use your iPhone's camera like a magnifying glass. When you enable this, you can triple-press the Side or Touch ID/Home button to activate it. You can also add its control to the Control Center using the steps provided earlier in the chapter.

‹ General	**Accessibility**	
VISION		
VoiceOver		Off ›
Zoom		Off ›
Magnifier		On ›
Display Accommodations		On ›
Speech		›
Larger Text		Off ›
Bold Text		
Button Shapes		
Reduce Transparency		Off ›
Increase Contrast		Off ›
Reduce Motion		Off ›
On/Off Labels		
Face ID & Attention		›

- **Display Accommodations**—
These options change how your
iPhone uses color. You can use
the Invert Colors function to
reverse the color on the screen
so that what is light becomes
dark and vice versa. The Color
Filters tool enables you to customize how colors appear on
the screen. The Auto-Brightness
switch controls whether the
iPhone's screen automatically
dims or not. The Reduce White
Point switch, when enabled,
reduces the intensity of bright
colors.

- **Speech**—Under the Speech
option, Speak Selection causes
a Speak button to appear when
you select text, and Speak Screen
provides the option to have the
screen's content spoken. You
can also determine whether you
hear feedback while you type,
and you can configure the voices
used, the rate of speech, and
pronunciations.

- **Larger and Bold Text**—These
increase the text size and add
bold; these are in addition to the
Text Size and Bold settings that
you learn about in Chapter 5.

- **Other options**—You can also
change button shapes, reduce
transparency, change contrast,
reduce motion, and turn labels
on or off.

❮ General	**Accessibility**	
VISION		
VoiceOver	Off	❯
Zoom	Off	❯
Magnifier	On	❯
Display Accommodations	On	❯
Speech		❯
Larger Text	Off	❯
Bold Text		⬤
Button Shapes		⬤
Reduce Transparency	Off	❯
Increase Contrast	Off	❯
Reduce Motion	Off	❯
On/Off Labels		⬤○
Face ID & Attention		❯

4

(5) Swipe up to see the INTERACTION section.

(6) Use the controls in this section to adjust how you can interact with the iPhone. The controls here include the following:

- **Switch Control**—The controls on this screen enable you to configure an iPhone to work with an adaptive device so that you can control the iPhone with that device.

- **AssistiveTouch**—These controls make an iPhone easier to manipulate; if you enable this, a white button appears on the screen at all times. You can tap this to access the Home screen, Notification Center, and other areas. You can also create new gestures to control other functions on the iPhone.

- **Touch Accommodations**— You can use the Touch Accommodations options to make it easier for you to use the touch screen. For example, you can change the amount of time you must touch the screen before it is recognized as a touch.

- **Side Button**—Use this switch to set the rate at which you press the Side button to register as a double- or triple-press. On non-X models, this is the Home Button, but it performs the same purpose, which is to configure how pushes on the Touch ID/Home button are registered.

< General   **Accessibility**

INTERACTION

Reachability

Swipe down on the bottom edge of the screen to bring the top into reach.

Switch Control   Off >

AssistiveTouch   Off >

Touch Accommodations   Off >

Side Button   >

Siri   >

3D Touch   On >

Tap to Wake

Keyboard   >

Shake to Undo   On >

Vibration   On >

Call Audio Routing   Automatic >

- **Siri**—You can determine if the Type to Siri function is active and when voice feedback is provided to you.

- **3D Touch**—This setting enables you to turn the 3D Touch feature off or on. If 3D Touch is on, you can determine how much pressure you need to apply to the screen to activate it.

- **Keyboard**—Using these options, you can show or hide lowercase letters and change how the keys react to your touches.

- **Tap to Wake**—Set this to off if you don't want to be able wake the phone by tapping the screen.

- **Shake to Undo**—This setting enables you to turn off the shake motion to undo a recent action.

- **Vibration**—This setting enables you to enable or disable vibrations. It overrides the vibration settings in other areas, such as notifications.

- **Call Audio Routing**—Use this to configure where audio is heard during a phone call or FaceTime session. If you select Automatic, the iPhone chooses the routing based on how it is configured. You can select Bluetooth Headset or Speaker to always use one of those options first instead. You can also have the phone automatically answer calls.

‹ General	**Accessibility**	
INTERACTION		
Reachability		◯
Swipe down on the bottom edge of the screen to bring the top into reach.		
Switch Control		Off ›
AssistiveTouch		Off ›
Touch Accommodations		Off ›
Side Button		›
Siri		›
3D Touch		On ›
Tap to Wake		⬤
Keyboard		›
Shake to Undo		On ›
Vibration		On ›
Call Audio Routing		Automatic ›

6

(7) Swipe up the Accessibility screen to see the HEARING section.

(8) Use the controls in this section to configure sounds and to configure the iPhone to work with hearing-impaired people. The controls in this section include the following:

- **MFi Hearing Devices**—When you activate this setting, you can pair an iPhone to work with MFi hearing aids and other devices. (You pair other types of hearing aids using Bluetooth.)

- **RTT/TTY**—These controls enable you to use your iPhone with an RTT or TTY device.

- **LED Flash for Alerts**—When you set this switch to on (green), the flash flashes whenever an alert plays on the phone.

- **Mono Audio**—This causes the sound output to be in mono instead of stereo.

- **Phone Noise Cancellation**—This switch turns noise cancellation on and off. Noise cancellation reduces ambient noise when you are using the Phone app.

- **Balance**—Use this slider to change the balance of stereo sound between left and right.

- **Hearing Aid Compatibility**—If you enable this switch, the sound quality is improved for some types of hearing aids. When you use hearing aids with your iPhone, try setting this switch to on (green) to see if you can hear more clearly.

< General   **Accessibility**

HEARING

MFi Hearing Devices   >   (7)

RTT/TTY   Off >

LED Flash for Alerts   Off >

Mono Audio   (8)

Phone Noise Cancellation

Noise cancellation reduces ambient noise on phone calls when you are holding the receiver to your ear.

L   R

Adjust the audio volume balance between left and right channels.

Hearing Aid Compatibility

Hearing Aid Compatibility improves audio quality with some hearing aids.

(9) Swipe up to see the MEDIA section.

(10) Use the controls in this section to add features to video playback, including the following:

- **Subtitles & Captioning**—Use these controls to enable subtitles and captions for video and choose the style of those elements on the screen.

- **Audio Descriptions**—This causes an audio description of media to be played when available.

(11) Use the Guided Access setting if you want to limit the iPhone to using a single app at a time.

(12) Use the Accessibility Shortcut control to determine what happens when you press the Side or Touch ID/Home button three times. For example, if you choose Magnifier, you can quickly magnify something by pressing the Side or Touch ID/Home button three times.

MEDIA	
Subtitles & Captioning	>
Audio Descriptions	Off >

LEARNING	
Guided Access	Off >

Accessibility Shortcut	Magnifier >

Customizing How Your iPhone Works with Apps

Installing apps on your iPhone enables you to add more functionality than you can probably imagine. As the old Apple ad use to proclaim, "There's an app for that." And in all likelihood, there probably is an app for a lot of what you would like to use your iPhone for. The App Store app enables you to find, download, and install apps onto your iPhone.

Before you jump into the App Store, take a few moments to ensure your iPhone is configured for maximum ease and efficiency of dealing with new apps.

Configuring Your iPhone to Download and Maintain Apps

To download apps from the App Store, you need an Apple ID (if you need help getting or configuring an Apple ID, see Chapter 3, "Setting Up and Using an Apple ID, iCloud, and Other Online Accounts"). With your Apple ID configured on your phone in the iCloud area, make sure it is also ready to go for the App Store and ensure you can use Face ID or Touch ID when you download apps (instead of typing your password).

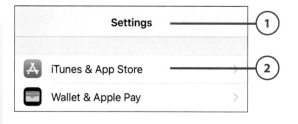

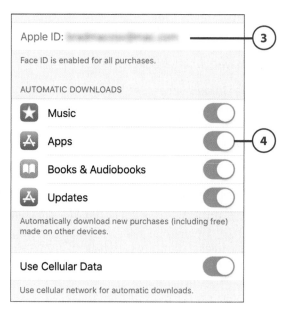

(1) Open the Settings app.

(2) Tap iTunes & App Store.

(3) Ensure the Apple ID you want to use to download apps is shown at the top of the screen; if it isn't tap the Apple ID shown, tap Sign Out, and then sign into your Apple ID.

(4) Ensure the Apps switch is on (green); this causes any apps you download to your iPhone to also automatically be downloaded to other devices (with which the apps are compatible, of course) that use the same Apple ID.

5 Ensure the Updates switch is on (green); this causes any updates to apps you have installed on your iPhone to be downloaded and installed automatically. I recommend you use this option so you can be sure you are always running the most current versions of your apps.

6 If you don't have an unlimited cellular data plan, you might want to set Use Cellular Data to off (white) so apps and other content are downloaded only when you are on a Wi-Fi network. If this is enabled (green), apps and content are downloaded to your iPhone when you are using a cellular network, which can consume significant amounts of your data plan. (Some apps or content are so large, they can only be downloaded when you are using a Wi-Fi connection.)

7 Use the information in the task "Configuring a Passcode and Face ID (X models)" or "Configuring a Passcode and Touch ID (non-X models)" to ensure the iTunes & App Store switch is enabled (green) so that you can use Face ID or Touch ID to download apps instead of typing your password. (If it isn't enabled, tap the switch, enter your Apple ID password, and tap OK to enable it.)

Apple ID:

Face ID is enabled for all purchases.

AUTOMATIC DOWNLOADS

Music

Apps

Books & Audiobooks

Updates — **5**

Automatically download new purchases (including free) made on other devices.

Use Cellular Data — **6**

Use cellular network for automatic downloads.

< Settings   **Face ID & Passcode**

USE FACE ID FOR:

iPhone Unlock

iTunes & App Store — **7**

Using the App Store App to Find and Install iPhone Apps

The App Store app enables you to quickly and easily browse and search for apps, view information about them, and then download and install them on your iPhone with just a few taps.

When you use the App Store app, you can find apps to download using any of the following options:

- **Today**—This tab takes you to apps featured in the App Store on the day you visit the store. When you tap any of the items on the Today screen, you move into the group or app on which you tapped.

- **Games**—Easily the most popular category of apps, Games enables you to find those critical games you need to prove your skills and pass the time. When you move into the Games area, the games are also grouped in various ways, such as Top Paid, Top Free, Top Categories, etc.

- **Apps**—This category leads you to apps that aren't games. On this screen, in addition to the Top Paid and Top Free lists, you can see apps organized by category, which is a useful way to find apps you want to use for specific purposes. Tap a category to explore the apps it contains.

- **Updates**—Through this option, you can update your apps (if you don't have automatic updates set as described earlier) or if you have automatic updates enabled, you see the list of updates made to the apps on your iPhone along with those that are pending.

- **Search**—This tool enables you to search for apps. You can search by name, developer, and other keywords.

Finding and downloading any kind of app follows this same pattern:

1. **Find the app you are interested in.** You can use the options described in the previous list to find apps by browsing for them, or you can use the search option to find a specific app quickly and easily.

2. **Evaluate the app.** The information screen for apps provides lots of information that you can use to decide whether you want to download an app (or not). The information available includes a text description, screenshots, ratings and reviews from users, and so on.

3. **Download and install the app.**

The following tasks provide detailed examples for each of these steps.

Searching for Apps

If you know something about an app, such as its name, its developer, its purpose, or just about anything else, you can quickly search the App Store to find the app. Here's how to search for an app:

① Move to the Home screen and tap App Store.

② Tap Search.

③ Tap in the Search box.

Follow the Trends?

Before you enter a search term on the Search screen, you see the Trending Searches, which are the searches that are being performed most frequently. You can tap one of these to use it to search for apps.

---

④ Type a search term. This can be the type of app you are looking for based on its purpose (such as *Travel*) or the name of someone associated with the app, its title, its developer, or even a topic. As you type, the app suggests searches that are related to what you are typing.

⑤ Tap the search you want to perform or tap the Search key on the keyboard to search for the term you entered in step 4. The apps that meet your search term appear.

6 Swipe up and down on the screen to review the apps in the search results.

7 If none of the apps are what you are looking for, tap Clear (x) in the Search box and repeat steps 4–6.

8 When you find an app of interest to you, tap it. You move to the app's information screen.

9 Use the app's information on the information screen to evaluate the app and decide if you want to download it. You can read about the app, see screenshots, and read other peoples' reviews to help you decide. If you want to download the app, see "Downloading Apps" later in this chapter for the details.

Browsing for Apps

If you don't know of a specific app you want, you can browse the App Store. To browse, you can tap any graphics or links you see in the App Store app. One of the most useful ways to browse for apps is by using categories.

App Store

1. Open the App Store app.

2. Tap Apps (browsing for games or using the Today option works very similarly).

3. Swipe up the screen until you see the Top Categories section.

4. Tap See All to browse all available categories.

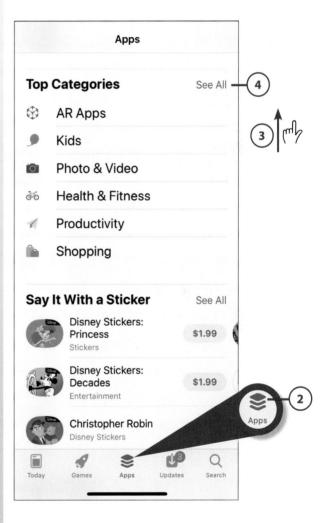

(5) Tap a category in which you are interested.

(6) Swipe up and down to browse the groupings of apps, such as Apps We Love, Top Paid, and so on.

(7) Tap See All for a grouping to browse the apps it contains.

(8) Swipe up and down to browse the apps in the group you selected in step 7.

(9) Tap an app in which you are interested. You move to that app's information screen.

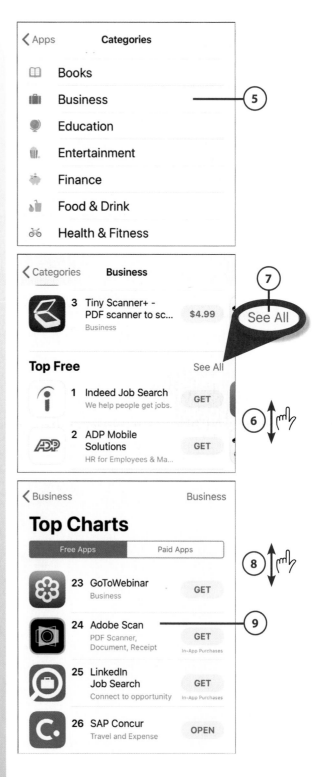

(10) Use the information on the information screen to decide whether you want to download the app. You can read about the app, see screenshots, and read other people's reviews to help you decide. If you want to download the app, see "Downloading Apps" later in this chapter for the details. Or, you can continue browsing by tapping the Back icon in the top-left corner of the screen to return to the category list.

>>>Go Further
MORE ON FINDING APPS

Following are a few pointers to help you use the App Store:

- When you see a + inside an app's price or Get button, that means the app is a universal app, which means it runs equally as well on iPhones or iPads.

- Some apps include video previews. When you see the Play icon on an image, it is a video preview. Tap the Play icon to watch it. Tap Done in the upper-left corner of the screen to move back to the screenshots.

- After you have used an app, you can add your own review by moving back to its Reviews tab and tapping Write a Review. You move to the Write a Review screen where you have to enter your iTunes Store account information before you can write and submit a review.

- You can read user reviews of the apps in the App Store. You should take these with a grain of salt. Some people have an issue with the developer or the type of app; are reviewing an older version of the app; or are commenting on issues unrelated to the app itself; and these issues can cause them to provide unfairly low ratings. The most useful individual user reviews are very specific, as in "I wanted the app to do x, but it only does y." It can be more helpful to look at the number of reviews and the average user rating than reading the individual reviews.

Downloading Apps

Downloading and installing apps is about as easy as things get, as you can see:

1. In the App Store, view the app you want to download.

2. Tap GET (for free apps) or the price (for apps that have a license fee). You're prompted to download and install the app.

Why Apple ID? Why?

At times, you might be prompted to enter your Apple ID password to download an app even if you have Face ID or Touch ID set up to work with the App Store. This can happen for a variety of reasons so don't be too surprised if it happens to you. After you've used Face ID or Touch ID for a while, you might find it annoying to have to actually type a password… at least I do.

(3) If you are using an X model and have Face ID enabled, press the Side button twice and look at the screen to confirm that you want to download and install the app. If you're using a non-X model and have Touch ID configured, touch the Touch ID/Home button (not shown in the figures). You see the Done message and the app starts to download.

You see the progress of the process.

When the process is complete, the status information is replaced by the OPEN button.

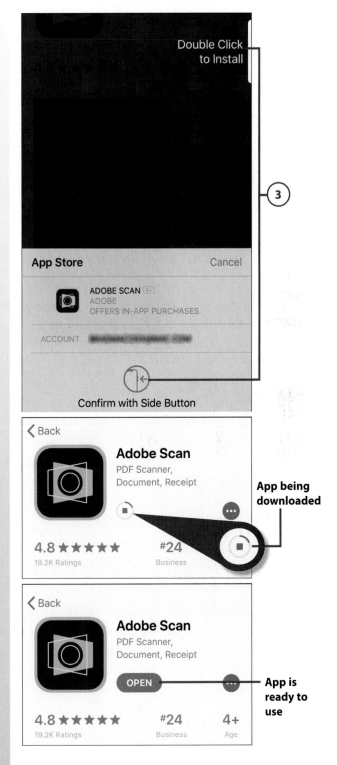

Double Click to Install

(3)

App Store   Cancel

ADOBE SCAN [4+]
ADOBE
OFFERS IN-APP PURCHASES

ACCOUNT

Confirm with Side Button

< Back

Adobe Scan
PDF Scanner,
Document, Receipt

App being downloaded

4.8 ★★★★★   #24
19.2K Ratings   Business

< Back

Adobe Scan
PDF Scanner,
Document, Receipt

OPEN

App is ready to use

4.8 ★★★★★   #24   4+
19.2K Ratings   Business   Age

>>>Go Further

MORE ON APPS

As you use the App Store app to install apps on your iPhone, keep the following hints handy:

- When you install an app, it is placed in the first "open" position on the Home screens. You can move it to a more convenient location as described in Chapter 5.

- Like other software, apps are updated regularly to fix problems, add features, or make other changes. If you set the Updates setting to on (green) as described earlier in this chapter, updates to your apps happen automatically in the background. Your apps are always current so you don't have to update them manually. (More information on updating apps is in Chapter 16, "Maintaining and Protecting Your iPhone and Solving Problems.")

- If you see the Download icon next to an app rather than GET or BUY, that means you have previously downloaded (and paid for if it isn't free) the app but it is not currently installed on your iPhone. Tap the icon to download and install it; if it is a paid app, you won't have to pay for it again.

- To let someone else know about an app, tap the Share icon and then tap how you want to let him know; the options include AirDrop, Message, Mail, Twitter, and Facebook. To buy an app for someone, tap Gift.

- Apps can work in the background to keep their information current, such as Weather and Stocks. To configure this, open the Settings app, tap General, and tap Background App Refresh. Tap Background App Refresh and tap Off to disable this, Wi-Fi to enable it only when your iPhone is connected to a Wi-Fi network, or Wi-Fi & Cellular Data to allow it any time your iPhone is connected to the Internet. Tap the Back icon (<), located in the upper-left corner of the screen, to see the list of apps installed on your iPhone. To enable an app to work in the background, set its switch to on (green). To disable background activity for an app, set its switch to off (white).

- After you install an app, move to the Settings screen and look for the app's icon. If it is there, the app has additional settings you can use to configure the way it works. Tap the app's icon in the Settings app and use its Settings screen to configure it.

Customizing How Your Phone Works with Shortcuts

Shortcuts enable you to perform a task or a series of tasks by speaking a phrase, tapping a button on the Shortcuts widget, or in a number of other ways. The great thing about shortcuts is that you can combine multiple apps so they work together. For example, you can have a shortcut that gives you directions to a location and starts a playlist for you to enjoy while you drive there.

There are two basic types of shortcuts:

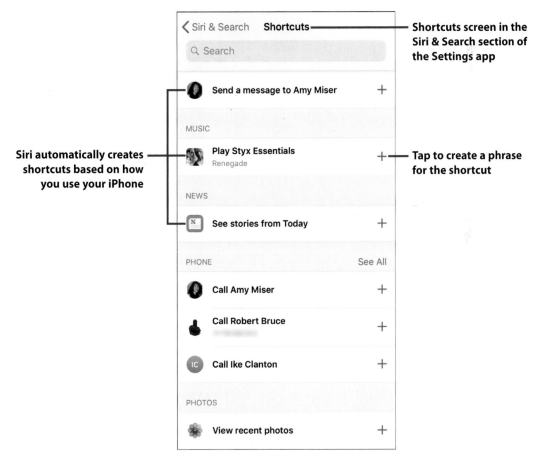

Shortcuts screen in the Siri & Search section of the Settings app

Siri automatically creates shortcuts based on how you use your iPhone

Tap to create a phrase for the shortcut

- **Siri Shortcuts.** Siri automatically creates shortcuts for you as you use it to perform tasks (unless you disable this in the Settings app). To use a shortcut Siri has created for you, all you need to do is enable the shortcut by associating a phrase with it; you can perform the task by speaking this phrase. Siri shortcuts are very handy and require very little effort for you to start using. See "Using Siri Shortcuts," in Chapter 11 for the details.

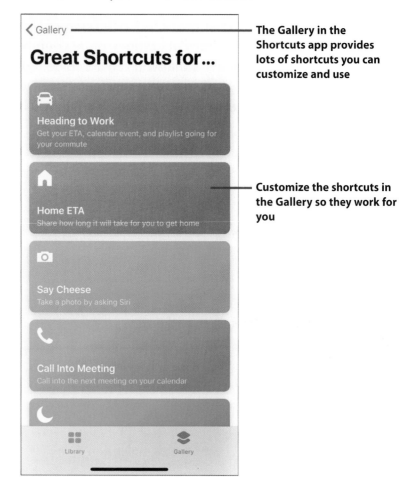

The Gallery in the Shortcuts app provides lots of shortcuts you can customize and use

Customize the shortcuts in the Gallery so they work for you

- **Shortcuts created with the Shortcuts app.** The Shortcuts app enables you to build your own shortcuts that can involve multiple apps. To build a shortcut, you combine actions in a series so that they work together to accomplish one or more tasks. For example, you might combine a message in the Messages app with travel time from the Maps app. Shortcuts doesn't require you to write code because the actions are like building blocks you can use to create a shortcut.

>>>*Go Further*

THE SHORTCUTS APP: DO I NEED IT?

You don't need to use the Shortcuts app to take advantage of Shortcuts. Siri Shortcuts are very easy to use, and you can accomplish a lot of different tasks with those shortcuts just by speaking to Siri directly.

The Shortcuts app is used to combine multiple apps to accomplish a sequence of steps with one command. It is a very powerful app, but can be daunting to learn if you've never programmed anything before. You can use your iPhone, including Siri shortcuts, just fine without ever using the Shortcuts app.

However, it can be fun and useful to take advantage of what the Shortcuts app can do. Shortcuts comes with a number of pre-made shortcuts you can tailor with your specific information to be able to run them. To get started, open the Shortcuts app and tap Gallery. Tap the category of shortcuts you want to see and then tap the shortcut you want to use. Tap Get Shortcut and follow the onscreen prompts to add your own information to the shortcut. You can then use that shortcut to accomplish the steps it contains.

You can also build shortcuts completely from scratch. To learn how to do this, start by working with some of the pre-made shortcuts so you can see how these shortcuts are constructed. This helps you understand how to connect steps together and pass information between them. There are also a lot of YouTube videos that provide more examples of how shortcuts can be built. After you understand these examples, you can start creating your own shortcuts.

Tap to configure your iPhone's screen and sounds

Customize the layout of the icons on your Home screens by placing icons where you want them

Place icons in folders to keep your Home screens organized

Choose the image you want as wallpaper

In this chapter, you learn how to make an iPhone look and sound the way you want it to. Topics include the following:

→ Getting started
→ Customizing your Home screens
→ Setting the screen's brightness, lock/wake, text, view, and wallpaper options
→ Choosing the sounds and vibratory feedback your iPhone uses

5

Customizing How Your iPhone Looks and Sounds

There are lots of ways that you can customize an iPhone to make it *your* iPhone so that it looks and sounds the way you want it to. You can design your Home screens; set the screen's brightness, text size, and wallpaper; and choose the sounds your iPhone makes.

Getting Started

In Chapter 4, "Customizing How Your iPhone Works," you learned how to change many aspects of how your iPhone works. This chapter focuses on how you can change the way you interact with your iPhone and how it interacts with you. Following are key areas you can configure to personalize your iPhone's personality:

- **Home screens**—The iPhone's Home screens are the starting point for most everything you do because these screens contain the icons that you tap to access the apps that you want to use. You see and use the Home screens constantly, so it's a good idea to customize them to your preferences. You can place icons on specific screens, and you can use folders to make your Home screens work better for you.

- **Screen brightness, Auto-Lock, Raise to Wake, text, view, and wallpaper options**—There are a number of ways you can change how your iPhone's screen looks and works. For example, you can set its brightness level and text size.

- **Sounds**—Sound is one important way your iPhone uses to communicate with you. The most obvious of these sounds is the ringtone that plays when you receive a call. However, there are many other sounds you can choose to help you know when something is happening. You can also choose to disable sounds so that your iPhone isn't so noisy. You can also have your iPhone vibrate in conjunction with, or instead of, making sounds.

Notifications

Notifications are the primary way your iPhone communicates with you and there are many options you can configure to change your iPhone's visual, auditory, and vibratory notifications. How to use notifications is explained in Chapter 2, "Using Your iPhone's Core Features," while in Chapter 4, you learn how to configure the types of notifications your iPhone uses to communicate with you.

Customizing Your Home Screens

The iPhone's Home screens are the starting point for anything you do because these screens contain the icons and folders of icons that you tap to access the apps that you want to use. You see and use the Home screens constantly, so it's a good idea to customize them to your preferences.

In the background of the Lock screen and every Home screen is the wallpaper image. In the section called "Setting the Wallpaper on the Home and Lock Screens," you learn how to configure your iPhone's wallpaper in both locations.

As you know, you can access apps on your Home screens by tapping them. The Home screens come configured with icons in default locations. You can change the location of these icons to be more convenient for you. As you install more apps on your iPhone, it's a good idea to organize your Home screens so that you can quickly get to the apps you use most frequently. You can move icons around the same screen, move icons between the pages of the Home screen, and organize icons within folders. You can even change the icons that appear on the Home screen Dock. You can also delete icons that you no longer need.

Moving Icons Around Your Home Screens

You can move icons around on a Home screen, and you can move icons among screens to change where they are located.

(1) If you aren't already on one, move to a Home screen by swiping up from the bottom of the screen (X models) or pressing the Touch ID/ Home button (non-X models).

(2) Swipe to the left or right across the Home screen until the page containing an icon you want to move appears.

(3) Touch (don't tap because if you do, the app opens instead) and hold on any icon. After a moment, the icons begin jiggling, which indicates that you can move icons on the Home screens. You also see the Delete symbol (x) in the upper-left corner of some icons, which indicates that you can delete both the icon and app (more on this later in this section).

(4) Touch and hold an icon you want to move; it becomes darker to show that you have selected it.

Touch But Don't Press (3D Touch Models)

If you are working with an iPhone 6s/6s Plus or later model that supports 3D Touch, don't press on icons when you want to move them; just touch your finger lightly to the screen. If you apply pressure, you might open the Quick Action menu instead. When you just touch an icon and leave your finger on the screen without any pressure, the icons become fuzzy briefly, and then start jiggling to indicate you can move them.

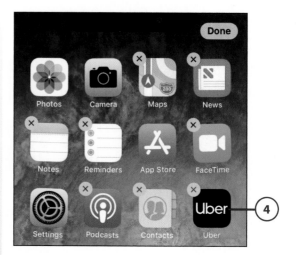

(5) Drag the icon to a new location on the current screen; as you move the icon around the page, other icons separate and are reorganized to enable you to place the icon in its new location.

(6) When the icon is in the location you want, lift your finger. The icon is set in that place. (You don't have to be precise; the icon automatically snaps into the closest position when you lift your finger off the screen.)

7 Tap and hold on an icon you want to move to a different page.

8 Drag the icon to the left edge of the screen to move it to a previous page or to the right edge of the screen to move it to a later page. As you reach the edge of the screen, you move to the previous or next page.

9 Drag the icon to its location on the new Home screen and lift your finger off the icon.

10 Continue moving icons until you've placed them in the locations you want; then tap the Done button (X models) or press the Touch ID/Home button (non-X models). The icons are locked in their current positions, they stop jiggling, and the Delete symbols disappear.

Another Way to Be Done

On an X model, you can lock icons in place by swiping up from the bottom of the screen (instead of tapping Done).

Creating Folders to Organize Apps on Your Home Screens

You can place icons into folders to keep them organized and to make more icons available on the same page. To create a folder, do the following:

1. Move to the Home screen containing icons you want to place in a folder.

2. Touch and hold an icon until the icons start jiggling; the Delete icons (x) appear on most icons.

3. Drag one icon on top of another one that you want to be in the new folder together.

4. When the first icon is on top of the second and a folder appears, lift your finger. The two icons are placed into the new folder, which is named based on the type of icons you place within it. The folder opens and you see its default name.

5. To delete the current name so you can create a completely new name, tap Delete (x); if you want to keep all or part of the current name, skip this step.

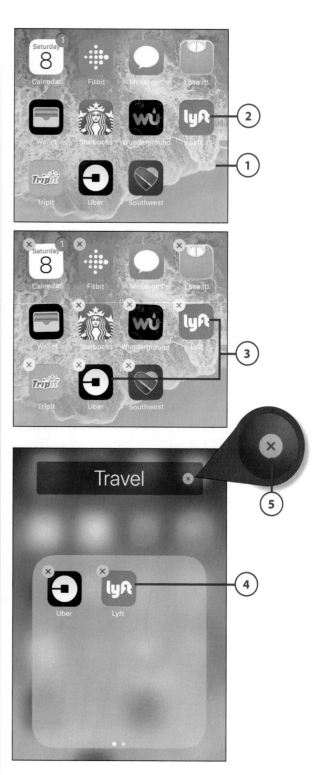

6 Change the default name for the folder or type a completely new name if you deleted the previous one.

7 Tap Done.

8 Tap outside the folder to close it.

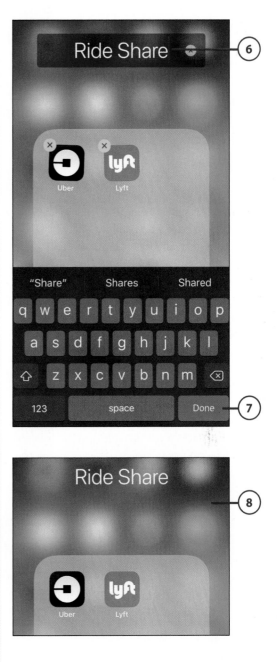

(9) If you're done organizing the Home screen, tap Done (X models) or press the Touch ID/Home button (non-X models). The icons are locked into place and stop jiggling.

Locating Folders

You can move a folder to a new location in the same way you can move any icon. Touch and hold (don't tap or it opens instead) the folder's icon until the icons start jiggling. Drag the folder icon to where you want it to be.

Placing Icons in Existing Folders

You can add icons to an existing folder like so:

(1) Move to the Home screen containing an icon you want to place in a folder.

(2) Touch and hold an icon until the icons start jiggling and the Delete icons (x) appear on most app icons.

(3) Drag the icon you want to place into a folder on top of the folder's icon so that the folder opens. (The icon doesn't have to be on the same Home screen page; you can drag an icon from one page and drop it on a folder on a different page.)

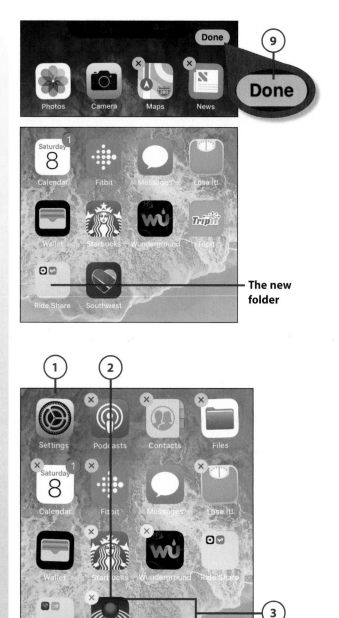

The new folder

(4) When the folder opens, lift your finger from the screen. The icon is placed within the folder.

Adding Apps to Folders Quickly

If you don't want to change the icon's location when you place it in the folder, lift your finger as soon as the folder's icon is highlighted; this places the icon in the folder but doesn't cause the folder to open. This is faster than waiting for the folder to open, but doesn't allow you to position the icon within the folder.

(5) Drag the new icon to its location within the folder.

(6) Tap outside the folder. The folder closes.

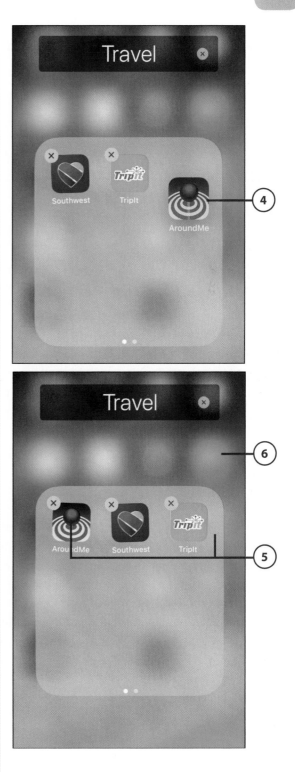

(7) When you're done adding icons to folders, tap Done (X models) or press the Touch ID/Home button (non-X models).

The folder now contains the app you placed in it

Removing Icons from Folders

To remove an icon from a folder, tap the folder from which you want to remove the icon to open it. Touch and hold the icon you want to remove until it starts jiggling. Drag the icon you want to remove from inside the folder to outside the folder. When you cross the border of the folder, the folder closes and you can place the icon on a Home screen.

Folders and Badges

When you place an icon that has a badge notification (the red circle with a number in it that indicates the number of new items in an app) in a folder, the badge transfers to the folder so that you see it on the folder's icon. When you place more than one app with a badge notification in the same folder, the badge on the folder becomes the total number of new items for all the apps in the folder. You need to open a folder to see the badges for the individual apps it contains.

Configuring the Home Screen Dock

The Dock on the bottom of the Home screen appears on every page. You can place any icons on the Dock that you want, including folder icons.

1. Move to the Home screen containing an icon you want to place on the Dock.

2. Touch and hold an icon until the icons start jiggling and the Delete icons (x) appear on most app icons.

3. Drag an icon that is currently on the Dock from the Dock onto the Home screen to create an empty space on the Dock.

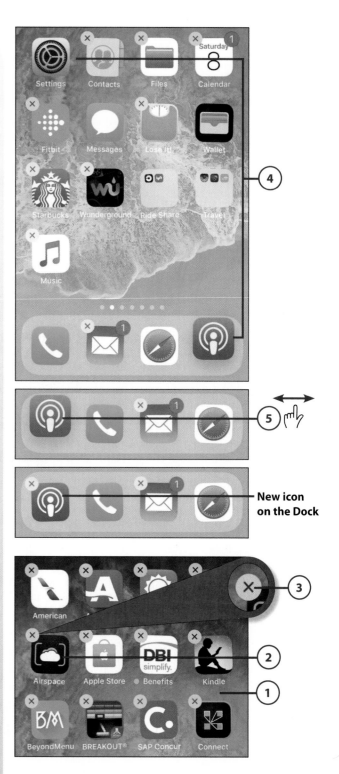

New icon
on the Dock

(4) Drag an icon or folder from the Home screen onto the Dock.

(5) Drag the icons on the Dock around so they are in the order you want them to be.

(6) If you're done organizing the Home screen, tap Done (X models) or press the Touch ID/Home button (non-X models). The icons are locked into place and stop jiggling.

Deleting Icons

You can delete most icons from a Home screen to remove them from your iPhone (there are exceptions as explained in "More on Organizing Home Screens"). When you delete an app's icon, its data is also deleted and you won't be able to use the app anymore (of course, you can download it again if you change your mind, but the data that the app was using is lost unless it is stored elsewhere).

(1) Move to the Home screen containing an icon you want to delete.

(2) Touch and hold an icon until the icons start jiggling and the Delete icons appear on most icons (you can delete icons that are inside folders, too).

(3) Tap the icon's Delete icon (x).

4 Tap Delete. The app and any associated data on your iPhone are deleted.

Delete "Airspace"?

Deleting this app will also delete its data.

Cancel   Delete —— **4**

>>>*Go Further*

MORE ON ORGANIZING HOME SCREENS

Organizing your Home screens can make the use of your iPhone more efficient. Here are a few more things to keep in mind:

- You can place many icons in the same folder. When you add more than nine, any additional icons are placed on new pages within the folder. As you keep adding icons, pages keep being added to the folder to accommodate the icons you add to it. You can swipe to the left or right within a folder to move among its pages, just as you can to move among your Home screens. You can also drag icons between pages in a folder, also just like on a Home screen.

- To change an existing folder's name, move to a screen showing the folder whose name you want to change. Touch and hold an icon until the icons jiggle. Tap the folder so that it opens, and then tap the current name. Edit the name, tap Done, and tap outside the folder to close it.

- To delete a folder, remove all the icons from it. The folder is deleted as soon as you remove the last icon from within it.

- You can delete icons for apps you've added to your iPhone or some of the default apps, such as the Stocks app. You can't delete some of the default apps, such as Safari, which is why their icons don't have Delete icons like apps that you install do. If you don't use some of these default apps that you can't delete, move them to pages of your Home screen that you don't use very often so they don't get in your way, or create a folder for unused icons and store them there, out of your way.

- To return your Home screens to how they were when you first started using your iPhone, open the Settings app, tap General, Reset (you might need to swipe up the screen to see this), Reset Home Screen Layout, and Reset Home Screen. The Home screens return to their default configurations. Icons you've added are moved onto the later pages.

Setting the Screen's Brightness, Lock/Wake, Text, View, and Wallpaper Options

There are a number of settings you can configure to suit your viewing preferences and how your iPhone locks/wakes:

- **Brightness**—Because you continually look at your iPhone's screen, it should be the right brightness level for your eyes. However, the screen is also a large user of battery power, so the dimmer an iPhone's screen is, the longer its battery lasts. You should find a good balance between viewing comfort and battery life.

- **True Tone**—This feature attempts to adjust the display so that colors appear the same despite changes to the ambient light around the phone.

The Models Don't Remain the Same

Different models of iPhones have different screen capabilities, so you might or might not see all of or the same options on your phone that are described in this section. If your iPhone doesn't have a specific capability, such as True Tone, you can just ignore information related to that topic.

- **Night Shift**—This feature changes the color profile of the screen after dark. It is supposed to make the light produced by the iPhone more suitable to darker conditions. You can set the color temperature to your preferences and can set a schedule if you want Night Shift to be activated automatically.

- **Auto-Lock**—The Auto-Lock setting causes your iPhone to lock and go to sleep after a specific amount of inactivity. This is good for security as it is less likely someone can pick up and use your phone if you let it sit for a while. It also extends battery life because it puts the iPhone to sleep when you aren't using it.

- **Raise to Wake**—This setting enables you to wake up the iPhone by lifting it up. This is useful because you don't even need to press a button, just lift the phone and you see the Lock screen, giving you quick access to the current time, the Audio Player, notifications, and widgets. However, some people find this feature more annoying than helpful so if the phone waking when you lift it up bothers you, disable this setting on your phone.

- **Text Size/Bold**—As you use your iPhone, you'll be constantly working with text so it's also important to configure the text size to meet your preferences. You can use the Bold setting to bold text to make it easier to read.

- **View**—Some non-X models offer two views. The Standard view maximizes screen space and the Zoomed view makes things on the screen larger, making them easier to see, but less content fits on the screen. You can choose the view that works best for you.

- **Wallpaper**—Wallpaper is the image you see "behind" the icons on your Home screens. Because you see this image so often, you might as well have an image that you want to see or that you believe makes using the Home screens easier and faster. You can use the iPhone's default wallpaper images, or you can use any photo available on your iPhone. You can also set the wallpaper you see on the iPhone's Lock screen (you can use the same image as on the Home screens or a different one). Although it doesn't affect productivity or usability of the iPhone very much, choosing your own wallpaper to see in the background of the Home and Lock screens makes your iPhone more personal to you and is just plain fun.

Setting Screen Brightness, True Tone, and Night Shift Using the Settings App

To set the screen brightness and Night Shift, perform the following steps:

1. In the Settings app, tap Display & Brightness.

2. Drag the slider to the right to raise the brightness or to the left to lower it. A brighter screen uses more power but is easier to see.

3. If you don't want the True Tone feature to be active, set the True Tone switch to off (white).

4. Tap Night Shift.

Settings

⚙ General   >

▣ Control Center   >

AA Display & Brightness   >   ①

◁ Settings   **Display & Brightness**

BRIGHTNESS

☀ ————————————— ☀   ②

True Tone   ⬤   ③

Automatically adapt iPhone display based on ambient lighting conditions to make colors appear consistent in different environments.

Night Shift ——————— Off >   ④

(5) To have Night Shift activate automatically, set the Scheduled switch to on (green); if you don't want it to activate automatically, skip to step 12.

(6) Tap the From/To setting.

(7) To have Night Shift on between sunset and sunrise, tap Sunset to Sunrise and skip to step 11.

(8) To set a custom schedule for Night Shift, tap Custom Schedule.

(9) Tap Turn On At and swipe up or down on the hour, minute, and AM/PM wheels to set the time when you want Night Shift to activate.

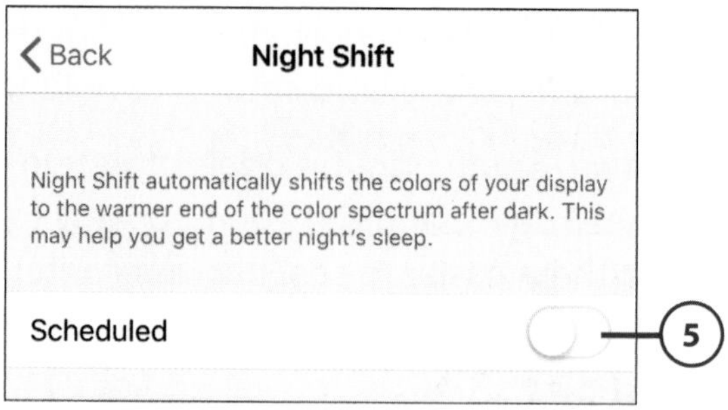

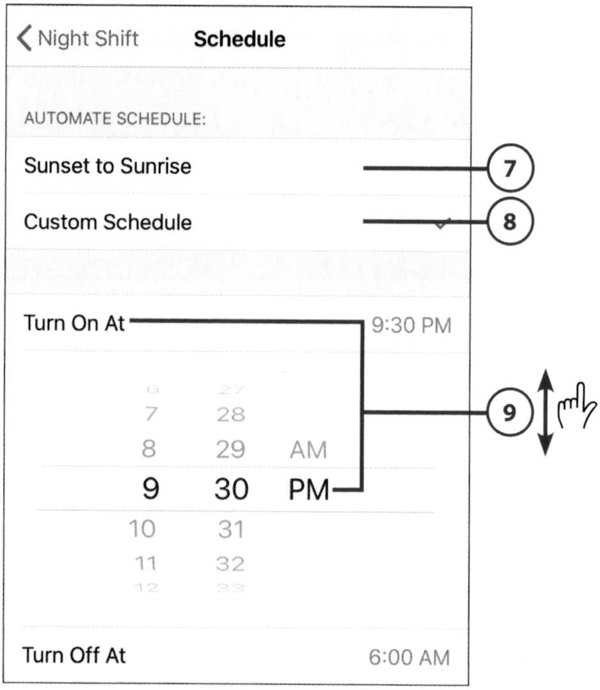

< Back   **Night Shift**

Night Shift automatically shifts the colors of your display to the warmer end of the color spectrum after dark. This may help you get a better night's sleep.

Scheduled   — **(5)**

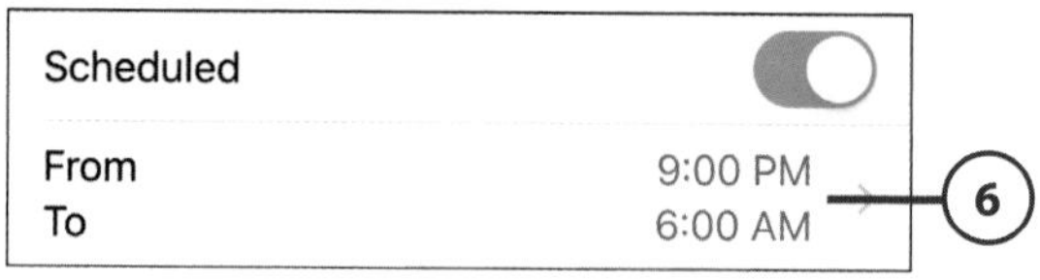

Scheduled

From   9:00 PM
To   6:00 AM   — **(6)**

< Night Shift   **Schedule**

AUTOMATE SCHEDULE:

Sunset to Sunrise   — **(7)**

Custom Schedule   — **(8)**

Turn On At   9:30 PM

6	27	
7	28	
8	29	AM
9	**30**	**PM**
10	31	
11	32	
12	33	

— **(9)**

Turn Off At   6:00 AM

10 Tap Turn Off At and use the time wheels to set when you want Night Shift to turn off.

11 Tap Night Shift.

12 To manually turn Night Shift on at any time, set the Manually Enable Until Tomorrow switch to on (green). Night Shift activates and remains on until sunrise when it shuts off automatically. (You can manually turn off Night Shift by setting the Manually Enable Until Tomorrow switch to off [white]).

13 Drag the COLOR TEMPERATURE slider to the right to make the Night Shift effect more pronounced or to the left to make it less warm. If Night Shift isn't active when you drag the slider, it goes into effect as you move the slider so you can see the effect the temperature you select has.

14 Tap Back.

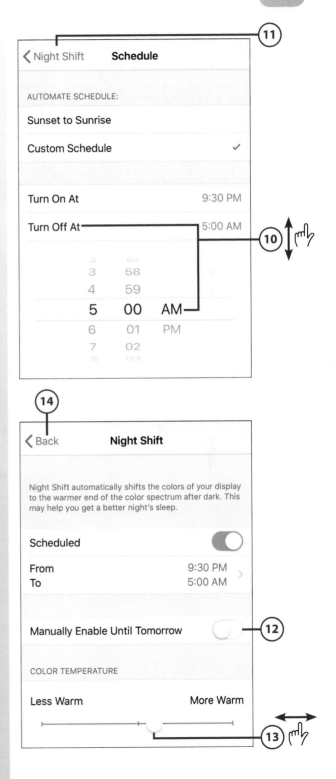

Setting the Screen Brightness and Night Shift Using the Control Center

You can use the Control Center to quickly adjust brightness and Night Shift as follows:

(1) Open the Control Center by swiping down from the upper-right corner of the screen (X models) or swiping up from the bottom of the screen (non-X models).

(2) Swipe up or down on the Brightness slider to increase or decrease the brightness, respectively.

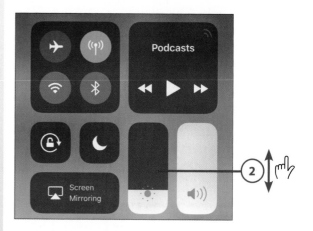

(3) To turn Night Shift on or off, press and hold on the Brightness slider.

(4) Use the Brightness slider to change the screen's brightness (this does the same thing as using the slider on the Control Center, but since it is larger here, it is a bit easier to use).

(5) To enable or disable True Tone, tap the True Tone icon. The current status is indicated under the icon so you know when it is on or off.

(6) Tap the Night Shift icon to turn Night Shift on. When on, the Night Shift icon is orange.

(7) Tap the Night Shift icon to turn Night Shift off. When off, the Night Shift icon is white.

(8) Tap outside the tools to return to the Control Center.

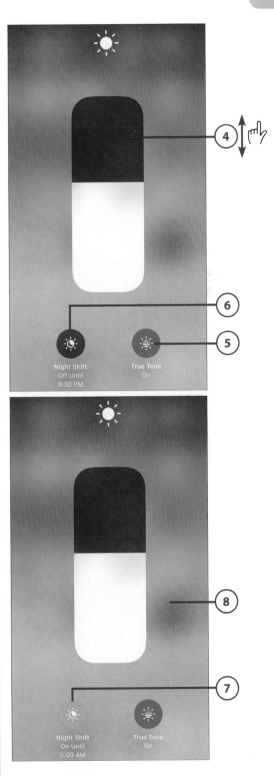

(9) Tap on any area on the background of the Control Center to
close it.

Setting Auto-Lock and Raise to Wake

To configure Auto-Lock or Raise to
Wake, perform the following steps:

(1) In the Settings app, tap Display &
Brightness to open the Display &
Brightness settings screen.

(2) Tap Auto-Lock.

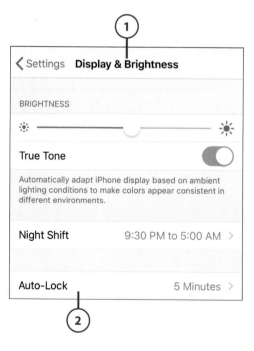

3 Tap the amount of idle time you want to pass before the iPhone automatically locks and goes to sleep. You can choose from 30 seconds or 1 to 5 minutes; choose Never if you want to only manually lock your iPhone. I recommend that you keep Auto-Lock set to a relatively small value to conserve your iPhone's battery and to make it more secure. Of course, the shorter you set this time to be, the more frequently you have to unlock your iPhone.

4 Tap Back.

5 If you want to be able to wake your phone by lifting it, set the Raise to Wake switch to on (green); to disable this feature, set the switch to off (white).

Setting Text Size and Bold

To change the text size or make all text bold, perform the following steps:

1 In the Settings app, tap Display & Brightness to open the Display & Brightness settings screen.

2 Tap Text Size. This control changes the size of text in all the apps that support the iPhone's Dynamic Type feature.

< Back   Auto-Lock

30 Seconds

1 Minute

2 Minutes

3 Minutes

4 Minutes

5 Minutes

Never

Attention is detected when you are looking at the screen. When attention is detected, iPhone does not dim the display.

Auto-Lock   4 Minutes >

Raise to Wake

< Settings   Display & Brightness

BRIGHTNESS

True Tone

Automatically adapt iPhone display based on ambient lighting conditions to make colors appear consistent in different environments.

Night Shift   9:30 PM to 5:00 AM >

Auto-Lock   4 Minutes >

Raise to Wake

Text Size

(3) Drag the slider to the right to increase the size of text or to the left to decrease it. As you move the slider, the text at the top of the screen resizes so you can see the effect of the change you are making.

(4) When you are happy with the size of the text, tap Back.

(5) If you want to make all of the text on your iPhone bold, set the Bold Text switch to on (green) and move to step 6. If you don't want to bold the text, skip the next step.

(6) Tap Continue. Your iPhone restarts. All the text is in bold, making it easier to read.

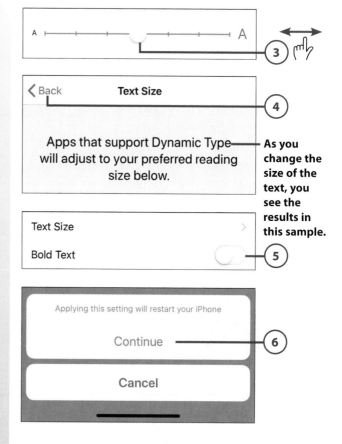

A ———————————— A — (3)

< Back   **Text Size** — (4)

Apps that support Dynamic Type — **As you change the size of the text, you see the results in this sample.**
will adjust to your preferred reading size below.

Text Size   >

Bold Text   ⬭ — (5)

Applying this setting will restart your iPhone

Continue — (6)

Cancel

Setting Text Size Using the Control Center

To change the text size with the Control Center, perform the following steps:

(1) Open the Control Center by swiping down from the upper-right corner of the screen (X models) or swiping up from the bottom of the screen (non-X models).

(2) Tap the Text Size icon. (If you don't see this icon, you need to add it to the Control Center. See Chapter 4 for details.)

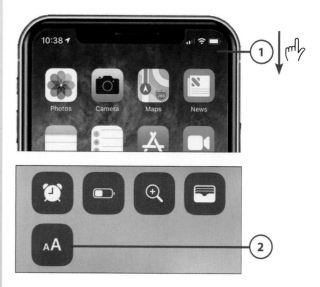

10:38

Photos   Camera   Maps   News — (1)

⏰   🔋   🔍⁺   💳

AA — (2)

3 Tap above the shaded area to increase the text size.

4 Tap below the shaded area to decrease the text size.

5 Tap outside the tool to return to the Control Center.

6 Tap on any area on the background of the Control Center to close it.

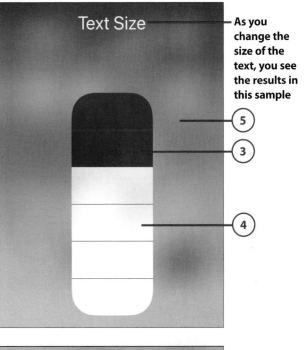

Text Size

As you change the size of the text, you see the results in this sample

Choosing a View

To configure the view you use, perform the following steps:

(1) In the Settings app, tap Display & Brightness to open the Display & Brightness settings screen.

(2) Tap View; if you don't see this option, your iPhone doesn't support it and you can skip the rest of these steps.

(3) Tap Standard.

(4) Look at the sample screen.

(5) Swipe to the left or right to see examples of what other screens look like in the Standard view.

What this screen looks like in Standard view

(6) Look at the next sample screen.

(7) Swipe to the left or right to see examples of what other screens look like in the Standard view.

(8) Tap Zoomed. The sample screens change to reflect the Zoomed view.

(9) Swipe to the left and right to preview the other sample screens in the Zoomed view.

(10) If you want to keep the current view, tap Cancel and skip the rest of these steps.

(11) To change the view, tap the view you want.

(12) Tap Set (if Set is grayed out, the view you selected is already set and you can skip the rest of these steps).

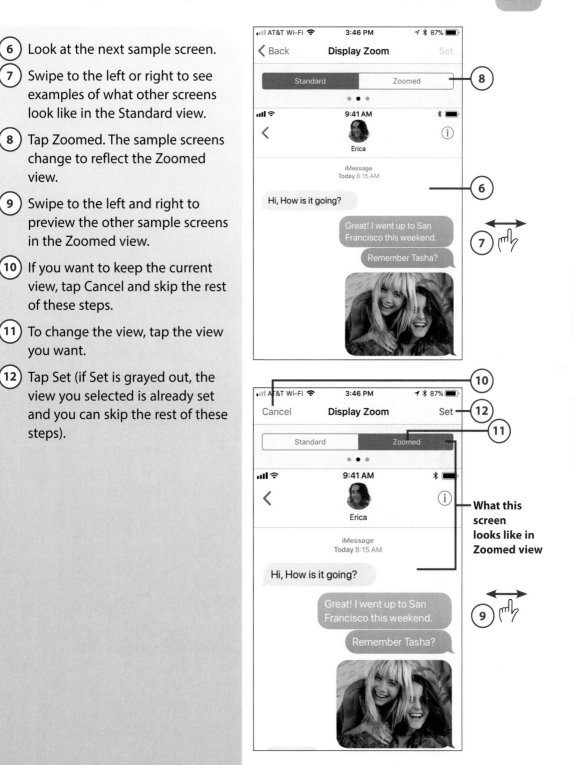

What this screen looks like in Zoomed view

(13) Tap Use Zoomed (this is Use Standard if you are switching to the Standard view). Your iPhone restarts and uses the new view.

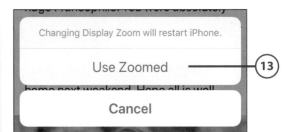

(13)

A Home screen in Zoomed view

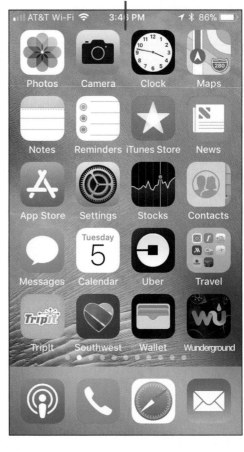

Setting the Wallpaper on the Home and Lock Screens

To configure your wallpaper, perform the following steps:

1 In the Settings app, tap Wallpaper. You see the current wallpaper set for the Lock and Home screens.

2 Tap Choose a New Wallpaper. The Choose screen has two sections. The top section enables you to choose one of the default wallpaper images (Dynamic, Stills, or Live), whereas the lower section shows you the photos available on your iPhone. If you don't have any photos stored on your iPhone, you can only choose from the default images. To choose a default image, continue with step 3; to use one of your photos as wallpaper, skip to step 8.

3 Tap Dynamic if you want to use dynamic wallpaper, Stills if you want to use a static image, or Live if you want to use a Live Photo. These steps show selecting the Stills option, but using a dynamic image or Live Photo is similar.

Current wallpaper on your Lock screen

Current wallpaper on your Home screens

(4) Swipe up and down the screen to browse the images available to you.

(5) Tap the image you want to use as wallpaper.

(6) Tap Perspective to use the Perspective view of the wallpaper, tap Still if you want a static version of the image, or tap Live Photo to use a Live Photo (you only see this option if you selected Live in step 3). (See the sidebar "More on View Options" for an explanation of these terms.)

(7) Tap Set and move to step 15.

Wallpaper Options Explained

Dynamic wallpaper has motion (kind of like a screen saver on a computer). Stills are static images. Live Photos show motion when you tap and hold on them. Live Photos are available only on iPhone 6s/6s Plus or later models. On other models, you see only the Dynamic and Stills options.

8 To use a photo as wallpaper, swipe up the screen to browse the sources of photos available to you; these include All Photos, Favorites, Selfies, albums, and so on.

Working with Photos

To learn how to work with the photos on your iPhone, see Chapter 14, "Viewing and Editing Photos and Video with the Photos App."

9 Tap the source containing the photo you want to use.

10 Swipe up and down the selected source to browse its photos.

11 Tap the photo you want to use. (If the photo is not currently stored on your iPhone, it downloads, which can take a few seconds.) The photo appears on the Move and Scale screen, which you can use to resize and move the image around.

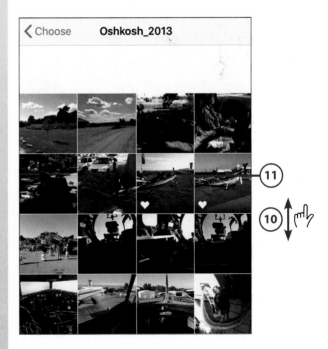

More on View Options

The Perspective view can be a bit difficult to describe because it is subtle. This view magnifies the wallpaper image when you tilt your iPhone. It is sometimes noticeable and sometimes not, depending on the image you are using for wallpaper. The best thing to do is to enable it to see if you notice any difference or disable it if you prefer not to use it for the specific images you use as wallpaper. You can enable or disable it at any time for your wallpaper on the Lock and Home screens. To change the view without changing the wallpaper, move to the Wallpaper screen and tap the wallpaper (tap the Lock or Home screen) you want to change. Tap Perspective to use the Perspective view or Still if you want the image to be static. To save the view, tap Set or to leave it as it is, tap Cancel.

When you choose a Live Photo as wallpaper, you can touch and hold on the screen to see the image's motion. Note that when you apply a Live Photo to the Home screen wallpaper, it becomes a static image for which you can choose the Still or Perspective view.

(12) Use your fingers to unpinch to zoom in or pinch to zoom out, and hold down and drag the photo around the screen until it appears how you want the wallpaper to look.

(13) Tap Perspective to use the Perspective view of the wallpaper (see the sidebar "More on View Options"), tap Still to use a static version of the image, or tap Live Photo to use a Live Photo (available only when you are working with a Live Photo on iPhone 6s or iPhone 6s Plus or later models).

(14) Tap Set.

(15) Tap Set Lock Screen or Set Home Screen to apply the wallpaper to only one of those screens; tap Set Both to apply the same wallpaper in both locations. The next time you move to the screen you selected, you see the wallpaper you chose.

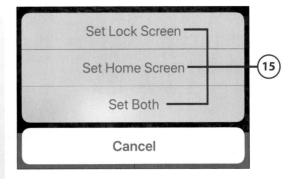

New wallpaper on the Home screen

(16) If you set the wallpaper in only one location, tap Choose (not shown on a figure) to move back to the Choose screen and repeat steps 3–15 to set the wallpaper for the other location.

New wallpaper on the Lock screen

Choosing the Sounds and Vibratory Feedback Your iPhone Uses

Sound and vibrations are two ways your iPhone uses to communicate with you. You can configure the sounds and vibrations the phone uses in two ways. One is by choosing the general sounds and vibrations your iPhone makes, which is covered in this section. You can also configure the sounds and vibrations that apps use for notifications about certain events (this is covered in Chapter 4) and for specific contacts (explained in Chapter 6, "Managing Contacts."

If you have an iPhone 7 or later model, it offers haptic feedback, which means the phone vibrates slightly when something happens, such as when you make a choice on a selection wheel. You can determine whether you want to feel this feedback or not. If you don't have one of these models, you won't see references to haptics on your Sounds screens.

To configure your iPhone's general sounds, do the following:

(1) On the Settings screen, tap Sounds & Haptics (iPhone 7 and later) or Sounds (earlier models).

(2) Set the Vibrate on Ring switch to on (green) if you want your iPhone to also vibrate when it rings.

(3) Set the Vibrate on Silent switch to on (green) if you want your iPhone to vibrate when you have it muted.

(4) Set the volume of the ringer and alert tones by dragging the slider to the left or right.

(5) Set the Change with Buttons switch to on (green) if you want to also be able to change the ringer and alert volume using the Volume buttons on the side of the phone.

(6) Tap Ringtone. On the resulting screen, you can set the sound and vibration your iPhone uses when a call comes in.

Settings

Notifications

Sounds & Haptics ——— **(1)**

< Settings   **Sounds & Haptics**

VIBRATE

Vibrate on Ring ————— **(2)**

Vibrate on Silent ————— **(3)**

RINGER AND ALERTS ————— **(4)**

Change with Buttons ————— **(5)**

The volume of the ringer and alerts can be adjusted using the volume buttons.

SOUNDS AND VIBRATION PATTERNS

Ringtone   Sweet Home Alabama → **(6)**

⑦ Swipe up and down the screen to see all the ringtones available to you. There are two sections of sounds on this screen: RINGTONES and ALERT TONES. These work in the same way; alert tones tend to be shorter sounds. At the top of the RINGTONES section, you see any custom ringtones you have configured on your phone; a dark line separates those from the default ringtones that are below the custom ones.

Individual Ringtones and Vibrations

The ringtone and vibration you set in steps 6–14 are the default or general settings. These are used for all callers except for people in your Contacts app for whom you've set specific ringtones or vibrations. In that case, the contact's specific ringtone and vibration are used instead of the defaults. See Chapter 6 to learn how to configure specific ringtones and vibrations for contacts.

⑧ Tap a sound, and it plays; tap it again to stop it.

⑨ Repeat steps 7 and 8 until you have selected the sound you want to have as your general ringtone.

❮ Back   **Ringtone**

Vibration   Heartbeat ❯

STORE

Tone Store

Download All Purchased Tones

This will download all ringtones and alerts purchased using the "bradmacosx@mac.com" account.

RINGTONES

Carry On Wayward Son

Kryptonite

Oh Where Is My Cell Phone?

Star Trek

Star Trek (Cover)

✓ Sweet Home Alabama

Reflection (Default)

⑦

❮ Back   **Ringtone**

✓ Carry On Wayward Son ——— ⑧

Kryptonite

Oh Where Is My Cell Phone?

Star Trek

Star Trek (Cover)

Sweet Home Alabama

Reflection (Default)

Apex

Beacon

10 If necessary, swipe down the screen so you see the Vibration section at the top.

11 Tap Vibration. A list of Standard and Custom vibrations is displayed.

12 Swipe up and down the screen to see all the vibrations available. The STANDARD section contains the default vibrations, and in the CUSTOM section you can tap Create New Vibration to create your own vibration patterns, as discussed in the "Sounding Off" sidebar at the end of this section.

13 Tap a vibration. It "plays" so you can feel it; tap it again to stop it.

14 Repeat steps 12 and 13 until you've selected the general vibration you want to use; you can tap None at the bottom of the Vibration screen below the CUSTOM section if you don't want to have a general vibration.

15 Tap Ringtone.

‹ Back   **Ringtone**

Vibration   Heartbeat ›   **11**

STORE

Tone Store

Download All Purchased Tones

This will download all ringtones and alerts purchased using the "bradmacosx@mac.com" account.

RINGTONES

✓ Carry On Wayward Son

Kryptonite

10

11:09 ⏎   ⚓ 🔋

‹ Ringtone   **Vibration**   Edit

15

STANDARD

Accent (Default)

Alert   **13**

Heartbeat

Quick

Rapid

S.O.S.

Staccato

Symphony

CUSTOM

My Vibe

Create New Vibration   ›

None

12

(16) Tap Back. The ringtone you selected is shown on the Sounds and Haptics (or Sounds) screen next to the Ringtone label.

(17) Tap Text Tone.

(18) Use steps 7–14 with the Text Tone screen to set the sound and vibration used when you receive a new text. The process works the same as for ringtones, though the screens look a bit different. For example, the ALERT TONES section is at the top of the screen because you are more likely to want a short sound for new texts.

(19) When you're done setting the text tone, tap Back.

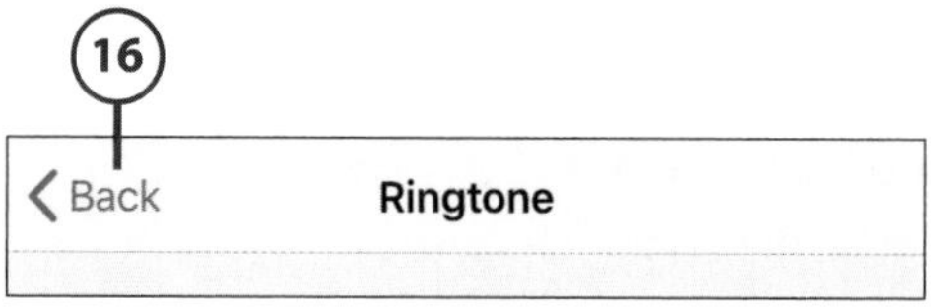

(16)

‹ Back	Ringtone

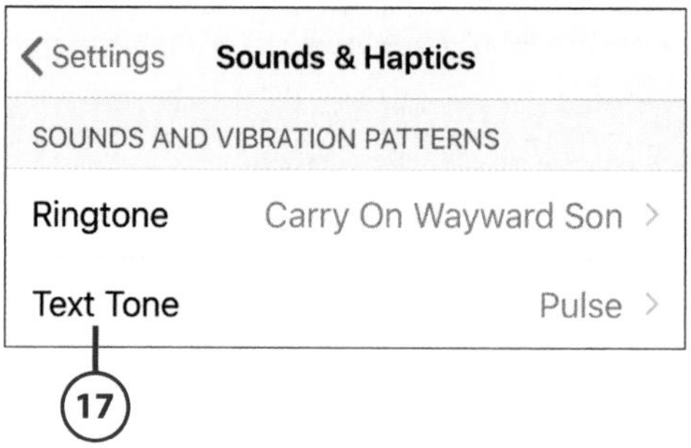

‹ Settings	**Sounds & Haptics**

SOUNDS AND VIBRATION PATTERNS

Ringtone	Carry On Wayward Son ›
Text Tone	Pulse ›

(17)

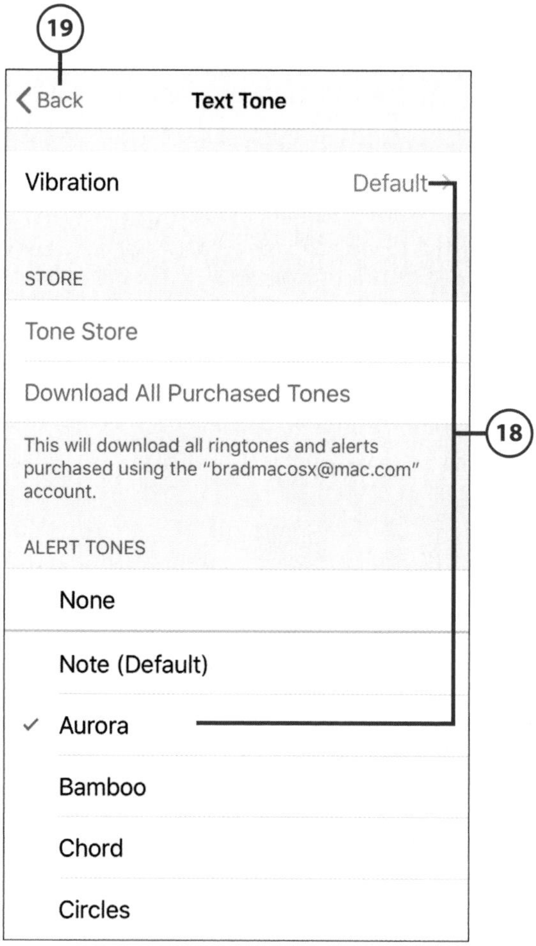

(19)

‹ Back	**Text Tone**

Vibration	Default →

STORE

Tone Store

Download All Purchased Tones

This will download all ringtones and alerts purchased using the "bradmacosx@mac.com" account.

ALERT TONES

None

Note (Default)

✓ Aurora

Bamboo

Chord

Circles

(18)

(20) Using the same process as you did for ringtones and text tones, set the sound and vibrations for the rest of the events on the list.

(21) If you don't like the audible feedback when you tap keys on the iPhone's virtual keyboard, slide the Keyboard Clicks switch to off (white) to disable that sound. The keyboard is silent as you type on it.

(22) If you don't want your iPhone to make a sound when you lock it, slide the Lock Sound switch to off (white). Your iPhone no longer makes this sound when you press the Side button to put it to sleep and lock it.

(23) Set the System Haptics switch to off (white) if you prefer not to experience vibratory feedback for events. (System Haptics are available on iPhone 7 or later models.)

‹ Settings   **Sounds & Haptics**

SOUNDS AND VIBRATION PATTERNS

Ringtone	Carry On Wayward Son ›
Text Tone	Aurora ›
New Voicemail	Tri-tone
New Mail	None ›
Sent Mail	Swoosh › — (20)
Calendar Alerts	Chord ›
Reminder Alerts	Chord ›
AirDrop	Pulse

Keyboard Clicks   ⬤ — (21)

Lock Sound   ⬤ — (22)

System Haptics   ⬤ — (23)

Play haptics for system controls and interactions.

>>>Go Further
SOUNDING OFF

Following are two more sound- and vibration-related pointers:

- You can tap the Store icon on the Ringtone, Text Tone, and other screens to move to the iTunes Store, where you can purchase and download ringtones and other sounds to your iPhone.

- You can create custom vibration patterns, too. On the Vibration screen, tap Create New Vibration. Tap the vibration pattern you want to create; when you're done tapping, tap Stop. Tap Record to start over if you don't like the one you created. When you're done, tap Save. Name the pattern and tap Save. The patterns you create are available in the CUSTOM section on the Vibration screen, so you can use them just like the iPhone's default vibration patterns. To remove a custom pattern, swipe to the left on it and tap Delete.

Use Settings to configure how contacts are displayed

Tap here to work with your contact information

Use your contact information in many apps

In this chapter, you learn how to ensure that your iPhone has the contact information you need when you need it. Topics include the following:

→ Getting started
→ Setting your Contacts preferences
→ Creating contacts on your iPhone
→ Working with contacts on your iPhone
→ Managing contacts on your iPhone

Managing Contacts

You'll be using your iPhone to make calls, get directions, send emails, and do many other tasks that require contact information, including names, phone numbers, email addresses, and physical addresses. It would be time-consuming and a nuisance to have to remember and retype this information each time you use it. Fortunately, you don't have to do either because the Contacts app puts all your contact information at your fingertips (literally).

Getting Started

The Contacts app makes using your contact information extremely easy. This information is readily available on your phone in all the apps in which you need it, such as Mail, Messages, and Phone. And, you don't need to remember or type the information because you can enter it by choosing someone's name, a business's name, or other information that you know about the contact. You can also access your contact information directly in the Contacts app and take action on it (such as placing a call).

To use contact information, it must be stored in the Contacts app. This can be accomplished in several ways. When you configure an online account on your iPhone—such as iCloud or Google—to include contact information, the contact information stored in that account is immediately available on your phone without you having to do anything else. (See Chapter 3, "Setting Up and Using an Apple ID, iCloud, and Other Online Accounts," for the steps to enable contact information in online accounts.) You can manually add new contact information to the Contacts app by capturing that information when you perform tasks (such as reading email). You can also enter new contact information directly in the Contacts app.

The Contacts app also makes it easy to keep your contact information current by doing such things as adding more information, updating existing contacts, or removing contacts you no longer need.

Setting Your Contacts Preferences

Use the Passwords & Accounts settings to configure the online accounts in which you store contact information. Refer to Chapter 3 for help setting up online accounts.

Using the Contacts settings, you can determine whether contact information can be used in Siri and other apps, how contacts are sorted and displayed, if or how names are shortened on various screens, your contact information, and which account should be the default for contact information. You can probably work with these settings just fine without making any changes to these Contacts settings, but if you want to make adjustments, open the Settings app and tap Contacts. Use the information in the following table to configure your contact settings.

Settings App Explained

To get detailed information on using the Settings app, see "Working with the Settings App" in Chapter 2, "Using Your iPhone's Core Features."

Contacts Settings

Setting	Description
Passwords & Accounts	Use the Passwords & Accounts settings to configure the online accounts you use to store contact information.
Siri & Search	Set the Search & Siri Suggestions switch to off (white) if you don't want to use contact information in searches or to allow Siri to access your contact information. Set the Allow on Lock screen to off (white) if you don't want contact information showing up on the Lock screen. Set Find Contacts in Other Apps to off (white) if you don't want contact information in the various apps to be suggested to you, such as to automatically complete addresses when you create emails, or try to identify callers when a number calling you is unknown. You typically should leave these on (green) unless you find the automatic contact suggestions annoying or not helpful or if you want to hide contact information when your iPhone is locked.
Sort Order	Tap First, Last to have contacts sorted by *first name* and then *last name* or tap Last, First to have contacts sorted by *last name* and then *first name*.
Display Order	To show contacts in the format *first name, last name,* tap First, Last. To show contacts in the format *last name, first name,* tap Last, First.
Short Name	You can choose whether short names are used and, if they are, what form they take. Short names are useful because more contact information can be displayed in a smaller area, and they look "friendlier." To use short names, move the Short Name switch to the on position (green). Tap the format of the short name you want to use. You can choose from a combination of *initial* and *name* or just *first* or *last name*. If you want nicknames for contacts used for the short name when available, set the Prefer Nicknames switch to on (green).
My Info	Use this setting to find and tap your contact information in the Contacts app, which it can insert for you in various places and which Siri can use to call you by name; your current contact information is indicated by the label "me" next to the alphabetical index.
Default Account	Tap the account in which you want new contacts to be created by default (which is then marked with a check mark). If you have only one account configured for contacts or if you only store contacts on your iPhone, you don't have this option.

Where Contacts Are Stored Matters

You should store your contacts in an online account (for example, iCloud or Google), because the information is accessible on many devices and it is also backed up. If you don't have an online account, contact information is stored only on your iPhone. This is not good because, if something happens to your phone, you can lose all of your contacts.

Creating Contacts on Your iPhone

You can create new contacts on an iPhone in a number of ways. You can start with some information, such as the email address on a message you receive, and create a contact from it, or you can create a contact by manually filling in the contact information. In this section, you learn how to create a new contact starting with information in an email message and how to create a new contact manually.

Creating New Contacts from Email

When you receive an email, you can easily create a contact to capture the email address. (To learn how to work with the Mail app, see Chapter 8, "Sending, Receiving, and Managing Email.")

1. On the Home screen, tap Mail.

2. Use the Mail app to read an email message (see Chapter 8 for details).

3. Tap the email address from which you want to create a new contact; if the address isn't in blue as shown, tap Details before tapping the address. The contact's Info screen appears. You see as much information as could be gleaned from the email address, which is typically the sender's name and email address.

4. Tap Create New Contact. The New Contact screen appears. The name, email address, and any other information that can be identified are added to the new contact. The email address is labeled with iPhone's best guess, such as other or home.

5. Use the New Contact screen to enter more contact information or update the information that was added (such as the label applied to the email address) and save the new contact by tapping Done. This works just like when you create a new contact manually, except that you already have some information—most likely, a name and an email address. For details on adding and changing more information for the contact, see the next task, "Creating Contacts Manually."

More Information for New Contacts

In some cases, such as when an email comes from an email server that includes full contact information, you see a bar at the top of the email message above the From and To section. This bar shows the sender's name and phone number. Under this, you see Ignore and Add to Contacts. Tap Ignore to ignore this additional contact information. Tap Add to Contacts to create a new contact with all of the information available; this does the same thing as steps 3 through 5 except the resulting new contact contains more information with the name and email address; for example, phone numbers.

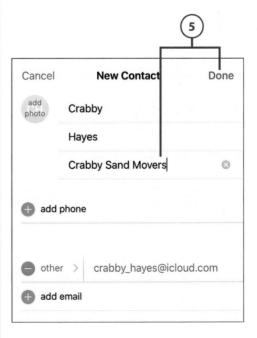

>>>Go Further
MORE ON CREATING CONTACTS FROM APPS

It's useful to be able to create contact information by starting with some information in an app. Keep these points in mind:

- Mail is only one of the apps from which you can create contacts. You can start a contact in just about any app you use to communicate, such as Messages, or get information, such as Maps. The steps to start a contact in these apps are similar to those for Mail. Tap the Info icon (i) for the person or address for which you want to create a contact, and then tap Create New Contact. The Contacts app fills in as much of the information as it can, and you can complete the rest yourself.

- You can also add more contact information to an existing contact from an app you are currently using. You can do this by viewing the contact information (such as a phone number) and tapping Add to Existing Contact (instead of Create New Contact). You then search for and select the contact to which you want to add the additional information. After it's saved, the additional information is associated with the contact you selected. For example, suppose you have created a contact for a company but all you have is its phone number. You can quickly add the address to the contact by using the Maps app to look it up and then add the address to the company's existing contact information by tapping the location, tapping Add to Existing Contact, and selecting the company in your contacts.

Creating Contacts Manually

Most of the time, you'll want to get some basic information for a new contact from an app, as the previous task demonstrated, or through an online account, such as contacts stored in your Google account. If these aren't available, you can also start a contact from scratch and manually add all the information you need to it. Also, you use the same steps to add information to or change information for an existing contact that you do to create a new one, so even if you don't start from scratch often, you do need to know how to do so.

The Contacts app leads you through creating each type of information you might want to capture. You can choose to enter some or all of the default information on the New Contact screen, or add additional fields as needed.

The following steps show creating a new contact containing the most common contact information you are likely to need:

1. On the Home screen, tap Contacts. (If you don't see the Contacts app on the Home screen, tap the Extras folder to open it and you should see the app's icon. You might want to move the Contacts icon from this folder to a more convenient location on your Home screen; see Chapter 5, "Customizing How Your iPhone Looks and Sounds," for the steps to do this.) The Contacts screen displays.

   If you see the Groups screen instead, tap Done to move to the Contacts screen. (Groups are covered later.)

2. Tap Add (+). The New Contact screen appears with the default fields. (You can add more data fields as needed using the add field command.)

3. To associate a photo with the contact, tap add photo. You can choose a photo already on your phone or take a new photo. These steps show using an existing photo. See the "Taking Photos" note for the steps to take a new photo.

4. Tap Choose Photo.

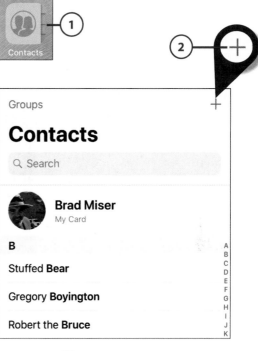

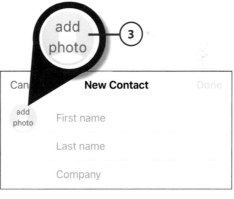

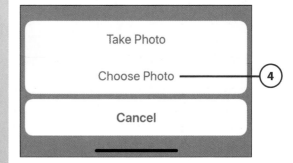

(5) Use the Photos app to move to, select, and configure the photo you want to associate with the contact (see Chapter 14, "Viewing and Editing Photos and Video with the Photos App," for help with the Photos app).

(6) Tap Choose. You return to the New Contact screen where the photo you selected is displayed.

(7) Tap in the First name field and enter the contact's first name; if you are creating a contact for an organization only, leave both name fields empty. (The Display Order preference in Settings determines whether the First name or Last name field appears at the top of the screen.)

(8) Tap in the Last name field and enter the contact's last name.

(9) Enter the organization, such as a company, with which you want to associate the contact, if any.

(10) Tap add phone to add a phone number. A new phone field appears along with the numeric keypad.

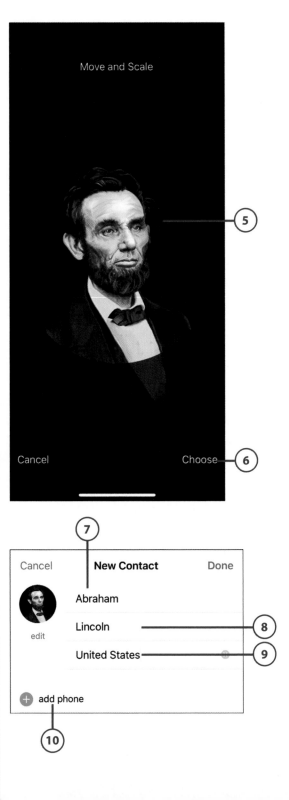

Taking Photos

To take a new photo for a contact, tap Take Photo in step 4 instead of Choose Photo. The Camera app's screen appears. Use the iPhone's camera to capture the photo you want to associate with the new contact (taking photos is covered in Chapter 13, "Taking Photos and Video with Your iPhone"). Use the Move and Scale screen to adjust the photo so it is what you want to use. Then, tap Use Photo. The photo is pasted into the image icon on the New Contact screen.

(11) Use the numeric keypad to enter the contact's phone number. Include any prefixes you need to dial it, such as area code and country code. The Contacts app formats the number for you as you enter it.

(12) Tap the label for the phone number, such as home, to change it to another label. The Label screen appears.

(13) Swipe up and down the Label screen to see all the options available.

(14) Tap the label you want to apply to the number, such as iPhone. That label is applied and you move back to the New Contact screen.

(15) Repeat steps 10–14 to add more phone numbers to the contact.

(16) Swipe up the screen until you see add email.

(17) Tap add email. The keyboard appears.

A Rose by Any Other Name Isn't the Same

The labels you apply to contact information, such as phone numbers, become important when a contact has more than one type of that information. For example, a person might have several phone numbers, such as for home, an iPhone, and work. Applying a label to each of these numbers helps you know which number is for which location. This is especially useful when you use Siri as you can tell Siri which number to use to place a call, such as "Call Abraham Lincoln home" to call the number labeled as home on Abraham's contact card.

(18) Type the contact's email address.

(19) Tap the label for the email address to change it.

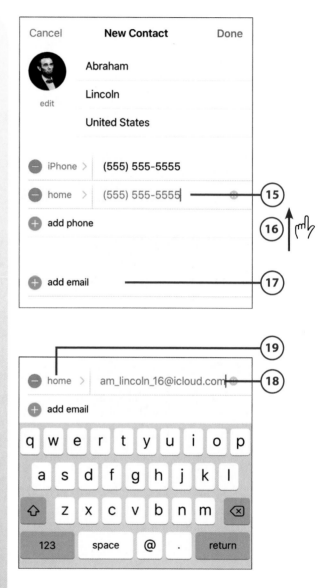

20. Tap the label you want to apply to the email address. You move back to the New Contact screen.

21. Repeat steps 17–20 to add more email addresses.

22. If necessary, swipe up the screen until you see Ringtone.

23. Tap Ringtone. The list of ringtones and alert tones available on your iPhone appears.

24. Set the Emergency Bypass switch to on (green) if you want sounds and vibrations for phone calls or new messages associated with the contact you are creating to play even when Do Not Disturb is on. (For more about Do Not Disturb, see Chapter 1, "Getting Started with Your iPhone" and for information about working with notifications, see Chapter 2.)

Cancel	**Label**	Edit
home		✓
work		
iCloud		
other		
Add Custom Label		
home 2		
primary		

⊖ work ›	am_lincoln_16@icloud.com ⊗	
⊕ add email		
Ringtone	Default	›

Cancel	**Ringtone**	Done
Emergency Bypass		⬤
Emergency Bypass allows sounds and vibrations from this person even when Do Not Disturb is on.		
Vibration		Default ›
STORE		
Tone Store		
Download All Purchased Tones		

(25) Swipe up and down the list to see all of the tones available.

(26) Tap the ringtone you want to play when the contact calls you. When you tap a ringtone, it plays so you can experiment to find the one that best relates to the contact. Setting a specific ringtone helps you identify a caller without looking at your phone. (For more on working with sounds and vibrations, see Chapter 5.)

(27) Tap Vibration and use the resulting screen if you want to set a specific vibration for the contact.

(28) Tap Done. You return to the New Contact screen.

(29) Using the pattern you have learned in the previous steps, move to the next item you want to set and tap it.

(30) Use the resulting screens to enter the information you want to configure for the contact. After you've done a couple of the fields, it is easy to do the rest because the same pattern is used throughout.

Cancel   **Ringtone**   Done ——(28)

Emergency Bypass   ◯

Emergency Bypass allows sounds and vibrations from this person even when Do Not Disturb is on.

Vibration   Default › ——(27)

STORE

Tone Store

Download All Purchased Tones

This will download all ringtones and alerts purchased using the "bradmacosx@mac.com" account.

DEFAULT

Sweet Home Alabama   (25) ↕

RINGTONES

✓ Carry On Wayward Son ——(26)

Kryptonite

Oh Where Is My Cell Phone?

Star Trek

Cancel   **New Contact**   Done

Text Tone   Default   ›

⊕ add url

1600 Pennsylvania Ave NW ——(29)

Street

⊖ work ›   Washington ——(30)

DC   20500

United States   ›

(31) When you've added all the information you want to capture, tap Done. The New Contact screen closes and the new contact is created and ready for you to use in Contacts and other apps. It is also moved onto other devices with which your contact information is synced. See the "Creating Contacts Expanded" Go Further sidebar for additional information on syncing and maintaining contacts.

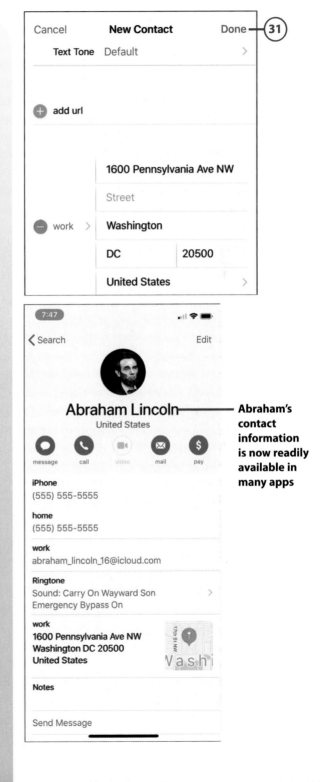

Abraham's contact information is now readily available in many apps

>>>Go Further

CREATING CONTACTS EXPANDED

Contacts are useful in many ways, so you should make sure you have all the contact information you need. Here are a few points to ponder:

- You can (and should) sync contacts on multiple devices (computers and other iOS devices) by using iCloud, Gmail, or other similar online accounts to store your contact information on the cloud where all your devices can access it. Refer to Chapter 3 for the details of setting up online accounts.

- Syncing your contacts works in both directions. Any new contacts you create or any changes you make to existing contact information on your iPhone move back to your other devices through the sync process.

- To remove a field in which you've entered information, tap Edit, tap the red circle with a dash in it next to the field, and then tap Delete. If you haven't entered information into a field, just ignore it because empty fields don't appear on a contact's screen.

- The address format on the screens in the Contacts app is determined by the country you associate with the address. If the current country isn't the one you want, tap it and select the country in which the address is located before you enter any information. The fields appropriate for that country's addresses appear on the screen.

- If you want to add a type of information that doesn't appear on the New Contact screen, swipe up the screen and tap add field to see a list of fields you can add. Tap a field to add it; for example, tap Nickname to add a nickname for the contact. Then, enter the information for that new field.

- When you add more fields to contact information, those fields appear in the appropriate context on the Info screen. For example, if you add a nickname, it is placed at the top of the screen with the other "name" information. If you add an address, it appears with the other address information.

- As you learn in Chapter 7, "Communicating with the Phone and FaceTime Apps," you can configure the Phone app to announce the name of callers when you receive calls. This can be even more useful than setting a specific ringtone for your important contacts.

Working with Contacts on Your iPhone

There are many ways to use contact information. The first step is always finding the contact information you need, typically by using the Contacts app. Whether you access it directly or through another app (such as Mail), it works the same way. Then, you select the information you want to use or the action you want to perform.

Using the Contacts App

You can access your contact information directly in the Contacts app. For example, you can search or browse for a contact and then view the detailed information for the contact in which you are interested.

(1) On the Home screen, tap Contacts. (If you don't see the Contacts app on the Home screen, tap the Extras folder to open it and you see the Contacts app. You might want to move the Contacts icon from this folder to a more convenient location on your Home screen; see Chapter 5 for the steps to do this.) The Contacts screen displays with the contacts listed in the view and sort format determined by the Contacts settings. (If the Groups screen appears, tap Done. You move back to the Contacts screen.)

You can find a contact to view by browsing (step 2), using the index (step 3), or searching (step 4). You can use combinations of these, too, such as first using the index to get to the right area and then browsing to find the contact in which you are interested.

2 Swipe up or down to scroll the screen to browse for contact information; swipe up or down on the alphabetical index to browse rapidly. When you see the contact you want to view, move to step 5.

3 Tap the index to jump to contact information organized by the first letter of the format you selected in the Contact Preferences (last name or first name). When you see the contact you want to view, move to step 5.

4 Use the Search tool to search for a specific contact; tap in the tool, type the name (you can type last, first, company, or nickname) of the contact you want to find.

5 Tap a contact to view that contact's information.

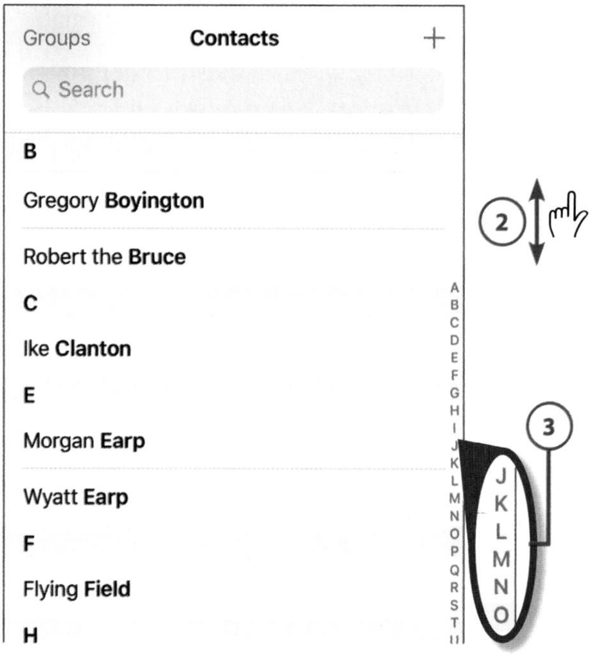

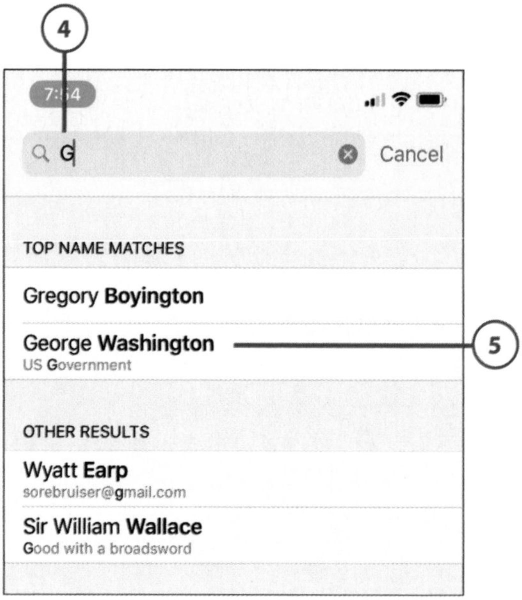

Groups   **Contacts**   +

Q Search

B

Gregory **Boyington**

Robert the **Bruce**

C

Ike **Clanton**

E

Morgan **Earp**

Wyatt **Earp**

F

Flying **Field**

H

A
B
C
D
E
F
G
H
I
J
K
L
M
N
O
P
Q
R
S
T
U

J
K
L
M
N
O

7:54

Q G   ⊗ Cancel

TOP NAME MATCHES

Gregory **Boyington**

George **Washington**
US **G**overnment

OTHER RESULTS

Wyatt **Earp**
sorebruiser@gmail.com

Sir William **Wallace**
Good with a broadsword

6. Swipe up and down the screen to view all the contact's information.

7. Tap the data or icons on the screen to perform actions, including the following:

- **Phone numbers**—Tap a phone number to call it. You can also tap one of the phone icons just under the contact's image to call that number. For example, to call the number labeled as iPhone, tap the iPhone icon.

- **Email addresses**—Tap an email address or the mail icon or the icon with the email address's label (such as other for the email address labeled as other) on it to create a new email message to that address.

- **URLs**—Tap a URL to open Safari and move to the associated website.

- **Addresses**—Tap a physical address to show it in the Maps app.

- **FaceTime**—Tap video or FaceTime to start a FaceTime call with the contact. (If an icon, such as video, is disabled, you don't have that type of information stored for the contact.)

- **Text**—Tap the message icon or tap Send Message and choose the phone number or email address to which you want to send a text message.

- **Share Contact**—Tap Share Contact. The Share menu appears. To share the contact via email, tap Mail; to share it via a text, tap Message; or to share it using AirDrop, tap AirDrop. You can also share via Twitter or Facebook. Then, use the associated app to complete the task.

- **Favorites**—Tap Add to Favorites and choose the phone number or email address you want to designate as a favorite. You can use this in the associated app to do something faster. For example, if it's the Phone app, you can tap the Favorites tab to see your favorite contacts and quickly dial one by tapping it. You can also quickly access favorites from the FAVORITES widget by swiping to the right when you are on the Lock screen. You can add multiple items (such as cell and work phone numbers) as favorites for one contact.

(8) To return to the prior screen without performing an action, tap the Back icon (<) located in the upper-left corner of the screen.

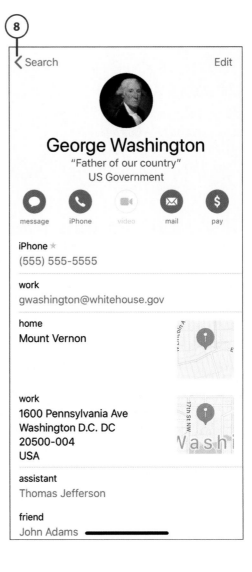

>>>Go Further

MAKE CONTACT

When working with your contacts, keep the following points in mind:

- **Last known contact**—The Contacts app remembers where you last were and takes you back there whenever you move into the Contacts app. For example, if you view a contact's details and then switch to a different app to send a message, and then back to Contacts, you are returned to the screen you were last viewing. To move back to the main Contacts screen, tap the Back icon (it is labeled with the previous screen's name, such as Search or Contacts) in the upper-left corner of the screen.

- **Groups**—In a contact app on a computer, such as Contacts on a Mac, contacts can be organized into groups, which in turn can be stored in an online account, such as iCloud. When you sync, the groups of contacts move onto the iPhone. You can limit the contacts you browse or search; tap Groups on the Contacts screen.

  The Groups screen displays the accounts (such as iCloud or Google) with which you are syncing contact information; under each account are the groups of contacts stored in that account. If a group has a check mark next to it, its contacts are displayed on the Contacts screen. To hide a group's contacts, tap it so that the check mark disappears. To hide or show all of a group's contacts, tap All *account*, where *account* is the name of the account in which those contacts are stored. To make browsing contacts easier, tap Hide All Contacts to hide all the groups and contacts; then, tap each group whose contacts you want to show on the Contacts screen.

  Tap Done to move back to the Contacts screen.

- **Speaking of contacts**—You can use Siri to speak commands to work with contacts, too. You can get information about contacts by asking for it, such as "What is William Wallace's work phone number?" If you want to see all of a contact's information, you can say "Show me William Wallace." When Siri displays contact information, you can tap it to take action, such as tapping a phone number to call it. (See Chapter 11, "Working with Siri," for more on using Siri.)

It's Not All Good

Managing Contact Groups

When you create a new contact, it is associated with the account you designated as the default in the Contacts settings and is stored at the account level (not in any of your groups). You can't create groups in the Contacts app, nor can you change the group with which contacts are associated. You have to use a contacts app on a computer to manage groups and then sync your iPhone (which happens automatically when you use an online account, such as iCloud) to see the changes you make to your contact groups.

Accessing Contacts from Other Apps

You can also access contact information while you are using a different app. For example, you can use a contact's email address when you create an email message. When you perform such actions, you use the Contacts app to find and select the information you want to use. The following example shows using contact information to send an email message; using your contact information in other apps (such as Phone or Messages) is similar.

$50 Off Lifetime Ends Now 😅 Your future self...

Updated Just Now

① Open the app from which you want to access contact information (this example uses Mail).

② Tap the Compose icon.

③ Tap Add (+) in the To field.

Cancel **New Message** Send

To: |

Cc/Bcc, From: bradmiser@icloud.com

Subject:

4 Search, browse, or use the index to find the contact whose information you want to use. You see the results of your search under the Search bar. The text that matches your search is shown in bold. For example, if you search for Wal, you see people named Wallace, Walker, Walken, etc., and "Wal" is shown in bold in each result. The search looks within the contact too. For example, when you search for an email address within Mail, the email addresses are searched in addition to the name information.

5 Tap the contact whose information you want to use. (If a contact doesn't have relevant information; for example, if no email address is configured when you are using the Mail app, that contact is grayed out and can't be selected.)

If the contact has only one type of the relevant information (such as a single email address, if you started in the Mail app), you immediately move back to the app and the appropriate information is entered, and you can skip to step 7.

6 If the contact has multiple entries of the type you are trying to use, tap the information you want to use—in this example, the email address. The information is copied into the app and entered in the appropriate location.

7 Complete the task you are doing, such as sending an email message.

Managing Your Contacts on Your iPhone

When you sync contacts with an iCloud, Google, or other account, the changes go both ways. For example, when you change a contact on the iPhone, the synced contact manager application, such as Outlook, makes the changes for those contacts on your computer. Likewise, when you change contact information in a contact manager on your computer, those changes move to the iPhone. If you add a new contact in a contact manager, it moves to the iPhone, and vice versa. You can also change contacts manually in the Contacts app on your iPhone.

Updating Contact Information

You can change any information for an existing contact, such as adding new email addresses, deleting outdated information, and changing existing information.

1. Use the Contacts app to find and view the contact whose information you want to change.

2. Tap Edit. The contact screen moves into Edit mode, and you see Unlock icons.

3. Tap current information to change it; you can change a field's label by tapping it, or you can change the data for the field by tapping the information you want to change. Use the resulting tools, such as the phone number entry keypad, to make changes to the information. These tools work just like when you create a new contact (refer to "Creating Contacts Manually," earlier in this chapter).

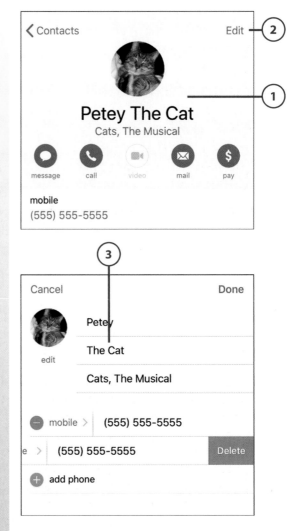

4 To add more fields, tap Add (+) in the related section, such as add email in the email address section; then, select a label for the new field and complete its information. This also works just like adding a new field to a contact you created manually.

5 Tap a field's Unlock (–) icon to remove that field from the contact.

6 Tap Delete. The information is removed from the contact.

7 To change the contact's photo, tap the current photo, or the word edit under the current photo, and use the resulting menu and tools to select a new photo, take a new photo, delete the existing photo, or edit the existing photo.

8 When you finish making changes, tap Done. Your changes are saved, and you move out of Edit mode.

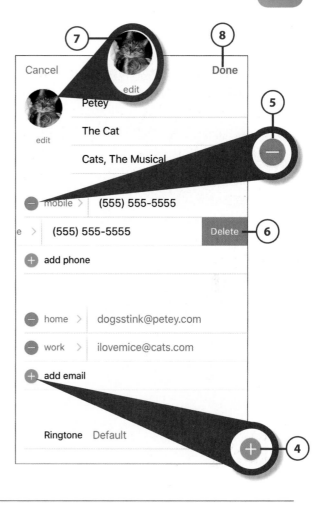

No Tones or Vibes?

If you leave the default tones or vibration patterns set for a contact, you won't see those fields when you view the contact. However, when you edit a contact, all the fields you need to add these to a contact become available.

Adding Information to an Existing Contact While Using Your iPhone

As you use your iPhone, you'll encounter information related to a contact that isn't currently part of that contact's information. For example, a contact might send an email to you from a different email address than the one you have stored for her. When this happens, you can easily add the new information to the existing contact. Just tap the information to view it (such as an email address), and then tap Add to Existing Contact. Next, select the existing contact to which you want to add the new information. The new information is added to the contact. Depending on your iPhone model, tap Update or Done (or Cancel, if you decide not to keep the new information) to return to the app you're working in.

Deleting Contacts

To get rid of contacts, you can delete them from the Contacts app.

1. Find and view the contact you want to delete.

2. Tap Edit.

3. Swipe up to get to the bottom of the Info screen.

4. Tap Delete Contact.

5. Tap Delete Contact to confirm the deletion. The app deletes the contact, and you return to the Contacts screen.

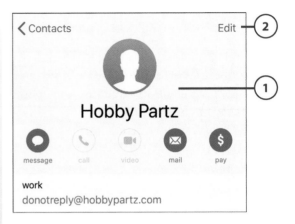

>>>*Go Further*

LINKING CONTACTS

When you enter Edit mode in a contact, the Linked Contacts section appears at the bottom of the screen. You can use this to combine contacts. For example, if you end up with two contacts for the same person, you can link them to combine their information into one contact. Or, you might want to link multiple people to a company. When you link contacts, information from all the linked contacts appears on one contact, which is the contact from which you start the link process.

To link a contact, tap Edit, swipe all the way up the screen to get to the bottom, and then tap link contacts. Find and tap the contact you want to link to the one you are editing. That contact's information displays. Tap Link.

The information from the second contact is linked to the first. You can repeat this as many times as you want. (Note that you have to have the group within which a contact is stored displayed to be able to link it.) When you are finished linking contacts, tap Done. The contact to which the others are linked is known as the *unified contact* (or card). It is labeled with the contact from which you started the linking process.

You can change how the information in the unified contact is displayed by viewing the unified contact, and then tapping one of the linked contacts. Tap the command you want to use, such as Use This Photo for Unified Card, which uses the image for the main contact in the unified contact.

To unlink contacts, edit the unified contact, tap the Unlock icon next to a linked contact, and tap Unlink. The contact information is separated as it was before you linked them.

Tap to configure Phone and FaceTime settings

Tap to hear and see the person you want to talk to

Tap to make calls, listen to voicemail, and more

In this chapter, you explore all the cell phone and FaceTime functionality that your iPhone has to offer. Topics include the following:

→ Getting started
→ Configuring phone settings
→ Making voice calls
→ Managing in-process voice calls
→ Receiving voice calls
→ Managing voice calls
→ Using visual voicemail
→ Communicating with FaceTime

Communicating with the Phone and FaceTime Apps

Although it's also a lot of other great things, such as a music player, web browser, email tool, and such, there's a reason the word *phone* is in iPhone. It's a feature-rich cell phone that includes some amazing features, two of which are visual voicemail and FaceTime. Other useful features include a speakerphone, conference calling, and easy-to-use onscreen controls. Plus, your iPhone's phone functions are integrated with its other features. For example, when using the Maps application, you might find a location, such as a business, that you're interested in contacting. You can call that location just by tapping the number you want to call directly on the Maps screen.

Getting Started

Some of the key concepts you'll learn about in this chapter include:

- **Phone app**—The iPhone can run many different kinds of apps that do all sorts of useful things. The iPhone's cell phone functionality is provided by the Phone app. You use this app whenever you want to make calls, answer calls, or listen to voicemail.

• **Visual Voicemail**—The Phone app shows you information about your voice-mails, such as the person who left each message, a time and date stamp, and the length of the message. The Phone app provides a lot more control over your messages, too; for example, you can easily fast forward to specific parts of a message that you want to hear. (This is particularly helpful for capturing information, such as phone numbers.) And if that wasn't enough, you can also read transcripts of voicemails so you don't have to listen to them at all.

• **FaceTime**—This app enables you to have videoconferences with other people (using iPhones or Mac computers) so that you can both see and hear them. Using FaceTime is intuitive so you won't find it any more difficult than making a phone call.

• **FaceTime Audio**—You can make FaceTime calls using only audio; this is simi-lar to making a phone call. One difference is that when you are using a Wi-Fi network to place a FaceTime audio call, there are no extra costs for the call, no matter if you are calling someone next-door or halfway around the world.

Configuring Phone Settings

Of course, we all know that your ringtone is the most important phone set-ting, and you'll want to make sure your iPhone's ringtones are just right. Use the iPhone's Sounds settings to configure custom or standard ringtones and other phone-related sounds, including the new voicemail sound. You can also config-ure the way your phone vibrates when you receive a call. These are explained in Chapter 5, "Customizing How Your iPhone Looks and Sounds."

You can also have different ringtones and vibrations for specific people so you can know who is calling just by the sound and feel when a call comes in (config-uring contacts is explained in Chapter 6, "Managing Contacts").

And you'll want to configure notifications for the Phone app. These include alerts, the app's badge, sounds, and vibrations. Configuring notifications is explained in Chapter 4, "Customizing How Your iPhone Works."

It is likely that you can use the Phone app with its default settings just fine. However, you might want to take advantage of some of its features by configuring the settings described in the following table. To access these settings, open the Settings app and tap Phone.

Provider Differences

The settings for the Phone app depend on the cell phone provider you use. The table lists most, but certainly not all, of the options you might have available. Depending on the provider you use, you may see more, fewer, or different settings than shown in the table. It's a good idea to open your Phone settings to see the options available to you.

Phone Settings

Section	Setting	Description
N/A	My Number	Shows your phone number for reference purposes.
CALLS	Announce Calls	When you enable this setting, the name of the caller (when available) is announced when the phone rings. Tap Always to always have the name announced, Headphones & Car to have the caller announced only when you are using headphones or your car's audio system, Headphones Only to have announcements only when you are using headphones, or Never if you don't want these announcements.
CALLS	Call Blocking & Identification	Tap this to see a list of people who you are currently blocking. You can tap someone on the list to see more information or swipe to the left and tap Unblock to unblock someone. Tap Block Contact to block someone in your Contacts app.
CALLS	SMS/Call Reporting	There are third-party apps that provide additional functionality to deal with phone calls and incoming text messages. For example, these apps can provide more sophisticated call blocking and message filtering than the iPhone apps have by default. These third-party apps have extensions that work with the Phone and Messages apps to provide information the third-party apps need to perform their function. If such apps and extensions are installed on your iPhone, you can choose the one you want to use on the SMS/Call Reporting screen or choose None to use only the default SMS/Call Reporting configuration.

Section	Setting	Description
CALLS	Wi-Fi Calling	When enabled, you can place and receive calls via a Wi-Fi network. This is particularly useful when you are in a location with poor cellular reception, but you have access to a Wi-Fi network. When you set the Wi-Fi Calling on This iPhone switch to on (green), you're prompted to confirm your information. When you do, the service starts and you see the Update Emergency Address option; this is used to record your address so if you can place emergency calls via Wi-Fi, your location can be determined. The Add Wi-Fi Calling For Other Devices switch enables you to take calls on other devices signed into your iCloud account even if they aren't in the same area as your iPhone.
CALLS	Calls on Other Devices	When enabled, and your iPhone is on the same network as other iOS devices (such as iPads) or Macs configured with your information, you can take incoming calls and place calls from those devices. This can be useful when you aren't near your phone or simply want to use a different device to have a phone conversation. It can also be annoying because when a call comes in, all the devices using this feature start "ringing." When the Allow Calls on Other Devices switch is on (green), you can choose the specific devices calls are allowed on by setting their switches to on (green). If you don't want a device to receive phone calls, set its switch to off (white).
CALLS	Respond with Text	When calls come in, you have the option to respond with text. For example, you might want to say, "Can't talk now, will call later." There are three default text responses or you can use this setting to create your own custom text responses.
CALLS	Call Forwarding	Enables you to forward incoming calls to a different phone number. Set the Call Forwarding switch to on (green) and enter the number to which you want calls forwarded. Set the switch to off (white) to stop your calls from being forwarded.
CALLS	Call Waiting	Enables or disables the call waiting feature.

Section	Setting	Description
CALLS	Show My Caller ID	Shows or hides your caller ID information when you place a call.
N/A	Change Voicemail Password	Use this option to change your voicemail password. Note that this only changes the password to access voicemail on your iPhone. This password must match the password for your voicemail account with your cell phone provider.
N/A	Dial Assist	Enable the Dial Assist feature if you want the correct country code to be added to numbers in your country when dialing those numbers from outside your country or if you want the correct area codes to be added when you dial a local number. For example, if you live in the United States and don't want the correct prefixes added to U.S. phone numbers when you dial them from outside the United States, turn off Dial Assist. You then have to add any prefixes manually when dialing a U.S. number from outside the United States.
N/A	SIM PIN	Your iPhone uses a Subscriber Identity Module (SIM) card to store certain data about your phone; the SIM PIN setting enables you to associate a personal ID number (PIN) with the SIM card in an iPhone. To use your account with a different phone, you can remove the SIM card from your iPhone and install it in other phones that support these cards. If you set a PIN, that PIN is required to use the card in a different phone.
N/A	*Provider* Services, where *Provider* is the name of your provider	This area provides information about your account, such as the numbers you can dial for checking balances, paying bills, and other account management. With some providers, you can also access your account by tapping the link at the bottom of the screen.

Making Voice Calls

There are a number of ways to make calls with your iPhone; after a call is in progress, you can manage it in the same way no matter how you started it.

Signal strength
(more filled-in
bars indicates
stronger signal)

All in One Place

If you use a non-X iPhone model, you see the signal strength, provider, and Wi-Fi Calling status at the top of the Home screen and on the Lock screen.

You can tell you are able to make a call or receive calls by the strength of the signal your phone is receiving, which is indicated by the number of shaded bars in the Signal Strength icon at the top of the Home or Lock screens. As long as you see at least one bar shaded in, you should be able to place and receive calls via the cellular network. More shaded bars are better because they mean you have a stronger signal, meaning the call quality will be better.

Provider name

Signal strength
(more filled-in
bars indicates
stronger signal)

To see who your provider is, move to the Lock screen (X models). You also see the Signal Strength icon here.

Provider name

Wi-Fi calling is available

Signal strength (more filled-in bars indicates stronger signal)

If the Wi-Fi calling feature is enabled and your phone is connected to a Wi-Fi network, you see the Wi-Fi calling icon for your provider at the top of the Lock screen (X models) or the Home or Lock screens (non-X models).

With a reasonably strong cellular signal or connection to a Wi-Fi network with Wi-Fi calling enabled, you are ready to make calls.

Which Network?

When you leave the coverage area for your provider and move into an area that is covered by another provider that supports roaming, your iPhone automatically connects to the other provider's network. When you are roaming, you see a different provider. For example, if AT&T is your provider and you travel to Toronto, Canada, the provider might become Rogers instead of AT&T, which indicates you are roaming. (In most cases, your provider sends a text message to you explaining the change in networks, including information about roaming charges.) Although the change to a roaming network is automatic, you need to be very aware of roaming charges, which can be significant depending on where you use your iPhone and what your default network is. Before you travel outside of your default network's coverage, check with your provider to determine the roaming rates that apply to where you are going. Also, see if there is a discounted roaming plan for that location. If you don't do this before you leave, you might get a nasty surprise when the bill arrives because roaming charges can be substantial.

Dialing with the Keypad

The most obvious way to make a call is to dial the number.

1. On the Home screen, tap Phone. The Phone app opens.

2. If you don't see the keypad on the screen, tap Keypad.

3. Tap numbers on the keypad to dial the number you want to call. If you dial a number associated with one or more contacts, you see the contact's name and the type of number you've dialed just under the number. (If you make a mistake in the number you are dialing, tap the Delete icon to the right of the call icon to delete the most recent digit you entered.)

4. Tap the call icon. The app dials the number, and the Call screen appears.

5. Use the Call screen to manage the call (not shown in the figure); see "Managing In-Process Voice Calls" later in this chapter for the details.

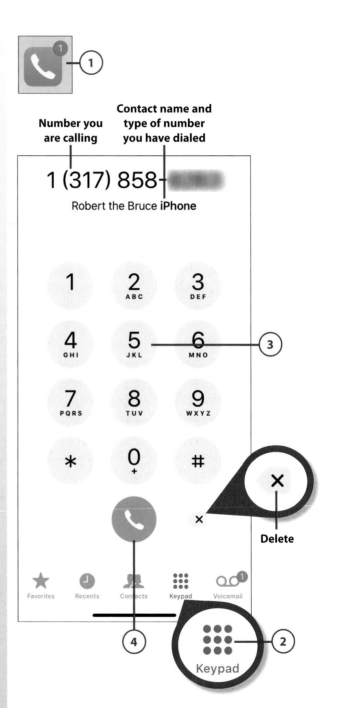

Number you are calling

Contact name and type of number you have dialed

Delete

Dialing with Contacts

As you saw in Chapter 6, the Contacts app is a complete contact manager so you can store various kinds of phone numbers for people and organizations. To make a call using a contact, follow these steps.

(1) On the Home screen, tap Phone.

(2) Tap Contacts.

(3) Browse the list, search it, or use the index to find the contact you want to call. (Refer to Chapter 6 for information about using the Contacts app.)

(4) Tap the contact you want to call.

(5) Tap the number you want to dial; or tap the call icon that is labeled with the type of number under the contact's name (if the person has more than one phone number, you are then prompted to tap the number you want to call). The app dials the number, and the Call screen appears.

(6) Use the Call screen to manage the call (not shown in the figure); see "Managing In-Process Voice Calls" later in this chapter for the details.

Call Icon

At the top of a contact's screen, you see the call icon (the Receiver icon). If a contact has only one number, this icon is labeled with the label applied to that number, such as iPhone or Work; tap the icon to call that number. If the person has more than one number, the icon is labeled with call; when you tap the call icon, you see all of the person's numbers and can tap the number you want to dial.

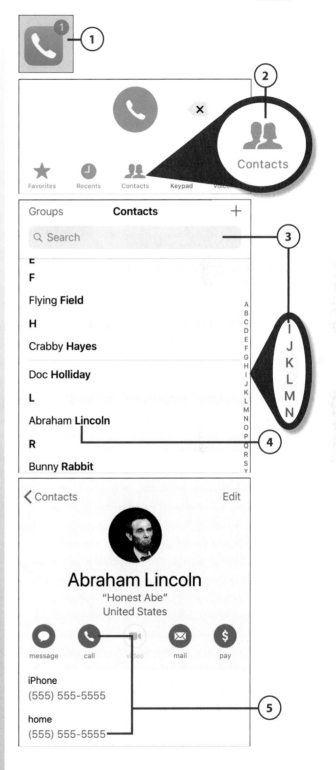

Dialing with Favorites

You can save contacts as favorites to make calling or videoconferencing them even simpler. (You learn how to save favorites in various locations later in this chapter. You learn how to make a contact into a favorite in Chapter 6.)

(1) On the Home screen, tap Phone.

(2) Tap the Favorites icon.

(3) Browse the list until you see the favorite you want to call. Under the contact's name, you see the type of favorite, such as a phone number (identified by the label in the Contacts app; for example, iPhone or mobile) or FaceTime.

(4) Tap the favorite you want to call; to place a voice call, tap a phone number (if you tap a FaceTime contact, a FaceTime call is placed instead). The app dials the number, and the Call screen appears.

(5) Use the Call screen to manage the call (not shown in the figure); see "Managing In-Process Voice Calls" later in this chapter for the details.

Nobody's Perfect

If your iPhone can't complete the call for some reason, such as not having a strong enough signal, the Call Failed screen appears. Tap Call Back to try again and maybe try moving to another location that might have a stronger signal or tap Done to give up. When you tap Done, you return to the screen from which you came.

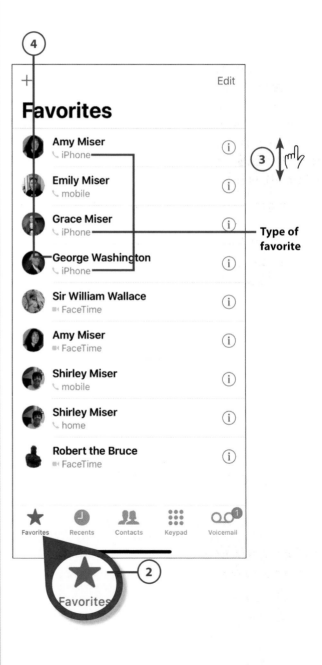

Type of favorite

Dialing with Recents

As you make, receive, or miss calls, your iPhone keeps tracks of all the numbers on the Recents list. You can use the Recents list to make calls.

1. On the Home screen, tap Phone.

2. Tap Recents.

3. Tap All to see all calls.

4. Tap Missed to see only calls you missed.

5. If necessary, browse the list of calls.

6. To call the number associated with a recent call, tap the title of the call, such as a person's name, or the number if no contact is associated with it. The app dials the number, and the Call screen appears. Skip to step 10.

7. To get more information about a recent call, for example, to see exactly what time yesterday they called, tap its Info icon. The Info screen appears.

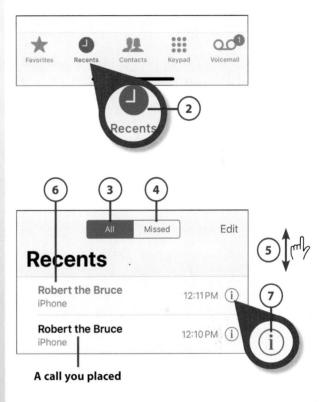

A call you placed

Info on the Recents Screen

If you have a contact on your iPhone associated with a phone number, you see the person's name and the label for the number (such as mobile). If you don't have a contact for a number, you see the number itself. If a contact or number has more than one call associated with it, you see the number of recent calls in parentheses next to the name or number. If you initiated a call, you see the phone icon next to the contact's name and label.

(8) Read the information about the call or calls. For example, if the call is related to someone in your Contacts list, you see detailed information for that contact. If there are multiple recent calls, you see information for each call, such as its status (Missed Call, Canceled Call, or Outgoing Call, for example) and time.

(9) Tap a number on the Info screen. The app dials the number, and the Call screen appears.

Going Back
To return to the Recents screen without making a call, tap Recents in the upper-left corner of the screen.

(10) Use the Call screen to manage the call (not shown in the figure); see "Managing In-Process Voice Calls" later in this chapter for the details.

Dialing from the FAVORITES Widget

Using the FAVORITES widget, you can quickly call a favorite. Use the following steps.

Managing Widgets
If you don't see the FAVORITES widget, you need to add it. See Chapter 4 for the steps to manage your widgets.

(1) From the Home or Lock screen, swipe all the way to the right to open your widgets.

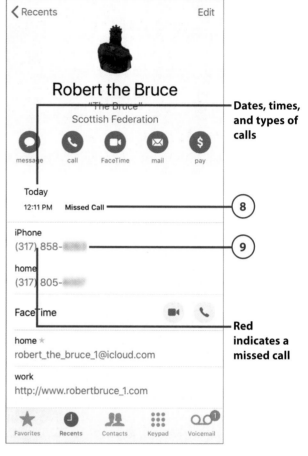

Dates, times, and types of calls

Red indicates a missed call

(2) Swipe up or down until you see the FAVORITES widget.

(3) Tap Show More to see the full list of favorites. The list expands.

(4) Tap the person you want to call.

(5) Use the Call screen to manage the call (not shown in the figure); see the next section for the details.

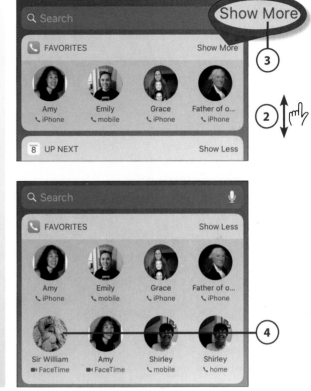

You've Got the Touch

If your iPhone supports 3D Touch (iPhone 6s/6s Plus and later), you can also place calls to favorites by pressing on the Phone app. The FAVORITES pane appears; tap a favorite to place a call. You can also access the most recent voicemail or see the most recent call.

Managing In-Process Voice Calls

When you place a call, there are several ways to manage it. The most obvious is to place your iPhone next to your ear and use your iPhone like any other phone you've ever used. As you place your iPhone next to your ear, the controls on its screen become disabled so you don't accidentally tap onscreen icons with the side of your face or your ear. When you take your iPhone away from your ear, the Call screen appears again and the Phone app's controls become active again.

When you are on a call, press the Volume buttons on the left side of the iPhone to increase (top button) or decrease (bottom button) its volume. Some of the other things you can do while on a call might not be so obvious, as you learn in the next few tasks.

Following are some of the icons on the Call screen that you can use to manage an active call:

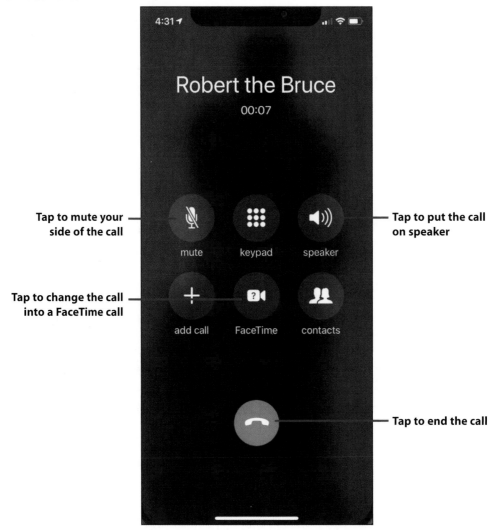

Tap to mute your side of the call

Tap to put the call on speaker

Tap to change the call into a FaceTime call

Tap to end the call

- Mute your side of the call by tapping mute. You can hear the person on the other side of the call, but he can't hear anything on your side.

- Tap speaker to use the iPhone's speakers to hear the call. You can speak with the phone held away from your face, too.

- Tap FaceTime to convert the voice call into a FaceTime call (read more on FaceTime later in this chapter).

- When you're done with the call, tap the Receiver icon to end it.

Contact Photos on the Call Screen

If someone in your contacts calls you, or you call her, the photo or other image associated with the contact appears on the screen (if there isn't an image for the contact, you only see the contact's name and label of the number being used to call, such as Home). Depending on how the image was captured, it either appears as a small icon at the top of the screen next to the contact's name or fills the entire screen as the background wallpaper.

Entering Numbers During a Call

You often need to enter numbers during a call, such as to log in to a voicemail system, access an account, or enter a meeting code for an online meeting.

(1) Place a call using any of the methods you've learned so far.

(2) Tap keypad.

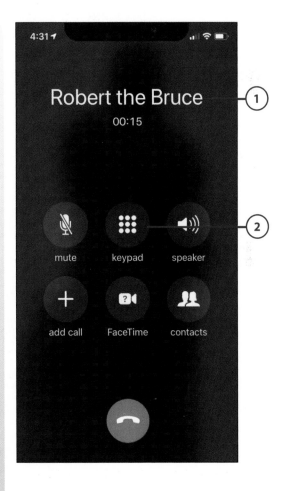

3. Tap the numbers you want to enter.

4. When you're done, tap Hide. You return to the Call screen.

Making Conference Calls

Your iPhone makes it easy to talk to multiple people at the same time. You can have two separate calls going on at any point in time. You can even create conference calls by merging them together. Not all cell providers support two on-going calls or conference calling, though. If yours doesn't, you won't be able to perform the steps in this section.

1. Place a call using any of the methods you've learned so far.

2. Tap add call.

3 Tap the icon you want to use to place the next call. Tap Favorites to call a favorite, tap Recents to use the Recents list, tap Contacts to place the call using the Contacts app, or tap Keypad to dial the number. These work just as they do when you start a new call.

4 Place the call using the option you selected in step 3. Doing so places the first call on hold and moves you back to the Call screen while the Phone app makes the second call. The first call's information appears at the top of the screen, including the word hold so you know the first call is on hold. The app displays the second call just below that, and it is currently the active call.

Similar but Different

If you tap contacts instead of add call, you move directly into the Contacts screen. This might save you one screen tap if the person you want to add to the call is in your Contacts app.

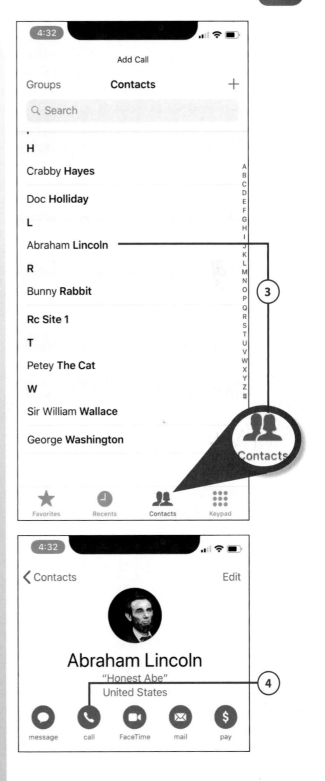

5 Talk to the second person you called; the first remains on hold.

6 To switch to the first call, tap it on the list or tap swap. This places the second call on hold and moves it to the top of the call list, while the first call becomes active again.

7 Tap merge calls to join the calls so all parties can hear you and each other. The iPhone combines the two calls, and you see a single entry at the top of the screen to reflect this.

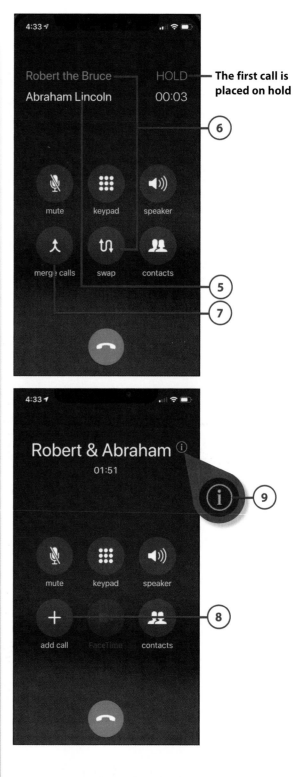

The first call is placed on hold

Merging Calls

As you merge calls, your iPhone attempts to display the names of the callers at the top of the Call screen. As the text increases, your iPhone scrolls it so you can read it. Eventually, the iPhone replaces the names with the word Conference.

Number of Callers

Your provider and the specific technology of the network you use can limit the number of callers you place in a conference call. When you reach the limit, the add call icon is disabled.

8 To add another call, repeat steps 2–7. Each time you merge calls, the second line becomes free so you can add more calls.

9 To manage a conference call, tap the Info icon (i) at the top of the screen.

10 To speak with one of the callers privately, tap Private (if the
Private icons are disabled, you
can't do this with the current
calls). Doing so places the conference call on hold and returns
you to the Call screen showing
information about the active call.
You can merge the calls again by
tapping merge calls.

11 Tap End to remove a caller from
the call. The app disconnects that
caller from the conference call.
When you have only one person
left on the call, you return to the
Call screen and see information
about the active call.

12 Tap Back to move back to the
Call screen. You move to the Call
screen and can continue working with the call, such as adding
more people to it.

13 To end the call for all callers, tap
the Receiver icon.

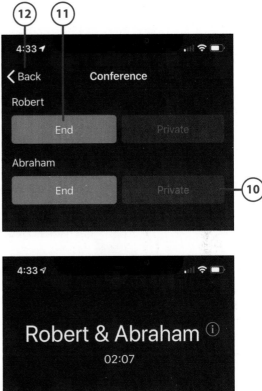

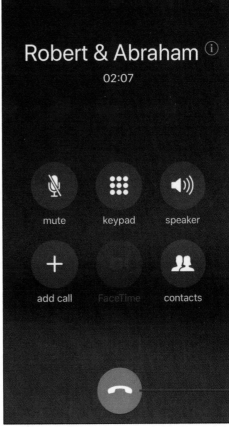

It's Not All Good

Watch Your Minutes

When you have multiple calls combined into one, depending on your provider, the minutes for each call can continue to count individually. So if you've joined three people into one call, each minute of the call might count as three minutes against your calling plan. Before you use this feature, check with your provider to determine what policies govern conference calling for your account.

Using Another App During a Voice Call

A call is active, and you can use other apps while still talking

Tap to return to the call

If your provider's technology supports it, you can use your iPhone for other tasks while you are on a call. When you are on a call, move to a Home screen by swiping up from the bottom of the screen (X models) or pressing the Touch ID/Home button

(non-X models), and then tap a different app (placing the call in speaker mode before you switch to a different app or using the headphones are best for this). Or, you can use the App Switcher to move into a different app. The call remains active and you see the active call information in a green oval in the upper-left corner of the screen (X models) or green bar across the top of the screen (non-X models). You can perform other tasks, such as looking up information, sending emails, and visiting websites. You can continue to talk to the other person just like when the Call screen is showing. To return to the call, tap the green oval or the green bar.

Receiving Voice Calls

Receiving calls on your iPhone enables you to access the same great tools you can use when you make calls, plus a few more for good measure.

Answering Calls

Person calling you — Robert the Bruce
Scottish Federation

Tap to decline and be reminded of the call later — Remind Me

Message — Tap to decline and respond with a message

Tap to decline and send the call to voicemail — Decline

Accept — Tap to answer

When your iPhone rings, it's time to answer the call—or not. If you configured the ringer to ring, you hear your default ringtone or the one associated with the caller's contact information when a call comes in. If vibrate is turned on, your iPhone vibrates whether the ringer is on or not. If you enabled the announce feature, the name of the caller is announced (if available). And if those ways aren't enough, a message appears on your iPhone's screen to show you information about the incoming call. If the number is in your Contacts app, you see the contact with which the number is associated, the label for the number, and the contact's image if there is one. If the number isn't in your contacts, you see the number only.

Wallpaper

If the photo associated with a contact was taken with your iPhone or came from a high-resolution image, you see the contact's image at full screen when the call comes in; if not, you see a small icon at the top of the screen instead.

Calls on Other Devices

By default, when you receive a call on your iPhone, it also comes to any iOS 8 or later devices or Macs running Yosemite or later that are on the same Wi-Fi network, and you can take the call on those devices. To disable this, set the Calls on Other Devices setting to off as described earlier in this chapter.

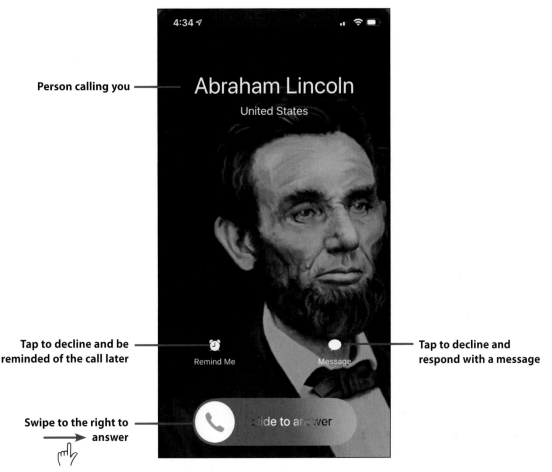

Person calling you ——— **Abraham Lincoln**
United States

Tap to decline and be ——— Remind Me   Message ——— Tap to decline and
reminded of the call later   respond with a message

Swipe to the right to ——— Slide to answer
answer

If your iPhone is locked when a call comes in, swipe the slider to the right to answer it or use the Remind Me and Message icons, which work just like they do when a call comes in when the iPhone isn't locked.

When you receive a call, you have the following options:

- **Answer**—Tap Accept (if the iPhone is unlocked) or swipe the slider to the right (if the iPhone is locked) to take the call (you don't have to unlock the phone to answer a call). You move to the Call screen and can work with the call just like calls you place. For example, you can add a call, merge calls, place the call on hold, or end the call.

- **Decline**—If you tap Decline (when the iPhone is unlocked), the Phone app immediately routes the call to voicemail. You can also decline a call by quickly pressing the Side button twice.

- **Silence the ringer**—To silence the ringer without sending the call directly to voicemail, press the Side button once or press either volume button. The call continues to come in, and you can answer it even though you shut off the ringer.

- **Respond with a message**—Tap Message to send the call to voicemail and send a message back in response. You can tap one of the default messages, or you can tap Custom to create a unique message (the table at the beginning of the chapter explains where to find the setting to create custom messages). Of course, the device the caller is using to make the call must be capable of receiving messages for this to be useful.

- **Decline the call but be reminded later**—Tap Remind Me and the call is sent to voicemail. Tap When I leave, When I get home, When I get to work, or In 1 hour to set the timeframe in which you want to be reminded. A reminder is created in the Reminders app to call back the person who called you, and it is set to alert you at the time you select.

Silencio!

To mute your iPhone's ringer, slide the Mute switch located above the Volume switch toward the back so orange appears. The Mute icon (a bell with a slash through it) briefly appears on the screen to let you know you turned off the ringer. To turn it on again, slide the switch forward. The bell icon appears on the screen to show you the ringer is active again. To set the ringer's volume, use the Volume controls (assuming that setting is enabled) when you aren't on a call and aren't listening to an app, such as the Music app.

Blocking Calls

You can block calls so that if someone attempts to call you from that number again, the call is prevented from coming to your phone. You can block voice calls, messages, and FaceTime calls. To learn how to block calls, see "Blocking Unwanted Calls, Messages, or FaceTime Requests," in Chapter 16, "Maintaining and Protecting Your iPhone and Solving Problems." If you change your mind and want to receive calls or messages from that person again, you can unblock them. This is also covered in Chapter 16.

Answering Calls During a Call

As mentioned earlier, your iPhone can manage multiple calls at the same time. If you are on a call and another call comes in, you have a number of ways to respond.

- **Decline incoming call**—Tap Send to Voicemail to send the incoming call directly to voicemail.

- **Place the first call on hold and answer the incoming call**—Tap Hold & Accept to place the current call on hold and answer the incoming one. After you do this, you can manage the two calls just as when you call two numbers from your iPhone. For example, you can place the second call on hold and move back to the first one, merge the calls, and add more calls.

- **End the first call and answer the incoming call**—Tap End & Accept to terminate the active call and answer the incoming call.

- **Respond with message or get reminded later**—These options work just as they do when you are dealing with any incoming phone call.

Auto-Mute

If you are listening to music, video, audiobooks, or directions from Maps when a call comes in, the app providing the audio, such as the Music app, automatically pauses. When the call ends, that app picks up right where it left off.

Managing Voice Calls

You've already learned most of what you need to know to use your iPhone's cell phone functions. In the following sections, you learn the rest.

Clearing Recent Calls

Previously in this chapter, you learned about the Recents tool that tracks call activity on your iPhone. As you read, this list shows both completed and missed calls; you can view all calls by tapping the All tab or only missed calls by tapping Missed. On either tab, missed calls are always in red, and you see the number of missed calls since you last looked at the list in the badge on the Recents tab. You also learned how you can get more detail about a call, whether it was missed or made.

Over time, you'll build a large Recents list, which you can easily clear.

(1) Tap Phone.

(2) Tap Recents.

(3) Tap Edit.

(4) Tap Clear to clear the entire list; to delete a specific recent call, skip to step 6.

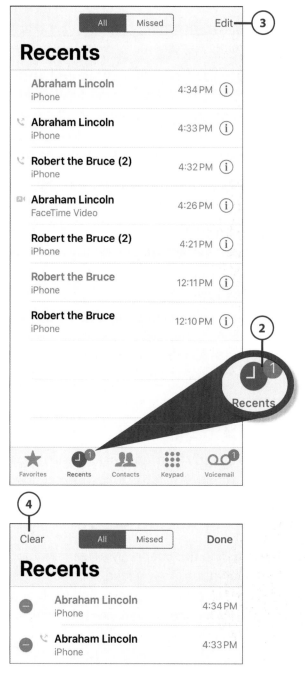

(5) Tap Clear All Recents. The Recents list is reset.

Delete Faster

On the Recents screen, you can delete an individual recent item by swiping all the way to the left on it (starting to the left of the i icon).

(6) Tap a recent item's Unlock (–) icon.

(7) Tap Delete. The recent item is deleted.

(8) When you are done managing your recent calls, tap Done.

Adding Calling Information to Favorites

Earlier you learned how simple it is to place calls to someone on your Favorites list. There are a number of ways to add people to this list, including adding someone on your Recents list.

(1) Move to the Recents list.

(2) Tap the Info icon (i) for the person you want to add to your favorites list. The Info screen appears. If the number is associated with a contact, you see that contact's information.

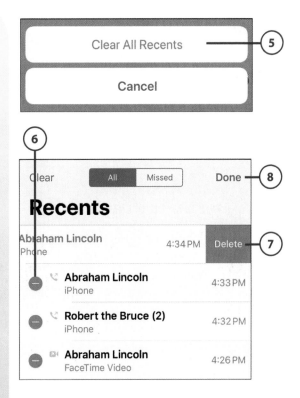

(3) Swipe up to move to the bottom of the screen.

(4) Tap Add to Favorites. If the person has multiple types of contact information, such as phone numbers, email addresses, and so on, you see each type of information available.

(5) Tap the type of information you want to add as a favorite, such as Call to make a phone number a favorite.

(6) Tap the number or email address you want to add as a favorite.

(7) Repeat steps 5 and 6 if you want to add the contact's other numbers or addresses to the favorites list. (If all the numbers and email addresses are assigned as favorites, the Add to Favorites icon doesn't appear on the contact's screen.)

Make Contact First

To make someone a favorite, he needs to be a contact in the Contacts app. Refer to Chapter 6 to learn how to make someone who has called you into a contact.

Add to Favorites
📞 Call iPhone ^
iPhone
home (555) 555-5555
FaceTime
Cancel

Using the iPhone's Headset for Calls

Your iPhone includes an EarPods headset with a microphone on one of its cords. The mic includes a button in the center of the switch on the right side of the EarPods' cable that you can use to do the following:

- **Answer**—Press the mic button once to answer a call.

- **End a call**—Press the mic button while you are on a call to end it.

- **Decline a call**—Press and hold the mic button for about two seconds. Two beeps sound when you release the button to let you know that your iPhone sent the call to voicemail.

- **Put a current call on hold and switch to an incoming call**—Press the mic button once and then press again.

- **End a current call on hold and switch to an incoming call**—Press the mic button once and hold for about two seconds. Release the button and you hear two beeps to let you know you ended the first call. The incoming call is ready for you.

- **Activate Siri**—Press and hold the mic button until you hear the Siri chime. This is useful when you want to make a call to someone without looking at or touching your phone.

Oh, That Ringing in My Ears

When you have EarPods plugged into your iPhone and you receive a call, the ringtone plays on both the iPhone's speaker (unless the ringer is muted, of course) and through the EarPods.

Using Visual Voicemail

Visual voicemail just might be the best of your iPhone's many great features. No more wading through long, uninteresting voicemails to get to one in which you are interested. You simply jump to the message you want to hear. If that isn't enough for you, you can also jump to any point within a voicemail to hear just that part, such as to repeat a phone number that you want to write down. Even better, the iPhone creates a transcript of voicemails, so you can read them instead of listening to them.

The Phone app can access your voicemails directly so don't need to log in to hear them.

Recording a New Greeting

The first time you access voicemail, you are prompted to record a voicemail greeting. Follow the onscreen instructions to do so.

You can also record a new greeting at any time.

1. Move to the Phone screen and tap Voicemail. If badge notifications are enabled for the Phone app, you see the number of voicemails you haven't listened to yet in the badge on the Voicemail icon.

2. Tap Greeting.

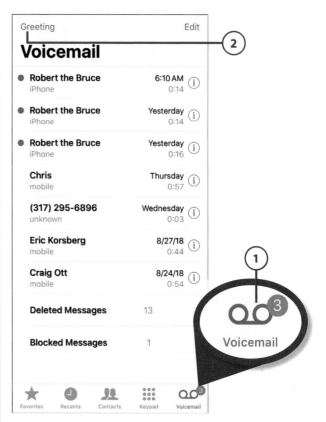

3. To use a default greeting that provides only the iPhone's phone number, tap Default and skip to step 10.

4. Tap Custom to record a personalized greeting. If you have previously used a custom greeting, it is loaded into the editor. You can replace it by continuing with these steps.

5. Tap Record. Recording begins.

6. Speak your greeting. As you record your message, the red area of the timeline indicates (relatively) how long your message is.

7. When you're done recording, tap Stop.

For the Very First Time

Some providers require that you dial into your voicemail number the first time you use it. If you tap Voicemail and the phone starts to dial instead of you seeing Visual Voicemail as shown in these figures, this is your situation. You call the provider's voicemail system, and you're prompted to set up your voicemail. When you've completed that process, you can use these steps to record your greeting.

Set your outgoing message.

Cancel   **Greeting**   Save

Default   ✓ — 3

Custom

Set your outgoing message.

Cancel   **Greeting**   Save

Default

Custom   ✓ — 4

Play   Record — 5

Set your outgoing message.

Cancel   **Greeting**   Save

Default

Custom   ✓

Play   Stop — 7

Your message being recorded

8. Tap Play to hear your greeting.

9. If you aren't satisfied, drag the Playhead (which is the circle that indicates the current position in the audio) to the beginning and repeat steps 5–8 to record a new message.

10. When you are happy with your greeting, tap Save. The Phone app saves the default or custom greeting as the active greeting and returns you to the Voicemail screen.

Set your outgoing message.

Cancel   **Greeting**   Save — 10

Default

Custom   ✓

Play   Record

8   Playhead
9

Adding to a Custom Message

To add onto an existing greeting, drag the Playhead to where you want to start recording and tap Record. Tap Stop when you're done.

No Visual Voicemail?

If your voicemail password isn't stored on your iPhone when you tap Voicemail, your phone dials into your voicemail instead of moving to the Voicemail screen. If that happens, something has gone wrong with your password and you need to reset the voicemail password on your iPhone. If you don't know your current voicemail password, follow your provider's instructions to reset the password. When you have the new password, open the Phone Settings screen, tap Change Voicemail Password, enter the reset password, create a new password, and re-enter your new password. (You need to tap Done after each time you enter a password.)

Change Greeting

To switch between the default and the current custom greeting, move to the Greeting screen, tap the greeting you want to use (which is marked with a check mark), and tap Save. When you choose Custom, you use the custom greeting you most recently saved.

Listening to, Reading, and Managing Voicemails

Unless you turned off the voicemail sound, you hear the sound you selected each time a caller leaves a voicemail for you. The number in the badge on the Phone icon and on the Voicemail icon on the Phone screen increases by 1 (unless you've disabled the badge). Note that the badge number on the Phone icon includes both voicemails left for you and missed calls, whereas the badge number on the Voicemail icon indicates only the number of voicemails left for you. (A new voicemail is one to which you haven't listened, not anything to do with when it was left for you.) If you've configured visual notifications for new voicemails (see Chapter 4), you see those on the screen as well.

If you receive a voicemail while your iPhone is locked, you see a message on the screen alerting you that your iPhone received a voicemail (unless you have disabled these notifications from appearing on the Lock screen). (It also indicates a missed call, which is always the case when a call ends up in voicemail.) Press (3D Touch iPhones) or swipe to the right (non-3D Touch models) on the notification to jump to the Voicemail screen so that you can work with your messages.

And in yet another scenario, if you are using your iPhone when a message is left, you see a notification (unless you have turned off notifications for the Phone app) that enables you to deal with the new message.

Missing Password

If something happens to the password stored on your iPhone for your voicemail, such as if you restore the iPhone, you are prompted to enter your password before you can access your voicemail. Do so at the prompt and tap OK. The iPhone signs you in to voicemail, and you won't have to enter your password again (unless something happens to it again, of course).

Contacts or Numbers?

Like phone calls, if a contact is associated with a number from which you've received a voicemail, you see the contact's name associated with the voicemail message. If no contact exists for the number, you see the number only.

Finding and Listening to Voicemails

Working with voicemails is simple and quick.

1. Move into the Phone app and tap Voicemail (if you pressed or swiped on a new message notification, you jump directly to the Voicemail screen).

2. Swipe up and down the screen to browse the list of voicemails. Voicemails you haven't listened to are marked with a blue circle.

3. To listen to or read a voicemail, tap it. You see the timeline bar and controls and the message plays.

4. Read the message if you don't want to listen to it.

5. Tap the Pause icon to pause a message.

6. Tap Speaker to hear the message on your iPhone's speaker.

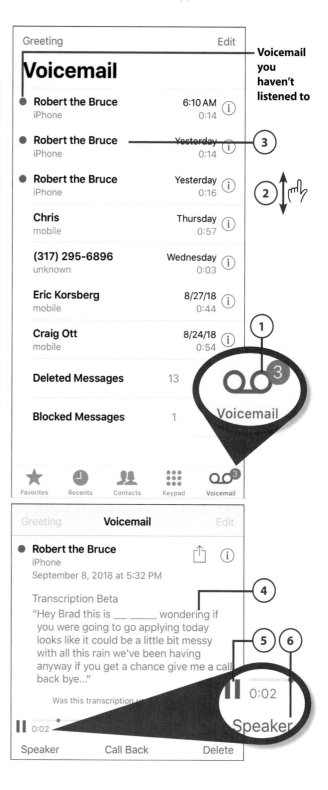

Voicemail you haven't listened to

7) To move to a specific point in a message, drag the Playhead to the point at which you want to listen.

Moving Ahead or Behind

You can also drag the Playhead while a message is playing to rewind or fast-forward it. This is also helpful when you want to listen to specific information without hearing the whole message again.

8) Tap Call Back to call back the person who left the message.

9) Tap Delete to delete the message.

10) Tap the Share icon to share the message, and then tap how you want to share it, such as Message or Mail. For example, when you tap Mail, you send the voicemail to someone else, so he can listen to the message.

11) Tap the Info icon (i) to get more information about a message. The Info screen appears. If the person who left the message is on your contacts list, you see her contact information. The number associated with the message is highlighted in blue.

12) Swipe up or down the screen to review the caller's information.

13) Tap Voicemail.

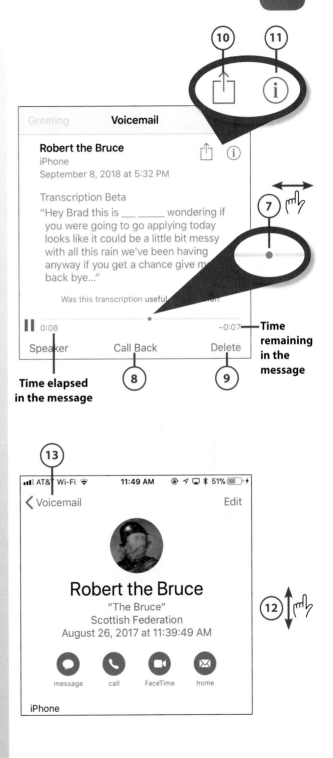

(14) To listen to a message you have listened to before (one that doesn't have a blue dot), tap the message and then tap the Play icon. It begins to play. You can also read its transcript (if available).

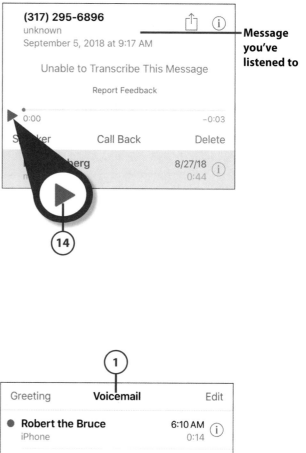

Message you've listened to

Deleting Messages

To delete a voicemail message that isn't the active message, tap it so it becomes the active message and then tap Delete. Or swipe to the left on the message you want to delete and tap Delete. Or swipe quickly all the way to the left on the message to delete it.

Listening to and Managing Deleted Voicemails

When you delete messages, they are moved to the Deleted Message folder. You can work with deleted messages as follows:

(1) Move to the Voicemail screen.

(2) If necessary, swipe up the screen until you see the Deleted Messages option.

(3) Tap Deleted Messages.

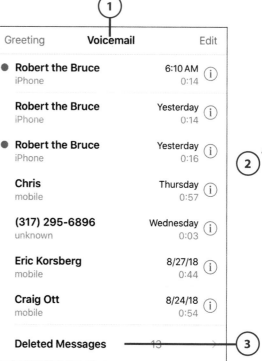

What's Missed?

In case you're wondering, your iPhone considers any call you didn't answer to be a missed call. So if someone calls and leaves a message, that call is included in the counts of both missed calls and new voicemails. If the caller leaves a message, you see a notification informing you that you have a new voicemail and showing who it is from (if available). If you don't answer and the caller doesn't leave a message, it's counted only as a missed call and you see a notification showing a missed call along with the caller's identification (if available).

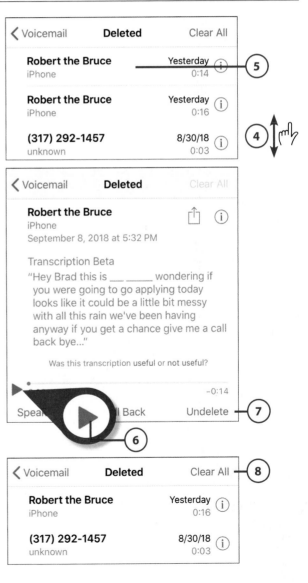

4 Swipe up or down the screen to browse all the deleted messages.

5 Tap a message to listen to it or to read its transcript.

6 Tap the Play icon to hear the message. You can use the other playback tools just like you can with undeleted messages.

7 Tap Undelete to restore the deleted message. The iPhone restores the message to the Voicemail screen.

8 Tap Clear All to remove all deleted messages permanently. (If this is disabled, close the open message by tapping it.)

9. Tap Clear All at the prompt. The deleted messages are erased and you return to the Deleted screen.

10. Tap Voicemail to return to the Voicemail screen.

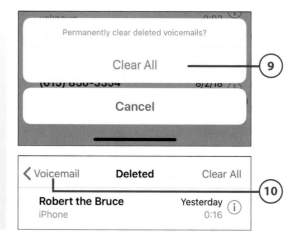

Lost/Forgot Your Password?

If you have to restore your iPhone or it loses your voicemail password for some other reason and you can't remember it, you need to reset the password to access your voicemail on the iPhone. If you don't know your current voicemail password with your provider, you need to reset it using your provider's support system. For most cell phone providers, this involves calling the customer support number and accessing an automated system that sends a new password to you via a text message. For AT&T, which is one of the iPhone providers in the United States, call 611 on your iPhone and follow the prompts to reset your password (which you receive via a text). No matter which provider you use, it's a good idea to know how to reset your voicemail password because it is likely you will need to do so at some point.

Blocked Messages

If you've blocked someone who previously left a message, you might see Blocked Messages on the Voicemail screen. Tap this to see messages from numbers you have blocked. You can work with these messages just like others—for example, tap Delete to move the message to the Deleted Messages area.

Communicating with FaceTime

FaceTime enables you to see, as well as hear, people with whom you want to communicate. This feature exemplifies what's great about the iPhone; it takes complex technology and makes it simple. FaceTime works great, but there are two conditions that have to be true for you and the people you want some FaceTime with. To be able to see each other, both sides have to use a device that has the required cameras (this includes iPhone 4s and newer, iPod touches third generation and newer, iPad 2s and newer, and Macs running Snow Leopard and newer), and have FaceTime enabled (via the settings on an iOS device that are explained on the next page or via the FaceTime application on a Mac). And each device has to be able to communicate over a network; an iPhone or cellular iPad can use a cellular data network (if that setting is enabled) or a Wi-Fi network while Macs have to be connected to the Internet through a Wi-Fi or other type of network. When these conditions are true, making and receiving FaceTime calls are simple tasks.

In addition to making video FaceTime calls, you can also make audio-only FaceTime calls. These work similarly to making a voice call except the minutes don't count against your voice plan when you use a Wi-Fi network (if you are making the call over the cellular network, the data does count against your data plan, so be careful about this).

Assuming you are in a place where you don't have to pay for the data you use, such as when you use a Wi-Fi network, you don't have to pay for a FaceTime call (video or audio-only) either.

Configuring FaceTime Settings

FaceTime is a great way to use your iPhone to hear and see someone else. There are a few FaceTime settings you need to configure for FaceTime to work. You can connect with other FaceTime users via your phone number or an email address.

1. Move to the Settings screen.
2. Tap FaceTime.

3 If the FaceTime switch is off (white), tap the FaceTime switch to turn it on (green). If the FaceTime switch is on and you see an Apple ID, you are already signed into an account; in this case, you see the current FaceTime settings and can follow along starting with step 7 to change these settings. You can sign out of the current account by tapping it, and then tapping Sign Out; proceed to step 4 to sign in with a different account.

4 To use your Apple ID for FaceTime calls, tap Use your Apple ID for FaceTime (if you haven't signed into an Apple ID account, see Chapter 3, "Setting Up and Using an Apple ID, iCloud, and Other Online Accounts" to do so and then come back here to enable FaceTime). If you don't sign in to an Apple ID, you can still use FaceTime, but it is always via your cellular connection, which isn't ideal because then FaceTime counts under your voice minutes on your calling plan or as data on your data plan.

5 Configure the email addresses you want people to be able to use to contact you for FaceTime sessions by tapping them to enable each address (enabled addresses are marked with a check mark) or to disable addresses (these don't have a check mark). (If you don't have any email addresses configured on your iPhone, you are prompted to enter email addresses.)

AT&T Wi-Fi	12:05 PM	56%

‹ Settings   **FaceTime**

FaceTime ◯ — **3**

People can contact you on all your devices with FaceTime, using your phone number or email address.

AT&T Wi-Fi	12:05 PM	56%

‹ Settings   **FaceTime**

FaceTime ⬤

Waiting for activation...

Use your Apple ID for FaceTime — **4**

AT&T Wi-Fi	12:06 PM	55%

‹ Settings   **FaceTime**

FaceTime ⬤

People can contact you on all your devices with FaceTime, using your phone number or email address.

Apple ID: @mac.com

YOU CAN BE REACHED BY FACETIME AT

✓

bradm3@me.com ——┐

✓   @icloud.com

          @mac.com —— **5**

          @me.com ——┘

✓ bradmiser@icloud.com

bradmiser@me.com

6 Tap the phone number or email address by which you will be identified to the other caller during a FaceTime call.

Blocking FaceTime

If you tap Blocked at the bottom of the FaceTime Settings screen, you see the names, phone numbers, and email addresses that are currently blocked from making calls, sending messages, or making FaceTime requests to your iPhone. To block someone else, tap Add New and then tap the contact you want to block. To unblock someone, swipe to the left on that person or number and tap Unblock.

CALLER ID

bradm3@me.com

@icloud.com

@me.com

✓ bradmiser@icloud.com — **6**

bradmiser@me.com

CALLS

Blocked >

Making FaceTime Calls

FaceTime is a great way to communicate with someone because you can hear and see him (or just hear him if you choose an audio-only FaceTime call). Because iPhones have cameras facing each way, it's also easy to show something to the person you are talking with. You make FaceTime calls starting from the FaceTime, Contacts, or Phone apps and from the FAVORITES widget. No matter which way you start a FaceTime session, you manage it in the same way.

Careful

If your iPhone is connected to a Wi-Fi network, you can make all the FaceTime calls you want (assuming you have unlimited data on that network). However, if you are using the cellular data network, be aware that FaceTime calls may use data under your data plan. If you have a limited plan, it's a good idea to use FaceTime primarily when you are connected to a Wi-Fi network. (Refer to Chapter 2, "Using Your iPhone's Core Features," for information on connecting to Wi-Fi networks.)

To start a FaceTime call from the Contacts app, do the following:

(1) Use the Contacts app to open the contact with whom you want to chat (refer to Chapter 6 for information about using the Contacts app).

(2) To place an audio-only FaceTime call, tap the FaceTime audio icon. (The rest of these steps show a FaceTime video call, but a FaceTime audio-only is very similar to voice calls described earlier in this chapter.)

(3) Tap the contact's FaceTime video or FaceTime icon. The iPhone attempts to make a FaceTime connection. You hear the FaceTime "chirping" and see status information on the screen while the call is attempted. When the connection is complete, you hear a different tone and see the other person in the large window and a preview of what she is seeing (whatever your iPhone's front-side camera is pointing at—most likely your face) in the small window. If the person you are trying to FaceTime with isn't available for FaceTime for some reason (perhaps she doesn't have a FaceTime-capable device or is not connected to the Internet), you see a message saying that the person you are calling is unavailable for FaceTime, and the call terminates.

Playing Favorites

If you've set a FaceTime contact as a favorite, you can open the Phone app, tap Favorites, and tap the FaceTime favorite to start the FaceTime session.

④ After the call is accepted, manage the call as described in the "Managing FaceTime Calls" task later in this chapter.

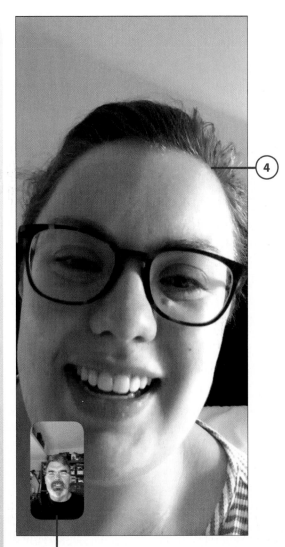

Preview window

>>>Go Further

MORE INFORMATION ABOUT FACETIME CALLS

As you make FaceTime calls, following are some other bits of information for your consideration:

- **Failing FaceTime**—If a FaceTime request fails, you can't really tell the reason why. It can be a technical issue, such as none of the contact information you have is FaceTime-enabled, the person is not signed into a device, or the person might have declined the request. If you repeatedly have trouble connecting with someone, contact him to make sure he has a FaceTime-capable device and that you are using the correct FaceTime contact information.

- **Leave a Message**—On the FaceTime Unavailable screen, you can tap Leave a Message to send a text or iMessage message to the person with whom you are trying to FaceTime.

- **Transform a call**—You can transform a voice call into a FaceTime session by tapping the FaceTime icon on the Call screen. When you transform a call into a FaceTime session, the minutes no longer count against the minutes in your calling plan because all communication happens over the Wi-Fi network or your cellular data plan if you enabled that option and aren't connected to a Wi-Fi network. (The voice call you started from automatically terminates when you make the switch.)

- **FaceTime app**—To use the FaceTime app to start a call, tap the FaceTime icon on the Home screen. Tap the Add (+) icon to enter a name, email address, or phone number in the bar at the top of the screen. If the information you enter matches a contact or someone you've communicated with before, tap the person with whom you want to FaceTime. If not, keep entering the information until it is complete to place the call. Then tap the Audio button to place an audio-only FaceTime call or tap Video to place a video FaceTime call. You also can tap a FaceTime call on the Recents list to place another FaceTime call to that person. Once you've connected, you manage the FaceTime session as described in the rest of this chapter.

- **FaceTime with Siri**—You can also place a FaceTime call using Siri by activating Siri and saying "FaceTime name" where name is the name of the person with whom you want to FaceTime. If there are multiple options for that contact, you must tell Siri which you want to use. After you've made a selection, Siri starts the FaceTime call.

- **FaceTime with the FAVORITES widget**—You can open the FAVORITES widget and tap the FaceTime icon for the person with whom you want to have a FaceTime conversation.

Receiving FaceTime Calls

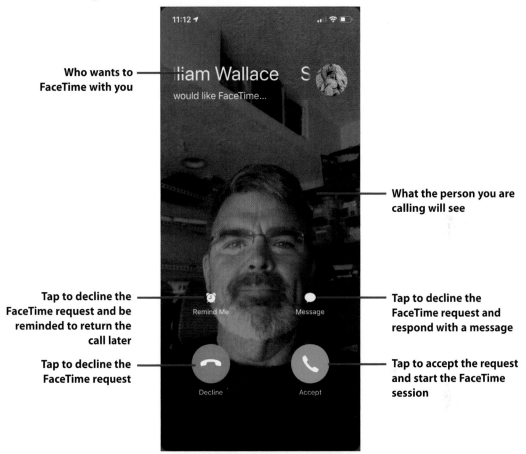

Who wants to FaceTime with you

liam Wallace S

would like FaceTime...

What the person you are calling will see

Tap to decline the FaceTime request and be reminded to return the call later

Remind Me

Message

Tap to decline the FaceTime request and respond with a message

Tap to decline the FaceTime request

Decline

Accept

Tap to accept the request and start the FaceTime session

When someone tries to FaceTime with you, you see the incoming FaceTime request screen message showing who is trying to connect with you and the image you are currently broadcasting. Tap Accept to accept the request and start the FaceTime session. Manage the FaceTime call as described in the "Managing FaceTime Calls" task.

Tap Remind Me to decline the FaceTime request and create a reminder or Message to decline the request and send a message. These options work just as they do for a voice call (you have the same custom message options). You can also press the Side button to decline the request.

When a FaceTime request comes in while your iPhone is locked, you swipe to the right on the slider to accept the call or use the Remind Me or Message options if you don't want to take the call (this is the same as when you receive a voice call via the Phone app).

If you decline the FaceTime request, the person trying to call you receives a message that you're not available (and a message if you choose that option). She can't tell whether there is a technical issue or if you simply declined to take the call.

Tracking FaceTime Calls

FaceTime calls are tracked just as voice calls are. Open the FaceTime app and you see the recents list. FaceTime calls are marked with the video camera icon. FaceTime audio-only calls are marked with a telephone Receiver icon. FaceTime calls that didn't go through are in red and are treated as missed calls. You can tap a recent call to place a FaceTime call to the same person.

Managing FaceTime Calls

During a FaceTime call (regardless of who placed the call initially), you can do the following:

Drag to change the location of the preview window

Tap to show the FaceTime controls

- Drag the preview window, which shows the image that the other person is seeing, around the screen to change its location. It "snaps" into place in the closest corner when you lift your finger up.

- Move your iPhone and change the angle you are holding it to change the images you are broadcasting to the other person. Use the preview window to see what the other person is seeing.

- Tap the screen to see the FaceTime controls. After a few minutes of not touching the screen, they disappear again. You can show them again at any time by touching the screen.

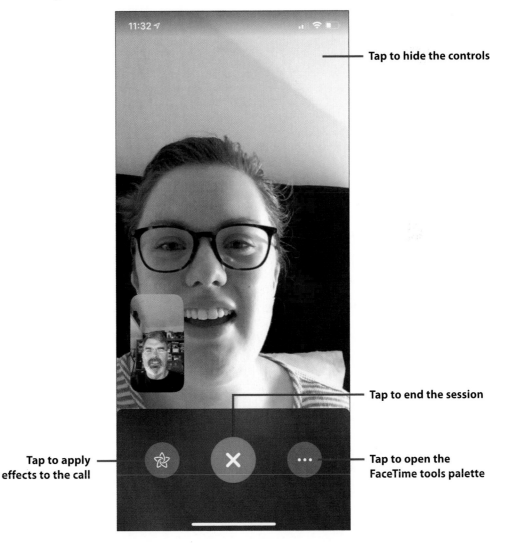

- Tap the x in the red circle to terminate the FaceTime session.
- Tap the Effects button to apply effects to the session (see the next section for details).
- Tap the Options icon (…) to open the FaceTime tools palette.

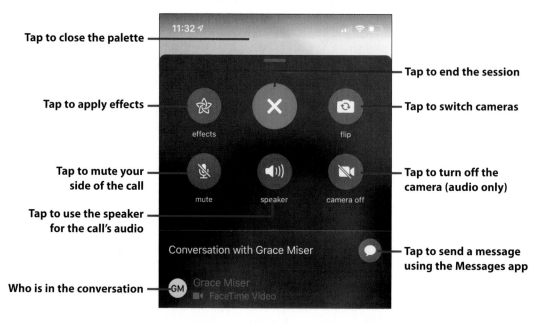

Tap to close the palette

Tap to end the session

Tap to apply effects — effects

Tap to switch cameras — flip

Tap to mute your side of the call — mute

Tap to turn off the camera (audio only) — camera off

Tap to use the speaker for the call's audio — speaker

Conversation with Grace Miser — Tap to send a message using the Messages app

Who is in the conversation — Grace Miser / FaceTime Video

- Tap mute to mute your side of the conversation. Your audio is muted and you see the mute icon in the preview window. Video continues to be broadcast so the other person can still see you.
- Tap speaker to use the speakerphone for the audio part of the session.
- Tap flip to change the camera you are using. If you are currently using the front-facing camera, the other person now sees the images from the back-facing camera.
- Tap camera off to turn off the camera. The audio portion of the session continues.
- Tap the conversation button to move into the Messages app so that you can send messages to the other person in the session.
- Tap above the palette or swipe down from the horizontal line at the top of the palette to close it and return to the FaceTime screen.

FaceTime works in landscape orientation too

The preview shows the landscape orientation

- Rotate your iPhone to change the orientation to horizontal. This affects what the other person sees (as reflected in your preview), but you continue to see the other person in her iPhone's current orientation.

Adding Animojis and Filters to FaceTime Calls

You can apply a wide variety of effects to FaceTime calls. These include animojis, filters, text, symbols, and so on. You can also add more effects by downloading apps that work within the FaceTime app itself.

X Model Required

Animojis and some of the other effects require an X model. If you are using an older version, you might see some or none of the features you see in this section. For example, instead of the effects icon, you might see the mute button on the FaceTime tools. On the tools palette, you might see other icons than shown in these images. In such cases, you might not be able to perform these tasks, but you might have another reason to upgrade.

The effects that you apply appear "on top" of the video part of the FaceTime session; filters change how the video itself appears. For example, when you apply an animoji, the animoji replaces your head in the video.

There are many options for these effects, but the following tasks show you how to apply animojis and filters. Using the other options is similar.

Apps Messages and FaceTime

The apps available in FaceTime are very similar to those available in the Messages app. These are covered in detail in Chapter 9, "Sending, Receiving, and Managing Texts and iMessages." See that chapter for information about installing and working with these apps.

Adding an Animoji to a FaceTime Call

To add an animoji to a FaceTime session, perform the following steps:

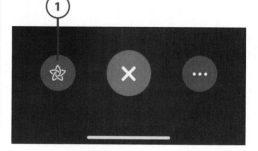

1. Tap the effects icon to open the effects tools. (If you don't see the effects icon, tap the FaceTime screen to cause the tools to appear.)

2. Tap the Animoji icon.

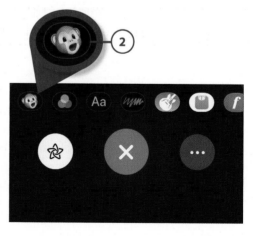

③ Swipe to the left and right to preview the available animojis.

The Animoji Menu

If you tap the top of the Animoji palette, the full menu of animojis appears; tap one to apply it. Tap the top of the menu to close it.

④ Tap the animoji you want to use. Your head is replaced by the animoji.

⑤ Tap Close (x) to close the animoji tools and return to the call.

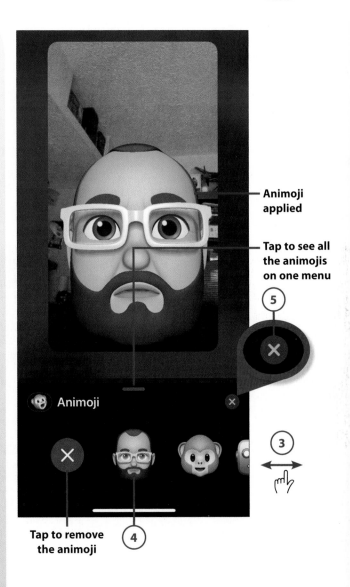

Animoji applied

Tap to see all the animojis on one menu

⑤

③

Tap to remove the animoji

④

(6) Tap the Effects icon to close the effects palette.

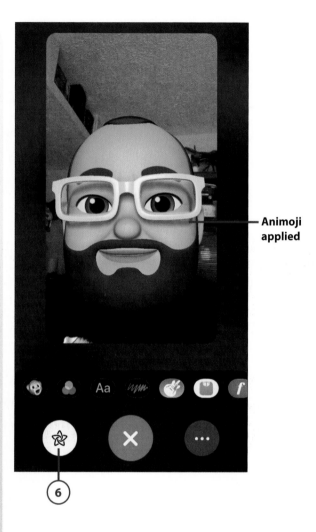

Animoji applied

(7) Continue the FaceTime session.

I Gotta Be Me

To remove the animoji, tap the x on the left end of the animoji toolbar.

I Gotta Be Someone Else

Creating your own animoji is explained in Chapter 9.

Applying a Filter to a FaceTime Call

Filters enable you to create interesting visual effects during FaceTime calls. To add filters, perform the following steps:

(1) Tap the effects button to open the effects tools.

(2) Tap the Filters icon.

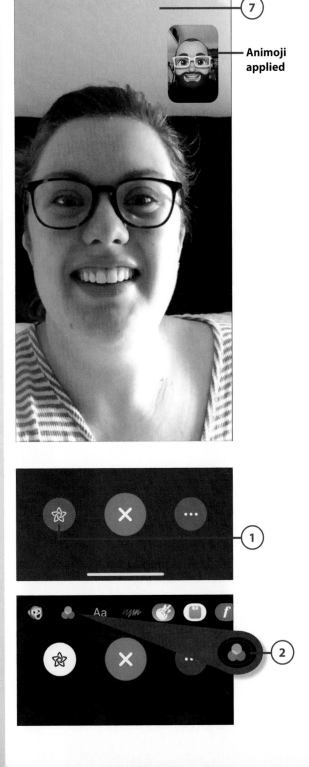

Animoji applied

(3) Swipe to the left and right to preview the available filters.

The Filter Menu

If you tap the top of the Filter palette, the full menu of filters appears; tap one to apply it. Tap the top of the menu to close it.

(4) Tap the filter you want to use. You see its name and a yellow box to highlight the current filter. The filter is applied to the image and you see the result.

Make It Stop

Select the Original filter to return to the unaltered image.

(5) Tap Close (x) to close the filter tools and return to the call.

Filter applied

Tap to see all the filters on one menu

Filters

Ink

6 Tap the Effects icon to close the
   effects palette.

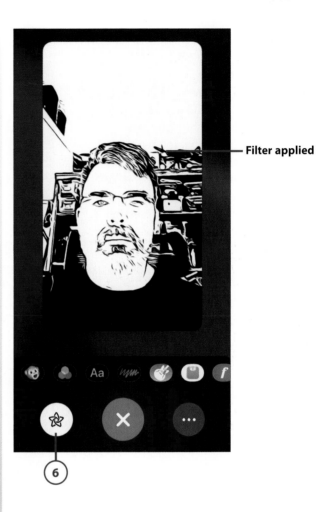

Filter applied

7 Continue the FaceTime session.

FaceTime Break

Just like when you are in a voice call, you can move into and use other apps (if your provider's technology supports this functionality). You see the green oval in the upper-left corner of the screen (X models) or the green bar across the top of the screen (non-X models). The audio part of the session continues, but the other person sees a still image with a camera icon and the word "Paused." As soon as you move back into the FaceTime session, the video resumes. Likewise, if the other person moves out of the FaceTime app, you see the Paused icon in the large part of the FaceTime window.

Filter applied

Working with Group FaceTime (Future iOS 12 Release)

Currently, FaceTime is limited to two people per session (with you as one of the two). Apple had announced that Group FaceTime, which allows for multiple participants in a single FaceTime session, would be part of iOS 12. However, this feature was not included in the initial release as planned. You can expect Group FaceTime to be added in a later release, at which point, you'll see new options that will enable you to add more people to a FaceTime session. The basic controls and features will work similarly to those in the version described in this chapter.

You will be able to start a Group FaceTime session from Messages, or by opening the FaceTime tools palette and choosing the option to add more participants. You will then enter the name, email address, or phone number of the person you want to add to invite the person into the session.

Each participant will have her own window. The window associated with the person currently speaking will be enlarged to indicate who that is.

It's not currently clear how many people will be able to participate in a single session, but it appears that it might be up to 32 people in one FaceTime call.

If this feature is of interest to you, keep your iOS software and apps updated (see Chapter 16) and be on the lookout for an update to the FaceTime app so you'll know when Group FaceTime is available.

Tap to configure
email settings

Tap to use email

In this chapter, you explore all the email functionality that your iPhone has to offer. Topics include the following:

→ Getting started
→ Configuring email accounts
→ Setting Mail app preferences
→ Working with email
→ Managing email

Sending, Receiving, and Managing Email

For most of us, email is an important way we communicate with others, both in our public and personal lives. Fortunately, your iPhone has great email tools so you can work with email no matter where you are.

Getting Started

To use email on your iPhone, you use the Mail app to access your email accounts over the Internet. The Mail app has lots of great features that help you really take advantage of all that email offers; you learn how to use these features throughout this chapter.

You configure your email accounts in the Mail app to be able to access them; configuring email accounts is described in the next section.

You need to be connected to the Internet through a Wi-Fi or cellular data connection to send or receive email—although you can read downloaded messages, reply to messages, and compose messages when you aren't connected. In Chapter 2, "Using Your iPhone's Core Features," you find out how to connect your iPhone to the Internet.

As you use email, it's helpful to understand that email isn't sent between devices; for example, from an email application on a computer to Mail on an iPhone. Rather, all email flows through an email server. When you send an email, it moves from your iPhone to an email server. From there, it moves from the server onto each device configured with the email account to which you sent it, such as an iPhone or a computer. The process is the same when someone sends email to you. The email travels from the device sending it to the email server that handles email for your email account. From there, it is available on every device configured with your email address. This means you can have the same email messages on more than one device at a time. You can determine how often email is moved from the server onto your iPhone.

Configuring Email Accounts

Before you can start using an iPhone for email, you have to configure the email accounts you want to access with it. The iPhone supports many kinds of email accounts, including iCloud, Gmail, and so on. Setting up the most common types of email accounts is covered in Chapter 3, "Setting Up and Using an Apple ID, iCloud, and Other Online Accounts," so if you haven't done that already, go back to that chapter and get your accounts set up. Then come back here to start using those accounts for email.

Setting Mail App Preferences

There are a number of settings that affect how the Mail app works. The good news is that you can probably use the Mail app with its default settings just fine. However, you might want to tweak how it works for you by making changes using the Settings app; you can use the information in the table that follows to understand the options available to you.

To access the settings in the table, first tap the Settings icon on the Home screen, tap the option listed in the Settings Area column, and then move to the location to make changes to the setting (for example, to change the amount of text shown in email previews, open the Settings app; tap Mail; move to the MESSAGE LIST section; and then tap Preview). For each setting, you see a description of what it does along with options (if applicable).

Settings App Explained

To get detailed information on using the Settings app, see "Working with the Settings App" in Chapter 2.

Mail and Related Settings

Settings Area	Location	Setting	Description
Passwords & Accounts	ACCOUNTS	Email accounts	You can configure the accounts used in the Mail app to determine which account can receive or send email on your iPhone (see Chapter 3 for details).
Passwords & Accounts	N/A	Fetch New Data	Determines when new email is downloaded to your iPhone (see Chapter 3 for an explanation of the options).
Mail	ALLOW MAIL TO ACCESS	Siri & Search	When the Siri & Suggestions switch is Enabled (green), Search, Siri, and other elements of the iOS can use information in the Mail app. For example, when you search for a person, the Search tool can search your email for relevant information. If you don't want your email information to be used, set the switch to off (white). Set the Allow on Lock Screen switch to on (green) if you want information about email to appear on the Lock screen. Tap Shortcuts to work with Siri shortcuts (see Chapter 4).
Mail	ALLOW MAIL TO ACCESS	Notifications	Configure the type of notifications the Mail app uses. See "Configuring Notifications" in Chapter 4, "Customizing How Your iPhone Works," for a detailed explanation.
Mail	ALLOW MAIL TO ACCESS	Cellular Data	When enabled (green), Mail can send and receive email when your iPhone is connected to the Internet using the cellular data network. Email typically doesn't use a lot of data, but if you receive many emails with very large attachments and have a limited data plan, you might want to set this switch to off (white).

Settings Area	Location	Setting	Description
Mail	MESSAGE LIST	Preview	Determines the number of lines you want to display for each email when you view the Inbox and in other locations, such as alerts. This preview enables you to get the gist of an email without opening it. More lines give you more of the message but take up more space on the screen.
Mail	MESSAGE LIST	Show To/Cc Label	Slide the switch to on (green) to always see a To or Cc label next to the subject line on messages in your inboxes. This helps you know when you are included in the To line or as a Cc, which usually indicates whether you need to do something with the message or if it is just for your information.
Mail	MESSAGE LIST	Swipe Options	Changes what happens when you swipe to the left or right on email when you are viewing an Inbox. You can set the Swipe Left motion to be None, Mark as Read, Flag, or Move Message. When you do a partial swipe to the left, you see the More icon, which leads to a menu of actions, and the option you configure for the Left Swipe setting. When you do a full swipe to the left, a message is deleted. You can set the Swipe Right motion to be None, Mark as Read, Flag, Move Message, or Archive. When you swipe all the way to the right on a message, the action you configure for the Swipe Right is performed. When you do a partial swipe, you see an icon that you can tap to perform the action. Note that you can't have the same option configured for both directions.

Settings Area	Location	Setting	Description
Mail	MESSAGE LIST	Flag Style	Determines how messages you flag are marked; you can choose a colored circle or a flag icon. Flagging messages marks messages that you want to know are important or that need your attention.
Mail	MESSAGES	Ask Before Deleting	When this switch is on (green), you're prompted to confirm when you delete or archive messages. When this switch is off (white), deleting or archiving messages happens without the confirmation prompt.
Mail	MESSAGES	Load Remote Images	When this switch is on (green), images in HTML email messages are displayed automatically. When this switch is off (white), you have to manually load images in a message. (If you receive a lot of spam, you should turn this off so that you won't see images in which you might not be interested.)
Mail	THREADING	Organize By Thread	When this switch is on (green), messages in a conversation are grouped together as a "thread" on one screen. This makes it easier to read all the messages in a thread. When this switch is off (white), messages are listed individually. (You learn more about working with threads in the "Working with Email" task later in this chapter.)
Mail	THREADING	Collapse Read Messages	When enabled and you read messages in a thread, the thread collapses so you see the thread rather than the individual messages in the thread.

Settings Area	Location	Setting	Description
Mail	THREADING	Most Recent Message on Top	With this switch set to on (green), the most recent message in a thread appears at the top of the thread and the messages move backward in time as you move down the list of messages. When disabled (white), the first message in the thread displays at the top with the next oldest message appearing next, and so on until the last message, which is the most recent message in the thread.
Mail	THREADING	Complete Threads	With this switch enabled (green), all the messages in a thread are displayed when you view the thread, even if you've moved messages to a different folder (other than the inbox).
Mail	COMPOSING	Always Bcc Myself	When this switch is on (green), you receive a blind copy of each email you send; this means that you receive the message, but you are hidden on the list of recipients. When this switch is off (white), you don't receive a blind copy. (Email you send is automatically saved in the Sent folder so you always have a record of emails you send.)
Mail	COMPOSING	Mark Addresses	This feature highlights addresses in red that are not from domains that you specify. You enter the domains (everything after the @ in email addresses, such as icloud.com) from which you do not want addresses to be marked (highlighted in red) when you create email. You can add multiple domains to the list by separating them with commas. All addresses from domains not listed will be marked in red. To disable this feature, delete all the domains from the list.

Settings Area	Location	Setting	Description
Mail	COMPOSING	Increase Quote Level	When this option is enabled (green), the text of an email you are replying to or forwarding (quoted content) is automatically indented. Generally, you should leave this enabled so it is easier for the recipients to tell when you have added text to an email, versus what is from the previous email messages' quoted content.
Mail	COMPOSING	Signature	Signatures are text that is automatically added to the bottom of new email messages that you create. For example, you might want your name and email address added to every email you create. You can configure the same signature for all your email accounts or have a different signature for each account. If you don't want to use a signature, delete any signatures that are currently configured. (Note that the default signature is "Sent from my iPhone.")
Mail	COMPOSING	Default Account	Determines which email account is the default one used when you send an email (this setting isn't shown if you have only one email account). You can override the default email account for an email you are sending by choosing one of your other email addresses in the From field.
Display & Brightness	N/A	Text Size	Changes the size of text in all apps that support Dynamic Type (Mail does). Drag the slider to the right to make text larger or to the left to make it smaller.
Display & Brightness	N/A	Bold Text	Changes text to be bold when the Bold Text switch is set to on (green).

Settings Area	Location	Setting	Description
Control Center	N/A	Text Size	Changes the size of text; you can add the Text Size tool to your Control Center to make it quicker and easier to use. See "Configuring the Control Center" in Chapter 4 for the steps to configure your Control Center.

More on Marking Addresses

When you configure at least one address on the Mark Addresses screen, all addresses from domains except those listed on the Mark Addresses screen are in red text on the New Message screen. This is useful to prevent accidental email going to places where you don't want it to go. For example, you might want to leave domains associated with your workplace off this list so that whenever you send email to addresses associated with your workplace, the addresses appear in red to remind you to pay closer attention to the messages you are sending.

Email Notifications and Sounds

If you want to be alerted whenever new email is received and when email you create is sent, be sure to configure notifications for the Mail app. These include whether unread messages are shown in the Notification Center, the type of alerts, whether the badge appears on the Mail icon, whether the preview is shown, the alert sound, and whether new messages are shown on the Lock screen. For a detailed explanation of configuring notifications, refer to Chapter 4.

Working with Email

The Mail app offers lots of great features and is ideally suited for working with email on your iPhone. This app offers a consolidated Inbox, so you can view email from all your accounts at the same time. Also, the Mail app organizes your email into threads (assuming you didn't disable this feature), which makes following a conversation convenient.

You've got email

When you move to a Home screen, you see the number of new email messages you have in the badge on the Mail app's icon (assuming you haven't disabled this); tap the icon to move to the app. Even if you don't have any new email, the Mail icon still leads you to the Mail app. Other ways Mail notifies you of new messages include by displaying visual notifications and the new mail sound. (You determine which of these options is used for each email account by configuring its notifications as explained in the "Email Notifications and Sounds" note earlier in this chapter.)

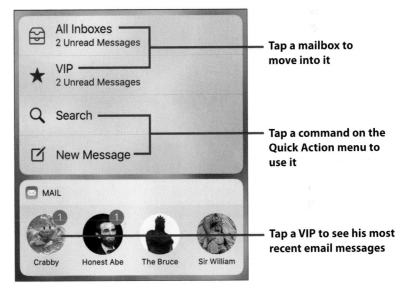

Tap a mailbox to move into it

Tap a command on the Quick Action menu to use it

Tap a VIP to see his most recent email messages

If you are using an iPhone that supports 3D Touch (6s/6s Plus or later models), you can press on the Mail icon to open the Quick Actions menu and choose an action you want to perform. For example, you can start a new email message by tapping New Message or move directly to your VIP email by tapping VIP. You can move to the most recent messages from one of your VIPs by tapping him in the MAIL widget.

VIP

You can designate people with whom you correspond as a Very Important Person (VIP). Mail has options specifically for your VIPs, such as a dedicated Inbox, the MAIL widget, and so on. You learn more about working with VIPs later in this chapter.

About Assumptions

The steps and figures in this section assume you have more than one email account configured and are actively receiving email from those accounts on your iPhone. If you have only one email account active, your Mailboxes screen contains that account's folders instead of mailboxes from multiple accounts and the Accounts sections that appear in these figures and steps. Similarly, if you disable the Organize by Thread setting, you won't see messages in threads as these figures show. Instead, you work with each message individually.

The Mail app enables you to receive and read email for all the email accounts configured on your iPhone. The Mailboxes screen is the top-level screen in the app and is organized into two sections.

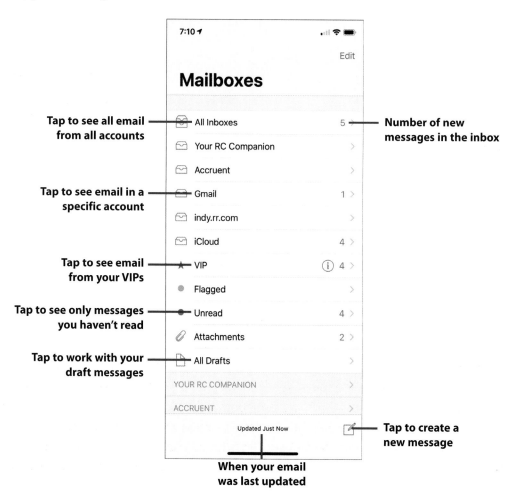

Tap to see all email from all accounts

Number of new messages in the inbox

Tap to see email in a specific account

Tap to see email from your VIPs

Tap to see only messages you haven't read

Tap to work with your draft messages

Tap to create a new message

When your email was last updated

The Inboxes section shows the Inbox for each account along with folders for email including from people designated as VIPs, your unread messages, and your draft messages (those you've started but haven't sent yet). Next to each Inbox or folder is the number of new emails in that Inbox or folder. (A new message is simply one you haven't viewed yet.) At the top of the section is All Inboxes, which shows the total number of new messages to all accounts; when you tap this, the integrated Inbox containing email from all your accounts is displayed.

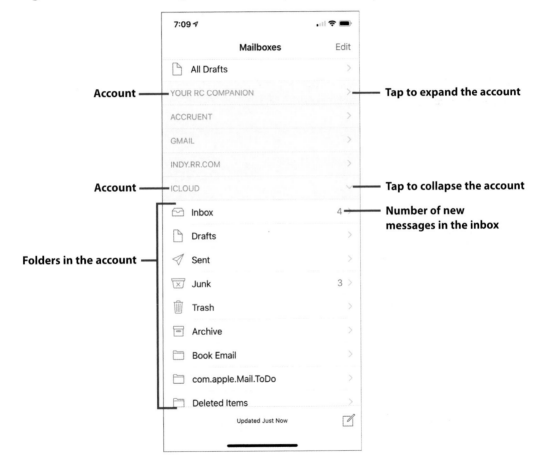

The Accounts section, which is underneath the Inboxes section on the screen, shows the set of inboxes and folders associated with each email account. The difference between these sections is that the Inbox options take you to just the Inbox for one or all of your accounts or specific folders (such as the VIP folder), whereas the Account options take you to all the folders under each account. Tap the right-facing arrow next to the account name to expand it so you can see the folders it contains.

You can tap any folder or inbox under an account to view the emails stored in that folder or inbox. Tap the downward-facing arrow to collapse an account so that you see only its name.

Receiving and Reading Email

To read email you have received, perform the following steps:

(1) On the Home screen, tap Mail. When you open Mail (assuming you didn't use the App Switcher to quit the app when you left it), you move back to the screen you were last on; for example, if you were reading an email you return to it. If the Mailboxes screen isn't showing, tap the Back icon (<) in the upper-left corner of the screen until you reach the Mailboxes screen.

(2) To read messages, tap the inbox that contains messages you want to read, or tap All Inboxes to see the messages from all your email accounts. Various icons indicate the status of each message, if it has attachments, if it is from a VIP, or if it is part of a thread. A message is part of a thread when it has double right-facing arrows along the right side of the screen—individual messages have only one arrow.

Edit

Mailboxes

📥	All Inboxes	6 >
✉	Your RC Companion	>
✉	Accruent	>
✉	Gmail	1 >
✉	indy.rr.com	>
✉	iCloud	6 >
★	VIP	ⓘ 6 >

3 Swipe up or down the screen to browse the messages. You can read the preview of each message to get an idea of its contents.

4 If a message you are interested in is in a thread, tap its arrows. (If it isn't part of a thread, skip to step 6.) The thread expands (the double arrows point down instead of to the right) and you can see the messages it contains. The first message in the thread appears in a gray bar. The responses to the message appear under it in a lighter shade of gray; the responses don't have a subject because they are all related to the subject of the thread.

Pulling on Threads

A thread is a group of emails that are related to the same subject. For example, if someone sends an email to you saying how wonderful the *My iPhone* book is, and you reply with a message saying how much you agree, those two messages would be grouped into one thread. Other messages with the same subject are also placed in the thread.

Collapsing Threads

To collapse an expanded thread, tap the downward-facing arrows at the top of the thread. You see only the most recent message in the thread again.

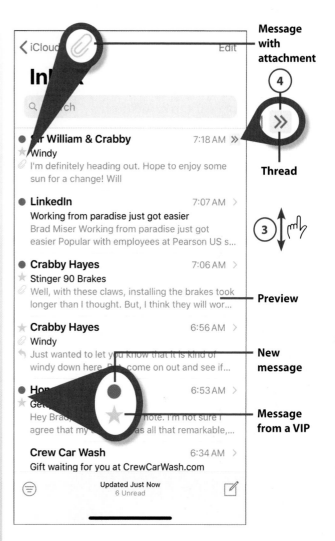

Message with attachment

Thread

Preview

New message

Message from a VIP

5 Swipe up or down the screen to browse the messages in the thread.

6 To read a message (whether in a thread or not), tap it. As soon as you open a message, it's marked as read and the new mail counter reduces by one. You see the message screen with the address information at the top, including whom the message is from and whom it was sent to. Under that the message's subject along with time and date it was sent are displayed. Below that is the body of the message. If the message has an attachment or is a reply to another message, the attachment or quoted text appears toward the bottom of the screen.

Title of thread

6

Expanded thread

Message thread

Messages in the thread

No subject indicates a message in a thread

(7) Swipe up and down the screen to read the entire message.

See More

When all of the information, such as for a quoted message, isn't being displayed, tap the related See More command. The section expands, and you can see the additional text. Tap the Back icon (<) located in the upper-left corner of the screen to return to your previous location.

< 3   **3 Messages**   ∧ ∨
Windy

⭐ **Sir William**   7:18 AM
To: Crabby   Cc: Brad   Details

Great. I'll be leaving soon.

Do you need me to bring anything?

Regards,

Will

On Aug 30, 2018, at 07:17 AM, Crabby Hayes <crabby_hayes@icloud.com> wrote: — **Quoted message**

See More from Crabby Hayes — **Tap to see the full quote**

(7) ↕ 🖐

📎 **Crabby Hayes**   7:17 AM
Looking good at the moment. Crabby

📎 **Sir William Wallace**   7:04 AM
I'm definitely heading out. Hope to enjoy som...

🏳   🗂   🗑   ↩   ✏

Standard Motions Apply

You can use the standard finger motions on email messages, such as unpinching or tapping to zoom, swiping directions to scroll, and so on. You can also rotate the phone to change the orientation of messages from vertical to horizontal; this makes it easier to type.

(8) If the message contains an attachment, swipe up the screen to get to the end of the message. Some types of attachments, most notably photos, appear directly in the message and you don't have to download them to the device. If an attachment hasn't been downloaded yet, it starts to download automatically (unless it is a large file). If the attachment hasn't been downloaded automatically, which is indicated by "Tap to Download" in the attachment icon, tap it to download it into the message. When an attachment finishes downloading, its icon changes to represent the type of file it is. If the icon remains generic, it might be of a type the iPhone can't display, and you would need to open it on a computer or other device.

(9) Tap the attachment icon to view it.

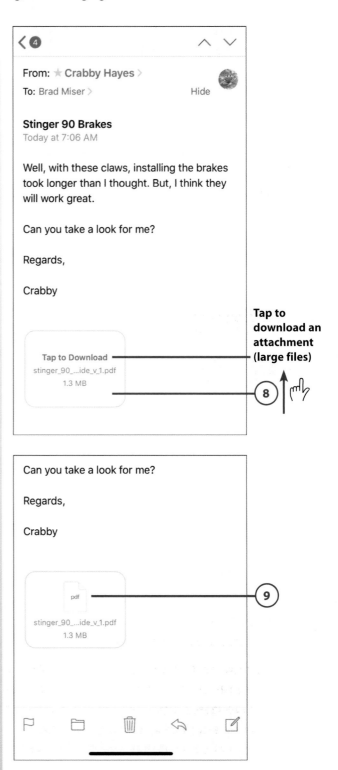

Tap to download an attachment (large files)

10 Scroll the document by swiping up, down, left, or right on the screen.

11 Unpinch or double-tap to zoom in.

12 Pinch or double-tap to zoom out.

13 Tap the Share icon to see the available actions for the attachment.

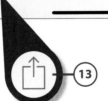

14 Swipe to the left or right to see all the available options.

15 Tap the action you want to take, such as opening the attachment in a different app, printing it, sharing it via email, and so on. Tap Cancel to return to the attachment if you don't want to do any of these. If you open the attachment in an app, work with the attachment in that app. To return to the email, tap Mail in the top-left corner of the screen to return to the Mail app (not shown in the figures).

16 Tap Done (depending on the type of attachment you were viewing, you might tap the Back icon (<) instead).

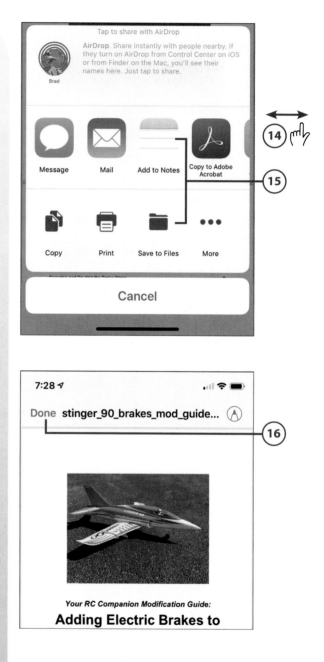

17 To view information for an email address, such as who sent the message, tap it. The Info screen appears. On this screen, you see as much information for the person as is available. If it is someone in the Contacts app, you see all of the information stored there, and you can place a call, send a message, etc. If it is not someone in the Contacts app, you see the person's email address along with actions you might want to perform, such as creating a contact for him or adding new information to an existing contact. (See Chapter 6, "Managing Contacts," for information about working with contacts.)

Details, Details

If the email address isn't in blue as shown in the figure, tap Details to show the details for the email. The addresses turn blue to show you can tap them to get more information. If you don't want them to be active, tap Hide and they turn black (which means you can't tap them to see more information).

18 Tap Done to return to the message.

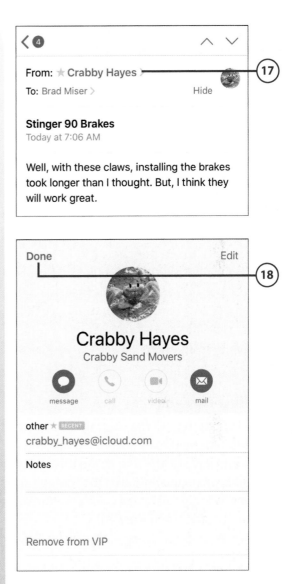

(19) To read the next message in the current inbox or thread, tap the down arrow. (If the arrow is disabled, you are viewing the most recent email in the inbox or thread.)

(20) To move to a previous message in the current inbox or thread, tap the up arrow. (If the arrow is disabled, you are viewing the oldest message in the inbox or thread.)

(21) To move back to see the entire inbox from where you came, tap the Back icon (<) , which shows the number of unread messages in that inbox (all your Inboxes if you were viewing them all).

(21) (20) (19)

< 4

From: ★ Crabby Hayes >

To: Brad Miser >   Hide

Stinger 90 Brakes
Today at 7:06 AM

Well, with these claws, installing the brakes took longer than I thought. But, I think they will work great.

Can you take a look for me?

Regards,

Crabby

Reading Threads

If you want to read all the messages in a thread instead of individual messages it contains, tap the thread (instead of tapping its arrows to expand it). The thread opens, and you see the title of the thread at the top of the screen in a gray bar. You can browse up and down the thread's screen to read all of the messages it contains. When you are done with the thread, tap the Back icon (<) located in the upper-left corner of the screen.

Two Other Ways to Open New Email

You can view a preview of email messages in notifications you receive and press or swipe on the notification to get to the full message. You can also use Siri to get and read new email. If those aren't enough ways, you can also use the MAIL widget to quickly get to email from your VIPs.

Receiving and Reading Email on an iPhone Plus

The larger screens on the iPhone Plus models (6, 7, 8, and Xs Max) provide some additional functionality that is unique to those models. You can access this by holding the Plus horizontally when you use the Mail app.

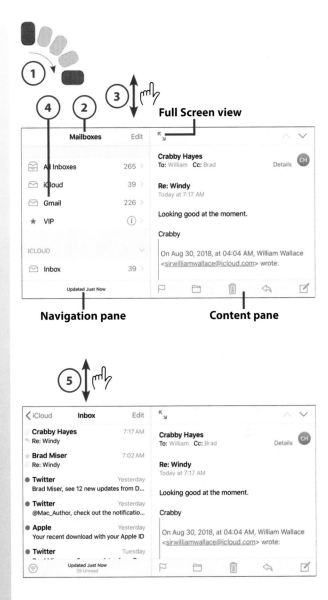

Full Screen view

Navigation pane   **Content pane**

(1) Open the Mail app and hold the iPhone so it is oriented horizontally. The mail window splits into two panes. On the left is the Navigation pane, where you can move to and select items you want to view. When you select something in the left pane, it appears in the Content pane on the right, which shows the email message you were most recently reading.

(2) In the left pane, navigate to the Mailboxes screen by tapping Back (<) until that icon disappears.

(3) Swipe up or down the Navigation pane to browse the mailboxes and accounts available to you. Notice that the two panes are independent. When you browse the left pane, the right pane doesn't change.

(4) Tap the mailbox or account whose contents you want to view.

(5) Swipe up and down the messages to browse all of them in the mailbox you selected.

6 Tap the message or thread that you want to read. If you tap a thread, the messages it contains appear in the left pane; browse the messages in the thread by swiping up and down the screen and then tap the message in the thread that you want to read. The message currently selected is highlighted in gray.

7 Read the message.

8 Use the other tools to work with it; these work just like they do on other models and when you hold the iPhone vertically. For example, tap the up arrow to move to the previous message in the current Inbox.

9 To read the message in full screen, tap the Full Screen icon. The Content pane uses the entire screen.

10 Work with the message.

11 When you're done, tap Back (<).

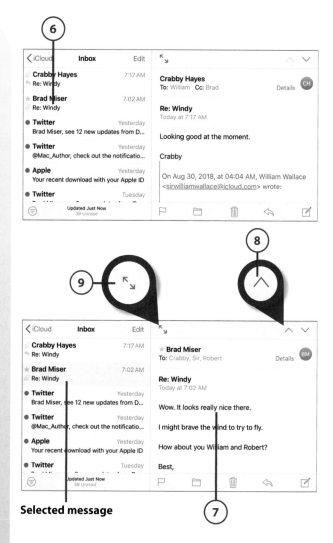

Selected message

12 Select and read other messages.

13 When you're done, tap Back (<), which is labeled with the name of the inbox or folder whose contents you are browsing.

Using 3D Touch for Email

You can use the 3D Touch feature (iPhone 6s/6s Plus or later models) for email as follows:

1 Browse a list of email messages.

2 Press and hold on an email in which you are interested. A Peek of that email appears.

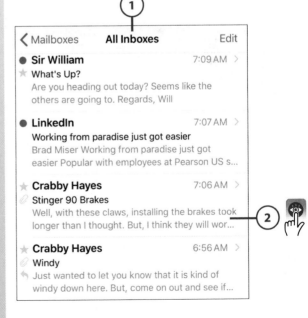

③ Review the preview of the email that appears in the Peek.

④ To open the email so you can read all of it, press down slightly harder until it pops open and use the steps in the earlier task to read it (skip the rest of these steps).

⑤ To see actions you can perform on the email, swipe up on the Peek.

⑥ Tap the action you want to perform, such as Reply, to reply to the email.

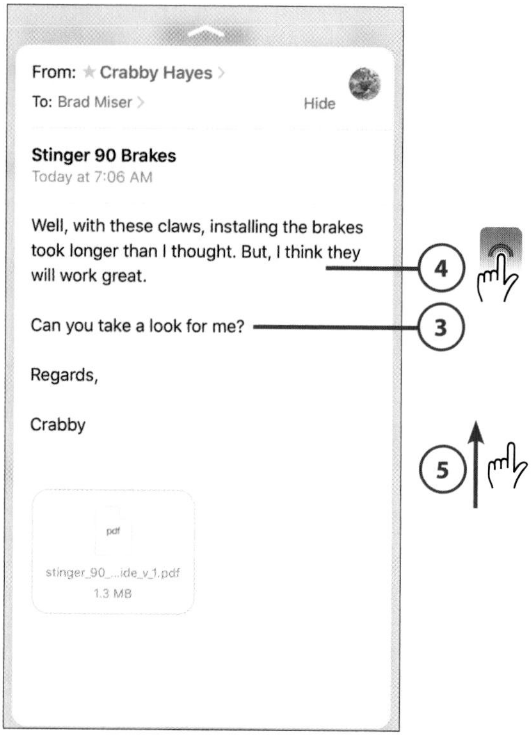

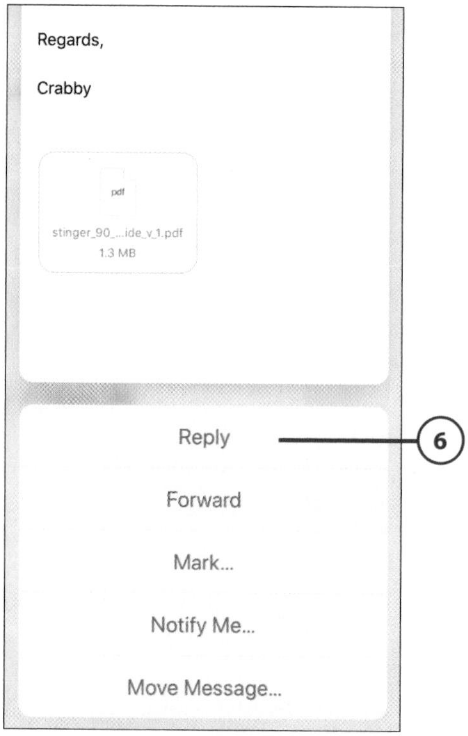

From: ★ Crabby Hayes ›
To: Brad Miser ›   Hide

Stinger 90 Brakes
Today at 7:06 AM

Well, with these claws, installing the brakes took longer than I thought. But, I think they will work great. ──── ④

Can you take a look for me? ──── ③

Regards,

Crabby

pdf

stinger_90_...ide_v_1.pdf
1.3 MB

⑤

Regards,

Crabby

pdf

stinger_90_...ide_v_1.pdf
1.3 MB

Reply ──── ⑥

Forward

Mark...

Notify Me...

Move Message...

>>>*Go Further*

MORE ON RECEIVING AND READING EMAIL

Check out these additional pointers for working with email you receive:

- If more messages are available than are downloaded, tap the Load More Messages link. The additional messages download to the inbox you are viewing.

- You can change the amount of detail you see at the top of the message screen by tapping Details to show all of the detail, such as the entire list of recipients, or Hide to collapse that information.

- A thread is started based on its subject and sender. As replies are made, the messages continue to be categorized by subject because Re: is appended to it. It even remains in the thread if the initial subject continues to be in the message but other words are added.

- If a message includes a photo, Mail displays the photo in the body of the email message if it can (if the image is large, you might have to download it to see it). You can zoom in or out and scroll to view it just as you can for photos in other apps.

- If you tap a PDF attachment in a message and the iBooks app is installed on your iPhone, you're prompted to select Quick Look or Open in iBooks. If you select Open in iBooks, the document opens in the iBooks app where you can read it using the powerful features that app offers for reading ebooks and other documents.

- Some emails, especially HTML messages, are large and don't immediately download in their entirety. When you open a message that hasn't been fully downloaded, you see a message stating that this is the case. Tap the link to download the rest of the message.

- If you have other apps with which an attachment is compatible, you can open the attachment in that app. For example, if you have Pages installed on your iPhone and are viewing a Word document attachment, you can tap the Share icon and tap Open in Pages to open the document in the Pages app. You can get the same options by touching and holding on the attachment's icon in the body of a message until the Share menu appears.

Sending Email

You can send email from any of your accounts. Follow these steps for a basic walk-through of composing and sending a new email message:

⭐ **Honest Abe**   Yesterday
Gettysburg Address
⊜   Updated at 8:11 AM
              1 Unread   ✎ ①

① Tap the Compose icon at the bottom of any Mail screen. (If you are using an iPhone that supports 3D Touch, you can press down on the Mail app's icon and choose New Message to create a new email from a Home screen.) A new email message containing your signature is created. (For an explanation of where to configure a signature, see the table at the beginning of the chapter.)

Cancel   **New Message**   Send

To: sir   ⊕ ②

Sir William Wallace
home sirwilliamwallace@icloud.com

Sir William Wallace
work sirwilliamwallace@me.com

Sir William Wallace,
Edward & The Bruce   ⓘ

Sir William & Edward   ⓘ

② Tap the To field and type the first recipient's email address. As you type, Mail attempts to find matching addresses in your Contacts list, or in emails you've sent or received, and displays the matches it finds. These can include individuals or groups with which you've emailed. To select one of those addresses, tap it. Mail enters the rest of the address for you. Or, just keep entering information until the address is complete.

Cancel   **New Message**   Send

To: Sir William Wallace,   ⊕ ③

Cc/Bcc, From: bradmiser@icloud.com

③ Address the email using your Contacts app by tapping Add (+).

4 Use the Contacts app to find and select the contact to whom you want to address the message. (Refer to Chapter 6 for the details about working with contacts.) When you tap a contact who has only one email address, that address is pasted into the To field and you return to the New Message window. When you tap a contact with more than one email address, you move to that contact's screen, which shows all available addresses; tap the address to which you want to send the message.

5 Repeat steps 2–4 to add other recipients to the message.

6 Tap the Cc/Bcc, From line. The Cc and Bcc lines expand.

7 Follow the same procedures from steps 2–4 to add recipients to the Cc field. Use this field to include people who might benefit from reading the email, but don't have any responsibility for it (information only).

Q Rob| ⊗ Cancel

TOP NAME MATCHES

Robert the Bruce
robert_the_bruce_1@icloud.com

Cancel   **New Message**   Send

To: Sir William Wallace, Robert the Bruce, | ⊕

Brad Miser
bradmiser@icloud.com

Crabby Hayes
crabby_hayes@icloud.com

Cc/Bcc, From: bradmiser@icloud.com

Subject:

Cancel   **New Message**   Send

Cc: Abraham Lincoln, | ⊕

Bcc:

Have Multiple Email Accounts?

If you have more than one email account, it's important to know from which account you are sending a new message. If you tap the Compose icon while you are on the Mailboxes screen or the Inboxes screen, the From address is the one for the account you set as your default; otherwise, the From address is the email account associated with the Inbox you are in.

Removing Addresses

To remove an address, tap it so it is highlighted in a darker shade of blue; then tap the Delete (x) icon on the iPhone's keyboard.

8 Follow the same procedures from steps 2–4 to add recipients to the Bcc field. Use the Bcc field for those people whom you want to receive the message, but that you don't want others on the distribution list to see have received it (hidden recipients).

9 If the account you want to send the email from is shown in the From section, skip to step 11; to change the account from which the email is sent, tap the From field. The account wheel appears at the bottom of the screen.

10 Swipe up or down the wheel until the From address you want to use is shown at the center of the wheel.

11 Tap in the Subject line. The account selection wheel closes.

12 Type the subject of the message.

13 If you want to be notified when someone replies to the message you are creating, tap the bell; if not, skip to step 15.

Cancel	**New Message**	Send

Bcc: Edward the Longshanks, | ⊕   — **8**

From: bradmiser@icloud.com   — **9**

Subject:

From: bradm3@me.com

Subject: — **11**

Best,

Brad

bradmacosx@icloud.com

bradmiser@me.com

bradm3@me.com

bradmiser@icloud.com

bradm3@icloud.com

10

13

From: bradm3@me.com

Subject: T-28   🔔

12

14 Tap Notify Me. When anyone replies to the message, you are notified with a banner alert that appears at the top of the screen (assuming you have notifications for Mail enabled).

Receive notifications when anyone replies to this email thread.

🔔 Notify Me ──── **14**

Cancel

15 If you don't see the body of the message, swipe up the screen and it appears.

16 Tap in the body of the message, and type the message above your signature. Mail uses the iOS's text tools, attempts to correct spelling, provides Predictive Text, and makes suggestions to complete words. (Refer to Chapter 2 for the details of working with text.)

17 To make the keyboard larger, rotate the iPhone so that it is horizontal.

18 When you finish the message, tap Send. The progress of the send process is shown at the bottom of the screen; when the message has been sent, you hear the send mail sound you configured, which confirms that the message has been sent. If you enabled the reply notification for the message, you are notified when anyone replies to it.

17

Cancel   T-28   Send ── **18**

Cc: Abraham Lincoln

Bcc: Edward the Longshanks

From:

Subject: T-28   🔔

The E-Flite T-28 is amazing. It's really big and flies very smoothly. Landings are uneventful too.│ ── **16**

Best,

Brad

15

Start Writing Now, Finish Writing and Send Later

If you want to save a message you are creating without sending it, tap Cancel. A prompt appears; select Save Draft to save the message; if you don't want the message, tap Delete Draft instead. When you want to work on a draft message again, touch and hold down the Compose icon. After a moment, you see your most recent draft messages; tap the draft message you want to work on. You can make changes to the message and then send it or save it as a draft again. (You can also move into the Drafts folder under the account from which you are sending the message to select and work with draft messages; moving among folders is covered later in this chapter.)

Using Mail's Suggested Recipients

As you create messages, Mail suggests recipients based on the new message's current recipients. For example, if you regularly send emails to a group of people, when you add two or more people from that group, Mail suggests others you might want to include. As you add others to the message, Mail continues suggesting recipients based on the current recipient list. You can use these suggestions to quickly add more recipients to a new message.

Mail's suggestions for more recipients for the new message

1 Create a new message.

2 Add at least two recipients. Just below the To line, Mail suggests additional recipients for the new message based on other messages you have created.

3 Tap the additional recipients you want to add to the new message. (Mail sometimes suggests multiple recipients as a group if you have emailed that group before.) As you select these recipients, Mail keeps making suggestions and new people appear in the gray bars.

4 When you're done adding To recipients, tap in the next field you want to complete and continue creating the new message.

Replying to Email

Email is all about communication, and Mail makes it simple to reply to messages.

(1) Open the message you want to reply to.

(2) Tap the arrow icon.

(3) Tap Reply to reply to only the sender or, if there was more than one recipient, tap Reply All to reply to everyone who received the original message. The Re: screen appears showing a new message. Mail pastes the contents of the original message at the bottom of the body of the new message below your signature. The original content is in blue and is marked with a vertical line along the left side of the screen.

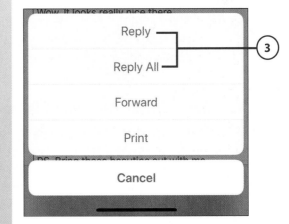

Re: Windy
Yesterday at 7:04 AM

I'm definitely heading out. Hope to enjoy some sun for a change!

Will

On Aug 30, 2018, at 07:02 AM, Brad Miser <bradmiser@icloud.com> wrote:

Wow. It looks really nice there.

I might brave the wind to try to fly.

How about you William and Robert?

Best,

Brad

PS. Bring these beauties out with m

Reply

Reply All

Forward

Print

Cancel

(4) Use the message tools to add or change the To, Cc, or Bcc recipients.

(5) Write your response.

(6) Tap Send. Mail sends your reply.

Cancel	**Re: Windy**	Send ── (6)

To: William Wallace   ⊕

Cc: Crabby Hayes, Robert the Bruce ──   ⊕ ── (4)

Bcc: ──

From: bradmiser@icloud.com

Subject: **Re: Windy**

No doubt about that! ☀ is awesome 🖐! ── (5)

Best,

Brad

I	I'm	The

1	2	3	4	5	6	7	8	9	0

-	/	:	;	(	)	$	&	@	"

Including a Photo or Video in a Message

To add a photo or video to a message you create (new, reply, or forward), tap twice in the body. Swipe to the left on the resulting toolbar (if you don't see it immediately) until you see the Insert Photo or Video command, and then tap it. Use the Photos app (see Chapter 14, "Viewing and Editing Photos and Video with the Photos App," for information about this app) to move to and select the photo or video you want to attach. Tap Choose. The photo or video you selected is added to the message.

Sending Email from All the Right Places

You can send email from a number of places on your iPhone. For example, you can share a photo with someone by viewing the photo, tapping the Share icon, and then tapping Mail. Or you can tap a contact's email address to send an email from your contacts list. In all cases, the iPhone uses Mail to create a new message that includes the appropriate content, such as a photo or link; you use Mail's tools to complete and send the email.

Print Email from Your iPhone

If you need to print a message, tap the arrow icon at the bottom of the screen and tap Print. To learn about printing from your iPhone, refer to Chapter 2.

Forwarding Emails

When you receive an email you think others should see, you can forward it to them.

(1) Read the message you want to forward.

(2) If you want to include only part of the current content in the message you forward, tap where you want the forwarded content to start. This is useful (and considerate!) when only a part of the message applies to the people to whom you are forwarding it. If you want to forward the entire message, skip to step 4.

(3) Use the text selection tools to select the content you want to include in your forwarded message.

(4) Tap the arrow icon.

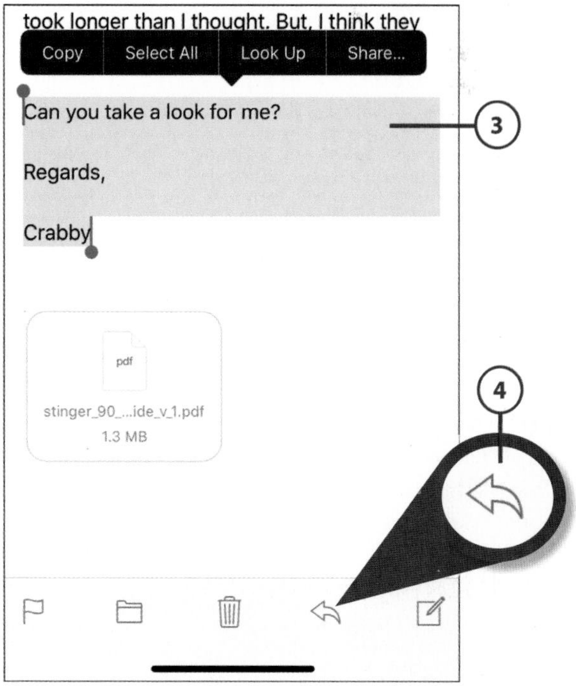

Yesterday at 7:06 AM

Well, with these claws, installing the brakes took longer than I thought. But, I think they will work great.

Can you take a look for me?

Regards,

Crabby

pdf

stinger_90_...ide_v_1.pdf
1.3 MB

took longer than I thought. But, I think they

Copy   Select All   Look Up   Share...

Can you take a look for me?

Regards,

Crabby

pdf

stinger_90_...ide_v_1.pdf
1.3 MB

(5) Tap Forward.

(6) If the message includes attachments, tap Include at the prompt if you also want to forward the attachments, or tap Don't Include if you don't want them included. The Forward screen appears. Mail pastes the contents of the message that you selected, or the entire content if you didn't select anything, at the bottom of the message below your signature. If you included attachments, they are added to the new message as well.

(7) Address the forwarded message using the same tools you use when you create a new message.

(8) Type your commentary about the message above your signature.

(9) Tap Send. Mail forwards the message.

Large Messages

Some emails, especially HTML messages, are so large that they don't immediately download in their entirety. When you forward a message whose content or attachments haven't fully downloaded, Mail prompts you to download the "missing" content before forwarding. If you choose not to download the content or attachments, Mail forwards only the downloaded part of the message.

Managing Email

Following are some ways you can manage your email. For example, you can check for new messages, see the status of messages, delete messages, and organize messages using the folders associated with your email accounts.

Checking for New Email

Swipe down to update your email

To manually retrieve messages, swipe down from the top of any Inbox or the Mailboxes screen. The screen "stretches" down and when you lift your finger, the Mail app checks for and downloads new messages.

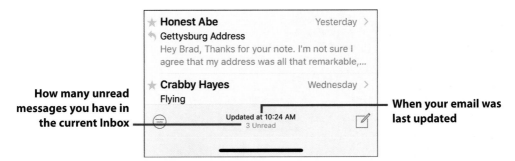

How many unread messages you have in the current Inbox

When your email was last updated

Mail also retrieves messages whenever you move into the app or into any Inbox or all your Inboxes. Of course, it also retrieves messages according to the selected Fetch New Data option. It downloads new messages immediately when they arrive in your account if Push is enabled or automatically at defined intervals if you've set Fetch to get new email periodically. (Refer to Chapter 3 for an explanation of these options and how to set them.)

The bottom of the Mailboxes or an Inbox screen always shows when email was most recently downloaded to your iPhone; on the bottom of Inbox screens, you also see the number of new email messages (if there are any unread messages).

Understanding the Status of Email

Message you've forwarded

Message from a VIP

Message to which you've replied

Message with attachments

Unread message

Message you've flagged

When you view an Inbox or a message thread, you see icons next to each message to indicate its status (except for messages that you've read but not done anything else with and that aren't from a VIP, which aren't marked with any icon).

Managing Email from the Message Screen

Tap to delete a message

To delete a message while reading it, tap the Trash icon. If you enabled the warning preference, confirm the deletion and the message is deleted. If you disabled the confirmation prompt, the message is deleted immediately.

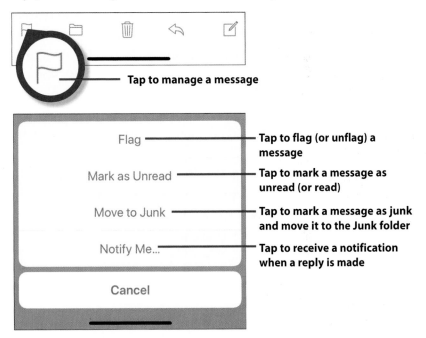

Tap to manage a message

Flag ————— **Tap to flag (or unflag) a message**

Mark as Unread ————— **Tap to mark a message as unread (or read)**

Move to Junk ————— **Tap to mark a message as junk and move it to the Junk folder**

Notify Me... ————— **Tap to receive a notification when a reply is made**

Cancel

To take other action on a message you are reading, tap the Flag icon. On the menu that opens, you can choose a number of commands. The action you select is performed on the message you are viewing.

Dumpster Diving

As long as an account's trash hasn't been emptied, you can work with a message you've deleted by moving to the account's screen and opening its Trash folder. Over time, a lot of deleted messages can accumulate in the Trash folder. To get rid of these messages, open the Trash folder under the account. Tap Delete All and tap Delete All again at the prompt. The deleted messages are removed from the folder and are gone forever. This frees up space on the cloud as well as on your iPhone.

Where Has My Email Gone?

When you send an email to the Archive folder, it isn't deleted. To access messages you've archived, tap the Back icon in the upper-left corner of the screen until you get to the Mailboxes screen. Tap the Archive folder under the account to which email you've archived was sent.

Managing Email from an Inbox

Previously in this chapter, you saw the settings options for swipe actions for email. You can use those to configure how right and left swipes affect your email from an Inbox screen, such as flagging a message with a left swipe. (Depending on the choices you set for the swipe preferences, the results you see when you swipe might be different than shown here. However, the swipe right or swipe left actions still reveal commands you can use unless you chose None in the settings, in which case nothing happens when you swipe on a message.)

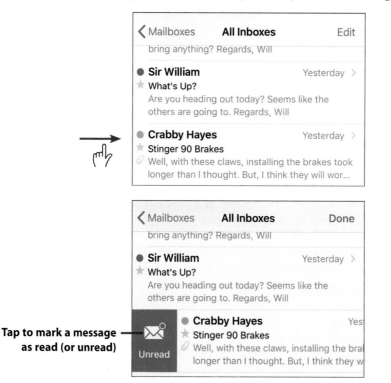

Swipe to the right on a message to change its read status. If the message has been read, you can reset its status to unread, or, if it hasn't been read, you can mark it as read.

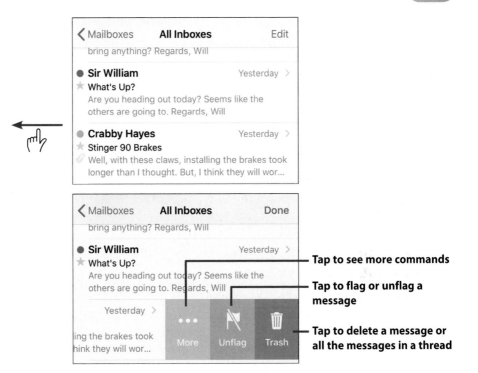

Tap to see more commands

Tap to flag or unflag a message

Tap to delete a message or all the messages in a thread

Swipe to the left on a message to see several options. Tap Trash to delete the message or messages if you swiped on a thread (the number of messages that will be deleted is shown in parentheses). Tap Flag to flag the message or Unflag to remove the flag. Tap More to open a menu of additional commands.

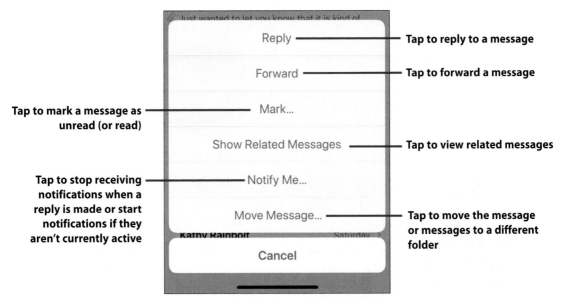

Tap to reply to a message

Tap to forward a message

Tap to mark a message as unread (or read)

Tap to view related messages

Tap to stop receiving notifications when a reply is made or start notifications if they aren't currently active

Tap to move the message or messages to a different folder

When you tap More, you see other commands for actions you can take on the message, such as replying to it or moving it to a different folder.

No-Stop Swiping to Delete

If you quickly swipe all the way to the left on a message on an Inbox screen, the message is deleted in one fell swipe.

Managing Multiple Emails at the Same Time

You can also manage email by selecting multiple messages on an Inbox screen, which is more efficient because you can take action on multiple messages at the same time.

1. Move to an Inbox screen showing messages you want to manage.

2. Tap Edit. A selection circle appears next to each message, and actions appear at the bottom of the screen.

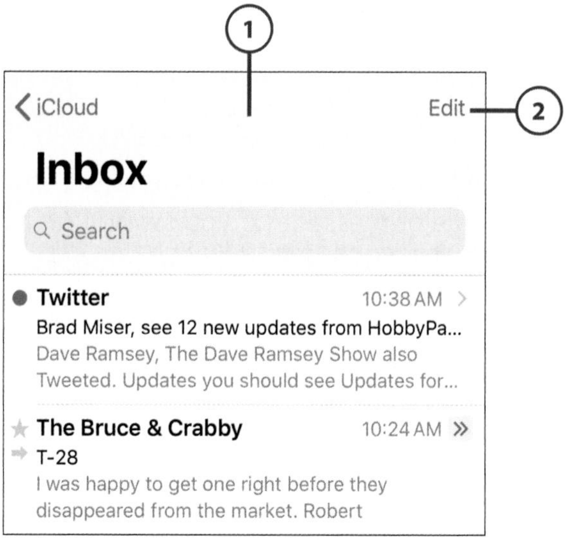

3 Select the message(s) you want to manage by tapping their selection circles. As you select each message, its selection circle turns blue and is marked with a check mark. At the top of the screen, you see how many messages you have selected.

Coming Unthreaded

When you select a collapsed thread, you automatically select all the messages in that thread. So, if you then delete what you selected, you delete the entire thread. If you expand a thread, you can select individual messages in that thread.

When you use an iPhone Plus in the horizontal orientation, you see the selection screen on the left and a preview of what you have selected in the right pane. Even though it looks a bit different, it works in the same way.

4 To delete the selected messages, tap Trash. Mail deletes the selected messages and exits Edit mode. (If you enabled the warning prompt, you have to confirm the deletion.)

5 To change the status of the selected messages, tap Mark.

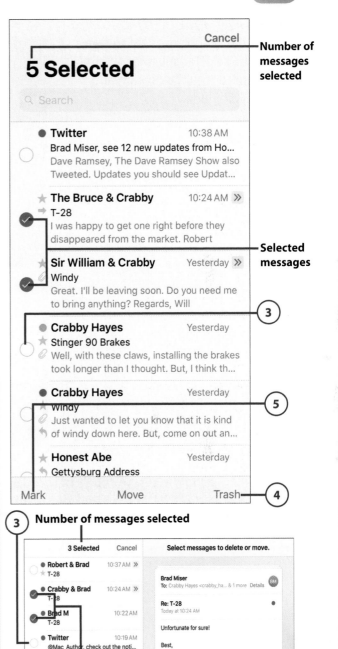

Number of messages selected

Selected messages

Number of messages selected

Selected messages

6) Tap the action you want to take on the selected messages. You return to the Inbox screen and exit Edit mode.

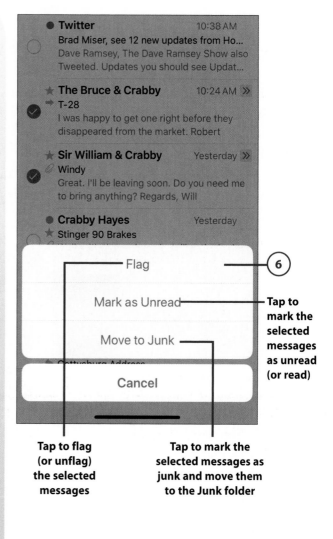

Tap to flag (or unflag) the selected messages

Tap to mark the selected messages as junk and move them to the Junk folder

Tap to mark the selected messages as unread (or read)

Organizing Email from the Message Screen

You can have various folders to organize email, and you can move messages among these folders. For example, you can recover a message from the Trash by moving it from the Trash folder back to the Inbox.

(1) Open a message you want to move to a different folder.

(2) Tap the Folder icon. The Mailboxes screen appears. At the top of this screen is the message you are moving. Under that are the mailboxes available under the current account.

Back to Where You've Been

If you repeatedly move messages into the same folder, you might see a prompt after step 2 that has two options. Tap Move to "*lastfolder*," where lastfolder is the name of the folder you've recently moved messages into, to move the selected messages into that folder; the selected messages are moved and you exit the move process. Tap Other Mailbox to move to step 3 to select a specific folder into which you want to move the messages.

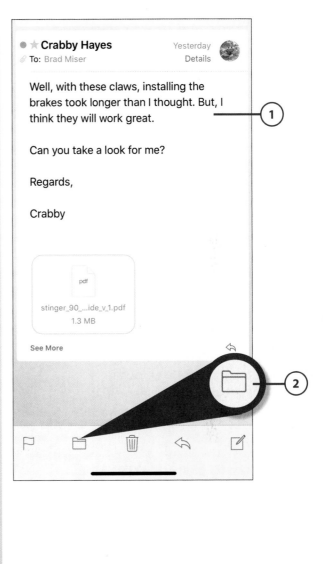

Move to Other Accounts

If you want to move selected messages to a folder under a different account, tap Accounts in the upper-left corner of the screen. Tap the account to which you want to move the message (not all accounts will be available; if an account is grayed out, you can't move a message to it). Then tap the mailbox into which you want to move the message.

Makin' Mailboxes

You can create a new mailbox to organize your email. Move to the Mailboxes screen and tap Edit. Then, tap New Mailbox located at the bottom of the screen. Type the name of the new mailbox. Tap the Mailbox Location and then choose where you want the new mailbox located (for example, you can place the new mailbox inside an existing one). Tap Save. You can then store messages in the new mailbox.

(3) Swipe up and down the screen to browse the mailboxes available in the current account.

(4) Tap the mailbox to which you want to move the message. The message moves to that mailbox, and you move to the next message in the list you were viewing.

When you use an iPhone Plus in the horizontal orientation, you see the list of folders you are navigating in the left pane and a preview of the messages you have selected in the right pane.

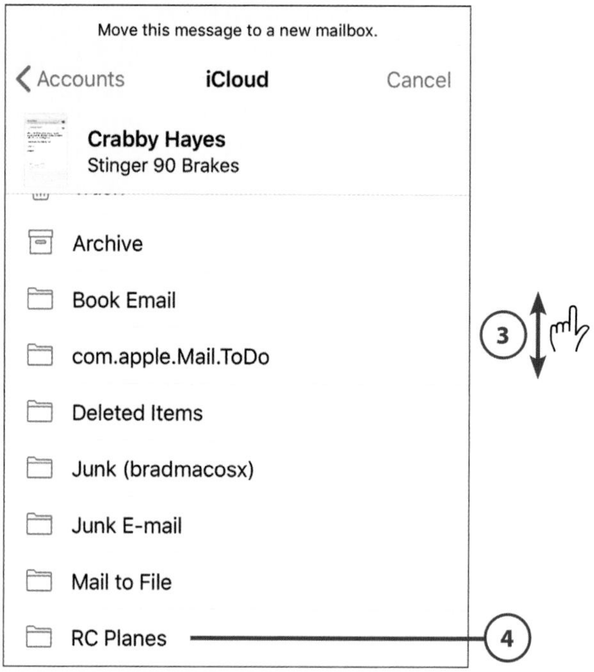

Organizing Email from the Inbox

Like deleting messages, organizing email from the Inbox can be made more efficient because you can move multiple messages at the same time.

(1) Move to an Inbox screen showing messages you want to move to a folder.

(2) Tap Edit. A selection circle appears next to each message. Actions appear at the bottom of the screen.

Move this message to a new mailbox.

‹ Accounts   **iCloud**   Cancel

Crabby Hayes
Stinger 90 Brakes

Archive
Book Email
com.apple.Mail.ToDo
Deleted Items
Junk (bradmacosx)
Junk E-mail
Mail to File
RC Planes

‹ iCloud   Edit

Inbox

Q Search

● **Twitter**   10:38 AM ›
Brad Miser, see 12 new updates from HobbyPa...
Dave Ramsey, The Dave Ramsey Show also Tweeted. Updates you should see Updates for...

● **Crabby & The Bruce**   10:24 AM »
☆ T-28
↰ I was looking at getting one. Too bad they are discontinued! Crabby

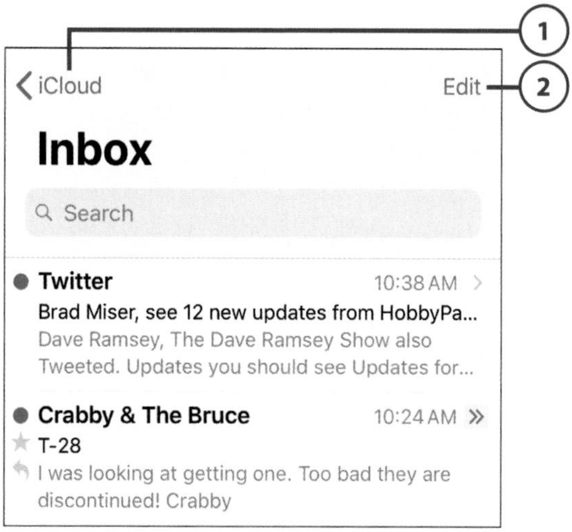

3 Select the messages you want to move by tapping their selection circles. As you select each message, its selection circle turns blue and is marked with a check mark.

4 Tap Move. You're prompted to move the messages into the folder you most recently moved messages into or to choose a different folder.

Going Where No Message Has Gone Before

If you haven't recently moved messages into a folder, you won't see the prompt in step 5. Instead, you move directly to the Mailboxes screen as described in step 7.

5 To move the messages into a folder you have previously used, tap Move to "*foldername*" where *foldername* is the name of that folder and skip the rest of these steps.

6 To move the message into a folder that wasn't the one you used most recently, tap Other Mailbox. The Mailboxes screen appears. At the top of this screen is the message you are moving. Under that are the mailboxes available under the current account.

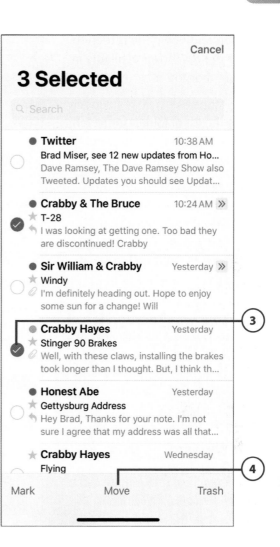

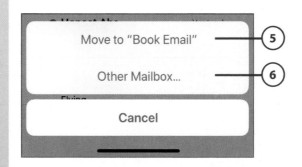

(7) Swipe up and down the screen to browse the mailboxes available in the current account.

On an iPhone Plus held horizontally, you see the list of folders in the left pane and a preview of the selected messages in the right pane.

(8) Tap the mailbox to which you want to move the selected messages. They are moved into that folder, and you return to the previous screen, which is no longer in Edit mode.

Threading Your Way Through Email

When you select a thread, you select all the messages in that thread. Whatever action you select is taken on all the thread's messages at the same time.

Viewing Messages in a Mailbox

You can open a mailbox within an account to work with the messages it contains. For example, you might want to open the Trash mailbox to recover a deleted message.

(1) Move to the Mailboxes screen.

(2) If necessary, swipe up the screen to see the email accounts you are using. Each account has its own section showing the mailboxes stored on that account.

Move these messages to a new mailbox.

‹ Accounts   **iCloud**   Cancel

Brad Miser, Crabby Hayes
3 messages

Archive

Book Email

com.apple.Mail.ToDo

Deleted Items

Junk (bradmacosx)

Junk E-mail

Mail to File

RC Planes ———————— (8)

(7)

Edit ———— (1)

Mailboxes

All Inboxes   8 >

Your RC Companion   >

Gmail   1 >

indy.rr.com   >

iCloud   7 >

★ VIP   (i) 7 >

● Flagged   1 >

● Unread   8 >

⫝ Attachments   3 >

All Drafts   1 >

YOUR RC COMPANION   >

GMAIL   1 >

INDY.RR.COM   >

(2)

3) If you don't see an account's mailboxes, expand the account by tapping its arrow.

4) Tap the folder or mailbox containing the messages you want to view. You see the messages it contains. In some cases, this can take a few moments for the messages to be downloaded if that folder or mailbox hasn't been accessed recently.

5) Tap a message or thread to view it. (If you want to move messages, such as to recover messages that are in the Trash, see "Organizing Email from the Inbox.")

Mailboxes		Edit
📎 Attachments		3
📄 All Drafts		1
YOUR RC COMPANION		⌄
📬 Inbox		>
📄 Drafts		>
✈ Sent		>
🗙 Junk		>
🗑 Trash		>
🗂 Junkmail		>
🗂 SentMail		>
🗂 Trash		>
GMAIL		1 >
INDY.RR.COM		>
ICLOUD		7 >

Updated Just Now   📝

Expanded account

Collapsed account

❬ Mailboxes   Edit

Sent

📎 **Brad Miser**   8/27/17 >
🔔 Plane Photos
Here are some nice shots of my fleet! Enjoy!
Robert Best, Brad Miser Your RC Companion y...

Brad Miser   8/25/17 >
Just Got Back
Hey Brad, Just returned from the mission. It was
very succesful! I tried that maneuver you sugg...

📎 **Janne Paananen**   1/18/17 >
Re: Mig 21 and Taranis
Hi Janne, I'm sorry for the long delay. It has
been a crazy travel month for me. Here is the e...

Changing Mailboxes

You can change the mailboxes that appear on the Mailboxes screen. For example, you can display the Attachments mailbox to make messages with attachments easier to get to. Move to the Mailboxes screen and tap Edit. To cause a mailbox to be visible, tap it so that it has a check mark in its circle. To hide a mailbox, tap its check mark so that it shows an empty circle. Drag the Order icon for mailboxes up or down the screen to change the order in which mailboxes appear. Tap Add Mailbox to add a mailbox not shown on the list. Tap Done to save your changes.

Saving Images Attached to Email

Email is a great way to share photos. When you receive a message that includes photos, you can save them on your iPhone.

1. Move to the message screen of an email that contains one or more photos or images.

2. Swipe up the message to see all the images it contains.

From: ★ Honest Abe 〉

To: Brad Miser 〉   Hide

Plane Photos ————————————— 1

Today at 11:22 AM

Hey Brad,

Here are some photos I took at the field.

Sincerely.

Abe

3 Touch and hold on an image (if you are using an iPhone that supports 3D Touch, don't press down when you touch or you Peek at the image instead). The Share tools appear.

4 Swipe to the left until you see the Save Image icons.

5 Tap Save Image to save just the image you touched or tap Save X Images, where X is the number of images attached to the message, to save all the attachments. (If there is only one image, the command is just Save Image.) The images are saved in the Photos app on your iPhone. (See Chapter 14 for help working with the Photos app.)

Filtering Email

You can quickly filter the email messages in an inbox as follows:

(1) Open the inbox you want to filter.

(2) Tap the Filter icon. The contents of the inbox are filtered by the current criteria, which is indicated by the terms under "Filtered by." The Filter icon is highlighted in blue to show the inbox is filtered.

(3) Tap the current filter criteria.

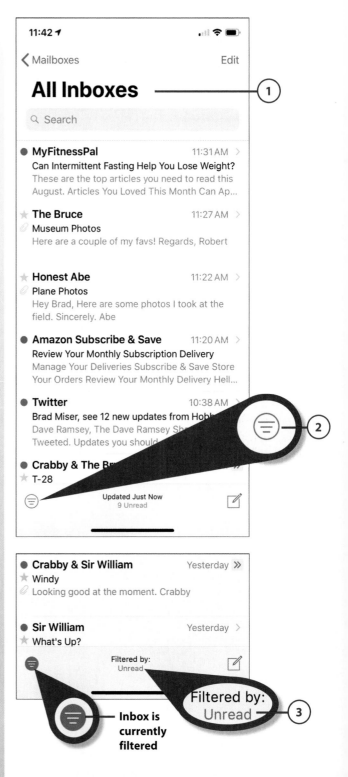

4 Set the criteria by which you want to filter the messages in the inbox; the current criteria are indicated by check marks or green switches. For example, tap To: Me to only show messages on which you are included in the To block.

5 Tap Done. You return to the inbox and only messages that meet your filter criteria are shown.

6 Tap the Filter icon to display all the messages again.

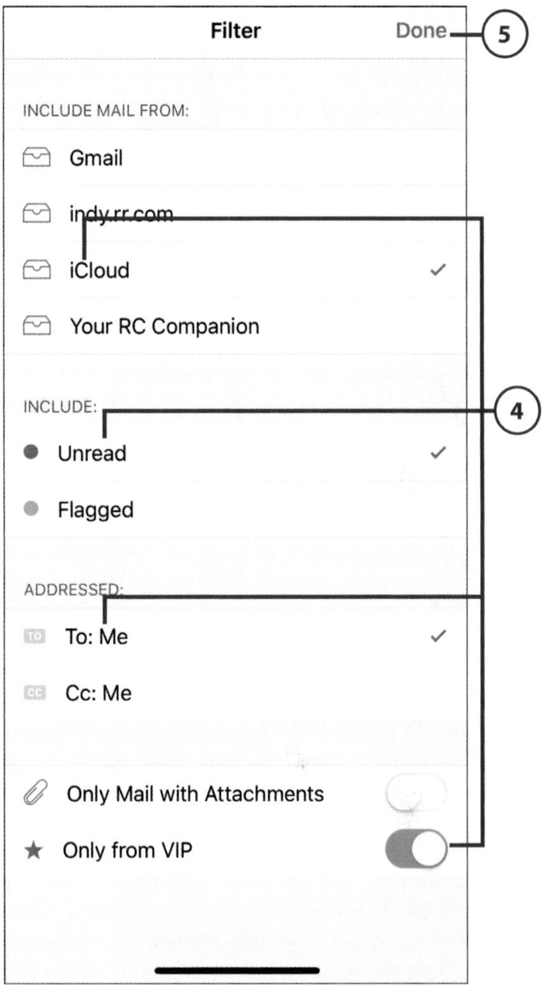

Filter	Done

INCLUDE MAIL FROM:

✉ Gmail

✉ indy.rr.com

✉ iCloud ✓

✉ Your RC Companion

INCLUDE:

● Unread ✓

● Flagged

ADDRESSED:

TO To: Me ✓

CC Cc: Me

🖉 Only Mail with Attachments

★ Only from VIP

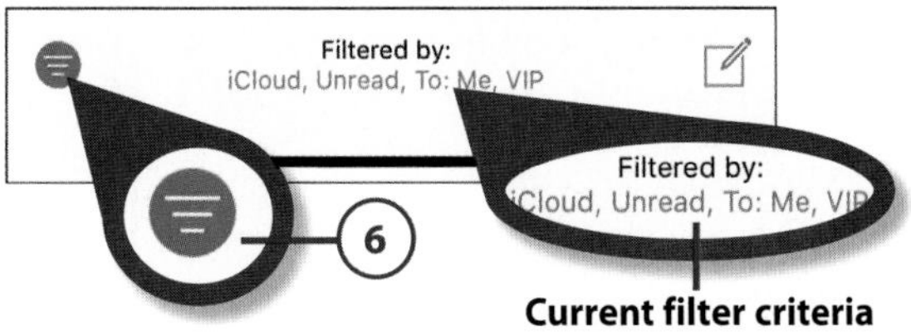

Filtered by:
iCloud, Unread, To: Me, VIP

Filtered by:
iCloud, Unread, To: Me, VIP

Current filter criteria

Searching Your Email

As you accumulate email, you might want to find specific messages. For example, suppose you want to retrieve an email message that was related to a specific topic, but you can't remember where you stored it. Mail's Search tool can help you find messages like this quite easily.

① Move to the screen you want to search, such as an account's Inbox or a folder's screen. (This is optional as you can choose an area to search later in the process.)

② If necessary, swipe down to move to the top of the screen to display the Search tool.

③ Tap in the Search tool.

④ Enter the text for which you want to search. As you type, Mail makes suggestions about what you might be searching for. These appear in different sections based on the type of search Mail thinks you are doing, such as People, Subjects, and more.

⑤ To use one of Mail's suggestions to search, such as a person, tap their name; or continue typing your search term and when you are done, tap Search. Mail searches for messages based on your search criterion and you see the results.

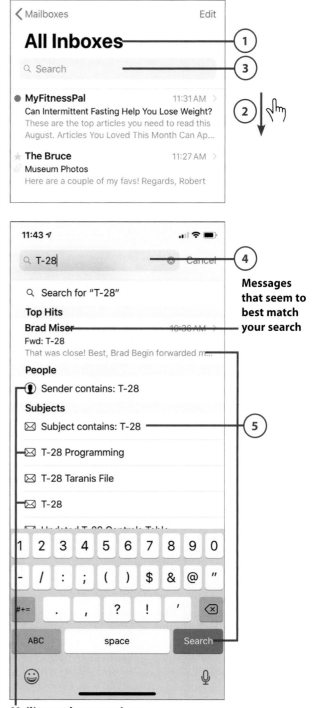

Messages that seem to best match your search

Mail's search suggestions

(6) To search for the term in the subject field, tap Subject, or to search in the body, tap Message.

(7) Tap Search.

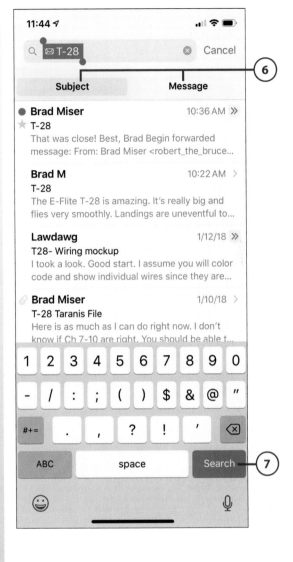

8 To search in all your mailboxes, tap All Mailboxes, or to search in only the current mailbox, tap Current Mailbox.

9 Work with the messages you found, such as tapping a message to read it. Tap the Back icon in the upper-left corner of the screen to return to the search results.

10 To clear a search and exit Search mode, tap Cancel.

11 To clear a search but remain in Search mode, tap Clear (x).

When you use an iPhone Plus horizontally, searching is even better, because you can select a found message in the search results in the left pane and read it in the right pane.

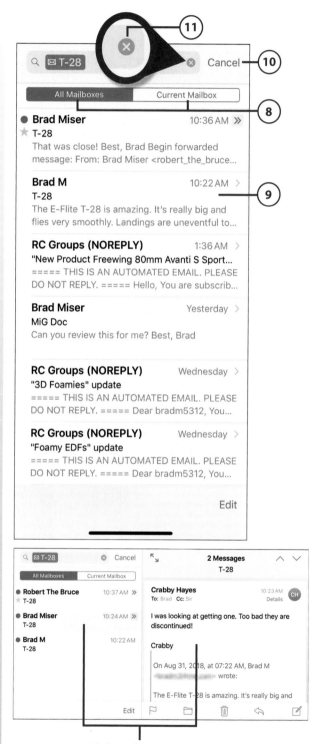

Selected message

Working with VIPs

The VIP feature enables you to indicate specific people as your VIPs. When a VIP sends you email, it is marked with a star icon and goes into the special VIP mailbox so you can access these important messages easily. You can also create specific notifications for your VIPs, such as a unique sound when you receive email from a VIP (see Chapter 4).

Designating VIPs

To designate someone as a VIP, perform the following steps:

(1) View information about the person you want to be a VIP by tapping his name in the From or Cc fields as described earlier in the chapter.

(2) Swipe up the Info screen.

(3) Tap Add to VIP. The person is designated as a VIP and any email from that person receives the VIP treatment.

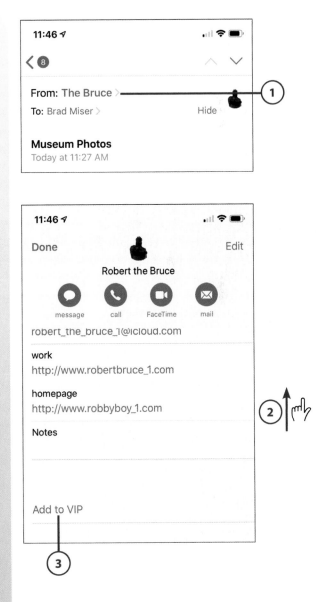

Accessing VIP Email

To work with VIP email, do the following:

(1) Move to the Mailboxes screen.

(2) Tap VIP.

(3) Work with the VIP messages you see.

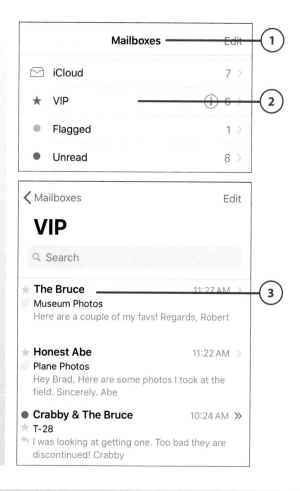

>>>Go Further
MORE ON VIPS

Here are a few more tidbits on VIPs:

- Messages from VIPs are marked with the gray star icon no matter in which mailbox you see the messages.

- To see the list of your current VIPs, move to the Mailboxes screen and tap the Info icon (i) for the VIP mailbox. You see everyone currently designated as a VIP. Tap Add VIP to add more people to the list. Tap VIP Alerts to create special notifications for VIPs.

- To return a VIP to normal status, view his information and tap Remove from VIP.

Managing Junk Email

Junk email, also known as spam, is an unfortunate reality of email. No matter what precautions you take, you are going to receive some spam emails. Of course, it is good practice to be careful about where you provide your email address to limit the amount of spam you receive.

Consider using a "sacrificial" email account when you shop, post messages, and in the other places where you're likely to get spammed. If you do get spammed, you can stop using the sacrificial account and create another one to take its place. Or you can delete the sacrificial account from your iPhone and continue to use it on your computer where you likely have better spam tools in place. If you have an iCloud account, you can set up and use email aliases for this purpose.

The Mail app on the iPhone includes a very basic junk management tool. However, if you use an account or an email application on a computer that features a junk mail/spam tool, it acts on mail sent to your iPhone, too. For example, if you configure spam tools for a Gmail account, those tools act on email before it reaches your iPhone. Similarly, if you use the Mail app on a Mac, its rules and junk filter work on email as you receive it; the results of this are also reflected on your iPhone. To change how you deal with junk email on your iPhone, change the junk email settings for your account online (such as for Gmail) or by changing how an email app on a computer deals with junk mail. The results of these changes are reflected in the Mail app on your iPhone.

Many email accounts, including iCloud and Gmail, have Junk folders; these folders are available in the Mail app on your iPhone. You can open the Junk folder under an account to see the messages that are placed there.

Marking Junk Email

You can perform basic junk email management on your iPhone by doing the following:

(1) When you view a message that is junk, tap the Flag icon.

(2) Tap Move to Junk. The message is moved from the inbox to the Junk folder for the account to which it was sent. Future messages from the same sender go into the Junk folder automatically.

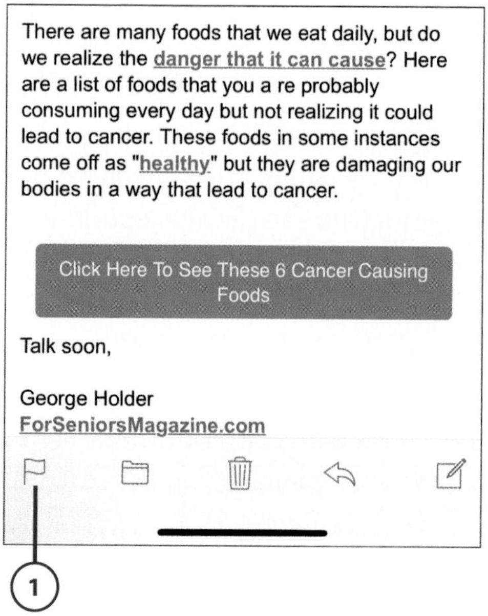

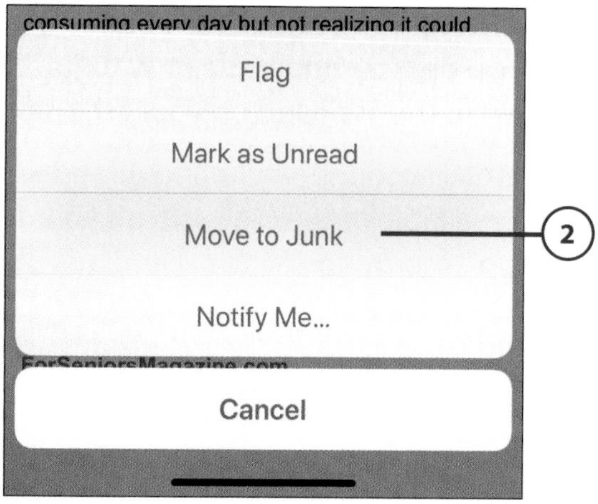

There are many foods that we eat daily, but do we realize the danger that it can cause? Here are a list of foods that you a re probably consuming every day but not realizing it could lead to cancer. These foods in some instances come off as "healthy" but they are damaging our bodies in a way that lead to cancer.

Click Here To See These 6 Cancer Causing Foods

Talk soon,

George Holder
ForSeniorsMagazine.com

consuming every day but not realizing it could

Flag

Mark as Unread

Move to Junk

Notify Me...

ForSeniorsMagazine.com

Cancel

Junk It

You can also move a message to the Junk folder by swiping slowly to the left on it, tapping More, and then tapping Move to Junk. If you swipe quickly all the way to the left side of the screen, you'll delete the message instead.

Junk It or Trash It?

The primary difference between moving a message to the Junk folder or deleting it is that when you mark a message as junk, future messages from the same sender are moved to the Junk folder automatically. When you delete a message, it doesn't change how future messages from the same sender are handled.

Send messages from
other apps too, such
as to share photos

Tap to configure
Messages

Tap to send and
receive text messages,
photos, video, and
more

In this chapter, you'll explore the texting and messaging functionality your iPhone has to offer. Topics include the following:

→ Getting started
→ Preparing the Messages app for messaging
→ Sending messages
→ Receiving, reading, and replying to messages
→ Working with messages

9

Sending, Receiving, and Managing Texts and iMessages

You can use the iPhone's Messages app to send, receive, and converse; you can also send and receive images, videos, and links with this app. You can enhance your messages in a number of ways, such as creating dynamic messages, sending Digital Touches, including animojis, and using apps. You can maintain any number of conversations with other people at the same time, and your iPhone lets you know whenever you receive a new message via audible and visible notifications that you can configure. In addition to conversations with other people, many organizations use text messaging to send important updates, such as airlines communicating flight status changes. You might find messaging to be one of the most used functions of your iPhone.

Getting Started

Texting, also called messaging, is an especially great way to communicate with others when you have something quick you want to say, such as an update on your arrival time. It's much easier to send a quick text, "I'll be there in 10 minutes," than it is to make a phone call or send an email. Texting/messaging is designed for relatively short messages. It is also a great way to share photos and videos quickly and easily. And if you communicate with younger people, you might find they tend to respond quite well since texting is a primary form of communication for them.

There are two types of messages that you can send with and receive on your iPhone using the Messages app.

The Messages app can send and receive text messages via your cell network based on telephone numbers. Using this option, you can send text messages to and receive messages from anyone who has a cell phone capable of text messaging.

You can also use the iMessage function within the Messages app to send and receive messages via an email account, to and from other iOS devices (using iOS 5 or newer), or Macs (running OS X Lion or newer). This is especially useful when your cell phone account has a limit on the number of texts you can send via your cell account; when you use iMessage for texting, there is no limit on the amount of data you can send when you are connected to the Internet using a Wi-Fi network and so you incur no additional costs for your messages. This is also really useful because you can send messages to, and receive messages from, iPad, Apple Watch, and Mac users. The limitations to iMessage are that it only works on those supported devices, and the people with whom you are messaging have to set up iMessage on their device (which isn't difficult).

You don't need to be overly concerned about which type is which because the Messages app makes it clear which type a message is by color and text. It uses iMessage when available and automatically uses cellular texting when it isn't possible to use iMessage.

You can configure iMessage on multiple devices, such as an iPhone and an iPad. This means you have the same text messages on each device. So, you can start a conversation on your iPhone, and then continue it on an iPad at a later time.

Preparing the Messages App for Messaging

Like most of the apps described in this book, there are settings for the Messages app you can configure to choose how the app works for you. For example, you can configure iMessage so you can communicate via email addresses, configure how standard text messages are managed, and so on. You can also choose to block messages from specific people.

Setting Your Text and iMessage Preferences

Perform the following steps to set up Messages on your iPhone:

1. Move to the Settings app and tap Messages.

2. Set the iMessage switch to on (green).

3. Set the Show Contact Photos switch to on (green) if you want images associated with your contacts to appear in messages.

4. Slide the Send Read Receipts switch to on (green) to notify others when you read their messages. Be aware that receipts apply only to iMessages (not texts sent over a cellular network).

5. Slide the Send as SMS switch to on (green) to send texts via your cellular network when iMessage is unavailable. If your cellular account has a limit on the number of texts you can send, you might want to leave this set to off (white) so you use only iMessage when you are texting. If your account has unlimited texting, you should set this to on (green).

6. Tap Send & Receive.

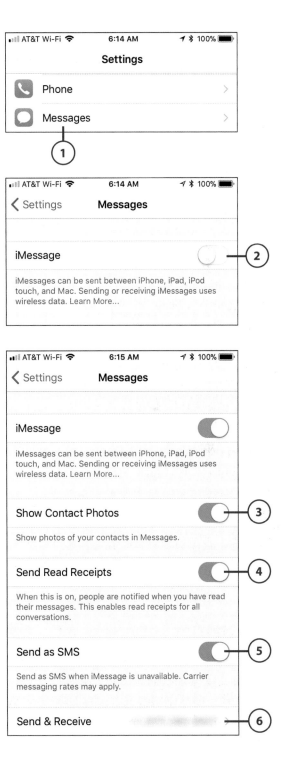

7 Tap Use your Apple ID for iMessage. You sign into your Apple ID. At the top of the iMessage screen, you see your Apple ID. You also see the phone number of your iPhone and the email addresses associated with your Apple ID that can be used in the Messages app.

8 To prevent an email address from being available to others to send you messages, in the YOU CAN RECEIVE IMESSAGES TO AND REPLY FROM section, tap it so it doesn't have a check mark.

9 To enable an address so it can be used for messages, tap it so it does have a check mark.

10 Tap the phone number or email address you want to use by default when you start a new text conversation in the START NEW CONVERSATIONS FROM section. Because there are no data or media limitations with iMessages, you usually want to choose your email address as the default way to start a conversation.

11 Tap the Back icon (<).

Apple ID?

These steps assume you are already signed into an Apple ID on your iPhone (see Chapter 3, "Setting Up and Using an Apple ID, iCloud, and Other Online Accounts" for help with an Apple ID). If you haven't, when you perform step 7, you're prompted to provide an Apple ID and password to sign into that Apple ID. If you are already signed into an Apple ID for Messages and see your Apple ID at the top of the iMessage screen, you can skip step 7. If you want to change the Apple ID currently being used for iMessage, tap Send & Receive, tap the Apple ID shown at the top of the iMessage screen, and then tap Sign Out. You can then sign in to a different Apple ID for Messages.

(12) Tap Text Message Forwarding; if you don't see this option, your cell phone carrier doesn't support it and you can skip to step 14.

(13) Set the switch to on (green) for devices on which you want to be able to receive and send text messages using your iPhone's cell phone function (this doesn't affect messages sent via iMessages because they go to all the devices on which your Apple ID is being used for iMessages automatically).

(14) Tap the Back icon (<).

Code Required?

In some cases, when you perform step 13, you are prompted to enter a code for that device. This code appears on the device you are enabling; for example, if you turned the switch for a Mac on, the code appears on that Mac. You need to enter that code at the prompt on your iPhone and tap Allow to finish the process.

Show Contact Photos	
Show photos of your contacts in Messages.	
Text Message Forwarding	1 Device >
Allow your iPhone text messages to also be sent and received on other devices signed in to your iMessage account.	

(12)

(14)

.ıll AT&T Wi-Fi 📶   6:16 AM   🢅 ✷ 100% ▬

< Back   **Text Message Forwarding**

Allow these devices to send and receive text messages from this iPhone.

Brad's Mac Mini (Mac)		— (13)
Brad M Miser's iPad (iPad)		
iPad (iPad)		

15 Swipe up the screen to see the SMS/MMS section.

16 Set the MMS Messaging switch to off (white) if you don't want to allow photos and videos to be included in messages sent via your phone's cellular network. You might want to disable this option if your provider charges more for these types of messages—or if you simply don't want to deal with anything but text in your messages.

17 Set the Group Messaging switch to on (green) to keep messages you send to a group of people organized by the group. When enabled, replies you receive to messages you send to groups (meaning more than one person on a single message) are shown on a group message screen where each reply from anyone in the group is included on the same screen. If this is off (white), when someone replies to a message sent to a group, the message is separated out as if the original message was just to that person. (The steps in this chapter assume Group Messaging is on.)

18 Set the Show Subject Field switch to on (green) to add a subject field to your messages. This divides text messages into two sections; the upper section is for a subject, and you type your message in the lower section. This is not commonly used in text messages, and the steps in this chapter assume this setting is off.

●ıl AT&T Wi-Fi 🔍	6:16 AM ⌁ ✴ 100% ▬
‹ Settings	**Messages**
Send & Receive	3 Addresses ›
SMS/MMS	
MMS Messaging	⬤○
Group Messaging	⬤○
Show Subject Field	○
Character Count	○
Blocked	›
MESSAGE HISTORY	
Keep Messages	Forever ›

15
16
17
18

19 Set the Character Count switch to on (green) to display the number of characters you've written compared to the number allowed (such as 59/160). When it is off, you don't see a character count for messages you send. Technically, text messages you send via the cellular network are limited to 160 characters, so showing the character count helps you see where you are relative to this limit (iMessages don't have a limit). I don't use this setting so you won't see it in the figures in this chapter, but if character count is important to you, you should enable this.

20 Use the Blocked option to block people from texting you (see the next task).

21 Tap Keep Messages.

22 Tap the length of time for which you want to keep messages.

23 If you tapped something other than Forever, tap Delete. The messages on your iPhone older than the length of time you selected in step 22 are deleted.

24 Tap the Back icon (<).

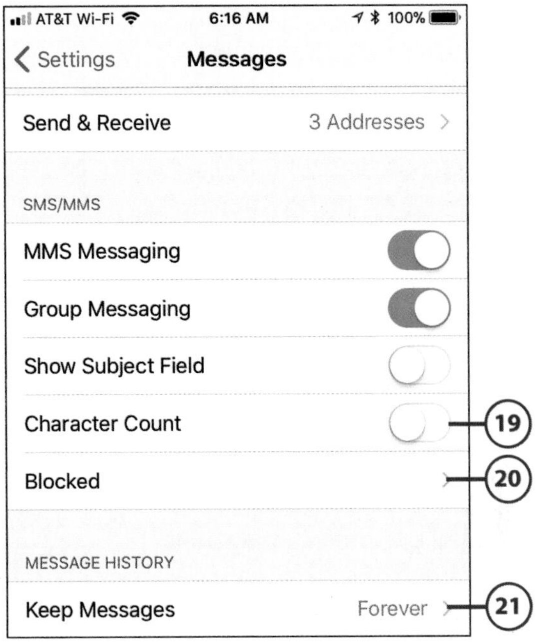

AT&T Wi-Fi	6:16 AM	100%

‹ Settings   **Messages**

Send & Receive   3 Addresses ›

SMS/MMS

MMS Messaging

Group Messaging

Show Subject Field

Character Count — **19**

Blocked › — **20**

MESSAGE HISTORY

Keep Messages   Forever › — **21**

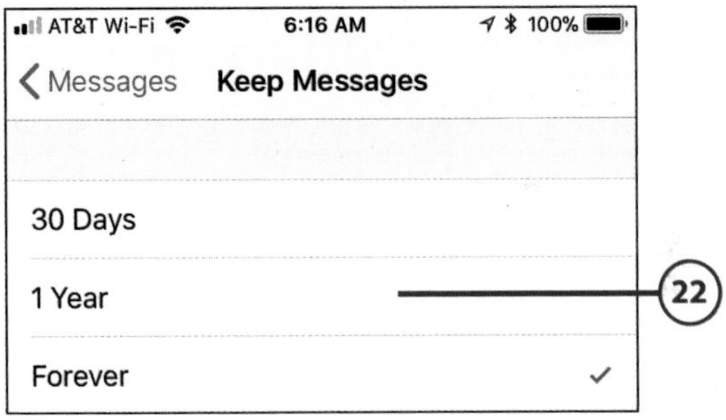

‹ Messages   **Keep Messages**

30 Days

1 Year — **22**

Forever ✓

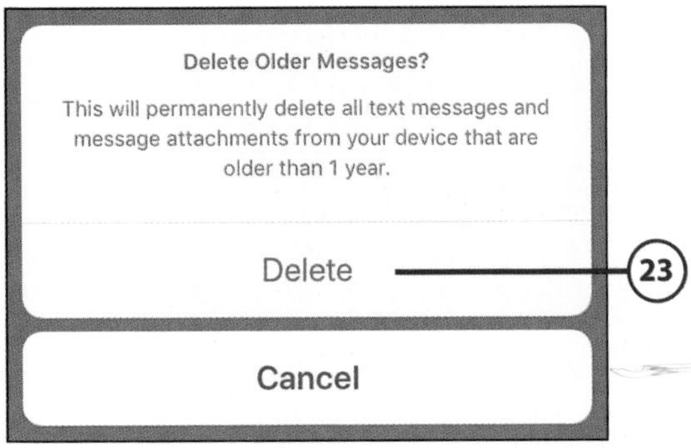

Delete Older Messages?

This will permanently delete all text messages and message attachments from your device that are older than 1 year.

Delete — **23**

Cancel

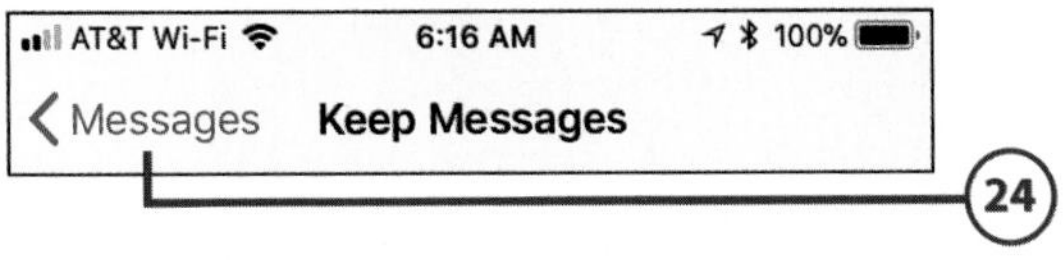

‹ Messages   **Keep Messages** — **24**

(25) If you want messages from people or organizations not in the Contacts app to be put on a separate list, set the Filter Unknown Senders switch to on (green). When this switch is on, you see a separate tab for messages from people you might not know; notifications for those messages are also disabled. This can be useful if you receive a lot of messages from people you don't know and don't want to be annoyed by notifications about those messages. (This feature is explained in the section "Working with Messages from People You Might Not Know" later in this chapter.)

(26) Tap Expire.

(27) Choose the time after which you want audio messages to expire and be deleted from your iPhone. The options you see depend on your cell phone provider. For example, if you tap After 2 Minutes, audio messages are automatically deleted two minutes after you listen to them. This is good because audio messages require a lot of storage space, and deleting them keeps that space available for other things. Other choices might be After 1 Year or Never (if you don't want audio messages to ever be deleted).

(28) Tap the Back icon (<).

MESSAGE HISTORY

Keep Messages   Forever >

MESSAGE FILTERING

Filter Unknown Senders   ⬤———(25)

Turn off notifications for iMessages from people who are not in your contacts and sort them into a separate list.

AUDIO MESSAGES

Expire   After 2 Minutes ›———(26)

---

(28)

📶 AT&T Wi-Fi 🛜   6:17 AM   ➤ ✶ 100% ▬

‹ Messages   **Expire**

After 2 Minutes ————————————— ✓ ———(27)

Never

When you send or listen to an audio message, it will automatically be removed from your conversation history after 2 minutes.

(29) To be able to listen to audio messages by lifting the phone to your ear, set the Raise to Listen switch to on (green). If you set this to off (white), you need to manually start audio messages.

(30) To have the images in your messages sent at a lower quality level, set the Low Quality Image Mode switch to on (green). This can be a useful setting if you or the other recipients of your messages have limited data plans because lower quality images require less data to transmit and receive. If you tend to use all or most of your data allowance each month and send a lot of images, you might want to enable this setting and see if that reduces your data use.

Expire	After 2 Minutes >
Raise to Listen	⬤ —(29)

Raise to Listen allows you to quickly listen and reply to incoming audio messages by raising the phone to your ear.

Low Quality Image Mode	◯ —(30)

When this is on, images sent will be lower quality.

One More Setting

When you use iCloud for messaging, you can store your messages on the cloud. This is good because you can access those messages from any device that can access your iCloud account. To enable this, open the iCloud Settings and set the Messages switch to on (green). See Chapter 3 for details of configuring iCloud.

Audio Messages

There are two types of audio messages you can send via the Messages app. Instant audio messages are included as part of the message itself. Audio, such as voice memos, can also be attached to messages. The Expire settings only affect instant audio messages. Audio that is attached to messages is not deleted automatically.

Blocking People from Messaging or Texting You

If you want to block someone before they send messages to you, configure that person's contact information so you can easily block his messages. Refer to Chapter 6, "Managing Contacts," for the steps to create contacts. (You can also block someone after you have received messages you don't want, which doesn't require that there be a contact first; those steps are provided later in this chapter.) Use the following steps to block a contact from sending messages to you:

1. Move to the Messages screen in the Settings app.

2. Swipe up the Messages screen.

3. Tap Blocked.

4. If necessary, swipe up the screen.

5. Tap Add New.

6. Use the Contacts app to find and tap the contact you want to block. (Note that contacts without email addresses or phone numbers that don't have the potential to send messages to you are grayed out and cannot be selected.) You return to the Blocked screen and see the contact on your Blocked list. Any messages, phone calls, and FaceTime requests from the contact, as long as they come from an email address or phone number included in his contact information, won't be sent to your iPhone.

>>>*Go Further*

MORE ON MESSAGES CONFIGURATION

Following are a few more Messages configuration tidbits for your consideration:

- You can use only one Apple ID for iMessages at a time. To change the account you are using, move to the iMessage screen by tapping Send & Receive on the Messages Settings screen. Then tap the Apple ID shown. Tap Sign Out. You can then sign in to a different Apple ID.

- SMS stands for Short Message Service, which is what text messages use. MMS stands for Multimedia Messaging Service, which adds the ability to include multimedia elements (photos, video, sound, and so on) in text messages. All text devices and accounts support SMS, but very old cellular phones might not support MMS (all smart phones do).

- In the Notifications settings, you can configure the notifications the Messages app uses to communicate with you. You can configure where notifications appear (Lock screen, Notification Center, Banners, or none), the banner styles (temporary or persistent), badges on the Messages icon to show you the number of new messages, sounds and vibrations when you receive messages, and so on. Messages also supports repeated alerts, which by default is to send you two notifications for each message you receive but don't read. Configuring notifications is explained in detail in Chapter 4, "Customizing How Your iPhone Works."

- To unblock someone so you can receive messages from them again, move to the Messages screen in the Settings app, tap Blocked, swipe to the left across the contact you want to unblock, and tap Unblock.

- You also can block someone without having a contact for them. To do this, move to the details screen for the conversation containing the person you want to block (you learn how to work with conversations later in this chapter). Tap the person, email address, or number you want to block. On the resulting screen, tap Block this Caller. Tap Block Contact at the prompt. That person is blocked from sending you messages.

Sending Messages

You can use the Messages app to send messages to people using a cell phone number (as long as the device receiving it can receive text messages) or an email address that has been registered for iMessage. If the recipient has both a cell number and iMessage-enabled email address, the Messages app assumes you want to use iMessage for the message.

When you send a message to more than one person and at least one of those people can use only the cellular network, all the messages are sent via the cellular network and not as an iMessage.

More on Mixed Recipients

If one of a message's recipients has an email address that isn't iMessage-enabled (and doesn't have a phone number), the Messages app attempts to send the message to that recipient as an email message. The recipient receives the email message in an email app on his phone or computer instead of through the Messages app.

Whether messages are sent via a cellular network or iMessage isn't terribly important, but there are some differences. If your cellular account has a limit on the number of texts you can send, you should use iMessage when you can because those messages won't count against your limit. Also, when you use iMessage, you don't have to worry about a limit on the number of characters in a message. When you send a message via a cellular network, your messages might be limited to 160 characters.

When you send messages to or receive messages from a person or a group of people, you see those messages in a conversation. Every message sent among the same people is added to that conversation. When you send a message to a person or group you haven't messaged before, a new conversation is created. If you send a message to a person or group you have messaged before, the message is added to the existing conversation.

Messages on an iPhone running iOS 10 or later can include lots of different elements, including effects, Digital Touches, content from apps, and more. When you include these items in your messages sent to other people using devices running iOS 10 or later, they'll be received as you intended. If they are using devices that aren't running iOS 10 or later or Macs running macOS Sierra or later, messages with these enhancements might or might not be what you intended. For example, if the recipient is using an older version of the iOS, a Digital Touch message comes in as a static image. If the recipient is using a device not running the iOS at all, such as an Android device, it can be hard to predict what will happen to messages if you enhance them. So, keep the recipients of your messages in mind and adjust the content you send to them accordingly.

Creating a New Message and Conversation

You can send messages by entering a number or email address manually or by selecting a contact from your contacts list.

(1) On the Home screen, tap Messages.

(2) Tap the Compose icon (if you don't see this icon, tap the Back icon (<) in the upper-left corner of the screen until you do). If you haven't used the Messages app before, you skip this step and move directly to the New Message screen in the next step.

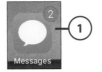

Edit

Messages

Q Search

| Contacts & SMS | Unknown Senders |

3 Type the recipient's name, email address, or phone number. As you type, the app attempts to match what you type with a saved contact or to someone you have previously messaged and shows you a list of suggested recipients. You see phone numbers or email addresses for each recipient on the list. Phone numbers or addresses in blue indicate the recipient is registered for iMessages and your message is sent via that means. Messages to phone numbers in green are sent as text messages over the cellular network. If a number or email address is gray, you haven't sent any messages to it yet; you can tap it to attempt to send a message. You also see groups you have previously messaged.

4 Tap the phone number, email address, or group to which you want to send the message. The recipients' names are inserted into the To field. Or, if the information you want to use doesn't appear, just type the complete phone number (as you would dial it to make a call to that number) or email address.

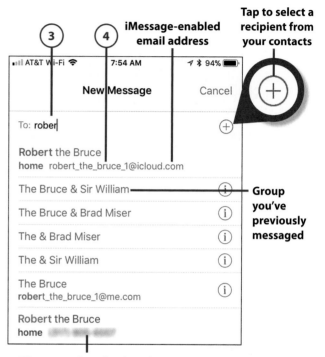

Tap to select a recipient from your contacts

iMessage-enabled email address

Group you've previously messaged

Phone number that hasn't been used for messaging

Straight to the Source
You can tap Add (+) in the To field to use the Contacts app to select a contact to whom you want to address the message (see Chapter 6 for the details of using the Contacts app).

Go to the Group
You can tap Info (i) next to a group on the suggested recipients list to see the people that are part of that group.

5 If you want to send the message to more than one recipient, tap in the space between the current recipient and Add (+) and use steps 3 and 4 to enter the other recipients' information, either by selecting contacts using Add (+) or by entering phone numbers or email addresses. As you add recipients, they appear in the To field. (If you addressed the message to a number or email address that matches a number in your contacts, the contact's name replaces the number in the To field. If not, the number or email address remains as you entered it.)

6 Tap in the Message bar, which is labeled iMessage if you entered iMessage addresses or Text Message if you entered a phone number. The cursor moves into the Message bar and you are ready to type your message.

7 Type the message you want to send in the Message bar.

8 Tap the Send icon (circle with an upward-facing arrow), which is blue if you are sending the message via iMessage or green if you are sending it via the cellular network. The Send status bar appears as the message is sent; when the process is complete, you hear the message sent sound and the status bar disappears.

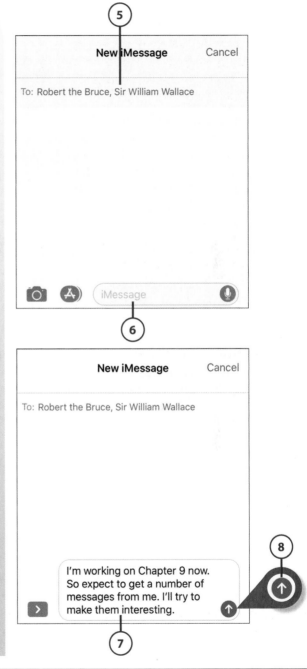

Change Your Mind?

To remove a contact or phone number from the To box, tap it once so it becomes highlighted in blue and then tap the Delete key on the keyboard.

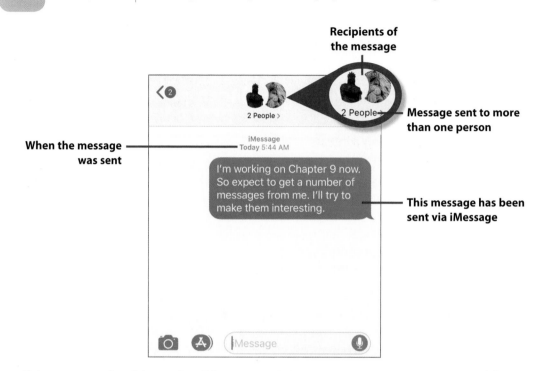

Recipients of the message

When the message was sent

Message sent to more than one person

This message has been sent via iMessage

If the message is addressed to iMessage recipients, your message appears in a blue bubble in a section labeled iMessage. If the person to whom you sent the message enabled his read receipt setting, you see when he reads your message.

Recipient of the message

Message has been sent via a cellular network

If you sent the message via the cellular network instead of iMessage, you see your message in a green bubble in a section labeled Text Message.

When you send a message, you see a new conversation screen if the message was not sent to someone or a group of people with whom you were previously messaging. If you have previously sent messages to the same recipient or recipients, you move back to the existing conversation screen and your new message is added to that conversation instead.

In a group conservation, you see icons and the names of each person who received the message; if there are more than two or three people, the icons "stack" on top of each other. (If you sent a message via a cellular text, you only see the person's name or number.)

>>>Go Further
TEXT ON

Following are some additional points to help you take your texting to the next level (where is the next level, anyway?):

- **iMessage or cell**—If the recipient has an iOS device or Mac that has been enabled for iMessage, text messages are sent via iMessage when possible even if you choose the recipient's phone number.

- **Group messaging**—If you've enabled the Group Messaging setting, when you include more than one recipient, any messages sent in reply are grouped in one conversation. If this setting isn't enabled, each reply to your message appears in a separate conversation.

- **Larger keyboard**—Like other areas where you type, you can rotate the iPhone to be horizontal where the keyboard is larger as is each key. This can make texting easier, faster, and more accurate.

- **Recents**—When you enter To information for a new message, included on the list of potential recipients are people being suggested to you by your iPhone. When a suggested recipient has an Info icon (i), tap that icon, tap Ignore Contact, and then tap Ignore at the prompt to prevent that person from being suggested in the future.

Sending Messages in an Existing Conversation

As you learned earlier, when you send a message to or receive a message from one or more people, a conversation is created. You can add new messages to a conversation as follows:

1. On the Home screen, tap Messages. You see a list of conversations on the Messages screen. If you were previously in a conversation, you see the messages in that conversation and the people involved at the top of the screen instead. Tap the Back icon (<), which is in the top-left corner of the screen to return to the conversation list on the Messages screen.

   On the list, the conversation containing the most recent message you've sent or received is at the top; conversations get "older" as you move down the screen.

2. Swipe up or down the screen or tap in the Search bar and type names, numbers, or email addresses to find the conversation to which you want to add a message.

3. Tap the conversation to which you want to add a message. At the top of the screen, you see the people involved in the conversation. Under that, you see the current messages in the conversation.

4 Tap in the Message bar.

5 Type your message.

6 Tap the Send icon. Your new message is added to the conversation and sent to everyone participating in the conversation.

Known Versus Unknown

If the Filter Unknown Senders setting is on, you see two tabs at the top of the Messages screen. The Contacts & SMS tab is where you see conversations with people in your contacts list or with whom you have communicated previously. The Unknown Senders tab is where messages from people with whom you haven't communicated before or aren't in your contacts are stored. The active tab is blue, and it defaults to the Contacts & SMS Messages list. You can tap either tab to make it active.

Who sent the message (group message only)

Prior messages in the conversation

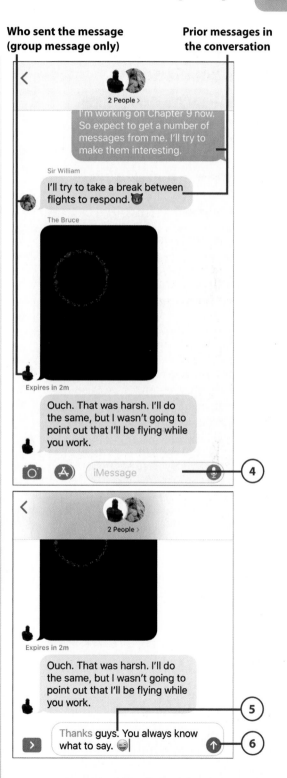

Applying Effects to Messages You Send

The Messages app enables you to apply effects to your messages. Bubble effects apply to the message you send, whereas Screen effects fill the screen when your message is read. There are quite a few effects you can use, and they are easy to apply using the following steps:

1. Create a new message or add a message to an existing conversation.

2. Tap and hold on the Send icon. The Send with effect screen appears.

No iOS 10 or later?

Recipients must be using devices running iOS 10 or later or Macs running macOS Sierra or later for these effects to play as you see them when you send them. You can send messages with effects to people not using iOS 10 or later devices or Macs not running macOS Sierra or later; the messages are delivered, but the effects are not.

3. Tap Bubble to apply a Bubble effect; to apply a Screen effect instead, skip to step 7.

4. Tap an effect. It is applied to the current message so you see how it will look.

5. Tap other effects to see what they do.

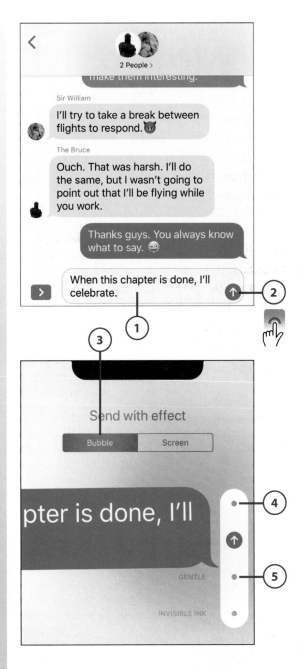

6 To send the message with the current Bubble effect, tap the Send icon and skip the rest of these steps. Your message is sent and the recipient sees the effect on the message's bubble when he opens the message.

Ah, Forget It

If you decide you don't want to add an effect, tap Delete (x) at the bottom of the screen and you return to your unadorned message, which you can then send without any bells or whistles.

7 Tap Screen to apply a Screen effect.

8 Swipe to the left or right. Each time you swipe, a new Screen effect is applied and you see it on the screen.

9 When you find the effect you want to use, tap the Send icon. Your message is sent and each recipient sees the effect in the background of the Messages screen when she opens the message. You also see the effect applied to the message on your iPhone.

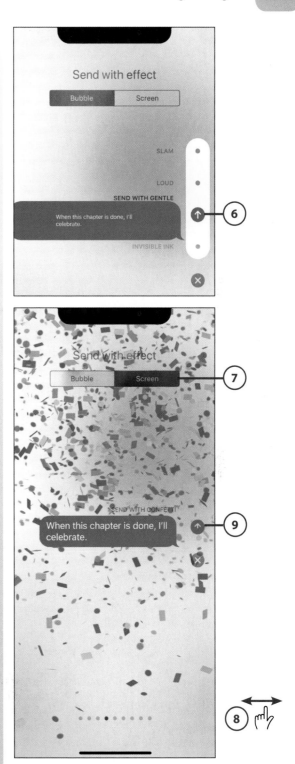

Including Photos or Video You've Recently Taken in Messages You Send

It's easy to use Messages to quickly send photos or video you've taken recently to other people as you see in the following steps:

1. Move into the conversation with the person or people to whom you want to send a photo, or start a new conversation.

2. Tap the Photos icon. If you don't see this icon, tap the App Drawer icon to open the App Drawer. If you don't see the App Drawer icon, first tap the right-facing arrow as shown in the second figure; the Camera and App Drawer icons appear. In the Photos pane, you see the photos and video you've taken recently.

Send a Video? No Problemo.

The steps in this task and the following two tasks show including photos in messages you send. You can send videos using very similar steps.

---

3. Swipe to the left or right on the photo panel to browse the recent photos and videos.

4. Tap the first photo or video you want to send. It is marked with a check mark and is added to the message you are sending.

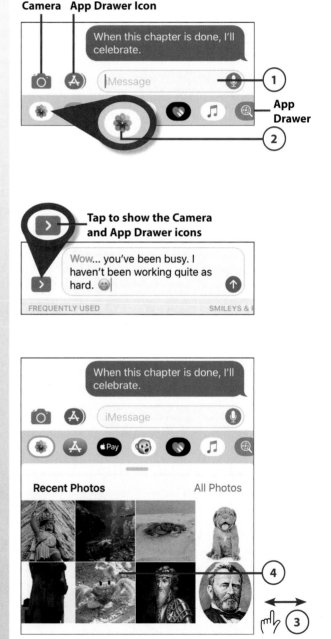

Camera   App Drawer Icon

When this chapter is done, I'll celebrate.

iMessage

1

App Drawer

2

Tap to show the Camera and App Drawer icons

Wow... you've been busy. I haven't been working quite as hard. 😄

FREQUENTLY USED   SMILEYS &

When this chapter is done, I'll celebrate.

iMessage

Recent Photos   All Photos

4

3

5 Swipe left or right to review more recent photos and videos.

6 Tap the next photo or video you want to send. It is also marked with a check mark and added to the message.

7 Repeat steps 5 and 6 until you've added all the photos and videos you want to send.

Limitations, Limitations

Not all cell carriers support MMS messages (the type that can contain images and video), and the size of messages can be limited. Check with your carrier for more information about what is supported and whether there are additional charges for using MMS messages. If you're using iMessage, you don't have this potential limit and are always able to include images and video in your texts. Also be sure your recipient can receive MMS messages before you send one.

8 Tap in the Message bar.

9 Type the comments you want to send with the photos or videos.

10 Tap the Send icon. The photos, videos, and comments are added to the conversation.

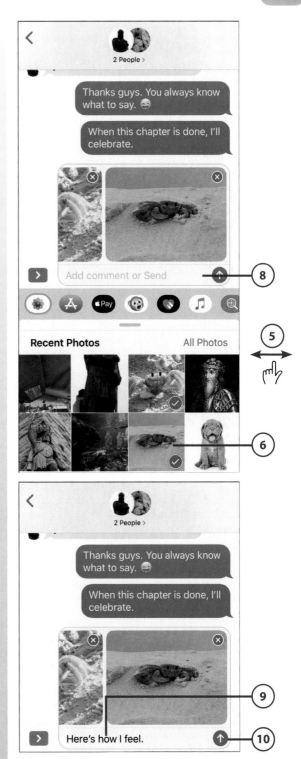

Including Photos or Video Stored in the Photos App in Messages You Send

You can add any image, photo, or video stored in Photos in a conversation by performing the following steps:

1. Move into the conversation with the person or people to whom you want to send a photo or video, or start a new conversation.

2. Tap the Photos icon. (You have to open the App Drawer if it isn't open already. If you don't see the App Drawer icon, tap the right-facing arrow so the App Drawer icon appears.)

3. Tap All Photos.

4. Swipe up or down the screen to find the source containing the photos or videos you want to send. (For more information about using the Photos app to find and select photos, see Chapter 14, "Viewing and Editing Photos and Video with the Photos App.")

5. Tap the source containing the photos or videos you want to send.

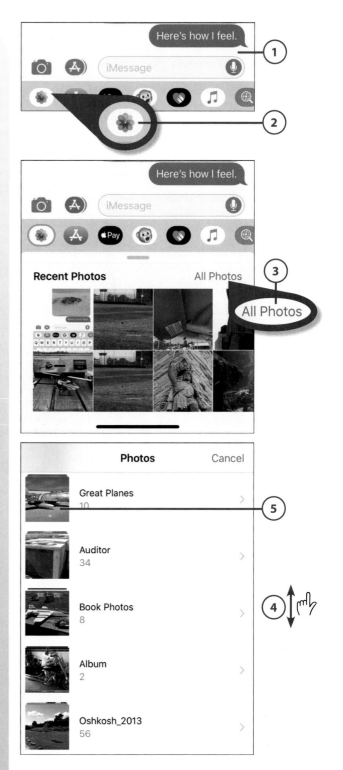

6 Swipe up or down the screen until you see the photo or video you want to send.

7 Tap the photo or video you want to send.

8 Tap Choose. You move back to the conversation and see the image or video in the Message bar.

9 Tap in the Message bar and type the message you want to send with the photo or video.

10 Tap the Send icon.

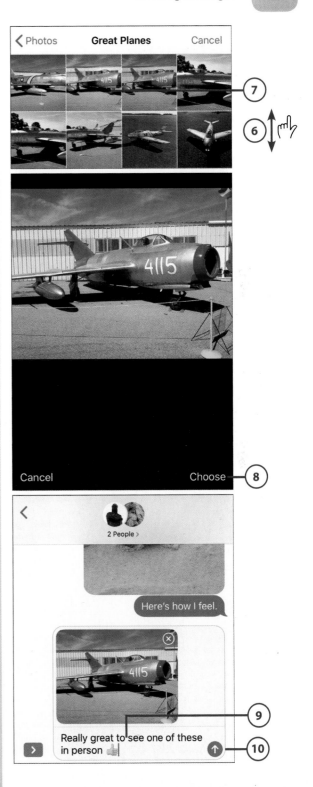

Taking Photos or Video and Sending Them in Messages

You can capture new photos and video using the iPhone's cameras and immediately send them to others via messages as follows:

1. Move into the conversation with the person or people to whom you want to send a photo or video, or start a new conversation.

2. Tap the Camera icon.

3. Use the Camera app to take the photo or video you want to send. (For more information about taking photos or videos, see Chapter 13, "Taking Photos and Video with Your iPhone.")

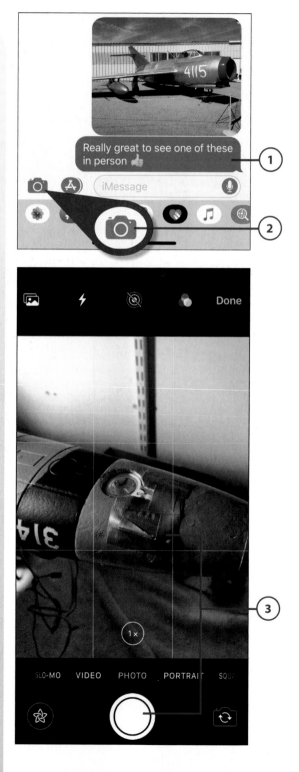

4 If you want to send the photo or video as is, tap the Send icon and skip to step 8.

5 Use the tools you see to modify the photo or video, such as to add effects, mark it up (such as drawing on it), or to edit it (see Chapter 14 for details).

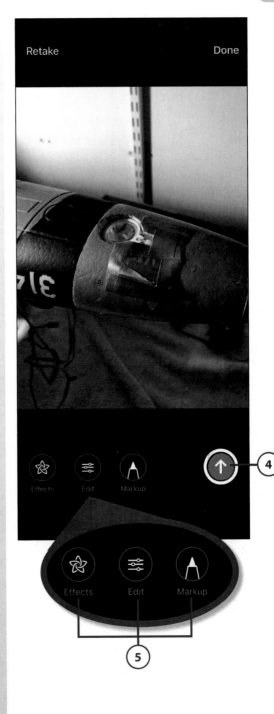

(6) Use the tools you selected in the previous step to make changes to the photo or video. This example shows adding a markup to a photo.

(7) Tap Save.

(8) Tap Done.

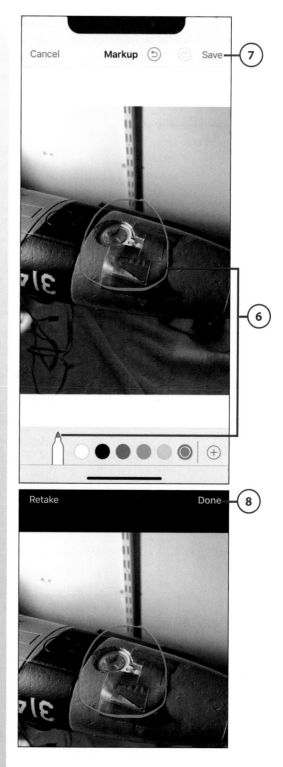

(9) Tap in the Message bar and type the message you want to send with the photo.

(10) Tap the Send icon. The photo (or video) and message are added to the conversation.

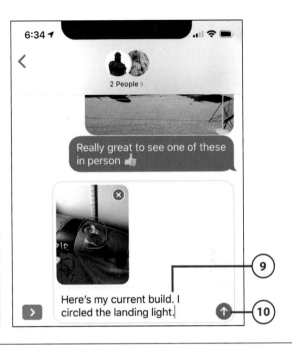

This Isn't Houston, but There Is a Problem

If a message you try to send is undeliverable or has some other problem, it is marked with an error icon, which is an exclamation point inside a red circle. The most common cause of this issue is a poor Internet connection. Tap the error icon and tap Try Again to attempt to resend the message. If it doesn't work again, you might need to wait until you have a better connection.

Sharing with Messages

You can share all sorts of information via Messages from many apps, such as Safari, Contacts, Maps, and so on. From the app containing the information you want to share, tap the Share icon. Then tap Messages. The information with which you are working is automatically added to a new message. Use the Messages app to complete and send the message.

Using Digital Touches in Messages You Send

You can enhance your messages with Digital Touches, which are dynamic images you draw with your fingers, or you can use the default images.

(1) Move into the conversation with the person or people to whom you want to send a Digital Touch.

(2) If you see the Digital Touch icon, skip to step 3; if not, tap the Apps icon.

(3) Tap the Digital Touch icon. The Digital Touch panel opens.

(4) Tap the line just above the Digital Touch panel to open the Digital Touch screen in full screen mode.

Use the Small Screen

You can create Digital Touches directly in the small Digital Touch panel that appears when you tap the Digital Touch icon. Putting it in full screen mode gives you more room to work but takes slightly longer. To create a touch directly in the panel, use the Digital Touch drawing tools directly in the small window and then tap the Send icon to send it.

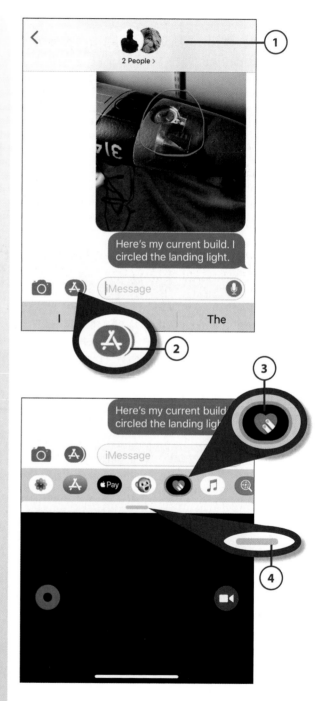

5 To send one of the default Digital Touches, move to step 8; to create your own Digital Touch, tap the color you want to use. The current color's icon has a dot in the center to show it's selected.

6 Use your finger to draw or write on the screen. You can change the color at any time; for example, you can use different colors in a drawing or for each letter in a word. Drawing on the Digital Touch screen is much like using colored pencils on paper.

7 Tap the Send icon to send it. The full screen mode digital pane collapses and you see a preview of your Digital Touch as it sends. To send a default Digital Touch, move back to step 4, or if you're done, skip the rest of these steps.

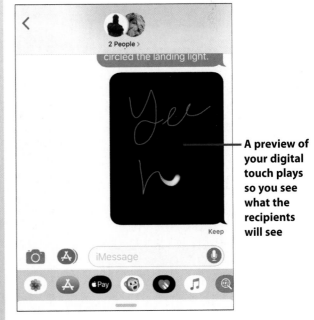

A preview of your digital touch plays so you see what the recipients will see

8. Tap Info (i). You see a list of all the gestures you can use to add a Digital Touch to a conversation. (This step is optional. If you know the gesture to create the Digital Touch you want to send, skip to step 11.)

9. Review the default Digital Touches.

10. Tap Close (x) to close the list.

iOS 10 Required

Like effects, the recipient must be using a device running iOS 10 or later or a Mac running macOS Sierra or later to receive Digital Touches as you see them when you send them. If you send a Digital Touch message to devices not running iOS 10 or later, they appear as a static image in the message.

Start Over

To get rid of the contents of the Digital Touch screen, tap Delete (x).

11. Use the finger gesture to add the default Digital Touch you want to the conversation. You see a preview in the Digital Touch pane, and the Digital Touch is immediately sent to the recipients and added to the conversation.

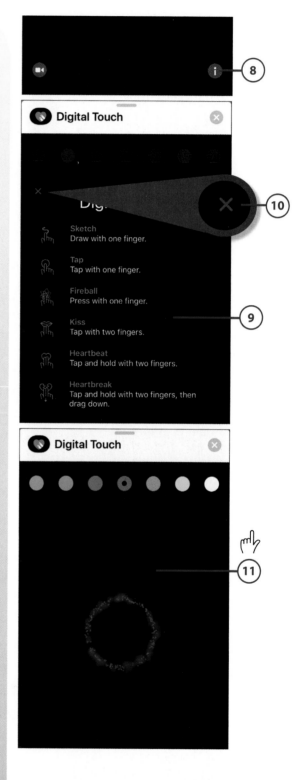

Digital Touch

Sketch
Draw with one finger.

Tap
Tap with one finger.

Fireball
Press with one finger.

Kiss
Tap with two fingers.

Heartbeat
Tap and hold with two fingers.

Heartbreak
Tap and hold with two fingers, then drag down.

Digital Touch

>>>Go Further
YOU'VE GOT THE TOUCH

Here are a few more touch-related tidbits:

- You can collapse the full screen Digital Touch pane by tapping the line located at the top, middle of the Digital Touch pane.

- By default, Digital Touch messages you send or receive expire after two minutes. If you want to keep a Digital Touch message, tap Keep, which appears at the bottom of the message as soon as you send it. The Digital Touch message remains until you delete it manually or it is deleted with the other messages based on the Messages app's settings.

- You can't stop a default Digital Touch once you make its gesture. As soon as you make the gesture, it is sent.

- You can take a video or photo and create a Digital Touch on top of it by tapping the Video Camera icon in the Digital Touch pane. The camera view opens and you can take a photo or video. You can draw on or apply a Digital Touch before or during a video capture. You can send the photo or video by tapping the Send icon.

Using Other Apps within Messages

You can use apps within Messages to add content to your messages. You can use the default apps installed in Messages (examples are provided later in this chapter) and you can add more apps as follows:

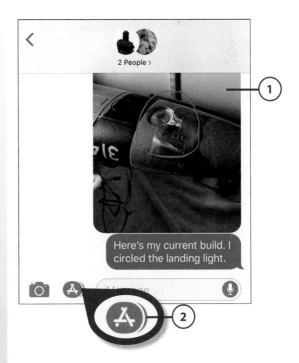

1. Open Messages and move into a conversation.

2. Tap the Apps icon. The App Drawer opens and you see the installed apps at the bottom of the screen. The app you used most recently is selected automatically.

3 Tap the App Store app (if you don't see this app, swipe to the left or right on the App Drawer until you do). You move into the App Store and see apps that work within Messages.

4 Browse or search within the App Store to find apps you want to add to Messages, such as stickers you can insert into your messages. This works very similarly to using the App Store app, which is covered in Chapter 4. Note that if you just browse you only see Messages-compatible apps, but if you search you see both "regular" apps and Messages apps.

5 Tap the Get icon for a free app or the price icon for an app with a license fee. Follow the prompts to download and install the app; for example, if you are using an X model with Face ID, press the Side button twice and look at the phone. Just like other apps, it is downloaded to your iPhone, but it's installed in the Messages App Drawer instead of on a Home screen.

After the app is downloaded, it appears in the App Drawer, and you can use it.

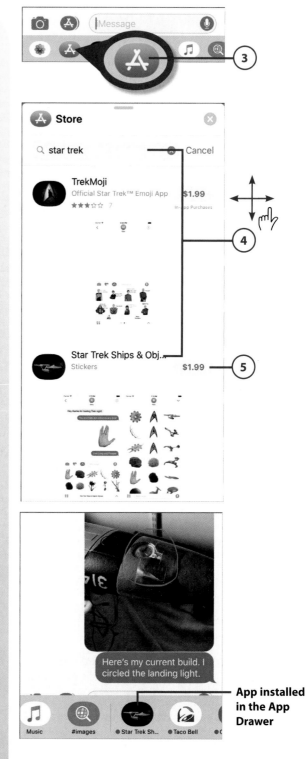

App installed in the App Drawer

Managing Apps Within Messages

You can configure the apps in the App Drawer by performing the following steps:

(1) Open Messages and move into a conversation.

(2) Tap the Apps icon. The App Drawer opens.

(3) Swipe to the left on the App Drawer until you see the More icon. As you swipe in the App Drawer, it enlarges so you can more clearly see the app icons.

(4) Tap More. You see apps currently installed in the App Drawer. There are two sections. FAVORITES are apps you've tagged as your favorites; these appear on the left end of the App Drawer and so are easier to access. In the MORE APPS section, you see the other apps in the App Drawer. You can use the apps in either section.

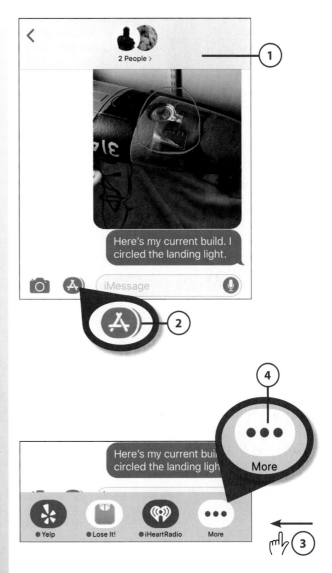

(5) Tap Edit.

(6) If you don't want to see an app in the App Drawer, set its switch to off (white). It no longer appears in the App Drawer, but remains available so you can re-enable it again.

Get Rid of It

If you want to remove an app from the App Drawer, perform steps 1 through 4. Swipe to the left on the app you want to remove. Tap Delete. The app is removed from the App Drawer.

(7) To move an app into the FAVORITES section, tap Add (+). It jumps up to the FAVORITES section and appears toward the left end of the App Drawer, making it faster to use.

(8) To move an app from FAVORITES to MORE APPS, tap its unlock (–) icon.

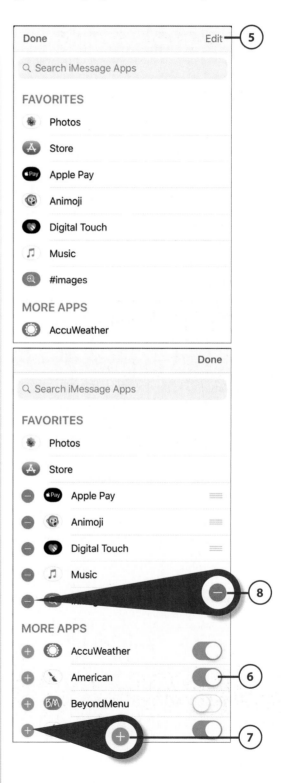

9 Tap Remove from Favorites. The app moves to the MORE APPS section of the screen, and it moves to the right side of the App Drawer. You can still use it, you just have to swipe on the App Drawer more to get to it.

10 To change the order of the apps in the FAVORITES section, drag apps up or down the list by their Order (three lines) icon. The apps you place toward the top of the list appear toward the left side of the App Drawer, making them faster to access. Therefore, place the apps you use the most often to be toward the top of the list.

11 When you're done managing apps, tap Done.

12 Tap Done.

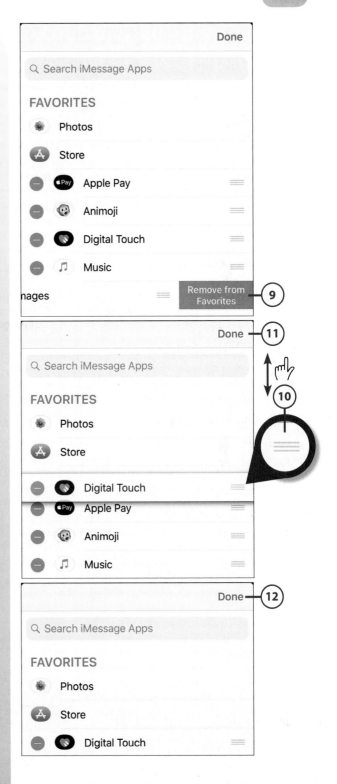

Adding Content from Apps to Messages You Send

You can use the apps in the Messages' App Drawer to add content to the messages you send. As you saw in the previous task, there are many different types of apps available and each works according to the type of content you can use. Some are quite simple, such as providing icons or images (sometimes called stickers) you can easily add to messages. Others are a bit more complicated, for example, you can use the #images app to search for and add images to your messages. Using any of these apps to add content to your messages follows a similar pattern, so once you see how to use one of them, you can use any of them fairly easily.

Adding Stickers to Messages

This example shows you how to use a sticker app to add icons or images to your messages:

1. Move into a conversation or start a new one.

2. If you don't see the App Drawer, tap the Apps icon to open it.

3. If you don't see the app you want to use, swipe to the left or right until you do.

4. Tap the app you want to use.

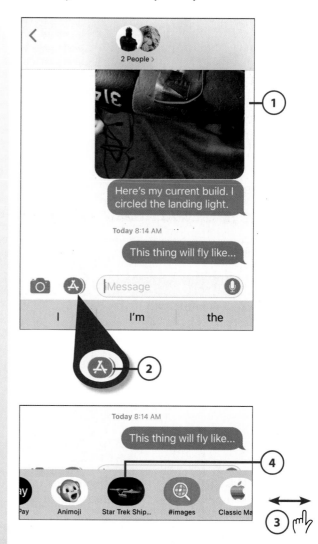

5 Tap the line to expand the app to full screen; this step is optional because you can use the app in the collapsed view in the same way.

6 Swipe up and down the screen to browse all the images that match your search.

7 Tap the image you want to add to the conversation.

8) Tap in the Message bar. In many cases, you'll skip adding a message (steps 8 and 9) and just send the content by skipping to step 10.

9) Type a comment you want to send with the content you added.

Delete It

To delete the content without sending it, tap Delete (x) on the content you've added to the conversation.

10) Tap the Send icon. The content (and comment if you made one) are added to the conversation.

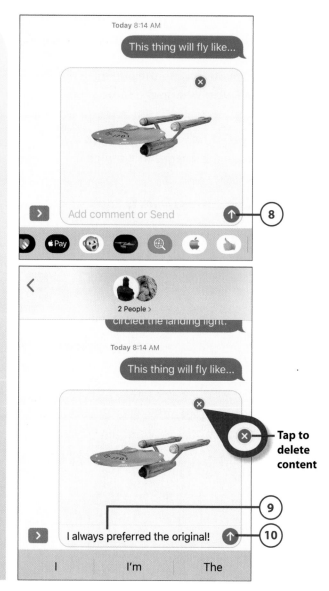

Tap to delete content

Adding Animojis to Messages

Animojis, which stands for Animated Emojis, enable you to capture your facial movements applied to an image, such as dog or alien, which then mimics your movements. You also can record sounds. After you've created an animoji, you can send it to others just like other kinds of text message content, such as photos, stickers, and so on.

X Only

Animojis are available only on iPhone X models.

To record and send an animoji, perform the following steps:

1. Move into an existing conversation or start a new one.

2. Tap the Animoji icon. (If you don't see it, you need to open and potentially swipe on the App Drawer as described earlier.)

3. Swipe left or right in the Animoji pane until the animoji you want to use appears in the center of the pane. If your face isn't recognized, you see a yellow frame over the animoji and the message to bring your face into view; if that happens, reposition the phone so your face is recognized.

4. Move your head and make facial expressions to see what the animoji does in response.

5. Look at the phone and tap the Record icon to start recording the animoji.

6. Move your head, smile, frown, wink, or make other facial expressions and speak the message you want to send. As you make these movements they are recorded along with the sounds made as you record. Your animoji can be up to 30 seconds long.

7. When you're done, tap the Stop icon. The animoji plays in the pane.

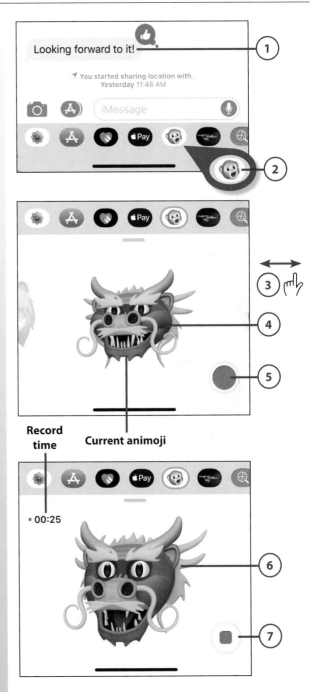

Record time

Current animoji

(8) To delete the animoji without sending it, tap the Trash icon.

(9) To send the animoji, tap the Send icon. It is added to the conversation and plays for you. When the recipients view the conversation in which you sent it, it plays for them (viewing animojis is covered in a later task).

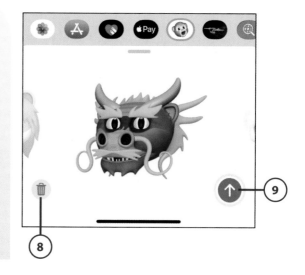

Watch It Again

After the animoji plays, the Replay icon appears. Tap that to play the animoji again.

I Gotta Be Me

You can create your own animoji by choosing a skin color, hairstyle, glasses, and so on. Open the Animoji pane and swipe all the way to the right. Tap Add (+) and use the resulting screens to create your version of you. When you're done, the animoji you created is available to use just like the default animojis.

Including Instant Audio in Messages You Send

You can send audio messages that you record via a message by performing the following steps:

(1) Move to the conversation to which you want to add an audio message, or start a new conversation.

(2) Tap and hold on the Microphone in the Message bar (not the one on the keyboard); if you are starting a new conversation, you need to add at least one recipient to make the Microphone icon appear. Recording starts.

(3) Speak your message; keep your finger touching the Microphone while you speak.

(4) When you're done recording, take your finger off the screen.

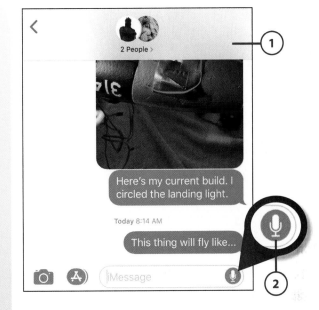

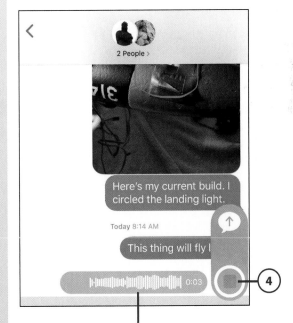

Your message is being recorded

5 Tap the Play icon to replay your message.

6 If you don't want to send the message, delete it by tapping Delete (x).

7 Tap the Send icon to send the message. The audio message is added to the conversation and the recipients are able to listen to it.

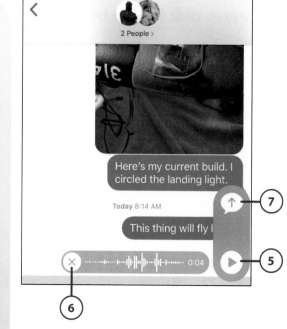

Adding Your Location to Messages You Send

Location information can be available for the participants in a conversation so you can see where others are, and they can see where you are. You can add your location information to a conversation as follows:

1 Move to the conversation to which you want to add your location information.

2 Tap the label under the icon or icons at the top of the screen. If the conversation is with one other person, this label is the person's name; if multiple people are involved, you see *X* People, where *X* is the number involved.

3 Tap Info (i).

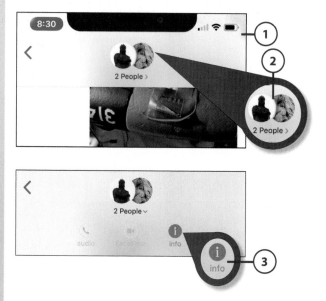

4. To share your current location as a snapshot, tap Send My Current Location. Your current location is captured and sent to the recipients of the message.

5. To dynamically share your location so that it updates as you move around, tap Share My Location.

6. Tap how long you want your location information to be shared.

Sharing Your Location

When you share your location, you are identifying where your iPhone (and likely you) are physically located. Someone with this information is able to come to where you are. Make sure you share only this information with people you know and trust. Be especially careful with the Share My Location option, because this allows others to dynamically track your movement. It's better to use the One Hour or End of Day options so that location sharing stops automatically.

Details   Done

NAME
Enter a Group Name

Robert the Br...

Sir William W...   — **Who you will be sharing your location with**

+ Add Contact

Send My Current Location   —— 4

Share My Location   —— 5

Share for One Hour   —— 6

Share Until End of Day

Share Indefinitely

Cancel

Current Locations

When a current location is added to a conversation, it is static, meaning it is only the location at that point in time. It appears as a map thumbnail in the conversation. Recipients can tap it to zoom in on the location, and then tap Directions to Here to generate directions from their location to the one sent as the current location.

Which Device?

If you have multiple devices that can provide your location, you can configure which device is used to determine your location by opening the Settings app, tapping Privacy, tapping Location Services, tapping Share My Location, tapping From, and then tapping the device that should be used for your position.

(7) To stop sharing your location, tap Stop Sharing My Location. If you selected to share it for one hour or until the end of the day, location sharing stops automatically at the time you selected.

(8) Tap Done to return to the conversation.

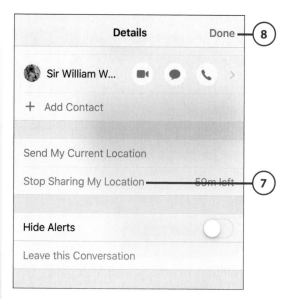

Using Quick Actions to Send Messages

You can use the Quick Actions feature on iPhones that support 3D Touch with the Messages app as follows:

(1) Press on the Messages icon. The Quick Actions menu appears.

(2) Tap the person to whom you want to send a message or tap New Message to send a message to someone not shown on the list. If you choose a person, you move into an existing conversation with that person or a new conversation is started. If you choose New Message, you move to the New Message screen.

(3) Complete and send the message.

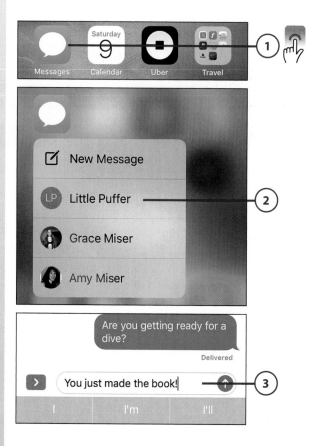

Receiving, Reading, and Replying to Messages

Text messaging is about communication, so when you send messages you expect to receive responses. People can also send new messages to you. As you learned earlier, the Messages app keeps messages grouped as a conversation consisting of messages you send and replies you receive to the same person or group of people.

Receiving Messages

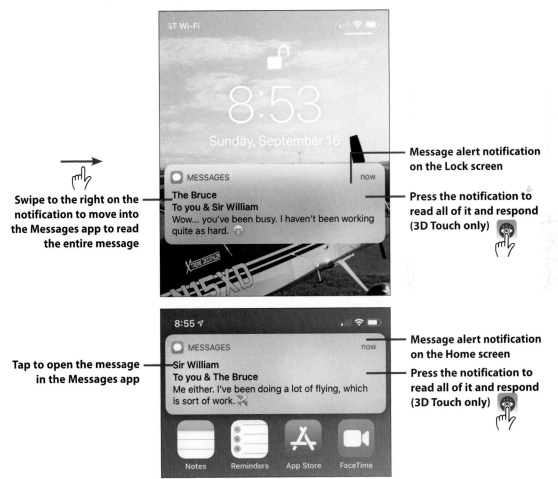

Swipe to the right on the notification to move into the Messages app to read the entire message

Message alert notification on the Lock screen

Press the notification to read all of it and respond (3D Touch only)

Tap to open the message in the Messages app

Message alert notification on the Home screen

Press the notification to read all of it and respond (3D Touch only)

When you aren't currently using the Messages screen in the Messages app and receive a new message (as a new conversation or as a new message in an ongoing conversation), you see, hear, and feel the notifications you have configured for the Messages app. (Refer to Chapter 4 to configure your message notifications.)

If you are on the Messages screen in the Messages app when a new message comes in, you hear and feel the new message notification sound and/or vibration, but a notification does not appear. On the conversation list, any conversations containing a new message are marked with a blue circle showing the number of new messages in that conversation.

If a new message is from someone with whom you have previously sent or received a message, and you haven't deleted all the messages to or from those recipients (no matter how long it has been since a message was added to that conversation), the new message is appended to an ongoing conversation. That conversation then moves to the top of the list of conversations in the Messages app. If there isn't an existing message to or from the people involved in a new message, a new conversation is started and the message appears at the top of that list.

Speaking of Texting

Using Siri to hear and speak text messages is extremely useful. Check out Chapter 11, "Working with Siri," for examples showing how you can take advantage of this great feature. One of the most useful Messages commands is to activate Siri and say, "Get new messages." Siri reads any new messages you have received.

Reading Messages

You can get to new messages you receive by doing any of the following:

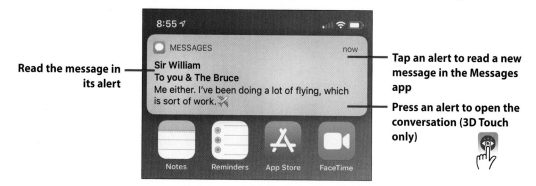

Read the message in its alert

Tap an alert to read a new message in the Messages app

Press an alert to open the conversation (3D Touch only)

- Read a message in its alert. Tap a banner alert notification from Messages to move into the message's conversation in the Messages app.

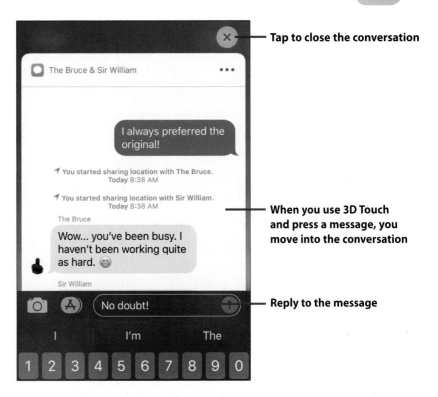

Tap to close the conversation

When you use 3D Touch and press a message, you move into the conversation

Reply to the message

- If you are using an iPhone that supports 3D Touch, you can press on an alert to open the conversation to which the message was added. You can read all the messages it contains and reply to those messages.

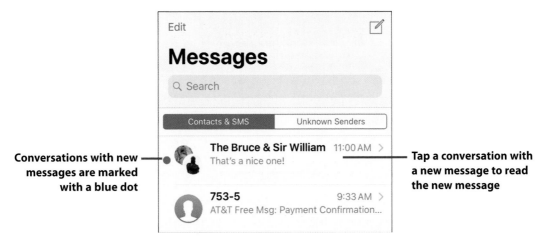

Conversations with new messages are marked with a blue dot

Tap a conversation with a new message to read the new message

- Open the Messages app and tap a conversation containing a new message; these conversations appear at the top of the Messages list and are marked with a blue circle. The conversation opens and you see the new message.

- Swipe to the right on a message notification when it appears on the Lock screen. You move into the conversation to which the message was sent (you might need to unlock your phone first).

- If you receive a new message in a conversation that you are currently viewing, you immediately see the new message.

However you get to a message, you see the new message in either an existing conversation or a new conversation. The newest messages appear at the bottom of the screen. You can swipe up and down the screen to see all the messages in the conversation. As you move up the screen, you move back in time.

Messages sent to you are on the left side of the screen and appear in gray bubbles. If the message is for a group, just above the bubble is the name of the person sending the message; if you have an image for the contact, that image appears next to his bubble. If the conversation is with just one other person, you see her image and name at the top of the screen. The color of your bubbles indicates how the message was sent: blue indicates an iMessage, whereas green indicates a cellular message.

Viewing Images or Video You Receive in Messages

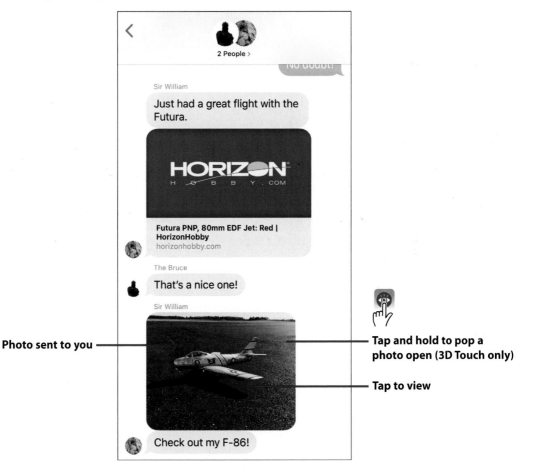

Photo sent to you

Tap and hold to pop a photo open (3D Touch only)

Tap to view

When you receive a photo or video as an attachment, it appears in a thumbnail along with the accompanying message.

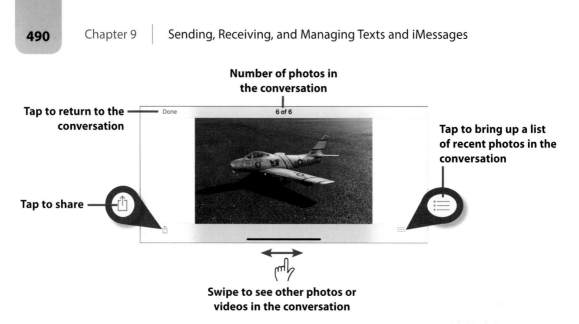

Number of photos in the conversation

Tap to return to the conversation — Done 6 of 6

Tap to bring up a list of recent photos in the conversation

Tap to share

Swipe to see other photos or videos in the conversation

To view a photo or video attachment, tap it. You see the photo or video at a larger size. You can rotate the phone, zoom, and swipe around the photo just like viewing photos in the Photos app (see Chapter 14 for details). You can watch a video in the same way, too.

Tap the Share icon to share the photo with others via a message, email, tweet, Facebook, and so on. (When you hold an iPhone Plus horizontally, all the icons are at the top of the screen.)

If there is more than one photo or video in the conversation, you see the number of them at the top of the screen. Swipe to the left or right to move through the available photos.

Tap the List icon to see a list of the recent photos in the conversation (this only appears if there is more than one photo in the conversation).

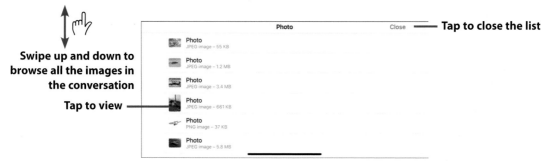

Swipe up and down to browse all the images in the conversation

Tap to view

Photo
Photo — JPEG image – 55 KB
Photo — JPEG image – 1.2 MB
Photo — JPEG image – 3.4 MB
Photo — JPEG image – 661 KB
Photo — PNG image – 37 KB
Photo — JPEG image – 5.8 MB

Close — **Tap to close the list**

Tap a photo on the list to view it. Tap Close to return to the photo you were viewing.

To move back to the conversation, tap Done.

Swipe up for options

Press to view

When you use an iPhone that supports 3D Touch and you press on a photo, it opens in a Peek. If you continue pressing on the photo, it opens in the view window just like when you tap on it in the conversation.

Tap to copy

Tap to save on your iPhone

Tap to forward in another message

When you are peeking at a photo, swipe up on it to reveal options. You can copy the photo so you can paste it elsewhere, save the photo in the Photos app, or forward it to others.

No 3D Touch?

If your iPhone doesn't support 3D Touch, you can save a photo by touching the photo (don't apply pressure) and using the Save Image command on the resulting menu. You can also copy or forward it from this menu.

Viewing Animojis You Receive in Messages

When someone includes an animoji in a message to you, you can watch and listen to it. (You can view an animoji on all iPhone models.)

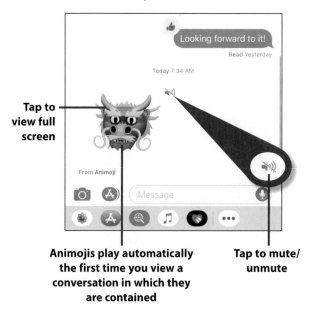

Tap to view full screen

From Animoji

Animojis play automatically the first time you view a conversation in which they are contained

Tap to mute/ unmute

When you receive an animoji, it plays automatically. Tap the speaker icon to mute or unmute it. To view it in full-screen mode, tap it.

Tap when you're done —— Done   2 of 2

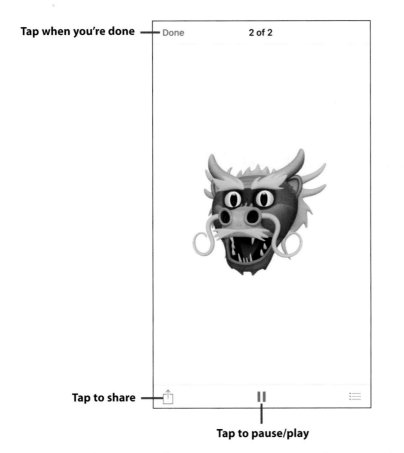

Tap to share ——

Tap to pause/play

You can tap the Pause/Play icon to start or stop the animoji, tap the Share icon to share it, or tap Done to close the full-screen view.

Every time you move into a conversation, the animoji plays and continues playing in an endless loop. Fortunately, they are automatically muted so at least you don't hear the same audio over and over. You can delete animojis as you can other messages (see "Deleting Messages and Conversations").

The Texts Remain the Same

You do other tasks with animojis that you can with other Messages content, such as copying them and forwarding them.

Listening to Audio You Receive in Messages

Audio message

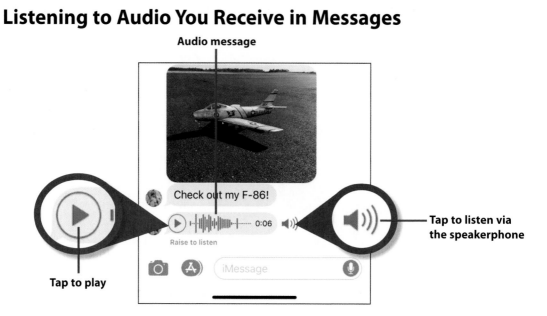

Tap to play

Tap to listen via
the speakerphone

When you receive an audio message, you can tap the Play icon to play it, or, if you enabled the Raise to Listen option, lift the phone to your ear and the message plays automatically. Tap the Speaker icon to hear the message via the iPhone's speakerphone.

Tap to pause

While the message is playing, you see its status along with the Pause icon, which you can tap to pause the audio message. After the message finishes, you see a message saying that it expires in 2 minutes or 1 year, depending on your settings. That message is quickly replaced by Keep.

Tap Keep to save the message on your phone. (Keep disappears indicating the audio is saved.)

Kept Audio Messages

When one or more of the recipients of an audio message that you sent keeps it, a status message is added to the conversation on your phone, so you know who keeps audio messages you have sent. And, others know when you keep their messages, too.

Replying to Messages from the Messages App

To reply to a message, read the message and do the following:

1. Read, watch, or listen to the most recent message.

2. Use the photos, Digital Touch, or App tools to reply with content of that type as you learned about earlier in this chapter.

3. Tap in the Message bar if you want to reply with text.

4. Type your reply or use the Dictation feature to speak your reply (this is translated to text; it's not recording and embedding an audio message).

5. Tap the Send icon.

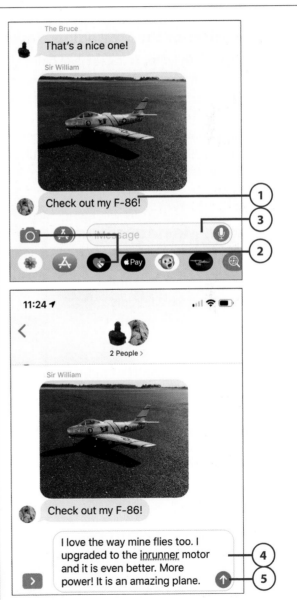

Mix and Match

The Messages app can switch between types of messages. For example, if you have an iMessage conversation going but can't access the iMessage service for some reason, the app can send messages as a cellular text. It can switch the other way, too. The app tries to send iMessages first if it can but chooses whichever method it needs to get the messages through. (If you disabled the Send as SMS option, messages are only sent via iMessage.)

More Tricks of the Messaging Trade

My Acquisitions Editor Extraordinaire pointed out that people can't receive messages when their phones aren't connected to the Internet (via Wi-Fi or cell). You don't see a warning in this case; you can only tell the message wasn't delivered because the Delivered status doesn't appear under the message. The message is delivered as soon as the other person's phone is connected to the Internet again, and its status is updated accordingly on your phone. Also, when an iMessage can't be delivered, you can tap and hold on it; then tap Send as Text Message. The app tries to send the message via SMS instead of iMessage.

Replying to Messages from a Banner Alert

If you have banner alerts configured for your messages, you can reply directly from the alert from either the Home or Lock screens:

1. Press on the notification (3D Touch) or swipe to the right (non-3D Touch). The conversation opens.

2. Type your reply or tap the right-facing arrow to add other types of content (such as a sticker from a Messages app) to your response.

3. Tap the Send icon. Your message is added to the conversation.

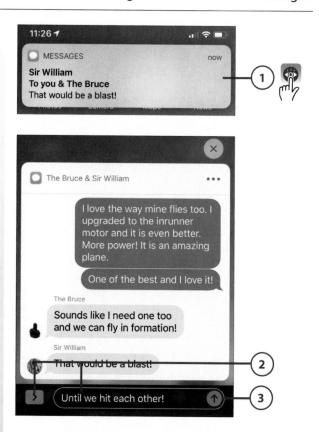

Having a Messages Conversation

Messaging is all about the back-and-forth communication with one or more people. You've already learned the skills you need, so put them all together. You can start a new conversation by sending a message to one or more people with whom you don't have an ongoing conversation; or you can add to a conversation already underway.

(1) Send a new message to a person or add a new message to an existing conversation. You see when your message has been delivered. If you sent the message to an individual person via iMessages and he has enabled his Read Receipt setting, you see when he has read your message and you see a bubble as he is composing a response. (If you are conversing with more than one person, the person doesn't have her Read Receipt setting enabled, or the conversation is happening via the cellular network, you don't see either of these.)

As the recipient composes a response, you see a bubble on the screen where the new message will appear when it is received (again, only if it is an iMessage with a single individual). Of course, you don't have to remain on the conversation's screen waiting for a response. You can move to a different conversation or a different app. When the response comes in, you are notified per your notification settings.

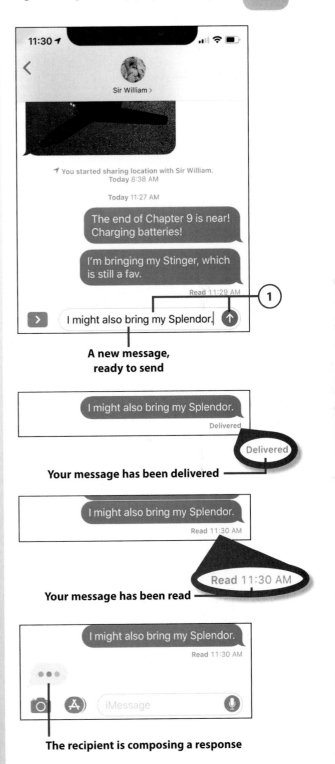

A new message, ready to send

Your message has been delivered

Your message has been read

The recipient is composing a response

2 Read the response.

3 Write and send your next message.

4 Repeat these steps as long as you want. Conversations remain in the Messages app until you remove them. Messages within conversations remain forever (unless you delete them, for one year, or for 30 days depending on your Keep Messages setting as shown earlier in this chapter).

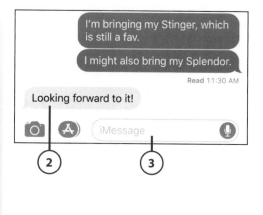

Seen But Not Read

Don't take the Read status too literally. All it means is that the conversation to which your message was added has been viewed. Of course, the Messages app can't know whether the recipient actually read the message.

The iMessage Will Be With You...Always

Messages that are sent with iMessage move with you from device to device, so they appear on every device configured to use your iMessage account. Because of this, you can start a conversation on your iPhone while you are on the move and pick it up on your iPad or Mac later.

Working with Messages

As you send and receive messages, the interaction you have with each person or group becomes a separate conversation. A conversation consists of all the messages that have gone back and forth. You manage your conversations from the Messages screen.

Multiple Conversations with the Same People

The Messages app manages conversations based on the phone number or email address associated with the messages in that conversation rather than the people (contacts) involved in the conversation. So, you might have multiple conversations with the same person if that person used a different means, such as a phone number and an email address, to send messages to you.

Managing Messages Conversations

Use the Messages screen to manage your messages.

1 On the Home screen, tap Messages.

The Messages screen showing conversations you have going appears, or you move into the conversation you were most recently using (tap the left-facing arrow at the top of the screen to move back to the conversation list). Conversations containing new messages appear at the top of the list. The name of the conversation is the name of the person or people associated with it, or it might be labeled as Group if the app can't display the names. If a contact can't be associated with the person, you see the phone number or email address you are conversing with instead of a name.

If you have the badge enabled, you see the number of new messages on the Messages icon

(2) Swipe up and down the list to see all the conversations.

(3) Tap a conversation you want to read or reply to. The conversation screen appears. If it's a group conversation, you see the number of people involved and an icon for each at the top of the screen. If there is only one other person involved, you see his name and image at the top of the screen instead. Note that if you use one of the smaller models, such as the iPhone SE, the images won't appear as described and shown; you'll just see people's names or conversation labels.

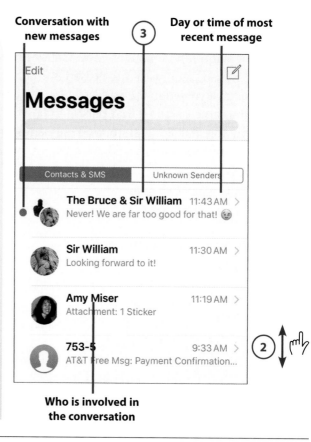

Conversation with new messages

Day or time of most recent message

Who is involved in the conversation

Information Messages

Many organizations use messages to keep you informed. Examples are airlines that send flight status information, retailers that use messages to keep you informed about shipping, and so on. These messages are identified by a set of numbers that don't look like a phone number. You can't send a response to most of these messages; they are one-way only. In some cases, you can issue commands related to the texts from that organization, such as "Stop" to stop further texts from being sent.

4 Read the new messages or view other new content in the conversation. Your messages are on the right side of the screen in green (cell network) or blue (iMessage), whereas the other people's messages are on the left in gray. Messages are organized so the newest message is at the bottom of the screen.

5 Swipe up and down the conversation screen to see all the messages it contains.

6 To add a new message to the conversation, tap in the Message bar, type your message or use an app to add content, and tap the Send icon.

7 Swipe down to scroll up the screen and move back in time in the conversation.

8 To see details about the conversation, tap X People, where X is the number of people in the conversation or the person's name if there is only one other person involved.

9 Tap Info (i). The Details screen appears. At the top of the screen, you see location information for the people with whom you are texting if it is available.

See the Time of Every Message

To see the time or date associated with every message in the conversation being displayed, swipe to the left and hold your finger down on the screen. The messages shift to the left and the time of each message appears along the right side of the screen. The date associated with each message appears right before the first message on that date.

(10) If you are working with a group message and want to give it a name, tap Enter a Group Name. If you are working with a conversation involving one other person or don't want to name the group, skip to step 12.

What's in a Name?

When you name a group (conversation), that name is applied to the conversation for all the participants.

(11) Enter the name of the group, and tap Done.

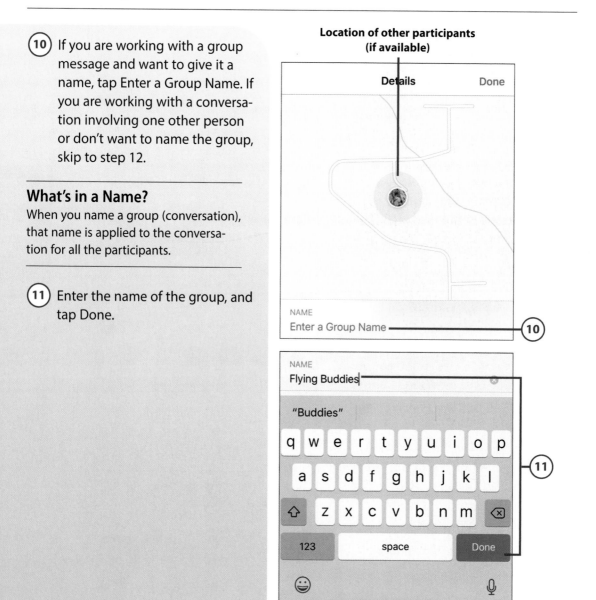

Location of other participants
(if available)

12 To place a voice call or audio-only FaceTime call to one of the participants in the conversation, tap the phone icon. If the person has a phone number config-ured, you're prompted to choose Voice Call or FaceTime Audio. When you make a choice, that call is placed. If the person only has an email address, an audio-only FaceTime call is placed over the Internet. You move into the Phone or FaceTime app and use that app to complete the call. (See Chapter 7, "Communicating with the Phone and FaceTime Apps," for the details about those apps.) Move to the Home screen and tap Messages or use the App Switcher to return to the Messages app.

13 Send a private message to one of the participants by tapping the Messages icon.

14 Place a FaceTime video call by tapping the Video Camera icon. You move into the FaceTime app to complete the call. When you're done, move to the Home screen and tap Messages or use the App Switcher to return to the Messages app.

15 To view a participant's contact information or send an email, tap the right-facing arrow for the per-son whose information you want to view.

New group name   **List of participants in the conversation**

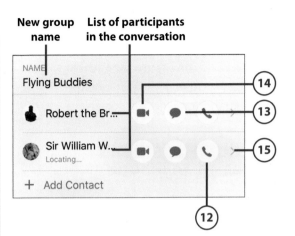

(16) Work with the contact information as described in Chapter 6.

(17) Tap the Back icon (<) to return to the Details screen and click Done to return to the conversation screen.

Receiving and Reading Messages on an iPhone Plus

The larger screen on the iPhone Plus provides some additional functionality that is unique to it. You can access this by holding the iPhone Plus horizontally when you use the Messages app.

(1) Open the Messages app and hold the iPhone so it is oriented horizontally. The window splits into two panes. On the left is the Navigation pane, where you can move to and select conversations you want to view. When you select a conversation in the left pane, its messages appear in the Content pane on the right.

(2) Swipe up or down the Navigation pane to browse the conversations available to you. Notice that the two panes are independent. When you browse the left pane, the right pane doesn't change.

(3) Tap the conversation containing messages you want to read. The messages in that conversation appear in the Content pane on the right.

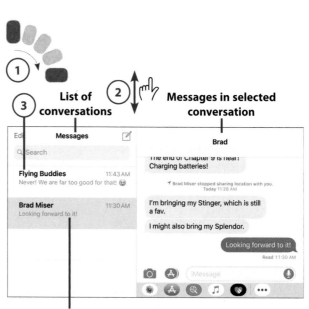

List of conversations

Messages in selected conversation

Selected conversation

4 Swipe up and down the Content pane to read the messages in the conversation.

5 Work with the messages in the conversation just like when the iPhone is held vertically.

6 To add a message to the conversation, tap in the Message bar, type your message, and tap Send. Of course, you can embed audio, attach photos or video, add content from apps, or send your location just as you can when using Messages when you hold the iPhone vertically.

7 Work with the conversation's details by tapping the name of the conversation to expose the Info icon (i) and then tap that icon.

8 Change conversations by tapping the conversation you want to view.

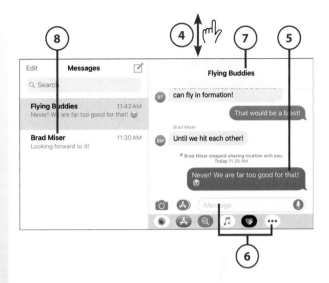

Using 3D Touch for Messages

You can use the 3D Touch feature (iPhone 6s and later models) with the Messages app as follows:

1 Browse your messages.

2 Press and hold on a conversation in which you are interested. A Peek of that conversation appears.

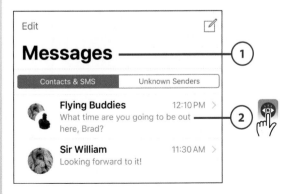

(3) Review the preview of the messages that appear in the Peek.

(4) Open the conversation so you can read all of its messages by pressing down slightly harder until it pops open. Use the steps in the earlier task to read it (skip the rest of these steps).

(5) See actions you can perform on the message by swiping up on the Peek.

(6) Tap the reply you want to make, which is based on the context of the previous message, and it is added to the conversation. If you tap Custom, you can create a custom reply to the message as you can when you view the conversation.

Browsing Attachments to Conversations

As photos, videos, and documents are added to a conversation, they are collected so you can browse and view them at any time:

(1) Move to the conversation in which you want to browse attachments.

(2) Tap the name of the conversation at the top of the screen.

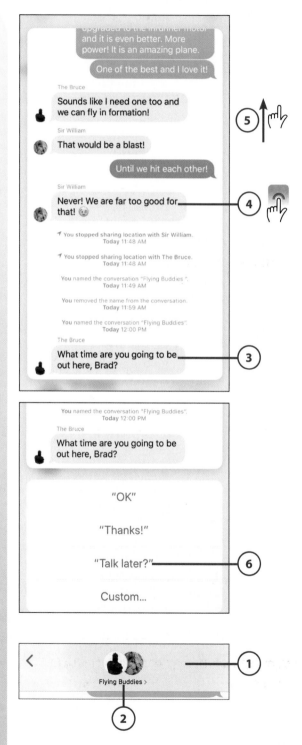

3. Tap Info (i).

4. Swipe up until you see the Images and Attachments tabs.

5. Tap Images to see images attached to the conversation or Attachments to work with other types of attachments (such as PDF documents).

6. Swipe up and down on the images or attachments until you see one you want to view.

7. Tap the image or attachment you want to view.

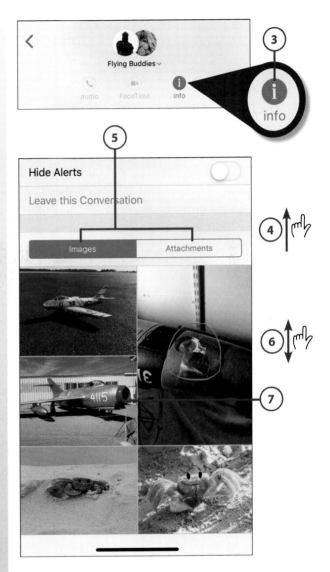

8 View the image or attachment, such as looking at a photo.

9 Tap Done to return to the Details screen.

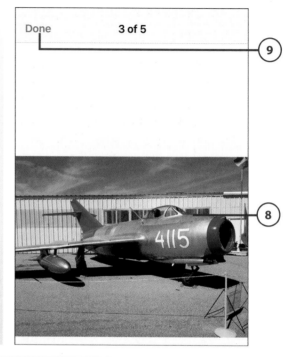

Done   3 of 5

Keep Quiet!

You can disable notifications for a specific conversation by moving to its Details screen. Set the Hide Alerts switch to on (green). You no longer are notified when new messages arrive in that conversation. Set the switch to off (white) to have notifications resume.

I'm Outta Here!

If you don't want to participate in a conversation any more, open the Details screen and tap Leave this Conversation. (You can't leave a conversation you started.)

Working with Messages from People You Might Not Know

As you use Messages, it is likely you'll receive messages from people who aren't in your contacts or who you haven't sent messages to before. Some of these will be legitimate contacts with whom you haven't messaged previously, whereas other messages will come from a person who made a mistake, such as not typing the phone number correctly; others will be made for nefarious purposes. The Messages app can filter messages from unknown people for you and put them on the

Unknown Senders tab so you can easily identify messages that are from people who you might not know.

To use this functionality, the Filter Unknown Senders switch on the Messages Settings screen must be turned on (green). (The details of configuring Messages settings are provided in "Setting Your Text and iMessage Preferences" earlier in this chapter.) When this switch is on, you see two tabs in the Messages app. The Contacts & SMS tab lists conversations with people who are contacts or with whom you have communicated previously. The Unknown Senders tab lists conversations from people who aren't contacts or with whom you haven't communicated previously. (If the Filter Unknown Senders switch is off, you don't see these tabs.)

If you enable the Filter Unknown Senders feature, you can work with "suspicious" messages as follows:

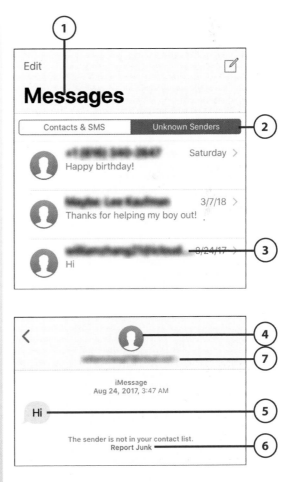

1. Open the Messages app.

2. Tap the Unknown Senders tab.

3. Tap a message to read it so you can determine if it is a legitimate message for you.

4. Review the identification of the sender as best Messages can determine it, such as an email address.

5. Read the message.

6. If the message is from someone you don't recognize and don't want to receive future messages from, tap Report Junk. The sender's message is deleted from the Messages app and the associated email address or phone number is blocked so you won't receive any more messages from the sender.

7. If you want to take other action on the sender, tap the label under the image at the top of the screen (which is a silhouette in most cases).

8 Tap Info (i).

9 Tap the contact information for the sender.

10 If you recognize the person, want to communicate with her, but don't have a contact configured for her, tap Create New Contact to create a new contact for the person. (For information about creating or updating contacts, see Chapter 6.)

11 If you recognize the person, want to communicate with her, and have a contact configured for her, tap Add to Existing Contact to update a current contact with new information.

12 If you don't want to receive future messages from the sender, tap Block this Caller.

13 Tap Block Contact.

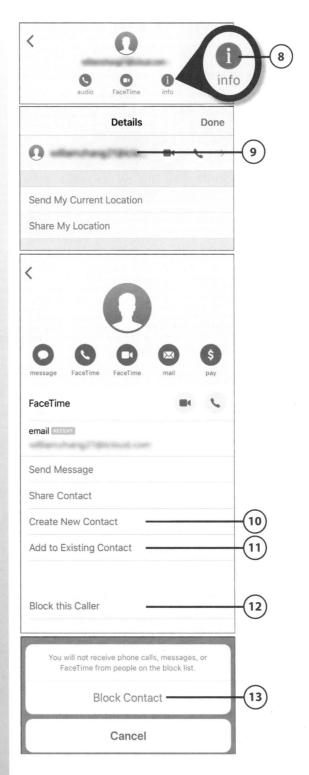

Junk or Block?

When you report a message as junk, the contact is blocked from communicating with you, but their information is not stored on your iPhone. When you block the contact instead, messages don't reach you, but the contact information is stored on the list of people you have blocked. You can unblock people from this list if you want to resume communicating with them. You can't resume communicating with someone whose messages you have marked as junk.

No Notifications

Be aware that you won't receive notifications for messages from unknown senders. So, it's a good idea to review this area periodically to make sure you aren't missing messages that you don't want to miss.

Responding to a Message with Icons

You can quickly respond to messages with an icon as follows:

 View a conversation.

 If you are using an iPhone with 3D Touch, press and hold on a message you want to respond to; if you are using a non-3D Touch phone, just touch and hold on a message. You can respond to any message, even if it's one you sent.

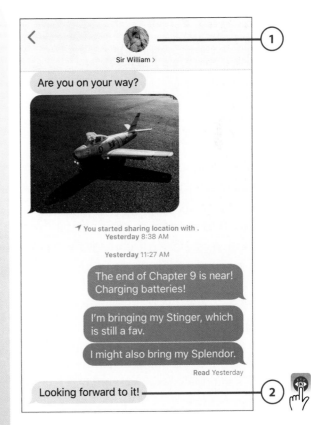

3 Tap the icon you want to add to the message; for example, tap the thumbs-up icon to indicate you like a message. The icon you select is added to the message. Others in the conversation receive notifications about what happened. For example, if you added a thumbs-up to a message, others receive a notification indicating that you liked it.

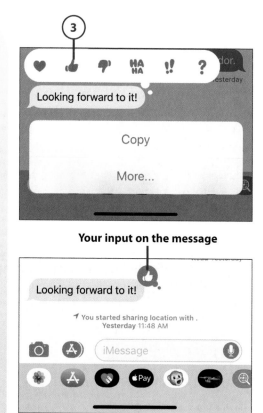

Your input on the message

Deleting Messages and Conversations

Old text conversations never die, nor do they fade away (if you have your Keep Messages setting set to Forever, that is). All the messages you receive from a person or that involve the same group of people stay in the conversation. Over time, you can build up a lot of messages in one conversation, and you can end up with lots of conversations. (If you set the Keep Messages setting to be 30 Days or 1 Year, messages older than the time you set are deleted automatically.)

Long Conversation?

When a conversation gets very long, the Messages app might not display all its messages. It keeps the more current messages visible on the conversation screen. To see earlier messages, swipe down on the screen to move to the top and earlier messages appear.

When a conversation gets too long, if you just want to remove specific messages from a conversation, or, if you want to get rid of messages to free up storage space, take these steps:

1. Move to a conversation containing an abundance of messages.

2. If you are using an iPhone with 3D Touch, press and hold on a message you want to delete; if you are using a non-3D Touch phone, just touch and hold on a message to be deleted.

3. Tap More. The message on which you tapped is marked with a check mark to show it is selected.

Be a Copycat

Tap Copy to copy a message so you can paste it in other messages or in other apps.

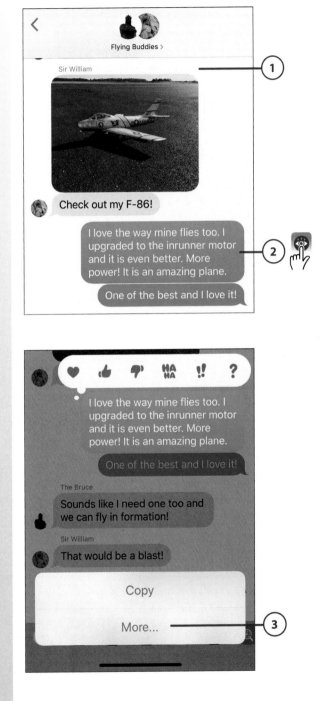

4 Tap other messages you want to delete. They are marked with a check mark to show you have selected them.

Delete Them All!

To delete all the messages in the conversation, instead of performing step 4, tap Delete All, which appears in the upper-left corner of the screen. Tap Delete Conversation in the confirmation box. The conversation and all its messages are deleted.

5 Tap the Trash Can.

6 Tap Delete X Messages, where X is the number of messages you have selected. The messages are deleted and you return to the conversation.

Tap to delete all the messages in a conversation

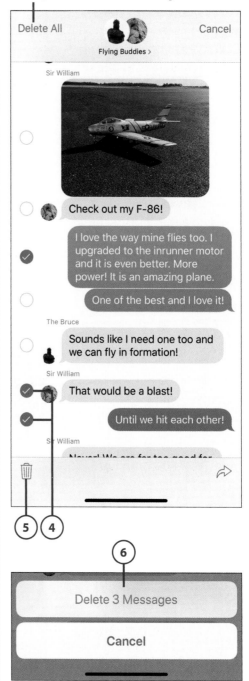

Pass It On

If you want to send one or more messages to someone else, perform steps 1–4. Tap the Forward icon that appears in the lower-right corner of the screen. A new message is created and the messages you selected are pasted into it. Select or enter the recipients to whom you want to send the messages, and tap Send.

Deleting Conversations

If a conversation's time has come, you can delete it.

1. Move to the Messages screen.
2. Swipe to the left on the conversation you want to delete.
3. Tap Delete.

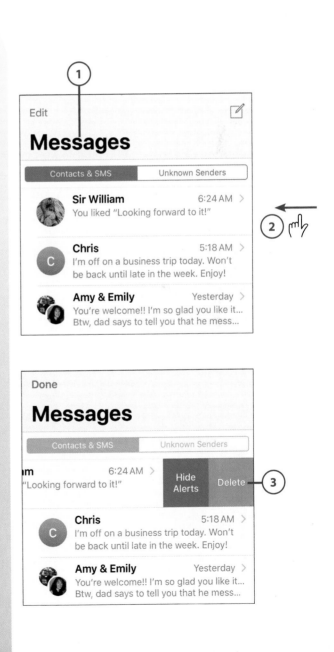

(4) Tap Delete at the prompt. The conversation and all the messages it contains are deleted.

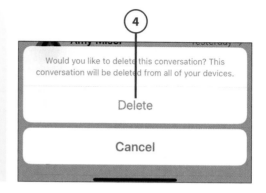

Would you like to delete this conversation? This conversation will be deleted from all of your devices.

Delete

Cancel

Gone, but Not Forgotten?

When you delete an iMessage conversation, it is removed from your iPhone and other devices. However, if you enable Messages for your iCloud account, the conversation remains in the cloud. If you send a message to the same person or people who were on the conversation you deleted, it is restored to your iPhone.

>>>Go Further
TEXTING LINGO

People frequently use shorthand when they text. Here is some of the more common shorthand you might see. This list is extremely short, but there are many websites dedicated to providing this type of information if you are interested. One that boasts of being the largest list of text message acronyms is www.netlingo.com/acronyms.php.

- **FWIW**—For What It's Worth
- **LOL**—Laughing Out Loud
- **ROTFL**—Rolling On the Floor Laughing
- **CU**—See You (later)
- **PO**—Peace Out

- **IMHO**—In My Humble Opinion
- **TY**—Thank You
- **RU**—Are You
- **BRB**—Be Right Back
- **CM**—Call Me

- **DND**—Do Not Disturb
- **EOM**—End of Message
- **FSR**—For Some Reason
- **G2G**—Got to Go
- **IDK**—I Don't Know
- **IKR**—I Know, Right?

- **ILU**—I Love You
- **NM or NVM**—Never Mind
- **OMG**—Oh My God
- **OTP**—On the Phone
- **P911**—Parent Alert
- **PLZ**—Please

Tap here to configure your date and time preferences

Go here to figure out where you're supposed to be and when to be there

In this chapter, you explore all the calendar functionality your iPhone has to offer. Topics include the following:

→ Getting started
→ Setting calendar, date, and time preferences
→ Working with calendars

Managing Calendars

When it comes to time management, your iPhone is definitely your friend. Using the iPhone's Calendar app, you can view calendars that are available on all your devices. You can also make changes to your calendars on your iPhone, and they appear on the calendars on your other devices so you have consistent information no matter which device you happen to be using at any time. You can also include other people in your events and manage events others invite you to attend.

Getting Started

The Calendar app does what it sounds like: It allows you to manage one or more calendars. This app has lots of features designed to help you work with multiple calendars and accounts, manage events that other people are invited to, and more. You don't have to use all these features, and you might just want to use the Calendar app's basic functionality, such as to record doctor appointments, dinner reservations, and similar events for which it is important to know the time and date (and be reminded when those times and dates are approaching).

Setting Calendar, Date, and Time Preferences

There are a number of time, date, and calendar settings that affect how you use your iPhone to manage your calendars and time. In most cases, you can leave these settings in their default configurations and start using the Calendar app right away (beginning with "Working with Calendars" later in this chapter).

Settings App Explained

To get detailed information on using the Settings app, see "Working with the Settings app" in Chapter 2, "Using Your iPhone's Core Features."

To be able to share your calendars among multiple devices, use an online account, such as iCloud or Google, to manage your calendar information. Before working with the calendar app, ensure you have at least one online account configured to manage calendar information on your iPhone. See Chapter 3, "Setting Up and Using an Apple ID, iCloud, and Other Online Accounts," for information about configuring online accounts.

To change the calendar settings, open the Settings app and tap Calendar. Use the settings described in the following list to make changes to how the app works.

- **Siri & Search**—Set the Search & Siri Suggestions switch to on (green) to allow information in your calendars to be searched and used by Siri. Set the Allow on Lock screen if you want calendar-related information (such as alerts) to appear on the Lock screen. Use the Shortcuts section to work with calendar-related shortcuts. Set the Find Events in Other Apps switch to on (green) if you want information that appears to be calendar related (such as someone mentioning a time and place to meet for lunch in an email) to be highlighted so you can easily add it to your calendars. These are both enabled by default.

- **Time Zone Override**—When disabled, the time for events is based on your current time zone. When enabled, the time zone for events on the calendars is overridden with the time zone for a city you select. This is useful if you always want event times to be based on a specific time zone. (See the Go Further sidebar at the end of this list for a more in-depth explanation of this setting.)

- **Alternate Calendars**—You can choose among different types of calendars, such as Chinese or Hebrew.

- **Week Numbers**—When this switch is on (green), week numbers appear on your calendars in the Month view.

- **Show Invitee Declines**—When enabled (the switch is green) and someone declines a meeting, they are shown on the Invitee list as having declined. When disabled (the switch is white), invitees who decline an event are removed from the list.

- **Sync**—Determines how far back events are synced onto your calendars. You can choose 2 weeks, 1 month (the default), 3 months, 6 months, or all events.

- **Default Alert Times**—Determines the default alert times for birthdays, events, and all-day events. When you set the Time to Leave switch to on (green), the Calendar app can use your travel time to configure an event's alert. You can change the alert time for any event on your calendar; these settings just determine the initial alert time.

- **Start Week On**—Determines the first day of the week.

- **Default Calendar**—Determines which calendar is used for new events by default (you can override this setting for any events you create). If you only have one calendar account or only store calendars on your iPhone, you won't see this option.

- **Location Suggestions**—When this switch is on (green), the Calendar app makes suggestions about the location of events when you create them. This is useful because you can use these suggestions to tag the event with a specific location, making it convenient to use the Maps app to generate directions and to configure a travel time for the event.

>>>Go Further
MORE ON TIME ZONE OVERRIDE

The Time Zone Override feature can be a bit confusing. If Time Zone Override is on, the iPhone displays event times according to the time zone you select on the Time Zone Override screen. When Time Zone Override is off, the time zone used for calendars is the iPhone's current time zone, which is set automatically based on your location or your manual setting. This means that when you change time zones (automatically or manually), the times for calendar events shift accordingly. For example, if an event starts at 3:00 p.m. when you are in the Eastern time zone, its start time becomes 12:00 p.m. if you move into the Pacific time zone.

When Time Zone Override is on, the dates and times for events become fixed based on the time zone you select for Time Zone Override. If you change the time zone the iPhone is in, no change to the dates and times for events is shown on the calendar because they remain set according to the time zone you selected for the Time Zone Override. Therefore, an event's actual start time might not be accurately reflected for the iPhone's current time zone because it is based on the fixed Time Zone Override city instead of the time zone where you are currently located.

To configure how your iPhone displays and manages the date and time, open the Settings app, tap General, tap Date & Time, and change the settings described in the following list:

- **24-Hour Time**—Turning this switch on (green) causes the iPhone to display 24-hour instead of 12-hour time.

- **Set Automatically**—When this switch is on (green), your iPhone sets the current time and date automatically based on the cellular network it is using. When it is off (white), controls appear that you use to manually set the time zone, time, and date.

Notifications

The Calendar app can communicate with you in various ways, such as displaying banners when something happens that you might want to know about; for example, you can be alerted with a banner when you receive an invitation to an event. The information you need to configure notifications is explained in Chapter 4, "Customizing How Your iPhone Works."

Working with Calendars

The Calendar app helps you manage your calendars. Notice I wrote calendars rather than calendar; that's because you can have multiple calendars in the app at the same time. To use the most cliché example, you might have a calendar for work and one for your personal life. Or, you might want a calendar dedicated to your travel plans, and then share that calendar with people who care about your location.

In most cases, you start by adding existing calendar information from an iCloud, Google, or similar account. From there, you can use the Calendar app to view your calendars, add or change events, and much more. Any changes you make in the Calendar app are automatically made in all the locations that use calendars from the same account.

Viewing Calendars and Events

You use the Calendar app to view and work with your calendars, and you can choose how you view them, such as by month, week, or day.

 The badge indicates how many invitations to events you have received

To get into your calendars, move to the Home screen and tap the Calendar app (which shows the current day and date in its icon and a badge if you have at least one new invitation). The most recent screen you were viewing appears.

There are three modes you use in the app. The mode in which you'll spend most of your time is the one that displays your calendars in various views, such as showing a month, week, day, or event. Another mode is the Calendars tool that enables you to choose and edit the calendar information that is displayed. The third mode is your Inbox, which you use to work with event invitations you receive.

Configuring Calendars

To configure the calendar information you see in the app, perform the following steps:

(1) If you have only one calendar, skip to step 2. Otherwise, tap Calendars to see all of your calendars. If you don't see this at the bottom of the screen, you are already on the Calendars screen (look for "Calendars" at the top of the screen) or you are on the Inbox, in which case, tap Done.

The Calendars screen displays the calendars available, organized by the account from which they come, such as ICLOUD or GMAIL (the names you see are the descriptions of the accounts you created on your iPhone). By default, all your calendars are displayed, which is indicated by the circles with check marks next to the calendars' names. Any calendars that have an empty circle next to their names are not displayed when you view your calendars.

(2) Tap a calendar with a check mark to hide it. The check mark disappears and the calendar is hidden. (The calendar is still available in the app, you just won't see it when you are viewing your calendars.)

(3) To show a calendar again, tap its name. It is marked with a check mark and appears when you are viewing your calendars.

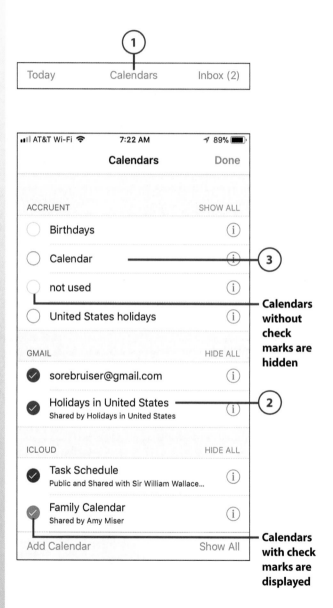

① ───

| Today | Calendars | Inbox (2) |

📶 AT&T Wi-Fi 📶   7:22 AM   🡥 89% ▬

Calendars   Done

ACCRUENT   SHOW ALL

◯ Birthdays   ⓘ

◯ Calendar ─────── ⓘ ── ③

◯ not used   ⓘ

    ── **Calendars without check marks are hidden**

◯ United States holidays   ⓘ

GMAIL   HIDE ALL

✓ sorebruiser@gmail.com   ⓘ

✓ Holidays in United States ─── ⓘ ── ②
    Shared by Holidays in United States

ICLOUD   HIDE ALL

✓ Task Schedule   ⓘ
    Public and Shared with Sir William Wallace...

✓ Family Calendar   ⓘ
    Shared by Amy Miser

Add Calendar   Show All

── **Calendars with check marks are displayed**

4 Tap Info (i) to see or change a calendar's settings. Not all types of calendars support this function, and those that do can offer different settings. The following steps show an iCloud calendar; if you are working with a calendar of a different type, such as a Google calendar, you might not have all of the same options as those shown here. In any case, the steps to make changes are similar across all available types of calendars.

5 Change the name of the calendar by tapping it and then making changes on the keyboard; when you're done making changes, swipe down the screen to close the keyboard.

6 To share the calendar with someone, tap Add Person, enter the email address of the person with whom you are sharing it, and tap Add. (Sharing calendars is explained in more detail later in this chapter.)

7 If the calendar is shared and you don't want to be notified when shared events are changed, added, or deleted, set the Show Changes switch to off (white). When this switch is enabled (green) and a change is made to a shared calendar, you receive notifications about the changes that were made. If the calendar is not shared, you won't see this switch.

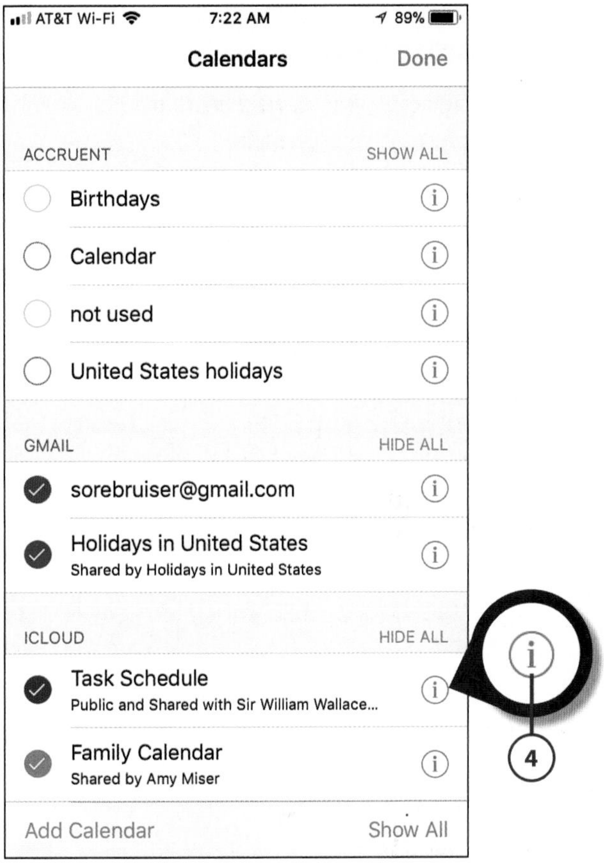

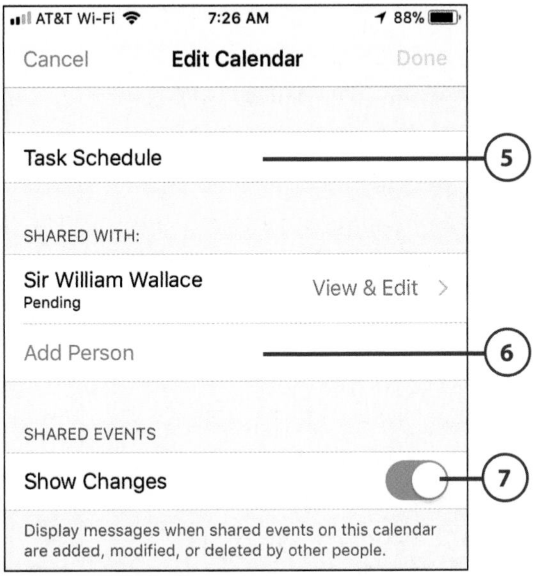

⑧ Swipe up the screen.

⑨ Tap the color you want events on the calendar to appear in.

⑩ If you want alerts to be enabled (active) for the calendar, set the Event Alerts switch to on (green).

⑪ To make the calendar public so that others can subscribe to a read-only version of it, set the Public Calendar switch to on (green), tap Share Link, and then use the resulting Share tools to invite others to subscribe to the calendar (more on this later in this chapter).

⑫ To remove the calendar entirely (instead of hiding it from view), tap Delete Calendar and then tap Delete Calendar at the prompt. The calendar and all its events are deleted. (It's usually better just to hide a calendar as described in step 2 so you don't lose its information.)

⑬ Assuming that you didn't delete the calendar, tap Done to save the changes you made.

⑭ Edit other calendars as needed.

⑮ Tap Done. The app moves into viewing mode, and the calendars you enabled are displayed.

·‖ AT&T Wi-Fi 🛜   7:28 AM   ⬈ 88% ⬛

Cancel   **Edit Calendar**   Done ⟵⑬

⬆ ⑧
🖑

● Green

● Blue

● Purple   ✓ ⟵⑨

● Brown

● Custom

NOTIFICATIONS

Event Alerts   ⬤◯ ⟵⑩

Allow events on this calendar to display alerts.

Public Calendar   ⬤◯
                 ⟵⑪
Share Link...

Allow anyone to subscribe to a read-only version of this calendar.

Delete Calendar ⟵⑫

·‖ AT&T Wi-Fi 🛜   7:31 AM   ⬈ 88% ⬛

Calendars   Done ⟵⑮

ACCRUENT   SHOW ALL

◯ Birthdays   ⓘ

◯ Calendar   ⓘ

◯ United States holidays   ⓘ ⟵⑭

GMAIL   HIDE ALL

✅ sorebruiser@gmail.com   ⓘ

✅ Holidays in United States   ⓘ
    Shared by Holidays in United States

>>>*Go Further*
ALL OR NOTHING

You can make all your calendars visible by tapping Show All at the bottom of the screen; tap Hide All to do the opposite. After all the calendars are shown or hidden, you can tap individual calendars to show or hide them. You can show or hide all the calendars from the same account by tapping the SHOW/HIDE ALL command at the top of each account's calendar list.

Navigating Calendars

The Calendar app uses a hierarchy of detail to display your calendars. The highest level is the year view that shows the months in each year. The next level is the month view, which shows the days of the month (days with events are marked with a dot). This is followed by the week/day view that shows the days of the week and summary information for the events on each day. The most detailed view is the event view that shows all the information for a single event.

Viewing Calendars

You can view your calendars from the year level all the way down to the day/week view. It's easy to move among the levels to get to the time period you want to see. Here's how:

1. Starting at the year view, swipe up and down until you see the year in which you are interested. (If you aren't in the year view, keep tapping the Back icon [<] located in the upper-left corner of the screen until that icon disappears.)

2. Tap the month in which you are interested. The days in that month display, and days with events are marked with a dot.

③ Swipe up and down the screen to view different months in the year you selected.

④ To see the detail for a date, tap it. There are two ways to view the daily details: the Calendar view or the List view. Steps 5 through 8 show the Calendar view, whereas steps 9 through 11 show the List view. Each of these views has benefits, and, as you can see, it is easy to switch between them.

⑤ To see the Calendar view, ensure the List icon is not selected (isn't highlighted). At the top of the screen are the days of the week you are viewing. The date in focus is highlighted with a red circle when that day is today and a black circle for any other day. Below this area is the detail for the selected day showing the events on that day.

⑥ Swipe to the left or right on the dates to change the date for which detailed information is being shown in the lower part of the screen. As you change the date being displayed the black circle indicates the date for which detail is shown.

⑦ Swipe up or down on the date detail to browse all its events.

⑧ Tap an event to view its detail and skip to step 12.

Today Is the Day

To quickly move to the current day, tap Today, which is located at the bottom-left corner of the screen.

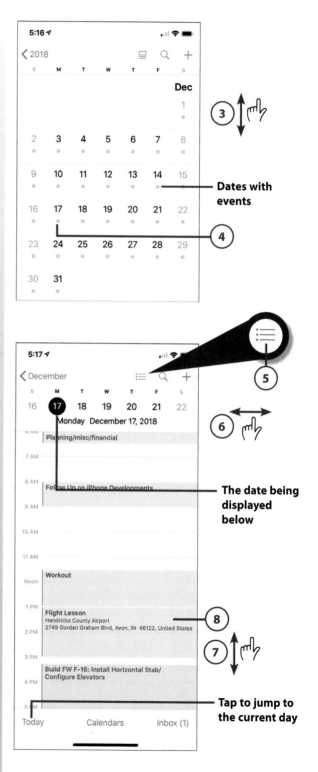

Dates with events

Monday December 17, 2018

The date being displayed below

Tap to jump to the current day

9 See the events in List view by tapping the List icon so it is highlighted.

10 Swipe up and down to see the events for each day.

11 Tap an event to view its detail.

12 Swipe up and down the screen to see all of the event's information.

13 View information about the event, such as its location, repetition, and relationship to other events on the calendar.

14 Tap the Calendar or Alert fields to change these settings; tap the Invitees area to get information about people you've invited to the event.

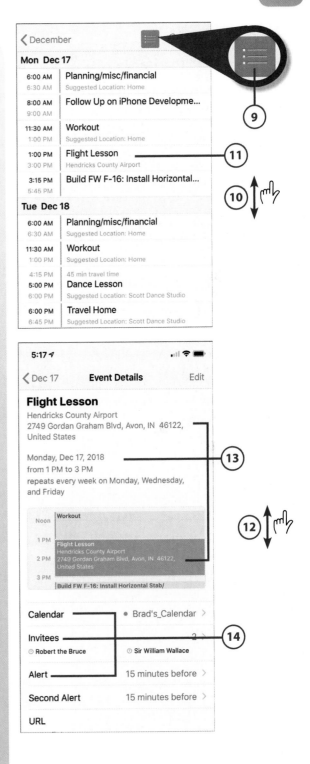

(15) If there is a second alert, tap Second Alert to change it.

(16) Tap any links to move to information related to the event.

(17) Read notes associated with the event.

(18) Tap a location to get directions to it.

(19) Use the Maps app to get directions (see Chapter 15, "Working with Other Useful iPhone Apps and Features," for more information).

(20) Tap Calendar to return to the Calendar app.

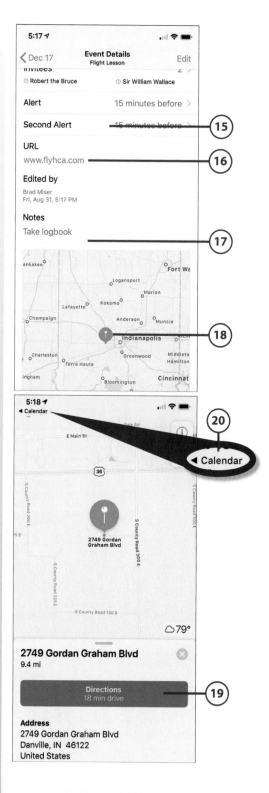

21. Tap the date to move back to the week/day view.

22. Tap the Back icon (<, which is also labeled with the month you are viewing) to move back to the month view.

23. To view your calendars in the multiday view, rotate your iPhone so it is horizontal. You can do this while in the week/day view or the month view.

24. Swipe left or right to change the dates being displayed.

25. Swipe up or down to change the time of day being displayed.

26. Tap an event to see its details.

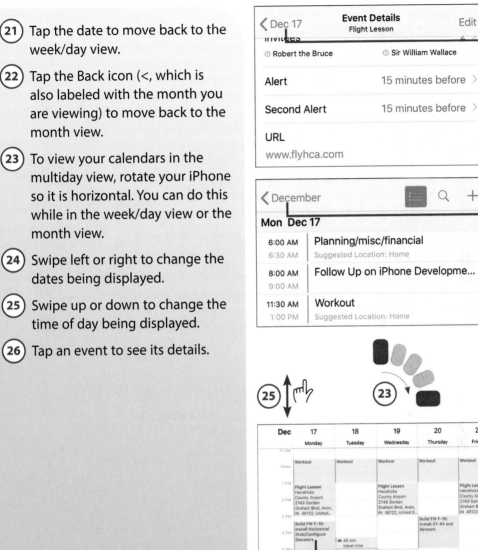

Current Time or Event

When you are viewing today in the Calendar view, the red line stretching horizontally across the screen indicates the current time, which is shown at the left end of that line. When you are viewing today in the List view, the current event is indicated by the text "Now" in red along the right edge of the screen.

Using 3D Touch for Events (iPhone 6s/6s Plus and Later)

You can use the 3D Touch feature on an iPhone 6s/6s Plus or later models with the Calendar app as follows:

1. Browse events, such as when you use the List view.

2. Tap and hold on an event in which you are interested. A Peek of that event appears.

3. Review the preview of the event that appears in the Peek.

4. To open the event so you can see all of its detail, press down slightly harder until it pops open and use the steps in the earlier task to work with it (skip the rest of these steps).

5. To see actions you can perform on the event, swipe up on the Peek.

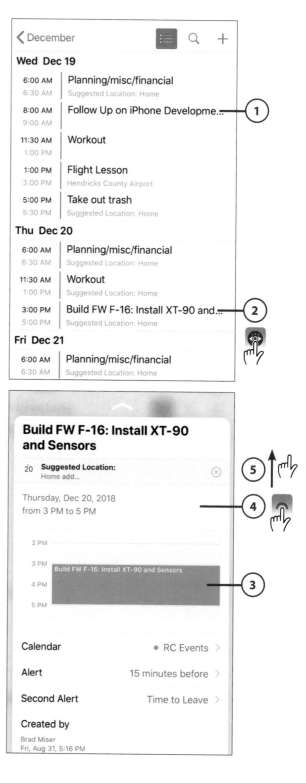

⑥ Tap the action you want to perform, such as Delete Event, to delete the event from your calendar.

What's Next?

To quickly see the next event on your calendar, move to a Home screen or the Lock screen and swipe to the right to open the Widget Center. Find the UP NEXT widget, which shows you the next event on your calendar; you might want to move this to the top of the Widget Center if you use it regularly. (For more on configuring your widgets, see Chapter 4.)

Build FW F-16: Install XT-90 and Sensors

20 Suggested Location:
    Home add...   ⊗

Thursday, Dec 20, 2018
from 3 PM to 5 PM

2 PM

3 PM   Build FW F-16: Install XT-90 and Sensors

4 PM

5 PM

Calendar	● RC Events >
Alert	15 minutes before >
Second Alert	Time to Leave >

Created by

Brad Miser
Fri, Aug 31, 5:16 PM

Delete Event ──────── ⑥

What's Next?...Even Faster

You can find out what's next even faster by activating Siri and saying, "What's next?" Siri shows you your next event and speaks the time and name of the event. Siri can also help with many other calendar-related tasks. (See Chapter 11, "Working with Siri," for the details.)

Adding Events to a Calendar

There are a number of ways you can add events to your calendar. You can create an event in an app on a computer, website, or other device and sync that event onto the iPhone through an online account. You can also manually create events in the Calendar app on the iPhone. Your events can include a lot of information, or they can be fairly basic. You can choose to create the basic information on your iPhone while you are on the move and complete it later from a computer or other device, or you can fill in all the details directly in the Calendar app. You can also add an event by accepting an invitation (covered later in this chapter).

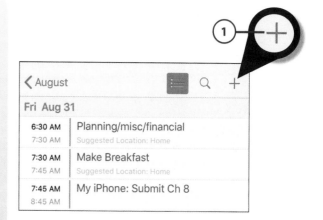

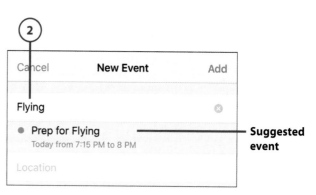

Suggested event

1. Tap Add (+), which appears in the upper-right corner of any of the views when your phone is vertical (except when you are viewing an event's details). The initial date information is taken from the date currently being displayed, so you can save a little time if you are on the date of the event before tapping Add.

2. Tap in the Title field and type the title of the event. As you type, events that are similar to the one you are creating are suggested; tap this to create the new event based on the suggestion. Then you can change the details to be specific to the event you are creating.

3 Tap the Location bar and type the location of the event; if you allow the app to use Location Services, you're prompted to find and select a location; if not, just type the location and skip to step 6.

4 Type the location in the Search bar. Sites that meet your search are shown below. The results screen has several sections including Recents, which shows locations you've used recently, and Locations, which are sites that the app finds that match your search criteria.

5 Tap the location for the event; tap Current Location if the event takes place where you are. You return to the New Event screen and see the location you entered.

6 To set the event to last all day, set the All-day switch to the on position (green); when you select the All-day option, you provide only the start and end dates (you don't enter times as described in the next several steps). To set a specific start and end time, leave this setting in the off position (white); you set both the dates and times as described in the following steps.

7 To set a timeframe for the event, tap Starts. The date and time tool appears.

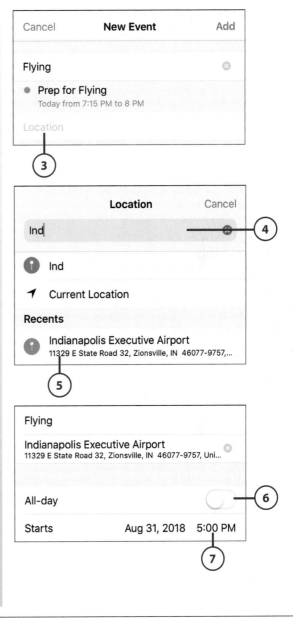

Location Prompt

The first time you create an event, you might be prompted to allow the Calendar app to access your location information. When you allow the app to use Location Services, you can search for and select event locations. The app can use this information to include an estimate of travel time for the event and to display events on a map when you view their detail.

8 Swipe up or down on the date wheel until the date on which the event starts appears in the center.

9 Swipe up or down on the hour wheel until the event's starting hour is shown.

10 Scroll and select the starting minute in the same way.

11 Swipe up or down on the hour wheel to select AM or PM.

12 If you want to associate the event with a specific time zone, tap Time Zone; if not, skip to step 14.

13 Search for and select the time zone with which the event should be associated.

14 Tap Ends.

15 Use the date and time wheels to set the ending date and time (if applicable) for the event; these work the same way as for the start date and time.

16 Tap Ends. The date and time tool closes.

17 To make the event repeat, tap Repeat and follow steps 18–23. (For a nonrepeating event, keep the default, which is Never, and skip to step 24.)

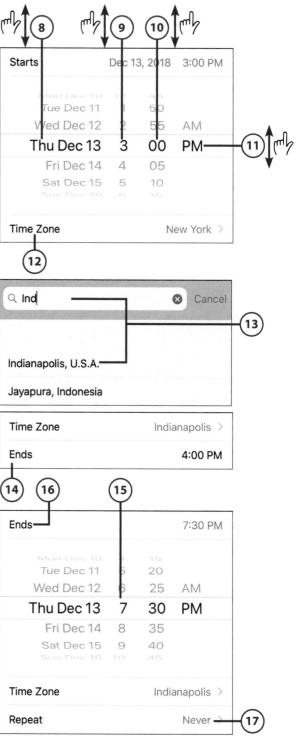

Your Results Might Vary

The fields and options available when you create a new event are based on the calendar with which the event is associated. For example, an iCloud calendar might have different options than a Google calendar does. If you aren't creating an event on your default calendar, it's a good idea to associate the event with a calendar before you fill in its details (to do that, perform step 30 before you do step 2).

Different Ending Time Zone?

The Calendar app assumes the time zone associated with the ending date and time is the same as for the starting date and time. If you want to set a different ending time zone, tap Time Zone below the Ends section and choose a different time zone as described in steps 12 and 13.

No Changes?

When you change a selection on most of the screens you see, you automatically return to the previous screen; for example, when you select a time zone, you immediately return to the New Event screen. If you don't make a change, you can return to the previous screen by tapping New Event in the upper-left corner of the screen. If you start to perform a search for something, such as time zone, but decide not to finish it, tap Cancel and then tap New Event.

(18) Tap the frequency at which you want the event repeated, such as Every Day, Every Week, etc.; if you want to use a repeat cycle not shown, tap Custom and create the frequency with which you want the event to repeat.

‹ New Event	Repeat
Never	✓
Every Day	
Every Week	—— (18)
Every 2 Weeks	
Every Month	
Every Year	
Custom	›

(19) Tap End Repeat to set a time at which the event stops repeating; if you want the event to continue indefinitely, skip to step 24.

(20) Tap Never to have the event repeat ad infinitum, and then skip to step 23.

(21) Tap On Date to set an end to the repetition.

(22) Use the date wheel to set the date for the last repeated event.

(23) Tap New Event.

Custom Repeat

To configure a custom repeat cycle for an event in step 18, such as the first Monday of every month, tap Custom on the Repeat screen. Then use the Frequency (Monthly for the example) and Every (for example, On the first Monday) settings to configure the repeat cycle. Tap Repeat to return to the Repeat screen and then tap New Event to get back to the event you are creating.

(24) To configure travel time for the event, tap Travel Time; if you don't want to configure this, skip to step 30.

(25) Set the Travel Time switch to on (green).

Ends	7:30 PM
Repeat	Weekly >
End Repeat	Never >

❮ New Event   **End Repeat**

Never	
On Date	

December	10	
January	11	2017
February	12	2018
March	**13**	**2019**
April	14	2020
May	15	2021
June	16	2022

End Repeat	Wed, Mar 13, 2019 >
Travel Time	None

❮ New Event   **Travel Time**

Travel Time	

Add travel time for this event to your calendar. Event alerts will take this time into account and your calendar will be blocked during this time.

26 To manually set a travel time for the event, tap it and skip to step 29.

27 Tap Starting Location to build a travel time based on a starting location.

No Change Needed

If you don't make a change to one of the settings, such as on the Repeat screen, tap the Back icon (<, which is also labeled New Event) in the upper-left corner of the screen to get back to the New Event screen.

28 To use your current location as the starting point, tap Current Location. Alternatively, use the search tool to find a starting location, and then tap it to select that location. This works just like setting a location for the event. The travel time is calculated based on the starting and ending locations entered for the new event. You can configure alerts based on this travel time as you see in later steps.

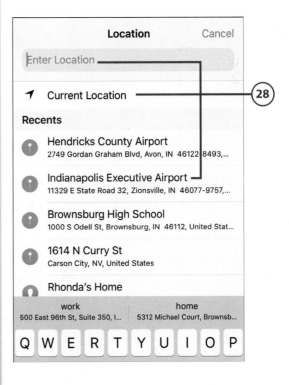

‹ New Event   **Travel Time**

Travel Time

Starting Location ——————→ **27**
None

Select a starting location to automatically determine travel time, or select a time below.

5 minutes

15 minutes ———————— **26**

✓ 30 minutes

1 hour

1 hour, 30 minutes

2 hours

Location   Cancel

Enter Location

➤ Current Location ————— **28**

Recents

Hendricks County Airport
2749 Gordan Graham Blvd, Avon, IN 46122-8493,...

Indianapolis Executive Airport
11329 E State Road 32, Zionsville, IN 46077-9757,...

Brownsburg High School
1000 S Odell St, Brownsburg, IN 46112, United Stat...

1614 N Curry St
Carson City, NV, United States

Rhonda's Home

work   home
500 East 96th St, Suite 350, I...   5312 Michael Court, Brownsb...

Q W E R T Y U I O P

29 Tap New Event.

30 To change the calendar with which the event is associated, tap Calendar (to leave the current calendar selected, skip to step 32).

31 Tap the calendar with which the event should be associated.

32 To invite others to the event, tap Invitees; if you don't want to invite someone else, skip to step 37.

33 Enter the email addresses for each person you want to invite; as you type, the app tries to identify people who match what you are typing. You can tap a person to add him to the event or keep entering the email address until it is complete. You can also tap Add (+) to choose people in your Contacts app (see Chapter 6, "Managing Contacts," for help using that app).

34 Repeat step 33 until you've added everyone you want to invite.

35 Tap Done. You move to the Invitees screen and see those whom you invited.

Automatic Sharing

When you add an event to a calendar that is shared with others, the people with whom the calendar is shared, see the event in their Calendar app automatically.

29

⟨ New Event   **Travel Time**

Travel Time   40 min ›

Calendar   • sorebruiser@gmail.com ⟶ **30**

⟨ New Event   **Calendar**

GMAIL

• sorebruiser@gmail.com   ✓

ICLOUD

• **Task Schedule**
  Public and Shared with Edward the Longshanks...

• **Family Calendar**
  Shared by Amy Miser

• **Brad's_Calendar**   **31**
  Shared with Robert Bruce and...

• **Books**
  Public and Shared with Robert Bruce...

• **RC Events**
  Shared by Brad Miser

• **Work**
  Public Calendar

Calendar   • Brad's_Calendar ›

Invitees   None ⟶ **32**

Cancel   **Add Invitees**   Done ⟶ **35**

To: Abraham Lincoln, will   ⊕
                                            33

Sir **William** Wallace
home sirwilliamwallace@icloud.com

Sir **William** Wallace
work sirwilliamwallace@me.com

36 Tap New Event.

37 To set an alert for the event that is different than the default, tap Alert; if you want to use the default alert, skip to step 39.

38 Tap when you want to see an alert for the event. You can choose a time relative to the time you need to start traveling or relative to the event's start time.

39 To set a second alert that is different than the default, tap Second Alert; to use the default, skip to step 41.

‹ New Event   **Invitees**

36

Add invitees   ›

NO RESPONSE

  Abraham Lincoln   ?

Sir William Wallace   ?

Invitees   2 ›

Alert   15 minutes before ⟶ 37

‹ New Event   **Alert**

None

At start of travel time

5 minutes before travel time

15 minutes before travel time   ✓

30 minutes before travel time

1 hour before travel time   ⟶ 38

2 hours before travel time

1 day before

2 days before

1 week before

Alert   1 hour before ›

Second Alert   Time to Leave ⟶ 39

40 Tap when you want to see a second alert for the event. If you have included travel time in the event, the At or before start of travel time options are useful because they alert you relative to when your journey should begin.

41 To indicate your availability during this event, tap Show As.

42 Tap the availability status you want to indicate during the event. If someone can access your availability through their calendar application, this is the status they see if they try to book an event at the same time.

43 Tap in the URL field to enter a URL associated with the event.

‹ New Event   **Second Alert**

None

Time to Leave   ✓

Calendar uses your location, this event's location, and traffic conditions to tell you when you need to leave.

At start of travel time   ——————**40**

5 minutes before travel time

15 minutes before travel time

30 minutes before travel time

1 hour before travel time

2 hours before travel time

1 day before

Second Alert   1 hour before ›

Show As   Busy ›

41

‹ New Event   **Show As**

Busy   ——————✓ **42**

Free

Show As   Busy ›

URL

43

44 Type the URL.

45 Tap Done.

46 Tap in the Notes field.

47 Type the information you want to associate with the event.

48 Tap Add. The event is added to the calendar you selected, and invitations are sent to its invitees. Alerts trigger according to the event's settings.

A Better Way to Create Events

Adding a lot of detail to an event in the Calendar app can be challenging. One effective and easy way to create events is to start with Siri. You can activate Siri and say something like "Create meeting with William Wallace in my office on November 15 at 10 a.m." Siri creates the event with as much detail as you provided (and might prompt you to provide additional information, such as which email address to use to send invitations). When you get to a computer or iPad, edit the event to add more information, such as website links. When your calendar is updated on the iPhone, via syncing, the additional detail for the event appears in the Calendar app, too. (See Chapter 11 for detailed information about using Siri.)

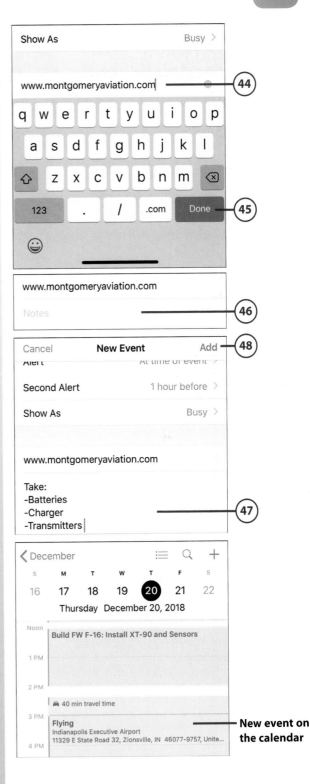

New event on the calendar

Using Quick Actions with the Calendar App (iPhone 6s/6s Plus and Later)

You can use the Quick Actions feature on an iPhone 6s/6s Plus or later models with the Calendar app as follows:

1. Press on the Calendar icon. The Quick Actions menu appears. At the top, you see the next event on your calendar.

2. To add a new event, choose Add Event and use the steps in the previous task to create the event.

3. Tap an event to view the event's details. You move to the event and can see all of its information.

Searching Calendars

You can search for events to locate specific ones quickly and easily. Here's how:

1. Tap the magnifying glass.

2. Type your search term. The events shown below the Search bar are those that contain your search term.

3. Swipe up or down the list to review the results.

4. Tap an event to see its detail.

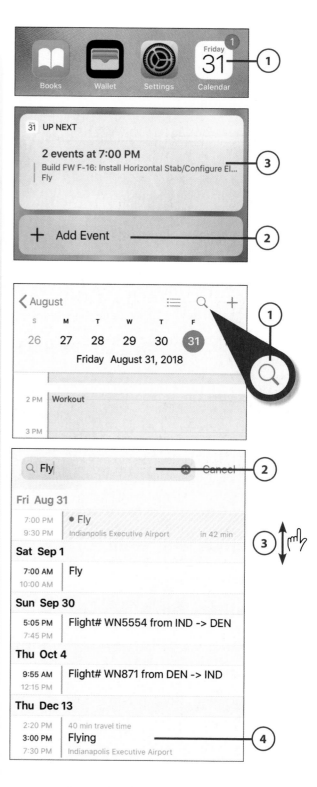

(5) Swipe up or down the event's screen to review its information.

(6) Tap Back (<) to return to the results.

(7) Continue reviewing the results until you get the information for which you were searching.

(8) Tap Cancel to exit search mode or Clear (x) to clear the search but remain in search mode.

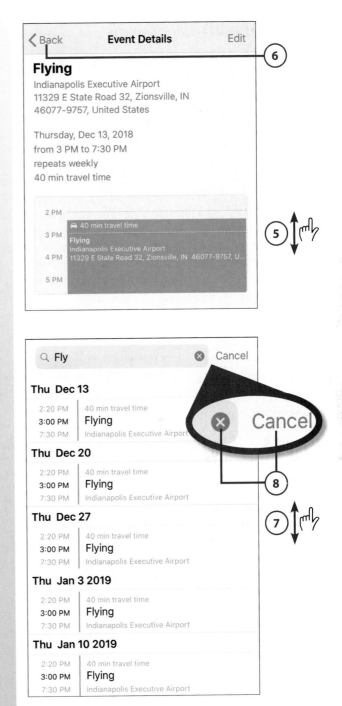

Working with Invitations

When someone invites you to an event, you receive an invitation notification in the Calendar app. You can accept these invitations, at which point the event is added to your calendar. You can tentatively accept, in which case the event is added to your calendar with a tentative status, or you can decline the event if you don't want it added to your calendar.

1. Tap the Calendar app icon when you see the badge on the app's icon indicating how many invitations you've received but not dealt with. (You may also receive notifications about new invitations according to your notification settings.)

2. Tap Inbox (the number in parentheses is the number of invitations you have received).

3. If you have multiple invitations, swipe up and down the screen to browse them.

4. If you see enough information about the event to be able to make a decision about it, tap Accept, Maybe, or Decline. The event is added to your calendar if you tap Accept or Maybe. If you tap Decline, it is not added to a calendar.

5. Tap an invitation to see its detail.

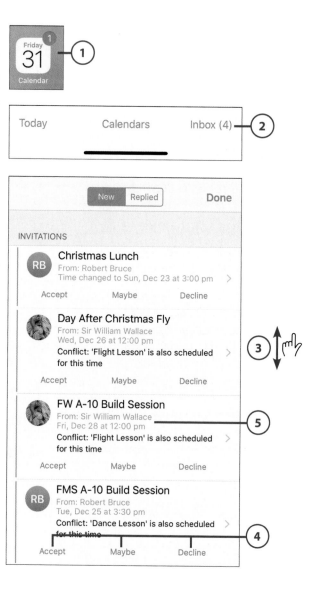

6 Swipe up and down the Event Details screen to see all its information.

7 To see how the proposed event relates to other events on the same date, look at the section of the calendar during which the event is being proposed. You see any events that might conflict with the one to which you have been invited.

8 If the time conflicts with another event or you want to propose a different time for some other reason, tap Propose New Time and use the resulting screen to configure a proposed date and time for the event. This goes back to the person who sent the invitation to you. If the change is accepted, you see the update and can accept the new time.

9 To choose the calendar on which the event should be shown, tap Calendar, and on the resulting screen, tap the calendar on which you want to store the event. Tap the Back icon (<) located in the upper-left corner of the screen to return to the Event Details screen.

10 To view details about whom the invitation is from, tap the Invitation from bar. You move to the person's contact information (from Contacts if her information is stored there or as much as can be gleaned from the invitation if it isn't). Tap the Back icon (<) located in the upper-left corner of those screens to return to the Event Details screen.

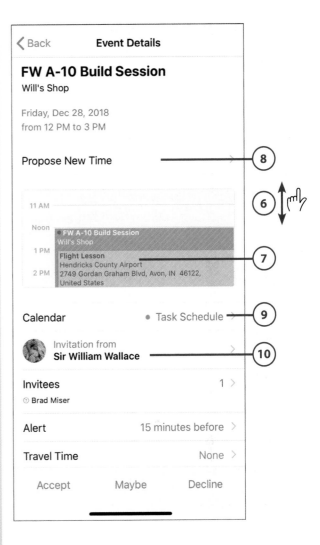

Invitation Notifications

You can use Notification settings to configure how the Calendar app informs you about invitations you receive. Refer to Chapter 4 for details. You can move to an invitation directly from its notification; for example, when a banner alert for an invitation appears on the screen, press it (3D Touch iPhones) or swipe it (non-3D Touch iPhones) to move to the invitation's details.

(11) Tap Invitees to see the status for each invitee to the event. You see a list of each person to whom the invitation was sent along with his or her current status. Tap Back (<) to return to the Event Details screen.

(12) If you want to change the event's alert, tap Alert and use the resulting Alert screen to choose an alert.

(13) Use the Travel Time option to configure your travel time to the event. This works just like when you create an event (see "Adding Events to a Calendar" earlier in this chapter).

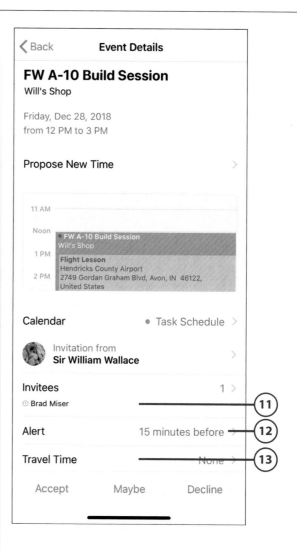

(14) Review any other information for the event, such as a website, attachments, or notes.

(15) To set your availability during the event, tap Show As and then tap your status during the event; in most cases, you tap Busy so others who want to schedule time with you will see that you aren't available.

(16) Indicate what you want to do with the event by tapping Accept, Maybe, or Decline. If you tap Accept or Maybe, the event is added to the calendar with the status you indicated. If you tap Decline, the event is not placed on a calendar, and the recipient receives a notice that you have declined.

After you make a decision, you move back to the Inbox. Any events you have accepted, indicated maybe, or declined disappear from the list of events on the New tab. Events that you have accepted from another device, such as from a computer, are shown with an OK icon, which you can tap to remove the invitation from the list.

(17) Use steps 5 through 16 to take action on other invitations you have received or tap OK to clear events you've dealt with on other devices.

(18) To review the invitations to which you've responded, tap Replied.

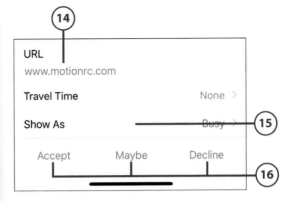

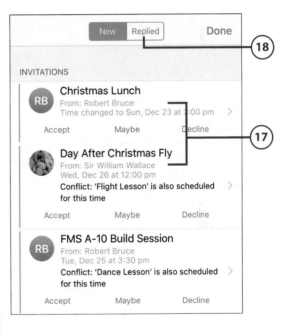

What You See Depends

Like when you create an event, the fields and options you see for an event to which you've been invited depend on the type of calendar the event is being sent from (for example, Google events may have different options than iCloud events do). Although the details for each type of calendar are slightly different, these steps help you deal with any invitations you receive.

(19) Swipe up and down the screen to review all the invitations to which you have responded. The highlighted box indicates your status for each event, such as Accept for those you have accepted or Decline for those you declined (these are also marked with a strikeout through their titles).

(20) Tap an event to see its details.

(21) To change your current status, tap one of the other status states. For example, to decline a meeting you previously accepted, tap Decline. The status changes immediately.

(22) When you are done reviewing invitations, tap Done to close the Inbox. You move back to the calendar. If you accepted or indicated maybe for any events, they are added to your calendars.

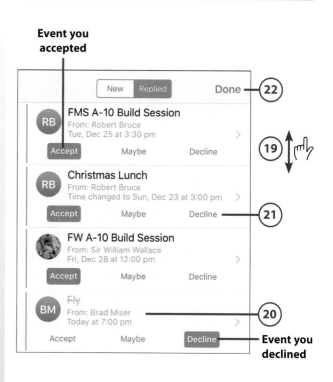

Event you accepted

Event you declined

Sharing Calendars

You can share your calendars with other people to enable them to both see and change your calendar, according to the permissions you provide. If you set the View & Edit permission, the person is able to both see and change the calendar. If you set someone's permission to View Only, she can see, but not change, the calendar.

(1) Move to the Calendars screen. Calendars you are sharing are indicated by the Shared with name, text just under the calendar name, where name is the name of the person with whom you are sharing the calendar.

(2) To see who is currently sharing a calendar, or to share a calendar, tap Info (i) for the calendar to be shared. If the calendar is currently being shared, the SHARED WITH section appears on the Edit Calendar screen. This section contains the names of and permissions granted to the people who are sharing the calendar. The status of each person's acceptance is shown under his name (Accepted, Pending, or Declined).

(3) Tap Add Person to share a calendar with someone else (whether it is currently shared or not).

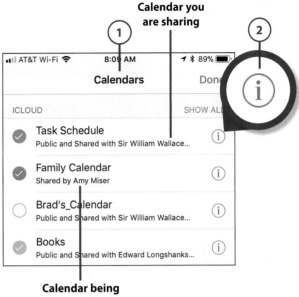

Calendar you
are sharing

Calendar being
shared with you

(4) Type a person's name or email address, tap a name or email address that the app suggests based on what you are typing, or use the Contacts app to choose the people with whom you want to share the calendar (you can add multiple people at the same time).

(5) Tap Add. You return to the Edit Calendar screen, and see the person you added on the SHARED WITH list. The person you invited receives an invitation to join the calendar you are sharing. If he accepts, the shared calendar becomes available in the calendar app he uses. As people make decisions about the calendar you are sharing, the status below each invitee's name changes to reflect the current status. You also see notifications when an invitee responds if you allow the app to provide notifications to you.

(6) If you don't want a person to be able to change the calendar, tap View & Edit.

(7) Slide the Allow Editing switch to off (white); the person will be able to view but not change the calendar.

(8) Tap Back (<).

(9) When you're done sharing the calendar, tap Done.

••ıll AT&T Wi-Fi 🔆	8:11 AM	🡥 ⚡ 88% 🔋
Cancel	**Edit Calendar**	Done ——(9)

(10) When you are finished configuring calendar sharing, tap Done.

••ıll AT&T Wi-Fi 🔆	8:11 AM	🡥 ⚡ 88% 🔋
	Calendars	Done ——(10)

Managing Calendars, Events, and Invitations

Following are some more points about the Calendar app you might find helpful:

- You can also use the List view when you are viewing the calendar in Month view. Tap the List icon (just to the left of the magnifying glass). The list opens at the bottom of the screen and shows the events on the day currently selected (the date is in a black circle unless the day selected is today, in which case the circle is red).

- You can see today's events at any time by opening the Widgets Center (move to a Home screen and swipe to the right) screen. In the UP NEXT widget, you see information about the next event on your calendar. You can view the current day's calendar in the CALENDAR widget; tap an event in the widget to see its detail. (See Chapter 2 for more information about working with the Widget Center and widgets.)

- When an event's alarm goes off, an onscreen notification appears (according to the notification settings for the Calendar app) and the calendar event sound you've selected plays. When an alert notification appears, the event's title, location (if one is set), and time appear. If it is a temporary banner, you can ignore it and it moves off the screen after a few moments. If it is a persistent banner, you have to take action on it (such as viewing it) to clear it from the screen. To take action on a banner notification (persistent or temporary), you can press (3D Touch) or tap (non-3D Touch) the notification to view its details; you can tap the details to move into the Calendar app or close the notification by tapping Close (x). You can swipe up from the bottom of a notification to manually close it without taking further action on it.

- If an event gets canceled after you accept it or indicated maybe, you receive a notification in your Inbox that displays a strikethrough through the event's title. Tap Delete to remove the event from your calendar.

- When you receive an invitation, the event is tentatively added to your calendar until you make a decision about it. The status changes as you accept, tentatively accept (Maybe), or decline invitations.

- Siri is useful for working with calendars, especially for creating events. See Chapter 11 for detailed information about using Siri.

- You can publish a calendar by making it public. When you do this, anyone who can access the shared calendar on the Web can view, but not change, the published calendar. To make a calendar public, move to its Edit Calendar screen and slide the Public Calendar switch to on (green). Tap Share Link. Then tap Mail to send the link via email, tap Message to send it via the Messages app, or tap Copy to copy the link so you can paste it elsewhere. Tap AirDrop, Twitter, or Facebook to share the link in those ways. The link can be clicked to view your calendar or, if the person uses a compatible application, to subscribe to it so it appears in her calendar application.

>>>Go Further

OTHER USEFUL APPS FOR MANAGING YOUR TIME

Your iPhone includes a couple more apps that can help you manage your time. The Clock app enables you to easily see the current time in multiple locations, set alarms, set a consistent time for sleep every day, use a stopwatch, and count down time with a timer. The Reminders app enables you to create reminders for events, tasks you need to perform, or just about anything else. You can learn a bit more about these apps in Chapter 15.

Use shortcuts to perform multiple tasks with one expression

Go here to set up Siri

Speak to Siri to send and hear messages, create and manage events, make calls, and much more

Dictate text input instead of typing

In this chapter, you learn about all the great things you can do with your iPhone by speaking to it. Topics include the following:

→ Getting started
→ Setting up Siri
→ Understanding Siri's personality
→ Learning how to use Siri by example
→ Using Siri with shortcuts
→ Using dictation to speak text instead of typing

Working with Siri

Siri is Apple's name for the iPhone's and iPad's voice recognition feature. This technology enables your iPhone to "listen" to words you speak so that you can issue commands just by saying them, such as "Send text message to Sam," and the iPhone accomplishes the tasks you speak. This technology also enables the iPhone to take dictation; for example, you can speak words that you want to send in a text or email instead of typing them on the keyboard.

Getting Started

Siri gives you the ability to talk to your iPhone to control it, get information, and to dictate text. Siri also works with lots of iPhone apps—this feature enables you to accomplish many tasks by speaking instead of using your fingers on the iPhone's screen. For example, you can hear, create, and send text messages; reply to emails; make phone and FaceTime calls; create and manage events and reminders; and much more. Using dictation, you can speak text into any supported app instead of typing. And, Siri can make suggestions as you perform tasks, such as searches, based on what you have done before.

You can even combine different tasks in a shortcut and then perform those tasks with a single expression. For example, you can generate directions to your home, send a text message saying you are on the way, and start music by saying "Head home." Based on that expression, Siri launches the shortcut and accomplishes each task it contains.

In fact, Siri does so many things, it's impossible to list them all in a short chapter like this one; you should give Siri a try for the tasks you perform and to get the information you need, and, in many cases, Siri can handle what you want to do.

Think of Siri as your personal, digital assistant to help you do what you want to do more quickly and easily (especially when you are working in handsfree mode).

You don't have to train Siri very much to work with your voice, either; you can speak to it normally and Siri does a great job understanding what you say. Also, you don't have to use any specific kind of phrases when you have Siri do your bidding. Simply talk to Siri like you talk to people (well, you probably won't be ordering other people around like you do Siri, but you get the idea).

Your iPhone has to be connected to the Internet for Siri and dictation to work. That's because the words you speak are sent over the Internet, transcribed into text, and then sent back to your iPhone. If your iPhone isn't connected to the Internet, this can't happen, and if you try to use it, Siri reports that it can't complete its tasks.

Because your iPhone is likely to be connected to the Internet most of the time (via Wi-Fi or a cellular network when you have cellular data enabled), this really isn't much of a limitation—but it is one you need to be aware of.

Just start speaking to your iPhone and be prepared to be amazed by how well it listens! You'll find many examples in this chapter to get you going with specific tasks; from there, you can explore to learn what else Siri can do for you.

Setting Up Siri

There are several settings that affect how Siri works. In most cases, you can leave these settings in their default positions (including those you selected the first time you turned your iPhone on) and start using Siri right away (beginning with "Understanding Siri's Personality" later in this chapter).

If you decide you want to make changes to Siri's settings, you can use the information in the table that follows to understand the options available to you.

To access Siri's settings, tap Settings on the Home screen and then tap Siri & Search. For each of these settings, you see a description of what it does along with options (if applicable).

The Settings App Explained

To get detailed information on using the Settings app, see "Working with the Settings App" in Chapter 2, "Using Your iPhone's Core Features."

Siri & Search Settings

Section	Setting	Description
SIRI SHORTCUTS	My Shortcuts	Takes you to a list of shortcuts you have created (shortcuts are covered in "Using Siri with Shortcuts" later in this chapter). You can edit or delete shortcuts from the My Shortcuts screen.
SUGGESTED SHORTCUTS	List of suggested shortcuts	In this section, you see a list of shortcuts that Siri has created for you. You can create a phrase for these shortcuts if you want to be able to activate them.
SUGGESTED SHORTCUTS	All Shortcuts	Takes you a list of all shortcuts on your iPhone, organized by the app with which they are associated most. You can search for shortcuts or add phrases for shortcuts to make them available (in which case, the shortcut is moved onto your My Shortcuts list).
ASK SIRI	Listen for "Hey Siri"	When this switch is on (green), you can activate Siri by saying, "Hey Siri" (you can still use the Side button or Ear-Pods switch to activate it). The first time you turned your iPhone on, you were prompted to speak the five phrases Siri uses to recognize when you want its attention. When this switch is off (white), you can only activate Siri with the other options. When you enable it again, you might have to go through the recognition process again.
ASK SIRI	Press Side Button for Siri	This switch enables (green) or prevents (white) you from activating Siri by pressing and holding on the Side button. On non-X models, you use the Touch ID/Home button instead.

Section	Setting	Description
ASK SIRI	Allow Siri When Locked	When this switch is on (green), you can activate and use Siri without unlocking your iPhone. This can be convenient, but it also makes your phone vulnerable to misuse because someone else may be able to activate Siri (for example, to send a text message) without unlocking the phone first. For some tasks, Siri requires the phone to be unlocked to complete them, but some can be done while the phone is still locked.
ASK SIRI	Language	Set the language you want Siri to use to speak to you.
ASK SIRI	Siri Voice	Choose the accent and gender of the voice that Siri uses to speak to you (the options you see depend on the language you have selected).
ASK SIRI	Voice Feedback	Choose when Siri provides verbal feedback as it works for you. When Always On is selected, Siri provides verbal feedback at all times. If you want to control Siri's voice feedback with the ring (Mute) switch, choose Control with Ring Switch. If you want voice feedback only when you are operating in handsfree mode, such as when you are using the iPhone's EarPods or a Bluetooth headset, tap Hands-free Only. Regardless of this setting, you always see Siri's feedback on the screen.
ASK SIRI	My Information	Choose your contact information in the Contacts app, which Siri uses to address you by name, take you to your home address, etc.
SIRI SUGGESTIONS	Suggestions in Search	When enabled (green), this switch allows Siri to make suggestions to you when you search. If you prefer not to have Siri make suggestions, set the switch to off (white).
SIRI SUGGESTIONS	Suggestions in Look Up	When enabled (green), this switch allows Siri to make suggestions when you use iOS's Look Up feature, which looks up information about a word or phrase you have selected on the screen. If you set this switch to off (white), Siri won't make suggestions when you use Look Up.

Section	Setting	Description
SIRI SUGGESTIONS	Suggestions on Lock Screen	When this is enabled (green), Siri's suggestions can appear on the Lock screen. If you don't want to see suggestions when your phone is locked, set this switch to off (white).
N/A	Apps	Toward the bottom of the Siri & Search screen, you see the list of apps installed on your iPhone. For each app, you can enable or disable Siri & Suggestions. When you enable this switch for an app, Siri can work within that app to make suggestions or learn from how you use the app. When you disable this switch, Siri is not able to work within the app for suggestions and search. You also have the option to Allow on Lock Screens for each app. When enabled, Siri information related to the app can appear when your iPhone is locked. When an app can use Siri shortcuts, you can tap Shortcuts to work with them (you learn more about this later in this chapter).

There are a couple of other settings that affect how you can speak to your iPhone:

- **Enable Dictation**—To access this setting, open the Settings app, tap General, and then tap Keyboard (you have to swipe up the screen to see it). At the bottom of the screen, you see the Enable Dictation switch. When this switch is on (green), you can tap the Microphone key on the keyboard to dictate text. When this switch is off (white), the Microphone key is hidden and you can't dictate text.

- **Cellular Data**—When enabled, this setting, located on the Cellular setting screen, allows your iPhone to access its cellular data network to connect to the Internet. This must be turned on for Siri to work when you aren't connected to the Internet via a Wi-Fi network.

Understanding Siri's Personality

Siri works in two basic modes: when you ask it to do something or when it makes suggestions to you.

Telling Siri What to Do

When you ask Siri to do something, Siri's personality is pretty simple because it follows a consistent pattern when you use it, and it always prompts you for input and direction when needed.

Activate Siri using one of the following methods:

- On the X models, press and hold the Side button for a couple of seconds until the Siri screen appears, you hear the Siri tone, and you feel the phone vibrate.

- On non-X models, press and hold the Touch ID/Home button until the Siri screen appears, you hear the Siri tone, and you feel the phone vibrate.

- Press and hold the center part of the buttons on the EarPods until the Siri screen appears and you hear the Siri tone.

- Say "Hey Siri" (if you've enabled this setting).

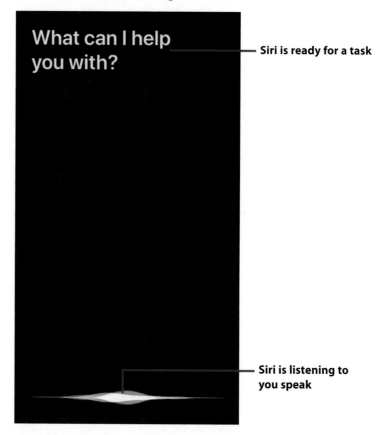

What can I help you with? —— Siri is ready for a task

—— Siri is listening to you speak

This puts Siri in "listening" mode and the "What can I help you with?" text appears along with a line at the bottom of the screen that shows when Siri is hearing you. This screen indicates Siri is ready for your command; if you used the "Hey Siri" option to activate it, you don't see this text because Siri goes directly into listening mode. If you don't speak within a second or two, Siri starts prompting you for a request and presents examples of what you can do.

Show me tomorrow's appointments — **What Siri heard you say**

Speak your command or ask a question. As you speak, the line at the bottom of the screen oscillates to show you that Siri is hearing your input, and Siri displays what it is hearing you say at the top of the screen. When you stop speaking, Siri goes into processing mode.

After Siri interprets what you've said, it provides two kinds of feedback to confirm what it heard: It displays what it heard on the screen and provides audible feedback to you (unless it's disabled through the settings you learned about earlier). Siri then tries to do what it thinks you've asked and shows you the outcome.

Tap to Edit >

Tap to edit the command

Show me tomorrow's appointments
Tap to Edit >

You have 16 appointments tomorrow:

CALENDAR — **Siri has completed the task**

Tue, Sep 11

6:00 AM 6:30 AM	Planning/misc/financial	in 11 hr
6:30 AM 7:45 AM	My iPhone: Submit Ch 11	in 12 hr
7:45 AM 8:30 AM	My iPhone for Seniors: Submit...	
8:30 AM 9:00 AM	Planning	
9:00 AM 10:00 AM	Nampa Demo Prep	
10:00 AM 10:30 AM	Brad	Clinton OOO MS Teams	
10:30 AM 11:00 AM	Sync up about upcoming dem... Microsoft Teams Meeting	
11:00 AM 11:30 AM	Book club check in #1 https://accruent.zoom.us/j/617672839	

? — **Listen icon**

If it needs more input from you, you're prompted to provide it, and Siri moves into "listening" mode automatically. If Siri asks you to confirm what it is doing or to make a selection, do so. Siri completes the action and displays what it has done; it also audibly confirms the result (again unless audible feedback is disabled as described earlier). If you want Siri to do more for you, tap the Listen icon at the bottom of the screen and speak your command. If you want to work with the object Siri created for you in its associated app, tap the object Siri presents.

In some cases, you can edit the information you spoke to Siri to change it. For example, suppose you are sending a text message to Sir William Wallace but Siri didn't get the name quite right; you can tap Tap to Edit on the Siri screen and then change the name; this can sometimes be easier and faster than redoing the task from the beginning. You can also change the content of actions, such as what you are texting via Siri; if it isn't what you intended, you can tap the message to edit it before you send it.

Also, how Siri interacts with you can depend on how it was activated. For example, if you started the interaction using the verbal "Hey Siri" option, Siri assumes you want to interact verbally and might respond with other options than you would see or hear when you activate Siri manually. When you ask Siri to show you your appointments for the day in this mode, you see the summary, but then Siri asks if you want to hear the details; if you say yes, Siri reads each event to you. When you activate Siri by using the Side or Touch ID/Home button with the same request, Siri stops after showing you the summary.

When you're done with Siri, swipe up from the bottom of the screen to move back to your previous location (X models) or press the Touch ID/Home button (non-X models) to move back to the Home screen or to the app you were using.

Siri uses this pattern for all the tasks it does, but often Siri needs to get more information from you, such as when there are multiple contacts that match the command you've given. Siri prompts you for what it needs to complete the work. Generally, the more specific you make your initial command, the fewer steps you have to work through to complete it. For example, if you say "Meet Will at the park," Siri might require several prompts to get you to tell it who Will is and what time you want to meet him at the park. If you say, "Meet William Wallace at the park on 10/17 at 10 a.m.," Siri can likely complete the task in one step.

The best way to learn how and when Siri can help you is to try it—a lot. You find a number of examples in the rest of this chapter to get started.

Following are some other Siri tidbits:

- If Siri doesn't automatically quit "listening" mode after you've finished speaking, tap the oscillating line. This stops "listening" mode and Siri starts processing your request. You need to do this more often when you are in a noisy environment because Siri might not be able to accurately discern the sound of you speaking versus the ambient background noise.

- If you are having trouble with Siri understanding commands, speak a bit more slowly and make sure you firmly enunciate and end your words. If you tend to have a very short pause between words, Siri might run them all together, making them into something that doesn't make sense or that you didn't intend.

- However, you can't pause too long between words or sentences because Siri interprets pauses of a certain length to mean that you are done speaking, and it goes into processing mode. Practicing with Siri helps you develop a good balance between speed and clarity.

- If Siri doesn't understand what you want, or if you ask it a general question, it often performs a web search for you. Siri takes what it thinks you are looking for and does a search. You then see the results page for the search Siri performed, and you might have to manually open and read the results by tapping the listing you want to see. It opens in the Safari app. In some cases, Siri reads the results to you.

- When Siri presents information to you on the screen, you can often tap that information to move into the app with which it is associated. For example, when you tap an event that Siri has created, you move into the Calendar app, where you can add more detail using that app's tools, such as inviting people to an event, changing the calendar it's associated with, and so on.

- When Siri needs direction from you, it presents your options on the screen, including Yes, Cancel, Confirm, or lists of names. You can speak these items or tap them to select them.

- Siri is very useful for some tasks, such as creating reminders, responding to text messages, getting directions, and so on, but not so useful for others, such as inputting search criteria, because it can take longer to use Siri than to type your input.

- Siri is not so good at editing text you speak. You have to manually edit what Siri hears you say by tapping Tap to Edit and then using the keyboard to change what Siri heard or by selecting an option that Siri recommends. When you've finished making changes, tap Done. If you changed a command, Siri replaces the prior command with the edited version. If you changed content, Siri updates the content. After you've made changes, you can continue with the task.

- Siri might ask you to help it pronounce some terms, such as names. When this happens, Siri asks you to teach it to pronounce the phrase. If you agree, Siri presents a list of possible pronunciations, which you can preview. Tap the Select icon for the option you want Siri to use.

- To use Siri effectively, you should experiment with it by trying to say different commands or similar commands in different ways. For example, when sending email, you can include more information in your initial command to reduce the number of steps because Siri doesn't have to ask you for more information. Saying "Send an email to Wyatt Earp home about flying" requires fewer steps than saying "Send email" because you've given Siri more of the information it needs to complete the task, and so it won't have to prompt you for who you want to send it to, which address you want to use, or what the subject of the email is.

- When Siri can't complete a task that it thinks it should be able to do, it usually responds with "I can't connect to the network right now," or "Sorry, I don't know what you mean." This indicates that your iPhone isn't connected to the Internet, the Siri server is not responding, or Siri just isn't able to complete the command for some other reason. If your iPhone is connected to the Internet, try the command again or try rephrasing the command.

- When Siri can't complete a task that it knows it can't do, it responds by telling you so. Occasionally, you can get Siri to complete the task by rephrasing it, but typically you have to use an app directly to get it done.

- If you have a passcode set to protect your iPhone's data (which you should), Siri might not be able to complete some tasks because the phone is locked. If that happens, Siri prompts you to unlock your phone, (which you can do by using Face ID, touching the Touch ID/Home button, or entering your passcode) and continue with what you were doing.

- Siri is really good at retrieving all sorts of information for you. This can include schedules, weather, directions, unit conversions, and so on. When you need something, try Siri first, as trying it is really the best way to learn how Siri can work for you.

- Siri sees all and knows all (well, not really, but it sometimes seems that way). If you want to be enlightened, try asking Siri questions, such as these:

  What is the best phone?
  Will you marry me?
  What is the meaning of life?
  Tell me a joke.

  Some of the answers are pretty funny, and you don't always get the same ones so Siri can keep amusing you. I've heard it even has responses if you curse at it, though I haven't tried that particular option.

Working with Siri Suggestions

When you enable the Suggestions in Search, Suggestions in Look Up settings, and the Search & Siri Suggestions setting for individual apps, Siri becomes proactive and provides information or suggestions for you based on what you are doing and what you have done in the past. Over time, Siri "learns" more about you and tailors these suggestions to better match what you typically do. For example, when you create a text message and start to input a name, Siri can suggest potential recipients based on prior texts you've sent. Similarly, when you perform a search, Siri can tailor the search based on your history.

Because Siri works proactively in this mode, you don't do anything to cause Siri to take action. It works in the background for you and presents information or options at the appropriate times.

Learning How to Use Siri by Example

As mentioned earlier in this chapter, the best way to learn about Siri is to use it. Following are a number of tasks for which Siri is really helpful. Try these to get some experience with Siri and then explore on your own to make Siri work at its best for you.

Using Siri to Make Voice Calls

You can use Siri to make calls by speaking. This is especially useful when you are using your iPhone in handsfree mode.

(1) Activate Siri (such as by pressing and holding the Side button [X models] or pressing and holding the Touch ID/Home button [non-X models]).

Speeding Up Siri

You can combine these steps by saying "Hey Siri, call Robert the Bruce iPhone." This is an example where providing Siri with more information when you speak gets the task done more quickly.

(2) Say "Call name," where name is the person you want to call. Siri identifies the contact you named. If the contact has only one number, Siri places the call and you move into the Phone app. If the person has multiple numbers, Siri lists the numbers available and asks you which number to use.

(3) Speak the label for the number you want to call, or tap it. Siri dials the number for you and you move to the Phone app as if you had dialed the number yourself.

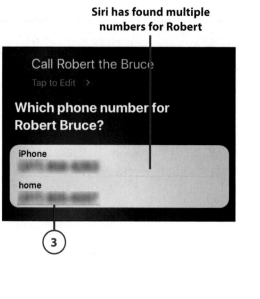

Siri has found multiple numbers for Robert

Siri Is Pretty Sharp

Siri can work with all kinds of variations on what you say. For example, if a contact has a nickname configured for him, you can use the nickname or the first name. If you want to call Gregory "Pappy" Boyington, you can say, "Call Pappy Boyington," or, "Call Gregory Boyington." If you say, "Call Pappy," and there is only one contact with that nickname, Siri calls that contact. If more than one contact has "Pappy" as part of their contact information, Siri presents a list of contacts and prompts you to select one.

Placing FaceTime Calls

You can also use Siri to make FaceTime calls by saying, "FaceTime name."

Composing New Email with Siri

To create email with Siri, do the following:

(1) Say "Hey Siri, send email to *name*," where *name* is the person you want to email. Siri creates a new email addressed to the name you spoke. (If the recipient has more than one email address, Siri prompts you to choose the address you want to use.) Next, Siri asks you for the subject of the email.

More Than One Recipient?

To send an email to more than one recipient, say "and" between each name as in, "Send email to William Wallace and Edward Longshanks." Siri adds each address before and after the "and."

(2) Speak the subject of the email. Siri inserts the subject, and then prompts you for the body of the message.

home:
sirwilliamwallace@icloud.com

What's the subject of the email, Brad?

MAIL

To: Sir William Wallace
Subject:

(3) Speak the body of the email. As you speak, you can include punctuation; for example, to end a sentence, say the word "period" or to end a question, say the words "question mark." When Siri completes the email, it displays the message on the screen and prompts you to send it.

(4) Review the message.

(5) Change the message by tapping Tap to Edit.

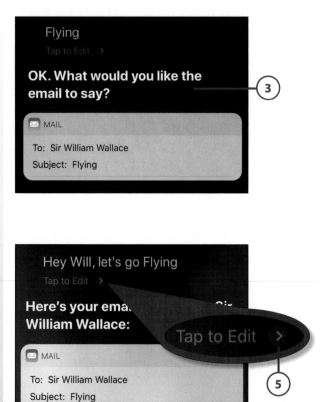

6. Tap a Siri suggestion to replace your message with the suggestion or use the keyboard to change the body of the email.

7. Tap Done. Siri updates the content based on your changes and presents the edited content to you; it again prompts you to send the message.

8. Say "send" to send the email or "cancel" to delete it. If you say "send," Siri sends the message, confirms it will be sent, and plays the sent mail sound when it is.

What Am I Editing?

When you tap Tap to Edit, you edit the last thing you spoke to Siri. If this was a command, you edit the command. If it was content, such as a text message, you edit the content. You can edit only the most recent thing you spoke.

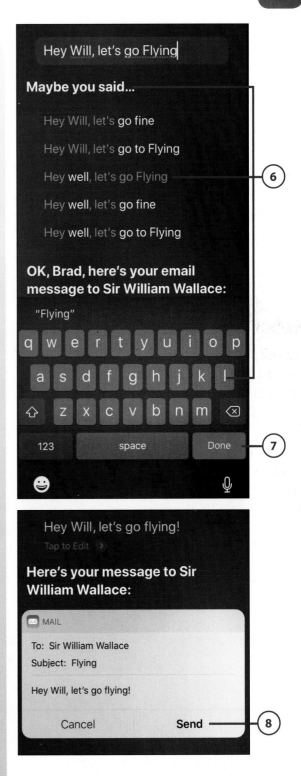

Replying to Emails with Siri

You can also use Siri to speak replies to emails you've read. Here's how:

(1) Open the message to which you want to reply.

(2) Say "Hey Siri, reply to this email." Siri prompts you for what you want your reply to say.

(3) Complete and send the reply; this works just like when you create a new message.

From: ★ The Bruce >
To: Brad Miser >   Hide

Hurry Up!
Today at 7:27 PM   (1)

Hey Brad,

Are you done yet? There isn't much wind and the sun is shining! It's time to fly!

Regards,

Robert

Pretty soon I'll be finished and then we can go

Tap to Edit >

Here's your message to Robert the Bruce:

MAIL

To: Robert the Bruce
Subject: Re: Hurry Up!

Pretty soon I'll be finished and then we can go

Cancel   **Send**   (3)

>>>Go Further
DOING MORE IN EMAIL WITH SIRI

Following are some other ways to use Siri for email:

- If you tell Siri to "Read email," Siri tells you how many emails are in your Inboxes and starts reading the time and date of the most recent email message followed by the subject and sender of the message. Siri then does the same for the next email until it has read a number of them. When it gets to the last message it reads, it prompts you to ask if you want to hear the entire list. On the screen, Siri lists the emails; you can tap an email message to read it yourself.

- Siri can read the content of email messages to you when you speak commands that tell it which email you want it to read, such as "Read most recent email," or "Read last email from William Wallace." Siri reads the entire message to you.

- To edit an email Siri created, say "Change." Siri prompts you to change the subject, change the message, cancel it, or send it. If you choose one of the change options, you can replace the subject or the body of the message. To change just some of the subject or body or to change the recipients, tap the message and edit it in the Mail app.

- You can start a new and completely blank email by saying "New email." Siri prompts you for the recipients, subject, and body.

- You can retrieve your email at any time by activating Siri and saying, "Check email." Siri checks for new email and then announces how many emails you have received since the oldest message in your Inboxes was received. If you don't have any new email messages, Siri announces how many emails you have previously received and that remain in your Inbox.

- If you just want to know about new email messages, say, "Check new email" instead. Siri reports back on new email you have received, but doesn't provide any information on email messages you've previously read.

- You can determine if you have emails from a specific person by asking something like, "Any email from William Wallace?" Siri's reply includes the number of emails in your Inboxes from William and displays them on the screen. Siri might also ask if you want it to read the email to you. Or, you can tap an email Siri found to read it.

- You can forward an email you are reading by saying "Forward this email" and then following Siri's lead to complete the process.

Having Messages Read to You

The Messages app is among the best to use with Siri because you can speak the most common tasks you normally do with messages. Especially useful is Siri's ability to read new messages to you. When you receive new text messages, do the following to have Siri read them to you:

1. When you receive a text notification, activate Siri.

2. Speak the command "Read text messages." (You can combine steps 1 and 2 by saying, "Hey Siri, read text messages.") Siri reads all the new text messages you've received, announcing the sender before reading each message. You have the option to reply (covered in the next task) or have Siri read the message again.

Siri reads each new message in turn until it has read all of them and then announces, "That's it," to let you know it has read all of them.

Siri only reads new text messages to you when you aren't on the Messages screen. If you've already read all your messages and you aren't in the Messages app, when you speak the command "Read text messages," Siri tells you that you have no new messages.

2

Hey Siri read new text messages
Tap to Edit >

Robert the Bruce sent you a new message...

Siri is reading a text message

Reading Old Messages

To read an old message, move back to the conversation containing the message you want to hear. Activate Siri and say the command "Read text message." Siri reads the most recent text message to you.

Replying to Messages with Siri

You can also use Siri to speak replies to messages you've received. Here's how:

 Listen to a message.

 At the prompt asking if you want to reply, say, "Yes." Siri prepares a reply to the message.

 Speak your reply. Siri displays your reply.

 Change the message before you send it by tapping Tap to Edit.

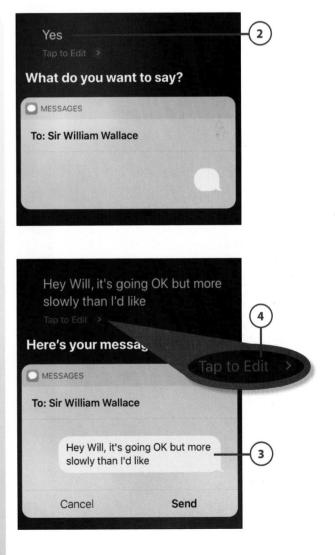

5. Use the keyboard to edit the message, or if you want to use Siri suggestions, skip to step 7.

6. Tap Done and skip to step 9.

7. Review Siri's suggestions for the message.

8. Tap a suggested message to use it.

9. At the prompt, say "Send" to send the message, "Cancel" to delete it, or "Change" to replace it. If you tell Siri that you want to send the message, Siri sends it and then confirms that it was sent.

Sending New Messages with Siri

To send a new message to someone, do the following:

1. Say "Hey Siri, send text message to *name*," where *name* is the person you want to text. Siri confirms your command and prepares to hear your text message.

2. Speak your message. Siri listens and then prepares your message.

3. If you want to send the message, say "Send." Siri sends the message.

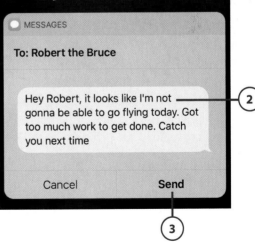

>>>*Go Further*

DOING MORE MESSAGING WITH SIRI

Following are some other ways to use Siri with messaging:

- If you say "Change" after you have created a new message, Siri prompts you to replace the message with a different one. If you say "Review" after creating a new message, Siri reads your message back to you. If you say "Cancel," Siri stops the process and deletes the message.

- You can use the Tap to Edit feature for any text message you are sending to manually edit it using the keyboard or to replace your message with one that Siri suggests.

- To send a text message to more than one recipient, say "and" between each name, as in, "Send text to William Wallace and Edward Longshanks."

- You can speak punctuation, such as "period" or "question mark" to add it to your message.

- You can tap icons that Siri presents on the screen, such as Send or Cancel, to take those actions on the message you are working on.

- Messages you receive or send via Siri appear in the Messages app just like messages you receive or send by tapping and typing.

- You can dictate into a text message you start in the Messages app (you learn about dictating later in this chapter).

Using Siri to Create Events

Siri is useful for capturing meetings and other events you want to add to your calendars. To create an event by speaking, use the following steps:

(**1**) Activate Siri.

(**2**) Speak the event you want to create. There are a number of variations in what you can say. Examples include, "Set up a meeting with William Wallace on Friday at 10 a.m." or "Doctor appt on Thursday at 1 p.m." and so on. If you have any conflicts with the event you are setting up, Siri lets you know about them and asks you if you want to schedule the new event anyway.

(**3**) Say "Confirm" if you don't have any conflicts or "Yes" if you do and you still want to have the appointment confirmed; you can also tap Confirm. Siri adds the event to your calendar. Say "Cancel" to cancel the event.

(**4**) To add more information to an event Siri has created for you, tap it on the confirmation screen. You move into the Calendar app and can edit the event just like events you create within that app (see Chapter 10, "Managing Calendars" for information about the Calendar app).

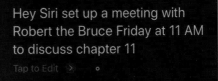

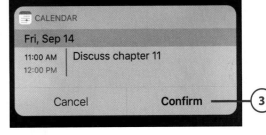

Invitees

If you include the name of someone for whom you have an email address, Siri automatically sends invitations. If you include a name that matches more than one contact, Siri prompts you to choose the contact you want to invite. If the name doesn't match a contact, Siri enters the name but doesn't send an invitation.

Using Siri to Create Reminders

Creating reminders can be another useful thing you do with Siri, assuming you find reminders useful, of course. Here's how:

1 Activate Siri.

2 Speak the reminder you want to create.

Here are some examples: "Remind me to buy the A-10 at Motion RC," "Remind me to finish Chapter 10 at 10 AM on Saturday," or "Remind me to buy milk when I leave work."

Siri provides a confirmation of what you asked. If you didn't mention a time or date when you want to be reminded, Siri prompts you to provide the details of when you want to be reminded.

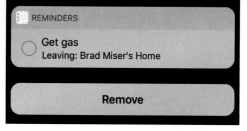

(**3**) Speak the date and time when you want to be reminded. If you included a date and time in your original reminder request, you skip this step. Unlike some of the other tasks, Siri creates the reminder without confirming it with you.

(**4**) If you don't want to keep the reminder, activate Siri and say "Remove" or tap Remove.

(**5**) To add detail to the reminder, tap it. You move into the Reminders app and can add more information to the reminder, as you can when you create one manually.

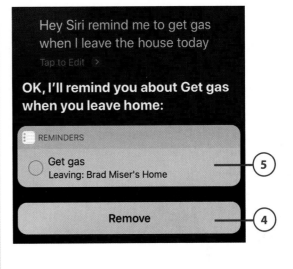

Hey Siri remind me to get gas when I leave the house today
Tap to Edit >

OK, I'll remind you about Get gas when you leave home:

REMINDERS

Get gas
Leaving: Brad Miser's Home ——————— (**5**)

Remove ——————— (**4**)

>>>*Go Further*
GOING FURTHER WITH SIRI TO MANAGE TIME

Following are some other ways to use Siri with the Calendar, Reminders, and Clock apps:

- You can change events with Siri, too. For example, if you have a meeting at 3 p.m., you can move it by saying something like, "Move my 3 p.m. meeting to Friday at 6 p.m."

- You can get information about your events with Siri by saying things such as

    Show me today's appointments.
    Do I have meetings on November 3?
    What time is my first appointment tomorrow?
    What are my appointments tomorrow?

    Siri tells you about the events and shows you what they are on the screen. You can tap any event to view it in the Calendar app.

- You can speak to your iPhone to set alarms. Tell Siri what you want and when you want the alarm to be set. For example, you can say something like, "New alarm *alarmname* 6 a.m.," where *alarmname* is the label of the alarm. Siri sets an alarm to go off at that time and gives it the label you speak. It displays the alarm on the screen along with a status icon so you can turn it off if you change your mind. You don't have to label alarms, and you can just say something like, "Set alarm 6 a.m." However, a label can be useful to issue other commands. For example, if an alarm has a name, you can turn it off by saying, "Turn off *alarmname*." Any alarms you create with Siri can be managed just like alarms you create directly in the Clock app. Note that alarms don't have dates associated with them so you can't set an alarm that's more than 24 hours in the future; if you request one further out than that, Siri offers to create a reminder for you instead.

- To set a countdown timer, tell Siri to "Set timer for x minutes," where x is a number of minutes (you can do the same to set a timer for seconds or hours, too); to make it even easier, you can just say, "Hey Siri, x minutes." Siri starts a countdown for you and presents it on the screen. You can continue to use the iPhone however you want. When the timer ends, you see and hear an alert. You can also reset the time, pause it, and so on by speaking.

- You can get information about time by asking questions, such as "What time is it?" or "What is the date?" You can add location information to the time information, too, as in "What time is it in London, England?"

- Tapping any confirmation Siri displays takes you back into the related app. For example, if you tap a clock that results when you ask what time it is, you can tap that clock to move into the Clock app. If you ask about your schedule today, you can tap any of the events Siri presents to move into the Calendar app to work with them.

- When you use Siri to create events and reminders, they are created on your default calendar (events) or reminder list (reminders).

Using Siri to Get Information

Siri is a great way to get information about lots of different topics in many different areas. You can ask Siri for information about a subject, places in your area, unit conversion (such as inches to centimeters), and so on. Just try speaking what you want to learn to best get the information you need. Here's an example looking for Chinese restaurants in my area:

(1) Activate Siri.

(2) Say something like, "Show me Chinese restaurants in my area." (Or a faster way is to combine steps 1 and 2 by saying, "Hey Siri, show me Chinese restaurants in my area.") Siri presents a list of results that match your query and even provides a summary of reviews at the top of the screen. (You must have Location Services enabled for this to work. Refer to Chapter 4, "Customizing How Your iPhone Works," for information about configuring Location Services.)

Siri prompts you to take action on what it found. For example, if you asked for restaurants, Siri tells you about the closest one and then asks if you want to try it. If you say yes, Siri offers to call it for you or gives you directions. You can tap other items on the list to get more information or directions.

If you like Chinese food (or just about anything else), Siri can help you find it

(2)

Hey Siri show me Chinese restaurants in my area

Tap to Edit   >

OK, one option I see is Asia Wok, which averages 3½ stars and is inexpensive.

MAPS

Asia Wok
Chinese · 1.9 miles · Closed Now
★★★★★ (68) on Yelp · $

Ho Wah Restaurant
Chinese · 1.5 miles · Closed Now
★★★★★ (25) on Yelp · $

China Best
Chinese · 1.7 miles · Closed Now
★★★★★ (18) on Yelp · $

Happy Wok
Chinese · 1.9 miles
No Reviews

3. Swipe up and down the results to see all of them.

4. To manually select a result, tap it.

5. Swipe up and down to see the details about what you selected.

6. Tap the screen to take action, such as tapping the Directions button to generate directions to the location using the Maps app.

Siri is also useful for getting information about topics. Siri responds by conducting a web search and showing you the result. For example, suppose you want to learn about the F-15 fighter plane. Activate Siri and say, "Tell me about the F-15 Eagle." Siri responds with information about your topic. You can have Siri read the information by activating Siri and saying "Read." Siri reads the results (this doesn't always work; it works best when the results are presented via Wikipedia or something similar).

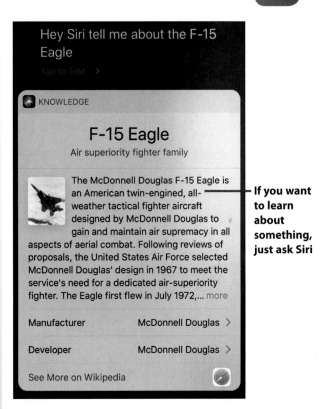

If you want to learn about something, just ask Siri

Using Siri to Play Music

You also can play music by telling Siri which music you want to hear.

(1) Activate Siri.

(2) Tell Siri the music you want to hear. There are a number of variations in what you can say. Examples include:

Play album Time of My Life.
Play song "Gone" by Switchfoot.
Play playlist Jon McLaughlin.

Siri provides a confirmation of what you asked and begins playing the music.

(3) Tap Open Music to move into the Music app to control the music with your fingers.

>>>Go Further

MORE SPOKEN COMMANDS FOR MUSIC

There are a number of commands you can speak to find, play, and control music (and other audio). "Play *artist*" plays music by the artist you speak. "Play *album*" plays the album you name. In both cases, if the name includes the word "the," you need to include "the" when you speak the command. "Shuffle" plays a random song. "Play more like this" uses the Genius to find songs similar to the one playing and plays them. "Previous track" or "next track" does exactly what they sound like they do. To hear the name of the artist for the song currently playing, say "Who sings this song?" You can shuffle music in an album or playlist by saying "Shuffle playlist *playlistname*." You can stop the music, pause it, or play it by speaking those commands.

Using Siri to Get Directions

With Siri, it's easy to get directions—you don't even have to stop at a gas station to ask.

(1) Activate Siri.

(2) Say something like, "Give me directions to the airport." If you want to find a specific location, include the details, such as, "Hey Siri, give me directions to the Indianapolis International Airport." If you want directions starting from someplace other than your current location, include that in the request, such as, "Get directions from the Eagle Creek Airpark to the Indianapolis International Airport."

(3) If Siri presents a list of possible locations, swipe up and down to review the list.

Hey Siri give me directions to the airport

Tap to Edit ›   ——————————— **(2)**

One option I found is Indianapolis International Airport on Col H Weir Cook Memorial Dr in Indianapolis.

MAPS

Indianapolis International Ai...
International Airport · 11 miles
★★★★★ (740) on Yelp

Fuller Field
Airfield · 5.0 miles
No Reviews

Eagle Creek Airpark
Airfield · 6.4 miles
★★★★★ (2) on Yelp   **(3)**

Indianapolis Executive Airp...
Airfield · 16 miles

④ Tap the location for which you want directions.

⑤ Tap Directions. Siri uses the Maps app to generate directions.

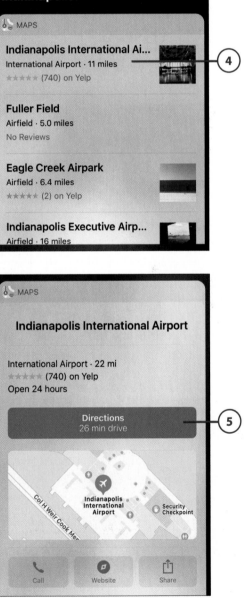

Hey Siri give me directions to the airport
Tap to Edit >

One option I found is Indianapolis International Airport on Col H Weir Cook Memorial Dr in Indianapolis.

MAPS

Indianapolis International Ai...
International Airport · 11 miles
★★★★★ (740) on Yelp ④

Fuller Field
Airfield · 5.0 miles
No Reviews

Eagle Creek Airpark
Airfield · 6.4 miles
★★★★★ (2) on Yelp

Indianapolis Executive Airp...
Airfield · 16 miles

MAPS

Indianapolis International Airport

International Airport · 22 mi
★★★★★ (740) on Yelp
Open 24 hours

Directions
26 min drive ⑤

Col H Weir Cook Mer
Indianapolis International Airport
Security Checkpoint

Call | Website | Share

(6) Tap Go to start turn-by-turn directions.

To Indianapolis International Air... ⊗
From My Location

26 min
22 mi · I-74 E
Fastest route

GO ──(6)

🚗 Drive   🚶 Walk   🚊 Transit   🏃 Ride

Using Siri to Open Apps

As you accumulate apps on your iPhone, it can take several taps and swipes to get to a specific app, such as one that is stored in a folder that isn't on the page of the Home screen you are viewing. With Siri, you can open any app on your phone with a simple command.

(1) Say "Hey Siri, open *appname*," where *appname* is the name of the app you want to open.

(2) If your phone needs to be unlocked to open the app, Siri prompts you to unlock it (such as by using Face ID or touching the Touch ID/Home button). Siri then opens the app for you, and you move to the last screen in the app you were using.

(1)

Hey Siri open Contacts
Tap to Edit >

You'll need to unlock your iPhone first.

It's Not All Good

When Siri Misunderstands

Voice commands to Siri work very well, but they aren't perfect. Make sure you confirm your commands by listening to the feedback Siri provides when it repeats them or reviewing the feedback Siri provides on the screen. Sometimes, a spoken command can have unexpected results, which can include making a phone call to someone in the Contacts app. If you don't catch such a mistake before the call is started, you might be surprised to hear someone answering your call instead of hearing music you intended to play. You can put Siri in listening mode by tapping the Listen icon, and then saying "no" or "stop" to stop Siri should a verbal command go awry.

Using Siri to Translate

Siri can translate words and phrases from the language you are using into other languages. Siri supports the translation of English into French, German, Italian, Mandarin, and Spanish among others. Try this translating function to see if it supports the language you need. Here's an example of translating an English phrase into Italian:

1. Say "Hey Siri, translate How do I get to the airport in Italian." Siri does the translation for you and speaks the translated phrase.

2. Tap the Play icon to have Siri speak the translation again.

> Hey Siri translate how do I get to the airport in Italian — 1
>
> Tap to Edit >
>
> **In Italian, 'how do I get to the airport' is:**
>
> TRANSLATION
>
> English
> how do I get to the airport ———— **The phrase Siri is translating**
>
> Italian
> Come si arriva all'aeroporto ▶
>
> **The translated phrase**
>
> 2 ▶

No Can Do

If Siri is unable to complete the translation you requested, it speaks what it can do. For example, it speaks a list of currently supported languages.

Using Siri with Shortcuts

Shortcuts enable you to do more by saying less. As you work with Siri, it automatically creates potential shortcuts for you; to enable those shortcuts, you need to tell Siri the phrase you want to use to do whatever the shortcut is. After that, you can perform the shortcut by speaking its phrase.

Do More with Shortcuts

You aren't limited to just those shortcuts that Siri creates for you. You can use the Shortcuts app to create multistep shortcuts. For example, you could create a shortcut that gets directions to your home, sends a text message that you are leaving, and starts music playing. You would just have to speak the shortcut's phrase to do all of these tasks. Multistep shortcuts are very powerful and you can use them to do a lot of things very quickly and easily. Working with the Shortcuts app is covered in "Customizing How Your Phone Works with Shortcuts," in Chapter 4.

Activating Siri Shortcuts

To review and activate shortcuts Siri has created for you, perform the following steps:

(1) Move to the Settings app.

(2) Tap Siri & Search.

(3) If you see a shortcut in the SUGGESTED SHORTCUTS section that you want to activate, tap Add (+) and skip to step 7.

(4) Tap All Shortcuts to see all of the shortcuts Siri has created for you.

(1)

Settings

Wallpaper >

Siri & Search > (2)

Tap to review shortcuts you've already activated

< Settings   **Siri & Search**

SIRI SHORTCUTS

My Shortcuts 2 >

(3)

SUGGESTED SHORTCUTS

Send a message to Amy Miser +

Create a new contact +

Start a timer for 10 minutes +

All Shortcuts > (4)

Add Shortcuts for things you frequently do so you can get them done just by asking Siri.

5 Browse the list of shortcuts, which are grouped by the apps with which they are associated, or search for a specific shortcut.

6 Tap Add (+) for the shortcut you want to activate.

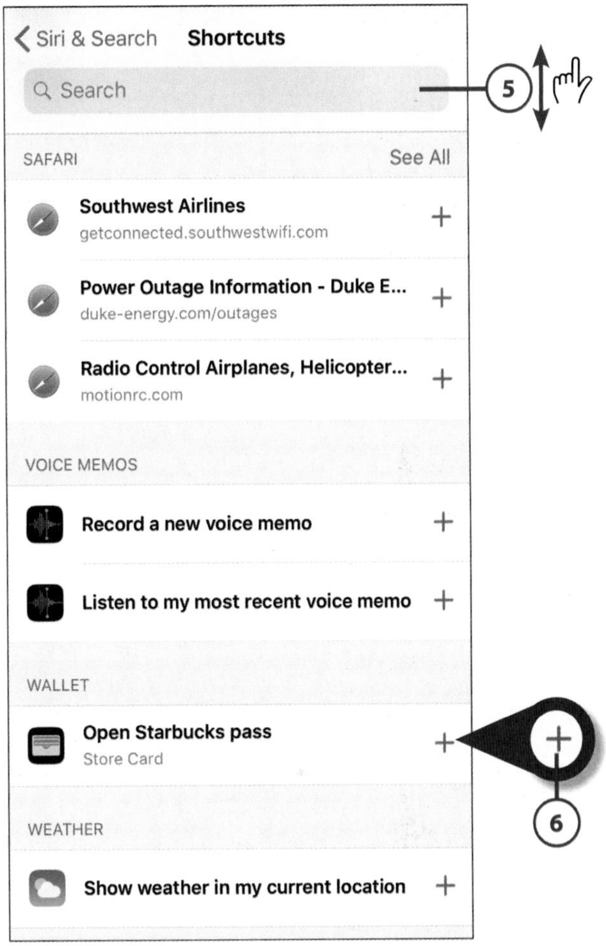

< Siri & Search   Shortcuts

Q Search ─────── ⑤

SAFARI   See All

🧭 **Southwest Airlines**   +
   getconnected.southwestwifi.com

🧭 **Power Outage Information - Duke E...**   +
   duke-energy.com/outages

🧭 **Radio Control Airplanes, Helicopter...** +
   motionrc.com

VOICE MEMOS

🎙 **Record a new voice memo**   +

🎙 **Listen to my most recent voice memo** +

WALLET

💳 **Open Starbucks pass**   +   ⊕
   Store Card   ⑥

WEATHER

☁ **Show weather in my current location** +

7 Tap the Record icon.

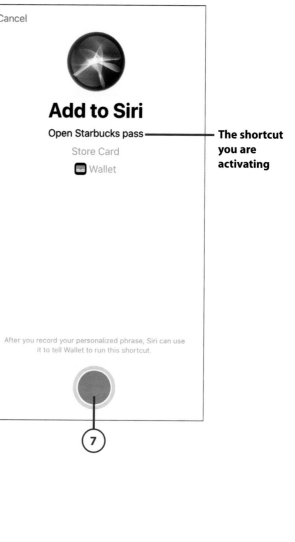

Cancel

Add to Siri

Open Starbucks pass ———————— The shortcut
you are
Store Card   activating

Wallet

After you record your personalized phrase, Siri can use
it to tell Wallet to run this shortcut.

7

8 Speak the phrase you want to use.

9 When you're done speaking the phrase, tap the Stop icon.

10 If you want to change the phrase, tap Edit and repeat steps 7 through 9.

11 When the shortcut is what you want, tap Done. You see the new shortcut on the My Shortcuts screen.

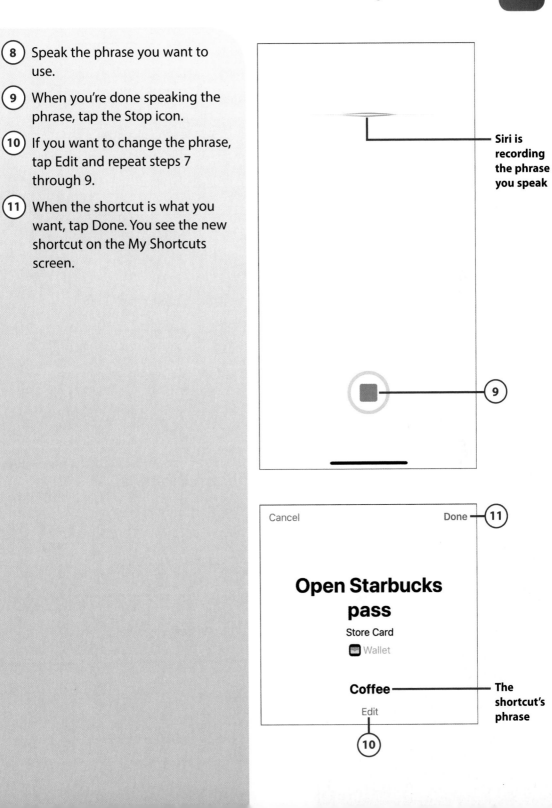

Siri is recording the phrase you speak

Cancel   Done —(11)

Open Starbucks pass

Store Card
Wallet

Coffee —————— The shortcut's phrase

Edit
(10)

Reviewing and Changing Your Shortcuts

To work with your shortcuts, perform the following steps

1. Move to the Settings app.

2. Tap Siri & Search.

3. Tap My Shortcuts.

4. Swipe up and down the screen to see all of the shortcuts you've activated.

5. Tap a shortcut you want to change or delete.

6. To change the phrase for the shortcut, tap Re-Record Phrase and follow steps 7 through 9 in the previous task.

7. If you're done working with the shortcut, tap Done and skip the rest of these steps.

8. To delete the shortcut, tap Delete Shortcut.

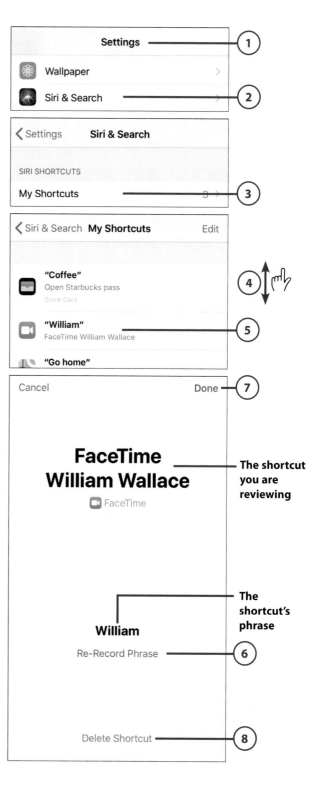

9 Tap Delete Shortcut. The shortcut is removed and you return to the My Shortcuts page. (Siri might re-create the shortcut again, but if you don't activate it again, it shouldn't get in your way.)

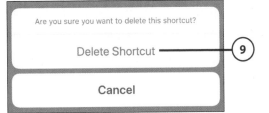

Using Shortcuts

Using shortcuts is as easy as easy gets:

1 Activate Siri and speak the shortcut's phrase.

2 Work with the result of the shortcut.

Siri Shortcuts Are Fun, But...

Most of the shortcuts Siri creates for you are relatively simple and, in many cases, it is easier just to speak the associated action than trying to remember the shortcut phrase. For example, Siri creates shortcuts for directions to addresses to which you navigate using the Maps app, such as for your home address. You can activate a shortcut for these directions with a phrase such as, "Home." However, since you can also say, "Siri, get me directions home," to do the same thing, you might not want to bother with activating a shortcut for it.

Using Dictation to Speak Text Instead of Typing

You can use the iPhone's dictation capability to speak text into any app, such as Mail, Messages, and so on. In fact, any time you see the Microphone key on the keyboard, dictation is available to you. Here's how this works:

(1) In the app you are using, put the cursor where you want the text you dictate to start. For example, if you are creating an email, tap in the body.

(2) Tap the Microphone key on the virtual keyboard. The dictation pane opens at the bottom of the screen. The oscillating line indicates Siri is listening to you and you can begin speaking.

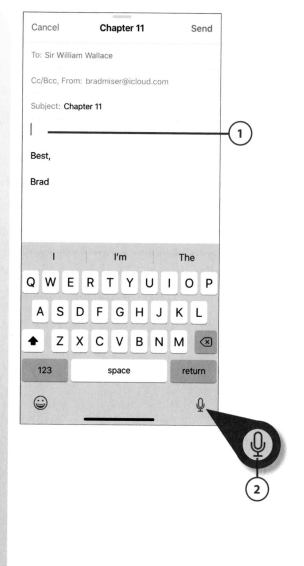

3 Speak the text you want to add. In addition to text, you can speak punctuation, such as saying "comma" when you want to insert a comma or "new paragraph" when you want to create a new paragraph. While you are speaking, you see the line that oscillates as you speak and the text you are speaking at the location of the cursor.

4 Tap the keyboard icon when you finish your dictation. The Dictation pane closes, and the keyboard reappears. The text you spoke is part of the message. From there, you can edit it just like text you've typed.

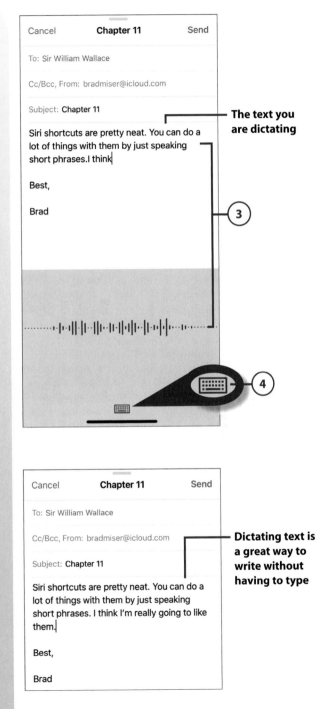

The text you are dictating

Dictating text is a great way to write without having to type

Tap to
configure
Safari

Tap to have the World Wide Web
in the palm of your hand

In this chapter, you explore the amazing web browsing functionality your iPhone has to offer. Topics include the following:

→ Getting started
→ Setting Safari preferences
→ Visiting websites
→ Viewing websites
→ Working with multiple websites at the same time
→ Searching the Web
→ Saving and organizing bookmarks
→ Using 3D Touch with Safari
→ Sharing web pages
→ Signing in to websites automatically

Surfing the Web

The Web has become an integral part of most of our lives. It is often the first step to search for information, make plans (such as travel arrangements), conduct financial transactions, shop, and so much more. Safari on the iPhone puts the entire Web in the palm of your hand. Safari is a full-featured web browser; anything you can do on a website in a browser on a computer can be done with Safari on your iPhone.

Getting Started

The World Wide Web, more commonly called the Web, is a great resource for finding information, planning travel, keeping up with the news, and just about anything else you want to do. Following are some of the more common terms you encounter as you use the Web:

- **Web page**—This is a collection of information (text and graphics) that is available on the Web. A web page is what you look at when you use the Web.

- **Website**—This is a collection of web pages that "go together." For example, most companies and other organizations have websites that contain information they use to help their customers or members, provide services, market and sell their products and services, and so on. A website organizes the web pages it contains and provides the structure you use to move among them.

- **Web browser**—This is the software you use to view web pages. There are many different web browsers available. Examples include Safari—which comes pre-installed on your iPhone—as well as Google Chrome, Internet Explorer, and Firefox. They all allow you to view and interact with web pages, and each has its own set of features. Some are available on just about every device there is, such as Safari and Google Chrome, while some are limited to certain devices, such as Internet Explorer that only runs on Windows computers.

- **Safari**—This is the default web browser on your iPhone; it is also the default web browser on Mac computers. You can download and install it on Windows computers, too.

- **URL**—A Uniform Resource Locator (URL) is a web page's or website's "address" on the Web. URLs allow you to direct your web browser to specific locations on the Web. Most URLs you deal with consist of text, such as www.apple.com or www.aarp.org. Some URLs are more complicated because they take you to specific web pages instead of a website. An example of this is www.aarp.org/health, which takes you to the Health web page on the AARP website. You seldom have to type URLs because you usually access web pages by tapping on links or using a bookmark, but it's good to know what they are and how to use them.

- **Link**—A link is a photo or other graphic, text, or other object that has a URL attached to it. When you tap a link, you move to the URL and open the web page associated with it. Most text links are formatted with a color so you can distinguish them from regular text. Links can also be attached to images, such as photos or other kinds of graphics.

- **Bookmark**—This is a saved location on the Web. When you visit a web page or website, you can save its URL as a bookmark so you can return to it with just a few taps instead of typing its URL. Safari allows you to save and organize your bookmarks on your iPhone.

- **Search engine or search page**—The Web contains information on every topic under the sun. You can use a search engine/page to search for information in which you are interested. There are a number of search engines available, with Google being the most popular. You access a search engine through a web browser. Safari uses Google by default, but you can choose Bing, DuckDuckGo, or Yahoo! as your default search engine if you prefer one of those instead.

Setting Safari Preferences

Like most apps, Safari offers settings you can use to adjust the way it works. You can likely use Safari with its default settings just fine; when the time comes that you want to tweak how Safari works for you, use the following table as a reference for the available settings. To access these settings, tap the Settings icon on the Home screen, and then tap Safari.

Safari Settings

Settings Area	Location	Setting	Description
ALLOW SAFARI TO ACCESS	Siri & Search	Search, Suggestions & Shortcuts	Set this switch to on (green) to allow information from Safari to be used in searches, when you perform lookups, and in other places. It also allows Siri to learn from how you use Safari to make better suggestions over time. And, you can include Safari in shortcuts. If you don't want Safari information to be used in this way, set the switch to off (white).
ALLOW SAFARI TO ACCESS	Siri & Search	Allow on Lock Screen	Set this switch to on (green) to allow information from Safari to appear on the Lock screen. If you don't want Safari information to appear there, set the switch to off (white).
ALLOW SAFARI TO ACCESS	Siri & Search	Shortcuts	Use this area to work with shortcuts related to Safari (shortcuts are covered in Chapter 4, "Customizing How Your iPhone Works").
SEARCH	Search Engine	Search Engine	Enables you to choose your default search tool; the options are Google (default), Yahoo, Bing, or DuckDuckGo.

Settings Area	Location	Setting	Description
SEARCH	N/A	Search Engine Suggestions	When this switch is on (green), Safari asks your default search engine for suggestions related to what you type in the Address/Search bar. This makes search easier because you can type your search term in the bar instead of first moving to the search web page.
SEARCH	N/A	Safari Suggestions	When this switch is on (green), Safari makes suggestions related to what you type in the Address/Search bar. This makes search easier because you can type a term in which you are interested in the bar instead of first moving to the search web page.
SEARCH	Quick Website Search	Quick Website Search	When this switch is on (green), you can perform a search at a specific website by typing its name before your search term. For example, you can type "wiki william wallace" in the Address/Search bar and the first section of the results will be entries in the Wikipedia related to William Wallace; this saves you the steps of moving to the search engine results, and then tapping the articles you want to read because you can do this directly from the Search screen instead.
SEARCH	N/A	Preload Top Hit	When this switch is on (green), the sites you move to or find more frequently are loaded while you search, making accessing them faster.
GENERAL	Autofill	Use Contact Info	Set the Use Contact Info switch to on (green) if you want to be able to automatically fill in your contact information (such as your address) on web forms.
GENERAL	Autofill	My Info	If you enable Use Contact Info, tap My Info and choose your card in the Contacts app. The information on this card will be used to automatically complete information on web forms.

Settings Area	Location	Setting	Description
GENERAL	Autofill	Credit Cards	Set the Credit Cards switch to on (green) to store and use credit cards on your iPhone so you can more easily enter their information to make purchases.
GENERAL	Autofill	Saved Credit Cards	Tap Saved Credit Cards to view or change existing credit card information or to add new credit cards to Safari.
GENERAL	N/A	Frequently Visited Sites	When this switch is on (green) and you move into the Address/Search bar, Safari shows a section of sites that you visit frequently, making them easier to return to.
GENERAL	Favorites	Favorites	Use this option to choose the folder of bookmarks for sites that you use most frequently. The bookmarks in the folder you select appear at the top of the screen when you move into the Address/Search bar, making them fast and easy to use.
GENERAL	Open Links	Open Links	This tells Safari the option you want to see when you tap and hold a link on a current web page to open a new web page. The In New Tab option causes Safari to open and immediately take you to a new tab displaying the web page with which a link is associated. The In Background option causes Safari to open pages in the background for links you tap so you can view them later.
GENERAL	N/A	Block Pop-ups	Some websites won't work properly with pop-ups blocked, so you can use this setting to temporarily enable pop-ups by sliding the switch to off (white). When the Block Pop-ups switch is on (green), pop-ups are blocked. You should usually leave this switch on and turn it off only in specific situations.

Settings Area	Location	Setting	Description
PRIVACY & SECURITY	N/A	Prevent Cross-Site Tracking	When enabled (green), this feature attempts to limit tracking of your browsing history by websites that you visit. Its purpose is to limit the exposure of your private information by websites that try to track you as you visit other sites to collect information about you.
PRIVACY & SECURITY	N/A	Block All Cookies	When enabled (green), Safari doesn't allow cookies to be stored; cookies are bits of information that websites store about you to use to tailor your experience at that website. If you block all cookies, some sites might not work correctly. Safari only accepts cookies for websites you visit, so, in general, you should leave this feature disabled (white) so websites you visit work correctly.
PRIVACY & SECURITY	N/A	Ask Websites Not To Track Me	Some websites track your activity in order to tailor the site based on your browsing history. When enabled (green), Safari includes a request not to track you to each website you visit. If the website honors that request, you won't be tracked. However, it's up to each website to implement this.
PRIVACY & SECURITY	N/A	Fraudulent Website Warning	If you don't want Safari to warn you when you visit websites that appear to be fraudulent, set the Fraudulent Website Warning switch to off (white). You should leave this switch enabled (green).
PRIVACY & SECURITY	N/A	Camera & Microphone Access	When this switch is on (green) Safari can access the iPhone's microphone and camera to enable you to present video and transmit and receive audio communication via a website.

Settings Area	Location	Setting	Description
PRIVACY & SECURITY	N/A	Check for Apple Pay	When you visit websites that support Apple Pay with this switch enabled (green), you can use your Apple Pay account to make payments for goods or services. (Refer to Chapter 15, "Working with Other Useful iPhone Apps and Features," for information about Apple Pay.)
PRIVACY & SECURITY	N/A	Clear History and Website Data	When you tap this command and confirm it by tapping Clear History and Data at the prompt, Safari removes the websites you have visited from your history list. The list starts over, so the next site you visit is added to your history list again—unless you have enabled private browsing. It also removes all cookies and other website data that have been stored on your iPhone.
READING LIST	N/A	Automatically Save Offline	The Reading List enables you to store web pages on your iPhone for offline reading. If you want to allow pages to be saved to your iPhone automatically, slide this switch to the on (green) position.
Advanced	Website Data	Website Data	Website Data displays the amount of data associated with websites you have visited; swipe up on the screen and tap Remove All Website Data to clear this data.
Advanced	N/A	JavaScript	Set this switch to off (white) to disable JavaScript functionality (however, some sites won't work properly without JavaScript).
Advanced	N/A	Web Inspector	This switch controls a feature that is used by website developers to see how their sites work on an iPhone.
Advanced	N/A	Experimental Features	This area contains a number of additional controls that can be enabled or disabled. You aren't likely to need to access these.

Where, Oh Where Are My Passwords?

As when you visit websites on a computer, you'll need to enter your username and password to log into your account on websites you visit with your iPhone. To enable Safari to store and enter this information for you automatically, open the Settings app and tap Passwords & Accounts. Set the AutoFill Passwords switch to on (green). If you don't want Safari to store this information (you'll have to enter it every time), set this switch to off (white).

When you enable Safari to save your passwords, you can access them by opening the Settings app and tapping Passwords & Accounts. Tap Website & App Passwords. On the Passwords screen, you see a list of websites and usernames stored on your iPhone sorted by the URL of the website with which they are associated. You can quickly search for a website by typing information about it in the Search bar.

You can manually add a website to the list by tapping Add (+) and filling in the information (URL, username, and password).

You can tap a URL to see the username and password for that site and a list of all websites using that information (looking up a password here can be handy if you've forgotten it). You can edit this information, or in some cases, you can tap Change Password on Website to visit the website to change the password associated with your account.

To remove a URL and its associated username and password from the list, move to the Passwords screen and swipe to the left on it and tap Delete. The next time you move to that site, you will need to manually enter your username and password again.

Visiting Websites

If you've used a web browser on a computer before, using Safari on an iPhone is a familiar experience. If you've not used a web browser before, don't worry because using Safari on an iPhone is simple and intuitive.

Syncing Bookmarks

Using iCloud, you can synchronize your Internet Explorer favorites or Safari bookmarks on a Windows PC—or Safari bookmarks on a Mac—to your iPhone so you have the same set of bookmarks available on your phone that you do on your computer and other devices, and vice versa (refer to Chapter 3, "Setting Up and Using an Apple ID, iCloud, and Other Online Accounts"). You should enable iCloud's Safari switch before you start browsing on your iPhone, so you avoid typing URLs or re-creating bookmarks. When you enable Safari syncing via iCloud, you can also view tabs open in Safari on other devices, such as a Mac or an iPad.

Using Bookmarks to Move to Websites

Using bookmarks you've synced via iCloud or created on your iPhone (you learn how later in this chapter) makes it easy to get to websites.

① On the Home screen, tap Safari.

② Tap the Bookmarks icon.

③ Tap the Bookmarks tab (the open book) if it isn't selected already. (If you don't see this tab, tap the Back icon (<), which is labeled with the name of the folder from which you moved to the current screen, in the upper-left corner of the screen until you see the Bookmarks icon.)

④ Swipe up or down the list of bookmarks to browse the bookmarks and other folders of bookmarks available to you.

⑤ To move to a bookmark, skip to step 10; to open a folder of bookmarks, tap it.

Back to the Bookmarks

The most recent Bookmarks screen is retained when you move away from Bookmarks and then come back. Each time you open your Bookmarks, you see the same screen you were using when you left it.

More Conditions

< > ⬆ 📖 ⬜

② 📖

③ ⑤

᎐᎐᎐᎐ AT&T Wi-Fi 📶   11:52 AM   ⏱ 79% ▮

Bookmarks   Done

📖   👓   🕐

☆ Favorites ——————————————— Your Favorites bookmark folder

📁 Bookmarks Menu

📖 Demo 1 VFA.facility List

📁 Cool Planes ④

📁 shopping_rental ——————————— Folder containing bookmarks

📁 travel

📖 VFA WebEx Enterprise Site

📖 VINCI Facilities Home

Bookmark

6. Swipe up or down the folder's screen to browse the folders and bookmarks it contains.

7. Tap a folder to see the bookmarks it contains.

Change Your Mind?

If you decide not to visit a bookmark, tap Done. You return to the website you were previously viewing.

8. To return to a previous screen, tap the Back icon (<) in the upper-left corner of the screen, which is labeled with the name of the folder you previously visited (the parent folder); this disappears when you are at the top-level Bookmarks screen.

9. Repeat steps 5–8 until you see a bookmark you want to visit.

10. Tap the bookmark you want to visit. Safari moves to that website.

11. Use the information in the section "Viewing Websites" later in this chapter to get information on viewing the web page.

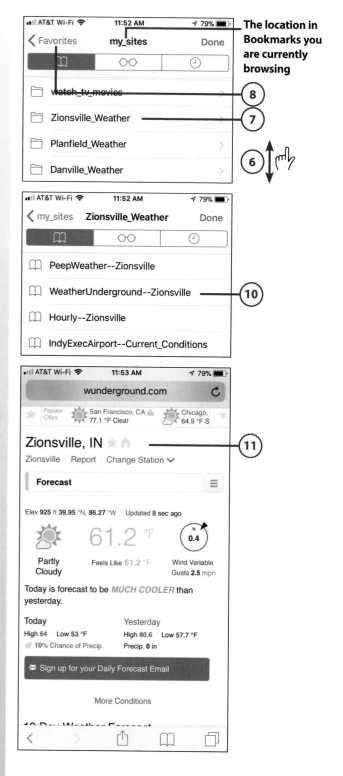

The location in Bookmarks you are currently browsing

Playing Favorites

You might see two Favorites folders on the Bookmarks screen. The folder marked with a star is the folder you designated, using the Safari settings described previously in this chapter, as the place to store Favorites on your iPhone. If you use Safari on a computer, you can also configure bookmarks and folders of bookmarks on its Bookmarks bar. When these bookmarks are synced from your computer to the iPhone, they might be stored in a folder of bookmarks also called Favorites and shown with the standard folder icon. If you set this synced folder in your iPhone's Safari settings to also be its Favorites folder, you won't have to deal with this potentially confusing situation of having two Favorites folders.

iPhone Web Pages

Some websites have been specially formatted for mobile devices. These typically have less complex information on each page, so they load faster. When you move to a site like this, you might be redirected to the mobile version automatically, or you might be prompted to choose which version of the site you want to visit. On the mobile version, there is typically a link that takes you to the "regular" version, too. (It's sometimes called the Desktop, Full, or Classic version.) Sometimes the version formatted for handheld devices offers less information or fewer tools than the regular version. Because Safari is a full-featured browser, you can use either version.

Using Your Favorites to Move to Websites

Using the Safari settings described earlier, you can designate a folder of bookmarks as your Favorites. You can get to the folders and bookmarks in your Favorites folder more quickly and easily than navigating to it as described in the previous section. Here's how to use your Favorites:

 On the Home screen, tap Safari. (If you are in Safari and have the Bookmarks screen open, tap Done to close it.)

2 Tap in the Address/Search bar (if you don't see the Address/Search bar, tap at the top of the screen to show it). Just below the Address/Search bar are your Favorites (bookmarks and folders of bookmarks). The keyboard opens at the bottom of the screen.

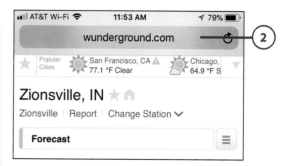

3 Swipe up and down on your Favorites. The keyboard closes to give you more room to browse.

4 To move to a bookmark, tap it and skip to step 8.

5 Tap a folder to move into it.

Folder of bookmarks

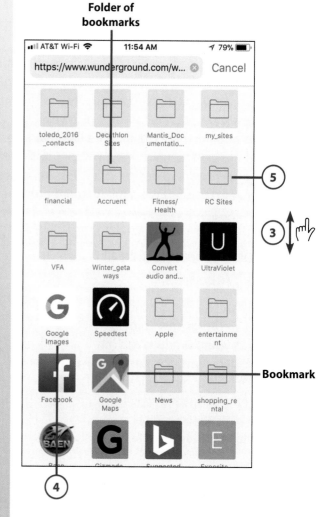

Bookmark

More Commands

At the top of the Favorites screen, you might see two more commands. Tap Add to Favorites to add a bookmark to the current site to your Favorites folder. Tap Request Desktop Site if you are currently viewing the mobile version of a site and want to see the "full" version; you move to that version after you tap the command.

(6) Continue browsing your Favorites until you find the bookmark you want to use. Like using the Bookmarks screen, you can tap a folder to move into it, tap a bookmark to move to its website, or tap the Back icon (<) to move to a previous screen.

(7) Tap the bookmark for the site you want to visit.

(8) Use the information in the section "Viewing Websites" later in this chapter to view the web page.

Typing URLs to Move to Websites

A Uniform Resource Locator (URL) is the Internet address of a web page. URLs can be relatively simple, such as www.apple.com, or they can be quite long and convoluted. The good news is that by using bookmarks, you can save a URL in Safari so you can get back to it using its bookmark (as you learned in the previous two tasks) and thus avoid typing URLs more than once. To use a URL to move to a website, do the following:

(1) On the Home screen, tap Safari. (If you are in Safari and have the Bookmarks screen open, tap Done to close it.)

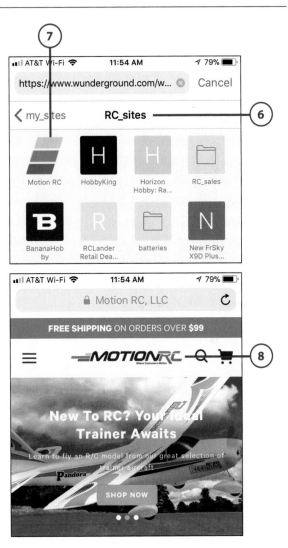

2 Tap in the Address/Search bar (if you don't see the Address/Search bar, tap at the top of the screen). The URL of the current page becomes highlighted, or if you haven't visited a page, the Address/Search bar is empty. Just below the Address/Search bar, your Favorites are displayed. The keyboard appears at the bottom of the screen.

3 If an address appears in the Address/Search bar, tap Clear (x) to remove it.

4 Type the URL you want to visit. If it starts with www (which almost all URLs do), you don't have to type "www." As you type, Safari attempts to match what you are typing to a site you have visited previously and completes the URL for you if it can. Just below the Address/Search bar, Safari presents a list of sites that might be what you are looking for, organized into groups, such as Suggested Websites.

5 If one of the sites shown is the one you want to visit, tap it. You move to that web page; skip to step 8.

6 If Safari doesn't find a match, continue typing until you enter the entire URL.

7 Tap Go. You move to the web page.

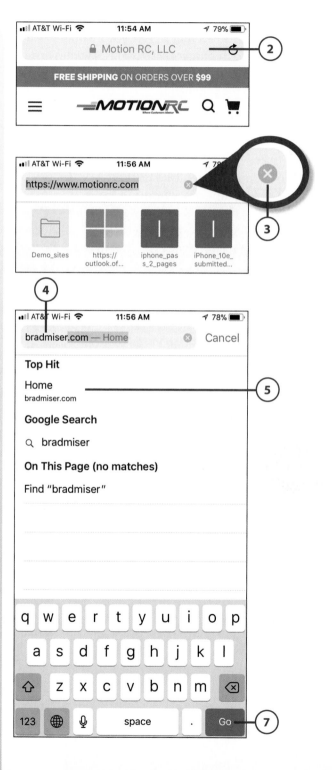

8 Use the information in the section "Viewing Websites" to view the web page.

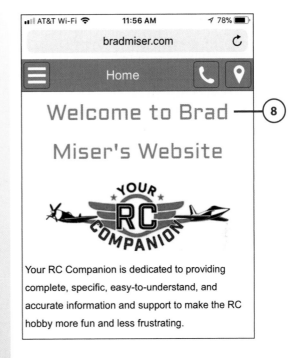

Shortcut for Typing URLs

URLs include a top-level domain code that represents the type of site (theoretically anyway) that URL leads to. Common examples are .com (commercial sites) and .edu (educational sites). To quickly enter a URL's code, tap and hold the period key to see a menu from which you can select other options, such as .net or .edu. Select the code you want on the keyboard, and it is entered in the Address/Search bar.

Using Your Browsing History to Move to Websites

As you move about the Web, Safari tracks the sites you visit and builds a history list (unless you enabled the Do Not Track option, in which case this doesn't happen and you can't use History to return to previous sites). You can use your browsing history list to return to sites you've visited.

1 Tap the Bookmarks icon.

2 Tap the History tab.

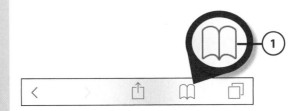

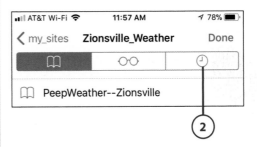

③ Swipe up and down the page to browse all the sites you've visited. The more recent sites appear at the top of the screen; the further you move down the screen, the further back in time you go. Earlier sites are collected in folders for various times, such as This Morning, or Monday Afternoon.

④ Tap the site you want to visit. The site opens and you can use the information in the section "Viewing Websites" to view the web page.

Erasing the Past

To clear your browsing history, tap Clear at the bottom of the History screen. At the prompt, tap the timeframe that you want to clear; the options are The last hour, Today, Today and yesterday, or All time. Your browsing history for the period of time you selected is erased. (Don't you wish it were this easy to erase the past in real life?)

Viewing Websites

Even though your iPhone is a small device, you'll be amazed at how well it displays web pages designed for larger screens.

1. Use Safari to move to a web page as described in the previous tasks.

2. To browse around a web page, swipe your finger right or left, or up or down.

3. Zoom in by unpinching your fingers.

Where Did the URL Go?

When you first move to a URL, you see that URL in the Address/Search bar. After you work with a site, the Address/Search bar and the toolbar are hidden and the URL is replaced with the high-level domain name for the site (such as sitename.com, site-name.edu, and so on). To see the Address/Search bar and toolbar again, tap the top of the screen. To see the full URL again, tap in the Address/Search bar.

4. Zoom out by pinching your fingers.

5. Tap a link to move to the location to which it points. Links can come in many forms, including text (most text that is a link is in color and underlined) or graphics. The web page to which the link points opens and replaces the page currently being displayed.

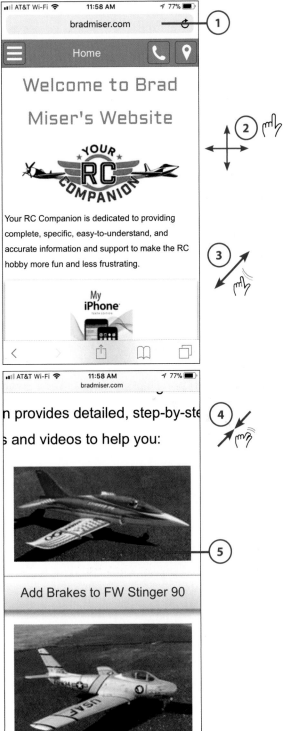

6 To view the web page in landscape orientation, rotate the iPhone so that it is horizontal.

7 Scroll, zoom in, and zoom out on the page to read it, as described in steps 2–6.

8 Tap Refresh to refresh a page, which causes its content to be updated. (Note: While a page is loading, this is Stop [x]; tap it to stop the rest of the page from loading.)

9 To move to a previous page you've visited, tap the Back icon (<). (If the arrow is grayed out, it means you are at the beginning of the set of pages you have visited.)

10 To move to a subsequent page, tap the Forward icon (>). (If the arrow is grayed out, it means you are at the end of the set of pages you have visited.)

11 As you move around, the Address/Search bar at the top of the page and the toolbar at the bottom of the page are hidden automatically; to show them again, tap the top of the screen.

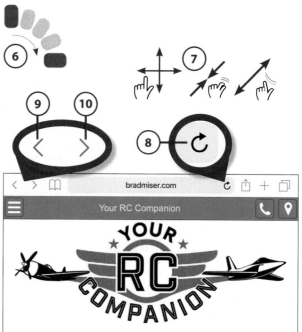

Do More with Links

To see options for a link, tap and hold your finger down for a second or so. (If you are using an iPhone that supports 3D Touch, this can be a bit tricky. If you apply pressure, a Peek appears instead of the menu. To see the menu, place your finger on the screen and hold it there, but don't put any pressure on the screen.) A menu appears. Tap Open to open the page to replace the current page at which the link points (this is the same as tapping a link). Tap Open in Background to open the page in a new Safari window that opens in the background, or tap Open in New Tab to open the new page in the new tab. (The command that appears depends on the Open Links Safari setting that you learned about earlier in this chapter.) Tap Share to open the Share menu that enables you to share the web page via email, a message, and so on. Tap Add to Reading List to add the page to your Reading List. If the link is an image, tap Save Image to save the image on your phone. Tap Copy to copy the link's URL so that you can paste it elsewhere, such as in an email message. Tap Cancel to return to the current page and take no action.

Different Phones, Different Look

The type of iPhone you are using to browse the Web affects how pages look and where controls are located. For example, when you use an iPhone 5s, you see black at the top and bottom of the screen whereas you see white there on an iPhone X. Also, when you rotate an iPhone 5s, the tools are at the top and bottom of the screen, but on an iPhone X, the controls are all at the top of the screen. Regardless of where the controls appear on the screen, they work in the same way.

Working with Multiple Websites at the Same Time

When you move to a web page by using a bookmark, typing a URL, or tapping a link on the current web page, the new web page replaces the current one. However, you can also open and work with multiple web pages at the same time so that a new web page doesn't replace the current one.

When you work with multiple web pages, each open page appears in its own tab. You can use the tab view to easily move to and manage your open web pages.

You can also close open tabs, and you can even open web pages that are open on other devices on which your iCloud account has been configured and Safari syncing enabled.

There are two ways to open a new web page in a new tab. One is to touch and hold on a link on the current web page; you can use the resulting Open command to open the new page. There are two options for this approach; the one you use is determined by the Open Links preference set as described earlier in this chapter. The In Background option causes the new page to open and move to the background. This is most useful when you want to read the new page at a later time, such as when you are done with the current one. The In New Tab option causes the new page to open and move to the front so you see it instantly while moving the current page and its tab to the background.

The second way to open a new web page in a new tab is by using the Tab Manager.

These options are described in the following tasks.

Tapping Without Holding

When you tap, but don't hold down, a link on a web page, the web page to which the link points opens and replaces the current web page—no new tab is created. When you touch and hold down on a link, the behavior is determined by the setting you chose in the preferences as covered in a task earlier in this chapter ("Setting Safari Preferences"). To make things a bit more complicated, if your phone supports 3D Touch (iPhone 6s/6s Plus and later), don't apply pressure to the screen when you tap; if you do, a Peek appears instead (you learn about this in "Using 3D Touch with Safari").

Opening New Pages in the Background

If you enabled the In Background option for the Open Links preference, you can open new web pages by doing the following:

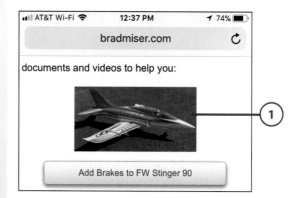

(**1**) Touch and hold (but don't press) on the link you want to open in the background.

2 Tap Open in Background. The page to which the link points opens. The only result you see is the page associated with the link you touched "jumping" down to the Tab Manager icon in the lower-right corner of the screen.

3 Continue opening pages in the background; see "Using Tab View to Manage Open Web Pages" to learn how to use the tab view to move to pages that are open in the background.

Opening New Pages in a New Tab

If you enabled the In New Tab option for the Open Links preference, you can open new pages by doing the following:

1 Touch and hold on the link you want to open in the background.

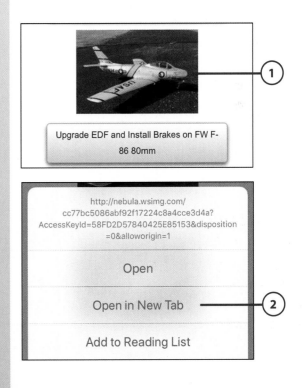

2 Tap Open in New Tab. The tab view appears briefly, and a new tab opens and displays the page to which the link points. The web page from which you started moves into the background.

3 Continue opening pages; see "Using Tab View to Manage Open Web Pages" to learn how to use the tab view to manage your open pages.

Just Open It

If you tap the Open command on the menu in step 2 of the previous tasks, the new web page replaces the one you were viewing on the current tab. This is the same as tapping a link on the page rather than touching and holding (but not pressing) on it.

Using Tab View to Manage Open Web Pages

As you open new pages, whether in the background or not, new tabs are opened. Safari's tab view enables you to view and work with your open pages/tabs. Here's how:

1. Tap the Tab View icon. Each open page appears on its own tab.

2. Swipe up or down on the open tabs to browse them.

3. Tap a tab/page to move into it. The page opens and fills the Safari window.

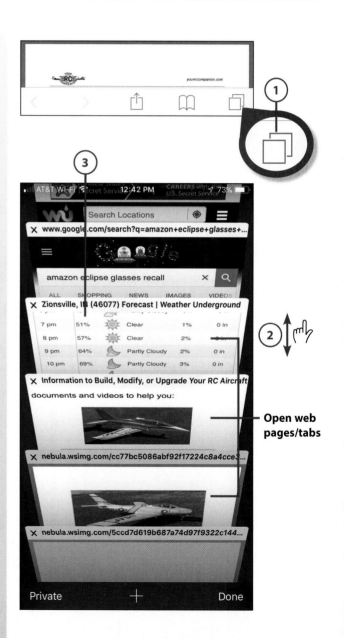

Open web pages/tabs

(4) Work with the web page.

(5) Tap the Tab View icon.

Tabs Are Independent

Each tab is independent. So, when you are working with a tab and use the back/forward icons to move among its pages, you are just moving among the pages open under that tab. Pages open in other tabs are not affected.

(6) Tap Close (x) to close a tab; alternatively swipe to the left on the tab you want to close.

(7) To open a new tab, tap Add (+) to create a new tab that shows your Favorites screen; navigate to a new page in that tab using the methods described in other tasks (tapping bookmarks or typing a URL).

(8) Tap Done to close the tab view. The tab view closes, and the page you were most recently viewing is shown.

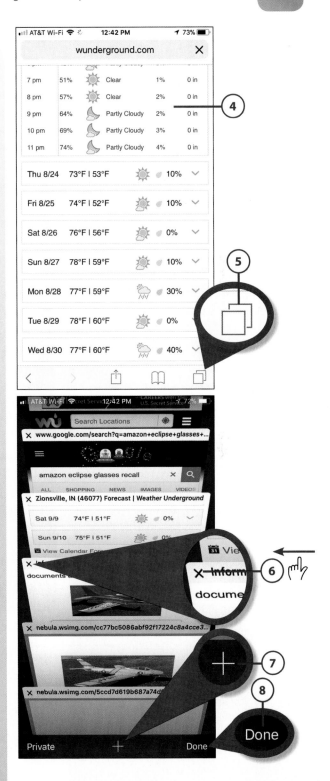

Opening Web Pages That Are Open on Other Devices

When you enable iCloud Safari syncing, iCloud tracks the websites you have open on all the devices on which you have Safari syncing enabled, including your iPhone, iPads, and Macs. This is really handy when you have pages open on another device and want to view them on your iPhone. (Web pages open on your iPhone are available on your other devices, too.) To view a page you have open on another device, do the following:

1. Open the tab view.

2. Swipe up the screen until you see the pages open on other devices. There is a section for each device; sections are labeled with the device's name. In each device's section, you see the pages open in Safari on those devices.

3. Tap the page you want to view. The page opens on the iPhone and becomes a new tab.

Keep Private Things Private

If you aren't browsing in Private mode and tap Private at the bottom of the tab view, Safari moves into Private mode and stops tracking the sites you visit. Tap Private again to return to the previous state. If you are browsing in Private mode, tapping Private shows or hides the tabs in the tab view.

A Mac with open web pages

Searching the Web

In the first section of this chapter, you learned that you can set Safari to search the Web using Google, Yahoo!, Bing, or DuckDuckGo. No matter which search engine you chose, you search the Web in the same way.

(1) Tap in the Address/Search bar (if you don't see this bar, tap at the top of the screen). The keyboard appears along with your Favorites.

(2) If there is any text in the Address/Search bar, tap Clear (x).

(3) Type your search word(s). As you type, Safari attempts to find a search that matches what you typed. The list of suggestions is organized in sections, which depend on what you are searching for and the search options you configured through Safari settings. One section, labeled with the search engine you are using (such as Google Search), contains the search results from that source. Other sections can include Bookmarks and History, or Apps (from the App Store). At the bottom of the list is the On This Page section, which shows the terms that match your search on the page you are browsing.

(4) To perform the search using one of the suggestions provided, tap the suggestion you want to use. The search is performed and you can skip to step 6.

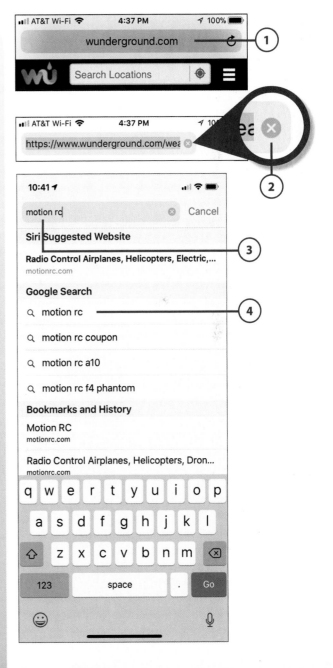

(5) If none of the suggestions are what you want, keep typing until you have entered the entire search term, and then tap Go. The search engine you use performs the search and displays the results on the search results page.

(6) Use the search results page to view the results of your search. These pages work just like other web pages. You can zoom, scroll, and tap links to explore results.

Searching on a Web Page

To search for words or phrases on a web page you are viewing, perform these steps, except in step 4, tap the word or phrase for which you want to search in the On This Page section (you might have to swipe up the screen to see this section). You return to the page you are browsing and each occurrence of your search term on the page is highlighted.

Quick Website Search

If you enabled the Quick Website Search feature, you can include the site you want to search in the Address/Search bar, such as "Wiki F-15." When you do this, the results from the site you entered appear at the top of the list and you can access them directly by tapping the information that appears (as opposed to having to move to the search engine site first as in these steps).

Saving and Organizing Bookmarks

In addition to moving bookmarks from a computer or iCloud onto your iPhone, you can save new bookmarks directly in your iPhone (they are synced onto other devices, too). You can also organize bookmarks on your iPhone to make them easier and faster to access.

Creating Bookmarks

When you want to make it easy to return to a website, create a bookmark with the following steps:

(1) Move to a web page for which you want to save a bookmark.

(2) Tap the Share icon.

(3) Tap Add Bookmark. The Add Bookmark screen appears, showing the title of the web page you are viewing, which will also be the name of the bookmark initially; its URL; and the Location field, which shows where the bookmark will be stored when you create it.

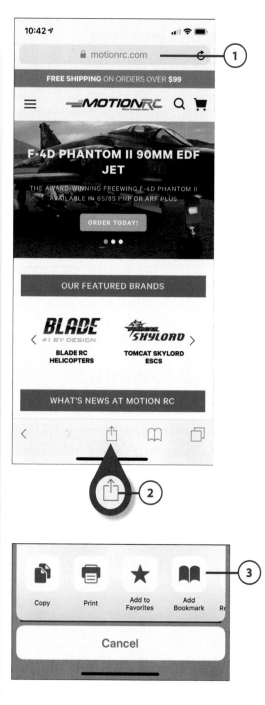

4 Edit the bookmark's name as needed, or tap Clear (x) to erase the current name, and then type the new name of the bookmark. The titles of some web pages can be quite long, so it's a good idea to shorten them so the bookmark's name is easier to read on the iPhone's screen.

5 Tap the current folder shown under Location. The Location section expands and you see all of the folders of bookmarks on your phone. The folder that is currently selected is marked with a check mark.

6 Swipe up and down the screen to find the folder in which you want to place the new bookmark. You can choose any folder on the screen; folders are indented when they are contained within other folders.

7 Tap the folder in which to store the new bookmark. You return to the Add Bookmark screen, which shows the location you selected.

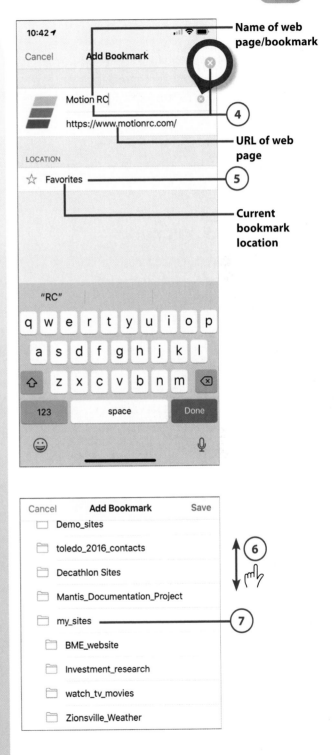

Name of web page/bookmark

URL of web page

Current bookmark location

8 Tap Save. The bookmark is created and saved in the location you specified. You can use the bookmark to return to the website at any time.

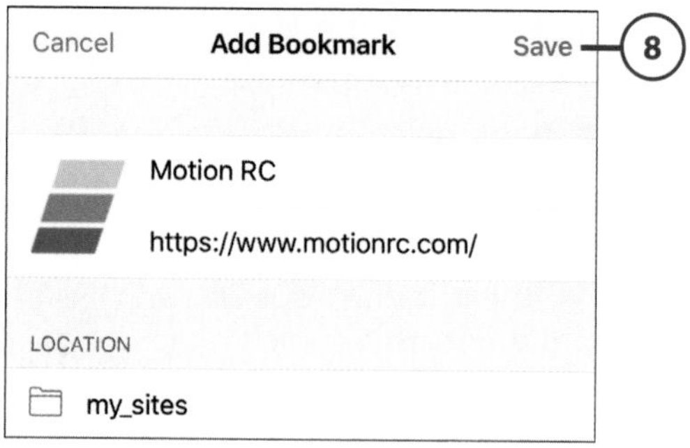

| Cancel | **Add Bookmark** | Save | **8** |

Motion RC

https://www.motionrc.com/

LOCATION

my_sites

Organizing Bookmarks

You've seen how bookmarks can be contained in folders, which is a good thing because you're likely to have a lot of them. You can change the names and locations of your existing bookmarks and folders as follows:

1 Move to the Bookmarks screen showing the bookmarks and folders you want to change. (You can't move among the Bookmarks screens while you are in Edit mode so you need to start at the location where the items you want to change are located.)

2 Tap Edit. Unlock icons appear next to the folders and bookmarks you can change (some folders can't be changed and you won't see controls for those folders). The order icons also appear on the right side of the screen, again only for folders or bookmarks you can change.

•ıll AT&T Wi-Fi 🛜   4:41 PM   ⚡ 100% ▬

‹ Bookmarks   **Favorites**   Done   **1**

📖   ∞   🕐

📖   Amazon.com: 100 Science Fiction & F...

📁   toledo_2016_contacts   ›

📁   Decathlon Sites   ›

📁   Mantis_Documentation_Project   ›

📁   my_sites   ›

📁   financial   ›

📁   Accruent   ›

📁   Fitness/Health   ›

📁   RC Sites   ›

📁   VFA   ›

📁   Winter_getaways   ›

Edit   **2**

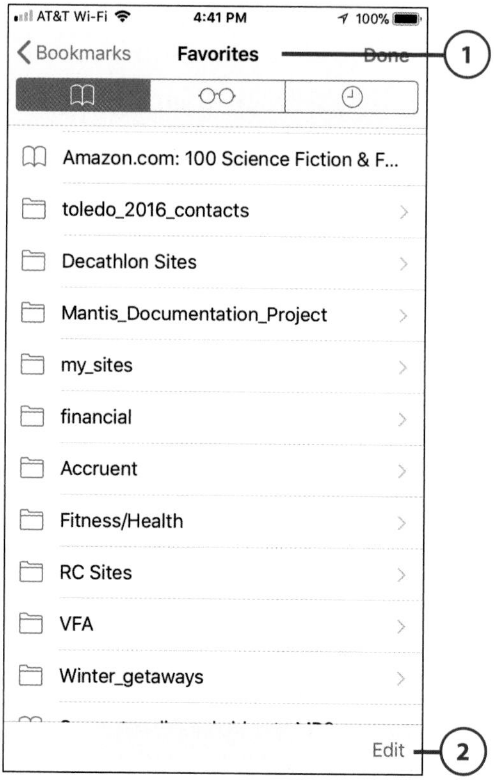

3. Drag the order icon next to the bookmark or folder you want to move up or down the screen to change the order in which it appears on the screen. When you drag a folder or bookmark between other items, they slide apart to make room for the folder or bookmark you are dragging. The order of the items in the list is the order in which they appear on the Bookmarks screen.

4. Tap a folder to change its name or location.

5. Change the name in the name bar.

6. To change the location of the folder, tap the LOCATION bar, which shows the folder's current location.

Can't Move?

If you have only one bookmark you've added, you can't move them around as described here because Safari won't let you "disturb" the default bookmarks and folders (such as Favorites). You can only delete default bookmarks.

---

7. Swipe up and down the list of folders until you see the folder in which you want to place the folder you are working with.

8. Tap the folder into which you want to move the folder you are editing.

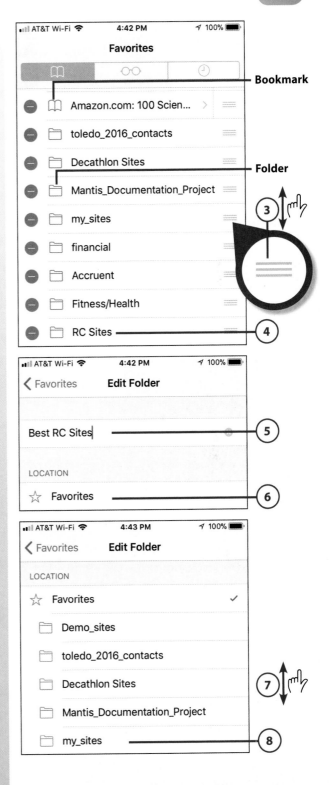

9 Tap the Back icon (<), which is labeled with the location from which you came. You move back to the prior Bookmarks screen, which reflects any changes you made.

10 Tap a bookmark you want to change.

Editing a Bookmark

If the bookmark you want to change isn't on the Bookmarks screen you are currently viewing, tap Done to exit Edit mode. Then open the folder containing the bookmark you want to change and tap Edit. You are able to change the bookmark.

11 Change the bookmark's name in the name bar.

12 If you want to change a bookmark's URL, tap the URL bar and make changes to the current URL. For example, you might want to change it to have the bookmark point to a site's home page rather than the specific page on that site you are viewing.

13 To change the location of the folder or bookmark, tap the LOCATION bar and follow steps 7 and 8.

14 Tap Done. You move back to the previous screen, and any changes you made—such as changing the name or location of a bookmark—are reflected.

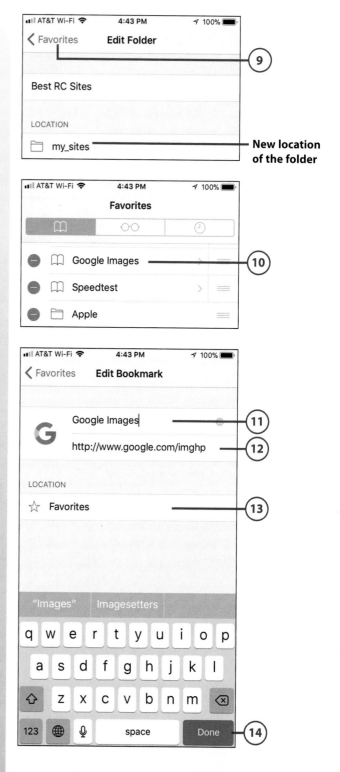

New location of the folder

15 Tap New Folder to create a new folder.

16 Enter the name of the folder.

17 Follow steps 6–8 to choose the location in which you want to save the new folder.

18 Tap Done. The new folder is created in the location you selected. You can place folders and bookmarks into it by using the LOCATION bar to navigate to it.

19 Tap Done. Your changes are saved, and you exit Edit mode.

Browsing Both Ways

As you browse, make sure you try both the horizontal and vertical orientations. Safari sometimes offers different features in the two orientations on different models. For example, when you open the Bookmarks screen and rotate an iPhone Plus or Xs Max, the screen is divided into two panes. On the left is the Bookmarks pane you are viewing and the right pane shows the web page you were browsing. If you tap a bookmark, the web page in the right pane becomes the page at which the bookmark points.

Deleting Bookmarks or Folders of Bookmarks

You can get rid of bookmarks or folders of bookmarks you don't want any more by deleting them:

1. Move to the screen containing the folder or bookmark you want to delete.

2. Swipe to the left on the folder or bookmark you want to delete.

3. Tap Delete. The folder or bookmark is deleted. Note that when you delete a folder, all the bookmarks it contains are deleted, too.

Using 3D Touch with Safari

Like other default iPhone apps, Safari supports 3D Touch (iPhone 6s and later models), which you can use in a couple of ways.

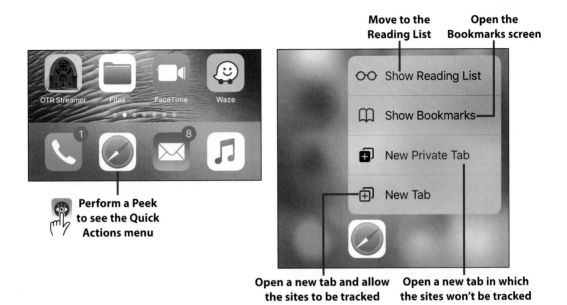

Move to the Reading List — OO Show Reading List

Open the Bookmarks screen — Show Bookmarks

Perform a Peek to see the Quick Actions menu

Open a new tab and allow the sites to be tracked — New Tab

Open a new tab in which the sites won't be tracked — New Private Tab

When you press and hold on the Safari app's icon, you see the Quick Actions menu. You can select from among its options to quickly perform actions in Safari. For example, choose New Tab to open a new tab in which you can navigate to a web page, or choose Show Bookmarks to jump to the Bookmarks page.

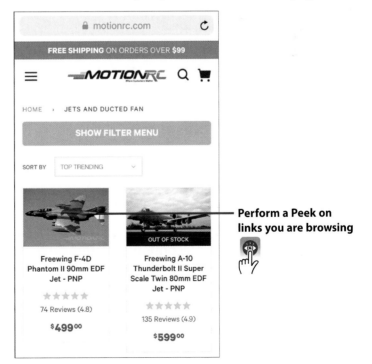

Perform a Peek on links you are browsing

When you see this, you can swipe up the screen to see options

Perform a pop to open the web page

Tap an action to perform it

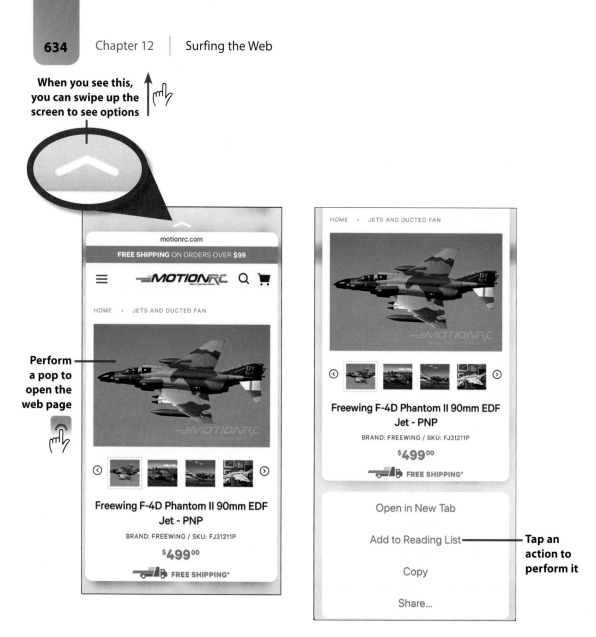

When you are browsing links, such as when you have performed a search, or your bookmarks, press on a link or a bookmark in which you are interested to perform a Peek on it. In the Peek window, you see the web page for the link or web page on which you peeked. If you continue to press on the Peek, it pops open so you can view the web page in Safari. When you perform a Peek on some screens, such as the links resulting from a search, you see an upward-facing arrow at the top of the screen; this indicates you can swipe up the screen to reveal a menu of commands. Tap a command to perform it. For example, tap Open in New Tab to open the web page in a new tab in Safari.

Sharing Web Pages

Safari makes it easy to share web pages that you think will be valuable to others. There are many ways to share, including AirDrop, Message, Mail, Twitter, and Facebook. A couple of examples will prepare you to use any of them.

Emailing a Link to a Web Page

You can quickly email links to web pages you visit.

(1) Use Safari to navigate to a web page whose link you want to email to someone.

(2) Tap the Share icon.

(3) Tap Mail. A new email message is created, and the link to the web page is inserted into the body. The subject of the message is the title of the web page.

4 Complete and send the email message. (Refer to Chapter 8, "Sending, Receiving, and Managing Email," for information about the Mail app.) When the recipient receives your message, he can visit the website by tapping the link included in the email message.

Messaging a Web Page

If you come across a page that you want to share with someone via Messages, Safari makes it easy.

1 Use Safari to navigate to a web page whose link you want to message to someone.

2 Tap the Share icon.

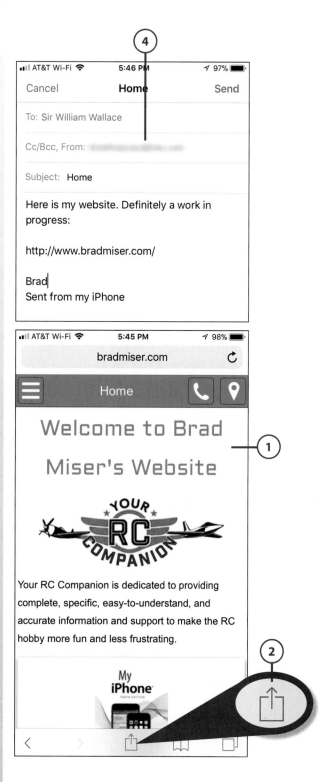

3. Tap Message. A new message is created, and the link to the web page is inserted.

4. Address the message.

5. Enter text you want to send along with the link to the web page.

6. Tap the Send icon. Your message is sent. The recipients can visit the web page by tapping the link included in the message.

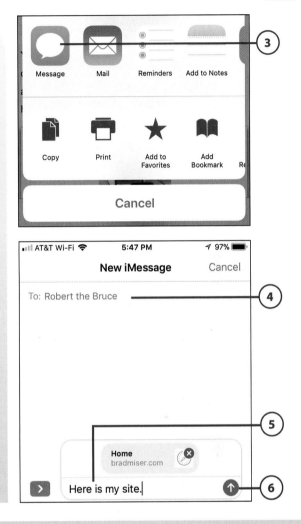

>>>Go Further

MORE WAYS TO SHARE THE WEB

If you want to share a web page in the old-fashioned way, you can print it by opening the Share menu and tapping Print (assuming you have your iPhone set up to print, as explained in Chapter 2, "Using Your iPhone's Core Features"). If you tap Copy, the web page's address is copied to the clipboard, so you can paste it into documents, emails, notes, or messages. You can also share via Twitter and Facebook.

Signing In to Websites Automatically

If you enable Safari to remember usernames and passwords with the AutoFill Passwords setting on the Passwords & Accounts screen, it can enter this information for you automatically. When Safari encounters a site for which it recognizes and can save login information, you are prompted to allow Safari to save that information. This doesn't work with all sites; if you aren't prompted to allow Safari to save login information, you can't use this feature with the site you are visiting. When saved, this information can be entered for you automatically.

1. Move to a web page that requires you to log in to an account.

2. Enter your account's username and password.

3. Tap the icon to log in to your account, such as Continue, Sign In, Submit, Login, and such. You are prompted to save the login information.

4. Tap Save Password to save the information. The next time you move to the login page, your username and password are entered for you automatically. Tap Never for This Website if you don't want the information to be saved and you don't want to be prompted again. Tap Not Now if you don't want the information saved but do want to be prompted again later to save it.

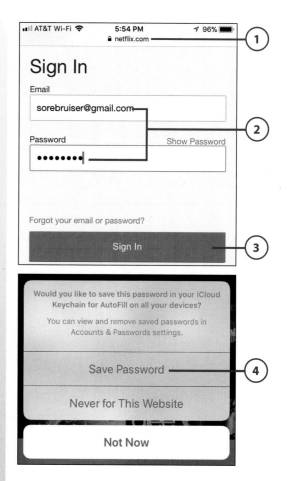

>>>*Go Further*

LETTING SAFARI CREATE PASSWORDS FOR YOU

If you have enabled the AutoFill Passwords setting, Safari can create passwords for you. Go to a website that requires you to create a password, such as when you register for a new account. When you tap in a field that Safari recognizes as requiring a password, tap Suggest Password. Safari presents a password for you; most of these are not easy to remember, but that doesn't matter because it is saved for you automatically so you won't have to enter it manually. If you want to use the recommended password, tap Use Suggested Password; Safari enters the password in the password and verify password fields. When syncing is enabled, the password is stored on the synced devices, too, so you are able to sign in from those devices just as easily.

Take photos and video

Configure camera settings

In this chapter, you explore all the photo and video functionality that your iPhone has to offer. Topics include the following:

→ Getting started
→ Setting Camera preferences
→ Using the Camera app to take photos and video with your iPhone

Taking Photos and Video with Your iPhone

The iPhone's cameras and Camera app capture high-quality photos and video. Because you'll likely have your iPhone with you at all times, it's handy to capture photos with it whenever and wherever you are. And, you can capture video just as easily.

Whether you've taken photos and video on your iPhone or added them from another source, the Photos app enables you to edit, view, organize, and share your photos. (To learn how to use the Photos app with the great photos and video you take, see Chapter 14, "Viewing and Editing Photos and Video with the Photos App.") You'll likely find that taking and working with photos and videos are among the most useful things your iPhone can do.

Getting Started

Each generation of iPhone has had different and more sophisticated photo and video capabilities and features than the previous versions. All current versions sport high-quality cameras; in fact, there is a camera on each side of the iPhone. One takes photos of what you are looking at (the back-facing camera, located on the backside of the phone), whereas the other takes photos of what the screen is facing (the front-facing camera, which is usually for taking selfies, located on the face of the phone).

Current generations also have a flash; can zoom; take burst, panoramic, and time-lapse photos; and have other features you expect from a high-quality digital camera. The iPhone 6s and later models can also take Live Photos, which capture a small amount of video along with the photo.

The iPhone 7 and later models have image stabilization, more resolution, and other enhancements to enable them to take even higher quality photos and video with both the back-facing and front-facing cameras.

The iPhone 7 Plus, 8 Plus, X, Xs, and Xs Max models have two back-facing cameras: one is the wide-angle camera that all models have (in different versions depending on the model), and the other camera has a telephoto lens. These two cameras give these models unique photo capabilities, which are a Telephoto mode that enables you to capture much better quality photos using both optical zoom and digital zoom. You can use a true optical zoom of up to 2x, and then an enhanced digital zoom of up to 10x for photos and 6x for videos. These models also enable you to take Portrait photos in which the subject is in very sharp focus and the background in a soft blur.

The Xs and Xs Max offer the most sophisticated photographic capabilities with the X model just slightly less powerful.

The iPhone's photo and video capabilities and features are probably the largest area of differences between the various models. Because of the fairly large variation in capabilities of iPhone models that can run iOS 12, it's impossible to cover all the differences in this chapter; the iPhone X and Xs models are used for most of the step-by-step tasks in this chapter. If you have a different model, some of the tasks described might not be applicable to you, or some of the details in this chapter might be different than what you see on your iPhone. However, all models can do most of the tasks in this chapter so even if you don't have an X, Xs, or Xs Max, you can still take lots of different (and great!) kinds of photos and videos using the information in this chapter.

The biggest grouping of model types from the photographic perspective is models that have telephoto capabilities and those that don't. Therefore, there is a section on taking photos for each type because once you know how to take photos, you can use the other options fairly easily.

Additionally, the iPhone's photo and video capabilities have been increasingly tied into iCloud. For example, you can store your entire photo library under your iCloud account; this offers many benefits, including backing up all your photos, making it easy to access your photos from any device, and being able to quickly share your photos with others. Therefore, I've assumed you are using iCloud and have configured it to work with photos as described in Chapter 3, "Setting Up and Using an Apple ID, iCloud, and Other Online Accounts." Like differences in iPhone camera capabilities, if you don't use iCloud with your photos, some of the information in this chapter doesn't apply to you and what you see on your phone might look different than what you see in this chapter.

Setting Camera Preferences

The following table describes options in the Settings app that you can access by tapping Settings on the Home screen, and then tapping Camera. The default settings allow you to take photos and video without making any changes to these settings, but it's good to know where they are and what they do if you decide to change how the Camera app works.

Settings App Explained

To get detailed information on using the Settings app, see "Working with the Settings App" in Chapter 2, "Using Your iPhone's Core Features."

Your Screen May Vary

The settings in the following table are for the iPhone Xs; other models might have slightly different settings.

Camera Settings

Section	Setting	Description
Preserve Settings	Camera Mode	When this switch is on (green), the Camera app retains the mode you most recently used, such as VIDEO or PANO. When off (white), the camera is reset to the PHOTO mode each time you move into the Camera app.
Preserve Settings	Creative Controls	When this switch is on (green), the Camera app retains the filters, light, or depth settings you most recently used, such as the DRAMATIC filter. When off (white), the camera is reset to the default settings for each of these adjustments each time you move into the Camera app.
Preserve Settings	Live Photo	When this switch is on (green), the Camera app retains the Live Photo setting you used most recently, such as Off. When off (white), Live Photo is turned on automatically each time you move into the Camera app.
N/A	Grid	When this switch is on (green), you see a grid on the screen when you are taking photos with the Camera app. This grid can help you align the subject of your photos in the image you are capturing.
N/A	Scan QR Codes	When this switch is on (green), you can use the Camera app to scan QR codes that provide information about the object to which they are attached or with which they are associated. For example, many zoos and museums put QR codes on their exhibits; you can use your iPhone's camera to quickly scan these QR codes to get information about what you are looking at. When this switch is off (white), this feature is disabled.
Record Video	Resolution and Frame Rate	Use these options to determine how video is recorded. The options available depend on the model of iPhone you have. You can choose from among different combinations of resolution and frame rate. Higher resolution and frame rates mean better-quality video, but also larger files. For example, 4K at 60 fps is very high quality, but the resulting video also has the largest file size.
Record Video	Auto Low Light FPS	When this switch is enabled (green), the frame rate of video recording is automatically lowered when videoing under low light conditions. This improves the quality of the image captured with less light.

Section	Setting	Description
Record Video	Lock Camera	The iPhone can switch cameras while recording to maintain the best image quality. With this switch enabled, the camera you used when you start recording is locked in and is used for the duration of the video session.
Record Slo-mo	Resolution and Frame Rate	The selections here determine the resolution and frame rate for slow-motion video. Like regular video, the higher the resolution and frame rate, the better quality the resulting video is and the file sizes are larger.
N/A	Record Stereo Sound	When enabled (green), your iPhone records audio in stereo. If you disable this, it records the audio in mono. Stereo provides better quality, but also larger file sizes.
Formats	CAMERA CAPTURE	Choose High Efficiency if you want your photos to be captured in the HEIF/HEVC format so they use less storage space. Not all devices and apps can use this format, but any that are related to the iPhone (such as iPads and Macs) should be able to. This format results in smaller file sizes so you can store more photos on your iPhone. If you use photos on other types of devices or if you want to make sure your photos are compatible with as many devices and apps as possible, choose Most Compatible instead.
HDR (High Dynamic Range)	Smart HDR	When enabled, Smart HDR, which is supported on Xs and Xs Max models, (read more about this in the Go Further sidebar at the end of the chapter) captures a series of images and blends them into one image. The intention is to produce higher quality images. Note that if Smart HDR is disabled, you won't be able to take HDR images at all. On iPhone X models, this is Auto HDR. On other models, this setting isn't available because you manually turn HDR on or off when you capture images.
HDR	Keep Normal Photo	When this switch is on (green), the HDR and the normal version of photos are stored. When this switch is off (white), only the HDR version of the photo is stored.

Photos Settings

You should use the Photos settings to determine what happens with your photos and videos after you capture them, such as if they are stored in your iCloud Photo Library and if photos are optimized for storage on your iPhone. See the section "Configuring Photos Settings" in Chapter 14 for a detailed explanation of these settings.

Using the Camera App to Take Photos and Video with Your iPhone

You use the Camera app to take photos and video with your iPhone. This app has a number of controls and features. Some features are easy to spot, whereas others aren't so obvious. By the end of this section, you'll know how to use these features to take great photos and video with your iPhone.

The general process for capturing photos or video follows:

1. Choose the type of photo or video you want to capture.

2. Set the options for the type of photo or video you selected.

3. Take the photos or video.

4. View and edit the photos or video you captured using the Photos app.

The information you need to accomplish steps 1 through 3 of this process is provided in tables and tasks throughout this chapter. The details for step 4 are provided in Chapter 14.

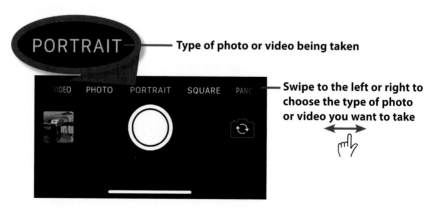

PORTRAIT —— Type of photo or video being taken

—— Swipe to the left or right to choose the type of photo or video you want to take

The first step in taking photos or video is to choose the type of photo or video that you want to capture. You do this by swiping to the left or right on the selection bar just above the large Shutter icon at the bottom of the Camera app's screen, as shown in the previous figure. The option shown in yellow at the center of the screen just above the Shutter icon is the current type of photo or video you are capturing. The options available in the Camera app are explained in the following table.

Types of Photo and Video iPhones Can Capture

Type of Photo or Video	Description
TIME-LAPSE	Captures a video with compressed time so that the time displayed in the video occurs much more rapidly than "real time." This is what is often used to show a process that takes a long time, such as a plant growing, in just a few seconds.
SLO-MO	Takes slow motion video so that you can slow down something that happens quickly.
VIDEO	Captures video at a real-time speed. The steps to take video are provided in the task "Taking Video," later in this chapter.
PHOTO	Captures still photos (or Live Photos on iPhone 6s/6s Plus or later models). Step-by-step instructions showing how to use this option are provided in the task "Taking Photos with Standard Zoom," later in this chapter. Using an iPhone's telephoto zoom capabilities is described in "Taking Photos with Telephoto Zoom."
PORTRAIT	Takes portrait photos of people using a sharp focus in the foreground on the subject and a soft blur in the background. Additionally, there are a number of lighting options that you can apply to the portrait photos. On the newest X models, you can also adjust photo depth. The steps to take portrait photos are in "Taking Portrait Photos."
SQUARE	Takes "square" photos in which the height and width are the same.
PANO	Takes panoramic photos that enable you to capture very wide images. An example of capturing a panoramic photo is provided in the task "Taking Panoramic Photos," later in this chapter.

When you choose the type of photo or video you want to take, there are quite a few options you can select (the options available to you depend on the type of photo or video you are taking and the specific model of iPhone you are using). When you select options, the icons you see on the screen change to reflect your selection. For example, when you choose a self-timed photo, the Self-timer icon changes to show the time delay you have selected. Not all options are available at the same time. For example, you can't set the flash and HDR to go on at the same time because you can't take HDR images with the flash. If you use a model that has Smart HDR, you don't turn it off or on for specific photos; it is set via the settings described earlier and works automatically if it is enabled.

The following table describes the icons and tools available on the Camera app's screen. (Remember that the specific icons and tools you see depend on the type of photo or video you are capturing and the model of iPhone you are using.)

Photo and Video Options and Icons

Icon	Description
⚡	**Flash**—When you tap this icon, you see a menu with the flash options, which are Auto (the app uses the flash when required), On (flash is always used), or Off (flash is never used). Tap the option you want to use and the menu closes. When the flash is set to on, the icon is yellow.
⚡	**Flash Being Used**—When this icon appears on the screen, it indicates the flash will be used when taking a photo or video.
HDR	**High Dynamic Range (HDR)**—Tap this to set the HDR options (only models that don't support Automatic or Smart HDR). (You learn more about HDR in the "More on Taking Photos and Video" Go Further sidebar later in this chapter.) The options are Auto, On, or Off. When the flash is set to on, this is disabled and you see a line through the HDR icon because you can't use the flash with HDR images.
◉	**Live Photo on**—When this feature is enabled, you take Live Photos (see the "Live Photos" note following this table) and the Live Photos icon is yellow. To turn Live Photos off, tap this icon.
◎	**Live Photo off**—When disabled, you take static photos and the Live Photos icon is white. To turn Live Photos on, tap this icon.

Icon	Description
	Self-timer—When you tap this icon, a menu appears on which you can choose (3s or 10s) a 3- or 10-second delay for photos. When you choose a delay, the icon is replaced with one showing the delay you set. When you tap the Shutter icon, the timer starts and counts down the interval you selected before capturing the image.
	Filter—When you tap this icon, a filter selection bar appears above the Shutter icon. You can swipe on this bar to see the filters available, with the name of the filter in the center box appearing above it. You can choose from such filters as Dramatic Warm and Vivid Cool. Then tap a filter to apply it to the photo or video you are capturing. For example, you can apply the NOIR filter to give the photo a cool Noir-movie look. When you apply a filter, you see the image with the filter applied and you see the name of the filter above its preview on the Filter selection bar. Generally, it's better to apply filters after you take a photo so that you have an original, unfiltered version of the photo (this is covered in the task "Applying Filters to Photos" in Chapter 14).
	Filter applied—When the Filter icon is in color, you know a filter is currently applied. You also see the filter highlighted on the selection bar. When you capture a photo using the filter, the filter preview is marked with a white dot. Tap the Filter icon to close the filter selection bar. To remove a filter, tap the Filter icon, select the Original filter, and tap the Filter icon.
	Change Camera—When you tap this icon, you toggle between the back-facing and front-facing camera (the front-facing camera is typically used for selfies).
◯	**Shutter**—This icon changes based on the type of photo or video you are taking. For example, when you are taking a photo, this button is a white circle as shown. When you take a video, it becomes red. It looks a bit different for other types as well, such as Time-Lapse. Regardless of what the button looks like, its function is the same. Tap it to start the process, such as to take a photo or start capturing video. If applicable, tap it again to stop the process, such as stopping video capture. To take burst photos, you touch and hold it to capture the burst.
00:00:06	**Timer**—When you capture video, the timer shows the elapsed time of the video you are capturing. The red dot on the left side of the time indicates you are currently capturing video.

Icon	Description
	Focus/exposure box—When you frame an image, the camera uses a specific part of the image to set the focus, exposure, and other attributes. The yellow box that appears on the screen indicates the focus/exposure area. You can manually set the location of this box by tapping on the part of the image that you want the app to use to set the image's attributes. The box moves to the area on which you tapped and sets the attributes of the image based on that area.
	Exposure slider—When you tap in an image you are framing, the sun icon appears next to the focus/exposure box. If you tap this icon, you see the exposure slider. Drag the sun up to increase the exposure or down to decrease it. The image changes as you move the slider so you can see its effect immediately.
AE/AF LOCK	**AE/AF Lock**—When you tap an image to set the location of the focus/exposure box and keep your finger on the screen after a second or so, the focus and exposure become locked based on the area you selected. This icon indicates that the exposure and focus are locked so you can move the camera without changing the focus or exposure that is used when you capture the image. Tap the screen to release the lock and refocus on another area.
	Faces found—When your iPhone detects faces, it puts this box around them and identifies the area as a face. You can use faces to organize photos by applying names to the faces in your photos.
	**Zoom slider**—You can unpinch on an image to zoom in or pinch on an image to zoom out. When you do, the Zoom slider appears on the screen except for models that support telephoto zoom, in which case you see the current level in the Zoom Level icon. The Zoom slider indicates the relative level of zoom you are applying. You can also drag the slider toward the – to zoom out or drag it toward the + to zoom in to change the level of zoom you are using.
	Zoom Level icon—On models that support telephoto zoom, this indicates the level of zoom currently applied to the image, such as 1x, 2x, etc. If you swipe or unswipe on an image to change the zoom level, you always see the current level in this icon.

Icon	Description
	**Digital Zoom slider**—On models that support telephoto zoom, this appears when you touch and hold on the Zoom Level icon. Dragging on the slider along the curve increases or decreases the level of magnification.
	Portrait Lighting Effect—Indicates the current lighting effect applied to an image when you are using the Portrait mode.
	Depth Level icon and slider—When you are using Portrait mode, you can set the depth level by tapping this icon. When active, it turns yellow and the Depth Level slider appears. Swipe to left and right on this slider to change the depth level. When you have manually set the depth level, you see the setting in the icon.

And Now a Few Words on Live Photos

The iPhone 6s/6s Plus and later models can capture Live Photos. A Live Photo is a static image, but it also has a few of what Apple calls "moments" of video around the static image that you take. To capture a Live Photo, you set the Live function to on (it is on by default and its icon is yellow) and take the photo as you normally would. When you are viewing a Live Photo you have taken (these photos have the LIVE icon on them), tap and hold on the photo to see the motion associated with that photo. When you aren't tapping and holding on a Live Photo, it looks like any other photo you've taken.

Like other types of photos, you can share Live Photos with others. If the recipient is using an iPhone model 6s or newer, they can view the motion part of the Live Photo too. If the recipient is using an older model or some other type of device (such as an Android phone), the recipient sees only the static image (what you see when you are looking at a Live Photo without pressing on it).

Taking Photos with Standard Zoom

You can use the Camera app to capture photos with all iPhone models like so:

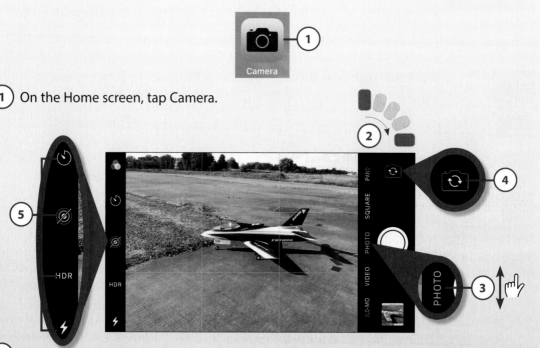

(1) On the Home screen, tap Camera.

(2) To capture a horizontal photo, rotate your iPhone so that it's horizontal; of course, you can use either orientation to take photos just as you can with any other camera.

(3) Swipe up or down (right or left if the phone is vertical) on the selection bar until PHOTO is in the center and in yellow.

(4) If you want to change the camera you are using, tap the Change Camera icon. When you change the camera, the image briefly freezes, and then the view changes to the other camera. The front-facing camera (the one facing you when you look at the screen) has fewer features than the back-facing camera has. These steps show taking a photo with the back-facing camera.

(5) Set the Flash, HDR, Live, and Self-timer options you want to use for the photo; see the previous table for an explanation of these options. (You won't see the HDR option on X, Xs, or Xs Max models.)

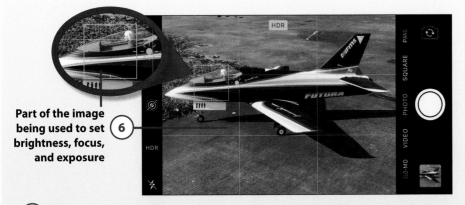

Part of the image being used to set brightness, focus, and exposure

(6) Frame the image by moving and adjusting the iPhone's distance and angle to the object you are photographing; if you have the Grid turned on, you can use its lines to help you frame the image the way you want it. When you stop moving the phone, the Camera app indicates the part of the image that is used to set focus, brightness, and exposure with the yellow box. If this is the most important part of the image, you are good to go. If not, you can set this point manually by tapping where you want the focus to be (see step 9).

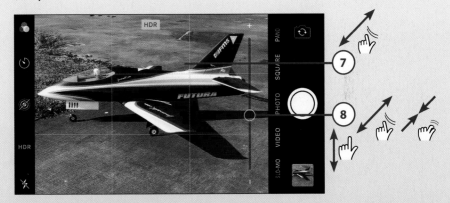

(7) Zoom in by unpinching on the image. The camera zooms in on the subject. If you're using a model that doesn't have telephoto capabilities, the Zoom slider appears. If you're using a model with telephoto capabilities, you don't see this slider; instead you see the current zoom level in the Zoom level icon (not shown in the figure, but is shown on figures in the next section).

(8) Unpinch on the image (all models) or drag the slider (non-telephoto models only) toward the + to zoom in or pinch on the image or drag the slider toward the – to zoom out to change the level of zoom until it's what you want to use.

⑨ Tap the screen to manually set the area of the image to be used for setting the focus and exposure. The yellow focus box appears where you tapped.

⑩ To change the exposure, swipe up on the sun icon to increase the brightness or down to decrease it.

⑪ Continue making adjustments in the framing of the image, the zoom, focus point, and brightness until it is the image you want to take.

⑫ Tap the Shutter icon on the screen, either Volume button on the side of the iPhone, or press the center button on the EarPods. The Camera app captures the photo, and the shutter closes briefly while the photo is recorded. When the shutter opens again, you're ready to take the next photo.

⑬ Tap the thumbnail to see the photo you most recently captured.

⑭ Use the photo-viewing tools to view the photo (see Chapter 14 for the details).

⑮ If you don't want to keep the photo, tap the Trash Can, and then tap Delete Photo.

⑯ Edit the photo by tapping Edit and using the resulting editing tools to make changes to the picture (see Chapter 14 for the details).

⑰ Tap the Back icon (<). You move back into the Camera app and can take more photos.

Taking Photos with Telephoto Zoom

You can use the optical and digital telephoto zoom features of the iPhone 7 Plus, 8 Plus, X, Xs, and Xs Max as follows:

(1) Select the PHOTO mode, set up the image you want to capture, choose the options (such as flash or Live), frame the image, and set the exposure as described in the previous steps.

(2) To zoom in at 2x using the optical zoom, tap the Zoom Level icon. The magnification level changes to 2x using the iPhone's optical zoom.

Just a Little Pinch Will Do You

The standard pinch and unpinch gestures to zoom or unzoom work, too. When you use a pinch or unpinch motion to zoom, the amount of magnification currently applied is shown in the Zoom Level icon. Using the pinch and unpinch motion to zoom is less precise than the method shown in these steps, but can be a bit faster.

3. Touch and hold on the Zoom Level icon. The Digital Zoom slider appears.

4. Drag the Digital Zoom slider to the left to increase the level of magnification or to the right to decrease it. As you drag, the amount of magnification is shown in the Zoom Level icon and of course, you see the magnified image on the screen. When you've set the magnification level and lift your finger from the screen, the slider disappears.

Telephoto Zooming Applies Everywhere—Almost

The zooming features shown in these steps apply to all modes except Portrait. However, there are different maximum levels of zoom in the various modes. For example, when using the VIDEO mode, you are limited to 6x, whereas in the SLO-MO mode, you are limited to 3x. In PANO mode, you only have the 1x and 2x options. Experiment with the zoom in the modes you use to see what zoom capabilities they have.

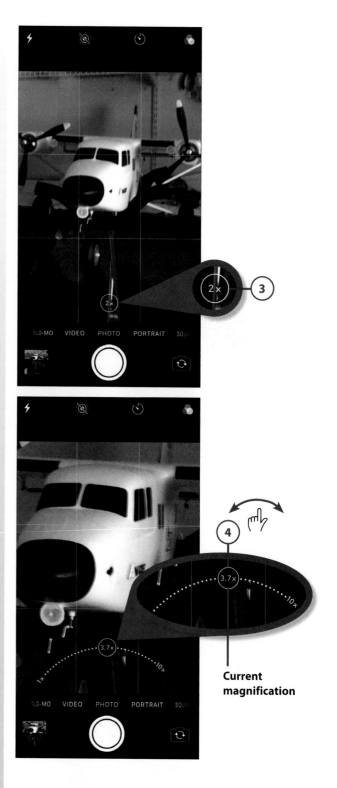

Current magnification

(5) Tap the Shutter icon to take the photo or video.

Quick Reset

To quickly return the magnification level to 1x, tap the Zoom Level icon.

Taking Portrait Photos

The Portrait mode (available on the iPhone 7 Plus, 8 Plus, X, Xs, and Xs Max) captures the subject in sharp focus and blurs the background. You can also apply various lighting effects and set the depth level. Use these steps to take portrait photos:

(1) Swipe on the Selection bar until you reach PORTRAIT mode.

(2) Make sure the subject is inside the yellow frame. Once the subject is recognized and captured inside the frame, the frame automatically stays on the subject even if she moves. If you're too close to the subject, you see a message indicating you should move further away.

(3) Touch and hold on the Lighting icon. The Portrait Lighting Effect slider appears.

Portrait Photos

When you take a portrait photo, you can use many of the Camera app's features, such as the self-timer. These work just like they do for other types of photos. You can't zoom or use HDR when you're taking portrait photos.

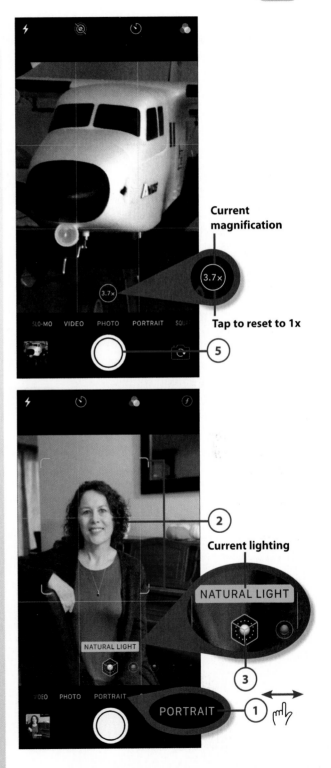

Current magnification

Tap to reset to 1x

Current lighting

NATURAL LIGHT

(4) Swipe the Portrait Lighting Effect slider to the left or right to change the lighting effect applied to the image. In some cases, such as STAGE LIGHT, you see a focus area that shows where the light will be focused; you can use this to set up the image you want to capture.

(5) To manually set the depth level, tap the Depth Level icon. The Depth Level slider appears.

(6) Swipe the Depth Level slider to the left to increase the depth or to the right to decrease it. You see the results of the changes on the screen.

(7) Tap the Shutter icon to take the photo.

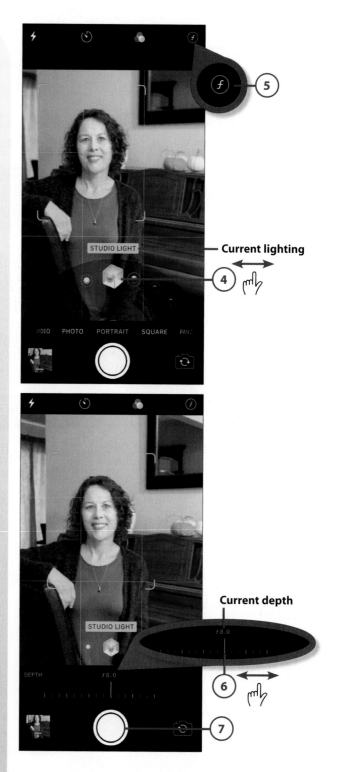

Current lighting

Current depth

Taking Panoramic Photos

The Camera app can take panoramic photos by capturing a series of images as you pan the camera across a scene, and then "stitching" those images together into one panoramic image. To take a panoramic photo, perform the following steps:

Camera — ①

Current position in the image

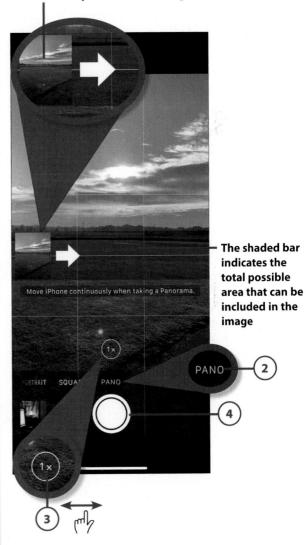

The shaded bar indicates the total possible area that can be included in the image

Move iPhone continuously when taking a Panorama.

PANO — ②

④

PORTRAIT   SQUARE   PANO

③

① Open the Camera app.

② Swipe on the selection bar until PANO is selected. On the screen, you see a bar representing the entire image that contains a smaller box representing the current part of the image that will be captured.

③ If you're using a model that has telephoto capabilities, you can zoom the image to 2x by tapping the Zoom Level icon.

④ Tap the Shutter icon. The app begins capturing the image.

5 Slowly sweep the iPhone to the right while keeping the arrow centered on the line on the screen. If you move the phone too fast, you see a message on the screen telling you to slow down. If the arrow goes too far above or below the line, you see a message telling you to move the phone to better align the arrow with the line. The better you keep the tip of the arrow aligned with the line, the more consistent the centerline of the resulting image will be.

6 When you've moved to the "end" of the image you are capturing or the limit of what you can capture in the photo, tap the Shutter icon. You move back to the starting point and the panoramic photo is created. You can tap the panoramic image's thumbnail to view, delete, or edit it just as you can with other types of photos.

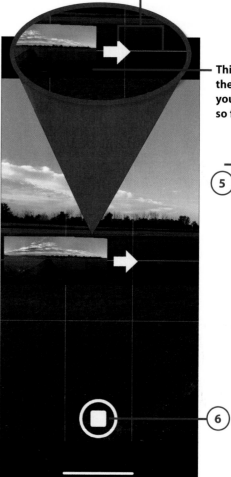

As you move the iPhone from the start of the image to the end, keep the arrow centered on the line

This box shows the image you've captured so far

Taking Video

You can capture video as easily as you can still images. Here's how.

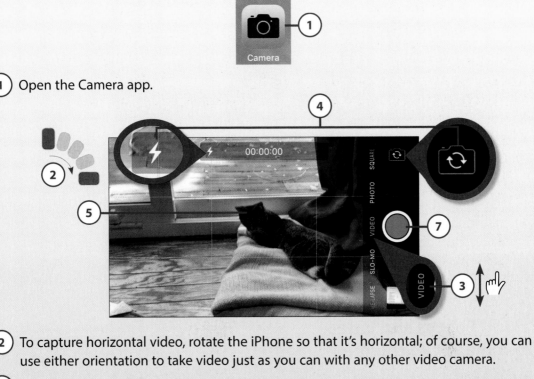

1 Open the Camera app.

2 To capture horizontal video, rotate the iPhone so that it's horizontal; of course, you can use either orientation to take video just as you can with any other video camera.

3 Swipe on the selection bar until VIDEO is selected.

4 Choose the back-facing or front-facing camera, configure the flash, or zoom in, just like setting up a still image. (The Self-timer, Filter, and HDR modes are not available when taking video.)

5 Tap on the screen where you want to focus.

6 If needed, adjust the exposure by sliding the "sun" icon up or down just like a still photo (not shown on the figure).

7 Tap the Shutter icon to start recording. You hear the start/stop recording tone and the app starts capturing video; you see the timer on the screen showing how long you've been recording.

Length of video

8 Take still images while you take video by tapping the white Shutter icon. (If the Live Photos preference is enabled, the photos you take are Live Photos. If not, you take static images.)

9 Stop recording by tapping the red Shutter icon again. Also, like still images, you can then tap the video's thumbnail to preview it as well as any still images you took while taking the video. You can use the Photos app's video tools to view or edit the clip. (These tasks are also explained in Chapter 14.)

Taking Photos and Video from the Lock Screen

Because it is likely to be with you constantly, your iPhone is a great camera of opportunity. You can use its Quick Access feature to quickly take photos when your iPhone is asleep/locked. Here's how:

1 When the iPhone is locked, press the Side button, tap the screen, touch the Touch ID/Home button, or lift your phone up (if you have a model that supports the Raise to Wake feature and it is enabled). The Lock screen appears.

2 Swipe to the left (all models) or press the Camera icon (X models). The Camera app opens.

(3) Use the Camera app to take the photo or video as described in the previous tasks. You can only view the most recent photos or videos you captured from within the Camera app when your iPhone is locked; you have to unlock the phone to work with the rest of your photos.

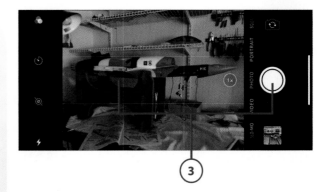

Taking Photos and Video from the Control Center

You can get to the camera quickly using the Control Center, too.

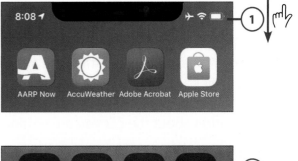

(1) Open the Control Center by swiping down from the upper-right corner of the screen (X models) or swiping up from the bottom of the screen (non-X models).

(2) Tap the Camera icon. The Camera app opens.

(3) Use the Camera app to take photos or video as you've learned in the previous tasks (not shown in the figures).

Taking Photos with Quick Actions (Models with 3D Touch)

On iPhone 6s/6S Plus and later models, the Quick Access menu offers a selection of photos and video commands that you can choose right from a Home screen.

1. Touch and hold on the Camera icon until the Quick Actions menu opens.

2. Tap the type of photo or video you want to take. The Camera app opens and is set up for the type you selected.

3. Use the Camera app to capture the photo or video (not shown in the figures).

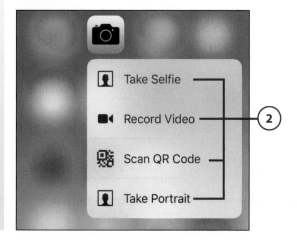

Scanning QR Codes

QR (Quick Response) codes provide information about or enable you to take action on objects to which they are attached or associated. A QR scanner reads these codes and presents the information they contain. For example, rental cars usually have a QR code sticker on a window; when you scan this code, you get information about the car you are renting.

QR codes also enable you to take action, such as scanning the QR code for a Wi-Fi network and then joining it, scanning the code for an email address and then creating an email, and so on.

The Camera app can scan QR codes. After the code is scanned, you are prompted to take action on it.

The following steps show scanning a QR code for a rental car; scanning other types of QR codes is similar:

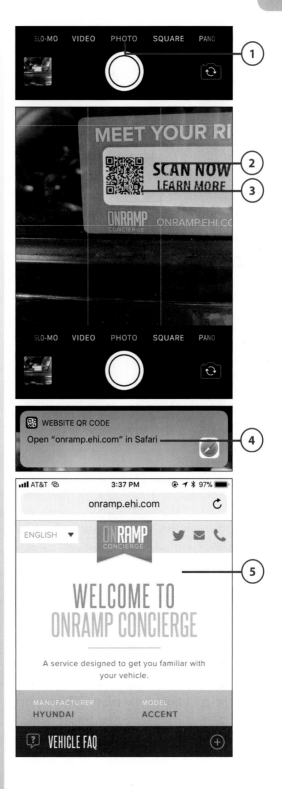

(1) Open the Camera app and put it in either Photo or Square mode.

(2) Frame the QR code in the camera.

(3) Tap on the code to focus on it. You see a prompt about the code you scanned.

(4) Tap the prompt to take action on it.

(5) Complete the task you started in step 4 based on the type of code you scanned. For example, when you scan the QR code on a rental car, you might move to a website with information about the vehicle you rented. If the code is for a Wi-Fi network, you join that network. If the code contains an email address, you move into Mail and can complete the email to that address.

>>>*Go Further*
MORE ON TAKING PHOTOS AND VIDEO

The Camera app enables you to do all sorts of interesting and fun things with photos and video. Following are some additional pointers that help you make the most of this great app:

- **Set and forget**—You need to set the Flash, HDR, and most other options only when you want to change the current settings because these settings are retained even after you move out of the Camera app and back into it. The Camera Mode, Creative Controls (such as filters), and Live Photo behaviors are controlled by the Preserve Settings described earlier in this chapter.

- **HDR**—The High Dynamic Range (HDR) feature causes the iPhone to take three shots of each image, with each shot having a different exposure level. It then combines the three images into one higher-quality image. HDR works best for photos that don't have motion and where there is good lighting. (You can't use the iPhone's flash with HDR images.) Also, HDR photos take longer to capture.

  Smart HDR is supported on Xs and Xs Max models. It uses more images than standard HDR and is a more sophisticated application of the technique to produce even higher quality images (for example, multiple exposures of the images are also used).

  When you are using an X model, HDR is either on and happens automatically, or it is off, which means it isn't used at all. This is controlled by the setting you read about at the start of the chapter. By default, HDR or Smart HDR is turned on.

  On other models, you choose to use HDR or not when you take photos. (In these cases, HDR photos display the HDR icon in the upper-left corner when you view them.)

  When the Keep Normal Photo switch in the Camera Settings is on (green), you see two versions of each HDR photo in the Photos app: One is the HDR version, and the other is the normal version. If you prefer the HDR versions, set the Keep Normal Photo switch to off (white) so that your photos don't use as much space on your iPhone, and you don't have twice as many photos to deal with.

- **Location**—The first time you use the Camera app, you are prompted to decide whether you allow it to use Location Services. If you allow the Camera app to use Location Services, the app uses the iPhone's GPS to tag the location where photos and video were captured. Some apps can use this information, such as the Photos app on your iPhone, to locate your photos on maps, find photos by their locations, and so on.

- **Sensitivity**—The iPhone's camera is sensitive to movement, so if your hand moves while you are taking a photo, it's likely to be blurry; iPhone 6 Plus and later models have image stabilization that mitigates this to some degree. Sometimes, part of the image will be in focus and part of it isn't, so be sure to check the view before you capture a photo. This is especially true when you zoom in. If you are getting blurry photos, the problem is probably your hand moving while you are taking them. Of course, because it's digital, you can take as many photos as you need to get it right; delete the rejects as you take them and use the Photos app to periodically review and delete photos you don't want to keep (see Chapter 14), so you don't have to waste storage room or clutter up your photo library with photos you don't want to keep.

- **Burst photos**—When you touch and hold on the Shutter icon while taking photos, a series of images is captured rapidly and you see a counter showing the number being taken. When you release the Shutter icon, a burst photo is created; the burst photo contains all of the images you captured but appears as a single image in the Photos app. You can review the images in the burst and choose to keep only the images you want to save (this task is also covered in Chapter 14). Burst photos are best suited to capturing action.

- **Self-timer**—When you set the Self-timer option, you choose either a 3- or 10-second delay between when you tap the Shutter icon and when the image is captured. Like the other settings, the Self-timer is persistent, so you need to turn it off again when you want to stop using it.

- **Self-timer and burst**—If you set the timer, and then tap and hold on the Shutter icon for a second or so, a burst of ten photos is captured when the timer expires.

- **Slow-motion video**—You can also take slow-motion video. Choose SLO-MO on the selection bar. Set up the shot and take the video as you do with normal speed video. When you play it back, the video plays in slow motion except for the very beginning and ending. (The speed of the video is determined by the Record Slo-mo setting, described earlier.)

- **Time-lapse video**—When you choose the TIME-LAPSE option, you can set the focus and exposure level and choose the camera you want to use. You record the video just like "real time" video. When you play it back, the video plays back rapidly so you seemingly compress time.

- **Screenshots**. You can take screenshots of your iPhone's screen by pressing and holding the Side button and upper Volume button (X models) or by pressing and holding the Touch ID/Home and Side buttons at the same time (non-X models). The screen flashes white and the shutter sound plays to indicate the screen has been captured. You see a thumbnail of the screen capture. You can tap this to open the screen capture to edit it; when you're finished editing it, tap Done to close the preview (tap Save to Photos to save it or Delete Screenshot if you don't want to save it). If you don't tap the thumbnail, after a couple of seconds, it disappears (you can swipe it off the screen to get rid of it immediately).

If you didn't preview the screenshot, it automatically is saved. If that happened or you chose to save the preview in the editor, the resulting image is stored in the Screenshots album in the Photos app. You can view the screen captures you take, email them, send them via Messages, or other tasks as you can with photos you take with the iPhone's camera.

View, edit, and share photos, slideshows, and video

Use Messages, Mail, and other apps to share your photos and video

In this chapter, you explore all the photo- and video-viewing and editing functionality that your iPhone has to offer. Topics include the following:

→ Getting started
→ Configuring Photos settings
→ Viewing, editing, and working with photos on your iPhone
→ Viewing, editing, and working with video on your iPhone
→ Using iCloud with your photos

Viewing and Editing Photos and Video with the Photos App

Chapter 13, "Taking Photos and Video with Your iPhone," explains how to take photos and video using the iPhone's Camera app. The photos and video you take with your iPhone's cameras are stored in your photo library, which you can access using the Photos app. In this chapter, you learn how to use the Photos app to view, organize, edit, and share those photos and videos.

Getting Started

The Photos app provides many useful tools that you can use to view and edit photos and video stored on your iPhone, whether you used the iPhone's camera to capture them or you downloaded them from another source, such as images attached to email messages.

As you take photos, capture video, and download photos or video onto your iPhone, you can quickly build up a large photo library. Fortunately, the Photos app automatically organizes your photos and video so that you can find specific photos or video you want to view, edit, or share quite easily. You can also manually organize photos in albums with just a few steps.

After you locate photos and video in which you are interested, you can view them in the app manually or you can use the amazing Memories feature to see collections of photos and video based on location, dates, people, and other factors.

You can edit photos and videos to fix mistakes or to just make improvements in them. You can even use additional photo editors, such as the Markup tool that enables you to draw on or add text to your photos.

You'll probably want to share photos and videos with others, and the Photos app makes that a snap, too. You can do that through other apps on your iPhone, such as Messages, or directly using iCloud's Photo Sharing tools.

Even though the Photos app provides lots of features you can use with your photos and video, it isn't hard to use, as you'll see throughout the rest of this chapter.

Configuring Photos Settings

The following table describes options in the Settings app that you can access by tapping Settings on the Home screen, and then tapping Photos. You can likely work with the Photos app without changing any of these, but it's good to know what and where these settings are in case you want to make changes.

Settings App Explained

To get detailed information on using the Settings app, see "Working with the Settings App" in Chapter 2, "Using Your iPhone's Core Features."

Photos Settings

Section	Setting	Description
Siri & Search	Siri & Search Suggestions	When this switch is enabled (green), information in the Photos app can be searched, used when you perform Look Ups on terms, and by Siri. If you set this switch to off (white), Photos information is not used for searches or Siri Suggestions.
Siri & Search	Allow on Lock Screen	When enabled (green), this switch allows information from the Photos app to appear on the Lock screen.
Siri & Search	Shortcuts	Tap this to see a current list of shortcuts you can use with the Photos app. On the resulting Photos Shortcuts screen, tap Add (+) to create a phrase you can speak to perform the shortcut.
N/A	iCloud Photos	When enabled, your photos and videos are stored in your iCloud account on the cloud so that they are backed up and you can access them from multiple devices. See Chapter 3, "Setting Up and Using an Apple ID, iCloud, and Other Online Accounts," for information about using iCloud with your photos and video.
N/A	Optimize iPhone Storage	If you select this option, only versions of your photos that are optimized for the iPhone are stored on your phone; this saves space so that you can keep more photos and videos on your iPhone. Full resolution photos are uploaded to the cloud.
N/A	Download and Keep Originals	This option downloads full resolution versions of your photos and videos on your iPhone. They consume a lot more space than optimized versions.
N/A	Upload to My Photo Stream	When enabled, all your photos are automatically uploaded to your iCloud Photo Stream when you are connected to the Internet with Wi-Fi. New photos are also downloaded from the cloud to your iPhone and other devices with this setting enabled.

Section	Setting	Description
N/A	Upload Burst Photos	This setting determines if all of the photos in a burst are uploaded to the cloud or only photos you tag as favorites are uploaded. Because burst photos can take up a lot of space, it's usually better to leave this disabled. If you leave this disabled, when you select favorite photos in a burst series, only those photos are uploaded.
N/A	Shared Albums	When enabled, you can share your photos with others and subscribe to other people's albums to access their photos.
Cellular Data	Cellular Data	When the Cellular Data switch is enabled (green), photos are copied to and from your iCloud account when you are using a cellular Internet connection. If you have a limited data plan, you might want to set this to off (white) so photos are copied only when you are using a Wi-Fi network.
Cellular Data	Unlimited Updates	When enabled, updates to your photos are made constantly, which uses much more data. With this disabled, updates are made periodically, which lowers the data use.
PHOTOS TAB	Summarize Photos	When this switch is on (green), you see thumbnails for only some of the photos in a collection and the timeframe of each group is larger. If you set this to off (white), you see a thumbnail of every photo in your collections, which takes up much more screen space and you have to scroll more to move among your collections. This setting affects how you see Collections view and Years view only.
HDR (HIGH DYNAMIC RANGE)	View Full HDR	When this switch is enabled (green), you always see the maximum quality of photos as created with the HDR feature.

Section	Setting	Description
MEMORIES	Show Holiday Events	With this switch enabled (green), the Photos app attempts to collect photos taken on the holidays in your country into memories. When disabled (white), the Photos app ignores holidays when it creates memories for you.
TRANSFER TO MAC OR PC	Automatic	If you select Automatic, when you sync photos to a Mac or Windows PC, the compatibility of the format is changed to improve compatibility with the computer you are transferring files to.
TRANSFER TO MAC OR PC	Keep Originals	If you choose Keep Originals, the files are transferred without checking compatibility.

iCloud Settings

The iCloud-related settings on the Photos settings screen are the same as the Photos settings under the iCloud settings area (see Chapter 3 for details).

Viewing, Editing, and Working with Photos on Your iPhone

When you work with your photos in the Photos app, you first find and view the photos that you are interested in. You can then view those photos in a number of ways including individually or in memories. Should you want to make changes to photos, a couple of taps get you into the app's amazing editing tools so you can make bad photos better, good photos great, and, well, you get the idea.

Finding Photos to Work With by Browsing

The first step in viewing, editing, or doing other tasks with photos is finding the photos you want to work with. When you open the Photos app, you see four ways to access your photos: Photos, For You, Albums, and Search. You can use these options to find photos in which you are interested.

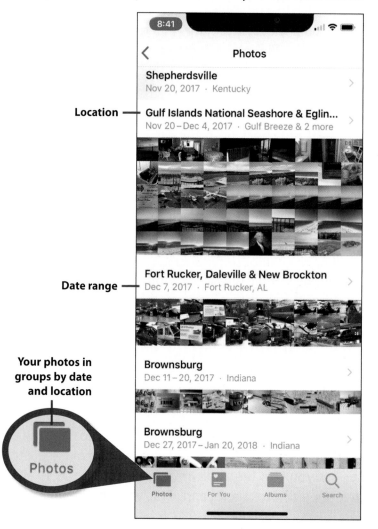

The Photos source automatically organizes photos based on the time and location associated with them (this information is embedded in the photos you take with the iPhone's camera, assuming you haven't disabled Location Services for it). The top level is Years, which shows your photos grouped by the year in which they were taken. You can then "drill down" into a year where you find memories (more about these shortly) and collections. Collections are photos that are organized by location and date ranges, which are determined according to the time, date, and location information on your photos. When you tap one of these collections, you drill down and see moments, which show you the detail of a collection. At the moment level, you see and can work with the individual photos in the collection.

Memories are based on people, locations, time periods, and other factors

Tap to see memories, featured photos, and shared albums

The For You source contains photos in Memories, Featured Photos, and Shared Album Activity. Memories are collections of photos the Photos app builds for you automatically. These collections can be based on a number of factors, such as time, location, holiday, and even people. You can view the photos in a memory individually, and the slideshows are created automatically to make viewing your photos more interesting.

Featured Photos shows photos the Photos app selects and presents to you. It's not clear how these photos are selected, but they change over time so you see different photos at different times. You can tap on Featured Photos to view them.

Shared Album Activity contains photo albums you are sharing with other people and photo albums other people are sharing with you. For each album being shared, you see the name of the album, who is sharing it (you, for photos you are sharing, or the name of the person sharing with you). When you tap a shared album, you see the photos it contains and can work with them. (Working with photo sharing is covered in detail in "Using iCloud with Your Photos" later in this chapter.)

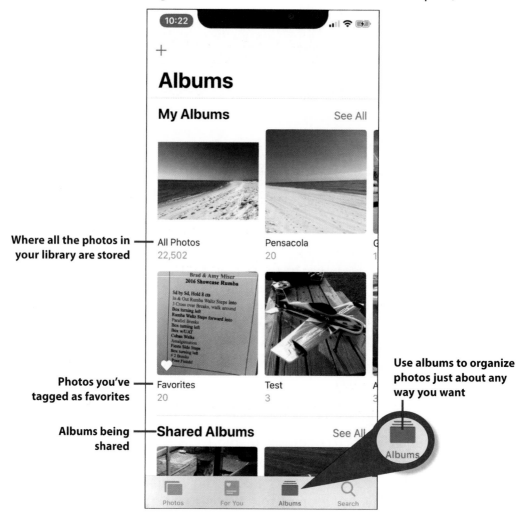

Where all the photos in your library are stored

Photos you've tagged as favorites

Albums being shared

Use albums to organize photos just about any way you want

The photos on the Albums screen are accessible in many ways:

- My Albums are albums you have created or that are default albums.
- Shared Albums are collections of photos you are sharing or that others are sharing with you.
- People & Places are albums created automatically based on the location of the photo (such as those captured with the iPhone's camera) or faces that are recognized by the iPhone's facial recognition system.
- Media Types are albums based on the type of media. For example, to see the videos stored in your library, you can open the Videos album, or if you want to see your selfies, tap Selfies.
- Other Albums contain collections of photos that you have imported, are currently hidden, or you have deleted recently (for a time, you can open this album to retrieve photos you have deleted).

In addition to the albums created for you, you can manually create albums to organize collections of photos or videos.

All Photos

One very useful album is called All Photos if you are using iCloud photos (it's called Camera Roll if you aren't using iCloud for photos). This is such a useful album because it automatically contains all the photos you take with the iPhone's cameras or any that you download onto your phone from other sources (such as from an email message). And, the photos you've most recently added to your iPhone are always at the bottom of this album so as soon as you open it, you see those photos. Because you will often want to work with photos you've taken recently, you can use this album to get to them quickly.

Your Albums May Vary

Some apps, such as Instagram, might add their own albums to the Albums tab.

Although each of these sources looks a bit different, the steps to browse them to find the photos you want to work with are similar for most of these sources. This example shows using the Photos source to browse for photos:

Photos

① On the Home screen, tap Photos.

② Tap Photos. On the Years screen, you see photos collected by the year in which they were taken. Under the year, you see a summary of the various locations where the photos were taken.

Start at the Beginning

If you don't see the years in bold as shown in the figure, tap the Back icon (<) located in the upper-left corner of the screen until you do.

③ Swipe up and down the screen to browse all the years.

④ Tap the thumbnails in the year that contains photos you want to work with. You move to the Collections screen that groups the selected year's photos based on locations and time periods.

Memories

If you want to jump directly to memories for the photos, tap a group's heading, such as the year or locations for a group of photos. You move into the memory view of those photos (covered later in this chapter).

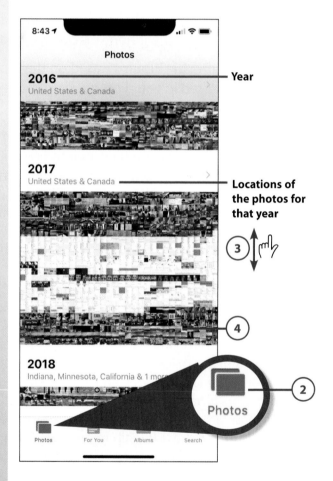

Year

Locations of the photos for that year

5 Swipe up and down the screen to browse all the collections in the year you selected.

6 Tap the collection that contains photos you want to see. Doing so takes you to the next level of your photos, which are moments that are collections of photos by the location where and the date on which they were taken.

7 Swipe up and down the screen to browse all the moments in the collection you selected.

8 Tap a photo to view it.

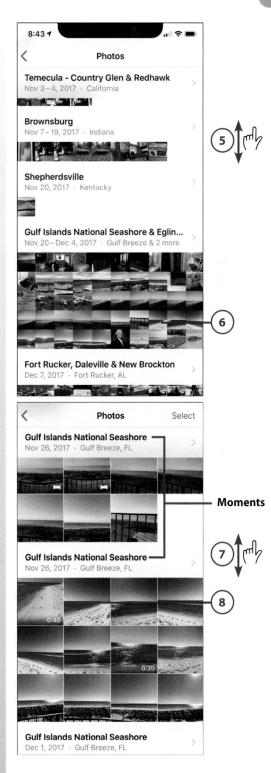

Moments

9 You're ready to view the photos in detail as described in the task "Viewing Photos Individually" later in this chapter.

Go Back

You can move back to the screens from where you came by tapping the Back icon (<), which is always located in the upper-left corner of the screen; this icon is sometimes named with the screen it takes you back to, it says Back, or it's just a left-facing arrow. It doesn't matter how it is identified, it always does the same thing, which is to take you back to the screen you were previously on. To choose a different source, you might have to tap the Back icon (<) a time or two as the Photos, For You, Albums, and Search icons at the bottom of the screen are visible only on some screens.

Finding Photos to Work With by Searching

Browsing photos can be a fun way to find photos, but at times you might want to get to specific photos more efficiently. The Search tool enables you to quickly find photos based on their time, date, location, content, and other factors.

(1) Continuing in the Photos app, tap the Search icon. At the top of the screen, you see the Search bar that you can use to perform a specific search. Below that are potential searches you might want to use; these are based on a variety of criteria, such as moments, people, places, and so on.

(2) Swipe up and down the current searches on the screen. For example, Places finds photos based on where they were taken.

(3) To use a current search, tap it and skip to step 6; if you don't want to use a current search, move to step 4.

(4) Tap in the Search bar.

(5) Type your search term. This can be any information associated with your photos. As you type, collections of photos that match your search criteria are listed under the Search bar. The more specific you make your search term, the smaller the set of photos that will be found.

(6) When you're done typing your search term, tap Search (this is optional, as you can work with the results as they appear when you do a search).

(7) Swipe up and down the screen to browse all the results.

(8) Tap the results you want to explore.

(9) Tap a photo to view it.

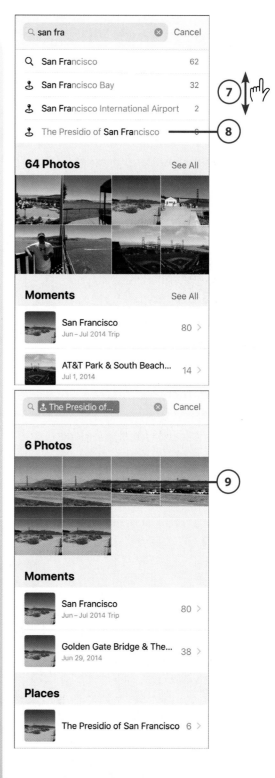

10 View the photo (covered in the next section).

11 Tap Search to return to the group of photos you were viewing.

12 Tap a different photo to view it.

13 Tap a different result to explore its photos.

14 To change the search, tap in the Search bar and change the current search term (you can delete the current term by tapping Delete [x]).

15 Tap Cancel to exit the search.

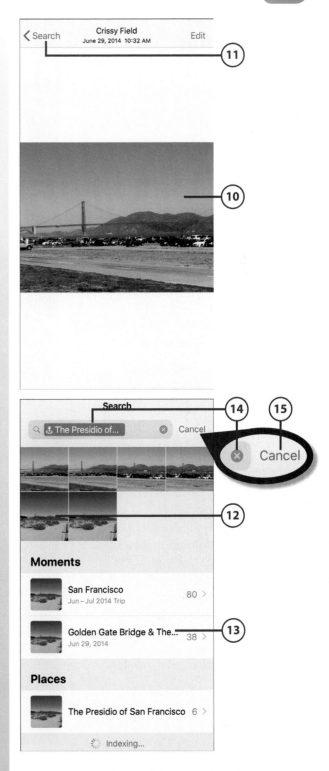

Viewing Photos Individually

The Photos app enables you to view your photos individually. Here's how:

1. Using the skills you learned in the previous tasks, open the group of photos that you want to view.

Orientation Doesn't Matter

Zooming, unzooming, and browsing photos works in the same way whether you hold your iPhone horizontally or vertically.

2. Swipe up and down to browse all the photos in the group.

3. Tap the photo you want to view. The photo display screen appears.

4. If it is a Live Photo, press down gently and hold on the screen to see the photo's motion.

My, Isn't That Special

If there is something unique about a photo, you see an icon indicating what it is on the photo when you view it. In this figure, you see the LIVE icon indicating it is a Live Photo. You might also see Burst for Burst photos, HDR for a photo captured with HDR, and so on. Keep an eye out for these icons as you explore your photos.

Live Photo

5 To see the photo without the app's toolbars, tap the screen. The toolbars are hidden.

6 Rotate the phone horizontally.

7 Unpinch or double-tap on the photo to zoom in.

8 When you are zoomed in, drag around the image to view different parts of the zoomed image.

9 Pinch or double-tap on the photo to zoom out. If you double-tap on the photo, all zoom is removed.

No Zooming Please

You can't have any zoom when you swipe to move to the next or previous photo, so make sure you are zoomed out all the way before performing step 10. If not, you move the photo around instead.

10 Swipe to the left to view the next photo in the group.

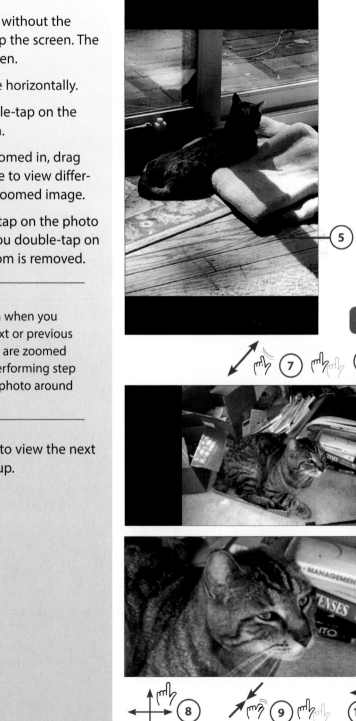

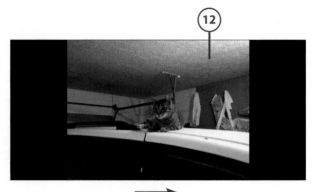

(11) Swipe to the right to view the previous photo in the group.

(12) When you're done viewing photos in the group, tap the screen to show the toolbars again.

(13) Swipe to the left or right on the thumbnails at the bottom of the screen to view all the photos in the current group. As you swipe, the photo you are viewing changes to be the one in the larger thumbnail at the center of the screen.

(14) Tap a photo to view it.

(15) Swipe up on the photo to get information about it and to see photos related to it.

(16) Tap Show Nearby Photos to see photos that were captured near the location associated with the photos you are viewing.

(17) Tap the photo on the map to move to the map view (using the map view is covered in the "Working with Memories" section later in this chapter).

(18) Swipe up the screen to see more related photos.

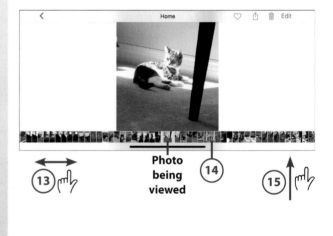

Photo being viewed (14)

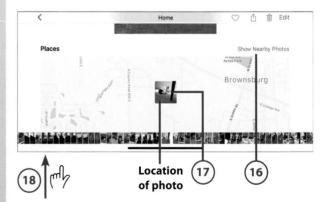

Location of photo (17)

(**19**) Tap a related memory to view it (details are provided later in this chapter).

(**20**) When you are done viewing the details, tap the Back icon (<).

Using 3D Touch with Photos

You can use 3D Touch (iPhone 6s and later models) to preview and open photos as follows:

(**1**) Browse a collection of photos in the Photos app.

(**2**) Tap and hold on a photo in which you are interested. A Peek of that photo appears.

(3) To open the photo, press down slightly harder until it pops open and use the steps in the previous task to view it. (If you pop the photo open, skip the rest of these steps.)

(4) To see actions you can perform on the photo preview, swipe up the image.

(5) Tap the action you want to perform, such as Favorite, to tag the photo as a favorite.

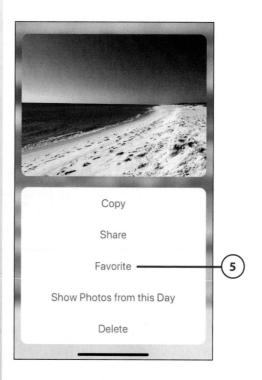

Copy

Share

Favorite

Show Photos from this Day

Delete

Working with Memories

The Memories feature automatically creates collections of photos for you to view in a number of ways. You can view them in a slideshow, individually, by selecting places, by selecting people, and so on. This feature provides lots of options and at times can be a very interesting way to view photos, because you might be surprised by some of the photos included in a particular memory.

There are a number of ways to access memories, including:

On the For You screen, tap See All for Memories to see all your memories

Tap to open the memory

Tap to access your photo memories

Memory based on location

- Tap the For You icon on the Dock at the bottom of the screen. The Memories section appears at the top of the For You screen. You can browse memories there or tap See All to see all your memories.

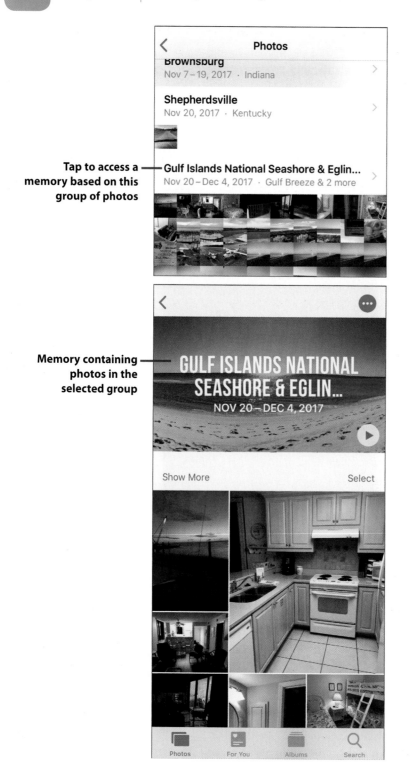

Tap to access a memory based on this group of photos

Memory containing photos in the selected group

- Tap a heading for a group of photos when viewing years, collections, or moments. You move into a memory associated with whatever you tapped on.

- When you are viewing a photo, swipe up the screen and tap a memory in the Related section.

- Tap a memory that appears as part of a search.

These are just some of the ways; memories pop up throughout the Photos app.

When you access a memory (no matter how you arrived), you see different options depending on the content of that memory. These can include:

- **Slideshow**—The photos collected in a memory play in a slideshow that plays using a theme, effects, and a soundtrack. You can change the theme and length of the slideshow, and you can also edit it.

- **Photos**—All memories enable you to view the photos they contain just like photos collected in other ways.

- **People**—If the photos in a memory include people, the app identifies those people by facial recognition and enables you to view other photos containing those people or groups of people.

- **Groups & People**—If the photos in a memory include people that are in consistent groupings, you can use these groups to view photos containing those groupings.

- **Places**—You can use the Places tool to view the photos in a memory on a map. You can tap locations on the map where photos were taken to view those photos.

- **Related**—This section of a memory presents other memories that are somehow related to the one you are viewing. This relationship can be based on location, people, and so on.

The Photos app creates memories for you dynamically, meaning they change over time as the photos in your library change. You can save memories that you want to keep as they are. Otherwise, the memories you see change as you take more photos or edit photos you have. This keeps memories a fresh and interesting way to view your photos.

You can work with memories in a similar way no matter how you open them or what kind of photos they contain. Following are examples showing how to use several of the sections you see in memories.

Watching and Changing a Memory's Slideshow

All memories have slideshows that you can watch using the following steps:

1. Open a memory using an option described previously. Slideshows appear at the top of a memory's screen.

2. Tap the Play icon. The slideshow begins to play. If some of the photos in the slideshow aren't currently stored on your iPhone, there might be a pause while they are downloaded (you see the Downloading status on the opening screen while this is done).

3. To view the slideshow in landscape orientation, rotate the iPhone. As the slideshow plays, you see effects applied to the photos; videos included in the memory also play.

4. Tap the screen to reveal the slideshow controls.

5. To pause the slideshow, tap the Pause icon. (When paused, this becomes the Play icon that you can tap to resume the slideshow.)

6. Swipe to the right or left on the theme bar to change the slideshow's theme. As you change the theme you might see changes on the screen, such as a different font for the title, and hear different music while the slideshow plays.

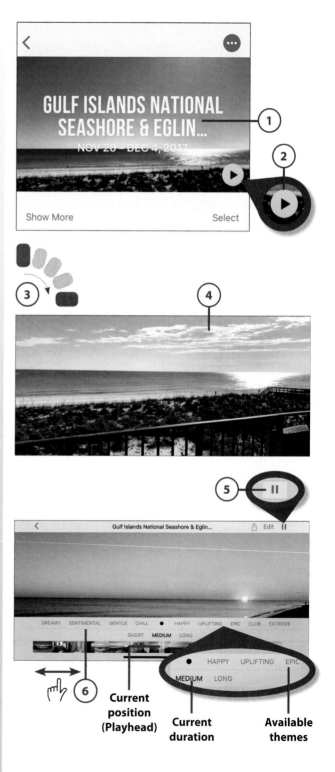

Current position (Playhead)

Current duration

Available themes

(7) Swipe to the right or left on the duration bar to change the slideshow's length. As you make changes, you see the slideshow's current length just above the theme bar.

(8) Swipe to the left or right on the thumbnails at the bottom of the screen to move back or forward, respectively.

(9) To restart the slideshow with the new settings, tap the Play icon (not shown on the figures).

(10) Tap Edit to make manual changes to the slideshow and save the memory (see the Go Further sidebar "Make Your Own Memories" for more information).

(11) Tap the Share icon and use the resulting menu to share the memory via AirDrop or an app; you can also save it to your iCloud Drive or Dropbox.

(12) Tap the Back icon (<) to return to the memory.

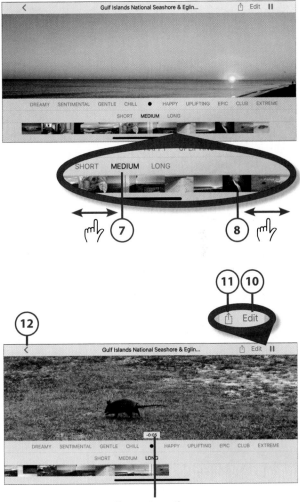

Current runtime

>>>*Go Further*
MAKE YOUR OWN MEMORIES

You can edit a memory's slideshow to change how it plays. Tap Edit; you might see a prompt indicating that the memory is saved to your memories, tap OK if you see this. Tap Title to change the slideshow's name and title style. Tap Title Image to change the image shown in the video's opening thumbnail. Tap Music to change its soundtrack; you can choose None to remove the soundtrack, Soundtracks to use one of the default soundtracks, or My Music to use music in your iTunes Music Library. Tap Duration to set the slideshow's playing time. Tap Photos & Videos to manually select the photos that are included; tap the Trash Can icon to remove a photo from the video (this doesn't delete the photo from your library, only from the slideshow) or tap Add (+) to include more of the memory's photos in the slideshow (tap the Back icon [<] when you are finished selecting photos). Tap Done to save your slideshow. When you play the slideshow, the options you selected are used. Choose Custom on the Theme bar to view the video you created.

Viewing a Memory's Photos

You can view the photos contained in a memory using the following steps:

(1) Open a memory using an option described previously.

(2) To see all of the memory's photos, tap Show More.

Show All, Tell All
If the memory has lots of photos, you might see only a summary view of them on the Photos section. Tap Show More to see all the photos. Tap Summary to return to the summary view.

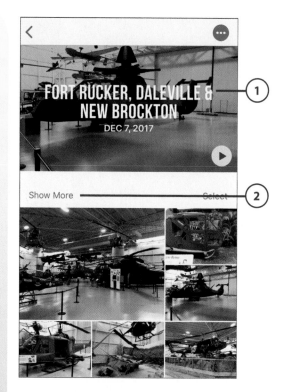

③ Swipe up and down the photos section to see all the photos the memory contains.

④ Tap a photo to view it.

⑤ Use the techniques you learned in "Viewing Photos Individually" earlier in the chapter to work with the photos in the memory.

⑥ Tap the Back icon (<) to return to the memory.

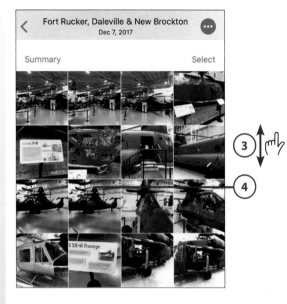

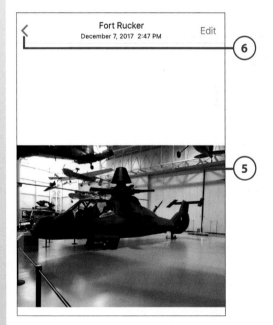

Viewing a Memory's Photos by Place

You can choose the photos in a memory to view based on the location using the Places section.

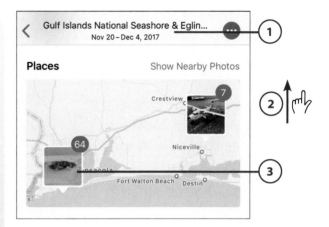

1. Open a memory using an option described previously.

2. Swipe up the screen until you see the Places section.

3. Tap a place. The map expands to fill the screen and you see more locations associated with photos in the memory.

Nearby Photos

Tap Show Nearby Photos to show other photos that were taken near the locations that you are viewing on the map, but that are not currently included in the memory. Tap Hide Nearby Photos to hide those photos again.

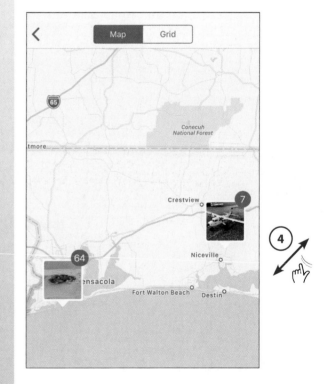

4. Unpinch your fingers on the screen to zoom in to reveal more detailed locations.

5 Swipe around the screen to move around the map.

6 Tap a location with photos to see the photos associated with it.

7 Swipe up and down the screen to browse the photos taken at the location.

8 Tap a photo to view it.

9 Use the techniques covered in "Viewing Photos Individually" earlier in the chapter to work with the photos you view.

10 Tap the Back icon (<) to return to the place.

11 Tap the Back icon to return to the map. (You might have to tap the Back icon an additional time to return to the map depending on whether the location you viewed has multiple moments associated with it.)

12 Tap other locations to view their photos.

13 Tap the Back icon (<) to return to the memory.

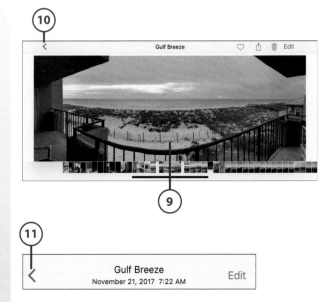

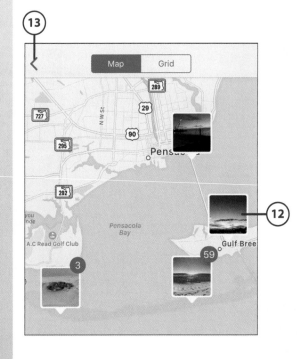

>>>Go Further

MAKING THE MOST OF YOUR MEMORIES

Here are a few more ways to make the most of your memories:

- To view memories based on people or groups of people, tap the person or group in the Groups & People or People section; you see a memory focused on the person or group you selected. (By the way, the Photos app can often identify pets in your photos and create memories focused on them.)

- Tap a memory in the Related section to see a memory that is related to the current one, such as one with photos containing the same people or in the same locations.

- Memories can change over time. If you want to save a memory as it is, view it and tap the Options icon (…) at the top of the screen. Then tap Add to Favorite Memories to add a memory you are viewing to the Favorite Memories album. Open the menu for a memory you've designated as a favorite and tap Remove from Favorite Memories to remove the memory from the Favorite Memories album.

- If you want to remove a memory, tap the Options icon (…) and tap Delete Memory and then confirm you want to delete a memory by tapping Delete Memory again; the memory is deleted. When you delete a memory, only the memory is deleted; the photos that were in that memory remain in your photo library. (However, if you delete a photo from within a memory, that photo is deleted from your photo library, too.)

>>>Go Further

ROLL YOUR OWN SLIDESHOWS

The Memories feature creates slideshows that include effects and soundtracks for you automatically, and, as you read in an earlier note, you can modify these slideshows. However, you can create your own slideshows manually too. View photos in a collection that you want to view as a slideshow; tap Select and then tap the photos you want to view in a slideshow. Tap the Share icon. Tap Slideshow. The slideshow plays. Tap the screen to show the slideshow controls. Tap Options to configure the slideshow, such as to choose music for it. When you're done configuring the slideshow, tap Done. Tap Done again when you are finished watching a slideshow.

Working with Burst Mode Photos

When you use the Burst mode to take photos, the Camera app rapidly takes a series of photos. (Typically, you use Burst mode to capture motion, where the action is happening too quickly to be able to frame and take individual photos.) You can review the photos taken in Burst mode and save any you want to keep as favorites; your favorites become separate photos just like those you take one at a time.

Here's how to identify which photos in a burst you want to keep:

1. View a Burst mode photo. Burst mode photos are indicated by the word Burst and the number of photos in the burst. (You can see all of the burst photos on your phone by opening the Bursts album.)

2. Tap Select. The burst is expanded. At the bottom of the screen, you see small thumbnails for the photos in the burst. At the top part of the screen, you see larger thumbnails of the photos; the photo in the center of the previews is marked with a downward-facing arrow. Photos marked with a dot are "suggested photos," meaning the best ones in the series according to the Photos app.

3. Swipe all the way to the right to move to the first photo in the series; swiping on the thumbnails at the bottom of the screen flips through them faster.

Burst mode photo · Number of photos in the series

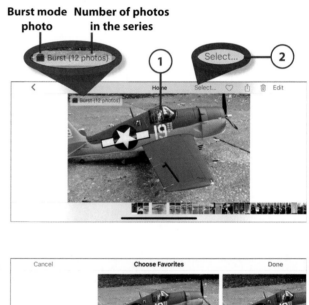

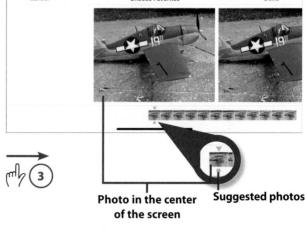

Photo in the center of the screen · Suggested photos

4 Tap a photo that you want to save. It is marked with a check mark.

5 Swipe to the left to move through the series.

6 Tap each photo you want to save.

7 Continue reviewing and selecting photos until you've gone through the entire series.

8 Tap Done.

9 Tap Keep Only *X* Favorites, where *X* is the number of photos you selected, or tap Keep Everything to keep all the photos in the burst. Each photo you keep becomes a separate, individual photo; you can work with these just like photos you take individually.

Total number of selected photos

Selected photos

Burst Mode Photos and Uploads to the Cloud

If the Upload Burst Photos switch on the Photos Settings screen is set to off, burst photos are not uploaded to the cloud until you go through these steps to select and save photos from a burst. The photos you selected to keep are then uploaded to the cloud just like individual photos you take.

Editing Photos

Even though the iPhone has great photo-taking capabilities, not all the photos you take are perfect from the start. Fortunately, you can use the Photos app to improve your photos. The following tools are available to you:

- **Enhance**—This tool attempts to automatically adjust the colors and other properties of photos to make them better.

- **Straighten, Rotate, and Crop**—You can rotate your photos to change their orientation and crop out the parts of photos you don't want to keep.

- **Filters**—You can apply different filters to your photos for artistic or other purposes.

- **Red-eye**—This one helps you remove that certain demon-possessed look from the eyes of people in your photos.

- **Smart Adjustments**—You can adjust the light, color, and even the black-and-white properties of your photos.

- **Markups**—You can add markups, such as redlines, drawings, and magnification to photos.

Enhancing Photos

To improve the quality of a photo, use the Enhance tool.

1. View the image you want to enhance.

2. Tap Edit.

3. Tap the Enhance icon. The image is enhanced and the Enhance icon turns orange.

4. If you don't like the enhancements, tap the Enhance icon again to remove the enhancements.

5. Tap Done to save the enhanced image.

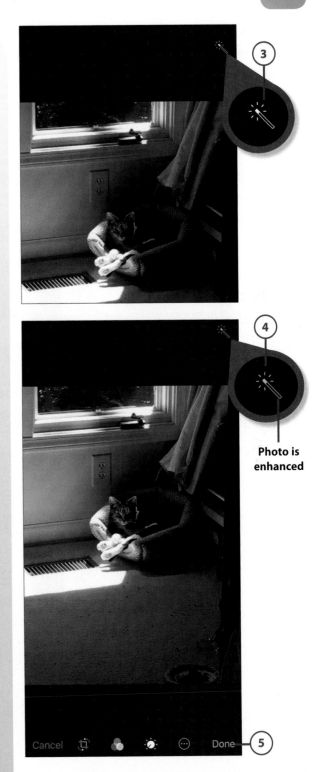

Photo is enhanced

Cancel   Done

Straightening, Rotating, and Cropping Photos

To change the alignment, position, and part of the image shown, perform the following steps:

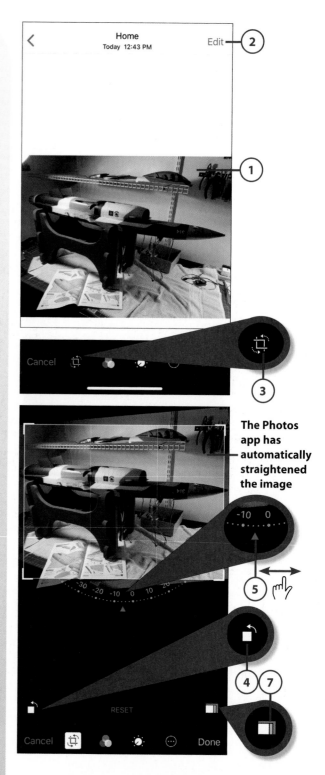

The Photos app has automatically straightened the image

1. View the image you want to change.

2. Tap Edit.

3. Tap the Rotate/Crop icon. The Photos app attempts to straighten the image if it detects it is not aligned according to the grid (because your phone wasn't vertical or horizontal when you took the photo).

4. To rotate the image in 90-degree increments, tap the Rotate tool. Each time you tap this icon, the image rotates 90 degrees in the counterclockwise direction.

5. If the automatic straightening isn't what you want, rotate the image within its frame by dragging the triangle to the left or right. This is often useful to straighten photos that aren't aligned quite right, but can be used for artistic effects too.

6. When the image is straightened, lift your finger from the screen. The dial shows how much you've rotated the image.

7. Crop the image proportionally by tapping the Constrain icon; to crop the image without staying to a specific proportion, skip to step 9.

8 Tap the proportion to which you want to crop the image. You use this to configure the image for how you intend to display it. For example, if you want to display it on a 16:9 TV, you might want to constrain the cropping to that proportion so the image matches the display device.

9 Drag the corners of the crop box until the part of the image you want to keep is shown in the box. If you performed step 8, the crop box maintains the proportion you selected.

10 Drag on the image to move it around inside the crop box.

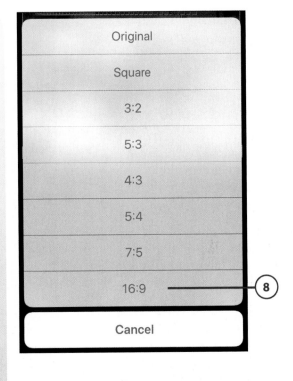

Part of image that will be cropped out   Part of image that will be kept

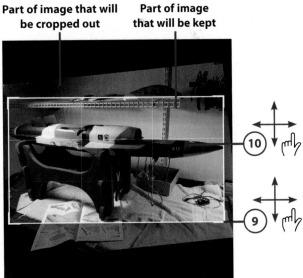

(11) When the image is cropped and positioned as you want it to be, tap Done. The edited image is saved.

More on Straightening and Cropping Photos

To undo changes you've made, tap RESET and the photo returns to the state it was in before you started editing it. To exit the Edit mode without saving your changes, tap Cancel.

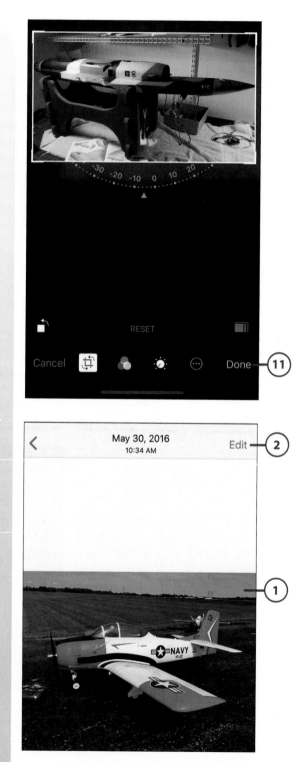

Applying Filters to Photos

To apply filters to photos, do the following:

(1) View the image to which you want to apply filters.

(2) Tap Edit.

(3) Tap the Filters icon. The palette of filters appears. If you haven't applied a filter, you see the current filter as Original.

(4) Swipe to the left or right on the palette to browse all of the filters.

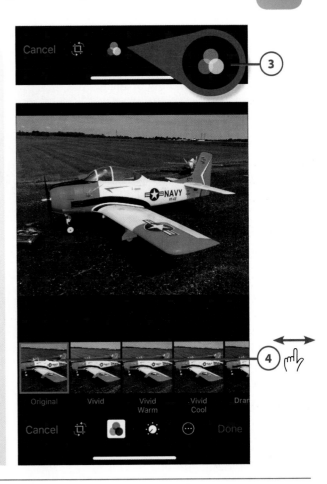

Undoing What You've Done

To restore a photo to its unedited state, tap Revert, which appears when you edit a photo that you previously edited and saved. At the prompt, tap Revert to Original, and the photo is restored to its "like new" condition.

The original version of photos is saved in your library so you can use the Revert function to go back to the photo as it was originally taken or added to the library, even if you've edited it several times.

However, you can't have the edited version and the original version displaying in your library at the same time. If you want to be able to have both an edited and original version (or multiple edited versions of the same photo), make a copy of the original before you edit it. To do this, view the photo, tap the Share icon, and tap Duplicate. You can do this as many times as you want. Each copy behaves like a new photo. If you edit one copy, the original remains available in your library for viewing or different editing.

(5) Tap the filter you want to apply. The filter is applied to the image and you see a preview of the image as it will be with the filter; the filter currently applied is highlighted with a blue box. Keep trying filters until the image is what you want it to be.

(6) Tap Done. The photo with the filter applied is saved.

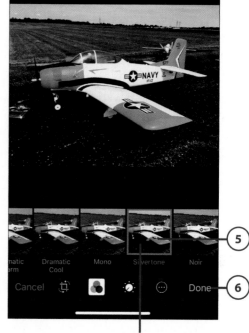

Filter currently applied

Removing Red-Eye from Photos

When you edit a photo with people in it, the Red-eye tool becomes available (if no faces are recognized, this tool is hidden). To remove red-eye, perform the following steps:

(1) View an image with people that have red-eye.

(2) Tap Edit.

(3) Tap the Red-eye icon.

4. Zoom in on the eyes from which you want to remove red-eye; as you zoom in, drag the photo to keep the eyes you want to fix on the screen.

5. Tap each eye containing red-eye. The red in the eyes you tap is removed.

6. Repeat steps 4 and 5 until you've removed all the red-eye.

7. Tap Done to save your changes.

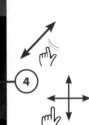

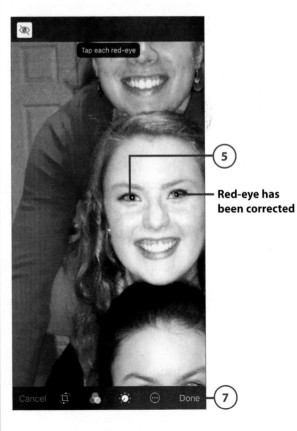

Red-eye has been corrected

Making Smart Adjustments to Photos

You can edit your photos using the Photos app's Smart Adjustment tools. Using these tools, you can change various characteristics related to light, color, and black-and-white aspects of your photos.

1. View the image you want to change.

2. Tap Edit.

3. Tap the Smart Adjust icon.

4. Tap the characteristic you want to change, such as Light.

Get Straight to the Point

To jump directly to a specific aspect of the area you are adjusting, tap the downward-facing arrow along the right side of the screen. On the resulting menu, tap the characteristic you want to adjust. For example, if you open the menu for Color, you tap Saturation, Contrast, or Cast to adjust those factors.

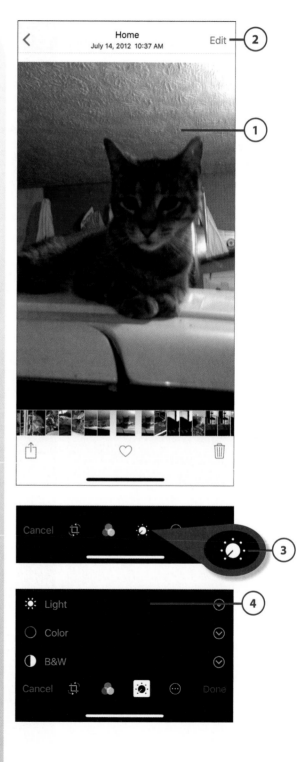

5 Swipe to the left or right to change the level of the parameter you are adjusting. As you make changes, you see the results of the change on the image.

6 When you're done adjusting the first attribute you selected, tap the List icon.

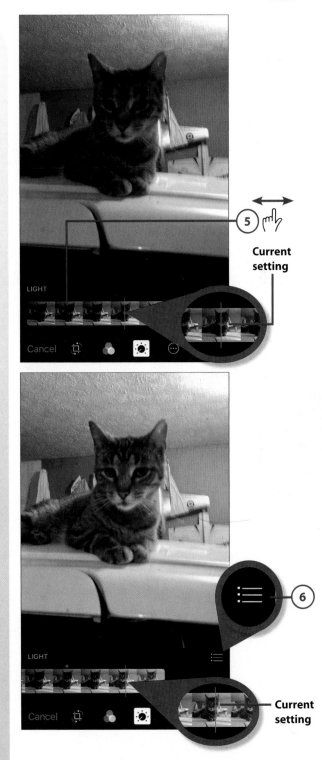

(7) Tap one of the options under the attribute you are already working with to adjust it; or tap the downward-facing arrow under one of the other attributes, and then tap the characteristic you want to change.

(8) Swipe to the left or right to change the level of the parameter you are adjusting. As you make changes, you see the results of the change on the image.

(9) Repeat steps 6 through 8 until you've made all the adjustments you want to make.

(10) Tap Done to save the adjusted image.

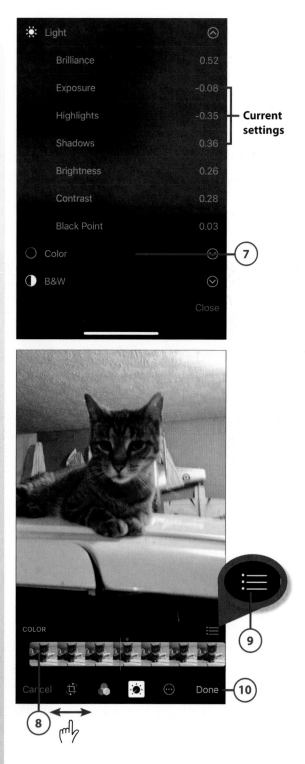

Marking Up Photos

You can add markups to photos, including:

- **Draw**—You draw directly on top of photos, such as to indicate areas of interest or highlight something.

- **Magnify**—This tool magnifies a section of an image in a circle that looks kind of like an image you see through a magnifying glass.

- **Add text**—You can use the text tool to add words to an image.

With the drawing and text tools, you can choose the format of the markup, such as its color.

The following steps show the magnification and text markup tools; the drawing and other tools work similarly.

1. View the image you want to mark up.
2. Tap Edit.
3. Tap the Options icon (…).

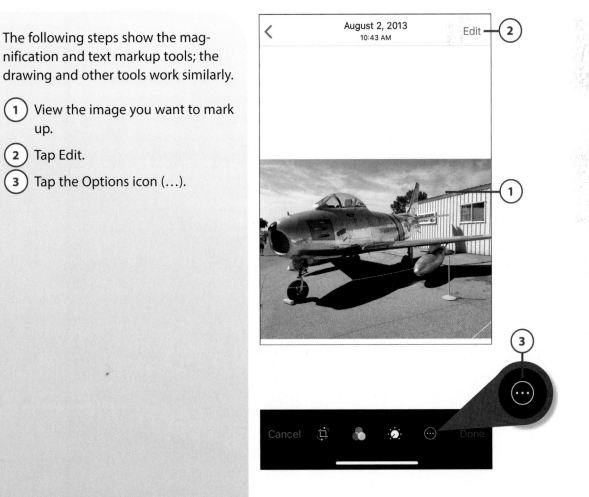

(4) Tap Markup.

(5) Tap Add (+).

(6) Tap Magnifier. The magnification circle appears.

(7) Drag the circle over the area of the image you want to magnify.

Drawing Tools

Tap the pen or pencil icons to draw on the photo. You can change the size and color of the lines and drag them on the screen similar to how these steps show using the text tool.

But Wait, There Might Be More

The Markup tool is the default photo editor that comes with the Photos app. Over time, other photo-editing tools might become available (check the App Store). When installed, you see them on the Photo Editing menu. Tap a tool to use it. Tap More (…) to configure the photo-editing tools you have installed—for example, set a tool's switch to off (white) to hide it. You can also change the order in which the tools are listed on the menu.

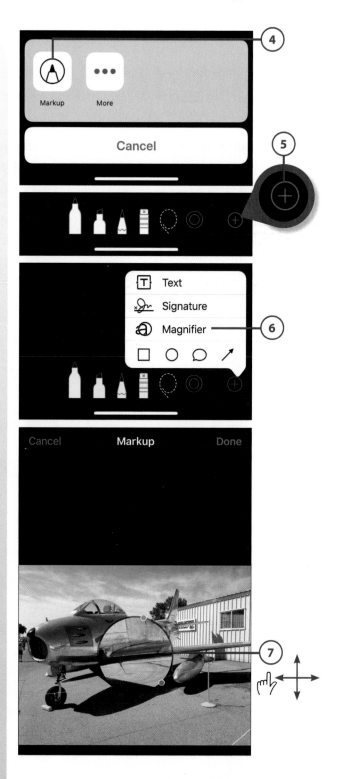

8 To change the size of the area being magnified, drag the blue dot away from the center of the circle to increase the area or toward the center to decrease the size of the area.

9 To change the amount of magnification being applied, drag the green dot clockwise around the circle to increase the magnification or counterclockwise to decrease it.

10 Tap Add (+).

11 Tap Text. A text box appears. The default text is black and kind of small, so it can be hard to spot. It appears in the center of the screen.

De-magnify

To remove a magnification markup, tap it and then tap Delete on the menu that appears.

12 Tap the text box.

13 Tap Edit.

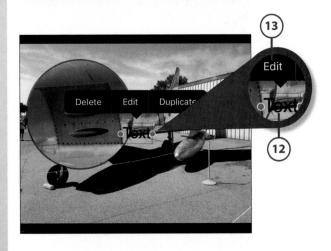

(14) Type the text you want to add.

(15) Tap on the screen to close the keyboard.

16 If it isn't selected already, tap the text.

17 Tap the font icon.

18 Use the font menu, size slider, and justification icons to format the text.

19 Tap outside the menu to close it.

(20) With the text still selected, tap the color icon (it starts as black so it is hard to see against the black background).

(21) Tap the color you want to apply to the text.

(22) Drag the text to where you want it to be on the photo.

(23) Tap Done.

Loose the Markups

If you tap the photo before tapping Done in step 24, you jump back to the original image without your markups. Tap it again to restore your markups.

(24) Tap Done to save your markups on the photo.

Editing Markups

To edit existing markups on a photo, edit the photo and open the markups tool using steps 1 through 4.

Working with Photos

Once you have photos on your iPhone, there are a lot of things you can do with them, including the following:

- Emailing one or more photos to one or more people (see the next task).
- Sending a photo via a text message (see Chapter 9, "Sending, Receiving, and Managing Texts and iMessages").
- Sharing photos via AirDrop (see Chapter 15, "Working with Other Useful iPhone Apps and Features").
- Sharing photos with others via iCloud (covered later in this chapter).
- Posting your photos on your Facebook wall or timeline.
- Assigning photos to contacts (see Chapter 6, "Managing Contacts").
- Using photos as wallpaper (see Chapter 5, "Customizing How Your iPhone Looks and Sounds").
- Sharing photos via tweets.
- Printing photos from your printer or (see Chapter 2).
- Deleting photos (covered later in this chapter).
- Organizing photos in albums (also covered later in this chapter).

Copy 'Em

If you select one or more photos and tap the Copy icon, the images you selected are copied to the iPhone's clipboard. You can then move into another app and paste them in.

You'll easily be able to accomplish any actions on your own that are not covered in detail here once you've performed a couple of those that are demonstrated in the following tasks.

Individual Versus Groups

Some actions are only available when you are working with an individual photo. For example, you might be able to send only a single photo via some apps, whereas you can email multiple photos at the same time. Any commands that aren't applicable to the photos that are selected won't appear on the screen.

Sharing Photos via Email

You can email photos via iPhone's Mail application starting from the Photos app.

① View the source containing one or more images that you want to share.

② Tap Select.

③ Select the photos you want to send by tapping them. When you tap a photo, it is marked with a check mark to show you that it is selected.

④ Tap the Share icon.

Too Many?

If the photos you have selected are too much for email, the Mail icon won't appear. You need to select fewer photos to attach to the email message.

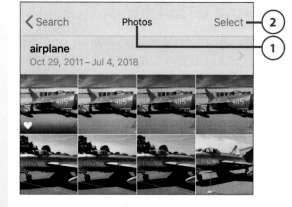

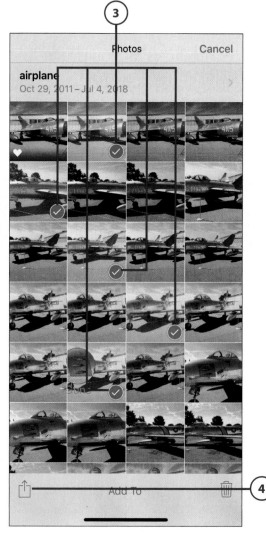

(5) Tap Mail. A new email message is created, and the photos are added as attachments.

(6) Use the email tools to address the email, add a subject, type the body, and send it. (See Chapter 8, "Sending, Receiving, and Managing Email," for detailed information about using your iPhone's email tools.)

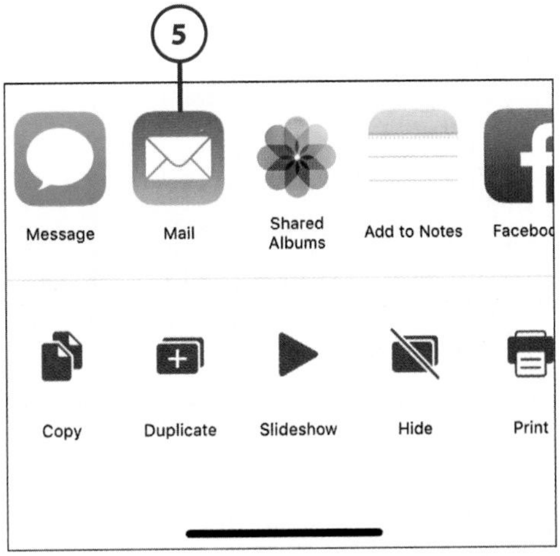

| Message | Mail | Shared Albums | Add to Notes | Facebook |

| Copy | Duplicate | Slideshow | Hide | Print |

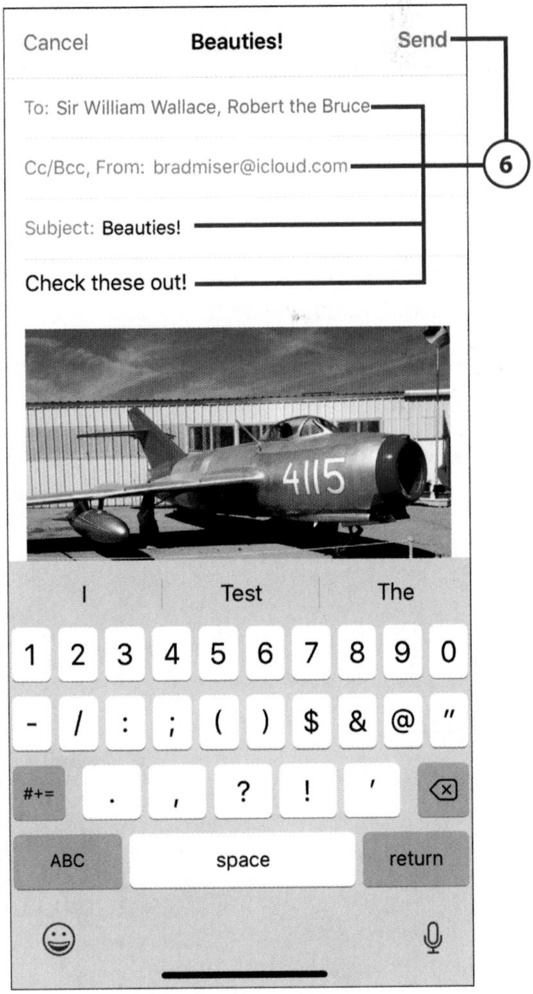

Cancel   **Beauties!**   Send

To: Sir William Wallace, Robert the Bruce

Cc/Bcc, From: bradmiser@icloud.com

Subject: **Beauties!**

Check these out!

| I | Test | The |
| 1 2 3 4 5 6 7 8 9 0 |
| - / : ; ( ) $ & @ " |
| #+= . , ? ! ' ⌫ |
| ABC | space | return |

7. Tap the size of the images you want to send. Choosing a smaller size makes the files smaller and reduces the quality of the photos. You should generally try to keep the size of emails to 5MB or smaller to ensure the message makes it to the recipient. (Some email servers block larger messages.) After you send the email, you move back to the photos you were browsing.

Images from Email

As mentioned in Chapter 8, when you save images attached to email that you receive, they are stored in the All Photos or Camera Roll photo album just like photos you take with your iPhone.

Organizing Photos in a New Album

You can create photo albums and store photos in them to keep your photos organized.

To create a new album, perform these steps:

1. Move to the Albums screen by tapping Albums on the toolbar.

2. Tap Add (+).

3. To create a personal album, tap New Album or to share an album, tap New Shared Album. These steps show a personal album; creating a shared album is covered later in this chapter.

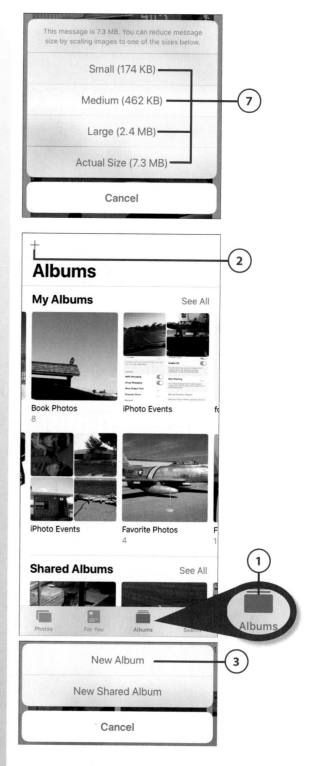

4 Type the name of the new album.

5 Tap Save. You're prompted to select photos to add to the new album.

6 Move to the source of the photos you want to add to the new album.

7 Swipe up and down to browse the source and tap the photos you want to add to the album. They are marked with a check mark to show that they are selected. The number of photos selected is shown at the top of the screen.

8 Tap Done. The photos are added to the new album and you move back to the Albums screen. The new album is shown on the list, and you can work with it just like the other albums you see.

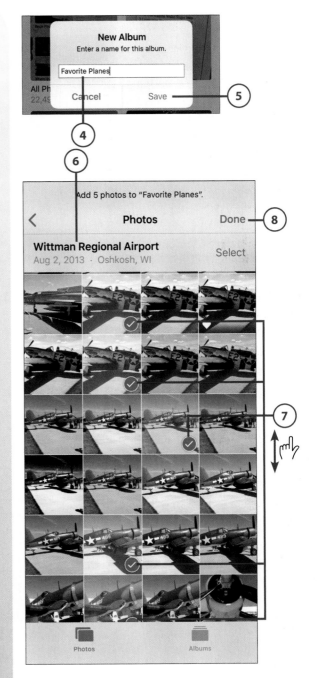

Playing Favorites

You can use the Favorite icon (the heart) to mark any photo or video as a favorite. It fills in with blue to show you that the item you are viewing is a favorite. Favorites are automatically collected in the Favorites album, so this is an easy way to collect photos and videos you want to be able to easily find again without having to create a new album or even put them in an album. You can unmark a photo or video as a favorite by tapping its Favorite icon again.

New album containing the photos you selected

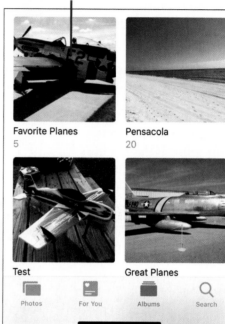

Adding Photos to an Existing Album

To add photos to an existing album, follow these steps:

1. Move to the source containing the photos you want to add to an album.

2. Tap Select.

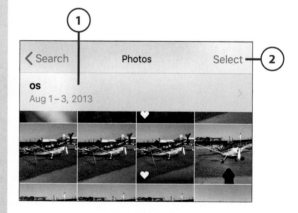

3 Tap the photos you want to add to the album.

4 Tap Add To.

5 Swipe up and down the list to find the album to which you want to add the photos.

6 Tap the album; the selected photos are added to the album. (If an album is grayed out and you can't tap it, that album was not created on the iPhone, so you can't change its contents.)

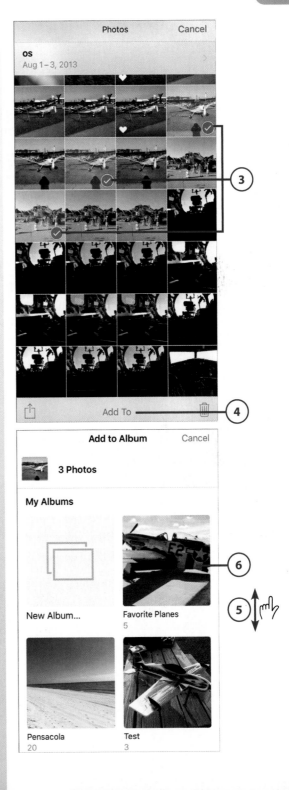

>>>Go Further

MORE ALBUM FUN

You can create a new album from photos you've already selected. Perform steps 1 through 5 and then tap New Album instead of tapping an existing album in step 6. Name the new album and save it. It's created with the photos you selected already in it.

You can change the order in which albums are listed on the Albums screen. Move to the Albums screen and tap Edit. Drag albums up or down the screen to reposition them. To delete an album that you created in the Photos app, tap its Unlock icon (red circle with a –) and then tap Delete Album. (This only deletes the album itself; the photos in your library remain there.) When you're done making changes to your albums, tap Done.

To remove a photo from an album, view the photo from within the album, tap the Trash icon, and then tap Remove from Album. Photos you remove from an album remain in your photo library; they are only removed from the album. (If you tap Delete instead, the photo is deleted from your photo library.)

Deleting Photos

You can delete photos and videos that you don't want to keep on your iPhone. If you use iCloud to store them, deleting photos from your phone also deletes them from your photo library and from all the other devices using your library. So, make sure you really don't want photos any more before you delete them.

① Open the source containing photos you want to delete.

② Tap Select.

3 Tap the photos you want to delete. Each item you select is marked with a check mark.

4 Tap the Trash icon.

5 Tap Delete *X* Photos, where *X* is the number of photos you selected. The photos you selected are deleted.

Deleting Individual Photos

You can delete individual photos that you are viewing by tapping the Trash icon, and then tapping Delete Photo.

Recovering Deleted Photos

As you learned earlier, photos you delete are moved to the Recently Deleted folder. You can recover photos you've deleted by opening this folder. You see the photos you've deleted; each is marked with the time remaining until it is permanently deleted. To restore photos in this folder, tap Select, tap the photos you want to recover, and tap Recover. Tap Recover *X* Photos, where *X* is the number of photos you selected (if you select only one, this is labeled as Recover Photo). The photos you selected are returned to the location from which you deleted them.

Deleted Means Deleted

Be aware that when you delete a photo from your iPhone, it is also deleted from your iCloud Library and all the devices sharing that library—not just from your iPhone. (After it has been deleted from the Recently Deleted folder of course.)

Viewing, Editing, and Working with Video on Your iPhone

As explained in Chapter 13, you can capture video clips with your iPhone. Once captured, you can view clips on your iPhone, edit them, and share them.

Finding and Watching Videos

Watching videos you've captured with your iPhone is simple.

1. Move to the Albums screen.

2. Tap the Videos album (swipe up the screen until you see the Media Types section to see it). Video clips display their running time at the bottom of their thumbnails. (Videos can also be stored in other albums, in collections, and in memories. This Videos album just collects videos no matter where else they are stored.)

3. Swipe up and down the screen to browse your videos.

4. Tap the video you want to watch.

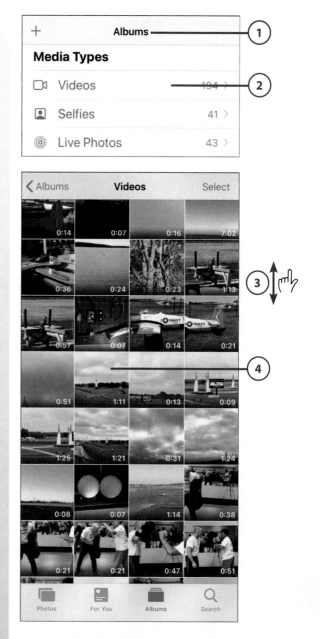

5) Rotate the phone to change its orientation if necessary.

6) Tap Play. The video plays. After a few moments, the toolbars disappear automatically.

7) Tap the video. The toolbars reappear.

Deleting Video

To remove a video clip from your iPhone (and all other devices that access your library), select it, tap the Trash icon, and then tap Delete Video at the prompt.

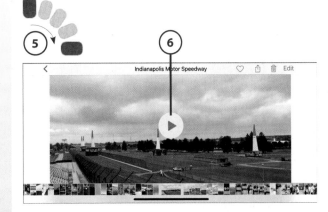

8) Pause the video by tapping Pause.

9) Jump to a specific point in a video by swiping to the left or right on the thumbnails at the bottom of the screen. When you swipe to the left, you move ahead in the video; when you swipe to the right, you move back in the video.

Watching Slow-Motion and Time-Lapse Video

Watching slow-motion video is just like watching regular speed video except after a few frames, the video slows down until a few frames before the end at which point it speeds up again. Watching time-lapse is similar except the video plays faster instead of slower than real time.

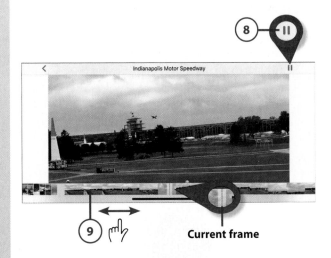

Current frame

Editing Video

You can trim a video clip to remove unwanted parts. Here's how you do it:

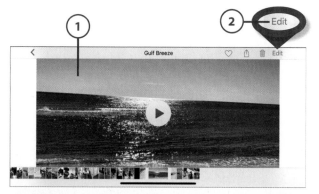

1. View the video you want to edit.

2. Tap Edit. If the video isn't stored on your phone, it is downloaded. When that process is complete, you can edit it.

3. Drag the left trim marker to where you want the edited clip to start; the trim marker is the left-facing arrow at the left end of the time-line. If you hold your finger in one place for a few seconds, the thumbnails expand so your placement of the crop marker can be more precise. As soon as you move the trim marker, the part of the clip that is inside the selection is highlighted in the yellow box.

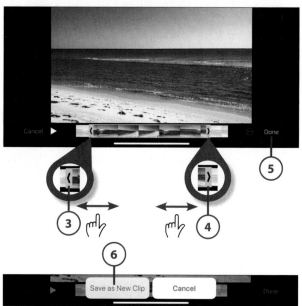

4. Drag the right trim marker to where you want the edited clip to end.

5. Tap Done.

6. Tap Save as New Clip to save the trimmed clip as a new clip or Cancel to leave the clip as it was. When you save it as a new clip, the frames outside the crop markers are removed from the clip and it is added to your library as a new clip.

There's an App for That

For more powerful video editing on your iPhone, download the iMovie app. This app provides a much more powerful video editor. You can use themes to design a video, add music, include titles and photos, and much more. After iMovie is installed on your iPhone, you can use it to edit a video. Select the video you want to edit, tap Edit, tap the Options icon (…), and then tap iMovie.

>>>*Go Further*

SHARING VIDEO

There are lots of ways to share your videos. Select the video you want to share. Tap the Share icon. Tap how you want to share the video. There are a number of options including Messages, Mail, iCloud, iCloud Photo Sharing, YouTube, and Facebook. Follow the onscreen prompts to complete the sharing process. The options available to you might depend on the size of the video; for example, you might not be able to email a large video.

Using iCloud with Your Photos

With iCloud, your devices can automatically upload photos to your iCloud account on the Internet. Other devices can automatically download photos from iCloud, so you have your photos available on all your devices at the same time. Using iCloud with your photos has two sides: a sender and receiver. Your iPhone can be both. Photo applications (such as the Photos app on a Mac) can also access your photos and download them to your computer automatically.

In addition to backing up your photos and having all your photos available to you on all your devices, you can also share your photos and videos with others and view photos and videos being shared with you.

Sharing Your Photos

You can share your photos with others by creating a shared album. This is a great way to share photos, because others can subscribe to your shared albums to view and work with the photos you share. When you share photos, you can add them to an album that's already being shared or create a new shared album.

To create a new, empty, shared album, do the following:

(1) Move to the Albums page.

(2) Tap Add (+).

(3) Tap New Shared Album.

(4) Type the title of the new album.

(5) Tap Next.

(6) Enter or select the email addresses of the people with whom you want to share the photos.

(7) Tap Create. The shared album is created and is ready for you to add photos. The recipients you included in the new album receive notifications that invite them to join the album.

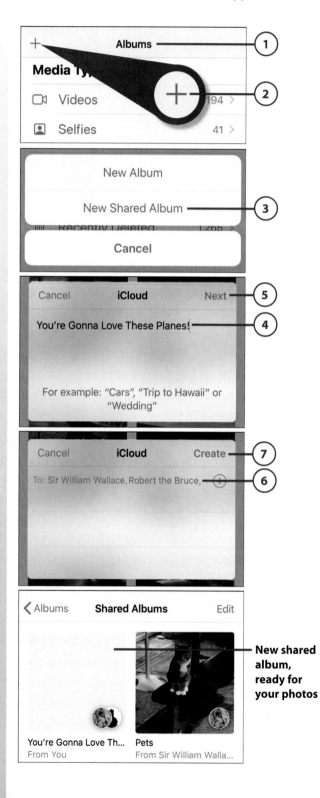

New shared album, ready for your photos

Adding Photos to a Shared Album

To add photos to an album you are sharing, perform the following steps:

(1) Tap the shared album.

(2) Tap Add (+).

(3) Open the source containing photos you want to share.

(4) Tap the photos you want to share.

(5) Tap Done.

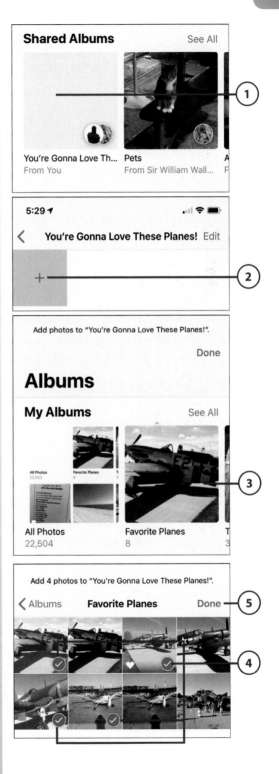

(6) Enter your commentary about the photos you are sharing. (Note, this commentary is associated only with the first photo you selected.)

(7) Tap Post. The photos you selected are added to the shared album. People who are subscribed to the album receive a notification that photos have been added and can view the new photos along with your commentary.

iCloud Account Required

The people with whom you share photos must have an iCloud account.

| Cancel | **iCloud** | Post — 7 |

I'm going to share my favorite plane photos. Please share yours too! — 6

4 Photos

Shared Album   You're Gonna Love Thes...

>>>Go Further
MORE ON iCLOUD PHOTO SHARING

Following are a few more pointers to help you use iCloud photo sharing:

- You can add comments to photos you are sharing. Open the shared album and tap the photo to which you want to add comments. Tap Add a comment. Type your comment and tap Send. People with whom you are sharing the photo receive a notification and can read your comments.

- To invite people to join a shared album, open the shared album. Tap the People tab at the bottom of the screen and then tap Invite People. Enter the email addresses of the people you want to invite and tap Add.

- You can configure various aspects of a shared album by opening it and tapping the People tab at the bottom of the screen. You can see the status of people you have invited, determine if the people with whom you are sharing the album can post to it, make the album a public website, determine if notifications are sent, or delete the shared album.

Working with Photo Albums Shared with You

You can work with albums people share with you as follows:

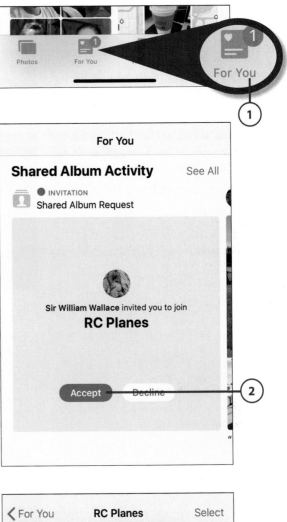

(1) Tap the notification you received, or tap the For You source when you see a badge indicating you have activity.

(2) Tap Accept for the shared album you want to join. The shared album becomes available in your Shared Albums area. You move into the new shared album.

(3) Tap a photo in the album.

(4) Tap the Thumbs-up icon to indicate you like the photo.

(5) Tap Add a comment. (If you previously liked the photo, you see the number of likes for it instead; tap that number to add a comment.)

(6) Type your comment.

(7) Tap Send. Your comments are added to the album.

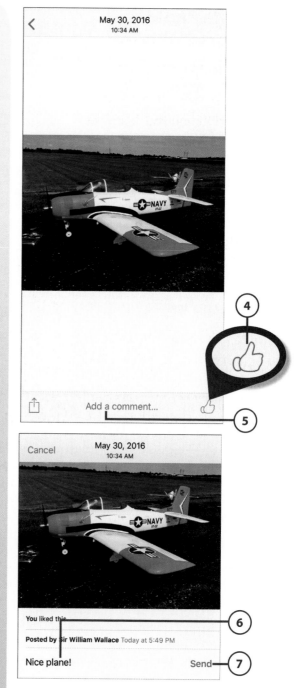

8 Tap the Back icon (<).

9 If you are allowed to add photos to the shared album by the person who shared it, tap Add (+) and post your own photos to the album you are sharing. This works just like posting to your own albums.

>>>Go Further

MORE ON PHOTOS SHARED WITH YOU

When you share other people's photos, keep the following points in mind:

- You can do most of the tasks with shared photos that you can with your own, such as emailing them, using them as wallpaper, and so on.

- To unsubscribe from an album, move to its People screen and tap Unsubscribe and confirm that is what you want to do. The shared album is removed from your iPhone.

- To see the activity associated with albums being shared with you, and those you are sharing, move to the For You screen and tap See All for the Shared Album Activity section. You see new postings to the albums, comments people have made, and so on.

Index

C

Answers to Your Technology Questions

The **My...For Seniors Series** is a collection of how-to guide books from AARP and Que that respect your smarts without assuming you are a techie. Each book in the series features:

- Large, full-color photos
- Step-by-step instructions
- Helpful tips and tricks

For more information about these titles, and for more specialized titles, visit informit.com/que

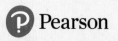